Providence and Empire

Religion, Politics and Society in Britain
Series editor: Keith Robbins

The Conversion of Britain: Religion, Politics and Society in Britain, c.600–800
Barbara Yorke

The Post-Reformation: Religion, Politics and Society in Britain, 1603–1714
John Spurr

Religion, Politics and Society in Britain, 1714–1815
Nigel Yates

Providence and Empire: Religion, Politics and Society in the United Kingdom, 1815–1914
Stewart J. Brown

Religion and Society in Twentieth-Century Britain
Callum G. Brown

Forthcoming

Religion, Politics and Society in Britain, 800–1066

Religion, Politics and Society in Britain, 1066–1272

Religion, Politics and Society in Britain, 1272–1485

Religion, Politics and Society in Tudor Britain

Providence and Empire

Religion, Politics and Society in the United Kingdom 1815–1914

Stewart J. Brown

PEARSON

Longman

Harlow, England • London • New York • Boston • San Francisco • Toronto
Sydney • Tokyo • Singapore • Hong Kong • Seoul • Taipei • New Delhi
Cape Town • Madrid • Mexico City • Amsterdam • Munich • Paris • Milan

Pearson Education Limited
Edinburgh Gate
Harlow CM20 2JE
United Kingdom
Tel: +44 (0)1279 623623
Fax: +44 (0)1279 431059
Website: www.pearsoned.co.uk

First edition published in Great Britain in 2008

© Pearson Education Limited 2008

The right of Stewart J. Brown to be identified as author of this work has been asserted
by him in accordance with the Copyright, Designs and Patents Act 1988.

ISBN: 978-0-582-29960-3

British Library Cataloguing-in-Publication Data
A CIP catalogue record for this book can be obtained from the British Library

10 9 8 7 6 5 4 3 2 1
12 11 10 09 08

Set by 35 in 10/13.5pt Sabon
Printed in Malaysia (CTP KHL)

The publisher's policy is to use paper manufactured from sustainable forests.

To Emmet Larkin
Historian, Mentor, Friend

Contents

Series Editor's Preface

No understanding of British history is possible without grappling with the relationship between religion, politics and society. How that should be done, however, is another matter. Historians of religion, who have frequently thought of themselves as ecclesiastical historians, have had one set of preoccupations. Political historians have had another. They have acknowledged, however, that both religion and politics can only be understood, in any given period, in a social context. This series makes the interplay between religion, politics and society its preoccupation. Even so, it does not assume that what is entailed by religion and politics remains the same throughout, to be considered as a constant in separate volumes merely because of the passage of time.

In its completed form the series will have probed the nature of these links from c.600 to the present day and offered a perspective, over such a long period, that has not before been attempted in a systematic fashion. There is, however, no straitjacket that requires individual authors to adhere to a common understanding of what such an undertaking involves. Even if there could be a general agreement about concepts, that is to say about what religion is or how politics can be identified, the social context of such categorisations is not static. The spheres notionally allocated to the one or to the other alter with circumstances. Sometimes it might appear that they cannot be separated. Sometimes it might appear that they sharply conflict. Each period under review will have its defining characteristics in this regard.

It is the Christian religion, in its manifold institutional manifestations, with which authors are overwhelmingly concerned since it is with conversion that the series begins. It ends, however, with a volume in which Christianity exists alongside other world religions but in a society frequently perceived to be secular. Yet, what de-Christianisation is taken to be depends upon what Christianisation has been taken to be. There is, therefore, a relationship between topics that are tackled in the first volume, and those considered in the last, which might at first sight seem unlikely. In between, of course are the 'Christian Centuries' which, despite their label, are no less full of 'boundary disputes', both before and after the Reformation. The perspective of the series, additionally, is broadly pan-insular. The Britain of 600 is plainly not the Britain of the early twenty-first century. However, the current political structures of Britain-Ireland have arguably owed as much to religion as to politics. Christendom has been inherently ambiguous.

It would be surprising if readers, not to mention authors, understood the totality of the picture that is presented in the same way. What is common, however, is a realisation that the narrative of religion, politics and society in Britain is not a simple tale that points in a single direction but rather one of enduring and by no means exhausted complexity.

Keith Robbins, November 2005

Acknowledgements

There are a number of debts of gratitude to record. Keith Robbins, the editor of this series, read through and corrected various drafts of the whole book and helped immensely in shaping the volume. I benefited from his broad historical knowledge, and from his encouragement at every stage of this project. Owen Dudley Edwards also read much of the book in draft and was extremely generous in sharing his wide-ranging expertise. Other colleagues at the University of Edinburgh, including Stephen Sutcliffe, Jack Thompson, Andrew Ross and Donald Bloxham, read and commented on portions of the typescript, and made valuable suggestions. Andrew Holmes assisted my research in Belfast on Ulster Presbyterianism, while Stephen Sutcliffe provided guidance on non-Christian faiths. I have also benefited from the assistance and conversation of Margaret Acton, Allan Anderson, David Bebbington, Eugenio Biagini, Arthur Burns, David Fergusson, Alvin Jackson, David Kerr, Hugh McLeod, Kirsty Murray, Andrew Porter, Mark Smith, Andrew Walls, and John Wolffe. The late Alec Cheyne was always magnanimous in sharing his knowledge and insights into Victorian religion. Over the years, I have gained much from the interactions with students in my advanced courses at the University of Edinburgh on religion, politics and society in nineteenth-century Britain and Ireland, and also from a number of able doctoral students.

I am grateful to the University of Edinburgh and the Arts and Humanities Research Council for a study leave in which to write much of the book. The Carnegie Trust for the Universities in Scotland provided a grant to support archival visits, and I profited from a period of research in the peace of St Deiniol's Library in Hawarden. The staffs of numerous research libraries have provided me with valuable assistance, and I wish particularly to express my appreciation to the staff of the University of Edinburgh's New College Library – one of the world's finest libraries for British religion and religious history. It is a special pleasure to record my

gratitude to my mentor, Emmet Larkin, the historian of the Roman
Catholic Church in nineteenth-century Ireland, who first aroused my fascination with nineteenth-century British and Irish history nearly 35 years
ago, and to whom this book is dedicated. My wife, Teri, has as always
shown great patience in living with this project – but more than that, she
has provided continual support and encouragement.

Introduction

This book relates the story of religion in the nineteenth-century United Kingdom of Great Britain and Ireland. It tells of men and women who sought to bring their conceptions of the divine to bear upon the world, and to shape their political and social institutions according to what they believed was God's will. It explores the fascinating interactions of the churches, the state, society and culture during the period of profound change associated with industrialisation, urbanisation and new scientific understandings of the universe.

Let me open this history with two observations. First, the period it covers marked the height of the United Kingdom's global power and influence. From the close of the Napoleonic Wars until the beginning of the Great War, the United Kingdom was *the* great world power. This point is sometimes lost amid our explorations of events and movements within these islands, and our discomfort with the imperial past. But it needs to be made. Britain's industrial revolution, for all its human suffering, also created immense wealth – and nineteenth-century British manufacturers, merchants, engineers, investors and entrepreneurs exercised a prodigious influence over the emerging world economy. As the world's first industrial society, Britain became the workshop of the world. The United Kingdom not only possessed the largest empire the world had ever seen, but its command of the oceans enabled it to project real power far beyond the borders of its formal empire. The great outward migration of British and Irish peoples that had begun in the seventeenth century continued; during the nineteenth century, millions of people left these shores and settled in North America, South Africa, Australia, New Zealand and beyond, bringing with them their language, culture and religion. The liberal political institutions of the nineteenth-century United Kingdom – parliamentary government, ministerial responsibility, an independent judiciary, recognition of individual rights, freedoms of speech and the press – were widely respected and emulated. Nineteenth-century London was the metropolis of the Western world, as well as the imperial capital for perhaps a fifth of the world's population. Along with this power and influence, to be sure, there was also cruelty, violence, insensitivity to other peoples and cultures, and racial arrogance. Much of the population of the United Kingdom, moreover, did not take much interest in the empire, except in times of crisis or of notable victories; and many, especially in Ireland, derived precious little benefit from the empire. None the less, the United Kingdom exerted an influence upon the world that was profound and extensive.

The second observation is that the nineteenth-century United Kingdom was highly religious. The overwhelming majority of its inhabitants viewed themselves as Christian and the churches were powerful and influential. The religious tone of the century had been set by the evangelical revival that swept through much of Protestant Europe and North America in the later eighteenth and early nineteenth centuries. Large numbers in the United Kingdom came to embrace an intense Christian faith – with a belief in human sin and depravity, in eternal damnation as the cost of sin, and in salvation from the fires of hell, and heavenly reward, only through acceptance of the divine grace purchased by Christ on the cross. A fervent faith, a 'vital religion', would come to infuse most existing Christian denominations and inspire the formation of new denominations. Vital religion called people to lead disciplined lives, to recognise the sovereignty of God over all the world, and to view this life as a preparation for eternity. It affected people in different ways. For some, vital religion meant an emphasis on the Bible as the direct word of God, on the need for personal conversion, and on the 'invisible' communion of the saved; for others vital Christianity meant veneration of the visible church as representing the authority of Christ on earth, of the sacraments as expressions of divine grace, and of the traditions of the faithful; for still others, vital religion meant pursuing the moral life, serving the needs of others, working for social regeneration, and seeking to follow the example of Jesus's earthly life. Some viewed this world as a place of evil and corruption, and looked for personal redemption in a life to come. Others had a profound sense of providence directing human history and governing human affairs. Many looked forward to a coming millennium, or the thousand-year reign of Christ and the saints on earth – a period of peace and light, that would be followed by the last judgement and the end of the world.

Vital religion could summon believers to action – to efforts to spread the Christian gospel at home and abroad, to end slavery and provide charity to the poor and the suffering, and to shape society in accordance with God's will. It inspired believers with an ethic of duty and work, and a sense that individuals were accountable to God for their talents and their every moment on earth. It infused them with a sense of divine purpose. In Britain there was a prevailing belief that theirs was a Protestant state, its strength rooted in the sixteenth-century Reformation. For some, the rise of the United Kingdom as a world power was connected to the religion of its people. They believed that the United Kingdom and its empire were God's instruments for the great work of spreading His gospel throughout the world. Some held that the inhabitants of these islands were a peculiar people – chosen by God as the ancient Hebrew people had been chosen. How else was it to be explained that the inhabitants of a group of islands off the northwest coast of Europe had come to exercise dominion over such vast territories and hundreds of millions of non-Christians? Not everyone, to be sure, followed this line of providentialist thinking. But many did. For them, world history was directed by the sovereign God, and as part of this history the United Kingdom was called to take a leading role in sending out Christian missionaries, spreading Christian and moral civilisation, and promoting righteousness in international affairs. Such beliefs lay behind political campaigns to bring 'commerce, Christianity and civilisation' into the heart of Africa, to champion the rights of oppressed Bulgarians and Armenians, or to promote a social gospel at home aimed at improving conditions for labouring people. And such perceptions of a national mission and providential purpose continued throughout our period. In 1914, belief in the higher responsibilities of the state led many to support warmly the United Kingdom's entry into the European war; it was a righteous crusade to defend, as they saw it, the rights of small nations, of Belgium and Serbia, and to maintain an international moral order.

Not all inhabitants, to be sure, embraced a vital religious faith. Of those who did, moreover, not everyone embraced the same beliefs. If one theme of this book is the strong sense of providential purpose, another theme is the growing diversity of religious beliefs in nineteenth-century Britain. As our period begins, the population was relatively homogenous in church adherence. In 1790, only about 10 per cent of the population of Great Britain were Dissenters, that is, Christians who chose to worship outside the churches that were established by the state – the Church of England or the Church of Scotland. This, however, changed significantly as the evangelical revival transformed religious life. The religious scene grew increasingly diverse. Existing Dissenting churches expanded greatly in numbers and missionary zeal, and new denominations emerged. More people left the established churches and joined Dissenting denominations. Society grew increasingly pluralistic. By the 1830s, an estimated one-third of British church-goers were members of a Dissenting body. Twenty years later, at the religious census conducted by the state in 1851, nearly half the church-going population of England, two-thirds of the church-going population of Scotland and four-fifths of the church-going population of Wales were Dissenters. Thereafter the percentages tended to stabilise, as the established churches grew more effective at home mission. But by 1914, a majority of the population were outside the established churches. They might be adherents of one of the large number of Protestant Dissenting denominations – General Baptists, Particular Baptists, Congregationalists, Wesleyan Methodists, New Connexion Methodists, Primitive Methodists, Bible Christians, Calvinistic Methodists, United Methodists, Unitarians, Free Church Presbyterians, United Presbyterians, Reformed Presbyterians, Free Presbyterians, Irvingites, Brethren, Salvation Army, Labour churches, or one of the hundreds of independent mission churches. They might be Roman Catholics, Orthodox Jews, or Reformed Jews. They might follow a non-Christian movement – spiritualism, Theosophy, Celtic religion, esoteric Buddhism. Or they might have no religious affiliation.

With this diversification, there were growing calls in Britain for the fullest possible freedom for different beliefs, and for equality under the law for all denominations. Many believed that the state had a responsibility to promote true religion and to impose civil disabilities on those outside the established churches. But others came to believe that the state was not competent to decide which among the many sincerely held versions of religious belief was true. For these others, religion was a personal matter, and religious practice should be a matter of individual free choice, with no element of state favour or coercion. And in time, and with the growing numbers of Dissenters, the arguments for religious freedom came to prevail. During the course of the century, the state gradually extended full civil rights first to the different Christian denominations, and then to non-Christian bodies as well. For some in Protestant Britain, this process raised questions about the nature of the United Kingdom as a Protestant state. For others, however, the extension of civil rights to religious minorities did not affect the essential Protestant nature of the state, or its obligation under God to use its power for righteous purposes.

Ireland followed a different path from that of Britain. In Ireland, the large majority of the population – between 75 and 80 per cent – remained solidly Roman Catholic throughout our period. There were efforts, especially in the early part of the century, to convert this Irish Catholic population to the established Protestant Church of Ireland, but these failed. During the course of the century Roman Catholicism became increasingly connected to the national identity of most Irish people. Thus, while the Protestantism of 'Protestant Britain' became emphatically plural, the Catholicism of 'Catholic Ireland' remained largely unified and communal. This, in turn, would lead to serious difficulties in legislating for the two parts of the United Kingdom. For while in Britain, growing numbers demanded religious freedom and a reduced role of the state in religious affairs, in Ireland, especially with the emergence of a nationalist movement in alliance with the Roman Catholic Church from the later 1870s, many came to argue that the state should legislate for a Catholic society and favour the church of the overwhelming majority of the Irish people.

This book explores religion, politics and society in the United Kingdom between 1815 and 1914, the period which corresponds to the height of its power and influence in the world. The emphasis is on the Christian religion, which was the dominant faith of the peoples of Britain and Ireland throughout the century – though other, non-Christian faiths also receive attention, particularly in Chapter 6. The account seeks to weave together the narratives of religious movements in England, Ireland, Scotland and Wales, and it recognises that the British Isles contained different nationalities with distinct religious histories. Ireland has a central place in this study, because Ireland formed an integral part of the United Kingdom throughout our period. Ireland was joined to Great Britain by the Act of Union of 1800, and it remained part of the United Kingdom until the treaty of 1922 granted dominion status within the British Commonwealth to 26 of its counties. Although nineteenth-century politicians and commentators would often behave as though Ireland were a separate country or an imperial province, constitutionally it was as much a part of the United Kingdom as Scotland, Wales, Sussex or Westminster. Similarly, this book gives attention to imperial developments and to efforts by the Christian public to influence imperial and foreign policy. The constraints of space have not allowed more than accounts of certain key episodes; and large areas of the empire, most notably in the Pacific and Canada, have not received attention. This is a history of religion, politics and society in the United Kingdom, and not of the British empire. Nonetheless, the religious history of the country during this period cannot be properly understood apart from the empire and the overseas missionary movement, and it is hoped that the discussion here will help promote further work on the inter-connections of religious movements in the United Kingdom and in the wider world.

CHAPTER 1

Evangelicalism, Empire and the Protestant State, 1815–1829

In 1815, the United Kingdom emerged victorious following over two decades of nearly uninterrupted warfare with revolutionary and Napoleonic France. It was now the great world power, its mastery of the seas unrivalled, and its main imperial rival, France, bled white and humbled. Developments in British manufactures, with the mechanisation of textile production, the growth of the factory system, the mobilisation of investment capital and the use of aggressive marketing techniques, were transforming the British economy and ensuring unprecedented levels of sustained economic growth. The quarter century before 1815 also witnessed a momentous expansion of British imperial dominion. The loss of the American colonies in 1783, following a prolonged and costly war, had been a blow to Britain's prestige as a world power. But during the subsequent three decades, the East India Company had greatly expanded and consolidated its control over the South Asian subcontinent, had seized Ceylon and the Cape of South Africa from the Dutch, planted a new colony in Australia and expanded trade with China. Where in 1792 there had been 26 colonies, by 1816 there were 43. The empire now became characterised by dominion over vast expanses of land, in Canada, India, Australia and South Africa, and the governance of immense numbers of non-Europeans and non-Christians, including some 87 million inhabitants of the Indian subcontinent. It was difficult for many inhabitants of the island kingdom not to view victory over revolutionary France and the acquisition of such territory and dominion as divinely ordained.[1]

Many in 1815 could not help but view the events of the quarter century of struggle in providentialist terms. The United Kingdom had triumphed over revolutionary and Napoleonic France, and established a great empire in the East. Surely the God who ruled the destinies of the world had raised the United Kingdom to such heights for a purpose? A hymn composed at the time of Britain's triumphs over Napoleonic arms expressed a sense of divine protection:

> Amidst our isle, exalted high,
> Do Thou our glory stand;
> And like a wall of guardian fire
> Surround Thy fav'rite land.[2]

There was a revival of the language of the inhabitants of Christian Britain as the Chosen People with a particular role. Admiral Nelson's famous victory at the Nile in 1799 had led to the freeing of the Holy Land from Napoleon's army – evidence of Britain's providential purpose, and linking Britain's imperial expansion with the biblical language of the Promised Land. It was in 1804 that William Blake penned his celebrated poem, 'Jerusalem', with its conception of England as the new Israel.[3] In his influential sermon, *The Star of the East*, first published in 1809, the Church of England clergyman, Claudius Buchanan, advanced a providentialist interpretation of Britain's expanding power. 'It should seem', he observed, 'as if God had selected this nation, as formerly his chosen people Israel, to preserve among men a knowledge of true religion'.[4] For some Christians, Britain's new power in the East was part of the divine plan for the spread of Christianity. 'In England', noted one clergyman in 1798, 'for some years past, the minds of christians have been unusually enlarged with a desire for the conversion of the heathen; which is a happy token that our blessed Lord is about to accomplish a glorious work in the earth'. 'Vigorous and persevering efforts', he added, 'are now making to send a cloud of missionaries to the East Indies, and to China'.[5] Some turned to prophecy to explain the events. They poured over Scripture, especially the Books of Daniel and Revelation, for explanations of the meaning of the rise of their island state, and they expressed their findings in such works as William Cunninghame's *Dissertations on the Seals and Trumpets* (1813), James Hatley Frere's *Combined View of the Christian Prophecies* (1814), and Lewis Way's *Letter to Basilicus* (1816). The London Society for Promoting Christianity among the Jews, formed in 1809, emerged as a major force from 1815 under the direction of Lewis Way – and reflected the belief that the conversion of the Jews and the second coming of Christ were fast approaching. For the London-based Scottish evangelical clergyman, Edward Irving, writing in 1826, God had been acting during the 'ominous years' of the revolutionary era to bring forth his 'long-awaited kingdom', and he 'hath chosen this nation, as he formerly made choice of Israel, to behold, declare, execute his righteous acts'.[6]

Others within the United Kingdom, however, could not share this confidence. For them, the prospects for their Christian state in 1815 seemed darker. The rapid industrialisation and urbanisation during the war years were bringing profound social dislocations. There was hardship and ruin for many handloom weavers, stocking-makers and other handicraft artisans who were now forced to compete with the new machinery. With the rapid growth of towns and cities came overcrowding, especially in decaying old town centres, and pollution, crime and disease. The end of years of warfare in 1815 also meant a severe downturn of the economy, as government military contracts ceased and tens of thousands of soldiers and sailors were demobilised. There were violent disturbances and widespread unrest and fears of revolution in a society that was becoming increasingly polarised between the rich and poor. These were the years of the Spa Fields riots of 1816, the march of the starving 'blanketeers' in 1817, the massacre at the political demonstration at St Peter's fields, Manchester, in 1819, the Cato Street conspiracy to murder the Cabinet in 1820, the 'Radical War' in the West of Scotland in 1820. This seemed far from the ideal of the chosen people, the new Israel, and the providential state.

There was still another difficulty with the notion of the providential state. In the view of many, the true greatness of the British state would be found in its Protestant constitution. It was, as the historian, Linda Colley, has emphasised, a 'Protestant state'.[7] In 1688–89, and again in 1745–46, many believed, God had delivered the British people from the danger of Continental despotism and an enforced return to Roman Catholicism. And yet, in 1801, the British state had entered into a parliamentary union with Ireland, an overwhelmingly Roman Catholic country. Of a total population of about 15,846,000 in the United Kingdom in 1801, some 5,216,000 were Irish, and of these, perhaps three-quarters were Roman Catholic. In short, about a quarter of the population of the Protestant United Kingdom was now Roman Catholic. The Government of William Pitt, moreover, had meant to follow up the Act of Union with a measure of Catholic emancipation that would have given Catholics nearly the same rights and privileges as Protestant subjects. For Pitt, this was the only way to reconcile the Irish Catholics to the Union. Pitt's plan had been thwarted in 1801 by the opposition of the king. Little more than a decade later, in 1813, Henry Grattan had brought forward another Catholic emancipation bill that had included the provision of state salaries for the Roman Catholic priests in

Ireland and that had broad support in Ireland. The bill had been abandoned. But a growing body of liberal opinion was coming to favour Catholic emancipation – and emancipation, for most Protestants, would undermine the Protestant constitution and the Protestant identity of the state.

The established churches in 1815

The United Kingdom in 1815 was a semi-confessional state, in which subjects were expected to conform to the worship, doctrine and discipline of the established church – that is, the church that was officially recognised and supported by the kingdom (England, Ireland or Scotland) in which they resided. The established churches were fundamental to the constitution of the state; they expressed the religious identity of the state, and represented the principle that society was dependent on divine favour. As the Tory politician and diarist, J. W. Croker, famously observed, 'Westminster Abbey is part of the British constitution'.[8] The established churches were responsible to the state for providing religious and moral instruction to the people. They were to provide pastoral care to parishioners, including visits to people in their homes. They offered the rites of passage – baptisms, first communions, marriages, burials – that shaped the lives of individuals within communities. There were two established churches in the United Kingdom in 1815 – the United Church of England and Ireland, and the Church of Scotland. The larger of the two, the United Church of England and Ireland, had been created by clause five of the Act of Union of 1800, which had united the established Churches of England and Ireland into 'one Protestant Episcopal Church', with a unified 'doctrine, discipline and government' which was to 'remain in full force for ever'. It was the established church of the overwhelming majority of inhabitants of the United Kingdom. The union, however, was still largely theoretical in 1815, and in the eyes of most observers, and for purposes of parliamentary legislation, the Churches of England and of Ireland remained two separate bodies.

The Church of England

The Church of England exercised ecclesiastical jurisdiction over both England and Wales. Episcopal in organisation, it included two archbishoprics, Canterbury and York, and 24 bishoprics, including four bishoprics in Wales. The British monarch was the supreme governor of the church, and the bishops, as 'lords spiritual', sat in the House of Lords, where they exercised both temporal and spiritual authority. In addition, the bishops were responsible for maintaining ecclesiastical discipline within their dioceses, for examining and ordaining new clergymen, for administering the rite of confirmation, and for conducting regular supervisory visits among the clergy. The official seat of the bishop in each diocese was the cathedral, which with its chapter house and library formed the administrative centre of the diocese. The cathedral buildings were imposing structures, towering over their cities, providing worship on a grand scale and serving as monuments to the nation's dedication to God, and as collective prayers in mortar and stone. They were served by a dean and chapter, including about a dozen prebendaries, clergymen who were expected to assist with worship and to defend and illuminate the faith through their theological scholarship and lives of conspicuous piety. The reality of early nineteenth-century cathedral life, to be sure, was somewhat less exalted. The journalist, William Cobbett, recalled attending mattins in Winchester cathedral on a Sunday in October 1825, with a total congregation of 15 women and four men in the vast empty space.[9] Many prebendaries were non-resident, taking the income but treating the office as a sinecure. Others might just as well have been non-resident, as they were quarrelsome, idle or eccentric. In 1815, there were about 780 chapter livings in the Church of England.

The church exercised pastoral supervision of the people of England and Wales through a parochial system. The country was divided into some 11,000 parishes, each with its incumbent clergyman and nearly all with a parish church. The parish clergyman was to provide regular Sunday services, to administer the sacraments, to help enforce ecclesiastical discipline and to provide pastoral care to the people of the parish. He was expected to know the boundaries of his parish, the condition of its inhabitants, the provision for the education of children and the local charities. His main responsibility was the moral and spiritual nurture of the parishioners. The parish clergy were supported from the tithes (a notional tenth of the value of agricultural produce), from rentals of church-owned property and from rents charged for seats in church. There were two main types of incumbents. Rectors were incumbents who possessed the right to all the tithes in a parish. In many parishes, however, the tithes had been granted, or appropriated, to another corporate body – for example, a college, school or cathedral. In these parishes, the clergyman was the rector's vicar, or substitute, and entitled to only a portion of the tithe. Whether he was a rector or vicar, the incumbent was under legal obligation to provide religious services to the parish population. If unable to perform the pastoral duties, he was required to provide a curate to act in his place.

The clergy were recruited mainly from the middle and lower middle social orders (substantial farmers, the urban middle classes), and large numbers were the sons of clergymen. A study of the social origins of the clergy in the diocese of London during the eighteenth century revealed that some 35 per cent were the sons of clergy, 32 per cent came from professional backgrounds, 13 per cent from the landed gentry, and 20 per cent from the labouring orders.[10] Most attended a 'public school' (independent, fee-paying school) where they were trained, often amid harsh discipline, in classical Greek and Roman literature. They then proceeded to Oxford or Cambridge University, where they continued their classical education, picking up some theology along the way. There was very little by way of what we might call professional training in liturgy, preaching or pastoral care. The more ambitious went out of their way to associate with the sons of the gentry and aristocracy and to cultivate connections with potential future patrons. Clerical incomes, meanwhile, rose steadily during the later eighteenth and early nineteenth centuries, along with the general rise in agricultural incomes which resulted from more commercial methods of agriculture, including the enclosures of estates, improved drainage of land and better crop rotations. By the early nineteenth century, many parish clergy were able to emulate the manners of the landed gentry, and were keeping carriages, riding to hounds, collecting books, and building spacious and comfortable residence houses. It was the 'age of the country rectory' and Augustus Hare's description of Alderley Rectory in early nineteenth-century Cheshire captures the idyllic comfort of many such homes: it was 'a low house with a verandah forming a wide balcony for the upper story, where birdcages hung among the roses; its rooms and passages filled with pictures, books, and old carved oak furniture'.[11] 'These were', recalled the novelist, Anthony Trollope, 'halcyon days' for the clergy, when 'the parson in his parsonage was as good a gentleman as any squire in his mansion or nobleman in his castle'.[12] Parsons were indeed becoming more socially respectable, better able to mix with the upper social orders, than their eighteenth-century predecessors, but they were also growing more distant from the majority of their parishioners.

The doctrine of the Church of England was defined loosely by the Thirty-nine Articles of Faith, a collection of short summaries of belief, open to broad interpretation and intended to represent an inclusive, comprehensive national faith, shaped from Scripture, the traditions of the church and the light of reason. More important than the Articles in defining the faith of the national church, however, was the Book of Common Prayer, rooted in pre-Reformation service books, produced during the sixteenth century and reaching its final form in 1662. Church-goers in England would have heard its sombre cadences and rich prose repeated Sunday after Sunday throughout their lives, until it was etched into their memories and informed their lives. The church was the largest and most imposing building in most parishes. It was often a time-honoured, medieval structure, whose worn stones had watched over generation after generation of worshippers, while in the churchyard, where parishioners gathered to gossip before and after Sunday services, were buried the ancestors. Most early nineteenth-century church interiors reflected the simple austerity of seventeenth-century Puritanism and eighteenth-century rationalism. They were dominated by the pulpit, often a high, triple-decked structure; the clergy dressed in black Genevan gowns. Walls were generally whitewashed, covering the richly coloured murals that might have once adorned the pre-Reformation interior. The naves were often obstructed by the high-backed, boxed private pews of the rich, and gradations of wealth and status were reflected in the seating arrangements within the church.

In their sermons and pastoral visiting, the parish clergy generally gave emphasis to the Pauline virtues of passive obedience and non-resistance to the powers that be, deference to social superiors, and acceptance of the existing social order as part of the providential plan. The parish formed the fundamental unit of local government. The parish vestry was made up of the incumbent and all the parishioners who owned or occupied property that was taxed for poor relief. It had the power to levy local taxes for poor relief and for the repair of roads and bridges, and it frequently had responsibility for administering endowments for schools or charity. The parish vestry appointed the two churchwardens, who collected the rate for the repair of the church building. Churchwardens also supervised discipline in the parish, and had the power to summon people to appear before the diocesan or bishop's court for such infractions as extra-marital sex, drunkenness, brawling in the churchyard, or libel – though by 1815 such summons had become rare. If the diocesan courts had declined in use, however, the parish clergy were exercising judicial authority through their role as magistrates. From about 1760, the clergy were increasingly appointed to the magistrates' bench in England and Wales, and shared in hearing civil cases and imposing civil penalties, including the death penalty. In 1815, perhaps a quarter of all magistrates in England and Wales were clergymen, and one clergyman in every six was a magistrate. Some were uncomfortable with the idea that clergymen, with a sacred responsibility for proclaiming the gospel of mercy and forgiveness, should also pass civil sentences and impose the penalty of death. Labouring people would not soon forget that two clerical magistrates signed the order for the yeomanry to attack the unarmed demonstrators on St Peter's field, Manchester, in 1819, killing 11, including two women, and wounding some 400, and that one of these clerical magistrates, the Revd W. R. Hay, assumed a leading role in defending the action, for which he was rewarded with the rich living of Rochdale and a stall in York Minster.[13] For others, however, the large number of clerical magistrates represented the union of church and state for the right ordering of the Christian commonwealth. It was proper that clergymen should use their wisdom and influence to help maintain the social order that God had ordained. In a sermon published in 1819, for example, J. W. Cunningham, the evangelical vicar of Harrow, called attention to the 'intimate alliance, in every age, between irreligion and disloyalty. The invaders of the altar are commonly the assailants of the throne'.[14]

In much of England and Wales, the social and religious order represented by the established Church of England had become severely weakened by 1815. The old ideal of the parish system was breaking down in parts of the country. For many people, the parish church had ceased to form a centre of their lives and the parish incumbent was not the pastor of their souls. One cause of this breakdown was the rigidity of the parish system. The parish boundaries had been largely fixed in the later middle ages; they reflected the patterns of population in late medieval England and Wales, and they were strictly defined by law. However, while the number and size of parish churches had remained largely unchanged, the general population of England and Wales had nearly doubled during the eighteenth century, with the result that a large and increasing portion of the population could not be accommodated in the parish church. Further, there had been considerable shifts in the population, with particular growth in London and the manufacturing and mining districts of the midlands and the north. In these areas, the existing parish system was often totally inadequate. There were, moreover, serious legal difficulties with subdividing parishes or erecting new churches in existing parishes; such changes required acts of Parliament, which could be extremely expensive to secure. In London, or Manchester, or Liverpool, there were parishes with populations of 15,000 to 20,000, far beyond the capacity of any parish incumbent to provide pastoral care. The parish of St Pancras, London, in 1815 had a population of 50,000, and a church that could seat 200.[15] In many parishes, moreover, the tithes and rentals were insufficient to provide a decent living for the incumbent. In 1809, according to returns by the bishops to Parliament, some 3,300 parish livings, nearly a third of the total, were worth less than £150 a year, hardly enough to support a married man with a family at a respectable level, while 860 parish livings were valued at less than £50 a year.

There were also problems with clerical discipline. Stories of clerical greed, laziness and sexual misconduct have been common to the church in all ages, and such stories were often greatly exaggerated. However, there was enough truth in the allegations about the Church of England clergy in 1815 to cause alarm among even the church's warmest supporters. There was widespread pluralism, or the holding of more than one church living. According to bishops' returns to Parliament in 1831, more than a third of the parish clergy in the Church of England held more than one living, and some 6 per cent held three or more livings. In many cases this pluralism was defensible; for example, it might be sensible to combine two small, neighbouring rural parishes by placing both under single clergyman. However, in many other cases, pluralism was simply the means for a clergyman to increase his income, the parishes were some distance apart, and there was a serious neglect of pastoral duties. There was also considerable non-residence among parish clergymen. In the parish ideal, the clergyman resided in the parish, shared in their communal life, inspired his neighbours by his example of righteous living and was available to visit the sick and the dying. In 1831, however, less than half of the parishes of England and Wales had a parish clergyman who resided within the parish boundaries. In many cases, the technically non-resident parish clergyman lived just outside the parish; but not a few clergy resided at considerable distances from the parishes and seldom if ever visited them. Excuses for non-residence generally related to health, and a considerable number of clerics felt obliged for medical reasons to live in fashionable spa towns, while their flocks managed somehow to survive in their unhealthy rustic surroundings.

When an incumbent could not, or would not, serve the parish, he was expected to provide a curate to perform the pastoral duties, and to pay the curate from the income of the parish living. Lord Harrowby's Curates' Act of 1813 provided some regulation of the conditions of employment for curates and eliminated the most scandalous abuses of curates by incumbents. None the less, the curate's lot was often a sad one. Poorly paid, frequently living in sparsely furnished rented rooms, with few books, threadbare clothes, and little prospect for advancement, they were the 'serfs' of the church, and frequently grew despondent or resentful. 'There is something', observed Sydney Smith, 'which excites compassion in the very name of a curate! A learned man in a hovel, with sermons and saucepans, lexicons and bacon, Hebrew books and ragged children . . . the first and purest pauper in the hamlet'.[16] Adding to the difficulties was the institution of patronage. Virtually every church living had its patron, who had the right to present an ordained clergyman to the office. The patronage of a living, or advowson, was a form of private property, which could be bought and sold. Advowsons were frequently advertised for purchase in the newspapers. About half were in the possession of corporate bodies or ecclesiastical dignitaries – colleges, cathedral chapters, bishops. But the other half were owned by private individuals, generally members of the landed classes. Patronage could lead to scandalous appointments, men more concerned to please their patrons than to serve as pastors to the common people and friends of the poor. Further, it was not uncommon for a clergyman to purchase an advowson and present himself to the living. All these factors combined to weaken the parochial establishment at a time when it needed flexibility and commitment to respond to the challenges of rapid industrialisation and urbanisation.

The Church of Ireland

If the Church of England was in difficulties in 1815, the situation of its sister establishment across the Irish Sea was even less enviable. The Church of Ireland, like its sister establishment, was Protestant and episcopal. Its doctrine was defined by the Thirty-nine Articles of Faith, and its worship by the Book of Common Prayer. Its clergy were recruited from the middling social orders, and educated mainly at Trinity College, Dublin, with its imposing neo-classical buildings. It ministered to its people through a parochial system, with parish vestries and churchwardens. There was, however, a major difference between it and the Church of England. While the established church in England and Wales could claim to minister to the majority of the population in the two countries in 1815, in Ireland the established church ministered to only a small minority, perhaps as little as 10 per cent of the Irish people – while some 80 per cent of the population was Roman Catholic and a further 10 per cent consisted of Protestant Dissenters, mainly Presbyterians. Although the established church, it was deeply resented as an alien presence by the overwhelming majority of the Irish people. It was in many respects the church of an imperial garrison.

There were four archbishops and 18 bishops in the Church of Ireland – representing a hierarchy nearly equal to that of the far larger Church of England. By the terms of the Act of Union, four Irish bishops sat in the

House of Lords, with a prescribed order of rotation. Most of the Irish dioceses had a cathedral, though these were generally modest structures. The cathedral chapters provided about 320 livings; these were mainly sinecures, with relatively few prebendaries actually performing the duties connected with their office. There were about 1,200 parish livings in Ireland, with the parish clergy supported from tithes and rentals. In Ireland, the burden of paying tithe fell overwhelmingly on the Catholic peasantry. In Munster and much of Leinster, even potatoes, the mainstay of the poorest classes, were subject to tithe. While legally responsible to provide religious services to the whole population, in practice, the Church of Ireland clergy restricted their ministry to adherents of their church, leaving the Catholics and Protestant Dissenters alone. There were parishes in Ireland, with well-paid incumbents, that had, apart from the incumbent's family, no more than two or three adherents of the established church, and in some cases, no adherents of the established church. It was not uncommon for the incumbent to preach on a Sunday to a congregation consisting of his own family and that of the Protestant landlord, if a service was held at all. This was scarcely an edifying picture, with one of the poorest peasantries in Western Europe forced to pay a heavy burden of tithe to support the clergy of a minority Protestant establishment – a clergy who, on the whole, felt little responsibility for their Roman Catholic parishioners.

Until the last decades of the eighteenth century, the Irish state had helped to maintain the Protestant establishment through the imposition of penal legislation directed against the Catholic majority. Passed by the Irish Parliament in the last years of the seventeenth and early years of the eighteenth century, following the defeat of the Jacobite rising of 1689–91 in Ireland, the penal laws had been intended to reduce the Irish Catholics to a position of permanent subservience, deprived of the legal right to own property, carry arms, serve in government or educate their children. The first three decades of the eighteenth century were the worst of the penal times and from about 1730, as the threat of a further Jacobite rising in Ireland diminished, the acts were not so rigidly enforced. Under the influence of Enlightenment ideas of toleration, the penal acts began to be repealed from the later 1770s, until by the mid-1790s most of the penal legislation had been withdrawn. None the less, it had left a permanent legacy of bitterness among the Catholic population, with communal memory recalling the days, for example, when Catholic children could be taught only in 'hedge schools', clustered against a hedge or escarpment for protection from the weather, while a watch had to look out for law officers or yeomanry. Such memories encouraged Irish Catholics to press all the more vigorously for full emancipation from all their remaining civil disabilities. The position of Irish Presbyterians was more ambiguous. On the one hand, since 1672 they had been granted (with occasional periods of lapse) a *regium donum*, or royal grant towards the payment of their clergy. This had been significantly increased after 1798, and was intended to promote Presbyterian loyalty to the state. On the other hand, as Dissenters from the established church, Presbyterians had also been subject to civil disabilities through much of the eighteenth century, at least until the repeal of the Irish Test Act in 1780, and they were also required to pay tithe to support an established church that they could not in conscience attend. As a result, probably most Irish Presbyterians also harboured deep resentments against the Church of Ireland.

The Irish establishment was becoming less and less defensible by 1815. It was not only a minority establishment, supported by tithes levied on Catholic and Presbyterian farmers who deeply resented its presence. It was also riddled with corruption. A survey of the Irish church, commissioned by the archbishop of Armagh in 1807, reported on 1,133 clergy. Of these, 561 were habitually non-resident and 274 were pluralists. A further survey in 1808 revealed that of 775 parishes for which reports were received, only 582 had churches in good repair and only 199 had glebe houses (residence houses) fit for habitation.[17] The Church of Ireland in 1815 did, to be sure, comprise many men and women of genuine commitment, who believed sincerely that theirs was the one true catholic and apostolic church in Ireland, and who viewed themselves as guardians of God's truth in a hostile land. There were church leaders of talent and commitment, among them John Jebb, the future bishop of Limerick, Alexander Knox, an influential lay theologian, William Magee, another prominent theologian and bishop of Raphoe, and Peter Roe, a committed evangelical pastor and rector of Odogh. None the less, the condition of the established church in Ireland as a whole was scandalous and, in the eyes of many, it was becoming an obstacle to the consolidation of the Union.

The Church of Scotland

The established Church of Scotland differed in fundamental ways from the established churches in England and Ireland. The churches of England and Ireland, as we have seen, were very similar in doctrine, liturgy and organisation, and they had been united in 1801. The Church of Scotland, however, was radically different in doctrine, liturgy and organisation – so much so, that the Church of Scotland and the United Church of England

and Ireland did not recognise each other as true churches of Christ. It was a curious situation: the same state recognised two churches as established within its territories, while those two churches viewed each other as in grave error. The established churches in England and Ireland were episcopalian in structure, with their doctrine defined by the Thirty-nine Articles and their liturgy by the Book of Common Prayer. In Scotland, however, the established church was Presbyterian in structure, its doctrine was defined by the Westminster Confession of Faith, and its worship by the Westminster Directory. The Scottish establishment had no bishops, cathedrals, cathedral chapters, rectors, vicars or curates. To travel north of the Tweed was to enter a different ecclesiastical world. This situation had developed because the Scottish Reformation had taken a different direction from that in England, and because the Stewart monarchs in the seventeenth century had been unsuccessful in their attempt to impose an episcopalian system upon Scotland.

The Church of Scotland was governed not by bishops, but by a hierarchy of church courts. One of the salient features of the Presbyterianism was the parity of ministers, with no single minister superior to, or exercising authority over, a fellow minister. Another feature was a commitment to imposing a godly discipline on the whole of society, so that the social order would approach a Scriptural model of justice and harmony. At the base of the Scottish Presbyterian system of courts was the parish kirk-session, made up of the minister and a number of elders, usually about 12, selected from among male heads of family in the parish on the grounds of their conspicuous piety and morality. Both the minister and elders were ordained, with the minister sometimes referred to as a 'teaching elder' and the others as 'ruling elders'. Only the minister was paid a stipend, or salary, drawn from the teinds (a Scottish form of the tithe, levied on the produce of agriculture and fishing), and from rentals on seats in the church. Ministers were drawn mainly from the sons of substantial farmers, urban merchants or professionals. They were educated at one of Scotland's five universities (St Andrews, Glasgow, Edinburgh, Marischal College, Aberdeen, and King's College, Aberdeen) – where they were expected to complete both a four-year Arts course and a four-year Divinity course. There were nearly 1,000 parishes in Scotland, each with its kirk-session of minister and elders, who were jointly responsible for providing religious and moral instruction to the parishioners, and for enforcing ecclesiastical discipline, summoning persons to appear before the session for such infractions as extra-marital sex, drunkenness, brawling and libel, hearing evidence, admonishing those found guilty, and imposing penances, which usually involved standing, dressed in sackcloth, before the congregation for a specified number of Sundays. Kirk-sessions also shared in the responsibility of providing parish poor relief (generally from collections taken at the church door before services) and supervising parish schools.

Above the kirk-session was the presbytery, which was made up of the minister and one ruling elder from several neighbouring parishes, and which was responsible for overseeing overall church life and public morals within the presbytery boundaries. There were 69 presbyteries in the Church of Scotland in 1815. Presbyteries could hear appeals against the decisions of kirk-sessions, and they were also responsible for examining and licensing candidates for the ministry, for ordaining new ministers and for supervising the work of the ministers within their boundaries. Presbyteries could also formulate 'overtures', or proposals for new church laws or policies, and submit these for consideration by the higher church courts. Above the presbytery was the synod, made up of all the members of several neighbouring presbyteries, and which met usually twice a year, in the spring and autumn, to oversee the activities of the kirk-sessions and presbyteries, hear appeals and recommend overtures. Finally, at the top of the system was the General Assembly, the supreme ecclesiastical court in Scotland, which met once a year in Edinburgh for a week-long session. It was made up of some 360 ministers and elders representing the presbyteries, royal burghs and universities of Scotland. It was the court of final appeal in all disciplinary cases, and also had the power to approve new church laws and policies.

The doctrine of the Church of Scotland was defined by the Westminster Confession of Faith, a statement of strict Calvinism, which placed emphasis on the power of God, salvation by grace alone, and 'election', or the doctrine that God had predestined from before all time only a limited number of souls for eternal salvation. Many Scots would have memorised from childhood the Shorter Catechism, a collection of questions and answers designed to present the doctrines of the Westminster Confession in a simplified form. Worship was defined by the Westminster Directory, with emphasis on the sermon, Scripture readings and the congregational singing of the Psalms, unaccompanied by musical instruments. By tradition, the Church of Scotland represented a highly communal faith. Kirk-session discipline was communal in character, and those guilty of infractions were publicly admonished and performed their penance before the assembled congregation. The celebration of holy communion was a social occasion, held twice a year in most parishes, with the ministers and congregations from neighbouring parishes invited to participate in an occasion which lasted up to four days. In the distribution of poor relief, kirk-sessions emphasised communal responsibility toward the aged and infirm, while they usually denied relief to the able-bodied, who were expected to pull their own weight. Scotland prided itself on its system of parish schools, which aimed at providing Christian primary education for all children of both sexes and at preparing boys (alas, only boys) of ability for university study, regardless of their incomes and status of their parents.

However, by 1815, this communal ideal was breaking down in much of Scotland. The eighteenth-century age of improvement had brought increased wealth to the country, but also increased the social divisions between rich and poor. An elite culture developed in Edinburgh, Glasgow, Aberdeen and other towns – with theatres, concert halls, debating clubs and private members clubs providing rival attractions to the pulpit and Bible. Urban kirk-sessions largely ceased trying to impose a strict Calvinist discipline, especially on the middle and upper classes, and increasingly restricted themselves to admonishing unmarried and pregnant young women who wished to have their children baptised. The Scottish universities, meanwhile, were gaining international reputations for excellence in teaching and scholarship, especially in the fields of moral philosophy and medicine. Many were imbibing the thought of the Enlightenment, with its emphasis on reason, progress and the harmonies of nature; as they did so, they grew uncomfortable with the rigid Calvinism of the Westminster Confession, and especially the doctrine of election, with its claim that only a limited number would be saved, and that they would be saved 'by grace alone' and not through their own merits. For enlightened thinkers, this appeared contrary to both reason and morality.

Among the clergy, a Moderate party emerged by the 1750s, made up of clergy who embraced much of the thought of the Enlightenment, contributed to the culture of improvement in Scotland through literary work, and played down the harsher aspects of Calvinism. In their sermons, they emphasised practical virtue and a reasonable faith. They supported the Patronage Act of 1712, which had restored the rights of patrons to present candidates to vacant parish livings in Scotland. Nearly every parish in Scotland had its patron, with about two-thirds of the church patronage belonging to the gentry and aristocracy and about one third to the crown. Although patronage was unpopular in Scotland (most parishioners believed that ministers should be elected by the godly people), Moderates maintained that patrons tended to present a better sort of minister, men of cultivated tastes and refined manners, who would exercise a civilising influence on their parishioners. They also believed patronage would strengthen connections between the clergy of the established church and the wealthy propertied elite in Scotland. The Moderate party, with the support of the state, dominated the upper church courts, especially the General Assembly, from the mid-1760s. Under Moderate influence, much of the clergy drew away from the traditional communal culture of Scottish Presbyterianism, and grew more distant from the majority of their parishioners. In response, many parishioners hated the Moderate ascendancy and the system of patronage. Some withdrew from the established church, to join one of the Dissenting churches in Scotland, and by 1790 perhaps 10 per cent of the Scottish population was outside the established church.

The evangelical revival and the growth of Dissent

Among the many difficulties facing established religion in 1815, perhaps the greatest was the haemorrhage of people out of the established churches, and the growing popular opposition to the very idea of state-maintained religious establishments. Throughout the North Atlantic world the eighteenth century had witnessed a resurgence of vital, evangelical religion. This evangelical revival was based upon an intense conviction of sin and of humankind's inability through their own merits ever to satisfy the demands of divine justice. It included a passionate belief that only by being 'converted' – only by accepting Jesus Christ as one's personal saviour, and truly believing that Christ had atoned for the sins of humankind by His crucifixion on the cross – could people hope to be saved from the everlasting torment of hell and to know the eternal bliss of heaven. Conversion set individuals free from the terrors and punishments of the divine law, and enabled them to know the saving power of divine grace. The experience of saving grace through Christ led converts to seek to lead disciplined, godly lives, to grow in the faith through personal Bible reading, and to strive to bring the gospel message of salvation to all people. Many of those affected by this fiery faith found the religious life of the established churches cold, formal and overly politicised. They grew convinced that the Christian faith was a warm, emotive, personal relationship between the sinful individual and the saving Christ, and that it was wrong for the state to attempt to enforce Christian faith or to give its support to any particular religious denomination. Had not Christ proclaimed that His kingdom was not of this world? The awakening of evangelical piety transformed religious life in the United Kingdom, especially during the years from 1790 to 1815, when the state was involved in the prolonged war with revolutionary and Napoleonic France, and when new ideas, not only about political organisation, but about the nature and destiny of humankind swirled about. These were years of enthusiasm, in both religion and politics.

As the historian W. R. Ward has argued, the evangelical awakening in the eighteenth-century North Atlantic world probably had its origins among displaced Protestants in Central Europe in the aftermath of the Thirty Years War.[18] The Peace of Westphalia in 1648 had drawn lines between Catholic, Lutheran and Calvinist Central Europe. However, some peoples had found themselves on the wrong side of the divide – for example, Calvinist remnants in Catholic Bohemia. Such peoples, marginalised and threatened with persecution, sometimes formed their own religious societies for prayer, worship and instruction. A heartfelt, strict, biblical and often highly personal piety developed within these communities. This intense piety spread through the North Atlantic community, carried by religious refugees, migrants and missionaries, and communicated by a growing print literature of tracts, published sermons, pious biographies, hymnbooks and devotional guides. In Britain, the emotive evangelical piety emerged first in Wales, where from the mid-1730s it was spread through itinerant preaching by the evangelical Anglicans, Howell Harris and Daniel Rowlands, who would preach in barns, cottages, roadsides and open fields, wherever they could gather a crowd. The England, the evangelical Anglicans, George Whitefield and John and Charles Wesley, began itinerant preaching from 1738, and their eloquence and passion for souls brought them followers, including other Anglican clerics who joined them in itinerant preaching. Soon Whitefield and John Wesley were gathering crowds of up to 20,000 at open-air services, and thousands were converted under their influence. Dubbed 'Methodists' for their strict and methodical style of Christian living, the followers of Whitefield and the Wesleys began forming separate 'class meetings' for prayer, Bible-reading and mutual support. The Methodist movement made its way to Ireland, mainly Ulster, in the 1740s. In Scotland, the first major manifestation of the evangelical awakening was a large-scale revival at Cambuslang and Kilsyth, near Glasgow, in 1741–42, which drew crowds of 20,000–30,000 for open-air preaching. Thousands were converted, often amid scenes of intense emotion, including convulsions, fainting, uncontrollable weeping and screams. In the aftermath of the revival, prayer meetings were formed in parishes across the Scottish Lowlands. The Presbyterian Scots did not, on the whole, warm to Whitefield or the Wesleys, and their evangelical movement did not take a Methodist direction. But many Scots embraced a similar heartfelt, Bible-based and conversionist faith.

Leaders of the evangelical awakening initially sought to keep their movement within the established churches. They were, for the most part, conservative in their thinking, and believed in the ideal of the Christian commonwealth, in which godly magistrates would co-operate with godly clergymen in providing religious instruction and spiritual discipline to all the inhabitants of the land. Their aim was to quicken the spiritual life in the established churches through itinerant preaching and prayer societies. But Methodist itinerant preachers also refused to allow parish boundaries to interfere with what they viewed as their higher calling to preach the gospel to all people, and this created tensions between their movement and the established church. Many parish clergy objected to the appearance of Methodist itinerants within their parish boundaries, and viewed the formation of prayer meetings among their parishioners as divisive and impertinent. The itinerants' insistence on the sinful nature of all humanity and the equality of all souls could even seem to threaten the social hier- archy. During the 1740s and 1750s, while the parish clergy and local magistrates turned a blind eye, mobs, often incited by a 'church in Danger' sermon and warmed with free ale at a public house, attacked Methodist gatherings and burned their meeting houses. John Wesley's journal recorded some 40 separate riots directed against Methodist meetings. Wesley hoped to keep his followers within the established church. But by the 1780s, the Methodists were being forced out of the Church of England, largely through the efforts of local magistrates, who forced them to register their society meeting houses as Dissenting places of worship under the terms of the Toleration Act of 1689. Wesley contributed to this growing breach between the Methodists and the established church when in the 1780s he began ordaining preachers for the Methodist movement in North America. As he was not a bishop in the Church of England, he had no authority to ordain, and his actions thus challenged Anglican ecclesiastical authority. The numbers of Methodists, meanwhile, continued to grow, reaching some 56,600 by 1791.[19]

The later eighteenth century also witnessed a significant growth in older Protestant Dissenting sects. These Dissenting sects were remnants of the radical religious groups that had emerged during the religious and civil strife of the seventeenth century. In England, the old Dissenters included Congregationalists, who were Reformed, or Calvinist, in theology and who believed that each local church should be autonomous, self-governing and independent, recognising only Christ as head of the church and seeking to reflect the simplicity of the early church. There were Baptists, who believed that only committed adult believers should be baptised and who generally practised baptism by immersion. Among the Baptists, the majority were General Baptists, who subscribed to an Arminian theology emphasising the freedom of the human will to accept the gospel offer, while a minority were Particular Baptists, who held to a predestinarian Calvinistic theology. There were English Presbyterians, who organised themselves on the Presbyterian model and subscribed to Calvinism of the Westminster Confession of Faith – though a growing number of Presbyterian churches during the eighteenth century were embracing an Arian theology, which denied that Jesus Christ was truly God. Further, there was the Society of Friends, or Quakers, who held that Christ spoke directly to each believer through the Holy Spirit, and that there was no need for an ordained clergy; at their meetings, friends, men and women, were encouraged to speak as the Spirit moved them. They emphasised pacifism, and a plainness of speech and dress. In Scotland, there were Episcopalians, who believed in church government by bishops and whose doctrine was defined by the Thirty-nine Articles. They had been driven from the Church of Scotland after the re-establishment of Presbyterianism in 1690. There were Reformed, or Cameronian, Presbyterians, who had separated in 1690 from a Church of Scotland which they viewed as insufficiently zealous for a godly discipline, and there were small bodies of Congregationalists and Baptists. In Ireland, there were separate communions of Presbyterians.

These Dissenting groups had grown inward-looking and sectarian in attitude during the early decades of the eighteenth century. They viewed themselves as chosen peoples, removed from the world – part of a succession of true believers called to preserve the purity of the faith that had been bequeathed to them by the parents and grandparents. They often insisted upon marriage within the communion. Theirs was often a deep, heartfelt piety, as expressed in the hymns of Isaac Watts or the theological learning of Phillip Doddridge or in meeting houses of austere dignity. They were not, however, active in evangelising, and their numbers fell through death and lapsing. By 1740, the Dissenters had declined to perhaps 5 per cent of the population of England, Wales and Scotland, and perhaps 10 per cent of the population of Ireland. Then, from the 1760s, amid the new fervour of the evangelical revival, there was a quickening of Dissent. A number of Congregationalists, Baptists, English Presbyterians, and other Dissenters came out of their 'walled gardens' and embraced a passion to save lost souls before they perished forever in the fiery pit. They followed the example of the Methodists and began preaching a pure and simple gospel, and they showed a new willingness to confront openly the authority of the established clergy.

The social and political unrest that followed the beginning of the French Revolution contributed further to the new evangelical zeal among the Dissenters. The democratic ideas associated with the events in France encouraged the notion that each individual, no matter how lowly the social status, was of equal value before God and had an eternal destiny. All, therefore, must be given the gospel message and must work out, in fear and trembling, their salvation. There was also a sense of millennial excitement, a belief that events in France marked indeed a new dawn for humankind. In 1793, the French Republic executed the king, overthrew the established Catholic church, and then embarked on a campaign to eradicate Christianity. When Britain went to war against the French Republic in 1793, many Christians viewed it as a war unlike previous wars, a struggle for the survival of Christian civilisation. In 1798 French Revolutionary armies overran the papal states, seized the infirm Pope Pius VI and removed him from Rome in captivity. Referred to by his captors simply as 'citizen Braschi', he died in Valence in the south of France in 1799, and his body lay unburied for months. After some months of confusion, a conclave of cardinals met near Venice and elected a new pope, Luigi Chiaramonti, who took the name Pius VII. But the election was controversial, and it was not clear that the new pope would be accepted by the whole church. Was this not a sign of a new dispensation, a working out of a providential plan? 'Rome', observed an English Protestant author in 1800, 'has felt the shocks of revolution, and its politico-ecclesiastical government is, at present, extinct. The kingdom of the beast is fast filling with darkness'.[20] The 1790s were also a time of economic distress, as the pressures of war exacerbated the tensions associated with the forces of industrialisation and urbanisation.

Amid this unrest, the numbers of Methodists and other evangelical Dissenters grew rapidly. Dissenters formed voluntary societies to support itinerant preaching. They were anxious to reach and convert the souls of labouring people, including those residing in the new industrial villages mushrooming about the countryside, often on the outskirts of parishes and at some distance from the parish churches. They were desperate to save the souls of the lowly and despised, souls which they recognised as having eternal value. Hundreds of itinerant preachers, many scarcely literate but filled with a burning passion to save souls, travelled through the villages, preached in fields, cottages or barns, lived on what the local labouring poor could provide them, made converts and gathered them into congregations.

The meetings were often loud, rowdy and coarse, with direct, homely and hellfire preaching, intense calls upon sinners to convert, and cries and convulsions among the hearers. 'To such a pitch of frenzy', noted an observer of such a meeting in 1820, 'are they at times wound up, that their gesture and actions assimilate nearer to the orgies of the Heathen, than to the dignified deportment... of the Christian worshipper'.[21] The itinerants brought a simple message of human sin and depravity, of the eternal torments of the damned, of salvation through the atoning sacrifice of Christ, and of sanctification under the influence of the Holy Spirit.

The movement of evangelical Dissent had particular success in areas where the parish structures of the established churches were weakest – in the north and west of England, in Wales and in the Highlands and islands of Scotland. It found fertile ground in mining areas, seaports and fishing villages, new factory towns and settlements by canals. The early itinerants included forceful women preachers, such as Ann, 'Praying Nanny' Cutler, Mary Barritt or Elizabeth Tomlinson (who was later portrayed as the character 'Dinah Morris' in George Eliot's novel, *Adam Bede*).[22] Moreover, a majority of members of the Methodist societies throughout England and Wales were women – about 58 per cent between 1759 and 1832.[23] In the early years of the nineteenth century, evangelists from North America, including the wild-eyed and black-bearded Lorenzo Dow, brought to Britain and Ireland the roughcast methods of religious revival from the western frontier, including the outdoor 'camp meeting' which would bring hundreds to an open field for several days of preaching and prayer. The first English camp meeting was held in 1807 at Mow Cop, in Staffordshire. The supporters of the camp meetings were expelled from the emerging Methodist church in 1811, but they formed themselves into a new denomination, the Primitive Methodists, and continued to pursue converts among the labouring poor. 'Our chapels', a founder of the Primitive Methodists, the millwright and lay preacher, Hugh Bourne, later recalled, 'were the coal-pit banks, or any other place; and in our conversation way, we preached the Gospel to all, good or bad, rough or smooth'.[24] Another Methodist preacher, the former draper, William O'Bryan, was expelled from the Methodist communion in 1815 for irregular evangelistic methods in rural Devon and Cornwall. He formed the denomination of Bible Christians, which was distinguished in its early years by admitting women to the ministry equally with men.

The growth of Dissent was staggering. In the decade 1781–1790, the registrars-general certified 738 Dissenting places of worship under the terms of the Toleration Act. This number increased to 2,065 for the decade

1791–1800 and 5,671 for the decade 1811–1820.[25] The Methodist membership, including secession groups, increased from some 56,600 in 1791 to 213,500 in 1821, while it is estimated that for every member, there were five more who regularly attended Methodist services. Baptists, Congregationalists and Presbyterian Seceders also experienced significant growth. For nervous members of the established churches, the growth of the various Dissenting sects could appear to form one large movement. 'These sectarists', complained the high church clergyman, H. H. Norris, to Lord Liverpool in 1813, 'consider the whole sectarian fraternity as embarked on one course'. 'There is', he added of his neighbourhood of London, 'one or other sectarian conventicle open for the purpose of poisoning the minds of the poor *every* night'.[26]

The rapid growth of evangelical Dissent was accompanied by new religious movements that looked for the imminent return of Christ in glory and the advent of the millennium of rule by the saints, in fulfilment of scriptural prophecy. The Church of the New Jerusalem, based on the writings of the Swedish mystic, Emanuel Swedenborg, was established in London in 1787, and 'New Jerusalemite' sects spread through England. There was a revival of the Muggletonians, an obscure seventeenth-century sect, with their belief that the age of the Spirit had begun and that the New Jerusalem would come to earth. In 1794, Richard Brothers, a retired naval officer, proclaimed himself to be the nephew of Christ and the king of the Hebrews. He insisted that only his direct intercession had spared London from utter destruction in January 1791 by the wrath of the righteous God.[27] He promised to gather all the Jews – including 'hidden Jews' who had assimilated into gentile society centuries earlier and lost their identity – and lead them back to the Holy Land to welcome Christ's return. In 1792, the former dairymaid and domestic servant, Joanna Southcott, claimed that she was 'the woman clothed with the sun' from the Book of Revelation and began preaching. By 1802, she had become the leader of a new religious movement, by which she claimed the power to 'seal' the 'true believers' for salvation, in anticipation of the imminent final judgement. By 1814, an estimated 20,000 had come forward to be sealed. She died in that year, after having failed in her promise to give birth to the messianic Shiloh, but her followers, or Southcottians, continued, believing that the birth of Shiloh had been a purely spiritual event and that the second coming was still imminent. In Ulster, there was a spread of prophetic and apocalyptic visions among the Presbyterians in the mid-1790s, associated with the social and political unrest in the North that contributed to the rising of 1798. Francis Dobbs announced in the Irish House of Commons in 1799 that Armageddon was soon be fought in County Armagh. It was an era of prophecies, fearsome visions and new hopes. It was a time, the poet Robert Southey observed in 1808, when

One madman printed his dreams, another his day-visions; one had seen an angel come out of the sun with a drawn sword in his hand, another had seen fiery dragons in the air, and hosts of angels in battle array . . . The lower classes . . . began to believe that the Seven Seals were about to be opened.[28]

Amid the excitement of these years, some rejected Christianity altogether. Many labouring people were attracted to the deism of the former Quaker and revolutionary pamphleteer, Tom Paine, especially his *Age of Reason* (1794–95), with its portrayal of established Christianity as a prop of the ruling elite. Robert Owen, the manager of a cotton mill at New Lanark in Scotland, developed a socialist vision of a society organised in small communities, with the means of production owned in common and decisions made by the adult members of the community as a whole. He sought to put his ideas into practice in his New Lanark mill community and published his ideas in *A New View of Society* (1813). In 1817, Owen announced his break with Christianity, and began preaching a new religion of socialism with a millenarian faith in a divine promise of social perfection in the present generation. He rejected all existing religions, in favour of his socialist faith. 'My conviction', Owen wrote candidly to the Scottish evangelical clergyman, Thomas Chalmers, in April 1820, 'is that they [existing religions] are directly calculated to destroy the first feelings of human nature and pervert the best faculties which belong to it and that while they should be taught men cannot become either good, wise or happy'.[29] In 1825, Owen's followers established a socialist community at Ormiston, near Glasgow, calling themselves the 'First Society of Adherents to Divine Revelation'. Other Owenite communities were established across Britain and North America. While some were attracted to this religion of socialism, others rejected any religious foundation to society and called for radical social reforms based on an essentially materialist view of the world. These Radicals included the Scottish writer for the East India Company, James Mill, the London tailor and journalist, Francis Place, the journalist, Richard Carlile, and the philosopher, Jeremy Bentham.

The 25 years between 1790 and 1815 had witnessed an unprecedented growth of Dissent. During these years, a significant portion of the population of the United Kingdom decided to remove themselves from the established order in church and state. They left the parish church, with all its historic associations – the often venerable building with its centuries of history, the church tower and bell which signified the communal life, the churchyard where the ancestors were buried and where neighbours met to exchange gossip, the rites of passage and the festival services – and found their way into a meeting house, perhaps only a hired room or a member's cottage. They became Dissenters, who deliberately took themselves outside the parish community in obedience to what they viewed as a higher call. In many cases, to be sure, they had never really been part of the established order; many of the poor and marginalised in society – miners, fisher folk, canal navvies, labouring women – embraced Dissent because an itinerant preacher or missionary had embraced them, had gone to them at their workplaces or in their homes, and had spoken in their own dialect of God's love for them. These labouring people were beginning to find their own voice. Some may have found their way to the new evangelicalism out of what the historian E. P. Thompson termed a 'chiliasm of despair', as a form of psychic escape from the intolerable conditions of their lives.[30] Others, however, found in the new religious beliefs hope for a better future, not only in the next world, but in this one as well. They looked for fundamental change in this world, as more and more people were renewed in the Spirit. There was an outpouring of religious literature to spread the religious commitments; over 100 new religious periodicals were founded between 1790 and 1820.[31] The new evangelical fervour led some to extreme views. There were millenarian expectations, new prophecies, and strange visions. Some were drawn by their visions to leave the Christian faith, to embrace Painite deism, Owenite socialism or Radical materialism. Religious fervour permeated through the social orders, and the religious landscape was transformed. In the 1790s, probably 90 per cent of the population of Britain were at least nominal adherents of the established churches. Dissent in Britain was still modest in numbers. By the early 1820s, however, this situation had fundamentally changed. Perhaps as much as a third of the population of Britain were now outside the established church, embracing a broad spectrum of different beliefs, from Wesleyan Methodism to Owenite socialism.

The evangelical awakening was not restricted to Protestant Dissenters. In Ireland, the Catholic masses were becoming politicised, and prophecies circulated that the Protestant ascendancy was soon to end and the Protestants were to be driven from the country forever. Within the established churches, moreover, some were drawn to the impassioned evangelical piety. John Wesley, as has been noted, had sought throughout his life to keep his movement within the established Church of England. Although

his Methodist movement had gradually separated from the church, many
of those touched by evangelicalism did not choose to leave the Church of
England. These church evangelicals sought to combine a warm, conversionist piety with respect for the established ecclesiastical order. During
the mid- to late-eighteenth century, evangelical clergymen in the Church
of England formed local clerical societies, such as the Eclectic Society in
London, for shared Bible study, prayer and mutual support. By the 1790s,
there were perhaps 300–500 evangelical clergy in the Church of England,
out of a total of about 10,000; they were a small but highly committed
group.[32] From the 1790s, these church evangelicals found influential support from a circle of wealthy lay supporters, based in the then-fashionable
London suburb of Clapham. They included the wealthy MP for Yorkshire
and anti-slavery campaigner, William Wilberforce, the former governor of
Sierra Leone, Zachary Macaulay, and the former society playwright and
now a popular author of religious tracts, Hannah More. An evangelical
movement developed within the Church of Ireland from the 1780s, with
evangelical clergy forming clerical societies for mutual support. The influential congregation of the Bethesda chapel in Dublin became a centre for
the evangelical movement in the Irish establishment, attracting students
from Trinity College, Dublin, who were in turn drawn into the evangelical
movement. In the Church of Scotland, an evangelical party emerged in the
church courts during the 1790s, rooted in the old anti-patronage popular
party, but embracing a new passion to gain individual converts. The developing evangelical party had particular strength in the North of the country, where there was a large unchurched population inhabiting the more
remote Highland glens and islands. Among the evangelical Church of
Scotland ministers active in the region was John Macdonald, the 'Apostle
of the North', who as minister of the Highland parish of Urquhart from
1813 to 1849, itinerated widely through the Highlands and islands,
preaching some 10,000 times, often to crowds of thousands at open-air
meetings.[33]

Overseas missions

The fervour for evangelising among the unchurched masses at home was
accompanied by a new zeal for overseas missions. The same imperatives
that drove men and women to preach the gospel to the labouring poor
in barns, cottages and open fields also called some to seek to bring
Christianity to the heathen masses in India, Africa or the Pacific islands.
There was widespread belief that the evangelical awakening and French

Revolution marked the beginning of a new era in world history – that all things might now be possible, and that Britain, with its expanding empire, had a particular responsibility before God. Missionary societies in connection with the established churches had been formed near the beginning of the eighteenth century. These included the Society for Promoting Christian Knowledge (1698), the Society for the Propagation of the Gospel in Foreign Parts (1701) and the Society in Scotland for Propagating Christian Knowledge (1709). However, the impact of these societies was limited. It was the rise of evangelicalism, combined with the sense of the approaching millennium, that gave a major impetus to overseas missions in Britain.[34]

In 1792, William Carey, a shoemaker and largely self-taught Baptist minister in Leicester, published a pamphlet making an impassioned appeal for overseas Christian missions. Christians, he proclaimed, were under an obligation to bring the gospel *now* to all the world, including distant lands sunk 'in the most deplorable state of heathen darkness'.[35] The English Baptists established a Missionary Society that same year, and in 1793, they sent Carey to Bengal, where he would conduct a ministry of some 40 years. His early years were burdened with sorrow, with first his five-year-old son and then his wife carried off by illness. It was seven years before he had his first convert. But he persevered, building an impressive knowledge of Indian languages and dialects, and translating the Bible into Bengali. In 1795, a group of Dissenters, mainly Congregationalists, with some evangelical Anglicans, united to form the Missionary Society, later called the London Missionary Society (LMS). 'This year', proclaimed the Congregationalist minister, David Bogue, at the inaugural meeting, 'will, I hope, form an epoch in the history of the world'. It was, he added, 'a new Pentecost'.[36] In 1796, inspired largely by the recently published account of Captain Cook's voyages in the South Pacific, the LMS sent its first group of some 30 missionaries to Tahiti and the neighbouring islands. Other LMS missionaries travelled to South Africa (1798), Ceylon (1804), Canton (1807), Demerara (1808), Malacca (1815) and Madagascar (1818). These early missionaries often came from the lower social orders – similar in background to many of the itinerating village preachers who were carrying a simple gospel message to the unchurched masses in Britain. One of the early LMS missionaries, for example, was John Philip (1777–1851), a weaver from the Scottish Lowland burgh of Kirkcaldy, who was converted through the influence of evangelical Dissenters, became a congregational minister in 1802 and was sent by the LMS to South Africa in 1819. Philip's background among the labouring orders, and his experiences as a minister to congregations of labouring people in England and Scotland, gave him a particular empathy for the Africans, and an abhorrence of slavery.[37] Many of the early missionaries died young, weakened by the changes in climate, carried away by diseases or accident; in some cases they suffered violent deaths. A few weeks after the first two LMS missionary families landed in Madagascar in 1818, for example, five out of the party of six had died.

Beginning in the later 1790s, supporters of missions outside London formed local missionary societies modelled on the LMS and in loose connection with it. These included the Glasgow, Edinburgh and Paisley Missionary Societies, all formed in 1796, and which united both Dissenters and adherents of the established Church of Scotland. The local societies spread information about the missionary fields, inspired commitment to the missionary enterprise, and collected funds to support missionary ventures. The effort of collecting funds for overseas missionaries, and the stories of martyrdom in the mission field, could serve to redouble missionary work at home. Many Anglican evangelicals, meanwhile, were uncomfortable with the formation of the LMS, believing that its Dissenting members were fundamentally unsound on church order and liturgy, and that Dissenting missionaries would export questionable beliefs and practices. In 1799, a group of Anglican evangelicals associated with the London-based Eclectic Society, formed their own missionary society, the Church Missionary Society (CMS). Three years later, it sent out its first missionaries, two German Lutherans, to Sierra Leone in West Africa. One of these, unfortunately, deserted the mission to become a slave trader. The CMS gained only modest support until 1813, when church evangelicals began forming auxiliary societies in towns and villages across the country, and mobilising considerable popular support. An Irish branch of the CMS was formed in 1814. Soon the CMS was sending missionaries to India and the Pacific, as well as West Africa. The Methodists also became active in the missionary outreach, forming the Wesleyan Methodist Missionary Society by 1818, and sending missionaries to West Africa, India, the Caribbean and the Pacific.

Probably the greatest of the missionary societies, however, was the British and Foreign Bible Society, which was formed in London in 1804 through the joint effort of Dissenters and church evangelicals. The aim of the Bible Society was both simple and grandiose – to provide every family in the world with a copy of the Bible, printed in their native language. The Society undertook to prepare the translations, print the Bibles and distribute them, at minimal cost. The work was financed by voluntary contributions and supervised by a London management committee. In order not to cause offence to any denomination of Christians, the Society proposed that its Bibles should contain only the Scriptures, without notes or commentary. During its first five years, the progress of the Bible Society was slow. From 1809, however, the Society took up the organisational techniques being adopted by other missionary societies, and began forming auxiliaries throughout the United Kingdom. The branch societies held regular meetings, raised funds for the parent society and distributed Bibles among the poor in their districts. Within seven years, the Society had formed 541 auxiliaries. During its first five years, from 1804 to 1809, it had printed and distributed some 150,000 Bibles; during the following five years, it printed and distributed 800,000 Bibles.[38] The Bible Society did not support missionaries or mission stations, and thus did not compete with the existing missionary societies. It gained broad support from Dissenters and evangelicals in the established church. But the Bible Society also stirred considerable controversy. Many non-evangelical Anglicans believed that the Society was subversive of due order in the established Church of England and Ireland. For them, the Bible Society promoted the notion that ecclesiastical organisation, doctrinal statements and liturgical practices were matters of indifference, and that the Bible alone was essential to the faith. They were unhappy seeing members of the established church co-operate with Dissenters, as though their differences were unimportant. From about 1810 and 1820, there was an intense conflict in England over the Bible Society, with high Anglicans seeking to halt the formation of local branches, and evangelicals insisting that the Society constituted no threat to church order. But the Bible Society weathered the storm and continued to expand, with auxiliary societies formed on the European continent as well as throughout Britain and Ireland.

By the 1820s the overseas missionary movement was still relatively modest in terms of money raised and numbers of missionaries sent forth; however, it had made a fair start. The missionary societies were gaining practical experience and growing in knowledge about the world. They issued regular reports and periodicals, such as the *Missionary Magazine*, which was published in Edinburgh from 1796. They established networks of local missionary societies throughout the country, in which people would gather regularly to hear stories of missionary exploits. These meetings brought colour and drama to people's lives, especially if they felt that they were contributing to the missions. Most of the early missionaries came from the ranks of the skilled artisans, with a disproportionate number coming from Scotland. They were in one sense ordinary men and women, with whom the middling social orders could identify; they were also heroic figures, carrying the gospel to exotic lands, experiencing adventures, and demonstrating the capacity of ordinary people to do extraordinary things. The evangelical Church of Scotland minister, Thomas Chalmers, a warm advocate of local associations for the support of missions, formed a missionary society in his Glasgow parish of St John's in 1819. At the monthly meetings, he would read out the missionary news for an hour or more. There was co-operation between the different missionary societies, which began holding their annual meetings in May in London. In about 1830, Exeter Hall was erected in the Strand in London to hold these annual meetings, and the name 'Exeter Hall' soon came to signify a recognisable moral and evangelical interest, especially with reference to the expanding empire. During the 1820s, the missionary movement was becoming respectable – too respectable for some. In 1824, the Scottish evangelical, Edward Irving, preached an anniversary sermon for the LMS in which he contrasted the Apostolic missionaries of the early church, with virtually no support apart from their faith, with the modern missionaries, backed by their extensive apparatus of parent and auxiliary societies, regular subscriptions and missionary publications, and with each new missionary venture carefully planned and organised, often with support from the imperial state.[39] Some were already associating the missionary interest with imperial expansion; the Bible was seen as following the flag. 'The same people', Thomas Duncan, Whig professor of mathematics at St Andrews University, observed to Chalmers in 1812, 'that subscribe so liberally for the propagation of the Gospel are equally forward in supporting schemes for the conquest of the most distant nations of the globe'.[40] Advocates of the missionary movement did often portray the empire as part of the divine plan to bring Christianity and civilisation to the non-European world. The British empire, observed Thomas Haweis in 1812, 'seems peculiarly destined to be the instrument . . . to carry [Christ's] salvation to the end of the earth'.[41]

The opening of India to missionaries and the providential empire

One of the greatest victories of the emerging missionary movement was to convince Parliament to open the territories of the East India Company on the Indian subcontinent to missionary activity in 1813. India was already the crown jewel of the British empire, the wealthiest and most heavily populated of Britain's possessions and the foundation of its power in the East. While the East India Company had permitted some limited missionary activity from the late seventeenth century, it severely restricted the entry of missionaries, believing, with good reason, that they would stir resentments on the part of the Hindu and Muslim populations. The Company governed vast territories and populations with a relatively small military force, made up largely of Indian sepoy recruits. It existed to promote trade between Britain and India and to make a profit for its shareholders. It would not risk antagonising the population and undermining its position in India. In 1806, a mutiny among sepoy troops in Vellore had been attributed to rumours that the Company intended to force them to convert to Christianity. There was, moreover, a widespread belief, rooted in Enlightenment ideas of toleration and promoted by a talented group of British scholars – the so-called 'Orientalists' – that India possessed rich and ancient religious and cultural traditions and that it would be immoral for Westerners to interfere with these traditions or to seek to impose their Christian religion.

This view of Indian civilisation, however, was challenged as evangelicalism spread in Britain. In 1792, Charles Grant, an official of the East India Company and an evangelical Christian, submitted a private memorandum to the Company directors, in which he presented a highly negative view of Hindu society based on his experience of some 20 years of living in Bengal.[42] Running through a catalogue of evils, including the caste system, mistreatment of women, cruel forms of worship, and pervasive dishonesty, Grant concluded that Indian society was 'in a very degraded and humiliated state'.[43] British supremacy in India would not be permanently established without reforming Indian society and this, Grant maintained, could only be achieved by Christianising the subcontinent.[44] At the renewal of the charter by Parliament of the East India Company in 1792, Grant pressed for the inclusion of a clause requiring the Company to support Christian education in India. There was, however, vehement opposition to the so-called 'pious clause' from the Company directors, and it was dropped.[45]

From about 1808, there were renewed calls for state support for Indian missions. A major figure behind this was Claudius Buchanan, a Cambridge-educated former East India Company chaplain, who travelled about Britain horrifying audiences with graphic descriptions of such practices as *sati* (the ritual burning alive of widows) and human sacrifice.[46] It was God's will that Britain should become a great missionary nation. In his influential *Memoir of the Expediency of an Ecclesiastical Establishment for British India*, published in 1805 and reprinted in 1812, Buchanan argued that Britain's conversion of India was part of the divine plan. 'Why should it be thought incredible', he asked, 'that Providence hath been pleased, in a course of years to subjugate this Eastern empire to the most civilized nation in the world, *for this very purpose?*'[47]

The East India Company charter was to be renewed in 1813, and Wilberforce and the Clapham sect acted to revive the 'pious clause' requiring support for the Christian mission. As it became clear that the Company directors remained opposed to the clause, the Clapham sect, with the assistance of the major missionary societies, organised a national campaign to arouse public opinion.[48] In 1813, supporters of a mission clause sent 895 petitions, with nearly half a million signatures, to Parliament.[49] In promoting the clause, there were further references to the providential character of Britain's conquests in India – for how else could Britain's control over a vast subcontinent, thousands of miles away, be explained? For the Baptist divine, Robert Hall, 'our acquisition of power [in India] has been so rapid, so extensive, and so disproportionate to the limits of our native empire, that there are few events in which the interposition of Providence may be more distinctly traced'.[50] 'In the course of Providence', observed the *Evangelical Magazine* in May 1813, 'Britain is become mistress of the East'.[51] For a speaker at a public meeting in Kingston-upon-Hull in April 1813, the conversion of India was only the beginning of God's plan, for 'if Christianity was established there, it might spread over the whole continent' of Asia.[52]

On 22 June 1813, Wilberforce spoke in support of the 'pious clause' in the House of Commons, in one of the most powerful speeches of his career.[53] For Wilberforce, the struggle for the conversion of India was one of light against darkness, of the kingdom of God against the kingdom of Satan. He presented chilling accounts of oppression of the poor, caste violence, infanticide, human sacrifice and mutilation, and the brutal and sexually explicit devotions associated with the Jaggernaut in Orissa. There could be no question of Britain's responsibility. 'Immense regions', he observed, '. . . have providentially come under our dominion. They are deeply sunk, and by their religious superstitions fast bound, in the lowest depths of moral and social wretchedness and degradation'.[54] The British state must grant missionaries its protection and its favour, and recognise that it bore a responsibility under God to bring Christian and moral instruction to its subjects in India.[55]

The petitioning campaign and the parliamentary efforts of Wilberforce and his supporters proved successful.[56] With the renewal of the charter in 1813, the East India Company was required to open its territories in India to Christian missionaries. Moreover, the Company was also obliged to provide financial support from its revenues for a small church establishment in India, with a bishop for India, and an archdeacon in each of the three presidencies of Calcutta, Madras and Bombay. The decision was a controversial one, and many in Britain continued to view it as dangerous folly which would enrage Indian Hindus and Muslims and foment rebellion. When the high church Thomas Middleton was consecrated the first bishop of Calcutta in 1814 in London, it was decided not to follow usual practice and publish the consecration sermon, as there was so much hostility to the creation of the bishopric.[57] None the less, it had been a great victory for the missionary movement. It had opened the vast subcontinent of India to missionary activity. Even more important, it had gained parliamentary support for the notion that the British empire was in some sense a trust held under God, and that Britain had the responsibility to exercise its expanding global power for a providential purpose.

Middleton arrived in India in late 1814, and was soon joined by four missionaries of the Anglican Church Missionary Society. The number of Protestant missionaries in British India increased to some 20 by 1816 and 100 by 1823.[58] With government support, an Anglican mission college, Bishop's College, was founded in Calcutta in 1820, while the interactions of missionaries and Hindu intellectuals such as Ram Mohan Roy contributed to a Bengali cultural renaissance. This, in turn, raised hopes of converting the intellectual castes and of the 'filtration' of Christianity down to the lower orders. In 1828, the arrival of a reforming governor-general with evangelical sympathies, Lord William Bentinck, began a new era of state and church co-operation and joint intervention aimed at spreading Christian and Western values in India. In 1829, amid growing pressure from the established churches, Bentinck prohibited the Hindu custom of *sati*, the burning of widows. In the same year, he established a government department under the direction of Captain William Sleeman for the eradication of rural gangs of robbers, or *thugs*, who strangled their victims in a ritual manner and operated in connection with temples to the Hindu goddess, Kali. By 1840, some 14,000 *thugs* had been hanged, imprisoned or transported. At the renewal of the East India Company charter in 1833 Parliament elevated the archdeaconries of Madras and Bombay into new Church of England bishoprics. Parliament also agreed that the Company would provide support for education in India, and this, it was decided by 1835, would be concentrated on English-language higher education. The character of the British rule in India, Bentinck asserted in January 1834, had been transformed. It was no longer concerned mainly with profits, but was now committed to ending 'the vices, the ignorance, the oppression, the despotism, the barbarous and often cruel customs that have been the growth of ages'.

The moral regeneration of this immense mass of our fellow-creatures – the communication to them [of] the blessings of the European condition, in knowledge, in domestic comfort, in security of person and property, in independence, in morals – these constitute the first duty of the Imperial Government.[59]

Britain, many believed, was now embracing the responsibilities of empire to which it had been called by providence.

The anti-slavery campaign

The global commitments of the evangelical awakening also found expression in the anti-slavery movement. While there had been expressions of revulsion over slavery and the slave trade from the early eighteenth century, it was in the 1780s, largely under the influence of the evangelical revival, that this revulsion was directed into an anti-slavery campaign, a campaign that initially focused on ending the slave trade. In 1787, opponents of slavery formed the London Committee for the Abolition of the Slave Trade. The Quakers, with their pacifism and their own history of suffering and oppression, took a leading role in the new movement, and Quakers made up 9 of the 12 members of the original London Committee. By the end of the 1780s, Wilberforce and the evangelical Clapham circle also joined in the struggle. The chances of success appeared slight. Britain's merchant fleet dominated the international slave trade. Between 1662 and 1807, British ships carried about 3,400,000 Africans to slavery, representing about half of all slave exports during the period; in the 1780s and 1790s alone, British ships carried 656,000 slaves.[60] A steady supply of African slaves was viewed as necessary to the prosperity of Britain's sugar-producing islands in the Caribbean. Port towns like Bristol and Liverpool thrived on the slave trade, and many of Britain's leading families owed their fortunes to slavery. The Scriptures seemed ambiguous about the legitimacy of slavery in a Christian social order, and many pointed to the story of Noah's curse on Ham as evidence that God had ordained the African race to be slaves. Others claimed that conditions for slaves were a considerable improvement over those they had known in the heathen wilderness of Africa. The first vote in the House of Commons on a motion to end the slave trade, in April 1791, resulted in an overwhelming defeat.

The anti-slavery campaigners now turned to extra-parliamentary methods, to mobilising what was known as 'opinion out of doors' – holding public meetings in taverns and chapels, publishing tracts and broadsheets, organising petitions to Parliament and appealing to common people with stories of the horrors on the slave ships during the infamous 'middle passage' across the Atlantic: the overcrowding, sickness, despair and death. The networks of missionary and evangelical societies helped to mobilise public opinion and organise petitioning campaigns. Those who had personally known injustice, undeserved suffering or exploitation, including many of those labouring men and women whose lives had been touched by the evangelical awakening, were often most forward in signing petitions and attending meetings. There was also a sense that the slave trade was an affront to God. It was, insisted one MP in the Commons in 1796, a 'foul iniquity' that would 'completely justify the avenging angel, in entirely extirpating [this nation] from the face of the earth'.[61] By the spring of 1792, a total of 519 petitions against the slave trade had been sent to Parliament, the largest number that had ever been submitted on a single subject. In 1792, meanwhile, the parliamentary state, fearful of the influences of the French Revolution, acted to suppress all popular reform movements and outlawed most public meetings. This effectively halted the popular agitation against the slave trade.

The abolitionists now directed their efforts to exerting pressure within Parliament.[62] Wilberforce was the most prominent opponent of the slave trade in Parliament, while his fellow Clapham evangelicals used their influence to convince members of the governing elite of the evils of the trade. The campaign also had considerable non-evangelical support, including that of worldly politicians like Charles James Fox. As the historian Roger Anstey has shown, opponents of the slave trade learned to make effective appeals to national interest, arguing, for example, that two-thirds of the British slave trade went towards supplying foreign territories with slaves, which enabled the plantations in those territories to undercut British-grown sugar in the Continental markets.[63] And there were further appeals to providence and the dangers of national sin. Granville Sharp warned in 1806 that continued toleration of slavery 'must finally draw down the Divine vengeance upon our state and nation!'[64] Finally in 1807, after a campaign of some 20 years, Parliament abolished the slave trade for British ships. Following the defeat of Napoleonic France, British leaders also worked to secure international agreements to end the slave trade altogether. The restored Bourbon monarchy agreed that France would not re-enter the trade, and at the Congress of Vienna in 1815, the Irish Tory

statesman, Viscount Castlereagh, secured a general declaration condemning the trade, which was followed over the next several years by more
specific agreements.

Beginning in 1808, the Royal Navy began stationing warships off the
coast of Africa to intercept slave ships – initially a 32-gun frigate and an
18-gun sloop to patrol over a thousand miles of coast. With the international agreements that allowed the navy to intercept slave ships of other
countries, the West Africa Squadron, as it was called, was increased to six
or seven warships during the 1820s.[65] Although the number of warships
was pitiably small, they did manage to capture some slave vessels. From
1808, the navy landed its freed human cargoes in Freetown, in the West
African crown colony of Sierra Leone. By 1814, there were some 10,000
'recaptives', or freed slaves, in the colony, making up four-fifths of the
total population. The number of liberated Africans in the colony then
began growing at a rate of about 3,000 a year. From 1814 to 1824, the
lieutenant governor (and later governor) of the colony was the Irish
Protestant, Sir Charles M'Carthy. With financial assistance from London,
he organised the liberated Africans into new villages surrounding
Freetown, with names like Leicester, Gloucester, Regent, Waterloo,
Hastings, and, of course, Wilberforce. M'Carthy was a strong supporter of
the established church, and in these villages, with their square-towered
Norman churches, the 'recaptives' (who had been cut off from their former
ancestral homes and identities) were to be given new identities – and
'civilised' under the influence of Anglican Christianity.[66]

In 1821–22, British opponents of slavery launched a new national campaign, now aimed at securing the abolition of slavery itself. Anti-slavery
activists, led by the Quaker, James Cropper, formed the Society for the
Amelioration and Gradual Abolition of Slavery in Liverpool in December
1822, and this was followed by the formation of a similar Anti-Slavery
Society in London in January 1823, with the Dissenter and MP, William
Smith, as chairman. Wilberforce's health was failing, and the leadership
of the anti-slavery forces (by now dubbed the 'Saints') in the House of
Commons fell to Thomas Fowell Buxton, Whig MP for Weymouth and an
Anglican evangelical, though with strong Quaker connections through his
mother's family. Buxton's sister-in-law, the Quaker minister, Priscilla
Gurney, had made an impassioned appeal to Buxton to take up the cause
of the slaves as she lay dying in March 1821, and Buxton received a letter
from Wilberforce asking him to take up the cause the day after his sister-
in-law's death. He could hardly refuse two such calls. While Buxton and
the 'Saints' pressed the issue in Parliament, abolitionists formed networks

of local branches of the Anti-Slavery Society throughout Britain and Ireland. A propaganda war raged after 1823, with the West Indies interest of planters, commercial agents and merchants circulating claims in the press and at public meetings that slaves were treated benevolently on the plantations, while abolitionists countered these claims with accounts of the cruelty of the slavery system, including the breakup of families at slave auctions, the floggings of men and women, the casual rape of women, and the frequents deaths through mistreatment. Crucial in this propaganda war, as Catherine Hall has noted, were the conflicting images of the slave. The planters claimed that Africans were fundamentally inferior to whites – lazy, violent, deficient in intellect and sentiment, and thus needing outside control. The abolitionists, on the other hand, portrayed Africans as their brothers and sisters, sharing with them a common humanity.[67] In 1823, there were 226 petitions calling for the abolition of slavery sent to the House of Commons, and in 1824, there were 460 abolitionist petitions sent. While the numbers of signatures on these petitions have not been preserved, the petition from Dundee in 1826 was reported in the press as measuring 63 feet in length, with five columns of signatures across the page.[68]

Dissenters played the leading role in the grass roots British anti-slavery campaign. Methodists and Baptists were especially active, largely because their denominations were sending missionaries to minister to the slaves in the West Indies. These Dissenting missionaries often spoke out against the abuse of slaves and as a result some suffered violence. The tragic fate of John Smith, a Congregational missionary with the LMS, was one such case. A black slave insurrection on the island of Demerara had evidently begun among members of his chapel congregation. Smith was arrested in 1823, tried by court martial and sentenced to death for having incited the rising, despite evidence that he had done all he could to prevent violence. He died of fever in prison in early 1824, before his sentence could be carried out. For Christian abolitionists in Britain, his was a martyr's death. As with the campaign against the slave trade, women took an active role in the movement for the abolition of slavery, with a Ladies' Anti-Slavery Society formed in almost every British town by 1830. The largest of these societies, in Birmingham, distributed some 35,000 items of propaganda each year.[69] Many evangelicals, like Wilberforce, opposed slavery primarily because they viewed it as an obstacle to the spread of the gospel. Their main concern was for the eternal fates of the slaves, who were often denied religious instruction. But for probably the great mass of evangelical abolitionists, the major motivation was humanitarian, rooted in concern for the freedom, dignity and potential for happiness of the African peoples. British labouring men and women, who were denied the vote, who felt everyday the realities of injustice, inequality and exploitation, could feel a special empathy for enslaved Africans, and such empathy were enhanced by evangelical teachings on the equality of all souls before God and the world as governed by providence. Through the missionary and anti-slavery movements, British evangelicals, and especially evangelical Dissenters, were becoming politicised and embracing a sense of national and international responsibility. The empire, they were coming to believe, must either become a force under God for the spread of Christianity and humanitarian reform, or risk bringing down upon it the wrath of God.

The reform and extension of the established churches

In 1815, Richard Yates, chaplain of Chelsea Hospital and rector of Ashen, published a lengthy pamphlet of some 226 pages entitled *The Church in Danger*, in which he outlined the portentous threats facing the established Church of England. Yates was deeply distressed over both the rapid growth of religious Dissent and the spread of popular irreligion during the past quarter century. Where the country had once known unity, stability and harmony within the parish structures of the national church, now there was, he believed, sectarian division, confusion, political unrest, increasing crime and a general breakdown of social order. Where people had once shared a sense of social belonging and mutual responsibility, and been united under an overarching national faith, now they pursued their selfish interests and followed diverse religious teachings, and society was losing all cohesion. The situation, Yates believed, was most ominous in the rapidly growing industrial towns and cities – 'the crowded assemblages which the extension of Manufactures and Commerce necessarily brings together', which bred, like a pestilence, 'the vicious and delusive principles of profligate infidelity and rash insubordination'. It was in the cities that religious Dissent, Painite deism, Owenite socialism, Radicalism and atheism seemed most widespread, and orthodox Anglicanism most beleaguered. A major cause of this desperate situation was the failure of the established church to expand its parish system in response to the rapid population growth in the new urban districts. In London, for example, the very heart of the empire and the headquarters of those missionary societies which were intent on Christianising the world, the established church was woefully inadequate and a large proportion of the population was without any religious instruction. Out of a total population of over 1,162,000 residing within an eight-mile radius of St Paul's cathedral, there was room in the churches and chapels of the Church of England for only 216,000, leaving some 946,000, or 81.5 per cent of the population, with no opportunity to attend public worship in the nation's religious establishment. 'Shut out, in fact', Yates observed:

from the Pale of the Church, from all participation in its benefits, these numbers are necessarily driven to join the ranks of injurious opposition, either in Dissent, and Sectarian Enthusiasm; – or in the infinitely more dangerous opposition of Infidelity, Atheism, and ignorant depravity. Such a Mine of Heathenism, and consequent profligacy and danger, under the very meridian (as it is supposed) of Christian illumination, and accumulated around the very centre and heart of British Prosperity, Liberty, and Civilization, cannot be contemplated without terror . . .[70]

To the north, in the industrialising city of Glasgow – soon to be recognised as the second city of the empire – the Church of Scotland minister, Thomas Chalmers, was coming to similar conclusions about the inadequacies of the Scottish establishment to meet the needs of the industrialising society. In a sermon published in 1817, he expressed his anxiety over the large percentage of the new industrial working class who were growing up outside the pale of the established church, subject to a 'thousand contaminations'. The expanding British empire was threatened with class warfare and revolutionary upheaval in its industrial heartland. 'If something be not done', he warned with reference to the industrial workers, 'to bring this enormous physical strength under the control of Christian and humanized principle, the day may yet come, when it may lift against the authorities of this land its brawny vigour, and discharge upon them all, the turbulence of its rude and volcanic energy'. The only effective means to preserve the Christian social order, he insisted, was to extend the parish system of the established church, and he called urgently for the creation of at least 20 additional parish churches in Glasgow alone.[71]

Yates and Chalmers were not isolated voices. Others had also become convinced that social order throughout the three kingdoms was under threat, and that what was needed was a strengthening of the established churches. There was concern among the governing elite in Britain over the long-term social effects of the explosive growth of religious Dissent, and over the large numbers who seemed to have no religious faith. 'It is no light evil', observed the *Quarterly Review* of the evangelical Dissenters in 1810, 'for a state to have within its bosom so numerous and active and increasing a party, whose whole system tends to cut them off from all common sympathy with their countrymen, and who are separatists not in religious worship alone, but in all the ordinary observances of life'.[72] The initiative for reforming and strengthening the established churches came largely from Parliament, and especially the Tory government of William Pitt and his successors, and the underlying force behind the initiative was mainly concern for the maintenance of the social order. From about 1809, Parliament began investing significant public money in the religious establishments, and working to diminish some of the worst abuses of non-residence and neglect on the part of the clergy. The primary aim of these initiatives was to strengthen the church at the parish, or grass roots, level. From 1805, Parliament began requiring the bishops of the Church of England to submit annual reports on the number of parish clergy who did not reside within their parishes. This put pressure on bishops to demonstrate at least some progress each year towards reducing the number of non-resident clergymen in their dioceses. In 1809, Parliament began taking action aimed at bringing the income of all parish livings in the country up to a minimum of £150 a year. This, it was hoped, would help bishops to curb pluralism, by eliminating any need for individual clergymen to multiply the number of parish livings they held in order to have an income sufficient to support their families in a respectable manner. Between 1809 and 1821, Parliament made 11 annual grants of £100,000, or a total of £1,100,000, to help raise the level of small livings in the Church of England.[73] The grants did not eliminate all small livings, but they did reduce their number, while they also demonstrated the new parliamentary commitment to strengthen the English church. In 1813, Parliament passed a Curates Act, requiring a non-resident parish clergyman to pay the curate a substantial proportion of the income of the parish living.

In 1818, Parliament provided a grant of £1,000,000 for building new parish churches in England and Wales. In introducing the motion for the grant in the House of Lords, the Tory prime minister, Lord Liverpool, insisted that it was 'the most important measure [he had] ever submitted to their lordships' consideration'.[74] This was the first major grant for church building in over a century. The money was to be distributed by a newly formed Commission for church-building, and the grants were intended to supplement funds that would be raised locally. In the parliamentary act governing the grant, preference was given to church building in the new urban districts, and at least a fifth of the seats in the churches were to be free of any rental, to enable the poor to attend. These new churches were conceived as forming a national monument to Britain's victory over

Napoleonic France; they were a collective prayer of gratitude, and symbols of the nation's rededication to God. The new churches, dubbed 'Waterloo churches', were soon rising across the land. In 1824, Parliament made a further grant of £500,000 to the church-building Commission. By 1831, a total of 188 new churches had been completed, with seating for some 260,000, over half of which was free.[75] Many of the new churches were grandiose, porticoed structures, in a classical Grecian style, with lavishly decorated interiors – too costly and often too large. The new church at St Pancras, for example, cost the princely sum of £76,000.[76] Some remained half-empty. None the less, the grant signified a new parliamentary commitment to revive the influence of the national church.

At the same time, Parliament acted to improve the parish ministry of the established Protestant Church in Ireland. From the 1770s, the Irish Parliament had given modest grants to the Protestant Church to help with the building and repair of parish churches and residence houses for the parish clergy, and following the Act of Union the United Kingdom Parliament continued these grants. The grants averaged about £10,000 a year during the first decade of the nineteenth century. But Parliament, keen to promote improvement in the Irish establishment, increased the grants to £60,000 a year between 1810 and 1816, then continued the grants at a smaller but still substantial level of £30,000 a year between 1817 and 1821. In 1808, moreover, Parliament passed legislation to strengthen the power of Irish bishops to improve residence among their parish clergy, with the result that the percentage of Irish clergy who resided in their parishes rose from 46 per cent in 1806 to 65 per cent by 1819. The number of clergymen in the Irish establishment increased from 1,253 in 1806 to 1,977 by 1826. Following the Union, moreover, Parliament began making grants to an educational society, the Association for Discountenancing Vice, connected with the established Church of Ireland; the grants began at a modest £300 a year in 1801, increasing to over £9,000 a year by 1823.[77]

The established Church of Scotland also benefited from Parliament's commitment to the religious establishments. From at least 1750, the Scottish clergy had sought, without success, to convince Parliament to legislate for a minimum stipend for all Church of Scotland ministers. Then in 1810, as part of the general effort to improve the parish ministry throughout the United Kingdom, Parliament passed legislation to require a minimum stipend of £150 a year for Church of Scotland parish ministers, and it provided an annual grant of £10,000 to supplement the teinds in poorer parishes, to enable local parish churches to pay the new minimum stipend.[78] In 1823, Parliament made a grant to extend the parochial system of the Church of Scotland in the Highlands and Islands, where mountains, lochs, moors and sea made communications extremely difficult, and much of the population was Gaelic-speaking and outside the established order of church and state. Over the next several years, the state built 43 new churches and endowed 42 new parish clergymen in the area, at a total cost of £180,000.[79] The new state investment encouraged the church for its part to undertake additional efforts. In 1824, the General Assembly created a Highlands and Islands Committee, to co-ordinate its mission in the region. Two years later, the General Assembly was supporting 39 missionaries and 23 catechists in the Highlands, and was establishing new parish schools.[80] The Church of Scotland also petitioned Parliament for a further grant for church-building in the growing industrial towns and cities of the Lowlands, and was encouraged to believe the money would be forthcoming.

Never before in their history had the established churches received direct financial aid from the state on such a scale as during the 15 years between 1809 and 1824. There was an enhanced spirit of co-operation between church and state. The Tories were in power during these years, first under Spencer Perceval (1809–12) and then, following his assassination, under Lord Liverpool (1812–27). It was mainly Tory politicians who were behind the policy of increased grants for the established churches. For them, the revived establishments would not only help to build national unity, but would also teach the lower social orders to respect the powers that be and accept their place in the existing social hierarchy. They hoped to roll back the gains made by Dissenters, deists, Owenite socialists and Radicals in recent decades and shape a conservative Christian social order. But this was not simply a matter of using the established churches for purposes of state-building. Both Perceval and Liverpool were sincere Anglican churchmen, and their governments included a number of other committed Anglicans, including Nicholas Vansittart, Lord Harrowby, Henry Goulburn and Sir Robert Peel. Such men believed in the benefits of a Christian social order, in which rich and poor would be united by ties of benevolence and deference within close-knit parish communities under the pastoral oversight of parish clergymen.

The increasing co-operation of church and state and the growing levels of state investment were accompanied by improvements in the leadership and internal management of the churches. In the United Church of England and Ireland, the crown used its patronage to promote men of exceptional talent and commitment to the episcopal bench, including William Van Mildert, Charles James Blomfield, John Kaye, and the brothers Charles and John Bird Sumner in England, and William Magee, John Jebb, Richard Mant and Power le Poer Trench in Ireland. These were men who had achieved reputations for scholarship, dedication to the pastoral ministry, and administrative ability, and who were prepared to use the new powers given them by Parliament to improve clerical residency, discipline and pastoral care within their respective dioceses. They became more regular than their predecessors in visiting the parishes within their dioceses and more careful about gathering accurate information about parish life. They strengthened administrative structures and appointed energetic archdeacons. They revived the office of rural dean, in order to provide leadership and inspiration to rural parish clergy. Further, they encouraged the formation of diocesan societies to promote church-building, school-building, and overseas missions. The 1820s witnessed the real beginnings of what the historian Arthur Burns has termed a 'diocesan revival' in the United Church of England and Ireland, a new internal dynamic of reform centred upon the church's revived episcopate.[81]

There was improvement in the pastoral work of the parish clergy, especially in the growing towns and cities. More and more parish clergy began regularly visiting their parishioners, to enquire into their moral and spiritual condition, to instruct them in the doctrines and teachings of the church, and to encourage regular church attendance and family devotion. From about 1812, some clergy began forming parish societies of district visitors – laymen and, increasingly, laywomen – who would visit parishioners in their homes, and, when needed, distribute charity. A leading proponent of such district visiting was the Church of Scotland clergyman, Thomas Chalmers, who in 1815 became minister of a crowded parish, with a population of some 12,000, in industrialising Glasgow. He recruited a large agency of committed lay supporters, subdivided his urban parish into smaller districts, and assigned a team of visitors to each district. The visitors were instructed to be 'aggressive' in their district visiting, regularly entering the homes of each family – Dissenters and Roman Catholics, as well as adherents of the Church of Scotland – and keeping careful records of the visits. The visitors included elders, who were to look after the moral and spiritual life of the community, deacons, who were to oversee the material needs of inhabitants and distribute poor relief, and sabbath school teachers, who were to look after the educational needs of children and form neighbourhood Sunday schools which would provide both religious instruction and training in reading. The full agency of visitors, which together numbered over 75, met monthly to discuss conditions in the parish and methods of visiting. Chalmers maintained that such systematic visiting could help to form close-knit communities in urban neighbour-hoods, reviving the religious unity and social harmony that he argued had prevailed in most rural parishes before the coming of industrialisation and the growth of Dissent. More than that, he was convinced that in such com-munities legal poor relief could be diminished and even abolished; it would be replaced by a communal charity, in which neighbours would assist one another freely out of a sense of benevolence and social responsibility. This last point had a particular appeal to the propertied social orders, who feared that the rising number of poor on the relief rolls would soon place an intolerable burden on the local property taxes that supported poor relief.

In 1819, Chalmers obtained the permission of the Glasgow town council and magistrates to conduct an experiment in a newly formed, working-class parish, St John's. He proposed to demonstrate, through a scientifically conducted social experiment, how legal poor relief could be eliminated by having district visitors promote self-sufficiency among able-bodied paupers, while encouraging families and neighbours to help the truly needy through purely voluntary giving. Over the next four years, the St John's deacons significantly reduced poor relief costs in the parish, and Chalmers's St John's experiment aroused considerable interest, not only in Scotland, but in England and Ireland as well. In a series of widely-read publications, Chalmers argued that his parish system could be emu-lated in parishes across England and Ireland as well as Scotland, bringing practical benefits, including a reduction of legal poor relief, crime and class tensions. There were critics of the scheme, who claimed that Chalmers achieved his results by depriving paupers of needed relief and forcing many to leave St John's parish and settle in other parishes; there was much truth in such criticisms. But for his supporters, Chalmers had given a set of new, pragmatic reasons for reviving the parish ministry of the established churches.[82]

Chalmers's writings on pauperism and his St John's experiment were also major contributions to an intellectual movement in early nineteenth-century Britain aimed at showing that the doctrines of political economy were compatible with Christian teachings, and indeed that the 'laws' of political economy were designed by a benevolent God for the good of humankind. From the early years of the century, a number of clergymen, mainly in the established churches and including Edward Copleston, John Bird Sumner and Richard Whately, endeavoured to show that the doctrines of the political economists – including the self-regulating market-place, the existence of the wage-fund, and the competition for scarce resources – were part of a providential world order which promoted individual responsibility and moral freedom.[83] As Peter Mandler has observed, 'For many Englishmen, Christian political economy *was* political economy'.[84] Of these Christian political economists, perhaps the most influential was the Church of England clergyman, T. R. Malthus. In his treatise on *The Principle of Population*, first published in 1798 and republished in an expanded version in 1804, Malthus argued that population always tended to grow at a faster rate than the growth in the food supply. Because population growth always pressed against the limits of the food supply, the large majority of humankind were destined to live close to the margins of subsistence – confirming Christ's words in Scripture that the poor would always be with us. Further, when population grew beyond the food supply, its numbers had to be diminished by the 'natural checks' of famine, epidemic disease or warfare. The only way for a society to avoid these cataclysmic natural checks was for individuals to exercise 'moral restraint', delaying marriage and limiting the number of their children. Chalmers had been converted to Malthusian principles as early as 1808, and became Britain's leading Malthusian – Malthus called him his 'ablest and best ally'.[85] One of the aims of Chalmers's parish ideal was to encourage 'moral restraint' among the poor by promoting communal responsibility and education in the principles of political economy. This would be to act within the providential laws of society to improve the moral and material condition of the poor.

Christian political economy was only one reflection of a new intellectual vitality within the religious establishments. There were also the influences of Romanticism, with its elevation of individual feeling and intuition, its veneration of history, and its celebration of community. Such works as William Wordsworth's *Ecclesiastical Sketches* of 1822, Robert Southey's *Book of the Church* of 1824, and John Keble's *Christian Year* of 1827 identified the established Church of England with the highest aspirations and ideals of the English nation, and celebrated the pastoral ministry and traditional parish community. In Scotland, Thomas McCrie's *Life of John Knox* of 1811 and *Life of Andrew Melville* of 1819 were immensely popular, Romantic depictions of the lives of two leaders of the Scottish Reformation. Although a member of a Secession Presbyterian Church, McCrie's histories portrayed the Church of Scotland as central to Scottish national life and history. And in the 1820s, as we have seen, Thomas Chalmers's writings were providing an idealised picture of the traditional Scottish rural parish, as an idyllic, stable and harmonious community united under the influence of the parish church.

The English and Scottish universities were experiencing expanding student numbers, with more and more students preparing for the Christian ministry. A greater moral earnestness took hold among the students. New Anglican colleges were founded in the 1820s – St David's College, Lampeter, Durham College, and King's College, London. At Oxford, Oriel College became home in the 1820s to a brilliant circle of Christian scholars, including Edward Copleston, Richard Whately, Thomas Arnold, John Keble, Richard Hurrell Froude and John Henry Newman. They combined interests in church history, theology, biblical studies and Christian political economy with a commitment to restore the influence of the Church of England, and their influence spread to the other colleges. At Cambridge, the evangelical Charles Simeon, minister of Holy Trinity Church, gathered a considerable following among the students and helped to spread a vital religion. The number of newly ordained Church of England clergymen rose from an average of 277 a year between 1800 and 1809, to an average of 387 a year between 1809 and 1819, to an average of 531 a year between 1820 and 1829.[86] When in 1824, Thomas Chalmers left his Glasgow parish ministry and took up an appointment as professor of moral philosophy at St Andrews University, many believed a new era for vital religion had commenced in the Scottish universities. 'Such a change' wrote one St Andrews student to his father in December 1824, 'I did not expect to see in my day. On the whole, our college seems at present to present an aspect something similar to that of the University of Oxford in the days of Hervey and Wesley'.[87] Four years later, Chalmers moved to the chair of divinity at the University of Edinburgh.

Across Britain, there was a new seriousness and vital Christianity among the middle and upper classes; Christianity was once again becoming intellectually respectable, even fashionable. It was a time when popular preachers became celebrities, attracting large congregations from among the governing elite. When in early 1823 the Tory Foreign Secretary, George Canning, praised the eloquence of a hitherto unknown Scottish preacher, Edward Irving, recently appointed minister of a small church in London, Irving became lionised by London high society, with the rich and the cultivated, Cabinet ministers and peers, crowding into his church each Sunday. Observers spoke of the row of coroneted coaches parked outside the church, and in July 1824, the foundation stone was laid for a magnificent twin-towered, neo-Gothic building in Regent Square to house his large and elegant following. Writing to a friend in 1824, Southey noted that those among his acquaintances who had been 'unbelievers some thirty years ago' were now 'settled in conformity with the belief of the national Church' and that there was 'less [infidelity] in the higher classes than at any time since the Restoration [of 1660]'.[88] In the 1820s, the Scottish novelist, Sir Walter Scott, observed that the reading public could no longer endure the lusty novels of the previous generation. His grand-aunt, he noted, had been deeply shocked at re-reading a novel, which she had loved in her youth and which had been 'read aloud for the amusement of large circles, consisting of the first and most credible society in London'.[89] It no longer seemed appropriate in a United Kingdom that was awakening to its moral and religious responsibilities, at home and in its expanding empire. The new spirit of co-operation of church and state, the increased investment in the established churches, and the ethos of church reform and renewal was having a decided impact on Protestant society. There was a growing hope that much of the British Dissenting population might be drawn back into the revived religious establishments; there was hope that religious unity would be restored to the parishes of Protestant Britain, and that the established churches would shape the character of the United Kingdom state, inculcate civic virtues among its inhabitants, inspire them with a shared sense of their religious and civilising mission in the world, and help to mould the diverse peoples of the British Isles into a single Protestant imperial state.

The struggle for the established church in Ireland

And what of Ireland? Was there also, on the wave of this revival of the established churches, a real hope of securing the conformity of the Catholic majority in Ireland to the established Protestant United Church of England and Ireland? For many supporters of the established churches, Ireland began to appear as the great mission field, the testing ground for the revival of established Protestantism. The Act of Union of 1800, it will be recalled, had 'for ever' united the Protestant establishments of England and Ireland, while the king, with firm support from the House of Lords, had refused to countenance the idea that the Union should be followed by a measure of Catholic emancipation. The United Kingdom was a Protestant state, and Irish Catholics were expected to conform to the Protestant establishment if they wished to share in the government of the United Kingdom and its growing empire. From about 1809, as we have seen, Parliament had begun investing unprecedented amounts of money in building and repairing churches, schools and residence houses for the Church of Ireland, and had given the Irish bishops enhanced powers to reduce non-residency, pluralism and pastoral neglect. By 1815, the new confidence affecting the established churches in Britain was also being felt within the Irish church. In the sixteenth century, the Protestant Reformation had failed to take hold in Ireland. But now with the revival in the established churches some began to hope there might be a 'Second Reformation' in Ireland, one that would bring much of the Catholic population into the Anglican establishment, and thus help to consolidate the Union of 1800 on the basis of a shared national faith.

Along with church building and improved pastoral care, the early nineteenth-century Protestant mission in Ireland included evangelical activity conducted by voluntary mission societies. In 1808, evangelicals in Dublin formed the Hibernian Bible Society, in association with the British and Foreign Bible Society. By the early 1820s, the Bible Society had established local branch societies in market towns throughout Ireland. These local societies purchased and distributed Irish-language Bibles among poor, mainly Catholic families; by 1829 they claimed to have distributed 209,000 Bibles in Ireland.[90] Other evangelical societies, moreover, concentrated on teaching the largely illiterate Irish peasantry to read their Bibles. A Hibernian Sunday School Society was established in 1809 to teach Irish children basic literacy as well as to provide religious knowledge; by 1825, it claimed to be assisting more than 1,700 Sunday schools, with over 150,000 pupils. A London Hibernian Society was formed by English evangelicals in 1806 to provide both English and Irish-language schools; the Bible formed the main text in these schools. By 1823, it claimed to be providing instruction to over 61,000 pupils.[91] In 1811, Protestants and Catholics in Dublin had jointly founded a Kildare Place Society for the purpose of providing non-denominational schools across Ireland, in which both Protestant and Catholic children would be educated together, without prejudice to anyone's faith. By 1819, however, Church of Ireland evangelicals had gained control of the management of the Society, and its schools began providing a type of Scripture-based education that many Catholics found offensive. Catholics now withdrew from the management committee and the Society was denounced by the Catholic hierarchy. None the less, by 1825 the Kildare Place Society claimed more than 1,400 schools with over 100,000 pupils, many of them Catholic children.[92] This Scripture-education movement, which received large-scale financial support from Britain, helped to spread the perception that Ireland was a mission field, its Catholic peasantry hitherto kept in darkness and superstition by their ignorance, by a lack of Bibles and by the pastoral failings of the established Protestant church. For most evangelicals, the Irish Catholics were no less 'heathens' than the Hindus or Muslims of India. But by the early 1820s, all this seemed to be changing, and the conversion of the Catholic majority of Ireland appeared as a real possibility.

In October 1822, William Magee, the newly consecrated archbishop of Dublin, sounded a call to arms when he delivered his first charge to the clergy of his archdiocese in St Patrick's cathedral. Magee was one of the new breed of bishops, from a lower middle-class home, earning distinction as a theologian and pastor, and appointed on the basis of merit rather than political connections. When he was first appointed to the see of Dublin he had been seen by many as a liberal, a friend to the Catholics and a supporter of toleration. But that perception quickly changed, as in his first charge he summoned his clergy to work for the conversion of the whole Irish people to the established church. For too long, he maintained, the established clergy, 'fearful of incurring the charge of bigotry', had declined to act to convert the Catholic masses. They had left those masses 'enslaved to a supposed infallible Ecclesiastical authority' which kept them from the 'Word of God'. The established church must now boldly go forward and fulfil their duty as the one true holy catholic and apostolic church in Ireland. They must confront the errors of both Catholics and Protestant Dissenters. They must carry the Bible to all the people of Ireland, Catholics as well as Protestants. They must build pastoral relationships with all their parishioners, and draw them into the true church.[93] Magee's charge aroused a storm of controversy. Catholics and liberal Protestants denounced the spirit of militancy and intolerance in Magee's charge; they also recognised that it was an expression of the new assertiveness which had been steadily gaining ground within the established church for over a decade.

Other leaders of the established church in Ireland took up Magee's call for mission. In his charge of 1823, John Jebb, bishop of Limerick, appealed to the clergy of his diocese to become leaders of local society, assuming direction of charities and educational ventures.[94] In the west, Power le Poer Trench, archbishop of Tuam, actively promoted the Bible societies. Leading members of the Protestant gentry in Ireland began openly patronising the Bible societies, Scripture education societies and other proselytising efforts. Dubbed by their critics the 'Bible gentry', they appointed 'moral agents' to oversee the religious life of the tenants on their estates and promote conformity to the established church. Women of the Protestant gentry class were especially active, teaching Sunday schools, distributing Bibles and tracts, and regularly visiting the homes of Catholic tenants to provide alms and advice.[95] Protestant clergy began showing a new militancy in their dealings with their Catholic parishioners. In 1824, for example, the evangelical, Richard Murray, was appointed vicar of Askeaton, west of Limerick, and immediately began aggressively proselytising among his Catholic parishioners. He refused to cultivate friendly relations with the local Catholic priest and insisted upon reading the Church of Ireland burial service at burials of Catholics in the parish churchyard. He promoted proselytising within the local schools. Such methods bore fruit, and within a year, he had brought over 40 Catholics into the established church. He actively encouraged neighbouring Protestant clergy to embrace his methods.[96]

In the autumn of 1826, the Tory Baron Farnham, owner of a 29,000-acre estate in County Cavan, claimed that he was approached by three Catholics school teachers who wished to convert to Protestantism but feared they would suffer retribution at the hands of the priests and Catholic peasantry if they did so. They therefore requested Farnham's protection. In response, Farnham announced that he would offer protection on his estate to any Catholics wishing to conform to the established church. Within weeks, over 250 Catholics had travelled to Cavan and conformed in the Cavan parish church. Evangelists hurried to Cavan.[97] The Protestant press in both Ireland and Britain grew excited, proclaiming the events in Cavan to herald the beginning of a 'Second Reformation', destined to achieve what the sixteenth-century Reformation had failed to accomplish – the conversion of the large majority of the Irish people to Protestantism. 'So rapidly is the spirit [of conversion to Protestantism] spreading in this Country', enthused the Protestant *Dublin Evening Mail* of 4 December 1826, 'that all we apprehend is the lack of shepherds to collect the straying flock and guide them to the fold. It is not now by individuals that we can record the recantations, but by families, by hamlets, nay by entire parishes'. 'Never, since the days of England's Reformation', it added, 'has such a scene been presented to the Empire, as that now in progress'.[98] In January 1827, a well-attended meeting on Farnham's Cavan estate inaugurated a Reformation Society to give direction to the movement. Branches were established in market towns throughout Ireland to support the Protestant mission. 'In Ireland', wrote William Krause, a Waterloo veteran turned Church of Ireland evangelist, to his sister in February, 'there is a shaking of dry bones and a stir throughout the country, such as never was known in this land'.[99] Through the first half of 1827, newspapers and broadsheets trumpeted the numbers of Catholics conforming. By April, there were 1,340 conversions.[100] The Reformation Society movement also spread to Britain, where supporters established branches, both to raise money for the Irish mission and to proselytise among Catholics, mainly Irish migrants, residing in Britain.[101]

The Roman Catholic community in Ireland seemed ill-equipped to meet the challenge of a revived established church and the New Reformation movement. Irish Catholics had only recently emerged from the penal times and many communities in the south and west still bore the scars of the defeated rising of 1798 and the reprisals inflicted in the aftermath. Although a prosperous Catholic mercantile middle class had emerged in Dublin, Cork and other Irish towns, the Catholic community also included the poorest sections of Irish society – small tenant farmers, landless rural labourers, unskilled town labourers. Catholic small tenants were burdened with tithes to the Protestant establishment, as well as heavy rents, and they struggled to contribute to the support of their own priests. These priests, struggling to gain needed financial support for their church, could seem overly concerned with money to the hard-pressed peasants making up their flocks. The priesthood, moreover, suffered from weaknesses in ecclesiastical discipline, with clerical factions dividing dioceses and some priests succumbing to alcoholism or sexual temptation. While the church had erected substantial stone chapels in most towns, in rural areas there was a severe shortage of chapel accommodation. In response, the practice of 'stations' – by which priests made use of private homes to hear confessions and administer communion – was prevalent in much of Ireland.[102] There was a shortage of schools for Catholic children, and many were still taught in 'hedge schools', conducted in barns or cottages, with a lack of books and slates, and often with incompetent teachers.[103] Catholic parents, therefore, frequently ignored the instructions of their priests and sent their children to Scripture education schools conducted by one of the Protestant societies.

Irish Catholics had little political power within the Protestant United Kingdom. Although the later eighteenth century had witnessed the repeal of much of the anti-Catholic penal legislation, Irish Catholics had not achieved full emancipation from their political and civil disabilities. A Dublin-based Catholic Committee had existed sporadically since the 1750s, and had organised occasional and moderate petitions for Catholic relief. The mainly middle-class Committee wished to appear respectable in the eyes of the governing elite, and had shown itself to be prepared to relinquish some of the independence of the Catholic Church in Ireland in order to provide the state with 'securities' (to ensure that Catholics would not abuse political power) in return for emancipation. These 'securities' included a state right to veto undesirable appointments to Irish Catholic bishoprics. In 1821, the House of Commons had passed a Catholic Emancipation bill, with the veto provision, but the bill was thrown out by the House of Lords, which voted overwhelmingly against emancipation. With public opinion in Britain strongly opposing it, and with the growing confidence in the Protestant establishment, the prospects for Catholic emancipation seemed to be fading.

Confronted by the militancy of established Protestantism, many Irish Catholics embraced apocalyptic visions. The traditional *Aisling* genre of Gaelic poetry portrayed Ireland as a beautiful woman, heavily burdened with sorrow, dominated by usurpers, and awaiting her deliverance. In the early nineteenth century, this poetry took on a sectarian dimension; the usurpers were increasingly portrayed as 'Calvin's hated breed' or 'the sons of Luther' and deliverance meant the overthrow of the Protestant land-lords, tithe-collectors, magistrates and clergy.[104] In the early 1820s there was a mass circulation of the prophecies of Pastorini, who had held that the Protestant churches would be overthrown and the Protestants expelled from Ireland in 1825.[105] But such dreams could seem the last gasps of a dying Gaelic civilisation, or the fading visions of a doomed Catholic culture, now destined to be transformed by a revived religious and educational establishment and integrated into a modern commercial, industrial and Protestant imperial state. The supporters of the Protestant mission had good reason to believe that they had providence on their side.

The seemingly inexorable advance of Protestantism in Ireland, however, was slowed, then halted, in the 1820s by an extraordinary popular agitation planned and led by a group of Dublin-based Irish Catholic lawyers and journalists – among them Richard Lalor Sheil, Thomas Wyse, and especially Daniel O'Connell. These leaders created within the Irish Catholic community a large-scale popular political movement – a movement employing essentially peaceful means to confront the Protestant missions, instil a new sense of pride and unity among Irish Catholics, and pressure Parliament into granting Catholic emancipation. The main figure behind the movement was Daniel O'Connell (1775–1847). Heir to a large Kerry estate and raised in a traditional Gaelic-speaking culture, O'Connell had subsequently been educated on the Continent and in London, thus striding both the old Irish world and the emerging world of industry, commerce and democratic politics. With an eloquent tongue, handsome presence and sharp legal mind, he became a successful barrister in Dublin. Embracing a warm Catholic piety about 1815, he was drawn into the political campaign for Catholic emancipation, but soon grew frustrated with the moderation of the middle-class Catholic Committee. In May 1823, O'Connell, together with his fellow barrister, Sheil, formed in Dublin a Catholic Association, to co-ordinate more resolute action for emancipation. By early 1824, the Association had decided to broaden its support, creating a new category of 'associate members' who pledged to contribute a penny a month in 'Catholic rent' to support the work of the Association. The Association funds were used to provide legal counsel for Catholic victims of political persecution, to subsidise pro-emancipation candidates for election to Parliament, and, most significantly, to support Catholic schools, build Catholic chapels and residence houses for the priests, and improve clerical incomes.[106] In short, the Association sought to mobilise voluntary giving to provide the Catholic Church with the same kinds of support that Parliament had been giving the established church.

In September 1824, O'Connell and Shiel set an example of open confrontation with the Protestant missions, when with a crowd of supporters they broke into a Bible Society meeting in Cork. They insisted upon a public debate with two visiting British agents of the Society. The agents accepted the challenge, and the debate was carried on over the next two days in a packed hall. O'Connell and Sheil vigorously challenged the assumption that Ireland was a mission field and that Irish Catholics were sunk in ignorance and irreligion. On the contrary, they insisted, Irish Catholics possessed the true ancient catholic and apostolic faith, and were heirs to a rich Christian national culture; their ancestors had been Christian long before the peoples of Britain.[107] The Cork debate aroused a sense of pride in the Catholic crowd, and inspired many similar disruptions of meetings of Protestant Bible and missionary societies across the south and west of Ireland. Local Catholic and Protestant leaders held numerous public debates, which frequently attracted large crowds and were widely reported in the press. The confrontations, dubbed the 'Bible war' by the newspapers, continued over the next few years.[108] Champions emerged on both sides. In April 1827, for example, Tom Maguire, a Leitrim priest, engaged the Protestant champion, the inaptly named Richard Pope, in a six-day debate in the Rotunda of Dublin before a large and respectable audience. The debate was carried on at a very high level of theological discourse.[109] The Catholic Association lavished honours upon Maguire for his performance, in which he showed Catholic theology to be intellectually sophisticated and firmly rooted in Scripture and the church fathers. Early in 1827, Dublin Catholics formed the Catholic Book Society, publishing and distributing inexpensive editions of Catholic theological and devotion writings. The beginning of the Bible war contributed to a significant increase in popular support for the Catholic Association. Catholic priests began joining in large numbers and assisted in the collection of the 'Catholic rent', which often took place at chapel doors after mass. Catholic bishops also began joining the Association; in time every bishop had joined. One of the first was James Doyle, the able bishop of Kildare and Leighlin, who had served as an interpreter with the British army in Portugal during the Napoleonic Wars. In pamphlets and letters to the newspapers, Doyle argued eloquently for an end to the notion of a confessional Protestant United Kingdom, and for its replacement by a liberal political order in which all inhabitants would be equal before the law, regardless of their religious beliefs. There should, he insisted in 1827, be 'no juggling of [religious] ascendancy – no corporate monopoly – no unhallowed commixture of what is human with what is divine'. Rather, the state should seek to ensure 'the liberties and happiness of all the people' and the freedom of every church or sect to 'hold its assemblies, preach the Gospel, and minister its rules in peace'.[110]

When Lord Farnham announced the beginning of the 'New Reformation' in Cavan in the winter of 1826–27, O'Connell and other Catholic leaders accused Farnham and the other 'Bible gentry' of attempting to buy conversions by offering impoverished Catholics bribes of food, clothing or money to sell out their religion and culture. 'The converts', insisted the O'Connellite *Dublin Evening Post* in July 1827, were 'starving and half-naked wretches [who] were bribed with a dinner, a pair of trowsers, or a petticoat, to foreswear themselves'.[111] Such claims served to discredit the New Reformation. Those Catholics who embraced Protestantism became objects of derision and were abandoned by their families and communities. The numbers prepared to conform to Protestantism dwindled, while many of those who had conformed now returned to the Catholic Church. In September 1827, for instance, a large body of converts renounced their defection amid tears before the Irish Catholic primate, Patrick Curtis, and a crowd of 5,000.[112]

Early in 1827, meanwhile, Lord Liverpool, champion of the revival of the established churches, and staunch opponent of Catholic emancipation, suffered a stroke, forcing his retirement. The Tories were thrown into disarray. By January 1828, a government had been formed under the leadership of the Duke of Wellington and Sir Robert Peel, neither of whom shared Liverpool's die-hard opposition to emancipation. The old religious constitution was tottering, and Catholics in Ireland were mobilised for the struggle against not only the Protestant missions, but the whole system of Catholic disabilities.

Opposition to the system of civil disabilities was growing in Britain as well. In 1827, Protestant Dissenters launched a campaign for the repeal of the Test and Corporation Acts, the seventeenth-century acts which disqualified non-Anglicans from holding many crown and municipal offices in England and Wales. Although these Acts had been rarely enforced since the later eighteenth century, they had a powerful symbolic importance. For Dissenters, they were emblems of their second-class citizenship, symbols of the notion that they could not be trusted to hold important state offices. In pressing the case for repeal of the Acts, Dissenting leaders emphasised that they were law-abiding and loyal citizens of the state, while they noted that neither Scotland nor Ireland maintained Test Acts against Protestant Dissenters. They also endeavoured to keep their cause separate from the Catholic question, and to argue that granting rights to Protestant Dissenters was not a precedent for granting rights to Catholics.[113] The Test and Corporation Acts proved to have relatively few defenders in Parliament. In the spring of 1828, the young Whig MP, Lord John Russell, brought before the House of Commons a motion to repeal the Test and Corporation Acts. It was, rather to everyone's surprise, adopted. The government now agreed to a repeal bill, which passed easily through both houses of Parliament. In the Lords, not a single bishop of the established church spoke against the repeal. The end of the Test and Corporation Acts had come swiftly, and for many, unexpectedly – removing a long-standing symbol of the established order in church and state. 'And so', Boyd Hilton has observed, 'the legislators casually cut down the sacred ivy that for nearly two centuries had graced the constitutional oak'.[114]

Catholic emancipation, however, proved more contentious. It was one thing to repeal largely unenforced seventeenth-century English acts against Protestant Dissenters; it was something else to admit Catholics into the House of Commons and high political offices. Most inhabitants of Britain viewed themselves as a Protestant people, with an identity forged in long struggle against Roman Catholic Spain and France. They believed that they had been blessed by providence as a Protestant power. There was considerable popular distrust of Catholics as resident aliens, who, it was believed, gave their first loyalty to Rome, did not honour agreements with 'heretics', and did not share in national rituals and religious services. In Britain, Catholics were not even allowed to vote in parliamentary elections. For probably most British people, it was the duty of the state to support the Reformation movement in Ireland, and not to abandon the Protestant constitution.

But in Ireland, the Reformation movement had been brought to a standstill, while the Catholic Association was gathering more and more popular support, holding mass meetings and processions, collecting Catholic rent and threatening to become violent, if their peaceful agitation proved unsuccessful. Then in May 1828, the country Clare election demonstrated just how dangerous the situation had become. There had been a Cabinet reshuffle and Vesey Fitzgerald, MP for county Clare, a popular Protestant landlord and, ironically, a supporter of Catholic emancipation, was appointed President of the Board of Trade. This required him to resign his parliamentary seat and stand again for election in his constituency. Daniel O'Connell now decided that he would himself stand for the Clare seat. He also announced that, if elected, he would not take the oath renouncing Catholicism that was required of all new MPs. In the election, the Catholic Association, with the support of local priests, marshalled the Catholic voters, including many of Fitzgerald's own tenants, to vote for O'Connell. Among the pro-O'Connell priests was the formidable Father Murphy, whose very glare was described as a form of intimidation. The result was a resounding victory of O'Connell, which sent tremors throughout Protestant Ireland. With the Catholic masses being mobilised as never before, the power of the Protestant landlords threatened and the Reformation movement largely halted, the Wellington government decided it had no real alternative but to introduce an emancipation bill if it wished to avoid civil war in Ireland.

In Britain, however, popular Protestant opinion was being aroused against Catholic emancipation. Mass anti-Catholic meetings were held, pamphlets poured forth from the press, and anti-emancipation petitions flowed into Parliament (some 720 petitions, many with tens of thousands of signatures, were received by the end of February 1829). But to no avail. The government would not risk civil war in Ireland. Further, the New Reformation movement was failing, the system of coercing Catholics through penal laws had failed, and many politicians believed it was time for a new direction for Irish policy. 'I would ask of those', stated Sir Robert Peel, the home secretary, in introducing the Emancipation Bill on 5 March 1829:

most strenuous for arguing [against emancipation] mainly upon religious grounds, what progress have we made in Ireland in the propagation and establishment of religious truth, under the system of penal and disqualifying laws? Where are our conversions?

'Be the cause what it may', he continued, 'the fact is certain, that the reformation in Ireland has hitherto made no advance. We lose nothing, we endanger nothing in this respect by the change of system'.[115] Many Protestant and ultra-Tory MPs strenuously resisted the government Bill. But the government held firm and by mid-April 1829, Parliament passed the Catholic Emancipation Act, enabling Catholics now to sit in

Parliament, to vote in parliamentary elections in Britain and to hold most state offices. There were, to be sure, 'securities' attached to the Act, most notably the disenfranchisement of the largely Catholic 40-shilling freehold voters in Ireland, and the subsequent reduction of the Irish electorate from about 100,000 to some 16,000. None the less, the constitutional order in church and state had been transformed, and a revolution accomplished.

'It is', O'Connell wrote to a colleague on the day the king signed the Emancipation Act, 'one of the greatest triumphs recorded in history – a bloodless revolution more extensive in its operation than any other political change that could take place'.[116] O'Connell had good reason to sound a triumphant note. Through an essentially non-violent agitation, a largely impoverished and despised Irish Catholic peasantry had convinced the imperial Parliament to adopt a fundamental constitutional change, granting Catholics almost full rights of citizenship. Irish Catholics had won a major victory and they had in the process found a new pride in their historic faith and culture. While Protestant societies would continue their mission activities in Ireland, the prospects of securing the conformity of the Irish Catholic majority to the established United Church of England and Ireland faded. The Union of 1801, it now became clear, was not to be secured by making the majority of the Irish people Protestant. On the contrary, the constitution of the United Kingdom had been changed to reflect its religiously diverse population, including its large Irish Catholic population. Catholic emancipation was a devastating blow to those who had hoped to consolidate the United Kingdom around the influence and authority of the established churches. The state had been investing unprecedented amounts of money in the established churches, including the established church in Ireland. And then, quite suddenly, all this changed. After 1829, the United Kingdom was no longer a semi-confessional state, in which all subjects were expected, though not forced, to adhere to the confession of faith of one of the established churches, and in which full civil rights were restricted to those who so adhered. There had indeed been a largely bloodless revolution – some Protestants would say an act of apostasy, a breaking loose from a divinely-ordained constitutional order. Where it would all lead was uncertain.

Notes

1 J. C. D. Clark, 'Providence, Predestination and Progress: or, did the Enlightenment Fail?', *Albion*, 35 (2003), 585–8.

2 Cited in E. Stock, *The History of the Church Missionary Society*, 3 vols (London, 1899), vol. i, 116.

3 E. Bar-Yosef, *The Holy Land in English Culture 1799–1917* (Oxford, 2005), 46–60.

4 C. Buchanan, *The Star in the East; A Sermon preached in the Parish-Church of St James, Bristol, on Sunday, February 26, 1809*, 2nd edn (Greenock, 1809), 39.

5 J. Suttcliffe, *A Treatise on the Universal Spread of the Gospel, the Glorious Millennium and the Second Coming of Christ* (Doncaster, 1798), 6.

6 E. Irving, *Babylon and Infidelity Foredoomed of God*, 2nd edn (Glasgow, 1828), 534–5.

7 L. Colley, *Britons: Forging the Nation 1707–1837* (New Haven, Conn., 1992), 11–54.

8 Quoted in H. W. Carless Davis, *The Age of Grey and Peel* (Oxford, 1929), 151.

9 P. Barrett, *Barchester: English Cathedral Life in the Nineteenth Century* (London, 1993), 1.

10 A. R. Holmes, 'The Protestant Clergies in the European World', in S. J. Brown and T. Tackett (eds), *The Cambridge History of Christianity*, vol. 7: *Enlightenment, Reawakening and Revolution 1660–1815* (Cambridge, 2006), 111–12.

11 Cited in M. H. Watt, *The History of the Parson's Wife* (London, 1943), 66.

12 A. Trollope, *Clergymen of the Church of England* (London, 1866), 59.

13 G. Best, *Temporal Pillars: Queen Anne's Bounty, the Ecclesiastical Commissioners and the Church of England* (Cambridge, 1964), 245–6; P. Virgin, *The Church in an Age of Negligence* (Cambridge, 1989), 120.

14 J. W. Cunningham, *The State of the Country: A Sermon* (London, 1819), 24.

15 N. Gash, *Aristocracy and People: Britain 1815–1865* (London, 1979), 61.

16 Cited in S. Baring-Gould, *The Church Revival* (London, 1914), 124.

17 E. Brynn, 'Some Repercussions of the Act of Union on the Church of Ireland, 1801–1820', *Church History*, 40 (Sept. 1971), 292–5; D. H. Akenson, *The Church of Ireland: Ecclesiastical Reform and Revolution, 1800–1885* (New Haven, Conn., 1971), 128–9.

18 W. R. Ward, *The Protestant Evangelical Awakening* (Cambridge, 1992), 54–92.

19 A. D. Gilbert, *Religion and Society in Industrial England* (London, 1976), 31.

20 J. Bicheno, *The Restoration of the Jews, the Crisis of all Nations* (London, 1800), 111.

21 Quoted in R. W. Ambler, *Ranters, Revivalists and Reformers: Primitive Methodism and Rural Society: South Lincolnshire 1817–1875* (Hull, 1989), 48.

22 D. M. Valenze, *Prophetic Sons and Daughters: Female Preaching and Popular Religion in Industrial England* (Princeton, 1985), 50–73.

23 G. M. Ditchfield, *The Evangelical Revival* (London, 1998), 101.

24 Cited in E. P. Thompson, *The Making of the English Working Class* (New York, 1963), 396.

25 Gilbert, *Religion and Society in Industrial England*, 34.

26 H. H. Norris to Lord Liverpool, 27 September 1813, Liverpool Papers, British Library, Add Mss 38254, fos 240–1.

27 R. Brothers, *A Revealed Knowledge of the Prophecies and Times* (London, 1794), 37–41.

28 Cited in Thompson, *Making of the English Working Class*, 383.

29 R. Owen to T. Chalmers, 24 April 1820, Thomas Chalmers Papers, New College Library, Edinburgh, CHA 4.16.21.

30 Thompson, *Making of the English Working Class*, 375–401.

31 L. Davidoff and C. Hall, *Family Fortunes: Men and Women of the English Middle Class 1780–1850*, 2nd edn (London, 2002), 78.

32 N. U. Murray, 'The Influence of the French Revolution on the Church of England and its Rivals' (Univ. of Oxford D.Phil., 1975), 5.

33 D. Ansdell, *The People of the Great Faith: The Highlands Church 1690–1900* (Stornoway, 1998), 50–51.

34 A. Porter, *Religion versus Empire? British Protestant Missionaries and Overseas Expansion, 1700–1914* (Manchester, 2004), 58–61.

35 W. Carey, *An Enquiry into the Obligations of Christians to Use Means for the Conversion of Heathens* (Leicester, 1792), 62.

36 R. Lovett, *History of the London Missionary Society 1795–1895*, 2 vols (London, 1899), vol. i, 36, 38.

37 A. C. Ross, *John Philip (1775–1851)* (Aberdeen, 1986), especially 52–115.

38 R. H. Martin, *Evangelicals United: Ecumenical Stirrings in Victorian Britain, 1795–1830* (Metuchen, New Jersey, 1983), 92.

39 M. Oliphant, *Life of Edward Irving*, 2 vols (London, 1862), vol. i, 195–207.

40 T. Duncan to T. Chalmers, 9 March [1812], Thomas Chalmers Papers, New College Library, Edinburgh, CHA 4.1.37.

41 Quoted in Porter, *Religion versus Empire?*, 61.

42 C. Grant, 'Observations on the State of Society among the Asiatic Subjects of Great Britain, Particularly with Respect to Morals, and on the Means of Improving It', *Parliamentary Papers* (Session 1812–23), vol. x, 1–112; A. T. Embree, *Charles Grant and British Rule in India* (London, 1962), 141–51; G. Carnall, 'Robertson and Contemporary Images of India', in S. J. Brown (ed.), *William Robertson and the Expansion of Empire* (Cambridge, 1997), 219–21.

43 Cited in Embree, *Charles Grant*, 145.

44 A. Porter, ' "Commerce and Christianity": The Rise and Fall of a Nineteenth-Century Missionary Slogan', *Historical Journal*, 28 (1985), 602.

45 P. Carson, 'The British Raj and the Awakening of the Evangelical Consciousness', in B. Stanley, ed., *Christian Missions and the Enlightenment* (Grand Rapids, Michigan, 2001), 55–6.

46 H. Pearson, *Memoirs of the Life and Writings of the Rev. Claudius Buchanan*, 2nd edn, 2 vols, (Oxford, 1817), vol. i, 173–86.

47 C. Buchanan, *Memoir of the Expediency of an Ecclesiastical Establishment for British India*, 2nd edn (London, 1812), 48.

48 R. I. Wilberforce and S. Wilberforce, *Life of William Wilberforce*, 2nd edn, 5 vols (London, 1839), vol. iv, 100–23; W. M. Howse, *Saints in Politics: The 'Clapham Sect' and the Growth of Freedom* (London, 1953), 82–8; C. W. Le Bas, *Life of Thomas Fanshaw Middleton, Late Lord Bishop of Calcutta*, 2 vols (London, 1831), vol. ii, 27–42.

49 Carson, 'The British Raj and the Awakening of the Evangelical Consciousness', 66–7.

50 R. Hall, *Considerations on a Most Important Subject Connected with the Question of the Renewal of the Charter of the East India Company* (Edinburgh, 1813), 20.

51 'Christianity in India', *Evangelical Magazine*, vol. xxi (May 1813), 172.

52 *Report of Speeches at a Meeting of Inhabitants of the Town of Kingston-upon-Hull, called to Consider the Duty of Petitioning Parliament for the Toleration of the Preaching and Profession of the Christian Religion in British India* (Edinburgh, 1813), 35–6.

53 *Hansard's Parliamentary Debates*, vol. xxvi (22 June 1813), cols 831–72.

54 Ibid., cols 833–4.

55 Ibid., col. 857.

56 I. Bradley, 'The Politics of Godliness: Evangelicals in Parliament, 1784–1832' (Univ. of Oxford D.Phil., 1974), 90–101; Howse, *Saints in Politics*, 82–93.

57 Le Bas, *Life of Middleton*, vol. ii, 52; M. E. Gibbs, *The Anglican Church in India 1600–1970* (Delhi, 1972), 57.

58 E. Storrow, *India and Christian Missions* (London, 1859), 43.

59 Quoted in J. Rosselli, *Lord William Bentinck: The Making of a Liberal Imperialist 1774–1839* (London, 1974), 210.

60 J. Oldfield, 'Britain and the Slave Trade', in H. T. Dickinson (ed.), *A Companion to Eighteeenth-Century Britain* (Oxford, 2002), 489.

61 Quoted in B. Hilton, *A Mad, Bad, and Dangerous People? England 1783–1846* (Oxford, 2006), 187–8.

62 J. Walvin, 'The Rise of British Popular Sentiment for Abolition, 1787–1832', in C. Bolt and S. Drescher (eds), *Anti-Slavery, Religion, and Reform* (Folkestone, 1980), 151–3.

63 R. Anstey, 'The Pattern of British Abolitionism in the Eighteenth and Nineteenth Centuries', in Bolt and Drescher (eds), *Anti-Slavery, Religion and Reform*, 21–4.

64 Quoted in D. B. Davis, 'The Emergence of Immediatism in British and American Anti-Slavery Thought', *The Mississippi Valley Historical Review*, 49 (1962), 219.

65 C. Duncan Rice, *The Rise and Fall of Black Slavery* (London, 1975), 236–7.

66 A. Hastings, *The Church in Africa 1450–1950* (Oxford, 1994), 184–8.

67 C. Hall, *Civilising Subjects: Metropole and Colony in the English Imagination 1830–1867* (Cambridge, 2002), 107–15.

68 I. Whyte, *Scotland and the Abolition of Black Slavery, 1756–1838* (Edinburgh, 2006), 182–3.

69 Colley, *Britons*, 278.

70 R. Yates, *The Church in Danger* (London, 1815), 51–2.

71 T. Chalmers, *Collected Works*, 25 vols (Glasgow, 1835–42), vol. xi, 17–53, quotation on 41.

72 'On the Evangelical Sects', *Quarterly Review*, vol. iv (1810), 510.

73 Virgin, *The Church in an Age of Negligence*, 17; W. L. Mathieson, *English Church Reform 1815–1840* (London, 1923), 18.

74 *Hansard's Parliamentary Debates*, vol. xxxvii (1818), col. 1125.

75 R. A. Soloway, *Prelates and People: Ecclesiastical Social Thought in England 1783–1852* (London, 1969), 298.

76 B. F. L. Clarke, *Church Builders of the Nineteenth Century* (London, 1938), 20–6.

77 D. H. Akenson, *The Church of Ireland: Ecclesiastical Reform and Revolution, 1800–1885* (New Haven, Conn. 1971), 113–27; E. Brynn, *The Church of Ireland in the Age of Catholic Emancipation* (New York, 1982), 127–35.

78 J. Cunningham, *Church History of Scotland*, 2 vols (Edinburgh, 1859), vol. ii, 608–10.

79 I. F. McIver, 'Unfinished Business? The Highland Churches Scheme and the Government of Scotland, 1818–1835', *Records of the Scottish Church History Society*, 25 (1995), 376–99; A. Maclean, *Telford's Highland Churches* (Inverness, 1989).

80 J. Sinclair, *Analysis of the Statistical Account of Scotland* (London, 1826), part ii, 55–6; D. Chambers, 'The Church of Scotland's Highlands and Islands Education Scheme, 1824–1843', *Journal of Educational Administration and History*, 7 (1975), 8–17.

81 A. Burns, *The Diocesan Revival in the Church of England c.1800–1870* (Oxford, 1999), especially 1–22.

82 S. J. Brown, *Thomas Chalmers and the Godly Commonwealth in Scotland* (Oxford, 1982), 91–151.

83 B. Hilton, *The Age of Atonement: The Influence of Evangelicalism on Social and Economic Thought 1785–1865* (Oxford, 1986), 36–70; A. M. C. Waterman, *Revolution, Economics and Religion: Christian Political Economy 1798–1833* (Cambridge, 1991).

84 P. Mandler, 'Tories and Paupers: Christian Political Economy and the Making of the New Poor Law', *Historical Journal*, 33 (1990), 103.

85 T. R. Malthus to T. Chalmers, 22 July 1822, Thomas Chalmers Papers, New College Library, Edinburgh, CHA 4.21.51.

86 Virgin, *The Church in an Age of Negligence*, 136, 165.

87 W. Orme, *Memoirs of John Urquhart* (Philadelphia, 1855), 69–70.

88 C. C. Southey, *Life and Correspondence of Robert Southey*, 6 vols (London, 1849), vol. v, 185–6.

89 J. H. Buckley, *The Victorian Temper* (Boston, 1951), 116.

90 D. M. Hempton and M. Hill, *Evangelical Protestantism in Ulster Society 1740–1890* (London, 1992), 52–5.

91 Ibid., 59–60; I. Whelan, *The Bible War in Ireland: The 'Second Reformation' and the Polarization of Protestant–Catholic Relations, 1800–1840* (Madison, Wisconsin, 2005), 92–107; H. R. Clayton, 'Societies formed to Educate the Poor in Ireland in the late 18th and early 19th Centuries' (Trinity College, Dublin, M.Litt., 1981), 68–99.

92 T. McGrath, *Politics, Interdenominational Relations and Education in the Public Ministry of Bishop James Doyle of Kildare and Leighlin, 1786–1834* (Dublin, 1999), 157–206; Whelan, *The Bible War in Ireland*, 134–7.

93 W. Magee, *A Charge delivered at his Primary Visitation, in St. Patrick's Cathedral, Dublin, on Thursday, the 27th of October, 1822* (London, 1822), 12–42.

94 J. Jebb, *A Charge delivered to the Clergy of the Diocese of Limerick* (Dublin, 1823), 37–8.

95 Whelan, *The Bible War in Ireland*, 161–72.

96 C. Forster, *Life of John Jebb*, 2 vols (London, 1836), vol. ii, 433–45; D. Massy, *Footprints of a Faith Shepherd: A Memoir of the Rev Godfrey Massy, Vicar of Bruff* (London, 1855), 112–55.

97 *Dublin Evening Post*, 3 February 1827; Lord Farnham to Sir R. Peel, 4 November 1826, British Library, Peel Papers, Add Mss 40389, fos 254–7.

98 'Progress of the Reformation', *Dublin Evening Mail*, 4 December 1826.

99 C. S. Stanford, *Memoir of the Late Rev. W. H. Krause* (Dublin, 1854), 168.

100 J. D. Sirr, *Memoir of Power le Poer Trench* (Dublin, 1845), 539.

101 J. Wolffe, *The Protestant Crusade in Great Britain 1829–1860* (Oxford, 1991), 36–61.

102 E. Larkin, *The Pastoral Role of the Roman Catholic Church in Pre-Famine Ireland, 1750–1850* (Dublin, 2006), especially 189–258.

103 P. J. Dowling, *The Hedge Schools of Ireland* (London, 1935), especially 35–98.

104 G. O. Tuathaigh, 'Gaelic Ireland, Popular Politics and Daniel O'Connell', *Journal of the Galway Achaeological and Historical Society*, 34 (1974–76), 21–34.

105 J. S. Donnelly, Jr, 'Pastorini and Captain Rock: Millenarianism and Sectarianism in the Rockite Movement of 1821–4', in S. Clark and J. S. Donnelly, Jr (eds), *Irish Peasants: Violence and Political Unrest* (Cork, 1988), 102–39.

106 F. O'Ferrall, *Catholic Emancipation: Daniel O'Connell and the Birth of Irish Democracy 1820–30* (Dublin, 1985), 52–3.

107 *Constitution or Cork Morning Post*, 10, 13, 15, 17, 27 September 1824.

108 Whelan, *The Bible War in Ireland*, 204–30.

109 *Authenticated Report of the Discussion which took place between the Rev Richard T. P. Pope and the Rev Thomas Maguire* (Dublin, 1827).

110 [J. Doyle], *A Reply by J.K.L. to the late Charge of the Most Rev Doctor Magee, Protestant Archbishop of Dublin* (Dublin, 1827), 91.

111 *Dublin Evening Post*, 31 July 1827.

112 A. Macaulay, *William Crolly, Archbishop of Armagh, 1835–49* (Dublin, 1994), 98.

113 R. W. Davis, 'The Strategy of "Dissent" in the Repeal Campaign of 1820–28', *Journal of Modern History*, 38 (1966), 374–87.

114 Hilton, *A Mad, Bad, and Dangerous People?*, 383.

115 *Hansard's Parliamentary Debates*, new series, vol. xx (1829), cols 753–4.

116 Quoted in O'Ferrall, *Catholic Emancipation*, 256.

CHAPTER 2

The Waning of the Church–State Connection, 1829–1845

Pessimism, prophecy and pre-millenarianism

The failure of the New Reformation campaign in Ireland and the passing of Catholic emancipation were, as we have seen, devastating blows to many Protestants, and especially to evangelicals within the established churches. Some viewed Catholic emancipation as an act of national apostasy; everywhere there was uncertainty. For Edward Irving, Catholic emancipation was 'a great evil in the sight of God', an act of 'national guilt' which now threatened to end forever Britain's status as the 'sealed' or elect nation. 'The crisis of this nation is come', he insisted, 'and upon the [Catholic] question now at issue in the kingdom ... depends the salvation or perdition of this island for ever'.[1] This sense of crisis contributed to a movement of prophecy and of dark visions of the approaching end of world that spread through both Britain and Ireland from the mid-1820s onwards, and was associated with the Albury Park conferences in England, the Rowite manifestations in Scotland and the Powerscourt conferences in Ireland.

The prophetic movement of the 1820s was associated with a pre-millenarian theology. For many Christians, and especially evangelicals, Scripture promised that there was to be a millennium, or a thousand-year reign of the saints on earth; this millennium would be followed by the resurrection of the dead and the last judgement. Most of those who looked for the coming millennium were 'post-millenarians'; that is, they believed that the world was advancing steadily, under the guidance of providence, towards the millennium. Theirs was an optimistic view of human prospects; they believed in gradual but steady improvement, until the world entered the millennium. Christ would come at the end of the millennium to judge the living and the dead. There was, however, another, darker strand of millenarian thought, that of the 'pre-millenarians'. For them, there was little prospect of real improvement in this world. Most people would spurn the gospel offer, and the world was destined to become ever more violent, selfish, cruel, confused, anarchic, and sinful – until, at the time prophesised in Scripture, Christ would come again in glory, to overcome the pervasive evil and usher in the millennium. Pre-millenarians thus had a gloomy view of the nature and destiny of humankind in this world, and saw little prospect of real human progress. They looked for signs of the Second Coming. One of these signs, they believed, would be a revival of the extraordinary gifts of the Holy Spirit, including prophecy, healing and inspired speech.

There were a number of pre-millenarian figures in the 1820s. The most prominent of these was Edward Irving, who in 1825 began preaching a pre-millenarian theology and prophesying the imminent Second Advent of Christ. Irving came to believe that with the cataclysm of the French Revolution the world had entered its 'end time' – a period that would be characterised by increasing unrest and also by extraordinary activity by the Holy Spirit in preparation for Christ's return, an event which he expected to occur in 1868. Another influential pre-millenarian was Henry Drummond, a wealthy banker, political economist, politician, and a member of the Church of England. Beginning in 1826, Drummond hosted a series of annual conferences, or retreats, at his country estate at Albury Park in Surrey for the study of 'unfulfilled prophecy' and the prediction of future events. About 50 clergymen and lay people, nearly all members of one of the established churches, attended these conferences, each of which lasted for six days.[2] The mood of the conferences was gloomy; the participants saw society steeped in sin and descending into anarchy and impiety. 'There is', insisted Drummond in his account of the conferences, 'division and disunion in every kingdom, in every shire, in every corporation, in every communion of men . . . All reverence is gone, all obedience forgotten'. The Albury conferences came to an end in July 1830. By then, other pre-millenarian circles for the study of prophecy were appearing in major cities, including London, Edinburgh and Dublin. From the autumn of 1827, Theodosia, Lady Powerscourt, a young widow, began hosting annual conferences for the study of prophecy on her large estate outside Dublin – drawing support from Church of Ireland evangelicals (among them an otherworldly, ascetic young curate with 'a fallen cheek' and 'a bloodshot eye' named John Nelson Darby). These evangelicals had become deeply disillusioned by the failure of the New Reformation campaign and they looked for a divine judgement on a faithless country. New journals appeared to give expression to the conservative, pre-millenarian ethos, including *The Record*, founded in 1828, and the *Morning Watch*, founded in 1829. The *Morning Watch* took the position that the Second Coming was fast approaching and that it would soon 'be necessary for the *Holy Ghost to make himself manifest* to God's children by visible signs, as it was in the first ages of Christianity'.[3] With the world now in its last days, Christians could expect to see 'signs and wonders'.

The anticipated manifestations of the Holy Spirit first appeared (in the view of many faithful) in the Scottish parish of Rhu (or Row), situated on the edge of the Western Highlands. There a young minister, John MacLeod Campbell, had been arousing parishioners with a powerful new gospel message emphasising the assurance of salvation through the testimony of the Holy Spirit. Edward Irving had visited the parish in 1828, and he had described his pre-millenarian visions and told of the approaching Second Advent. Then, in March 1830, the parish experienced an outbreak of the Spirit gifts. They included faith healing, trances, visions, telepathic communications, and prophecy. Among the manifestations, perhaps the most dramatic was the speaking in 'tongues', by which gifted individuals would exclaim or write strings of strange words which purported to be utterances in an unknown language. Or, gifted persons would speak with the 'power', by which they would make unnaturally loud and forceful exclamations, which had an eerie effect.[4] For believers, the Holy Spirit was speaking through the gifted individuals, reproducing the miracle of Pentecost and giving special messages to help prepare the world for Christ's return. Large numbers of inquirers now made pilgrimages to Rhu to witness the phenomena at first hand. They included the Scottish theologian, Thomas Erskine of Linlathen, who was convinced they were the work of the Spirit. 'These things which are now taking place', he observed in a pamphlet, 'are just signs of the times – listen to the voice of the sign. It tells of the near coming of Christ'.[5] In London, Irving's congregation – now housed in their grand church in Regent Square – sent a deputation to Rhu to observe the manifestations. They also prayed together for the Spirit to visit them as well. In April 1831 individuals began disrupting services in Irving's church by speaking in tongues or with the power. Irving initially sought to halt the disruptions, but then became convinced that he must not attempt to silence the Holy Spirit in his church and he allowed them. The result was pandemonium, with continual disruptions of the services by the 'gifted' and with large numbers of curious onlookers, believers and scoffers alike, crowding the services to watch the spectacle.

The Church of Scotland acted swiftly to suppress the radical new teachings. Macleod Campbell, the minister of Rhu, was deposed for heresy by the General Assembly of the church in May 1831. Several more ministers involved in the movement were deposed in the next few years, including Irving, who was deposed by the Church of Scotland for heresy in early 1833. A number of those involved in the prophetical movement, meanwhile, including Henry Drummond, became convinced that they were now called by the Spirit to form a new church – a church for the world's last days, that would gather the believers together to welcome Christ back in glory. The Catholic Apostolic Church emerged in late 1832. It was led by 12 'Apostles' who, it was claimed, had been called by the Holy Spirit to lead the true church in its last days, just as the original 12 Apostles had been called to lead the church at the beginning of the Christian era. Drummond became one of the Apostles, and they ordained 'angels' to care for congregations of the faithful. Edward Irving, who never claimed to exercise the Spirit gifts, did not become an Apostle, but was ordained as an angel – and for many the new church became known as the 'Irvingites'. Irving died, of consumption, in Glasgow in 1834, and was buried in a tomb donated by an admirer in the crypt of Glasgow cathedral, while a number of women in white kept vigil, confident that he would rise again from the dead.[6]

In Ireland, meanwhile, the prophetic movement also contributed to a breaking away from the established church and the formation of a new denomination. In the later 1820s, a number of Church of Ireland evangelicals, convinced that the world was in its last days, began seeking to revive the practices of the primitive church. This group, which included Anthony Groves and John Bellett, formed in Dublin informal circles for worship and the mutual celebration of holy communion, which they termed simply 'breaking bread'. These circles rejected bishops, an ordained priesthood, infant baptism, and many of the structures of the historic church. They were joined by the former Church of Ireland curate and member of the Powerscourt circle, John Nelson Darby, who soon asserted his leadership over the movement. Calling themselves the 'Brethren', they carried the movement to Plymouth, and then across Britain and Ireland. The Brethren did not claim any special gifts of the Holy Spirit and their denomination remained relatively small in numbers – but they did help to spread pre-millenarian beliefs and an expectation that the return of Christ was imminent.[7]

The prophetic movement of the late 1820s and 1830s reflected the sense of profound unsettlement in society. The New Reformation movement to convert the Irish Catholics to the true Protestant faith had failed. The Protestant constitution had been undermined by Catholic emancipation, and what appeared as a triumph for the Roman Catholic Church. For many Protestants, and especially evangelicals, the United Kingdom was now in spiritual crisis, and the future was uncertain. The sense of crisis was, as we will see, deepened by the social and political unrest spreading through the three kingdoms at this time. From the 1830s, the evangelical movement in Britain became increasingly split between a liberal, largely post-millenarian section, which believed in incremental progress in the world, and a conservative, pre-millenarian strand, which saw little prospect for improvement and viewed the world as in its last days. Some of the pre-millenarians entered the Catholic Apostolic or the Brethren churches. But many others pre-millenarians remained within the established churches or the main Dissenting denominations. They included Church of England clergymen, Lewis Way, Joseph Wolff, William Marsh (later known as 'Millennial Marsh'), Hugh McNeile, Daniel Wilson (later bishop of Calcutta), Edward Bickersteth and Thomas Rawson Birks, and the Church of Scotland clergymen, Robert Story of Roseneath, and Andrew and Horatius Bonar.[8] They read the *Record*, worked for the conversion of the Jews, interpreted the signs of the times, sought to win as many souls as possible during what they viewed as the world's end time, and watched for the return of Christ.

The Reform Act of 1832

The passing of Catholic emancipation not only led to unsettlement in Protestant conceptions of the world, but it also opened the way for further reforms in church and state. The constitutional order suddenly seemed more fluid. Catholics were now eligible to hold most offices of trust in the state. Could not other forms of exclusion also be ended and other social and religious groups be brought within the pale of the constitution? Some believed that the emancipation of Catholics should be followed by that of Jews. O'Connell, for example, had written to Isaac Goldsmid, the leader of the English Jewish community, near the end of 1829, offering his support for a campaign to secure Jewish emancipation. 'I think every day a day of injustice', he noted, 'until . . . civil equality is attained by the Jews'.[9] Others looked for the extension of the franchise, so that a larger proportion of the population would be allowed to vote in parliamentary elections and help to shape the destinies of the state and empire.

In December 1829, Thomas Attwood, a banker and former 'church and king' Tory who had opposed Catholic emancipation and who was now profoundly disillusioned with the existing political order, took a leading role in founding the Birmingham Political Union to work for the expansion of the franchise. The first meeting of the Union, in January 1830, attracted an estimated 12,000–15,000, and similar political unions were formed in other cities. There was a sense of a new beginning in politics. The Whigs, as the party of reform, found new confidence and growing popular support. The Tory party, after decades in power, was divided and indecisive. For many Protestants, the Tory leaders, Wellington and Peel, had betrayed the most fundamental principles of the Protestant constitution by giving their support to Catholic emancipation, and they could no longer be trusted. The general election that followed the death of George IV in June 1830 left the Wellington government in office, but fatally weakened. In July, the news of a revolutionary outbreak in Paris sent tremors through British society. In August, the atmosphere grew still more tense as agrarian disturbances – the 'Captain Swing' riots – spread through rural England. Hungry and desperate agricultural labourers burned ricks and destroyed new threshing machinery which they believed threatened their livelihoods. The rioters often turned upon the rural clergy, who were portrayed as growing rich and fat on the tithe while the poor around them starved. In November 1830, Wellington's government was brought down by a combination of disaffected Tories, Whigs, Radicals and independents, and the veteran Whig politician, Earl Grey, formed a government that was committed to parliamentary reform. By March 1831, over 1,000 petitions calling for reform of the franchise had been presented to Parliament.[10]

In early 1831, the government brought forward its Reform Bill, which then proceeded through months of intense parliamentary debate. The Bill provided for the suppression of a number of small borough constituencies, the increase of representation for the counties and new urban centres, and an expansion in the franchise to include most of the urban middle classes. For its supporters, it promised a more egalitarian and more just social order. For its opponents, it was a step toward revolution and threatened the end of venerable institutions – the monarchy, the aristocracy and the established churches. The mounting political tensions increased with the arrival of a devastating epidemic of cholera from the Continent in October 1831. That same month, the House of Lords rejected the Reform Bill by a majority of 41 votes. Reformers focused on the fact that 21 bishops in the House of Lords had voted against the Bill, and that these votes had been decisive in its defeat. As rioting spread across the country, the bishops and clergy of the Church of England were singled out as enemies of the people and self-interested defenders of a corrupt political order. Popular denunciations of the alleged greed, laziness and corruption of the clergy reached new levels, and the extent of popular animosity caught the church by surprise. Not since the civil warfare of the 1640s, complained the bishop of Peterborough in 1831, had the clergy been 'assailed with so much calumny and violence as they are at present'.[11] During riots in Bristol on 29–31 October, a drunken mob looted and then burned to the ground the bishop's palace and library, along with a number of other buildings. For their role in the riot, four men were later hanged – watched by a silent crowd. In Exeter, the bishop's palace had to be defended by yeomanry from a similar fate. On Guy Fawkes Day, effigies of Anglican bishops replaced effigies of the pope on many bonfires. Mobs attacked bishops in their carriages on the streets, or chalked threats on church walls. Finally, after months of crisis and with the country seemingly threatened with revolution, the House of Lords grudgingly approved the Reform Bill, which became law in June 1832. Although the number of bishops voting against reform had by now fallen to 12, many reformers promised to wreak vengeance on the established churches. 'The fatal vote given on the Reform Bill', wrote the Radical, John Wade, in 1832, in reference to the established clergy, 'has sealed your doom, and no depth of repentance can again establish you in the estimation of the people'.[12] For the Duke of Wellington, the Reform Act was ominous for the Church of England. 'The revolution is made', he wrote in March 1833, 'that is to say, that power is transferred from one class of society, the gentlemen of England, professing the faith of the Church of England, to another class, the shopkeepers, being Dissenters from the Church, many of them Socinians [who denied the divinity of Christ], others atheists'.[13]

Popular disillusionment with the established churches was further revealed when a group of evangelical MPs convinced Parliament to proclaim a National Day of Fasting for 21 March 1832 in response to the cholera epidemic. Many of the disaffected in Britain looked with contempt upon the churches' attempt to mark the day; they disdained to view the epidemic as a visitation from God and insisted it would be far better to look for scientific explanations and devise rational medical responses to the epidemic. For the Radical MP Joseph Hume, the Day of Fasting was all 'cant, humbug and hypocrisy! Ostentatious sanctity!' Given that many of those who succumbed to cholera had first been weakened by malnutrition, reformers insisted that Parliament should proclaim instead a National *Feast* Day and distribute food to the hungry. The Political Union of

London held a parody on the day, which they called the National Farce Day. As part of the dark humour, they let it be known that they would mark the fast by distributing free food in Finsbury Park. The humour became still darker when 25,000 appeared to receive the food, and then rioted when they discovered that there was none. Many of the established churches, meanwhile, were largely empty for the special services of national penitence.[14]

The abolition of slavery

In the late 1820s, with national attention focused on the Catholic emancipation controversy and the threat of civil war in Ireland, there had been relatively little public interest in the plight of the slaves. In 1827, only nine petitions against slavery were sent to the House of Commons, and in 1829, there were only six petitions. The celebrated evangelical abolitionist, William Wilberforce, was now aged and frail, and the Anglican evangelical with strong Quaker connections, T. F. Buxton, led the small anti-slavery group in Parliament. But they faced both popular indifference and powerful vested interests. The West Indies planters insisted that slavery was necessary for the running of their lucrative sugar plantations and that the abolition of slavery would mean their ruin. The planters were supported in Britain by the many merchants who derived profits from the sugar trade, and by the British landowners, of whom a considerable number owned, in whole or in part, West Indies plantations. The prospects of abolition seemed distant; and even committed abolitionists spoke of the end of slavery as a gradual process, to be achieved only after a long period of time.

But then, beginning about 1830, amid the popular agitation over parliamentary reform and a revival of the rhetoric of human rights and liberty, the popular movement for the abolition of slavery was revived. There were new appeals to public opinion. In May 1830, there was a large public anti-slavery meeting in London, chaired by Wilberforce; 2,000 people packed the hall and another 1,000 stood outside. Further packed meetings were held across the country. There was also a movement away from gradualism and a new call for the immediate abolition of slavery. In the autumn of 1830, at two large and heated meetings in Edinburgh, the Presbyterian clergyman and acknowledged leader of the Evangelical party in the Church of Scotland, Andrew Thomson, demanded, in the name of God and all things holy, *immediate* abolition. He argued passionately against any talk of gradual elimination. Slavery, he insisted, was an absolute evil, an offence against God that threatened to bring divine wrath down upon a guilty empire; and there must be no more compromise with sin and iniquity. The slaves must be freed now. God, he proclaimed, 'commands us to let the oppressed go free and to break every yoke'. 'If there must be violence', he continued, 'let it come. Give me the hurricane rather than the pestilence'.[15] Thomson died of a heart attack in February 1831, but his call for immediate abolition soon became a general one, giving the movement the character of a religious crusade.

The brutal suppression of a slave rebellion in Jamaica in 1831–32 was accompanied by planter-led attacks on missionaries and mission stations, including the destruction of 14 Baptist and 6 Methodist chapels. A number of Dissenting missionaries were imprisoned, and when released, they returned to Britain with harrowing stories, which incensed Christian opinion.[16] With the passing of the Reform Act, much of the fervour of the Reform agitation was transferred to the abolition movement. The Baptist missionary, William Knibb, returned from his imprisonment in Jamaica just as the parliamentary Reform Act became law. On learning the news, Knibb responded, 'Thank God, now I'll have slavery down'.[17] In a great public meeting at Carrs Lane Congregational church in Birmingham, Knibb portrayed slavery as 'a great national crime', which could not coexist alongside Christianity.[18] The Anti-Slavery Society sent paid lecturers on circuits and deluged the country in tracts – over a half million in 1830 alone. Public meetings were held in churches and halls throughout the country, and a total of 5,020 petitions, bearing nearly 1,310,000 signatures, flooded into Parliament in the first months of 1833. Some 56 per cent of these petitions originated in Christian churches.[19] At the first general election following the Reform Act, in December 1832, Dissenting ministers instructed their flocks to vote only for candidates pledged to abolition, and between 140 and 200 'pledged' MPs were returned. 'I have served a long apprenticeship to agitation, my young friend', Daniel O'Connell told one of the younger evangelical anti-slavery activists, 'but you are my master'.[20]

In May 1833, the government introduced an abolition bill in the reformed House of Commons. 'The nation', insisted Lord Stanley, in introducing the bill, 'have now loudly, and for a length of time declared that the disgrace of slavery should not be suffered to remain part of our national system'.[21] Wilberforce, who had devoted most of his life to the anti-slavery cause, died on 29 July 1833, the very night that a crucial clause of the Emancipation Bill was approved by the House of Commons, ensuring its success. 'The day which saw the termination of his labours', Buxton observed, 'saw also the termination of his life'.[22] The Emancipation Act was passed in August 1833 and went into effect in August 1834. It abolished slavery in the West Indies, though it imposed on all slaves over the age of six an apprenticeship period of up to six years, during which they were to continue working for their masters. (In the event, further agitation led to legislation that ended the apprenticeship system and granted full emancipation with effect from August 1838.) A massive £20,000,000 was paid in compensation to the slave owners. It was a defining moment for the developing imperial state. To be sure, the sugar islands of the West Indies were no longer as vital as they once were to the prosperity of industrialising Britain. Moreover, the Act, with its apprenticeship clauses and compensation to the slave owners, was disappointing to many abolitionists. None the less, the Act freed some 800,000 slaves, at an immense cost to the British taxpayer. Countless lives were no doubt made better; untold human misery alleviated. And perhaps most important, as the historian Linda Colley has observed, emancipation had a profound symbolic importance, which endowed the British imperial state with an enhanced sense of moral purpose.[23] There was no pressing economic interest in abolishing slavery; on the contrary, slavery had been proving profitable. Slavery had been abolished largely because of a popular Christian and humanitarian crusade, led by evangelical Christians. After 1833, the abolition of slavery became central to the idea of the empire as a providential agent in the world. As the empire spread, its apologists would argue, slavery would decline and the sphere of human liberty would expand. Such a view could, and did, serve as a justification for imperialist expansion. But awareness of the later ambiguities in the struggle against slavery must not tarnish the very real humanitarian achievement in 1833.

Religious liberty and the assault on the established churches

The constitutional changes of 1828–32 – the repeal of the Test and Corporation Acts, Catholic emancipation and the Reform Act – together represented what the historian Geoffrey Best has termed a 'constitutional revolution'.[24] Dissenters were now fully eligible to hold crown and municipal office, and Catholics could sit in Parliament and hold most state offices. British Catholics were no longer excluded by their religion from voting in parliamentary elections. The franchise in parliamentary elections had been expanded to include much of the middle class, and this also had the effect of increasing the political power of Dissenters. These changes raised questions about the future of the established churches. Would Dissenters and Catholics be content to continue paying church rates and tithes to support established churches that they could not in conscience attend? Would a more representative Parliament continue to insist that the Anglican and Presbyterian establishments must be maintained by the British and Irish people as a whole?

For many in Britain and Ireland, the answer to these questions was clear: the established churches should now be brought to an end. Their very existence, many believed, was an affront to the new ideals of religious liberty and equality. The early 1830s witnessed a popular movement throughout the three kingdoms aimed at ending the established churches. The movement reflected a growing popular belief that the reformed parliamentary state should no longer promote or encourage any particular system of religious beliefs and practices. This movement began in Ireland, where the Roman Catholic majority had long resented the burden of paying tithe to support the established Protestant Church of Ireland and where the New Reformation campaign of the 1820s had greatly intensified Catholic hostility to that church. In 1829, there had been a widespread belief among Irish Catholics that Catholic emancipation would be followed swiftly by the end of the established Protestant church. Why, they asked, should the Protestant tithe continue to be collected from a Catholic people who had been emancipated?

The tithe war and church reform in Ireland

The movement of non-payment of tithe began in the autumn of 1830 in the Leinster parish of Graiguenamanagh. Although the parish had a population of 4,779 Catholics and only 63 Protestants, the Catholics had been paying their tithe to support the Protestant Church of Ireland relatively peacefully for decades. Trouble erupted when Luke McDonnell, the Church of Ireland curate in the parish and a militant member of the Reformation Society, attempted to force the local Roman Catholic priest, Martin Doyle, to pay tithe. There was an informal convention in most of Ireland that Catholic priests were not made to pay tithe, and McDonnell's action was deliberately provocative. Doyle was also a militant, who had been active in the Bible war and Catholic emancipation campaign of the 1820s, and he not surprisingly refused to pay. But more than this, he now organised the local tenants in a campaign of non-payment. It was now a year since Catholic emancipation had been passed, and the tenants apparently believed (as some of them told the magistrates) that 'Daniel

O'Connell will get the tithes taken off us, as he got us emancipation'. Some months later, in March 1831, a military force of some 600 arrived in the parish to seize the cattle of those refusing to pay. The authorities, however, were not permitted by law to seize cattle that were locked in pens or barns, and the tithe resisters took advantage of this. Through an elaborate system of signals, villagers were warned of the approach of troops in time to get their cattle into pens. After two months of such 'cat and mouse' tactics, the military had managed to collect only a third of the tithe arrears.[25] The movement of non-payment, meanwhile, spread to other Irish parishes. There were confrontations between the tenants and the troops, and these led to bloodshed. In June 1831, at Newtownbarry, troops fired on a body of hostile but unarmed tithe-resisters, killing 34. In December, local inhabitants ambushed a detachment of police near Knocktopher, killing 13.[26] There were more fatalities in the following months and much of the public grew appalled and sickened by the sight of people being killed over the collection of tithe to support a Christian church. 'Must the Protestant Clergy', asked the *Dublin Evening Post* in June 1831, '. . . be under the necessity of killing and slaying the People, in order to exact the last penny of their dues?'[27] The movement of non-payment spread. By the end of 1832, little more than half the tithe had been collected in most of Ireland. Circumstances for the clergy of the established church in Ireland grew desperate. By now many incumbents had received no income for months, and some were being forced by poverty or intimidation to leave their parishes.

The Whig government found itself in an increasingly difficult position. It was difficult not to sympathise with a largely impoverished Irish Catholic peasantry, forced to pay tithes to a church they did not attend. However, if the peasantry could get away with not paying tithe, would they not cease to pay their rents as well? The tithe war, meanwhile, was not only impoverishing the Irish clergy and threatening the collapse of the established Church of Ireland; it was also calling the attention of the British public to the very real defects of that church. As the tithe war raged, and the cost in lives and money of trying to collect the tithe mounted, the glaring abuses of the Irish establishment became more and more evident, and a growing number began openly questioning the legitimacy of the Protestant establishment in Ireland. The Irish establishment had 22 well-paid bishops, which was only four fewer than the number of bishops in the Church of England. Yet, the Irish establishment ministered to only about 850,000 Irish Protestants, while the English establishment ministered to some 8,000,000 adherents. There were parishes in Ireland with a Church of Ireland clergyman but no Protestant parishioners; there

were churches in which services had not been held for years because there
was no congregation. And yet an impoverished Catholic peasantry was
forced to pay tithe to support this establishment, and some were now being
killed for resisting. For the English Radical, John Wade, the established
church in Ireland represented a 'revolting spectacle of inordinate incomes,
of lax discipline . . . and of an immense ecclesiastical revenue levied under
circumstances of . . . insult, partiality and oppression'.[28] This 'odious
system', Wade insisted, was a travesty of religion.

The Whig government responded to the Irish tithe war by securing two
major parliamentary acts. First, in 1831 it secured an act to end the state
subsidies to the Protestant Scripture-education schools, subsidies which,
as we have seen, had been a key element in the effort to make Ireland
Protestant. In a dramatic reversal of previous state policy, the state now
abandoned the Scripture education movement and instead agreed to provide subsidies, initially £20,000 a year, to support a national system of primary schools at which Catholic and Protestant children would be taught
together. In these schools, religious instruction, including Bible study,
would be offered only outside of normal school hours. Despite strenuous
protests from British Protestants, the state persevered. As the Irish
Secretary, Edward Stanley, explained to Chalmers in 1832, in Ireland 'we
are legislating . . . for a Catholic country [and] we are anxious to extend
our instruction into that country as widely as possible'.[29] By 1835, the new
national system of education in Ireland comprised 1,106 schools with
145,521 pupils.[30]

Secondly, in 1833, the Whig government secured the passage of a parliamentary act – the Irish Church Temporalities Act – which significantly
diminished the size of the Irish establishment. Of the 22 Irish bishoprics,
10 were abolished on the deaths of their incumbents. The incomes of the
two richest sees, Armagh and Derry, were significantly reduced. Sinecure
cathedral positions were abolished. Parishes in which no Protestant services had been held for at least three years before the passing of the Bill
were suspended. The Irish church rate, a property tax for the maintenance
of ecclesiastical buildings, was abolished, and replaced with a graduated
income tax imposed on all clerical livings valued at more than £300 a
year.[31] With the Irish Church Temporalities Act, Parliament acknowledged
that the Protestant Church of Ireland would never become the church of
the whole Irish people. In thus abolishing bishoprics and suspending
parishes of the established church in Ireland, Parliament did not claim to
be legislating on the grounds of any religious principle, or adjudicating
between different versions of religious truth. Rather, it was responding to

Catholic political pressure in Ireland, as expressed through the anti-tithe campaign. Five years later, in 1838, Parliament abolished the tithe in Ireland, replacing it with a rent charge equal to 75 per cent of the value of the tithe and payable by the landlords. O'Connell and other Irish Catholic leaders had also pressed Parliament to appropriate the property of the established church in Ireland and apply it to poor relief and education; and they were disappointed that Parliament had not done so.[32] None the less, the Church of Ireland had been significantly reduced in size and income, and it no longer represented any kind of threat to Ireland's Catholic majority. The fate of the established church in Ireland, meanwhile, raised questions about the future of its sister established churches in Britain. For if Parliament was prepared thus to weaken the Church of Ireland in response to agitation by the Catholics, it might also be prepared to weaken, or even end, the religious establishments in England or Scotland in response to a similar agitation by British Dissenters.

The Voluntary campaign in Britain

A major British movement to end the established churches and sever all ties between church and state took shape in 1832, in the wake of the passing of the Reform Act. The movement began in Scotland, where early in 1832, the United Secession Church, Scotland's largest Dissenting denomination, formed a committee to organise a national campaign to disestablish the Church of Scotland. Their aim was to end the connection of church and state, and usher in an era in which religious adherence would be based solely on the 'voluntary' decision of individuals. They called their campaign the 'Voluntary movement' to signify its ideal of freedom of choice in religion. By late 1832, Dissenters had formed Voluntary church associations in both Glasgow and Edinburgh. The movement spread quickly in the months following the passing of the Reform Act, and Voluntary societies appeared in towns and villages across Lowland Scotland. In March 1833, Glasgow Dissenters founded the monthly *Voluntary Church Magazine* to provide publicity for the cause, while Dissenting clergymen – among them Andrew Marshall, Ralph Wardlaw and Hugh Heugh – issued a stream of Voluntary pamphlets.

The Scottish Voluntary campaign was based primarily on their principle of freedom of conscience. Scottish Voluntaries had no pressing grievances against the Church of Scotland. The Scottish teinds levied on agricultural produce for the support of the established church were paid half by the landlord and half by the tenant; this meant they did not bear too heavily on small tenant farmers, as did the tithes in Ireland. Most of the Scottish Voluntaries were Presbyterian Seceders, who had no real objections to the doctrine, organisation or liturgy of the Church of Scotland. Their objection was to the very idea of a connection of church and state, which for them introduced an element of coercion into religion. How, they argued, could an individual make a free and genuine decision to accept the gospel offer of salvation by faith, if the state put pressure on them to attend an established church? Freedom of conscience meant a great deal to those Scots who had been educated in the philosophical traditions of the Scottish Enlightenment. Scottish Voluntaries also appealed to the teachings of the political economists, especially Adam Smith, who argued that competition between churches for membership in a free religious marketplace would bring forth maximum missionary exertion. They looked to the example of the early church. The church, they argued, had experienced its greatest era of commitment and missionary expansion in its first three centuries, before the Roman emperor Constantine had given Christianity his imperial favour. They also looked to the example of the American republic, where the separation of church and state had been made a fundamental principle of the Federal Constitution and where the churches seemed to be thriving. Above all, they appealed to a liberal idea of society, in which each individual would be free to follow his or her conscience in religious matters, and where no Christian denomination would be raised by the state to a privileged position.

Beginning in early 1833, the Voluntaries in Edinburgh embraced a new tactic in their campaign against the religious establishment. This was a campaign of civil disobedience focusing on non-payment of the Annuity Tax. The Annuity Tax was a local tax of six per cent on the rental value of houses and shops within the Edinburgh boundaries, with the revenues used to help maintain the city's several established churches. To demonstrate their conscientious opposition to the established church, Edinburgh Dissenters now began refusing to pay the tax. They were joined in this tax revolt by many nominal adherents of the established church, who objected to the tax for other reasons (many believed it fell disproportionately on shopkeepers and small businessmen, while wealthy lawyers and judges were exempt from it). The result was what one observer termed an 'Irish Anti-Tithe' campaign in Edinburgh. By April 1833, the city had managed to collect only £173 of the Annuity Tax for the year, while an estimated £11,000 went unpaid.[33] The city was unable to pay the stipends of the established clergymen in the city parishes, and the magistrates were forced to begin seizing the household goods of non-payers and threatening them with imprisonment. In a series of public meetings, the Edinburgh Voluntaries vowed to fill the prisons rather than submit to the 'tyranny' of the unjust tax. During 1833, 846 persons submitted to prosecution for non-payment, and several were imprisoned.[34] For the Voluntaries, these were martyrs to the cause of religious liberty. The liberal journalist, William Tait, was briefly imprisoned for non-payment in August 1833. On his release, he was conveyed home by a procession of 8,000 persons, with banners, pipes and drums. Later that month, a procession of 10,000 greeted the release of another man imprisoned for non-payment.[35] By the end of 1833, the city council and magistrates were being forced to consider reducing the number of established clergymen in the city. Established church leaders were outraged by any such proposals, seeing them as a first step toward the end of the Church of Scotland.

The Scottish Voluntary movement, meanwhile, was spreading to England, assisted by a flow of Scottish Voluntary speakers and literature southwards. In England, the Voluntary movement received support from the party of Radical reformers, followers of Thomas Paine, Jeremy Bentham and James Mill, who called for sweeping reforms in the constitution aimed at making government more rational, utilitarian and efficient. The aim of government, for the Radicals, should be the 'greatest good for the greatest number', with 'goodness' defined in a this-worldly sense of maximising pleasure and minimising pain. The more extreme Radicals tended towards deism or atheism. For them, religious establishments performed no useful function, while they believed that the march of intellect was destined to relegate the 'superstition' of Christianity to the dustbin of history. As early as 1818, Bentham had called for the abolition of the established Church of England by the removal of its endowments. It would, he insisted, be an easy death, of an institution that had passed its useful life. 'The life of this Excellent person being in her gold', Bentham insisted, '– taking away her gold, you take away her life'. 'But that death', he added, 'is a most easy one . . . a death which no one will feel: – a death for which all men will be better, and scarcely a man the worse'.[36] The Radical journalist, Richard Carlile, who embraced atheism in 1822, railed against Christianity, denouncing the Bible as an 'obscene, voluptuous, false, scandalous, malicious and seditious book' and the clergy as 'enemies of mankind'.[37] For James Mill, writing in 1835, the established church was a prop of a corrupt political order. 'The Church of England', he insisted, 'exists in no other character than that of a state engine; a ready and ever-willing instrument in the hands of those who desire to monopolize the powers of government – that is, to hold them for the purpose of abusing them'.[38] Fortunately, he added, the established clergy had 'lost their influence among a people improving, now at last improving rapidly, in knowledge and intelligence'.[39] For his son, the young prodigy, John Stuart Mill, writing in the *Jurist* in 1833, the endowments of the established churches should now be appropriated to support a system of national education. Those endowments, he argued, had been given by individuals in an earlier age, when Christianity was all pervasive, to support the moral and intellectual cultivation of the nation. However, in the present more enlightened age, it was time to remove those endowments from an institution that could no longer provide cultivation for modern men and women.[40] 'We are exhorting the laity', he insisted, 'to *claim* their property out of the hands of the clergy'.[41]

In London, the official voices of the main English Dissenting denominations joined in the call for religious liberty. They could not, of course, identify with the anti-Christian views of the extreme Radicals, nor would they support the demands of the Scottish Voluntaries for the abolition of the established churches. While they wanted full civil rights for Dissenters, they had no wish to promote civil strife with attacks on the established churches or to be viewed as mere 'political dissenters', who diluted their spiritual message with political self-interest.[42] But they did believe that the time had come for the official leadership of English Dissent to speak out. In May 1833, the Dissenting Deputies in London, a long-standing body which represented the English Baptists, Congregationalists and Presbyterians, agreed to petition the government for the redress of six specific grievances of English Dissenters. The six grievances were:

1   the compulsory marriage ceremony in the Church of England;

2   the mandatory payment of church rates;

3   the imposition of the poor rate on Dissenting chapels;

4   the lack of a civil registration for births and deaths (which meant that these records continued to be kept in the parish church);

5   the requirement that Dissenters be buried according to Anglican rites in parish churchyards; and

6   the exclusion of Dissenters from Oxford and Cambridge Universities.

The redress of these six grievances, the Dissenting Deputies insisted, was a matter of fairness and would not threaten the survival of the established churches.[43]

For many English Dissenters, however, this programme was far too moderate. A growing number now embraced the Voluntary cause and called for an end, not only to Dissenters' grievances, but to the source of their grievances, the established church. In late 1833, for example, the able young Congregational preacher, Thomas Binney, announced his conversion to the Voluntary cause in a sermon in London. He had come to a 'deep, serious religious conviction' that the established Church of England was 'a great national evil', whose end was 'most devoutly to be wished by every lover of God and man'.[44] Outside of London, especially in the north and midlands, other Dissenters, many of them of Scottish ethnic background, also embraced Voluntaryism. In September 1833, Dissenters in Newcastle founded a Voluntary Church Society, and during 1834, Voluntary Church Associations were formed in Birmingham, Liverpool and other towns and cities.

The English Voluntaries now declared war on the church rate, the property tax levied in English parishes to maintain church buildings and provide communion elements. The level of church rate was decided each year by the parish vestry, a body consisting of the parish clergyman and all the ratepaying inhabitants of the parish. Dissenters who paid the church rate were eligible to vote at vestry meetings, even though they were not members of the established church. In most large towns and cities, there was one general vestry, which acted for all the parishes. From early 1834, Voluntaries began organising resistance to the levying of the church rate. Vestry meetings in many towns and cities became scenes of angry confrontations between Churchmen and Dissenters, while demonstrators with banners, pipes and drums massed outside the meeting halls. During 1834, the church rate was voted down at vestry meetings in Manchester, Leeds, Rochdale and Birmingham. Across England, a vital source of funding for the established church came under increasing threat.[45]

For many Dissenters, this campaign against the church rate was part of the larger effort to bring down the established church. Provincial meetings to protest the church rate would frequently end with a motion for disestablishment.[46] In May 1834, English and Scottish Voluntaries jointly formed a British Voluntary Society, to co-ordinate a British campaign for disestablishment. There seemed a real possibility that the established churches would be brought down, and the connection of church and state ended. For the Voluntaries, this would be a logical consequence of the constitutional changes of 1828–32 and would usher in a new era of religious liberty and equality. It would end the efforts by the state to impose a religious conformity on the population from above, and it would break up the 'unholy alliance' of crown, Parliament and established church. The property of the established churches could be applied to pressing social needs, providing improved poor relief or popular education. All this, the Voluntaries insisted, would not diminish, but would rather strengthen real religion in society. Church membership would become based on sincere conviction, and the United Kingdom would find strength in diversity as a liberal, multi-denominational Christian state.

The defence and reform of the established churches

'The Church, as it now stands', wrote the liberal Anglican headmaster of Rugby, Thomas Arnold, to a clerical friend in June 1832, 'no human power can save'.[47] The prospects for the established churches in the years immediately after the passing of the Reform Act did indeed seem bleak. The wave of popular hostility to the clergy during the Reform Bill crisis, the tithe war in Ireland and Parliament's consequent reduction of the Irish established church, the Voluntary movement in Britain and the campaign against the church rate – all seemed to point to one conclusion: the imminent end of the established churches in the three kingdoms.

Supporters of the established churches, however, rallied to resist the Voluntary onslaught. The 1810s and 1820s, it will be recalled, had been a period of revival for the established churches, and the achievements of those years – not least the recruitment of a number of exceptionally able and committed clerics – now helped the churches in confronting the Voluntary challenge of the early 1830s. In response to their critics, church leaders recognised that they would need to continue the work of church reform. They would need to continue reducing pluralism, non-residence, pastoral neglect and other abuses, and to show themselves to be effective stewards of their tithes, endowments and church rates. But they would have to do more, if they were to save the established churches. Church leaders had to show that the established churches had a vital role to play in society, that they were churches of the whole people (including the labouring orders) – that they were 'popular' churches, committed to conducting a home mission among the poor. In the early 1830s, there was a steady stream of pamphlets outlining various programmes for the reform of the established churches. These authors focused on the need to strengthen the parochial system of the churches by building additional parish churches and providing more parish clergymen, especially in the growing industrial towns and cities. 'The state of the Church', observed the *Edinburgh Review* in 1832, 'has never, at any period since the Reformation, excited more general and more anxious solicitude'.[48]

The Church of Scotland

The Church of Scotland took the lead in this effort to make the established churches more popular, vital and active in home mission. At the General Assembly of May 1834, the Evangelical party for the first time gained a majority of the commissioners, achieving a control over the Church of Scotland's highest court that they would retain until 1843. The Evangelical party was led by the uncompromising champion of established religion, Thomas Chalmers, and it was committed to reviving the influence and authority of the Church of Scotland over the whole Scottish nation. The General Assembly of 1834 passed three acts aimed at strengthening the church for this national mission.

First, the General Assembly reformed the system of lay patronage in the appointment of parish ministers in the Church of Scotland. Patronage, it will be recalled, enabled patrons, who were for the most part members of the landed classes, to present ministers to parish livings in the established Church of Scotland. Each parish had its patron, and patronage was a property right. It had long been a highly contentious issue within the Scottish church, and most Presbyterians objected to the manner in which lay patrons could name ministers with no concern for the wishes of the parishioners. Since it had been reimposed on the church by Parliament in 1712, tens of thousands of conscientious Presbyterians had left the established church in protest. The General Assembly did not have the power to end patronage, which was a legal right enshrined in the Patronage Act of 1712. But the Assembly believed it had the authority to minimise the harmful effects of patronage. To do this, it passed the Veto Act. This Act permitted a majority of male heads of family in a congregation to reject a patron's candidate, obliging the patron either to present another candidate or to allow the heads of family to select their own minister. The Veto Act did not end patronage but rather sought to regulate it in the interests of the parishioners. It was aimed at enhancing the influence of the popular voice in the selection of ministers.

Secondly, the Assembly of 1834 passed the Chapels Act, which empowered the Church of Scotland to create new parish churches where they were needed for a revitalised home mission. Only the state could create new civil parishes (because of the legal responsibilities for poor relief and education that were attached to civil parishes). But the Chapels Act permitted the church to create new churches that would have pastoral and spiritual oversight over a defined territorial district, and that would be parish churches in the eyes of the church, with full representation in the church courts. Thirdly, the General Assembly inaugurated a national campaign for church extension – aimed at building new parish churches, increasing the church's pastoral role, and thus reviving the national influence and authority of the Church of Scotland.

To head its church extension campaign, the Assembly looked to the evangelical leader, Thomas Chalmers, who had achieved fame in the early 1820s for his St John's experiment in the urban ministry. Chalmers was now professor of theology at the University of Edinburgh. A staunch supporter of the established church principle, he had led the resistance to proposals to reduce the number of clergymen in Edinburgh in response to the Voluntary agitation against the Annuity Tax. In January 1834, after giving a heated speech against the Voluntaries, he had suffered a stroke, from which he had not been expected to recover. None the less, only four months after his stroke and while he remained seriously ill, he accepted the call to lead the church extension campaign – believing that he had been spared from death for the mission of saving the Church of Scotland. 'Nor can I regard it as otherwise than a gracious providence', he informed a meeting in June 1834, 'that having been unhinged, enfeebled, and well-nigh overborne in an arduous conflict with those who would despoil our beloved Church of her endowments, and abridge the number of her ministers, I should now be called upon, in the hour of my returning strength . . . to enlarge her means and multiply her labourers'.[49]

Under his leadership, the church extension campaign moved forward on two fronts. First, the church appealed for popular support for church building. It organised local church extension societies across the country and it called on all inhabitants to contribute as much as they could to the costs of building new churches. The wealthy were asked for substantial sums; the poor were asked for penny-a-week contributions. The aim was to unite rich and poor in common support for church extension. Chalmers was particularly concerned that the poor of Scotland should feel that they had a stake in the established church. 'Every man whom you succeed in gaining as a penny-a-week contributor to our cause', Chalmers explained to a supporter in July 1834, 'you will succeed in reforming as a friend to the Church of Scotland'.[50] Such a scheme of penny contributions had, in 1824, enabled Daniel O'Connell to transform the Catholic Association into an Irish national movement for emancipation; now, ten years later,

Chalmers hoped to create a Scottish national movement for the revival of a godly commonwealth, rooted in Scotland's Presbyterian traditions and represented by the established church.

Secondly, the church petitioned Parliament for a grant of public money to provide endowments for the new churches. The people of Scotland would build the churches, but Parliament would be asked to endow the churches. The endowments would help to pay the ministers' salaries. They would ensure that the new churches were not dependent on the contributions of middle and upper-class church members, and would thus enable those churches to conduct a vigorous home mission among the very poorest inhabitants. The revived Church of Scotland was to be a 'poor man's church', a popular church for the whole nation. The church extensionists proposed to build hundreds of new parish churches, until the entire population of Scotland was organised into closely-knit parish communities of no more than 2,000 inhabitants. In these communities, the people would regain a sense of religious unity; under direction from the national church, they would embrace again the same spiritual and moral values. The extensionists' aim was to reach the unchurched masses, the large outcast population, and bring them into the Christian commonwealth. 'It is on this', Chalmers maintained in 1835, 'and this alone . . . that our plea for an Establishment . . . is founded – on the moral and spiritual desolation of all remoter hamlets and villages in large country parishes, and on the outcast thousands and tens of thousands in large towns – only to be assailed by the territorial methods of an Establishment, and by the aggressive forces which belong to it'.[51]

The church extension campaign captured the imagination of the Church of Scotland. Its celebration of traditional parish communities appealed to the romantic sentiment of the times. Younger ministers, many of them Chalmers's former students, threw themselves into the great work. By May 1835, a year after the campaign began, the church had raised over £65,000 and had either built or nearly completed 64 new churches. Most of the contributions had come in small gifts to local church extension societies. It was an impressive achievement for a small nation, and demonstrated that the established church still had broad support in Scotland. After months of reeling under the Voluntary onslaught, the Church of Scotland had moved to the offensive, and there was now a real prospect that it would restore its former influence in the nation. Chalmers and his supporters, meanwhile, had opened negotiations with the Whig government at Westminster for the grant of public money to provide endowments for the new churches being erected by the contributions of the Scottish people. It was true that there had been no new grants of public money to the established churches in the United Kingdom for over a decade. However, many Scots believed, this would surely change now that the established Church of Scotland was showing itself to be a popular church, committed to its mission to the labouring classes. The Church of Scotland's hopes were raised even higher when in December 1834, the Whig government, divided and exhausted, resigned, and the king called the liberal Tory, Sir Robert Peel, to form a government. The son of a successful cotton manufacturer, wealthy, cultivated, intelligent, with a broad-minded Christian faith, Peel firmly supported the principle of national religious establishments for the moral instruction of the people. In January 1835, Peel assured Chalmers that he was 'favourably disposed' to the proposals for the state grant, and would take them 'into very early consideration'.[52] At the same time, Peel was also turning his attention to the reform and extension of the Church of England.

The Church of England

The Church of England had been working to raise popular support in response to the Voluntary onslaught. In August 1833, supporters had formed an Association of Friends of the Church. Early in 1834, the Association organised a petition to the King in defence of the established church that was signed by 7,000 clergymen, and a similarly worded address by the laity, signed by 230,000 heads of family. The militant evangelical *Record* newspaper gave its strong support to the establishment principle.[53] By 1834, several Church of England dioceses had formed church-building societies and were raising money for church extension.

Peel's government sought to encourage and support the church's efforts by forming a new body, the Ecclesiastical Commission. Appointed by Parliament, its membership was made up of clergymen and lay members of the Church of England. The Commission was instructed to study the revenues and organisation of the church and recommend reforms aimed at strengthening its home mission, especially among the poor of the manufacturing towns and cities. The Commission's recommendations were then to form the basis of parliamentary legislation. With the Voluntary campaign growing in force, the Ecclesiastical Commission was, as Peel informed Henry Phillpotts, bishop of Exeter, in December 1834, 'possibly the last opportunity' for the Church of England to work with 'its true friends in the cause of judicious reform'.[54] The Commission began its work in February 1835. Charles James Blomfield, the energetic, pragmatic and commanding bishop of London, soon emerged as the Commission's dominant figure.

For Sidney Smith, canon of St Paul's cathedral, Blomfield's dominance was no surprise: he is, Smith observed, 'passionately fond of labour, has certainly no aversion to power, is of quick temper, great ability, thoroughly versant in ecclesiastical law, and always in London'.[55] 'Till Blomfield comes', wrote one member of the Commission, 'we all sit and mend our pens, and talk about the weather'.[56] Blomfield's main concern was to strengthen the practical work of the church – by which he meant its pastoral care and outreach. 'If any changes can be made in the actual distribution of [the Church's] resources', he observed, 'which would have a clear and unquestionable tendency to increase its usefulness . . . we ought surely to carry them into effect, even if it be at the expense of some of those ornamental parts of the system'. The aim of church reform must be 'to enhance and give lustre to the true beauty of the church – the beauty of its holy usefulness'.[57]

By late March 1835, the Commission had produced its first report. Peel's minority government fell from power in early April, but the incoming Whig government reappointed the Commission (with some changes in membership), and it produced three more reports by the summer of 1836. The reports revealed serious weaknesses in the church's pastoral outreach. To begin with, there was an insufficient number of parish clergy and parish churches, especially in the expanding industrial and commercial cities. This resulted in urban parishes of 20,000 inhabitants or more, far too many to be accommodated in the parish church or given pastoral care by the parish clergyman. Moreover, many parish clergymen were paid starvation wages; as a result, some grew disheartened and neglected their duties. At the same time, there were numerous sinecure offices and church livings that commanded princely incomes; and these plums were pursued by ambitious and worldly-minded clerics.

In response, the Commission proposed three draft bills for church reform, aimed at redistributing the existing ecclesiastical resources, eliminating many sinecures and strengthening the parish ministry. The guiding principle was that the church should do all it could with its existing resources to address the glaring lack of parish churches and parish ministers. Once it had done so, it could then look to the state for additional grants of money for church extension.

Parliament passed the first of the Commission's three proposed acts in August 1836. This 'Established Church Act' redistributed the incomes of the Church of England bishops, reducing the largest incomes and increasing the smaller, with the aim of ensuring greater equality of income among the bishops. One aim was to reduce the temptation for a bishop to curry political favour in order to gain advancement to a better paid diocese. Instead, bishops would now be encouraged to remain in their dioceses for life and devote themselves to improving pastoral care and worship within its boundaries. The bill also redrew diocesan boundaries in order to make them both more manageable and more equal in size. It called for the creation of two new dioceses, Ripon and Manchester, in areas of major population growth. Finally, it made the Ecclesiastical Commission into a permanent advisory body to assist in the financial management of the Church of England. Parliament passed the second of the Commission's proposed acts, the 'Plurality Act', in 1838. The Plurality Act made it illegal for any clergyman to be appointed to more than one parish living, except by special dispensation of the archbishop of Canterbury. Even with this dispensation, a clergyman could hold no more than two parish livings. These could not be more than ten miles apart, neither could have a parish population of more than 3,000, and the combined income of the two livings could not be more than £1,000 a year. The Act also gave bishops authority to require two full Sunday services in each parish church.

Parliament enacted the third and most controversial of the Commission's proposed acts in 1840. The 'Dean and Chapter Act' reduced what Blomfield had referred to as 'the ornamental parts of the system', in order to make more resources available for the parish ministry. It called for the gradual suppression of all non-resident prebendaries, or cathedral livings, and it called for the gradual reduction of the number of resident prebendaries at each cathedral from an average of twelve per cathedral to no more than four, with some exceptions (two cathedrals were to be permitted five prebends and two cathedrals to be allowed six prebends). The Act would in time eliminate a total of some 400 prebendaries, and would eventually free up more than £130,000 a year, money that could be used to enhance the urban parish ministry.

Many Anglicans were deeply unhappy about reducing the number of clergy attached to the cathedrals. They believed this would severely weaken the work of the cathedrals in scholarship, music and worship. For their Anglican critics, Blomfield and the Ecclesiastical Commission had become too utilitarian in their approach to church reform, too willing to sacrifice time-honoured institutions for the new cause of multiplying urban churches. The cathedrals, after all, represented places of meditation; their prebendaries were often men of learning, whose scholarship over the centuries had helped to preserve Christian orthodoxy. They were beacons of spiritual light; their grandeur, worship and learning served to inspire the working clergy as they laboured away in their parishes. Behind the protests against the treatment of the cathedral chapters was a growing dislike of the Ecclesiastical Commission itself, which for many clergy was becoming too powerful, threatening to absorb the authority of the bishops and become the effective governing body of the church. 'If things go on thus', complained Edward Pusey, '. . . we shall live under the supremacy of the Commission; it will be our legislature, executive, the ultimate appeal of our bishops; it will absorb our Episcopate'.[58]

Blomfield, however, would not back down over the cathedrals. The extent of irreligion, ignorance and misery in the expanding towns and cities was for him appalling. The church must do all that it could for church extension, even if this meant sacrificing some of its 'ornamental parts'. Speaking in support of the Dean and Chapter Bill in the House of Lords in July 1840, Blomfield directed attention to the social dangers of England's large irreligious, immoral and disaffected underclass. The work of cathedrals was certainly valuable. But far more pressing, he insisted, were 'the evils resulting from the want of sufficient provision for the religious teaching and pastoral superintendence of the people':

If am asked what those evils are? I reply, look at the examples of Newport, and Birmingham, and Sheffield. Inquire at the gaol, the hulk, the penitentiary, what are the fruits of religious destitution and neglect. Read the calendars at every gaol delivery. Hear the charges of our venerable judges, and then determine whether, when we have the means of remedying those evils, in part at least, we shall suffer thousands and thousands of our fellow creatures to live in ignorance and sin, debarred from those privileges which are their birthright as members of Christ's holy Catholic Church.[59]

With the passing of the Dean and Chapter Act, the programme of legislation called for by the reports of the Ecclesiastical Commission was complete. The Church of England had submitted to every aspect of the Commission's reform programme, including the diversion of endowments from the cathedrals to church extension. The reforms had been painful, but the church was now making more efficient use of its existing resources. It now looked to Parliament for further grants of public money to help it to build and endow new churches for the rapidly growing population of England and Wales.

Parliament, meanwhile, had been passing other legislation, aimed at addressing the specific grievances of Dissenters and at reducing the popular opposition to the established church. In 1836, Parliament reformed the tithe system in England and Wales, addressing an issue that had long created resentment among small farmers and agricultural labourers. By this tithe act of 1836, parishes were permitted to replace the tithe with a simpler cash charge on rent, computed at the average price of grain over the previous seven years. Most of the tithe was commuted into a rent charge over the next two decades, and there was a considerable improvement in the relations of the established clergy and their rural parishioners. In 1836, Parliament passed the Civil Marriage Act for England and Wales, which legalised the celebration of marriages outside the parish church. Marriages could now be solemnised in Dissenting or Roman Catholic chapels, or they could take place before a civil registrar. That same year, Parliament passed the Civil Registration Act, which moved the registration of births, marriages and deaths from the parish churches to civil register offices. While efforts to remove the religious tests from Oxford and Cambridge Universities were thwarted by determined resistance from Anglicans, Parliament did, in 1836, grant a charter to the University of London. This non-denominational University was now authorised to award degrees, enabling Dissenters to earn university qualifications in England. Many in the established churches hoped that these reforms would serve to draw moderate Dissenters away from the Voluntary campaign.

Members of the Church of England were also showing a new confidence and zeal for the home mission, especially in the towns and cities. In 1836, Bishop Blomfield of London set up a Metropolis Churches Fund, with the aim of building 50 new churches in the London slums. The parish system, he maintained, was breaking down under the pressure of London's rapidly growing population. In the east and north-east of the city, there were only 18 established churches for a population of over 350,000, or an average of one church for 19,000 people. For Blomfield, thousands of souls were being lost, while social order was breaking down amid crime, drunkenness, prostitution, poverty and despair. Citing the example of Chalmers and the church extensionists in Scotland, Blomfield appealed for private donations. By the end of 1836, £106,000 had been raised, and new churches were being built, including an eventual ten new district churches in the deprived East End district of Bethnal Green.[60] A similar urban church-building campaign was launched that year in Manchester, while by 1839, diocesan church-building societies had been formed in 15 of the church's 26 dioceses.[61] Between 1831 and 1841, 667 established churches were built in England and Wales, as opposed to only 276 in the previous decade.[62]

The church-building effort was not simply about stone and mortar, but it also involved providing more pastoral care. Because there were not enough clergymen for the growing urban population, efforts were made to give them assistance. Since the 1820s, church evangelicals had been active in setting up district visiting societies, which subdivided impoverished districts into smaller neighbourhood districts, and assigned a voluntary lay visitor to each. The lay visitors, of whom a majority were women, would regularly and systematically visit the households in the proportion, distributing tracts, giving advice and sometimes charity, and encouraging church attendance. Church evangelicals increased these efforts in the mid-1830s, and began bringing the lay district visitors under the closer supervision of the parish clergy. J. B. Sumner began promoting such district visiting societies in his diocese of Chester in 1832, and Blomfield was giving district visiting schemes cautious support in London from 1834. In 1836, evangelicals formed the Church Pastoral-Aid Society to assist the hard-pressed parish clergy. The Society paid for additional curates to assist parish ministers. It also promoted the appointment of lay assistants to help the ordained clergy with non-ministerial duties. The first president was Lord Ashley, a well-connected young Evangelical aristocrat and Tory politician, who combined an abhorrence of human suffering with a paternalistic commitment to provide charity to the labouring poor. By 1838, the Society was supporting 137 curates and 24 lay assistants.[63] The Society's decision to employ lay assistants angered its high church members, who believed that only properly ordained clergy should provide religious instruction to the people. These high church members, including another young Tory politician, William Ewart Gladstone, broke away in 1837 to form the Additional Curates Society – which restricted itself to the employment of ordained curates to assist the parish clergy.

The church's new confidence was also expressed in efforts to expand its role in primary education. In 1833, Parliament had begun making an annual grant of £20,000 a year to assist primary education in England and Wales. The money was to be used for building schools and it was channelled into the two main educational societies – the National Society, which was connected with the Church of England, and the British and Foreign Schools Society, which was aligned with Dissent. Half the money for each new school was to be raised by the society, and the amount of state money a society received would depend on how much money it raised from private sources. The Church of England proved especially zealous in raising money for school building, and by 1838 the Church's National Society was winning over 70 per cent of the state grants, and building and maintaining hundreds of schools. In that year, the National Society adopted an ambitious plan for a national system of education controlled by the established church, with a hierarchy of infant schools, primary schools and middle schools, and with teacher training schools in every diocese.[64] By 1845, 22 diocesan teacher training colleges had been established.[65] The archbishop of Canterbury, moreover, recommended the formation of diocesan boards of education, and there were 24 such boards by 1839.

As the revival of the established churches in England and Scotland proceeded, the churches drew closer to the Tory party, which was also being revived in the later 1830s under Sir Robert Peel's leadership. A practising Anglican, but one who also admired the Presbyterian Church of Scotland, Peel made the revival of the parochial system of the established churches a key element of his party's programme. The Whigs, meanwhile, became increasingly identified with Dissent and increasingly dependent on the political support of Voluntaries and Radicals. As a result, the Whigs became widely viewed as the enemies of the established churches. 'Bishop of Ripon', King William IV had loudly proclaimed to Charles Thomas Longley after his consecration in 1836, 'I charge you, as you shall answer before Almighty God, that you never by word or deed give encouragement to those damned Whigs who would upset the Church of England'.[66]

The Oxford Movement

One powerful expression of the renewed sense of mission within the Church of England was a religious movement that emerged in Oxford in the late 1820s and early 1830s, and that was associated with a series of tracts on the church published between 1833 and 1841. The Oxford Movement began largely as a response to the threats to the established church posed by British Voluntaries and Irish Catholics and also by those Whig and Radical politicians who were prepared to weaken the established church. Supporters of the Oxford Movement were determined to reassert the influence of the national church as a spiritual society, rooted in the practices and beliefs of the ancient church, preserving and teaching doctrinal truth, and representing an independent spiritual authority. Among the Oxford scholars and clerics providing leadership to the movement were John Keble, Richard Hurrell Froude, and John Henry Newman. Some of the early leaders of the Movement had come from evangelical backgrounds, but had been drawn to high views of the authority of the church largely through their reading of the Caroline divines (seventeenth-century high Anglican apologists) and their studies of the early church and the history of liturgy. A few of the early leaders had connections to the prophetical movement of Edward Irving and Henry Drummond, and were influenced by the sense of a heightened spiritual presence at large in the world.[67] Accustomed to common room discussion and debate, they first began to act together politically in 1829, when they organised the opposition to Sir Robert Peel, the Home Secretary and MP for the University of Oxford, in a special by-election held after Peel had announced he would support Catholic emancipation. For the Oxford divines, Peel's reversal on the Catholic question amounted to an assault upon the United Church of England and Ireland, which represented the one true church within the United Kingdom. They were successful in organising Peel's defeat in the by-election, humiliating him and forcing him to find another seat.

In 1833, as Parliament passed the Irish Church Temporalities Act and as the Voluntaries began agitating for disestablishment in Britain, the Oxford divines began issuing their series of *Tracts for the Times*. These were initially short, racy statements of aspects of church authority, doctrine, worship, and pastoral work, which sold for a penny and were intended to provoke thought and stir emotion. The tracts were the idea of John Henry Newman, who had returned in the late summer of 1833 from a tour of Italy, where he had nearly died of a fever in Sicily. He now believed that his life had been spared for a purpose, and this was to call the church to an understanding of its true nature as the image of Christ on earth. Newman rejected the suggestions that there should be an editorial committee to ensure a degree of uniformity in the content and approach of the tracts. Rather, he envisaged them as free expressions on the part of individuals who shared high church beliefs. They were calls to action in defence of the church.

A dominant theme of the early tracts was that the church had not been created by the state and did not exist to serve the interests of the state. The United Church of England and Ireland was nothing less than the true branch within these islands of the holy, catholic and apostolic church, which had been instituted by Christ, guided through time by the Holy Spirit, directed by the apostles and then by their episcopal successors, preserved in doctrinal truth by the church fathers, renewed by the blood of the martyrs, venerated by generations of the faithful, and destined to abide until the return of Christ in glory. A defining mark of the United Church was that its bishops were part of the apostolic succession, the mystical chain through which authority in the true church was passed from Christ to the apostles, from the apostles to the first bishops and then from bishop to bishop, generation after generation. The clergy of the United Church thus possessed the authority to teach doctrine and administer the sacraments because they were commissioned to do so by the successors of the apostles.

'The Lord JESUS CHRIST', Newman explained in the first of the tracts, 'gave his Spirit to His Apostles; they in turn laid their hands on those who should succeed them; and these again on others; and so the gift has been handed down to our present Bishops, who have appointed us [the properly ordained clergy] as their assistants, and in some sense representatives'.[68] Through the apostolic succession, the United Church was preserved in the purity of the ancient apostolic church for each new generation. It spoke in the name and by the authority of Christ. The doctrine of apostolic succession was not new in the Anglican tradition. However, it had been largely neglected within the church – Bishop Blomfield had once famously said that he could easily count the number of Anglican clerics holding the doctrine – until it was revived by the tracts.

During the course of 1834, the tracts grew weightier and more scholarly in tone, and the Oxford divines expanded their forms of publication, including a series of 'Records of the Church', which explored the history and practice of the apostolic church. The Tractarians, as they became known, began to act together as a party within the church. In 1834, for example, they played a leading role in the defence of the religious tests that excluded Dissenters from Oxford University.[69] There could, they argued, be no compromise with the errors of Dissenters, who, in their view, placed their own private judgements above the authority vested by Christ in His Church through the apostolic succession. The Tractarians also became increasingly concerned to assert the catholicity of the Church of England, that is, with their church's identity as a branch of the one universal church. In this they received valuable support from a new adherent, Edward Bouverie Pusey, regius professor of Hebrew and canon of Christ Church cathedral. From a prominent aristocratic family, Pusey brought to the movement his political connections and his profound learning in Scripture and the Greek and Latin Fathers. He also brought an intense devotional life and rigorous self-discipline, and a commitment to the church as the mystical body of Christ and to the sacraments as visible expressions of divine grace.

After 1834, the Tractarians took a growing interest in the traditions of the church. Just as they insisted that the Church of England was not a creation of the state, so they maintained it had not come into being at the Reformation. Rather, their church derived its spiritual life from the whole history and witness of the church through the centuries. For the Tractarians, the Church of England was both Reformed and catholic; it was the via media, the middle way between the extremes of the Reformation and of Roman Catholicism, between Geneva and Rome.

The English church avoided the errors of both Calvinist and Roman Christianity, and it benefited from what was true in both traditions. The church must not neglect the traditions of its whole past, early, medieval and modern, but should treasure those traditions as its spiritual inheritance. Early in 1837, Newman published a volume of *Lectures on the Prophetical Office of the Church*, in which he developed a theological understanding of tradition. For Newman, tradition in the Anglican Church took two forms. First, there was what he termed the 'Episcopal Tradition', the creeds and liturgical practices in the church, which were conveyed from bishop to bishop through the apostolic succession. Second, there was what he called the 'Prophetical Tradition'. This consisted of the whole body of church teachings through the centuries, including the writings of the Fathers and of the doctors of the church, but also of the stories, legends, customs, folk memories and popular beliefs, that had been passed lovingly from generation to generation of the faithful. The 'Prophetical Tradition' was made up of that 'body of Truth, pervading the Church like an atmosphere, irregular in its shape from its very profusion and exuberance . . . at times melting away into legend and fable, partly written, partly unwritten'.[70] The various aspects, to be sure, were not all of equal value, but taken together they formed an atmosphere surrounding the church, an atmosphere pervaded by the Holy Spirit and not to be rejected or despised.

Some Tractarians began directing their attention to the practices, beliefs and architecture of the medieval church. In this, their thought reflected a general revival of interest in the Middle Ages, which was also finding expression in Romantic literature, especially the novels of Sir Walter Scott, in the cult of chivalry promoted in such works as Kenelm Digby's *The Broad Stone of Honour*, and in the fascination with gothic architecture associated with the work of Augustus Welby Pugin and also with the Cambridge Camden Society, founded in 1839 to revive the principles of medieval church architecture. Some became attracted to more elaborate ceremonial, saints' days, festivals, and liturgical dress. They were drawn to ornate church decoration – including stone altars, lighted candles, reredos, crosses, pointed arches, tapestries, stained glass, wall murals; and under their influence there was a movement of church restoration, aimed at reviving the original beauty and symbolism of medieval structures. Many others, however, were attracted most to the idea of a church that was separate from the world and a priesthood committed to a selfless service. Some, like Newman himself, embraced the ideal of clerical celibacy. The veneration of the medieval church, meanwhile, was by 1838 raising doubts in many Protestant minds about the Oxford Movement, which seemed to be drawing dangerously close to Rome.

There were, however, few doubts about the sincerity and commitment of the Tractarians. Those students who, under Tractarian influence, now sought ordination were deeply serious about their vocation as priests and strengthened by their love of tradition and the beauty of holiness. Many followed the example of the refined and gentle John Keble, the poet of *The Christian Year*, who in 1836 had become vicar of the rural parish of Hursley, near Winchester, where he remained for the next 30 years of his life, a devoted pastor to his rural parishioners. Keble represented what was perhaps the most important characteristic of the Oxford Movement – the dedication of its adherents to the parish ministry and their high sense of responsibility, before God, for the souls of those assigned to their pastoral care. Those young clerics caught up in the Oxford Movement were often prepared to accept the most difficult parishes, including those in the urban slums, and commit themselves to serve the impoverished underclass. The Tractarians could be fiercely intolerant of what they viewed as doctrinal error. They had all too little charity towards their ecclesiastical opponents. For their evangelical critics, they placed too much emphasis on clerical authority and historic traditions, to the neglect of the simple gospel of Jesus of Nazareth and his call to faith and repentance. Yet their elevated view of the Church of England and especially of the responsibilities of its clergy contributed in no small way to the Anglican revival of these years.

The defeat of church extension grants in Scotland and England

The Voluntary opponents of the religious establishments fiercely resisted the efforts to extend the influence and authority of the established churches. They rejected the claims of the established churches in England and Scotland to have broad popular support, and they insisted that the majority in Britain wanted to see an end to the connection of church and state. The Voluntaries opposed any moves to reform the established churches, viewing such changes as simply means to preserve ecclesiastical ascendancy. There could, they insisted, be no peace without justice. And for them justice would only be achieved when all Christian denominations were equal under the law, when none was privileged by the state, and when no individual was forced, against the dictates of their conscience, to pay for the support of a state church or felt under any state pressure to attend its services.

In Scotland, the Voluntaries vigorously opposed Chalmers's church extension campaign. They strenuously opposed this effort to revive the influence and authority of the national church, or to organise the population into close-knit parish communities. The Scottish Central Board of Dissenters, which had been founded in December 1834, began sending paid agents around the country, to conduct public meetings, give lectures, distribute tracts and organise petitions to Parliament. The agents collected statistics, aimed at demonstrating that there were already enough churches for the population and that there was no need for any state grants for church extension. But more important for the Voluntaries than statistics was their argument that the very existence of an established church was an affront to liberty of conscience. Voluntary champions included the Revd John Ritchie, a minister of the United Secession Church and a dapper man with a coarse, devastating wit, who could entertain crowds of 3,000 for three or four hours at a time with jokes and invective directed against the established church. In September 1835, the Irish agitator, Daniel O'Connell, toured Scotland, speaking before huge crowds and calling for an alliance of Scottish Voluntaries and Irish Catholics to bring down the established churches. Voluntaries were especially keen to thwart the efforts of the established Church of Scotland to gain new state endowments for church extension. The established church was, for them, to be ended, not extended.

For Chalmers and the church extensionists, on the other hand, the state endowments were absolutely essential to the success of their movement. The endowments would ensure that the ministers of the new churches were not dependent on the support of middle and upper-class congregations; they would give ministers a degree of independence, allowing them to concentrate on gaining working-class adherents, who might not be able to afford to pay for the support of the minister or the upkeep of the church. Without the state endowments, Chalmers maintained, the new churches would be forced to operate in a free market for religion, in which the poor and marginalised in society – those who could not afford to pay for religious services – would be neglected. The endowments would demonstrate the state's commitment to ensuring that the established church was the church of the whole people of Scotland, the poor as well as the middle and upper classes. In May 1835, following the considerable success of the first year of the church extension campaign, the General Assembly of the Church of Scotland increased the size of the Church Extension Committee to 130 members, making it the largest and most powerful standing committee in the church's history. In July, Chalmers led a deputation from the church to negotiate with Melbourne's Whig government for the endowment grant.

Confronted by the conflicting claims of the church extensionists and Voluntaries about the real need for additional churches, Melbourne's government was uncertain. In the summer of 1835, it appointed a Royal Commission on Religious Instruction to enquire into religious conditions in Scotland. It seemed sensible to find out the facts before making any decision about endowments. The Commission bore some resemblance to the Ecclesiastical Commission for the Church of England, which had been formed several months earlier. Like the English Ecclesiastical Commission, the Scottish Royal Commission on Religious Instruction was not only to explore the need for church extension, but was also to consider whether the Church of Scotland had resources of its own that it might apply to church extension. Both the church and the Voluntaries were unhappy with the government's decision to appoint the Commission. The church extensionists believed that they had already made a strong case to the government of the need for more churches. The Voluntaries, for their part, believed that the Commission's investigation into the extent of church accommodation was irrelevant. The government should, they believed, focus on the essential principle – that an established church was a form of coercion of conscience and should no longer be continued.

The Royal Commission moved slowly around Scotland over the next few years, calling witnesses and hearing evidence. Meanwhile, both the Voluntaries and the church extensionists continued to agitate. The Church of Scotland began emulating the formidable organisation of the Voluntaries. It employed 20 agents who travelled about the country holding church extension meetings, distributing tracts and organising petitions to Parliament. It made effective use of the press, supporting pro-church extension newspapers and magazines, and issuing a series of *Tracts on Religious Establishments* modelled on the Oxford *Tracts*.

The Scottish Voluntaries, meanwhile, grew more militant. In 1836, they revived the campaign of non-payment of the Annuity Tax for the upkeep of the established churches in Edinburgh, forming an Edinburgh Annuity Tax Abolition Society. Soon there were more Voluntary prisoners in Edinburgh's Calton Hill gaol. Early in 1838, the *Voluntary Church Magazine* announced that if Parliament were to provide endowments for the new established churches, the Voluntaries would organise a national campaign of non-payment of taxes, filling the prisons and 'plunging the country into a state of confusion from which it may not soon be recovered'.[71] The unrest was growing serious. 'Never had any question of domestic policy', asserted Lord Aberdeen in the House of Lords in March 1838, 'so much agitated the people of Scotland since the union of the two kingdoms'.[72]

In England, the Voluntaries were also becoming more militant. In the later 1830s, growing numbers of English Dissenters refused to pay the church rate, and in some towns any effort to collect the rate had to be abandoned. Several prominent Dissenters were imprisoned for refusing to pay the rate, among them John Childs, a Congregational printer from Bungay, Suffolk, who was imprisoned from May to September 1835. Others, like Edward Miall in 1836 in Leicester, had their goods seized and sold. They saw themselves as martyrs for religious freedom. Voluntaries denounced those moderate Dissenters who declined to work for disestablishment. In Leicester, a hotbed of resistance to the church rate, Voluntaries expressed scorn for moderate Dissenters who were 'so satisfied with mere toleration that they hardly dreamt of religious equality'.[73] At a public meeting in 1839, one Leicester Congregational minister denounced in no uncertain terms the 'white-livered, pigeon-hearted, addle-headed, power-worshipping, rank-admiring, money-loving, knee-cringing, mealy-mouthed, lick-spittle dissenters' of London.[74] New associations were formed to co-ordinate action. In 1839, the Voluntary Church Societies across England were united to form the Evangelical Voluntary Church Society. In May 1839, London-based Voluntaries and Radicals inaugurated a still more militant Religious Freedom Society, and branches were formed in many towns and cities.

The deep hostility felt by English Voluntaries towards the established church was not simply a matter of ideological opposition to establishments. For many, the memories of actual persecution at the hands of established clergy or magistrates were still very much alive. 'Those Nonconformist ministers who began their work early in this century', observed the Birmingham Congregational minister, Robert Dale, in 1861, 'had to struggle against persecutions of which we know nothing. When they went out into country villages to preach the gospel, they were not infrequently assaulted by brutal mobs, who knew that the clergy and the magistrates were looking on with scarcely concealed delight, and that the Methodist would appeal for protection in vain to the local preservers of the peace'.[75] Militant Dissenters were now determined to ensure that there would be no revival of a national church with the power to persecute. In Wales, where the large majority of the population were Dissenters, there had been a tradition of non-involvement in politics, especially among the Calvinistic Methodists. This, however, changed during the later 1830s, as a number of Welsh Dissenters were imprisoned for non-payment of the church rate. By the early 1840s, some Welsh Dissenters were embracing Voluntaryism, and calling for disestablishment.[76]

Early in 1838, the Royal Commission on Religious Instruction in Scotland issued its first report. There was, it found, a serious shortage of churches relative to Scotland's population, especially in the growing towns and cities. Several weeks later, in March 1838, Melbourne announced his government's response to the report and the calls for state funding for Scottish church extension. The news was devastating for the Church of Scotland. The government, Melbourne informed Parliament, would not provide state endowments for the new churches or support any new grants of public money for the Scottish church. If the Church of Scotland needed money for church building, the government recommended that it apply to the civil courts to try to recover certain church properties which had been appropriated during the sixteenth-century Reformation by the landed gentry and aristocracy.[77] Everyone knew that any such effort would fail, and for the church even to make an attempt would have the effect of antagonising the landed classes.[78] It was a cruel blow after so much effort. 'Gentleman', the Duke of Wellington explained to a Church of Scotland deputation after Melbourne's announcement, 'you will get nothing . . . I am sorry for it; but so you will find it'. 'The real question which now divides this country', he added, 'is just this – Church or no Church . . . and the majority in the House of Commons – a small majority, it is true, but still a majority – are practically against it'.[79] When challenged in the House of Lords on his refusal to support a state grant for Scottish church extension, Melbourne observed that the question in Scotland must be viewed in conjunction with that in England. The English need for church extension, he argued, was far greater than that of Scotland, and the state could not provide endowment grants for the one without providing for the other. In both countries, the population was growing rapidly and the costs of providing all inhabitants with seats in a parish church would be immense – far beyond what the state could reasonably afford.[80]

Chalmers now travelled to London to try to change the government's policy. In late April and early May 1838 he delivered a series of lectures on the national religious establishments under the auspices of the Evangelical Church Interests Society to an elite audience of leaders in church and state. He hoped to arouse combined action in support of church extension for both the English and Scottish religious establishments.[81] In his lectures, he played down the differences between the episcopal Church of England and Presbyterian Church of Scotland, and emphasised instead their shared commitment to the parish ministry and to organising all social orders into close-knit parish communities. He denied any intention to suppress Dissent, but insisted that only endowed national churches could bring Christianity to the impoverished and ignorant masses who had no real desire for religious instruction and no money to pay for it. Only established churches could preserve a Christian United Kingdom against the forces of industrialisation and urbanisation. He warned of the dangers of not supporting church extension and allowing irreligion to spread among the lower social orders. 'Unless the emollients of Christian kindness and Christian instruction be brought to bear on the turbulence of the popular mind, a smouldering fire, which now lies at the bottom of the social and political edifice, will at length burst forth, and explode it into fragments'.[82] All Chalmers's eloquence, however, proved unavailing. Melbourne's government would not support an endowment grant for Scottish church extension.

In England, the advocates of extension now redoubled their efforts to arouse public support for their cause. Public meetings were held in 1839 and 1840, and the Church Interests Society sponsored a further series of lectures in defence of church establishments by the fiery pre-millenarian Liverpool preacher, Hugh McNeile, who focused particular attention on the role of church extension in combating 'Socialism'.[83] In mid-1840, it will be recalled, Parliament passed the last of the acts recommended by the Ecclesiastical Commission – that reducing the size of the cathedral establishments – and the Church of England believed that, having submitted to Parliament's programme of reform, it now had every right to expect a fresh grant of public money for church extension. A petitioning campaign for the English church extension grant was mounted, and by June 1840, 2,546 petitions bearing 213,580 signatures had been sent to Parliament.[84] The motion for the English church extension grant was introduced in the House of Commons on 30 June 1840 by Sir Robert Inglis, MP for Oxford and a committed churchman, who emphasised the importance of the parish system for the preservation of the social order. 'Who, then, are the opponents of a grant?' he asked: 'The Papist and the Dissenter, in unholy alliance with the Infidel and the Socialist'.[85] Inglis was answered on behalf of the Whig government by Lord John Russell, who focused on the deep hostility towards any state money for church extension felt among large sections of the community. In the event, Inglis's motion was narrowly defeated by a vote of 166 to 149, or a majority of 17.

The English church extensionists were incensed. The vote seemed to them a betrayal of the arrangement by which the Church of England would submit to reform, on the understanding that the state would then provide additional money for church extension. 'It can scarcely now be said, as heretofore', observed the *Christian Guardian* after the vote, 'that the State must wait till the Church has first done her duty in the matter'.[86] Church extensionists vowed to renew the agitation, and drew some comfort from the closeness of the vote. They found further comfort in knowing that the Tory leader, Sir Robert Peel, had voted with the minority in support of the church extension grant.

Peel's return and the social crisis

In June 1841, Melbourne's Whig government was brought down on a vote of no confidence, and in the general election that followed, Peel's Conservative party was returned to power with a majority of almost 80 in the Commons. For many, this was a victory for the established churches. 'When the nation's eyes, tho' late, were at last opened to this enormous danger which threatened them', enthused the evangelical *Record* on 15 July 1841, 'down have gone Whigs, Radicals, Dissenters and Papists together'.[87] There was an expectation that Peel's government would now secure the church extension grant. That the new government, noted *Fraser's Magazine* in October 1841, 'will promote a system of church-extension, by erecting many edifices for public worship in our populous and needy districts, we have not the slightest doubt'. Peel, *Fraser's Magazine* further argued, had the confidence of nine-tenths of the clergy of the Church of England.[88] Many recalled Peel's expressions of commitment to shaping a common national identity among the peoples of England, Ireland and Scotland through the influence of the established churches. 'I mean to support', he had affirmed at a public meeting in Glasgow in 1837, 'the National Establishment which connects Protestantism with the state in the three countries'.[89] On coming to office, Peel renewed his close working relationship with his friend, Bishop Blomfield of London, consulting him about ecclesiastical appointments and plans for church extension.

British society, however, was now being confronted by a new set of challenges, before which the Voluntary and church extension conflicts faded in importance. By 1841, industrial Britain was deep in a serious economic crisis and this was contributing to growing social misery and unrest. Beginning in 1837, there had been a series of four poor harvests, which drove bread prices to famine levels. Rising food prices had been combined with a trade recession, which was connected to an economic downturn in the United States. From 1838 to 1842, tens of thousands were thrown out of work, while for those in work wages fell sharply. Conditions for many labouring people grew desperate – their gaunt faces, emaciated bodies and rags haunted the landscape – and there was a growing popular rage over the condition of England.

As more and more people needed poor relief, increasing anger was directed against the harsh new English Poor Law enacted in 1834. This controversial Act had called for the ending of 'outdoor' poor relief to persons in their homes and the building of workhouses across England and Wales. In order to be eligible for relief, the poor were to be required to give up any possessions they might have and enter the workhouse. There, according to the principle termed 'less eligibility', conditions were to be made worse than for the poorest paid labourers outside. In practice this meant a prison-like regimentation, the break-up of families, the separation of males and females, menial tasks, drab uniforms, coarse food and loss of civil rights. Although the Act was only gradually and partially implemented, 'Poor Law bastilles', as the new workhouses were widely known, were being built in many districts by the late 1830s. They became symbols of a political order that, despite the supposed victory of the people in the Reform Act of 1832, seemed insensitive to the widespread unemployment, poverty and social misery. As Peter Mandler has argued, the new Poor Law had been influenced largely by the teachings of Christian political economy, including the belief that competition for scarce resources helped to develop the individual discipline that was vital to human progress, and that it would be disastrous for the government to undermine this discipline with indiscriminate poor relief. The propertied classes, moreover, shared the belief that a harsh Poor Law was necessary to discourage applications for relief; the alternative, they feared, would be the Malthusian nightmare in which the poor would multiply until the growing poor rate swallowed up all the property in the land.[90] In 1838 Parliament passed a Poor Law for Ireland, similar to that in England, and by 1840 some were arguing for the extension of the new Poor Law system to Scotland. The Poor Law and the workhouse discipline, meanwhile, were hated by most labouring people.

With the economic distress and anti-Poor Law movement came a new popular agitation for fundamental political and social reform. The movement began in 1837, when the London Workingmen's Association drafted the People's Charter, a set of demands intended to establish a democratic House of Commons that would truly represent the needs and aspirations of the labouring masses. The People's Charter gave its name to the new movement, and the predominantly working-class Chartist agitation spread rapidly through England, Wales and Scotland. Chartists organised petitions, processions, and mass meetings, and issued tracts and journals. In some areas, Chartists focused their agitation on the established churches, viewing them both as props of an unjust political order and as symbols of a middle-class Christian respectability that professed concern for the poor but herded them into workhouse 'bastilles'. Many Chartists were products of Christian homes, and had learned to read their Bibles in Sunday schools. The language they found in the Bible – the frequent denunciations of the corruptions of the rich and the oppression of the poor – seemed far from the message of passive obedience and non-resistance proclaimed to the labouring poor from the pulpits and the Christian press. In the summer of 1839, Chartists broke into churches in Stockport, Bolton, Sheffield and other Midland towns, occupying the rented pews of middle-class families and disrupting Sunday services with demands that the ministers preach a gospel of social justice.

Following a number of violent confrontations, most notably a clash between armed Chartists and troops at Newport in South Wales in November 1839, Chartism was forcibly suppressed and 500 leaders arrested. As the economic distress worsened, however, Chartism quickly revived. A National Charter Association was formed in the summer of 1840, which developed a national organisation of local societies and penny-a-week subscriptions aimed at mobilising mass support. The Chartists presented a petition bearing over 3,300,000 petitions to Parliament in May 1842, but Parliament refused to receive it. Frustrated at the lack of political progress, and suffering increasing economic misery, Chartists in the Midlands returned to violent action in the summer of 1842. Marauding bands armed with clubs and staves forced the closure of factories and called for a general strike that would bring down the social order. These bands were suppressed by the military, but conditions remained volatile.

For many middle- and upper-class Christians, the social crisis of the early 1840s was a divine message to the nation, a warning of the dangers of class war and a call to return to a common national faith. Many perceived Chartism and Socialism as forms of rebellion against a social order ordained by God. For them, the crisis provided still further evidence of the need for church extension and a revival of the established churches. It was, they believed, only through parish churches and parish schools that the labouring classes would be taught patience and humility in times of

adversity; it was only through the influence of the national religious establishments that social harmony could be restored and preserved. Some
believed that Chartism and Socialism were outgrowths of Dissent. 'What
are those . . . forms of evil which we have seen gathered into the common
head of Socialism', asked Samuel Wilberforce, archdeacon of Surrey, in his
Charge of 1842, 'but the outgrown religious dissent of the previous generation? What are they, but the moral history of those who have run through
all sects, until, in the vexation of their weary spirits, they believe that all
religion is sectarian?'[91] For Bishop Blomfield in his *Charge* of October
1842, it was to church extension 'that the country must look, under God,
for the cure of its most dangerous diseases'.[92]

The Disruption of the Church of Scotland

In Scotland, however, the established church was by 1842 in no position
to provide any cure for a diseased social order. The Church of Scotland
was itself deeply divided and distracted, and on the verge of being broken
in two. The confidence of the mid-1830s, when the church had united
behind the church extension movement, was now gone, and instead nearly
half the membership was preparing to leave the national church, believing
that it was being fatally corrupted and losing its identity as a church of
Christ. How had this come to be?

The crisis threatening the break-up of the established Church of
Scotland had grown out of the church's attempt in 1834 to make the selection of its ministers more popular, by reforming the system of church
patronage. More particularly, the crisis had emerged from the Church's
Veto Act. This Act, it will be recalled, had been passed by the General
Assembly of the Church of Scotland in May 1834, as part of its programme of internal reforms. The Veto Act had given the parishioners – or
rather the majority of male heads of family in communion with the church
and living within the parish – the power to veto a candidate who had been
presented for the ministry of the parish church by the patron. The intention had been to protect parish churches from the 'intrusion' of patron's
candidates who were disliked by the parishioners for whatever reason. A
minister who was disliked by most parishioners, it was argued, could not
be an effective pastor in that parish, and 'intruding' him into a parish
church against the will of the majority of parishioners would lead to division and bitterness.

Difficulties regarding the Veto Act began to emerge in October 1834,
when the Earl of Kinoull, patron of the Perthshire parish of Auchterarder,

presented Robert Young, a recently-licensed probationer minister, to be minister of the parish. Young was not an inspiring preacher, and after hearing him preach, the male heads of family vetoed the presentation by a vote of 287 votes to 2. Young believed that the veto was the result of prejudice (he was slightly lame) and he appealed against the veto in the upper church courts. In May 1835, however, the General Assembly, as the highest ecclesiastical court of appeal, upheld the veto. At this point, Young decided to carry his case to the civil courts, and challenge the legality of the Veto Act under civil law. His civil rights, he believed, were affected by what he viewed as an unjust and illegal veto. Three years later, on 8 March 1838, the Court of Session, as the highest civil court in Scotland, delivered its verdict on Young's case. It found for Young, and pronounced the Church's Veto Act to be an illegal infringement on the civil rights of patrons and their presentees. Church patronage, the Court of Session argued, was part of the civil law, and the Church of Scotland did not have the authority to set aside rights that were guaranteed by civil law. The Church of Scotland immediately appealed against the Court of Session's decision to the House of Lords, the supreme civil court in the United Kingdom. But in May 1839, the House of Lords ruled in favour of the Court of Session, and against the church.

The leaders of the dominant Evangelical party in the church, and especially Thomas Chalmers, were in no mood to back down. The issue, in their view, involved the authority of the Church of Scotland to decide who should be appointed to its ministry; it was a question of who should appoint people to the spiritual office of pastor of souls. At the General Assembly in May 1839, Chalmers argued in an impassioned speech that there were two fundamental principles at stake in the Auchterarder case. First, there was the principle of 'non-intrusion'. To set aside the Veto Act would be to allow patrons, many of whom were not even members of the Church of Scotland, to 'intrude' unpopular ministers into parish livings, undermining the pastoral relationship between minister and parishioners, and weakening all the efforts of recent years to revive the influence of the national church. Second, and more important, there was the principle of 'spiritual independence'. For Chalmers and his evangelical supporters, the appointment of a minister to a pastoral charge was a spiritual act. If the civil courts were allowed to tell the church who it must place in its pastoral charges, it would compromise the church's independence in a vital spiritual matter. It would set the state over Christ as spiritual head of the church, and render the church little more than a department of state. It would be a confirmation of what the Voluntaries had been arguing – that the established church was controlled by the state and its clergy were state hirelings.

Not all within the Church of Scotland, however, supported the position taken by Chalmers and the evangelical 'non-intrusionists'. The Moderate party in the church, led by Professor George Cook of St Andrews University, had never been happy with the Veto Act, which moderates felt was too 'democratic' and potentially unfair towards patrons and their candidates. They now insisted that the church, as an established church, must accept the judgement of the civil courts that the Veto infringed on civil rights and had to be set aside. For them, the high flown claims by Chalmers and his evangelical supporters that the state was seeking to end the church's spiritual independence were exaggerated and irresponsible. The moderates, however, were a minority within the church, and their calls for compromise lacked the passion and impressive oratory of the evangelical non-instrusionists.

A few weeks later, in the summer of 1839, another patronage case came to a climax, adding further heat to the conflict. This involved the parish of Lethendy, in the Perthshire presbytery of Dunkeld. A few years earlier, in 1835, the crown, which was the legal patron of Lethendy, had presented Thomas Clark to be the assistant and successor to the infirm minister of the parish. However, the male heads of family vetoed Clark's presentation, and the church courts sustained the veto. The patron then presented a second candidate, Andrew Kessen, who was acceptable to the parishioners, and the presbytery of Dunkeld prepared to ordain him.

The vetoed candidate, however, had carried his case to the civil courts. In 1838, the Court of Session, having by now decided that the Veto Act was illegal, issued an interdict, or decree, forbidding the presbytery of Dunkeld to ordain the second candidate as minister of the parish. The presbytery turned to its superior ecclesiastical court, the General Assembly, for instructions, and the Assembly instructed them to proceed with the ordination. The members of the presbytery of Dunkeld were placed in a dilemma – whether to obey the Court of Session, as the supreme civil court in Scotland, or the General Assembly, as the supreme ecclesiastical court. Were they to obey Caesar or Christ? The presbytery decided to obey the supreme ecclesiastical court, and in September 1838, they ordained Kessen as minister of Lethendy. The Court of Session responded in June 1839 by summoning the presbytery to appear before them for the civil crime of breach of interdict. By a narrow majority, the Court decided not to imprison the ministers for participating in the ordination. But it did censure the presbytery and impose heavy court costs, and warned that in any future breach of interdict, a presbytery should expect to be imprisoned. The Lord President of the Court of Session, Charles Hope, issued, with the arrogance of power, a solemn admonition to those ministers who claimed their conscience would not permit them to accept the supremacy of the civil courts in the Church of Scotland. 'As for those ministers of the Church', he asserted, 'whose conscience cannot submit to the law . . . I am afraid nothing remains for those ministers but to retire from the Established Church. It is impossible that they should remain ministers of the Established Church, and yet reject the law by which they have become an Established Church'.[93] The evangelical non-intrusionists could not accept a legal judgement by the supreme civil court of Scotland which held that their church was the creation of the state (rather than of Christ), and the prospect of a breakup of the established Church of Scotland began to loom.

In early 1840, the evangelical leaders in the church looked to Parliament for a legislative solution to the conflict. The Tory Lord Aberdeen, a member of the Church of Scotland and a close friend of Peel, attempted to frame a bill that would allow a modified version of the Veto Act, provided that the civil courts had the authority to review any contested veto cases. But Chalmers and the Evangelical party in the church could not approve Lord Aberdeen's compromise, as they believed it left the civil courts with too much power over the church, and an angry Lord Aberdeen withdrew his bill. Melbourne's Whig government, meanwhile, refused to make any attempt to find a solution. Melbourne had developed a personal dislike for Chalmers, believing him to be a 'madman' and a 'rogue', while Chalmers, for his part, was open about his 'moral loathing' for the Whigs.

The conflict now moved to its final crisis – the tortuous case involving the Banffshire parish of Marnoch, in the presbytery of Strathbogie. In 1837, the Earl of Fife, as patron, had presented John Edwards, a 44-year-old schoolmaster and probationer minister, to the vacant parish of Marnoch. Edwards had previously served as an assistant minister in Marnoch, but had proved so unpopular that he had been dismissed at the request of the parishioners. Not surprisingly, then, his presentation was overwhelmingly vetoed – with 261 male heads of family voting to veto, and only one, a local innkeeper, supporting Edwards. The patron then presented another candidate, who was acceptable to the parishioners. Edwards, however, took his case to the Court of Session, which in July 1839 instructed the presbytery of Strathbogie to ordain Edwards to the ministry of Marnoch. The Veto Act, the Court of Session declared, was null and void, and the wishes of the parishioners were irrelevant to Edwards's civil right to the living. The General Assembly, however, instructed the presbytery not to ordain Edwards; in its view the Veto Act was still legal and binding within the Church of Scotland, and the unpopular Edwards must not be intruded on the people of Marnoch. Again, a presbytery was confronted with a dilemma: obey the supreme civil court or obey the supreme ecclesiastical court. This time, a majority of ministers on the presbytery of Strathbogie decided they would obey the civil court. The General Assembly tried to convince them to desist through 'brotherly consultation', but the presbytery held firm and ordained Edwards on a snowy January day in 1841. Before the ordination ceremony began, the congregation solemnly rose up and departed from the church, never to return; their place was then taken by an unruly crowd, including boys who pelted the presbytery members with snowballs from the balcony. The 'Marnoch intrusion' caused outrage among church evangelicals. A few months later, in May 1841, the General Assembly deposed the seven ministers of the Strathbogie presbytery for having ignored its solemn instruction not to ordain Edwards. With this act, a disruption of the Church of Scotland became virtually inevitable. The Moderate party rallied to the support of the deposed ministers, refusing to recognise the decision of the General Assembly, while the deposed ministers refused to leave their churches. Church order was breaking down amid passionate denunciations. Adding to the unrest, a religious revival movement had begun in 1839 in the Scottish church and reached its height in 1840–41. Many evangelicals came under millenarian influence, and believed that the world was now in its last days, which made them less open to compromise.[94]

Sir Robert Peel, whose government came to power in the summer of 1841, was incensed that ministers of the Church of Scotland should be deposed for obeying the civil law. He now decided that his government would do nothing to assist the Church of Scotland in its crisis. He became convinced that the General Assembly was seeking to suppress individual civil rights, place themselves above the civil law, and establish a theocratic tyranny in Scotland. Evangelical opponents of patronage would either have to submit to the civil laws which governed the established church in Scotland, or leave the church. In the event, most of the evangelicals chose to leave. In May 1843 the Church of Scotland experienced the great Disruption. Over 470 ministers and probationers – more than a third of the total number of clerics – and perhaps half the lay membership followed Chalmers out the established church to form the Free Church of Scotland. They left what they viewed as a compromised church to form a free, popular and national church. The outgoing ministers included men of great commitment and ability. They received significant financial support from

urban middle classes, many of whom had long resented the political dominance of the landed classes in Scotland. The outgoing laity also included
many independently-minded labouring people – artisans, tenant farmers,
rural labourers, fisherfolk – who resented the traditional hierarchical social
order dominated by the landed gentry and aristocracy.[95] In response, most
of the Scottish landed classes viewed adherents of the new Free Church as
rebels against the established order in church and state. Many landlords
denied the Free Church sites on which to build churches and manses, and
dismissed tenants and agricultural labourers who joined it.

Despite such victimisation, the Free Church flourished, creating through
considerable sacrifice a national ecclesiastical organisation. Within five
years, the Free Church had built 730 new churches, 400 manses, and 500
primary schools, while they were also in the process of building the New
College in Edinburgh for the training of the clergy. It became active in overseas missions. Under Chalmers's inspiration, it also launched an innovative
home mission movement in Scotland's industrial towns and cities. It was
an astonishing achievement, and the Free Church now emerged as the most
dynamic of Scotland's competing denominations.

To be sure, many committed Christians, including a number of able
clergymen, remained within the established church. Some of those who
remained sincerely believed that aristocratic and crown patronage was the
best means of appointing ministers. Some believed that the evangelical
non-intrusionists had provoked the crisis by their excessive zeal and intolerance of other views. Still others believed that whatever the rights and
wrongs of the patronage dispute, it was not worth breaking up Scotland's
national church. None the less, the established Church of Scotland was in
1843 reduced to a remnant, which could claim the adherence of less than a
third of the Scottish population.

The Church of Scotland had until 1838 been effectively restoring its
influence in Scotland's industrialising society. Thomas Chalmers had been
arguably the leading British champion of the principle of an established
church, and under his leadership there had been a great popular movement
aimed at building new churches and extending the authority of the religious establishment. Now Chalmers and half the members of the Church
of Scotland had departed. The established Church of Scotland, like the
Church of Ireland, was now a minority church. For most of the outgoing
ministers and laypeople, the Disruption was a glorious moment in the history of the Scottish church, when Scottish Presbyterians had taken a stand
for the principle of the church's spiritual independence from the state and
had been prepared to sacrifice for that principle. Many others viewed the

Disruption as a tragedy, and a devastating blow to the ideal of a national church.

The Oxford Movement in crisis

The beginning of Peel's government in 1841 also coincided with a growing crisis within the Church of England, associated with the Oxford Movement. From the later 1830s, as we have seen, some Tractarians were seeking to recover the ecclesiastical traditions of previous centuries, and especially the Middle Ages. There was a growing interest in the pre-Reformation church, and in the Catholic identity of the Church of England as a branch of the universal church. Some began looking upon the Reformation not as the triumph of national and Protestant religion, but as a tragic shattering of the unity of Latin Christendom – leading to the breakdown of religious authority, increased state control over national churches and the growth of Dissent. For such Tractarians, Voluntaryism, including its insistence on individual choice and a free market in religion, was the logical and unfortunate culmination of the Reformation emphasis on private judgement. In 1838, the Tractarians, John Henry Newman and John Keble, published two volumes of the writings of Richard Hurrell Froude, the Tractarian leader who had died of consumption two years earlier. Froude's *Remains* contained expressions of hatred for the Protestant Reformation and veneration for the medieval Catholic Church – which caused revulsion among many Anglicans. The following year, Isaac Williams's Tract 80, *On Reserve in Communicating Religious Knowledge*, aroused further distrust. Williams suggested that certain Christian teachings should be held back from the common people and kept in 'reserve'. For most Protestants, however the idea of 'reserved', or secretive doctrine resonated with perceptions of an authoritative Roman Catholic Church imposing spiritual tyranny through fear and superstition.

Evangelicals and liberal Anglicans grew increasingly suspicious of what they viewed as 'Romanising' tendencies in the Oxford Movement. In 1836, the liberal Anglican Thomas Arnold had published an attack on the Tractarians in the *Edinburgh Review* under the none too subtle title of 'The Oxford Malignants'. Such attacks grew more frequent after 1838. Opponents began insisting that the Tractarians did not belong in a Protestant Church of England, while some advanced Tractarians began contemplating seceding to the Roman Catholic Church. Early in 1841, John Henry Newman added fuel to the conflict with the publication of Tract 90, *Remarks on Certain Passages in the Thirty-Nine Articles*. His intention, he later insisted, was to halt secessions to Rome by demonstrating to advanced Tractarians that the Thirty-nine Articles, which defined Anglican doctrinal orthodoxy, could be interpreted in a Catholic sense. They had originally been formulated, he insisted, to be inclusive of both Protestants and Catholics – and 'Catholics', he added, 'will not now be excluded'.[96] But most Anglicans were enraged by what they viewed as a denial of the Protestant identity of their church, and Tract 90 aroused a storm of opposition. Many believed that in Tract 90, the Tractarians had revealed their real purpose, which was to corrupt the Church of England from within and bring England again into subjection to Rome. The Heads of Houses at Oxford University formally censured Tract 90 in March 1841, and over the coming months, 13 bishops criticised the Tracts in their diocesan charges. In response to a request from the bishop of Oxford, Newman agreed in late March 1841 to bring the series of Tracts to an end.

The Tractarians, however, continued to work for the revival of Catholic practices and beliefs within the Church of England, and to denounce Protestant influence. In the summer of 1841, they organised opposition to the plan of the British and Prussian governments to establish a joint Anglo-Prussian bishopric in Jerusalem aimed at promoting ecumenical co-operation in the expansion of Christian mission in the Near East. Although the scheme had the warm support of the young Queen Victoria and her German consort, Prince Albert, the Tractarians, and especially Newman, condemned any co-operation with the 'Protestant' Prussian Church. (Tractarian opposition was unavailing and the first Anglo-Prussian bishop of Jerusalem, Michael Soloman Alexander, was consecrated in November 1841.[97]) Advanced Tractarian 'Romanisers', most notably W. G. Ward, an affable, rotund, opera-loving fellow of Balliol College, Oxford, entered into discussions with leaders of the Roman Catholic Church in England, including Bishop Nicholas Wiseman, and dreamed of achieving a corporate union of the Anglo-Catholic section of the Church of England and the Roman Catholic Church. The Tractarian *British Critic* published a series of articles in 1841–42 that were highly favourable to Roman Catholicism. In the parishes, some advanced Tractarians adopted 'ritualistic' devotional practices modelled on those of Rome – decorating communion-tables with candles and flowers, using incense, holding daily communion, chanting the liturgy, praying with their faces turned eastwards, hearing private confessions, observing fast days, and wearing the white surplice rather than black gown. Other Tractarians established religious houses organised in a monastic manner. These included Newman's religious community at Littlemore (begun in early

1842), F. W. Faber's house at Elton (1843), and Robert Aitken's house at Leeds (1843).

Such practices elicited a furious reaction from evangelicals and other avowed Protestants within the church. For them, the Romanisers were giving ammunition to the Voluntary opponents of the church, and undermining the efforts to make the established church more popular. 'It is vain', insisted the Tory John Wilson Croker in the *Quarterly Review* of May 1843, '. . . that persons who have adopted these practices may tell us that they have no leaning to Popery'.[98] Such behaviour was especially dangerous in the excited state of the country, and their opponents called for vigorous action against the Tractarians. And such action was not long in coming. In May 1843, the Oxford University authorities convicted the leading Tractarian Edward Pusey of heretical teaching on the eucharist and suspended him from preaching within the University for two years. Although not a Romaniser, Pusey had become a symbol of the Oxford Movement, and his suspension was a humiliating blow. Parishioners were encouraged to report to the bishops or the press concerning any 'popish' words or deeds coming from the Tractarian clergy, and this created the atmosphere of a witch-hunt. According to the liberal Anglican F. D. Maurice, 'men employ themselves in the house of God in observing the tones and gestures of their pastors, that they may report something evil of them in next week's newspapers'.[99] In September 1843, Newman resigned his position as vicar of St Mary's church in Oxford and the following month the Tractarian *British Critic* ceased publication. In the summer of 1843, popular resistance to Tractarian innovations in ritual began in London, encouraged by the evangelical *Record*, with people walking out of services or loudly protesting against what they viewed as 'Roman' ceremonies. Such protests spread through the country, culminating in riots against ritualistic church services in Exeter in late 1844. In February 1845, a special meeting of the Oxford University Convocation condemned a provocative book by the Tractarian Romaniser, W. G. Ward, and stripped him of his degrees.

Some individual Romanisers, recognising that there was no real hope of bringing a substantial part of the Church of England into communion with Rome, now began joining the Roman Catholic Church. The numbers leaving the Church of England were not large, and certainly not comparable to the great Disruption of the Church of Scotland. But those going over to Rome included men and women of unquestioned devotion, moral character, and intellectual attainment, and their loss was felt deeply. The converts included most famously John Henry Newman, who entered the Catholic

Church in October 1845 and was sent to Rome to prepare for ordination. Other Tractarians, among them Pusey and Keble, remained in the Church of England and continued working for the preservation of Catholic traditions and the revival of Catholic devotional practices within that church. Distrusted by church leaders and with little hope of ecclesiastical advancement, the Anglo-Catholic clergy none the less often proved to be dedicated pastors in some of the most difficult parishes of the land. The Tractarians had contributed significantly, by their thought and their example, to the Anglican revival of the 1830s and 1840s. They had served to reawaken the Church of England to its identity as the spiritual body of Christ. They had, however, also contributed to deepening divisions within the Church of England.

Tory measures for church extension and national education

In 1843, Peel's government finally brought forward its long-awaited measure for English church extension. The Church of England, it will be recalled, had submitted to a parliamentary programme of reforms between 1836 and 1840. It had accepted Parliament's decision to take revenues from its ancient cathedrals to support church extension. It now expected a large grant of public money – Sir Robert Inglis called for a grant of two to three million pounds – to support its efforts at church building, especially in the crowded urban parishes.

By late 1842, however, Peel had decided that Parliament's vote of June 1840 against any further grants of public money for English church extension should be viewed as binding. The population, he had come to believe, was too diverse in its Christian beliefs; it could not be organised into parish communities under the direction of the established church. The old Tory notion of shaping a Christian United Kingdom around the established churches, which had been so prevalent 20 years before, was now gone forever. English and Welsh Dissenters, representing more than a third of the population, bitterly opposed any extension of the established church. The Scottish church extension campaign had collapsed and the Church of Scotland was now breaking up. In Ireland, the Roman Catholic majority would loudly condemn any calls upon the public purse for Anglican church extension. A proposal for an English church extension grant, Peel confided to a supporter in January 1843, 'would meet with powerful and persevering opposition from large classes of the House of Commons; from the representatives of Ireland; . . . from the representatives of Scotland; from all the representatives of Dissent in its various forms; from combinations for party purposes; from, in short, all the elements of which a powerful opposition could be formed'.[100] The days of large grants of public money to the established churches were over.

Peel introduced a modest church extension measure in May 1843. His Populous Parishes Bill was meant to stimulate the church to raise its own money for church extension. The Bill would permit the church to borrow money from Queen Anne's Bounty, a fund based on certain revenues that had been gifted to the church by Queen Anne in the early eighteenth century. The borrowed money would be used to provide incomes for new clergymen, who would be assigned districts in overcrowded parishes. Each new clergyman would be expected to gather a congregation in his district and then raise local funds for the building of a district church. The money borrowed from Queen Anne's Bounty would gradually be repaid from savings generated through church reform. The Bill, in short, simply allowed the church to borrow from itself to promote church extension. It encountered no resistance and was passed without debate. But members of the Church of England were greatly disappointed. Peel had relinquished the principle that the state had an obligation to provide a religious establishment commensurate with the growing population, and he had done so without even a fight. He had reversed his position of June 1840 when he had supported Inglis's motion for the church extension grant. As the evangelical *Record* observed in August 1843 of Peel's Bill, 'there are many who profess not to be able to distinguish any material distinction between the principles of a Conservative and a Whig-Radical Government'.[101]

The weakened position of the Church of England was further demonstrated that same year during the debates over a Factory Education Bill for England and Wales. In February 1843, the government brought forward a Bill aimed at limiting the number of hours children could work in factories and providing primary schooling for factory children three hours each workday. The schools for factory children would be supported by local rates and small deductions from the children's pay. The schools would include religious instruction, which would be Anglican in content, though Dissenting parents would be permitted to remove their children during the periods of religious instruction or, under certain conditions, they could have a licensed Dissenting minister give their children religious instruction. Each school would have a board of seven trustees. The chairman would be a Church of England clergyman, and two other members would be Church of England parish churchwardens. While the Bill would initially affect only about 30,000 factory children, it was hoped that it would form the foundation upon which a rate-supported system of universal primary education would develop in England and Wales. And this system would be directed largely by the Church of England.

The Dissenters recognised the threat that the Bill posed to them. It would lay the foundations for an Anglican-controlled system of national education, giving the Church of England the means to educate future generations of children. Having been defeated over church extension, it seemed that the established church now hoped, with the assistance of Peel's government, to gain control over national education. 'The state schoolmaster', observed one Voluntary newspaper, 'was to do the work which the state priest was unable to effect'.[102]

The Dissenters responded by organising the largest public petitioning campaign Britain had ever seen. The movement was orchestrated in large part by Edward Miall, a Congregational minister who had embraced the Voluntary cause in 1834 after witnessing imprisonments over non-payment of the church rate. In 1841 Miall had founded *The Nonconformist* newspaper, adopting on its masthead the strident slogan, 'The Dissidence of Dissent and the Protestantism of the Protestant Religion'. Between March and June 1843, 25,205 petitions bearing 3,988,633 signatures were sent to Parliament.[103] Wesleyan Methodists, who until now had largely shunned political action against the established church, were drawn into the campaign against the Factory Education Bill. They alone submitted 8,945 petitions with 910,000 signatures. In June 1843 the government felt forced to withdraw the Bill. It was a humiliating defeat for the principle of church-directed education, and a further blow to the established church.

Re-energised by the triumph over the Factory Education Bill, Voluntaries and Radicals followed up their victory with further action aimed at bringing down the religious establishments. Late in 1843, Miall and other Voluntaries began planning a national conference on the 'State Church question'. On 30 April 1844, over 700 delegates from Dissenting denominations and societies convened at the Crown and Anchor Hotel in London, where during the next three days they agreed to the constitution of a new society, the 'Anti-State Church Association', aimed at dissolving the 'unholy alliance' of church and state. The new Association had a council of 500, an executive committee of 50 members, and a parliamentary committee which worked to secure the election of MPs committed to disestablishment. Branches were formed throughout the country, and the Anti-State Church Association, renamed in 1853 the Society for the Liberation of the Church from State Control – or in short, the Liberation

Society – became the major body in the Victorian era working for the disestablishment of the Church of England.[104]

Irish Repeal and the Maynooth crisis

In Ireland, the early 1840s found the Peel government facing a major challenge to the existence of the United Kingdom. This was the campaign for the Repeal of the Act of Union of 1800, and the restoration of an Irish parliament in Dublin. The Repeal movement was conceived and led by the Irish 'liberator', Daniel O'Connell, who had championed Catholic emancipation and given a new pride to Irish Catholics. By the late 1830s, O'Connell had grown disillusioned with the United Kingdom parliamentary state. Catholic emancipation, he believed, had not brought full and equal civil rights for the Roman Catholic majority in Ireland. There had, certainly, been some achievements for Catholics in the 1830s. The most important of these was an Irish Tithe Act in 1838; this had replaced the hated tithe with a rent charge and brought an end to years of bitter conflict. However, the gains were modest when compared to the great hopes that had been raised by emancipation. And much in Ireland remained the same. The minority Church of Ireland was still the legal religious establishment and it held on to most of its property and income. Protestants remained ascendant in Irish landownership, the professions and government offices. Most Irish Catholics remained poor and most continued to feel like second-class citizens in the United Kingdom. The solution, O'Connell decided, would be to repeal the Act of Union and to restore the Irish parliament in Dublin. Unlike the eighteenth-century Irish parliament, however, the new parliament would be made up of mainly of Catholic MPs representing the overwhelming Irish Catholic majority. It would give expression to the Irish nation. In 1840, O'Connell had formed a Repeal Association, with branches throughout the country. He promised to secure Repeal through a peaceful agitation. Elected Lord Mayor of Dublin in late 1841, O'Connell had served his year-long term with great aplomb, determined to show that an Irish Catholic was capable of governing a great city. When his term came to an end late in 1842, O'Connell threw himself into the Repeal agitation, proclaiming that 1843 would be the 'great Repeal year', the year in which the moral force of the Irish people would secure the repeal of the Union, just as in 1829 it had secured Catholic emancipation.

Throughout the spring and summer of 1843, Ireland was ablaze. Local branches of the Repeal Association collected money and distributed literature. In addition to numerous Repeal meetings and dinners, some 40 great outdoor meetings – dubbed 'monster meetings' by the British press – were held across Ireland, gathering crowds of 100,000 or more. These meetings had the character of revivalist camp meetings, or of religious fairs. The vast numbers were marshalled by the Repeal wardens, or 'O'Connell's police', who had a quasi-military appearance. Roman Catholic priests were active in the campaign, assisting the local Repeal Associations, speaking at Repeal dinners, and leading processions of parishioners to the great outdoor gatherings. For many priests, Repeal would be the culmination of Catholic emancipation, giving Ireland a representative parliament that would legislate for a Catholic people. Of the 27 Irish Catholic bishops, 15 publicly supported the Repeal movement. The support of the priests helped give the movement the character of a religious crusade. In mid-August, for example, a great Repeal meeting was held on the historic hill of Tara on the feast of the Assumption, and attracted, some claimed, a million people. During the morning, a temporary altar was erected on the hill and four masses were held.[105] With very few exceptions, Irish Protestants opposed the Repeal movement, fearing for their fate under a Catholic-dominated Irish parliament. There were growing fears that the agitation would lead to sectarian warfare.

Peel's government had no intention of granting Repeal. It turned a blind eye to the demonstrations and monster meetings through the summer. Then in early October it suddenly moved to suppress the agitation, banning at the last minute a planned monster meeting at Clontarf, outside Dublin, and arresting O'Connell and several other leaders of the Repeal Association. O'Connell and the others were convicted of seditious conspiracy by a packed Protestant jury, and imprisoned. Several months later, in September 1844, these 'Repeal martyrs' were released, after a successful judicial appeal to the House of Lords. However, O'Connell had aged considerably under the strain of the trial and imprisonment. He resumed his work for Repeal following his release, but did not attempt to revive the methods of mass agitation. Many of his younger supporters – especially a 'Young Ireland' group of romantic literary nationalists associated with *The Nation* newspaper – had lost faith in their leader's fiery rhetoric and non-violent methods and dreamed of an armed struggle for Irish freedom.

Peel, meanwhile, followed up his government's suppression of the Repeal agitation with conciliatory measures, aimed at weakening support for the Repeal movement by addressing some of the Irish Catholic grievances.[106] The government introduced the first of these measures, the Charitable

Bequests Bill, in June 1844. It was a modest measure that was intended to help the Irish Catholic Church by making the legal procedures simpler and fairer for Catholics wishing to donate money to the church at their deaths. The Bill was opposed by some Catholic leaders who were offended by certain provisions, most notably the continued prohibition of donations to Catholic religious orders and the strict regulation of deathbed bequests. However, a number of Catholic bishops, including the archbishops of Armagh and Dublin, gave the measure guarded support, and Parliament passed the Bill. Both Catholic archbishops also agreed to serve on the government board to oversee bequests, marking a small but significant step towards greater co-operation between the Catholic Church and the United Kingdom state.[107]

The government's next measure won a far warmer approval from Irish Catholics. This was the Maynooth Bill, which proposed to increase the state grant to the Roman Catholic seminary at Maynooth, outside Dublin. The College of St Patrick at Maynooth had been founded in 1795 with financial assistance from the Irish Parliament, in part to ensure that most Catholic priests would be educated in Ireland, rather than on the continent, where they might be infected with revolutionary ideas. It received an annual grant from Parliament. The grant, however, was inadequate for the college's needs and over time the buildings had become overcrowded and dilapidated. Further, the Maynooth grant had to be approved by Parliament each year, giving extreme Protestant MPs a regular opportunity to denounce and abuse Catholicism from the floor of the Commons. To placate Catholic feelings, the government now proposed to triple the amount of the annual parliamentary grant and to provide additional money for repairs to the college buildings. Further, to avoid the need for annual approval, the government proposed to make the grant a permanent charge on the treasury, or in other words, to provide a state endowment for the college. It was a generous gesture. Even O'Connell (who had once nearly fought a duel with Peel) welcomed the measure when his old foe introduced it in the Commons in early February 1845.

It was otherwise, however, with Protestant opinion in Britain. For many Protestants, the proposed Maynooth endowment was but a first step towards the endowment and establishment of the Roman Catholic Church in Ireland. Peel, who in 1829 had supported Catholic emancipation, was now, it was widely believed, moving towards making the Catholic Church an established church in Ireland. The same government that had refused to intervene to save the Protestant Church of Scotland from Disruption now proposed to placate disloyal Irish Catholics who supported Repeal. The same government that had refused to provide endowment grants to the Church of England after it had submitted to the programme of reform imposed by Parliament, would now provide an endowment grant to the Irish Catholic Church, which refused to allow any parliamentary interference in its ecclesiastical arrangements. Anglicans contrasted the favourable treatment of the Irish Catholic Church in 1845 with the harsh treatment of the Church of Ireland in 1833. Voluntaries opposed what they viewed as a move to strengthen the alliance of church and state, by bringing millions of Irish Catholics into that alliance. Evangelical and high church Anglicans, Free Church Scots, Voluntaries, moderate Dissenters, Wesleyan Methodists and anti-Catholic zealots of various hues came together in a loose but potent alliance, determined to thwart the Government's Maynooth Bill. In late February, a Central Anti-Maynooth Committee was formed to co-ordinate national action. The recently formed Anti-State Church Association threw itself into the campaign, while Miall's *Nonconformist* newspaper fanned the fires. Meetings were held throughout the country. Between February and May 1845, 10,204 petitions, bearing 1,284,296 signatures, were submitted to Parliament against the Maynooth Bill.[108] A great Anti-Maynooth conference was held in London between 30 April and 3 May 1845; it drew over 1,000 delegates from various Protestant churches and societies throughout the United Kingdom.

The government was now in serious difficulty. Peel would not back down in the face of the anti-Maynooth agitation. The Bill was too important, involving, he believed, the preservation of the union of Great Britain and Ireland. 'You must break up', he insisted in his speech introducing the second reading of the Maynooth Bill, 'in some way or other, that formidable confederacy which exists in that country against the British government and the British connection. I do not believe you can break it up by force . . . You can do much to break it up by acting in a spirit of kindliness, forbearance, and generosity'.[109] He would preserve the union of Britain and Ireland, even if this meant further damaging the union of church and state. At least one junior minister, the rising Tory politician and high Anglican, William Ewart Gladstone, resigned from the government over the Maynooth issue. Another Tory, the extravagant society novelist, Benjamin Disraeli, pressed the beleaguered prime minister mercilessly over his Irish policy. 'Explain to us', he asked, 'why . . . you are now setting England on fire for the purpose of ingratiating yourself with the Irish'.[110] Although Peel staked his government's future on the passing of the Bill, over half the Tory MPs voted against it at the third reading, and it was only with Whig support that the Bill passed through both houses of Parliament and became law at the end of June. 'The Bill will pass, but our party is destroyed', wrote Sir James Graham, the home secretary, to Lord Heytesbury on 12 April.[111] 'What a strange ignorance', wrote the evangelical Lord Ashley of Peel in his diary on 7 April, 'or haughty contempt of the deep, solemn Protestant feeling in the hearts of the British people! Can a statesman, ought a statesman, to force a measure, by dint of a legislative majority, utterly hateful to the great mass of the nation?'[112]

A month later, Peel's government introduced their third measure aimed at conciliating Irish Catholic opinion. This was the Queen's Colleges Bill, which proposed to establish and endow three new colleges, in Belfast, Galway and Cork, aimed at increasing opportunities for higher education among both Catholics and Presbyterian Dissenters. In order to avoid sectarian controversy, there was to be no state endowment of theological chairs in the colleges. The Bill seemed to satisfy no one. The Tory evangelical, Sir Harry Inglis, MP for Oxford, claimed that the Bill would establish 'a gigantic scheme of godless education' in Ireland, further undermining both the established church in Ireland and the true Christian faith. The Catholic Church in Ireland agreed that these were 'godless colleges'. The Bill passed, but in 1846 the papacy officially condemned the measure and the Irish Catholic hierarchy forbade Catholics to attend the new colleges. This was the last of the measures of the Peel government to conciliate Catholic Ireland.

Pre-millenarianism and the Evangelical Alliance

The tensions of the 1840s, and especially the resurgence of Roman Catholicism in Ireland and England, contributed to a revival of the prophetical movement within Protestant evangelicalism. In 1842, millenarian evangelicals, including Edward Bickersteth and T. R. Birks, formed the Prophecy Investigation Society and in 1843, the Society began organising a series of Lenten lectures in London on millenarianism.[113] The evangelical Henry Melvill, said to be the most popular preacher in London, regularly preached on prophecy, the restoration of the Jews and the Second Coming during the 1840s. In 1844, Edward Elliot published his influential pre-millenarian treatise, *Horae apolypticae*. Pre-millenarianism became fashionable, and influential politicians, among them William Cowper (later Cowper-Temple), Lord Morpeth, and Lord Ashley, were converted.[114] Pre-millenarian evangelicalism increasingly emphasised the confrontation between Protestantism and Roman Catholicism. 'Our present temptations and delusions', Bickersteth proclaimed in a sermon in November 1842, '. . . should warn us of THE POSSIBLE PREVALENCE OF THE ROMAN CHURCH FOR A SHORT TIME'. This, however, would not prove lasting and it was a further sign that the Second Coming approached.[115] In July 1845, Bickersteth began publishing a series of letters 'On Christian Union' in the *Record*, calling for a union of all evangelicals.

In August 1845, a group of evangelicals issued a call to Protestant denominations 'to associate and concentrate the strength of an enlightened Protestantism against the encroachments of Popery and Puseyism'.[116] Leading figures in the initiative included the pre-millenarians, Bickersteth, Birks, James Hatley Frere, William Marsh and Hugh McNeile. A meeting of 216 delegates from 17 Protestant denominations was held in Liverpool in October 1845, which formed the Evangelical Alliance. The ageing Thomas Chalmers, now of the Scottish Free Church, could not attend the meeting but warmly supported the initiative. In a pamphlet in 1846, he defined a two-fold mission for the Alliance. It should, he insisted, 'stand forth in the character, first of a great Anti-Popish Association; and secondly, of a great Home Mission'. First, the Alliance should unite Protestants of all denominations against the twin threats of Tractarianism and Roman Catholicism – 'not only at home, but in America and the British Colonies, and the Continent of Europe, and every other place where Jesuitism is plying her wiles'. Second, the various Protestant denominations should co-operate in a vigorous home mission aimed at converting the new industrial working classes in the urban districts and overcoming the threats of Socialism and Radicalism.[117] Others were drawn to the movement in a mood of millenarian expectation, believing the Alliance would help to restore Zion and that the Alliance would be a fulfilment of prophecy.[118] In August 1846, an international gathering of over 900 delegates from British, American and European Protestant churches met in London with the aim of making the Alliance a great international association for combating not only Roman Catholicism but a number of heresies. The London conference was marred by conflict over whether or not to include Protestants from the slave-holding states of the American South.[119] None the less, though weakened by the slavery controversy, the Evangelical Alliance survived, representing a new spirit of national and international co-operation on the part of British evangelicals. As the old alliance of church and state within the United Kingdom waned, some were envisioning a new international Protestantism, united in a great global struggle against Roman Catholicism, and also working to convert as many as possible, before the Second Advent.

Conclusion

'The day of authority in its rightful exercise is over', lamented the *Church of England Quarterly Review* in July 1845, 'the constitution and preservation of society by rule and obedience as ordained from God are no more; the office of the Church, as an authoritative teacher, is almost repudiated'.[120] The religious composition of the United Kingdom had been transformed between the passing of Catholic emancipation in 1829 and the passing of the Maynooth Bill in 1845. The established churches in all three kingdoms had lost much of their political influence and authority, and the bonds between church and state were frayed and stretched. In Ireland, the established church in Ireland had been reduced in size and deprived of state support for any mission to convert the Roman Catholic population. In Scotland, the established Church of Scotland had broken up at the Disruption of 1843, and only about a third of the Scottish population now adhered to the established church. In England, Parliament's refusal to provide grants for church extension had left many Anglicans disillusioned with the old alliance of church and state. The hopes that Peel's government would revive the influence and authority of the established churches had been dashed, especially with the Maynooth grant – which was viewed by many as Peel's second great betrayal of the Protestant constitution, comparable to his betrayal over Catholic emancipation.

The 1830s and early 1840s had been, on the whole, a good time for Dissenters. These years had witnessed the continued growth in numbers, confidence and political influence of Dissent. Dissenters were proving highly effective in evangelism, especially urban evangelism, planting new churches where needed without concern for historic parish boundaries, and appealing to common people with a simple gospel message. There had been an astounding growth in Dissent during these decades. The number of Dissenting churches increased ten-fold between 1770 and 1850.[121] R. Tudur Jones calculated that between 1800 and 1850 in Wales alone, Dissenters were opening on average one new chapel every eight days. Alan Everitt has identified some 100 separate religious denominations in mid-Victorian England and Wales.[122] Dissenters had also developed methods of effective political agitation, as demonstrated in their successful campaigns against the church extension grants and the Factory Education Bill of 1843. The Voluntary agitation, to be sure, was bitter and divisive. It had shattered the co-operation between Dissenters and church evangelicals that had been so important in the campaign against slavery. But at the same time, the Voluntary agitation had given most Dissenters a new pride in their identity and an enhanced status in society. They were no longer a tolerated minority, their presence in Britain viewed as the unfortunate result of insufficient church accommodation in the religious establishments. They were increasingly referred to, not as Dissenters (a negative term), but by the more respectable title of 'Nonconformists', or even (as many preferred) 'Free Churches'.

But the conflicts of the 1830s and early 1840s had also not been without their benefits for the established churches. After 1832, those churches had been forced by the new political climate to identify more with the aspirations of the people, to accept the movement towards more representative and democratic government, and to portray themselves as popular bodies. Their leaders began describing established churches as the 'poor men's churches', churches that provided religious observances – baptisms, marriages, burials, as well as regular religious services – to the people regardless of their ability to pay. The established clergy no longer expected people passively to accept their teachings on authority, as they might have accepted the commands of the landlord or magistrate. Rather, the established churches became increasingly reliant upon the efforts and giving of their members, and this proved (rather unexpectedly) to be a great boon. When Parliament ceased providing the established churches with grants for church extension, they forced those churches to turn for support to their lay membership, and the lay members provided far more resources than the state had done. 'Fifteen years ago', observed Henry Manning, Archdeacon of Chichester, in his *Charge* of 1845, 'the Church of England rested upon its old constitutional foundations. It was privileged and protected by the whole force of the Statute Book; Acts of Parliament were passed; grants of public money voted for its extension; the whole weight and influence of the state went with it'.[123] Manning admitted that recent years had seen the church stripped of many of its state privileges, and that it was difficult not to look back on the 1820s with 'fond regret'. And yet, Manning argued, the Church of England was in fact a more effective missionary church in 1845 than it had been in 1829. 'What', he asked, 'have been the fruits of these fifteen years of adverse events?'

A thousand Churches; a work of almost universal restoration, never to be estimated; an increase of clergy, probably far exceeding the increase of Churches; a number of congregations newly formed; . . . more than half-a-million of money in the last five years offered to the work of national education; a whole system of institutions for training school teachers; the reorganization of nearly every diocese on the principle of its spiritual unity and government . . .

If this was the fruit of struggle, Manning concluded, 'may the shadows of worldly adversity for ever hang upon the Church of England!'[124] In truth, during the 1830s and 1840s, over 2,000 new churches had been added to the Church of England. Even in the established churches in Ireland and Scotland, there were the signs of recovery by the later 1840s. The Church of Ireland was, if small in numbers, more efficiently organised than in 1829 and was proving successful in raising money for building and repairing churches. By 1844, moreover, it was maintaining through voluntary dona-tions 1,647 schools with 99,165 pupils – which was equal to about a quar-ter of the number of pupils in the state-supported national system.[125] By the late 1840s, the Church of Scotland was recovering from the trauma of the Disruption – reviving a sense of its mission as Scotland's national church and returning to the work of raising its own funds for church extension. When the efforts of the established churches are viewed in conjunction with the dynamic growth and activism of the Dissenting churches, it is clear that, along with the conflicts of the 1830s and 1840s, there had been a significant increase in vital religion. The United Kingdom was, in many respects, more actively Christian by the late 1840s than it had been for centuries.

Notes

1 E. Irving, *The Church and State Responsible to Christ, and to One Another* (London, 1829), 16, 300–1.

2 E. Miller, *The History and Doctrines of Irvingism*, 2 vols (London, 1878), vol. i, 30–46.

3 Quoted in A. L. Drummond, *Edward Irving and his Circle* (London, 1937), 135.

4 Ibid., 136–51; Miller, *History and Doctrines of Irvingism*, vol. i, 51–61.

5 [T. Erskine], *On the Gifts of the Spirit* (Greenock, 1830), 23.

6 Drummond, *Edward Irving*, 227–8.

7 T. C. F. Stunt, *From Awakening to Secession: Radical Evangelicals in Switzerland and Britain 1815–35* (Edinburgh, 2000), 147–81; H. H. Rowdon, *The Origins of the Brethren, 1825–1850* (London, 1967).

8 E. R. Sandeen, *The Roots of Fundamentalism* (Chicago, 1970), 3–41.

9 Quoted in O. MacDonagh, *O'Connell: The Life of Daniel O'Connell 1775–1847* (London, 1991), 301.

10 Hilton, *A Mad, Bad, and Dangerous People*, 420.

11 Quoted in Mathieson, *English Church Reform*, 45.

12 [J. Wade], *The Extraordinary Black Book*, new edn (London, 1832), 95.

13 Clark, *English Society 1688–1832*, 413.

14 O. Chadwick, *The Victorian Church, Part One* (London, 1971), 37–8; B. Hilton, *The Age of Atonement: The Influence of Evangelicalism on Social and Economic Thought, 1785–1865* (Oxford, 1986), 214–5.

15 Whyte, *Scotland and the Abolition of Black Slavery*, 195–8.

16 C. Duncan Rice, 'The Missionary Context of the British Anti-slavery Movement', in J. Walvin (ed.), *Slavery and British Society 1776–1846* (London, 1982), 160.

17 Quoted in E. F. Hurwitz, *Politics and the Public Conscience: Slave Emancipation and the Abolitionist Movement in Britain* (London, 1973), 53.

18 Hall, *Civilising Subjects*, 310–11.

19 Watts, *The Dissenters*, vol. ii, 450; S. Drescher, 'Public Opinion and the Destruction of British Colonial Slavery', in Walvin (ed.), *Slavery and British Society*, 35–6.

20 E. M. Howse, *Saints in Politics: The 'Clapham Sect' and the Growth of Freedom* (London, 1953), 163.

21 Quoted in Colley, *Britons*, 360.

22 Howse, *Saints in Politics*, 165.

23 Colley, *Britons*, 356–60.

24 G. F. A. Best, 'The Constitutional Revolution, 1828–32, and its Consequences for the Established Church', *Theology*, vol. 52 (1959), 226–34.

25 P. O'Donoghue, 'Causes of the Opposition to Tithes, 1830–38', *Studia Hibernica*, 5 (1965), 7–28; P. O'Donoghue, 'Opposition to Tithe Payment in 1830–31', *Studia Hibernica*, 6 (1966), 69–72.

26 *Dublin Evening Post*, 23, 25, 28, 30 June, 2, 5 July 1831, for reports on the inquest into the Newtownbarry killings; *Dublin Evening Post*, 17 December 1831, for the report on the Knocktopher killings.

27 *Dublin Evening Post*, 25 June 1831.

28 [Wade], *Extraordinary Black Book*, 139.

29 E. G. Stanley to T. Chalmers, 19 May 1832, quoted in W. Hanna, *Memoirs of Dr Chalmers*, 4 vols (Edinburgh, 1849–52), vol. iii, 337.

30 D. H. Akenson, *The Irish Educational Experiment: The National System of Education in the Nineteenth Century* (London, 1970).

31 O. J. Brose, 'The Irish Precedent for English Church Reform: The Church Temporalities Act of 1833', *Journal of Ecclesiastical History*, 7 (1956), 204–25.

32 A. Macintyre, *The Liberator: Daniel O'Connell and the Irish Party 1830–1847* (New York, 1965), 188–200.

33 H. Cockburn to T. Chalmers, 22 April 1833, New College Library, Edinburgh, Chalmers Papers, CHA 4.202.18.

34 G. I. T. Machin, *Politics and the Churches in Great Britain 1832 to 1868* (Oxford, 1977), 115.

35 *Scotsman*, 22 June, 13, 17 July 1833; *Voluntary Church Magazine*, 1 (December 1833), 427–34; Machin, *Politics and the Churches*, 115.

36 J. Bentham, *Church of Englandism and its Catechism Examined* (London, 1818), 397.

37 F. Knight, 'Did Anticlericalism exist in the English Countryside in the Early Nineteenth Century?', in N. Aston and M. Gragoe (eds), *Anticlericalism in Britain, c.1500–1914* (Stroud, 2000), 167–8.

38 [J. Mill], 'The Church and its Reform', *London Review*, vol. 1 (July, 1835), 272.

39 Ibid., 271.

40 J. S. Mill, 'The Right and Wrong of State Interference with Corporation and Church Property' (1833), in J. S. Mill, *Dissertations and Discussions: Political, Philosophical, and Historical*, 2 vols (London, 1859), vol. i, 1–41.

41 Ibid., 17.

42 T. Larsen, *Friends of Religious Liberty: Nonconformist Politics in Mid-Victorian England* (Woodridge, Suffolk, 1999), 24–30.

43 N. Gash, *Reaction and Reconstruction in English Politics 1832–1852* (Oxford, 1965), 66.

44 T. Binney, *An Address delivered on Laying the First Stone of the New King's Weigh House*, 5th edn (London, 1834), 34.

45 J. P. Ellens, *Religious Routes to Gladstonian Liberalism: The Church Rate Conflict in England and Wales, 1832–1868* (University Park, Pa., 1994), 23–41; R. Brent, 'The Whigs and Protestant Dissent in the Decade of Reform: The Case of Church Rates, 1833–1841', *English Historical Review*, 102 (1987), 887–910.

46 E. Halévy, *The Triumph of Reform 1830–1841*, trans. E. I. Watkin, 2nd edn (London, 1950), 151.

47 A. P. Stanley, *Life and Correspondence of Thomas Arnold*, 8th edn, 2 vols (London, 1858), vol. i, 264.

48 'Lord Henley on Church Reform', *Edinburgh Review*, vol. 56 (October 1832), 203.

49 T. Chalmers, *First Report of the Committee of the General Assembly on Church Extension* (Edinburgh, 1835), 20.

50 T. Chalmers to J. Cook, 9 July 1834, Church Extension Letterbook 1834–1836, New College Library, Edinburgh, Ms X13b 6/3, 2.

51 T. Chalmers, *The Cause of Church Extension and the Question Shortly Stated, between Churchmen and Dissenters in Regard to It* (1835), in Chalmers, *Collected Works*, xviii, 136–7.

52 Sir R. Peel to T. Chalmers, 24 January 1835, British Library, Peel Papers, Add MS 40411, fol. 200.

53 D. M. Lewis, *Lighten their Darkness: The Evangelical Mission to Working-Class London, 1828–1860* (New York, 1986), 17–27.

54 Sir R. Peel to H. Phillpotts, 'Most Private', 22 December 1834, Exeter Cathedral Archives, Phillpotts Papers, ED 11/49/4.

55 S. Smith, *A Letter to Archdeacon Singleton, on the Ecclesiastical Commission*, 2nd edn (London, 1837), 42.

56 A. Blomfield, *A Memoir of Charles James Blomfield*, 2nd edn (London, 1864), 167.

57 C. J. Blomfield, *A Charge delivered to the Clergy of the Diocese of London at the Visitation in July 1834* (London, 1834), 16–17.

58 [E. B. Pusey], 'The Royal and Parliamentary Ecclesiastical Commission', *British Critic*, vol. 28 (April 1838), 526.

59 30 July 1840, *Hansard's Parliamentary Debates*, 3rd ser., vol. 55, col. 1143.

60 P. J. Welch, 'Bishop Blomfield and Church Extension in London', *Journal of Ecclesiastical History*, 4 (1953), 203–15.

61 A. Burns, *The Diocesan Revival in the Church of England, c.1800–1870* (Oxford, 1999), 116.

62 [H. Mann], 'Report of the Census, 1851 – Religious Worship', *Parliamentary Papers*, vol. lxxxix (Session 1852–53), xl.

63 W. Dealtry, *Obligations of the National Church: A Charge delivered at the Visitation in Hampshire* (London, 1838), 14.

64 R. J. W. Selleck, *James Kay Shuttleworth* (Ilford, 1994), 144–5; D. G. Paz, *The Politics of Working-Class Education in Britain, 1830–50* (Manchester, 1980), 62–5.

65 Gash, *Reaction and Reconstruction in English Politics*, 78, n. 2.

66 Quoted in R. T. Davidson, *Life of Archibald Campbell Tait*, 2 vols (London, 1891), vol. i, 206–7.

67 S. J. Brown, *The National Churches of England, Ireland and Scotland 1801–46* (Oxford, 2001), 271, 292.

68 [J. H. Newman], *Thoughts on the Ministerial Commission*, Tract 1 (London, 1833), 2.

69 P. B. Nockles, '"Lost Causes and . . . Impossible Loyalties": The Oxford Movement and the University', in *The History of the University of Oxford*, vi, *Nineteenth-Century Oxford, Part 1*, ed. M. G. Brock and M. C. Curthoys (eds) (Oxford, 1997), 212–22.

70 J. H. Newman, *Lectures on the Prophetical Office of the Church, viewed relatively to Romanism and Popular Protestantism*, 2nd edn (London 1838), 305–6.

71 'Passive Resistance', *Voluntary Church Magazine*, vol. 4 (January 1838), 25.

72 30 March 1838, *Hansard's Parliamentary Debates*, 3rd ser., xliii, col. 112.

73 Quoted in Machin, *Politics and the Churches in Great Britain 1832 to 1868*, 105.

74 Quoted in W. R. Ward, *Religion and Society in England 1790–1850* (London, 1972), 132.

75 R. W. Dale, *Life and Letters of John Angell James* (London, 1861), 168–9.

76 R. Tudur Jones, 'The Origins of the Nonconformist Disestablishment Campaign 1830–1840', *Journal of the Historical Society of the Church in Wales*, 20 (1970), 39–76.

77 *Hansard's Parliamentary Debates*, 3rd ser., xli (1838), cols 707–11.

78 S. J. Brown, 'Religion and the Rise of Liberalism: The First Disestablishment Campaign in Scotland, 1829–1843', *Journal of Ecclesiastical History*, 48 (1997), 699–701.

79 N. L. Walker, *Robert Buchanan: An Ecclesiastical Biography* (London, 1877), 76–7.

80 *Hansard's Parliamentary Debates*, 3rd ser., xlii (1838), cols 124–9.

81 T. Chalmers, *Lectures on the Establishment and Extension of National Churches* (1838) in *Collected Works of Thomas Chalmers*, vol. xvii, 187–336.

82 Ibid., 281–2.

83 *Christian Observer*, vol. 40 (March 1840), 190; (April 1840), 253–4; (May, 1840), 319–20; Lewis, *Lighten their Darkness*, 81–2.

84 30 June 1840, *Hansard's Parliamentary Debates*, 3rd ser., vol. 55, cols 273–4.

85 R. H. Inglis, *Church Extension: Substance of a Speech delivered in the House of Commons on Tuesday, the 30th June 1840* (London, 1840), 84.

86 *Christian Guardian* (December 1840), cited in Lewis, *Lighten their Darkness*, 82.

87 Quoted in Lewis, *Lighten their Darkness*, 83.

88 'Sir Robert Peel's Claim to the Confidence of the Clergy', *Fraser's Magazine*, vol. 24 (October 1841), 387.

89 G. Kitson Clark, *Peel and the Conservative Party*, 2nd edn (London, 1964), 328.

90 P. Mandler, 'Tories and Paupers: Christian Political Economy and the Making of the New Poor Law', *Historical Journal*, 33 (1990), 81–103.

91 S. Wilberforce, *A Charge, delivered at the Ordinary Visitation of the Archdeaconry of Surrey* (London, 1842), 31.

92 C. J. Blomfield, *A Charge delivered to the Clergy of the Diocese of London at the Visitation in October 1842*, 2nd edn (London, 1842), 63–4.

93 H. Watt, *Thomas Chalmers and the Disruption* (Edinburgh, 1943), 190.

94 D. Chambers, 'Prelude to Last Things: The Church of Scotland's Mission to the Jews', *Records of the Scottish Church History Society*, 19 (1977), 43–58.

95 For this aspect of the disruption, see William Alexander's novel, *Johnny Gibb of Gushetneuk* (Aberdeen, 1871).

96 J. H. Newman, *Remarks on Certain Passages in the Thirty-Nine Articles*, Tract 90 (London, 1841), 101–2.

97 R. W. Greaves, 'The Jerusalem Bishopric, 1841', *English Historical Review*, vol. 64 (1949), 328–52; P. J. Welsh, 'Anglican Churchmen and the Establishment of the Jerusalem Bishopric', *Journal of Ecclesiastical History*, 8 (1957), 193–204.

98 [J. W. Croker], 'Rubrics and Ritual of the Church of England', *Quarterly Review*, vol. 72 (May 1843), 287.

99 F. D. Maurice, *On the Right and Wrong Methods of Supporting Protestantism* (London, 1843), 13.

100 Peel to Henry Hobhouse, 21 January 1843, in C. S. Parker, *Sir Robert Peel*, 3 vols (London, 1899), vol. ii, 563.

101 *Record*, 5 August 1843, cited in Lewis, *Lighten their Darkness*, 87.

102 A. Miall, *Life of Edward Miall* (London, 1884), 90.

103 D. Hempton, *Methodism and Politics in British Society 1750–1850* (London, 1984), 170.

104 D. M. Thompson, 'The Liberation Society 1844–1868', in P. Hollis (ed.), *Pressure from Without in early Victorian England* (London, 1974), 210–38.

105 J. F. Broderick, *The Holy See and the Irish Movement for the Repeal of the Union with England 1829–1847* (Rome, 1951), 144–53.

106 For the government's programme of concessions to the Catholic Church in Ireland, see D. A. Kerr, *Peel, Priests and Politics: Sir Robert Peel's Administration and the Roman Catholic Church in Ireland, 1841–1846* (Oxford, 1982).

107 D. A. Kerr, *Peel, Priests and Politics: Sir Robert Peel's Administration and the Roman Catholic Church in Ireland*, 110–51.

108 G. I. T. Machin, 'The Maynooth Grant, the Dissenters and Disestablishment, 1845–1847', *English Historical Review*, 82 (1967), 64.

109 Quoted in D. Read, *Peel and the Victorians* (Oxford, 1987), 139.

110 Quoted in E. Hodder, *Life and Work of the Seventh Earl of Shaftesbury*, new edn (London, 1893), 325.

111 C. S. Parker, *Life and Letters of Sir James Graham*, 2 vols (London, 1907), vol. ii, 10.

112 Hodder, *Shaftesbury*, 327.

113 Lewis, *Lighten their Darkness*, 101–2; Sandeen, *Roots of Fundamentalism*, 24–5.

114 B. Hilton, 'Whiggery, Religion and Social Reform: The Case of Lord Morpeth', *Historical Journal*, 37 (1994), 838–9, 844–50.

115 E. Bickersteth, *The Divine Warning to the Church* (London, 1842), 34, 43.

116 J. Wolffe, 'The Evangelical Alliance in the 1840s', *Studies in Church History*, 23 (1986), 338.

117 T. Chalmers, *On the Evangelical Alliance* (Edinburgh, 1846); Hanna, *Memoirs of Dr Chalmers*, 384–90.

118 Wolffe, 'The Evangelical Alliance in the 1840s', 341.

119 E. R. Sandeen, 'The Distinctiveness of American Denominationalism: A Case Study of the 1846 Evangelical Alliance', *Church History*, 45 (1976), 222–34.

120 'The Prospects of the England Church', *Church of England Quarterly Review*, vol. 18 (July 1845), 105.

121 Watts, *The Dissenters*, vol. ii, 24.

122 Tudur Jones, 'Origins of the Nonconformist Disestablishment Campaign', 41; A. Everitt, *Patterns of Rural Dissent: The Nineteenth Century* (Leicester, 1972), 6.

123 H. E. Manning, *A Charge delivered at the Ordinary Visitation of the Archdeaconry of Chichester in July 1845* (London, 1845), 50.

124 Ibid., 52, 53.

125 'The Church Education Society', *Dublin University Magazine*, vol. 23 (1844), 639.

CHAPTER 3

Commerce, Christianity and Civilisation, 1840–1863

Christianity and commerce: the Niger expedition

In 1837, on the death of her uncle, King William IV, the 18-year-old Princess Victoria came to the throne of the United Kingdom and its empire. It was the beginning of a reign that would last for nearly 64 years. Her coronation took place on 28 June 1838. An estimated 400,000 people came to London to witness the event, some (a first for a coronation) travelling by railway. The ceremony in Westminster Abbey lasted nearly five hours and was rich in religious ritual. The archbishop of Canterbury, William Howley, presided; he anointed her with holy oil, administered the sacrament of communion and presented her with the crown and regalia. Other bishops of the established Church of England assisted in the service (with varying degrees of competence: one caused the queen considerable irritation by jamming a ring on the wrong finger). The ceremony concluded with Handel's 'Hallelujah Chorus'. For the Unitarian political economist, Harriet Martineau, the service 'erred both in endowing the Queen with divinity and the Almighty with royalty'.[1] For others, however, it was a reverent expression of the providential monarchical state.

The young queen, as Walter Arnstein has observed, did not share the intense religious convictions that were causing such division and turmoil in the 1830s. Her early religious upbringing had been at the hands of her mother, the duchess of Kent, and her governess, Baroness Lehzen, both German Lutherans. Her tutor between the ages of 8 and 18 had been a moderate evangelical clergyman, George Davys, who gave her a firm grounding in the essentials of the Anglican faith, but also inculcated in her ideas of toler-ance. In the early months of her reign, she came under the influence of her Whig prime minister, the learned and urbane Viscount Melbourne, a man who enjoyed the intellectual stimulation of reading theological works but whose own faith was cool and detached. Melbourne told her to focus on the 'simple truths' of Christianity and to avoid contentious theology. He also 'cautioned her against both the Low Church evangelical enthusiasts and the High Church doctrinaires who were seeking to remodel the Church of England' – advice which she took to heart. In 1840, Victoria married Albert, prince of Saxe-Coburg-Gotha. A German Lutheran by upbringing, Albert shared Victoria's liberal Protestant faith and her emphasis on the 'simple truths', though he also helped her to a greater appreciation for the moral and social teachings of the faith.[2] These moral teachings, for the young royal couple, included the great Christian campaign against slavery and the dream of the regeneration of the African continent.

Slavery and the international slave trade were flourishing in the 1830s. Despite the agreement of the great powers in 1815 to end the slave trade, and despite the abolition of slavery in the British empire in 1833, tens of thousands of Africans each year suffered the horrors of the middle passage to become slaves in the Americas. In Cuba, Brazil and other countries that continued to import slaves, the demand for slave labour was increasing. It was being met by a large number of slave ships, which included some of the fastest sailing vessels afloat. Profits were huge, some 200 per cent or more for each voyage. Britain's West Africa Squadron, now numbering about 30 ageing warships and assigned to patrol over 3,000 miles of coast, was largely ineffective in intercepting the slave ships, managing to liberate probably fewer than 10 per cent of the human cargoes. The Squadron's crews showed great fortitude, and many died on duty off the African coasts. But their best efforts often led to tragedy. In September 1831, for example, a royal naval vessel, the unfortunately named *Black Joke*, approached two slave ships in the Bight of Benin. 'During the chase', a wit-ness observed, 'they were seen to throw their slaves overboard, by twos, shackled together by the ankles, and left in this manner to sink or swim . . . Men, women and children were seen in great numbers, struggling in the water' – while sharks tore them apart.[3] There were, meanwhile, growing questions in Britain about the financial costs of maintaining the West Africa Squadron, and powerful calls for its withdrawal.[4]

In the late 1830s, anti-slavery campaigners, led by the veteran anti-slavery leader, Thomas Fowell Buxton, began to develop a bold new plan for eradicating the trade, by striking at its source, deep in the interior of the African continent. It was here, amid tribal warfare and lawlessness, that the slavers seized their human prey and marched them to the coasts. It was here, Buxton and his supporters believed, that slavery must be stopped. Their solution was to bring the benefits of settled agriculture, peaceful commerce and Christian civilisation into the interior of Africa. It would be 'developed' under European supervision, and with this economic development would come villages and towns, paid labour, rule by law, schools and churches. Their plan would commence with an expedition, to be financed largely by the state, which would develop model agricultural settlements, similar to British landed estates but managed by Africans, along the Niger River, a great potential artery for inland communication that penetrated deep into the interior and reached the edges of the Sahara. The model farming settlements would promote and spread habits of settled industry among Africans. Their produce, including palm oil and cotton, would be traded for European manufactures. The settlements would include churches and schools for the religious and moral instruction of the Africans. Soon the people themselves would emulate the model settlements, and would open their hearts to Christian influence. Through such means, argued Buxton, Africa would not only be economically transformed, but 'would present the finest field for the labours of Christian missionaries which the world has yet seen'.[5] The Christian agricultural settlements would help to end forever the violence and anarchy in the interior where people were captured and enslaved, and show Africa the way to a new future. 'It is', insisted Buxton, 'the Bible and the plough that must regenerate Africa'.[6]

On 1 June 1840, a great public meeting was held in London's Exeter Hall, the meeting-place for evangelical and missionary societies, to mark the first anniversary of the Society for the Extinction of the Slave Trade and for the Civilisation of Africa – or the African Civilisation Society, as it was known. At this meeting, the Society inaugurated the grand Niger River plan. The plan had already captured the public imagination and the meeting was one of the largest ever held in Britain, drawing an audience of 5,000 from nearly all the British churches and from across the political spectrum. In the midst of the bitter ecclesiastical conflicts, between Voluntaries and church extensionists, evangelicals and Tractarians, Protestants and Catholics, here was a cause that could unite all people of faith. In the chair was Prince Albert, the new consort of the young Queen Victoria, in his first major public engagement. He was flanked on the platform by nine aristocrats and nine Anglican bishops. Prince Albert, a German by birth, opened the meeting by expressing his admiration for Britain's great military traditions. However, he continued, 'there is a road to glory more noble, more illustrious, purer, and grander, than the battles of Waterloo or Trafalgar'. There was a greater campaign 'to arrest the destruction of mankind; to pour a blessing upon a continent in ruins; to send civilisation and the mild truths of the gospel over a region in comparison with which Britain herself is but a speck upon the ocean'. 'This', he insisted, 'is the road to true and lasting renown'.[7] In introducing the great scheme, Buxton focused on Africa as a continent of darkness and misery. 'What is the state of Africa?' he asked. 'Why, it is a universal slaughterhouse . . . What is its trade? The bodies of its inhabitants. What is its religion? The sacrifice of human flesh.'[8] Other speakers included the evangelical Charles Sumner, bishop of Winchester, the high church clergyman Samuel Wilberforce (son of the great evangelical abolitionist), the Tory leader, Sir Robert Peel, and the Quaker philanthropist, Samuel Gurney. In the hall were the Irish 'liberator', Daniel O'Connell, the high church Tory, William Gladstone, the Roman Catholic Duke of Norfolk, and the Evangelical Lord Ashley. There was also a young candidate medical missionary, David Livingstone, who was profoundly moved by Buxton's appeal to the civilising effects of 'Christianity and commerce'.

Among those present, there was a fervent belief both that Africa could be redeemed through peaceful commerce and that it was Britain's duty to do so. The money to be spent by the British people on the expedition would be recompense for the damage inflicted on Africa through the slave trade. It was a way in which Britain could use its growing industrial and commercial wealth and power to promote peace, freedom and Christian morality in the wider world. Several days later, on 12 June, London also hosted the 'World's Anti-Slavery Convention'. Sponsored by the recently formed British and Foreign Anti-Slavery Society, it brought together over 400 delegates from anti-slavery societies throughout the world to co-ordinate anti-slavery action. The convention agreed that slavery was a 'sin against God' and it appealed to the world to end this evil in the name of 'God and humanity'.[9] Further large public meetings on the Niger expedition, meanwhile, were held in September 1840 in Glasgow, Manchester and Norwich.

The Niger expedition departed with great fanfare from England in April 1841. It included scientists, physicians and agricultural experts as well as missionaries, and every aspect was carefully planned. The state provided three specially designed and constructed flat-bottomed iron steamships – the *Albert*, the *Wilberforce* and the *Soudan* – to carry the expedition members up the Niger River. The crown empowered the steamship captains to make treaties with African tribal chiefs for the abolition of the slave trade. Aware of the dangers of malaria, the planners had equipped the ships with expensive ventilation systems, while the vessels were to steam through the marshlands at the mouth of the Niger as rapidly as possible. These safeguards, however, proved unavailing. The expedition reached the mouth of the Niger by August and moved quickly through the coastal marshes. None the less, malaria soon made its appearance and began cutting the Europeans down. By September, with most of the Europeans ill or dying, the chain of command disintegrated and the grand hopes for the new Africa turned into a fevered nightmare. After making its way some 300 miles up the river and setting up one model farming settlement, the expedition was forced to turn back, and the boats struggled with skeletal crews, mainly Africans who proved stronger against the fever, to reach the coast. Out of the 145 Europeans, 130 had fallen ill of fever and 40 had died.[10] The public was horrified.

The *Wilberforce* made a return journey up the Niger River the following year, but found the model farm in a state of collapse. It evacuated the survivors and withdrew, convinced by the ghastly experience that no Europeans could survive the climate and oversee the proposed agricultural, commercial and religious development of the Niger basin. After all the great hopes, the failure cut deep into the Christian nation. There was severe criticism in the press, including a disparaging article by Charles Dickens in the *Examiner*.[11] (Dickens would later ridicule the ill-conceived aspirations of the Niger expedition's supporters in his novel, *Bleak House*, published in 1852–53.) Buxton, who felt a personal responsibility for the tragedy, was devastated, and died not long afterwards. None the less, although disappointed by the failure, many British Christians refused to submit to despair for Africa's future. They continued to believe that the providential laws of the free market would one day penetrate the interior of Africa, and indeed all the world, and bring an end to slavery at its source. These Christians, who included the young Livingstone, retained their faith in Buxton's grand idea that Africa's regeneration would come through commerce and Christianity.

Christianity and commerce: the Opium War

A few years earlier, in November 1839, Britain had commenced hostilities with the imperial state of China in order to force that vast country open to British trade. In this case, the expeditionary forces sent were not so peaceful nor were their aims so benign. The main cause of the first so-called 'Opium War' was the opposition of the Chinese authorities to the importation of opium into China. British merchants had found opium a lucrative trading commodity, and one of the few British 'goods' for which there was a ready market in China – something to exchange for the Chinese tea, silks, and fine manufactures that were so desired in Britain. The opium was produced in India and the trade thus brought large profits to the East India Company. The imperial government in China, justifiably concerned about the destructive physical and psychological effects of widespread opium use among its population, prohibited the trade. British merchants then endeavoured to smuggle the drug into the country, and the Chinese authorities responded by confiscating some twenty thousand chests of opium. The British government promised the merchants compensation, and went to war to force the Chinese to pay. There were, certainly, other causes of the war, including the high-handed behaviour of Chinese officials towards British merchants and the claims of the Chinese to have legal jurisdiction over British subjects residing in China. But the main cause was the British insistence that China open its ports to their trade, including trade in opium.

There was only a small Protestant missionary presence in China in the late 1830s, perhaps a dozen or so Protestant missionaries for the vast Chinese empire. (There were a larger number of Roman Catholic missionaries, but the Protestant missionaries scarcely recognised them as fellow Christians.) The first British Protestant missionary, Robert Morrison of the London Missionary Society, had arrived in 1807, and by 1823 he and a fellow worker, the Scot, William Milne, had produced a Chinese translation of the Bible. But over the following years, the Protestant missions achieved precious little. Largely confined by the Chinese authorities to the Western trading factories of Canton and Macao and barred from preaching by Chinese law, the Protestant missionaries had by 1835 made fewer than 20 Chinese converts. They distributed tracts and portions of the Scriptures in Chinese, but these went unread, and were used to wrap candy in the bazaars or to wallpaper houses. They sought to engage groups of Chinese in earnest discussion, but met with, at best, polite indifference. It was difficult to understand this apparent failure of the Protestant gospel. Missionaries became convinced that it was the result of the obstacles placed by the Chinese government on the free movement of missionaries. They therefore welcomed the outbreak of the war. It was not that they did not recognise the damaging effects of opium. But they believed that the war had a far more important purpose. As well as to open China to free trade, it would open China to the free movement of the gospel.[12]

The Opium War was brief, and China was soon forced to sue for peace. By the Treaty of Nanking in 1842, Britain received the island of Hong Kong, and its merchants gained free access to four other 'treaty ports' in China. China was also forced to pay compensation for opium confiscated by the Chinese authorities and for the costs of the war. They now had to allow the importation of opium. The terms of the treaty also opened the so-called 'treaty ports' to Christian missionary activity. Missionaries, some of whom had served as interpreters with the British forces, welcomed the victory. China, wrote the missionary, William Lockhart, to the London Missionary Society in October 1842, was now 'in very truth a land of promise', while the Society held a special service of thanksgiving that month in England for the opening of China.[13] Soon a growing number of British and American missionaries were at work bringing Christianity to the treaty ports and surrounding districts. For many, this was providential – evidence that British commerce and Christianity were meant to advance together to transform the world. Contributions to missionary societies increased significantly between 1843 and 1846 in recognition of the new mission field.[14] Some Christians, to be sure, including the evangelical Lord Ashley, bitterly condemned the immorality of the opium trade. But others believed that God was using the spread of trade, even the iniquity of the opium trade, in order to open China to Christian influence. By a curious logic, they would explain that Christian influence was now destined to end the scourge of opium in China. At its anniversary meeting in September 1845, the Leeds auxiliary of the LMS recorded their 'indefinable impression of awe and amazement' over 'how Providence has suddenly opened China, with its third of the human race, to Missionary enterprize'. In 1846, Bishop Samuel Wilberforce assured a missionary meeting that it was an affront to the divine government of the world to believe that Britain had gone to war with China merely over trade rights. Providence had clearly brought British trade and British arms to China, so that it would be opened to Christianity.[15] For John Bowring, a Manchester businessman who became consul of the treaty port of Canton in 1847 and governor of Hong Kong in 1854, the message of providence was clear: 'Jesus Christ is Free Trade and Free Trade is Jesus Christ'.[16]

The two episodes – the Niger expedition of 1841 and the Opium War of 1839–42 reflected different Christian responses to British imperial power in the world. But they shared this in common: they represented the belief that Britain had the responsibility, under God, to bring free trade to the non-Western world – and that free trade would bring in its wake other benefits, among them the end of slavery and the spread of Christian missions. For a growing number of British Christians, commerce and Christianity were part of God's plan for the regeneration and conversion of Africa and Asia. Such providentialist conceptions of Britain's global role were exercising a growing influence on public opinion in the late 1830s and early 1840s. They included the belief that Britain's growing industrial and commercial supremacy had been bestowed upon it by God for a purpose, and that Britain had a responsibility to use its power and influence to benefit the larger world. They included the belief that the slave trade and slavery would only be eradicated through the economic development of the African interior under Christian influence. Above all, there was the belief that the growing networks of trade and communication would also promote the spread of Christianity to the entire world. For ultimately, in their view, it was Christianity that defined Britain's imperial power. In 1848, several West African chiefs sent a petition to the queen, in which they renounced slavery and pledged their support to free trade. In her response to the chiefs, the queen acknowledged that it was good to end the abominable slave trade and engage in the free commerce between nations, which 'is blessed by God'. 'But commerce alone', she added, 'will not make a nation great and happy like England: England has become great and happy by the knowledge of the true God and Jesus Christ'.[17]

The Anti-Corn Law League

While Buxton had been preparing the Niger plan for the opening of the African interior, a group of merchants and manufacturers based in Manchester had been developing another initiative aimed at advancing commerce and freedom. This was the movement for the abolition of the Corn Law (or the heavy duties imposed on the importation of grain into the United Kingdom). The Corn Laws had long been part of British economic policy. The most recent Corn Law had been enacted in 1815 by a Parliament dominated by the landed interest, and it had been intended to protect British agriculture from being overwhelmed by imports of cheap Continental grain following the end of the Napoleonic Wars. Initially, the Corn Law prohibited all imports of foreign grain unless domestic grain prices reached famine levels. In 1828, Parliament revised the Law, easing these draconian restrictions on the importing of grain, but continuing to impose heavy duties on foreign grain.

For its Manchester critics, the Corn Law restricted the growth of British industry by not allowing the free exchange of British manufactured goods for grain produced in other countries. It also did harm to working-class families, by forcing them to pay artificially high prices for bread, their main food. The Corn Law was, for them, a piece of class legislation, which enriched the landed classes at the expense of the rest of society. In March 1839, the Manchester group formed the Anti-Corn Law League, to co-ordinate a national agitation aimed at abolishing the Corn Law. Within six years, 225 affiliated associations had been formed in England alone. The League sponsored journals, including the *Anti-Bread-Tax Circular* and *Anti-Corn-Law Circular*, and issued mountains of tracts; during one week alone in February 1843, it sent out over nine million tracts. Its paid lec-turers travelled around the country, while local branches held mass meet-ings, banquets, fancy-dress balls, tea parties, and dramatic performances aimed at educating the public.[18]

An Anglican partner in a cotton printing company, the 35-year-old Richard Cobden, was one of the founding members of the League and soon emerged as the leading spokesman for the cause. He was elected to Parliament at the general election of 1841. A gentle, sympathetic man, who had known poverty in his youth and who abhorred privilege and dis-trusted authority, Cobden had embraced the cause of free trade with a reli-gious fervour. For him, the Corn Law was an immoral interference with God's gift of food to humankind and with God's intention that all should be fed; it was a national sin against the laws of providence. Cobden believed that abolishing the Corn Law would help to restore the divinely ordained order, and would thus bring benefits for all. It would promote trade and manufactures; it would reduce the price of bread for working men; and it would benefit agriculturalists by obliging them to adopt improved farming methods in order to compete with foreign suppliers. Moreover, abolishing the Corn Law would be a first step towards the elim-ination of all tariff barriers and the inauguration of an era of free trade for Britain, and through Britain's example, for the whole world. Free trade, Cobden insisted, was 'God's diplomacy', the 'grand panacea' for the world.[19] It would unite the nations in peaceful commerce and mutual dependence, bringing an end to warfare and uniting the peoples of all the world's societies in a great division of labour. Some would supply raw materials, some would engage in manufactures, and some would facilitate the transporting of goods – while all would benefit from the free movement of goods and services. There was an element of post-millennial enthusiasm to the free trade movement, a belief that free trade would gradually usher in the kingdom of God. 'Free Trade – what is it?' asked Cobden at a large meeting in September 1843:

Why, breaking down the barriers that separate nations; those barriers behind which nestle the feelings of pride, revenge, hatred and jealousy, which every now and then break their bonds and deluge whole countries with blood; those feelings which nourish the poison of war and conquest . . . which foster that lust for conquest and dominion which send forth your warrior chiefs to sanction devastation through other lands, and then calls them back that they may be enthroned securely in your passions, but only to harass and oppress you at home.[20]

The Anti-Corn Law League found particular support among Nonconformists, for whom there seemed an obvious connection between the privileges of the protectionist landlords and the privileges of the established church. Nor was the perceived connection entirely fanciful. The Tithe Commutation Act of 1836 for England and Wales had linked clerical incomes to the price of grain, and as a result the rural Anglican clergy benefited from the high grain duties. Although Cobden was an Anglican, his closest associate, John Bright, was a Quaker, and the overall membership of the Anti-Corn Law League was made up mainly of Dissenters. In August 1841, the League held a conference of clergymen in Manchester, which attracted 645 ministers to a forum which pronounced the Corn Law to be 'opposed to the law of God . . . anti-scriptural and anti-religious'. The conference was made up almost exclusively of Nonconformist ministers; only two clergymen of the Church of England and two of the Church of Scotland attended. Similar conferences for clergymen were held in Wales in December 1841 and in Scotland in January 1842, and again were almost exclusively composed of Nonconformist ministers.[21]

The abolition of the Corn Law

Peel's Tory government had come to office in August 1841 firmly committed to maintaining the Corn Law as the foundation of the wealth and influence of the landed classes. For most Tories, the Corn Law was inviolable: without it, the social influence of the landed classes, and with it the whole social hierarchy, would be undermined, and social order collapse. They had the support of much of the Anglican clergy. For the *Church of England Quarterly Review* of October 1841, the Corn Law was part of the providential order of church and agriculture. 'We are convinced', it asserted, 'that the two great elements of national peace and welfare set before us in the word of God, are the culture of the soil, and the culture of the human heart'. The repeal of the Corn Law would subject the country to 'the artificial, mercenary, and feverish spirit of trade' and thus be a 'step in a precipitate descent to national ruin'.[22] However, for Peel, the son of a Lancashire cotton manufacturer, the Corn Law did not have the same aura. While he disliked the theatrical methods and extravagant language of the Anti-Corn Law League, he was convinced by many of their economic arguments, and he was drawn to their claims of the moral and religious benefits of free trade. In 1842, in response to the economic distress in Britain's manufacturing districts, Peel's government brought forward a bold and controversial budget, which began moving the country in the direction of freer trade. In an effort to promote economic growth, the budget reduced the duties on about 750 of the 1,200 items for which customs duties were levied, including reductions in the duties on imported grain. To cover the shortfall in revenues, the government introduced Britain's first peacetime income tax. This was as far toward free trade as the Tory party would allow the government to go, and it was too far for many landowners.

The situation changed in the cold, wet summer of 1845, when the potato crop across northern Europe was devastated by a fungal blight. In Ireland, where perhaps a third of the population, mainly in the west and south, was dependent on the potato for survival, the loss of the crop was disastrous. The blight made its appearance in Ireland in September 1845, and rapidly spread, destroying a third of the crop and leaving millions vulnerable to starvation. In this sudden appearance of famine, many discerned the hand of God. 'It is awful to observe', wrote the home secretary, Sir James Graham, to Peel on 18 October, 'how the Almighty humbles the pride of nations. The Sword, the Pestilence, and Famine are the instruments of his displeasure . . . he gives the word, a single Crop is blighted, and we see a nation prostrate, and stretching out its Hands for Bread'.[23] Peel recognised that extreme measures would be needed to avoid mass starvation. In the late autumn, he used £100,000 in treasury funds to purchase American maize, which was offered for sale at cheap prices in Ireland. More significantly, he also suspended the Corn Law, believing this would help to promote the free flow of grain to Ireland. The government, he believed, should remove the artificial barrier to the movement of food to Ireland, and allow the laws of God to operate and help alleviate the catastrophe. Indeed, he confessed to his Cabinet on 2 December that he been converted in principle to the total repeal of the Corn Law. The Cabinet, however, was divided over suspending the Corn Law, and a few days later, Peel and the government resigned. The Whig leader, Lord John Russell, who also supported repealing the Law, was unable to form a government, and near the end of December 1845, Peel returned to office, now determined to secure repeal.

The large majority of the Tory party, committed to maintaining the Corn Law, turned upon their leader. Peel, they believed, had entered office pledged to maintain the Law, and it was a betrayal of trust for him now to seek repeal. For many Tories, Peel's reversal demonstrated contempt for the views of the party rank and file. For a party already deeply disturbed over Maynooth, Peel's abandonment of the Corn Law seemed further evidence of his lack of principle. In the Commons, two-thirds of the Tory party opposed the government's bill to repeal the Corn Law, and the measure could only be carried with Whig and Radical support. The House of Lords only passed repeal when it became clear that, if they broke constitutional convention and rejected what was in effect a finance bill, the government would ask the crown to create a sufficient number of new peers to vote the measure through. Tory supporters of the Corn Law had expected the established Church of England to rally behind the landed classes in support of protection. In the event, however, they were disappointed. In the House of Lords, the bishops of the established church split on the issue, with 16 bishops voting in favour of repeal and 9 voting against. Connop Thirlwall, bishop of St David's, and Samuel Wilberforce, bishop of Oxford, both spoke eloquently in support of repeal, arguing that a policy of free trade would not only help the victims of famine in Ireland, but also bring long-term benefits to the working classes in Britain.

The bill repealing the Corn Law became law in late June 1846, and two days later Peel's government was brought down. Peel would never again hold office, and the Tory party was broken up. For many of his critics, the repeal of the Corn Law was his second great betrayal of conservative principles, the first being his support for Catholic emancipation in 1829. And yet, as Boyd Hilton has argued, Peel himself believed that in repealing the Corn Laws he was placing the welfare of the nation above the interest of the landed classes. He was sacrificing his political career for a higher good – the feeding of the poor. He would seek to shape Britain's economic policy around the divine laws, and this, he believed, would mean the avoidance of mass starvation in Ireland, the improvement of the lot of the labouring classes, and the promotion of peaceful commerce among nations.[24] Three years after the repeal of the Corn Laws, in 1849, Parliament abolished the Navigation Acts, which had provided protection for British shipping. The duties on other imported goods, moreover, were steadily eliminated, until by 1860, nearly all protective duties had been repealed. As Britain moved towards free trade, many looked to the gradual spread of its example, until all nations were bound together by networks of trade, communications and mutual understanding. Some infused the spread of commerce and communication with a millennial aura. In his charge of 1848, Julius Charles Hare, liberal archdeacon of Lewes, enthused over 'the wonders of the steam-engine . . . [and] the wonders of the electric telegraph, whereby the North and the South are brought together, and the East and the West are almost joined into one'. 'Surely', he added, 'these wonders were meant to prepare the way for the restoration of the Unity of Mankind'.[25]

Many of those who embraced the providentialist vision of free trade, including Richard Cobden and the Birmingham Quaker anti-slavery activist, Joseph Sturge, also became active in the international movement for peace. The belief that the nations were being providentially drawn together through commerce led many British Christians to envisage inter-national forums that would arbitrate disputes between nations. Such ideas had a post-millenarian aspect, reflecting the belief that the world was advancing towards the promised era of universal peace, love and harmony. The mid-nineteenth-century peace movement was largely an Anglo-American initiative. The key figure was the evangelical 'learned blacksmith' of Connecticut, Elihu Burritt, who travelled to Britain in 1846 to proclaim his belief that God had chosen the 'Anglo-Saxon race' to perform 'his great work of love to the human family in spreading the light of civilisation and Christianity over all the habitations of men'. For Burritt, Britain's decision to embrace free trade was the 'Commercial Harbinger of the Millennium'. He founded a League of Universal Brotherhood, which by July 1848 had over 30,000 members and 400 branches throughout the Anglo-American world. Largely through Burritt's efforts, a series of four international peace congresses were held – in Brussels in 1848, Paris in 1849, Frankfurt in 1850 and London in 1851. These called for universal disarmament, arbitration of disputes, and a code of international law.[26] Free trade, arbitration and peace were, it seemed, advancing together under Britain's leadership. When revolution swept across Europe in 1848, Britain had been spared from the bloodshed and social upheavals. Was this not further evidence of its role as an elect nation, chosen by God to dispense the bless-ings of commerce, Christianity and civilisation? Was this not evidence, asked Charles Thomas Longley, the bishop of Ripon (and a future arch-bishop of Canterbury), that God was 'pleased to look upon our land with an eye of favour'?[27]

The great famine in Ireland

But there was a shadow over this vision. In Ireland, the repeal of the Corn Laws had no effect in alleviating the famine; and free trade did not feed the starving or halt the spread of disease. To be fair, Peel's government had not expected repeal to bring an immediate flow of foreign grain into Ireland to replace the blighted potatoes. Rather, they had believed that repeal would lead to long-term benefits to Ireland, by promoting the cultivation of grain for both domestic use and export, by ending the excessive dependence upon the potato and diversifying the Irish diet, by generating surplus wealth through grain exports, and by using that wealth to invest in the economic infrastructure. In the short term, Peel's government had recognised that the Irish poor would need to be fed through the famine period, and it had planned to do this with American maize and with public works projects until the famine had run its course. As Peter Gray has argued, Peel and some of his close colleagues were imbued with a providentialist belief that human affairs were regulated by God for human good. The famine was a visitation from God, and as such would have an ultimately beneficent purpose. Rather like the Opium War, long-term good could be expected to come out of short-term evil. The famine would lead to a more diversified economy, ensuring long-term prosperity and social stability.[28] And in the meantime, the public works projects would keep people from starving.

Despite the good intentions, however, Irish people did starve, and the Irish famine proved one of the great tragedies of the nineteenth century. The potato crop, which had fallen about one-third short in 1845, was devastated in 1846, with three-quarters of the crop lost through blight. By early 1847, people were dying in massive numbers from starvation and from the epidemic diseases which spread through the weakened population. The Whig–Liberal government of Lord John Russell, which came to power following Peel's fall in June 1846, had no clear policy to deal with a prolonged famine of such magnitude. Russell's government, like Peel's, was influenced by providentialist thinking, though for some the famine seemed to be less a divine summons to long-term reform and more a divine punishment of the Irish. The leading figure in the management of famine relief was the career civil servant, Sir Charles Trevelyan, a man dogmatically opposed to interference with *laissez faire* doctrine, hostile to public works, and convinced that the free distribution of food would be destructive to both public morals and the state. The famine, Trevelyan believed, should teach the Irish the importance of hard work, foresight and self-reliance, and the state must avoid indiscriminate relief that would create a permanent culture of dependency. He regarded deaths by famine as a form of 'discipline', providing a hard lesson to those who survived.[29]

In the spring of 1847, Russell's government resolved to end the public works projects, which by now were supporting 750,000 people. In place of public works, the government proposed to set up soup kitchens to feed the starving in the west and south of the country. There was, however, a hiatus of a few months between the closing of the works and the opening of the kitchens, and during this time many more people starved. In the summer of 1847, the government decided to shift the main provision of relief from soup kitchens to an extended Irish poor law, which Parliament had enacted in the spring of 1847. The new law provided both outdoor relief and indoor relief in workhouses, with the relief to be supported by local rates on property. The aim was to shift the burden of relief from the British taxpayers as a whole to the local Irish ratepayers, especially the Irish landed classes.[30] Included in the new law was the notorious Gregory clause, which specified that no tenant occupying more than a quarter acre would be eligible for relief. In order to qualify for relief, a starving tenant and his family had to surrender their holding to the landlord.[31]

Much of Ireland, especially the south and west, descended into a nightmare of death, disease, evictions and despair. 1847, or the 'Black '47', would be etched into the folk memory as the 'famine year'. The district around Skibbereen in the southwest gained international notoriety through a series of articles in the *Illustrated London News* which appeared in late 1846 and 1847 – but many other districts also suffered grievously. The accounts from Ireland were chilling. Bodies lay unburied by the roadsides, and whole families were found dead in more remote cabins. Thousands were evicted from their smallholdings, with landlords burning their cabins to ensure they would never return; many of those evicted died of exposure in the winter cold and rain. The number of families evicted rose from about 3,600 in 1846 to 6,026 in 1847 and 9,657 in 1848.[32] Those who could make their way into the overcrowded workhouses often died there of typhus, or 'famine fever'. Others managed to escape the country, some coming across to Britain, others to North America, packed into the holds of overcrowded ships. They brought typhus with them, which quickly spread through the holds, turning them into 'coffin ships'. Under the famine conditions, parents were frequently forced to make choices of which of their children could be fed and survive, and which must die. Survivors would be haunted with guilt. It is generally accepted that a million died of starvation or famine-related disease and another million emigrated, though some reputable historians estimate that the number of dead was much higher. The tragedy was heightened by the fact that the famine took place within the wealthiest state in the world. It was also restricted to Ireland and especially to the Irish Catholic population. Although the failure of the potato crop had also brought famine conditions to the Highlands and Islands of Scotland, where the mainly Presbyterian crofters were also dependent on potatoes, relief efforts there – especially those mounted by the new Free Church – were sufficient to avert starvation. This contributed to the widespread belief in Ireland that a 'British' Protestant state had allowed massive starvation as a means of reducing the Irish Catholic population and strengthening its control over the country. The providentialist language of public figures added to this perception.

In truth, many British and Irish Protestants were distressed by the tragedy, and placed the immediate relief of human suffering above attempts to anticipate the workings of providence. In his last major work, which appeared in May 1847 (the month in which he died), Thomas Chalmers called for massive governmental and private contributions for famine relief. Throughout his career, Chalmers had staunchly opposed state involvement in poor relief, preferring it to be voluntary and personal. He believed, however, that the famine was so 'extraordinary' and 'overwhelming', as to summon the united efforts of the nation. He called for increased direct taxation in Britain to support massive relief efforts, so that they could end 'the great national outrage upon humanity which has been perpetrated within our own shores' and which has scandalised 'the whole civilized world'. Chalmers discerned the hand of providence in the horrors, but as a divine judgement upon Britain for its misgovernment of Ireland. There was a need now for 'acts of princely, but well-directed munificence to repair the accumulated wrongs of many generations'.[33] A similar view was expressed by the high Anglican Tory MP, William Gladstone. 'Here is a calamity most legibly Divine', he wrote to his friend, Henry Manning, on 9 March 1847:

There is a total absence of such second causes as might tempt us to explain it away; it is the greatest horror of modern times, that in the richest age of the world, and in the richest country of that age, the people should be dying of famine . . . No mere giving of money will do, it can only be met by national and personal humiliation.

'How', he added, with reference to the Old Testament story of Belshazzar's feast (Daniel 5: 25), 'can the handwriting be made clear against us, if it is not clear now'.[34]

In Ireland, hundreds of Protestant clergymen of the Church of Ireland and other churches remained in their neighbourhoods, serving on local relief committees, distributing food at soup kitchens, writing letters to the newspapers or to wealthy relatives begging for financial aid, visiting the sick and dying, conducting funerals, consoling the bereaved – and often succumbing to famine fever. They included such people as James Burrowes, Church of Ireland vicar in Killala, who with his wife and children regularly distributed food to 400 families at his glebe house. But the crowds brought with them famine fever, and Burrowes's wife and daughter died in 1847, and Burrowes followed them to the grave in 1849.[35] Some 40 Church of Ireland clergymen died of famine fever in 1847 alone. The Society of Friends, or Quakers, took a leading role in relief efforts; from November 1846 they conducted soup kitchens in distressed districts. Their efforts in publicising the suffering they encountered – with their accounts given added credibility by their reputation for scrupulous honesty – did much to raise awareness of actual conditions and generate donations. In early January 1847, the queen issued a letter, calling for collections in all the parish churches of the United Kingdom for famine relief. The money raised – nearly £435,000 – was channelled into a newly created British Association for the Relief of Extreme Distress, and used primarily to assist the hard-pressed Poor Law unions. When the government proclaimed a national day of fast and humiliation for Wednesday, 24 March 1847, it was widely observed, with well-attended services in most churches.[36]

There was, however, another side to the Protestant response to the famine. Noting that the worst effects of the famine were restricted to mainly Roman Catholic districts, some zealous evangelicals viewed it as a divine punishment of Catholics. Still others discerned in the famine a call to revive the Second Reformation movement of the 1820s, and secure at last the conversion of the Roman Catholics to Protestantism. The horrors of the famine, they reasoned, would undermine Irish Catholic confidence in their church, and open them to Protestant influence. Starving Catholics would be still more likely to convert as they saw Protestants working to relieve their hunger and distress. For these evangelicals, bringing desperate Irish Catholics to the true faith, for the eternal welfare of their souls, was far more valuable than mere temporal relief that might prolong their lives. The evangelical effort to combine relief and proselytising focused on the west of Ireland. From 1845, Alexander Dallas, an English evangelical and rector of Wonston in Hampshire, had begun forming mission stations in the west, receiving support from sympathetic Protestant landlords. Convinced that the famine had been sent by God to open the Irish people to Protestant influence, Dallas and his supporters increased their missionary efforts, turning the famine-stricken west into a sectarian battleground. There were widespread rumours, often encouraged by local Catholic priests, that the proselytisers were offering food and clothing in return for conversions, and those who converted were described, in popular parlance, as having 'taken the soup'. While there is no evidence that the evangelicals restricted their relief efforts to actual or potential converts, it is clear that converts were often well cared for in Protestant 'colonies' in the west of Ireland, such as that on Achill Island. The charge of 'souperism' became embedded in the folk memory of the famine years, and permanently damaged both the reputation of the Church of Ireland and Protestant–Catholic relations. In 1849, Dallas and his fellow Evangelicals founded the Society for Irish Church Missions to Roman Catholics. With considerable financial support from Britain, the Society established over 100 mission stations in Ireland, and by 1851 claimed that it had gained 35,000 converts.[37] The Catholic hierarchy was, for a time, concerned about the proselytisers. However, in the following years, as the famine ran its course, the number of conversions rapidly declined, and most of the famine converts returned to Catholicism.[38]

The famine had a profound effect on Roman Catholicism in Ireland. In the mid-1840s, as we have seen, the Catholic hierarchy had been moving towards a greater accommodation with the British state, co-operating with the Charitable Bequests Act and supporting the Maynooth endowment. Lord John Russell, who headed the government after June 1846, was regarded as a friend to Irish Catholics, and his government had been warmly welcomed by the Irish leader, Daniel O'Connell. As the famine deaths and evictions mounted, however, Catholic priests grew disillusioned with Russell and his government. O'Connell died in May 1847 while on pilgrimage to Rome. In the parishes, priests were daily confronted with the horrors, serving on relief committees, visiting the sick and dying, performing last rites, and burying the dead, often, too often, in mass graves. It was difficult for the priests not to denounce the government for failing to do more. The Roman Catholic hierarchy in Ireland, meanwhile, was placed in a dilemma. If the bishops remained silent, it could seem to the parish priests and suffering flocks that the church feared to stand up against injustice and needless death, and might even be keeping silent in the hope of currying the favour with the state and the landlords. However, if the bishops spoke out against the inadequate relief efforts or evictions, the church could be seen as fomenting violence among a desperate people. In November 1847, a Catholic priest denounced from the pulpit the Irish landowner, Major Denis Mahon, who was responsible for evicting 3,000 people from his estates. Shortly after, Mahon was murdered, and the Irish Catholic Church was widely denounced in Britain for incitement to murder. This, in turn, harmed efforts in Britain to raise money for famine relief. In the summer of 1848, there was an abortive rising led by the Young Ireland group of romantic nationalists. Although the Catholic Church gave no support to the rising, many in Britain assumed a connection between Catholicism and Irish rebellion, and reduced their relief contributions in the face of Irish 'ingratitude'. All of this contributed to a growing distance between the communities in Ireland. During the famine, Irish Catholic and Protestant clergy had often co-operated on local relief committees, but afterwards, such co-operation became rare.

In December 1848, the Irish church received uncompromising new leadership when Paul Cullen, formerly rector of the Irish College in Rome, was appointed archbishop of Armagh and primate of Ireland by Pope Pius IX. The son of a staunchly anti-British Kildare farmer, Cullen had spent most of his adult life in Rome, where he had worked to counter British influence at the Vatican. He had also witnessed at first hand the revolution of 1848 in Rome, and would throughout his life harbour a deep distrust of nationalism and liberalism. On returning to Ireland, Cullen – devout, authoritarian, suspicious, and deeply Roman in orientation – was determined to reassert the independent influence of the Catholic Church. To strengthen the Irish hierarchy, he organised the first formal conference of the Irish episcopacy to be held since 1642. The Synod of Thurles met in late August and early September 1850.[39] Although many Irish bishops disliked Cullen and his ways, which seemed more Roman than Irish, Cullen none the less managed to exert his authority over the Synod and achieve his aims. The bishops agreed to insist upon stricter administration of the sacraments and closer discipline of the parish clergy. They agreed to cease any efforts to secure a compromise with the government over the 'godless colleges' set up in 1845 and instead they began plans for a Catholic university. Significantly, the Synod also spoke out boldly on the sufferings of the poor during the famine. 'We behold our poor', the Synod proclaimed:

not only crushed and overwhelmed by the awful visitation of Heaven, but frequently the victims of the most ruthless oppression that ever disgraced the annals of humanity. Though they have been made to the image of the living God, and are purchased by the blood of Calvary, though the special favourites and representatives of Jesus Christ, we see them treated with a cruelty that would cause the heart to ache if inflicted on the beasts of the field.[40]

The Synod of Thurles marked the beginning of what Emmet Larkin has described as a 'devotional revolution' – a revolution that would see the Catholic Church become greatly strengthened in its clerical discipline and institutional organisation, and Catholic Ireland achieve probably the highest levels of regular church attendance in Christendom.[41] There were, to be sure, signs of a revival of Catholic devotion before the famine, for example, in the Temperance movement led by Father Mathew or the popular devotions associated with the O'Connellite campaigns for Catholic emancipation and repeal. Larkin has shown that the Catholic Church in Ireland made impressive achievements in providing pastoral care in pre-famine Ireland through the use of private homes as 'stations' for hearing confessions and celebrating communion.[42] But the two decades after 1850 witnessed a profound transformation in expressions of popular piety, as the Irish people embraced new, mainly Roman devotions, including 'the rosary, forty hours, perpetual adoration, novenas, blessed altars, *Via Crucis*, benediction, vespers, devotion to the Sacred Heart and to the Immaculate Conception, jubilees, triduums, pilgrimages, shrines, processions and retreats'.[43] The church exercised an increased influence over all aspects of the lives of Irish Catholics – marriage, sexual behaviour, the raising of children, family devotions, the care of the aged, and bequests. In part, this enhanced pastoral role was a matter of numbers. The famine had swept away, through death or emigration, over two million people out of a population of nearly seven million in 1846, and the Irish population continued to decline during the 1850s and 1860s. Even without any increase in the number of priests, each priest would have had a decreasing number of Catholics to supervise. But the number of priests was increasing, and the result was a dramatic decrease in the ratio of priests to population. In 1840, there had been one priest for every 3,000 people in Ireland. This ratio had fallen to one to 2,100 in 1850 and one to 1,250 by 1870.[44] Priests were thus able to exercise greater pastoral supervision over their smaller flocks. Cullen, meanwhile, steadily expanded his power over the Irish episcopacy and strengthened the internal discipline and order of the Irish church.

The trauma of the famine, meanwhile, undermined popular confidence in magical practices to protect crops and livestock or stave off disease and death. It swept away the legions of poor tenants and landless labourers in the west and south who had been the repositories of Gaelic lore and traditions. As old Gaelic folk beliefs died away amid the holocaust, the famine survivors became more susceptible to the new devotional influences coming from Rome.[45] Ireland emerged from the famine as a self-consciously Roman Catholic society and one which associated Protestant relief efforts with 'souperism'. There was a widespread belief that the deaths and evictions of the famine years had been largely preventable, and had been allowed to happen by a Protestant British state which embraced free trade as its faith and looked upon a million mainly Catholic deaths as providential. This was a simplification, but the perception took hold of British culpability, and not entirely without grounds. In response to the providentialist views of free trade and the Protestant British empire, there emerged in Ireland a devotional revolution, a disciplined Roman Catholic Church, and a growing Irish Catholic identity.

Religion and industrial society in Britain

In Britain, as we have noted, there was no mass famine during the 1840s. However, behind Britain's growing industrial supremacy, and the grand visions of commerce and Christianity, there were dark shadows. Although their deaths were often concealed by the smoke of the factories, darkness of the mines or squalor of the urban slums, thousands died unnecessarily each year in industrial Britain through malnutrition, exposure, contaminated food or water, industrial accidents, or overwork. In the textile factories, men, women and children over 13 worked up to 16 hours a day, 6 days a week, the pace of work driven by steam-powered machinery, the air polluted with cotton dust which destroyed the lungs. In the coal mines, half-naked women and children dragged coal wagons on their hands and knees through the dark and damp passages, or carried heavy baskets of coal up ladders to the surface. Children as young as five years of age were left alone in the darkness for 16-hour shifts, working the trap doors that were necessary to provide ventilation in the mines. In the urban slums, needlewomen and tailors worked for 16 hours or more a day making garments, and still failed to earn enough to feed themselves and their families. Men and women found escape in cheap gin, and widespread drunkenness brought domestic abuse, loss of employment and financial ruin. People sometimes starved to death rather than enter the hated workhouses established by the poor law of 1834 – with their penal atmosphere, drab uniform and diet, and separation of family members. The economic conditions throughout Britain were bleak during the later 1840s. There was a further sharp downturn in the economy in 1847, and in 1848–49, cholera struck Britain for a second time, claiming tens of thousands of lives.

The dominance of political economy, with its bleak doctrines of the inevitability of mass deprivation, meant that many looked upon the suffering as part of the divinely ordained order. As we have seen, such Christian political economists as Thomas Malthus, Edward Copleston or John Bird Sumner viewed mass poverty, like epidemic disease or crop failures, as part of the providential order of society – forms of divine chastisement, which provided harsh but necessary lessons to the labouring poor concerning the importance of sexual abstinence before marriage, delayed marriage, thrift, hard work and foresight.[46] It was not, these Christian political economists insisted, beneficial in the long term for the government to interfere with the natural operations of the market-place. Such interference would prove ineffective, while it would promote overpopulation, reduce productivity, and spread 'pauperism', or a culture of dependency among the labouring orders. It would also diminish individual freedom and the sense of personal responsibility.

Christian paternalism: Young England and Lord Ashley

While many viewed Britain's industrial and commercial growth as providential, there were also a number of influential figures who were highly critical of the expanding industrial society of the 1840s. They saw industrial society as anarchic, materialist and uncaring; for them, its brick and iron cities, tenements, factories and smoke were ugly and soul-destroying. They recalled with longing the 'world they had lost', the world before the onset of industrialisation – which they envisaged as a green, pleasant, orderly, Christian, caring and hierarchical society. In pre-industrial society, they believed, people had known their place within the social hierarchy, showing benevolence to those below them on the social ladder, and deference and respect to those above; in this society, the common people had lived communally, sharing tools and oxen and assisting one another in times of adversity, while the aristocracy had governed fairly and the clergy had instructed the people in moral and religious values.

One such critic of industrial society was the Scottish historian and man of letters, Thomas Carlyle. From a family of strict Lowland Presbyterian Seceders, Carlyle had given up plans to enter the ministry while a student at Edinburgh University and had lost much of his Christian faith – though he retained the stern Dissenting morality of his parents. In his *Chartism* of 1840, Carlyle had portrayed the Chartist movement as misguided and immoral, but also an understandable protest by labouring people against a social order that seemed indifferent to their needs. The real root of the social problem, he believed, was the creed of political economy, with its doctrine of *laissez faire*, or the belief that government should interfere as little as possible in the economy. Political economy, he insisted, was little more than a justification for the exploitation of the poor by the rich, and *laissez faire* was 'an abdication on the part of the governors; an admission that they are henceforth incompetent to govern, that they are not there to govern at all, but to do – one knows not what'. He denounced the prevalent view that employers had no responsibility to their employees beyond the payment of wages. 'Cash Payment', he protested, must not become 'the universal sole nexus of man to man'.[47] What society needed, he insisted, was not less, but more government: it needed more guidance, more instruction, and more authority; it needed an aristocracy that would lead the people, and a clergy that would instruct them in spiritual and moral values.

Within the Church of England, a group of young laymen responded to the social unrest of the 1840s with calls for a Christian paternalism, in which the governing elite would act as caring parents to society, and treat their wealth and influence as a trust held under God for the service of others. The group included the young Cambridge-educated aristocrats Lord John Manners and George Smythe, both of whom had come under Tractarian influence. Together with a third friend, Alexander Baillie-Cochrane, they were elected in 1841 to Parliament, where they formed an alliance with the flamboyant Tory society novelist and politician, Benjamin Disraeli, with his ringlets of black hair, jewels and perfumed handkerchiefs. Embracing the name 'Young England', they acted as a pressure group within the Tory party. Influenced by the romantic novelist, Sir Walter Scott, and the Anglican poet and historian, Robert Southey, Young England advocated a hierarchical social order, a responsible aristocracy, paternalist government, harmony among the social orders, a close alliance of aristocracy and people, rejection of *laissez faire* political economy, and the maintenance of the Corn Laws as a bulwark of aristocratic order.[48] They were inspired by visions of medieval society. In a volume of verse published in 1841, Lord John Manners celebrated the ideal of a medieval paternalistic society, in which

> Each knew his place – king, peasant or priest,
> The greatest owed connexion with the least,
> From rank to rank the generous feeling ran,
> And linked society as man to man.

Young England looked to an Anglo-Catholic Church of England, with its rituals, prayer book, saints' days, choral music, cathedrals, parish churches, churchyards and harvest services, to provide the moral values and communal devotion needed to knit the different social orders together. Young England, Disraeli later recalled, looked on 'the Anglican Church as the main machinery by which these results might be realised. There were few great things left in England, and the Church was one'.[49] In the mid-1840s, Disraeli published three novels, *Coningsby; or the New Generation* (1844), *Sybil; or the Two Nations* (1845), and *Tancred; or the New Crusade* (1847), intended to convey to a broader public the political, social and religious ideals of the movement. Young England provided Disraeli with the ideological base from which he launched his attack on Sir Robert Peel, after the Tory leader had decided to repeal the Corn Laws.

Perhaps the greatest of the aristocratic paternalists, however, had no part in the Young England movement, although he sometimes co-operated with them and shared much of their social ideal. Lord Ashley (who in 1851 became the seventh Earl of Shaftesbury) was arguably the foremost philanthropist of the nineteenth century.[50] Born in 1801 into a prominent aristocratic family with estates in Dorset, Ashley had suffered a lonely childhood, experiencing little affection from his distant parents. After gaining a first-class degree at Christ Church, Oxford, Ashley entered Parliament in 1826 as Tory MP for the pocket borough of Woodstock, which was in the gift of his uncle, the Duke of Marlborough. In the mid-1830s, largely through his friendship with Edward Bickersteth, he embraced a strict evangelical faith, including pre-millenarian views about a world destined to remain perverted by sin until the second coming of Christ. He served on various evangelical societies for home and overseas missions from the mid-1830s, taking a particular interest in the conversion of the Jews and their restoration to the holy land, events which would, he believed, presage Christ's return.

Ashley became, however, best known for his parliamentary work to secure improved conditions for industrial workers and miners. The aristocratic Ashley despised the growing power and influence of the urban mill-owners, and the harsh conditions they imposed on their labourers. In 1833, in part at the urging of his wife, Emily, he agreed to become a parliamentary spokesman for the Ten Hours Movement, which sought to secure legislation to reduce the hours of factory labourers to no more than ten a day. He devoted himself to the cause, mastering economic theory, statistics and the practical details of factory life. His outspoken criticism of the industrial middle classes probably cost Ashley office in Peel's government in 1841 (as Peel viewed Ashley's impassioned advocacy of factory reform as a potential political liability). Although deeply hurt at being passed over for office, however, Ashley would not be deflected by what he saw as a duty before God to help the labouring orders. In 1842, he played a leading role in the parliamentary fight to secure legislation to remove women and children from working in the mines. Here his efforts were assisted by a parliamentary report which shocked public opinion with revelations of women and girls stripped to the waist and working alongside men in the pits, and of young children working the traps alone in the darkness. Then in 1847, Ashley's years of struggle for factory reform were rewarded when Parliament passed the Ten Hours Act, limiting the work of women and young persons between the ages of 13 and 18 in the textile mills to ten hours a day for five days a week and eight hours on Saturday. By working the women and youths in relays, mill-owners were able to keep the men working longer hours, until in 1853, Parliament also abolished the relay system.

Ashley's fervent desire to help industrial labourers drew him into move-ments to improve living conditions in the towns and cities. After 1842, he took a prominent role in the sanitary reform movement, working closely with the sanitary pioneer, Edwin Chadwick, in struggling against vested interests and public ignorance to provide clean water and adequate sewage systems. He served as first president of the General Board of Health set up by the Public Health Act of 1848. His interest in public health drew him to the problems of urban slum housing, and in 1851 he steered through Parliament a series of lodging houses acts. These acts provided for the licensing and inspection of lodging houses to safeguard against overcrowd-ing and ensure proper sanitation, and they empowered local authorities to build model lodging houses for working people, to be subsidised from the rates. In addition to his parliamentary work, Ashley also embraced from 1844 the cause of ragged schools (schools established by private philanthropists to provide basic education and meals to neglected and abandoned children in the cities). In all this varied activity, he was driven largely by his sense of aristocratic paternalism. Ashley had no desire to level the existing social hierarchy, which he viewed as ordained by God. He opposed Chartism, socialism and democracy, and did not believe that working-class children should receive more than five years of primary schooling. Behind his work on behalf of the urban workers, there was a desire to revive aristocratic leadership in society and put the new captains of industry in their place. But his evangelical faith was also an important motivation. It instilled in him the ever-present sense that he would be personally held to account by God for his wealth, his privilege, his status, his political influence, his talents and his every moment of time in this world. As a pre-millenarian, moreover, he believed that the return of Christ was imminent, and that at any moment he might find himself called to his final accounting.

Christian socialism

In 1848, yet another conception of Christian social reform emerged, promoted by a group of young, London-based Anglican intellectuals. This was the Christian Socialist movement, a movement which sought fundamental change in the structures of industrial capitalism in the interest of securing richer, more fulfilling lives for labouring people. The Christian Socialist movement shared elements of the Christian paternalism of Young England and of Lord Ashley – including emphases on community, harmony between the social orders, and the responsibilities of wealth. According to Edward Norman, the Christian Socialist 'concern for the conditions of the working men was like that of most old-fashioned paternalist clergy who hated the middle-class manufacturers and the industrial England they had created'.[51] However, the Christian Socialists also accepted that England's urban-industrial society could not be reversed and that a return to a feudal social order of paternalistic landowners and deferential, contented peasants was not an alternative. It was time, they believed, for the national Church of England to look forward, and develop new social teachings for England's urban-industrial society.

The Christian Socialist movement first emerged during the revolutionary upheavals that shook Europe in 1848. In late February, there was a revolution in Paris, which overthrew the French monarchy and established a republic. The movement was dominated by middle-class reformers who received, in the early months at least, broad support from the urban labouring orders. The new republic proclaimed the 'right to work' as a fundamental human right, and it set up national workshops in an effort to ensure full employment and promote humane working conditions. The revolutionary movement, meanwhile, spread from France across Western and Central Europe, overthrowing governments and finding particular support from urban labourers who were suffering acutely amid the social dislocations of early industrialisation. In Britain, the Chartists revived their hope of securing national acceptance of their 'people's charter' for fundamental democratic reform, and they planned a great demonstration in London for 10 April 1848. A mass procession was to carry a huge petition in support of the Charter, bearing two million signatures, to Parliament. The authorities feared that this demonstration would be the occasion for revolutionary action. Thousands of special constables were sworn in and armed, and public buildings were fortified. In the event, the day passed quietly, amid a heavy rainfall. The Chartist leaders held their mass meeting, but called off the planned march to Parliament to avoid possible bloodshed. However, the resentments simmered, and many Chartists felt betrayed by what they viewed as the timidity of their leaders.

On the evening of 10 April, three friends, Frederick Denison Maurice, Charles Kingsley and John Malcolm Ludlow – the first two Church of England clergymen and the third an Anglican barrister – met in London to consider a response to the Chartist crisis. All three had opposed the Chartist demonstration. Yet they were also sensitive to the sufferings of the urban poor and they were anxious over the growing chasm that separated rich from poor. The leading figure among the three was Maurice, chaplain of Lincoln's Inn and professor of history and literature at King's College, London. Raised as a Unitarian, Maurice had joined the Church of England as a young adult and was ordained in 1834. He was a gifted though obscure theologian, whose first major work, *The Kingdom of Christ*, published in 1838, explored what would be the dominant theme of his life's work – the unity of society under the spiritual and moral influence of the national church. The other clergyman was Charles Kingsley, the young, Cambridge-educated vicar of Eversley, who extolled the virtues of cold baths and outdoor sports, spoke with a stutter and suffered chronic poor health, and was a keen amateur naturalist. Loving the English countryside and influenced by the romantic paternalism of Young England, Kingsley shared Maurice's view of the Church of England as a force for social cohesion. Having as a child seen the charred bodies of those who died in the Bristol Reform Bill riot and fire of 1831, he deplored violent protest – and yet he also understood the sense of oppression and injustice that could drive labouring people to violence. He denounced what he perceived to be the excessive individualism of free trade capitalism. 'Our selfish commercial spirit', he proclaimed in a sermon on 30 April 1848, 'has infected our very religion. It has made men fancy that a man's spiritual business was merely to save his own soul, and that he owed no absolute duty to the souls of others'.[52] The third member of the group, John Malcolm Ludlow, had been raised in Paris by his mother, the widow of a British military officer. Moving to London in 1838, he had read law and been called to the bar in 1843. While in Paris, Ludlow had been attracted to French radical and socialist thought, and claimed to understand the appeal of socialism to the working classes.

In their meeting on 10 April, the three men agreed that members of the Church of England must seek dialogue with Chartists and working-class radicals. To initiate such dialogue, they agreed to found a weekly penny journal, directed to working-class readers. *Politics for the People* began publication on 6 May 1848. The aim of the new journal, its promoters insisted, was to demonstrate that politics cannot be separated from religion in a world where God was sovereign; and also that God was not on the side of property and against reform. 'The world is governed by God; this is the rich man's warning; this is the poor man's comfort; . . . this is the pledge that Liberty, Fraternity, Unity, under some conditions or other, are intended for every people under heaven'.[53] The journal contained much strong and forceful writing, and provided a Christian commentary on the revolutionary movement on the Continent and the demands at home for political and social reform. To be sure, its authors were middle-class men of their times, and their message was not revolutionary in tone or content. They used organic and hierarchical metaphors for society, portraying working people, for example, as making up the muscles and sinews of the social body.[54] They sought to convince working-class readers of the futility of violent revolution, while they promoted the virtues of temperance, thrift, hard work and independence. But the authors also demanded that the upper classes use their political power to reform social abuses, including slum housing, contaminated water supplies, poor sanitation, and sweated labour. Above all, the journal sought to portray Christianity as committed to achieving social justice as well as social harmony. Some of the most forceful writing came from Charles Kingsley, who asserted that, in his view, the 'people's charter' of the working-class Radicals did not go far enough in its demand for social reform, and that a more radical reform agenda would be found in the Bible. It was, he also believed, largely the fault of the clergy that the Bible's radical reform message was not better known. 'We have', he observed of his fellow clerics, 'used the Bible as if it was a mere special constable's handbook – an opium-dose for keeping beasts of burden patient while they were being overloaded'. This was clearly wrong. 'Instead of being a book to keep the poor in order', he insisted, 'it is a book, from beginning to end, written *to keep the rich in order*'. This was 'the poor man's comfort and the rich man's warning'.[55] *Politics for the People* failed to gain a large circulation and was soon in financial difficulties – closing, after only 17 issues, in July 1848. However, by now several other clerics and writers had joined Maurice's little brotherhood, and it was gaining national attention.

The brotherhood began hosting public lectures, and conducting evening classes for labouring men and women. Beginning in April 1849, moreover, they organised meetings between clergy and Chartists in a London coffee house. The atmosphere at these meetings was often tense, as there was considerable bitterness among Chartists toward the upper-classes in general and the clergy in particular. But the organisers persevered, and in time feelings of mutual respect developed. The meetings became weekly events. What was perhaps most impressive in these gatherings was the willingness of the middle-class clerics to listen to working men, to seek to understand their frustrations and their aspirations, rather than simply preach to them. In June 1849, the group was joined by Thomas Hughes, a London barrister and well-known cricketer and boxer, whose sporting reputation, physical prowess and unaffected manner won respect among working men. When, during one difficult meeting, Hughes leapt on a chair and threatened to fight the next man who hissed the queen, he was not obliged to make good his threat.

In the summer of 1849, there was considerable concern about the return of cholera, which claimed thousands of lives, especially in the urban slums. Beginning in October, moreover, the London public was appalled by a series of articles by Henry Mayhew in the *Morning Chronicle*, exposing low wages, long hours, squalid living conditions, hunger and general misery among London artisans, dockworkers and garment workers. Perhaps most shocking to middle-class readers were the revelations of widespread prostitution among female garment workers, a prostitution practiced by married as well as single women, because money was needed to feed and clothe their families. Distressed by Mayhew's revelations, members of the brotherhood, including Kingsley, undertook their own investigations of slum conditions. Kingsley's observations of the fetid and fever-ridden hovels along the Thames provided the graphic descriptive passages in his novel of social criticism, *Alton Locke* – a disturbing account of sweated labour in the garment industry – which he published in August 1850. For the Christian Socialists, society was an organic whole, and the suffering of slum dwellers would infect the health of all, if only because infectious disease, bred in urban squalor, could not be contained there. In a sermon of 1849 on the cholera epidemic, Kingsley related an anecdote that conveyed this sense of mutual dependence. 'A wise man', he observed:

tells a story of a poor Irish woman who came to Liverpool, and no one would take her in or have mercy on her, till, from starvation and bad

lodging . . . she caught typhus fever, and not only died herself, but gave
the infection to the whole street, and seventeen persons died of it. 'See,'
says the wise man. 'the poor Irish woman was the Liverpool people's
sister after all'.[56]

Social responsibility, argued the Christian Socialists, was part of God's law –
no less so than the economic laws governing free trade and the market-place.

Early in 1850, the group began issuing a series of 'Tracts on Christian
Socialism', which were modelled on the Oxford Tracts of the 1830s and
intended to define a programme of co-ordinated Christian social action.
Maurice chose the name, which was deliberately provocative. Socialism
was at this time associated with atheism, materialism and revolution, and
the phrase 'Christian socialism' seemed to many a contradiction in terms.
Maurice recognised that the name would alienate many, but, as he wrote
to Ludlow, it would also 'commit us at once to the conflict we must engage
in sooner or later with the unsocial Christians and the unchristian
Socialists'.[57] In November 1850, they began a new journal, *The Christian
Socialist*, which gained a circulation of 3,000 before it closed in June 1852.

The group's commitment to Christian socialism was not restricted to
publications and meetings. Early in 1850, they began experimenting with
new forms of economic activity, based on co-operation rather than competition, and thus challenging the dominant free trade, *laissez faire* ideology.
They formed a number of producers' co-operatives, bringing together
teams of workers engaged in the same craft for the purpose of sharing the
cost of tools, materials and workplace. The co-operatives worked together
under their own management, and shared the profits. The main force
behind these producers' co-operatives was Ludlow, who had spent part of
early 1849 in Paris, observing co-operative associations being established
by workers there. The producers' co-operatives also had roots in medieval
craft guilds. The co-operatives required heavy initial investment of capital,
and here the movement was fortunate in gaining the support of Edward
Vansittart Neale, a lawyer with a vast family fortune, a loose religious
faith and a tortured conscience. Neale, it was said, invested £60,000 of his
personal fortune in the various co-operative associations.[58] In the spring of
1850, the group established a Co-operative Society, with a governing
council and central board, paid staff and central offices in London. There
were by now nine producers' associations – a tailors' association, three
shoemaking associations, two builders' associations, a printers' association, a bakers' association and a needlewoman's association. Two more
associations were added in 1851. The associations were modest in size,

with between 20 and 40 members in each. As their members had little experience in management, advertising or book-keeping, the associations were soon in difficulties. Hopes for co-operative production soared briefly when in 1851 the newly formed Amalgamated Society of Engineers, which included among its members pattern-makers, machinists, millwrights and other skilled workers in heavy metals, embraced the principles of co-operation and made plans for the purchase of a foundry. However, an industrial dispute in 1852 devastated the finances of the new Amalgamated Society and plans for the co-operative foundry collapsed. Co-operation remained limited to small-scale production and services. In 1851, the Christian Socialists also began promoting the co-operative distribution of goods, through the establishment of co-operative stores, at which goods were sold at a fair price and profits were shared among consumers in the form of dividends.

In 1851, the British imperial state celebrated its industrial achievements and heralded the benefits of free trade by hosting a great world exhibition in London. The exhibition, which was largely the inspiration of Albert, Prince Consort, was housed in a vast structure of iron and plate glass, the Crystal Palace, erected in Hyde Park. Over 1,800 feet long, 400 feet wide and high enough to enclose the mature elm trees in the park, the Crystal Palace contained exhibitions of manufactures from nations throughout the world. It opened to the public on 1 May, and attracted hundreds of thousands of visitors through the summer. For many, the exhibition marked the end of the 'hungry forties', with its economic distress, Chartism and Irish famine, and the beginning of a new era of prosperity, as promised by the proponents of free trade. In the midst of this festival of trade and industry, the Christian Socialist Charles Kingsley delivered a sermon in London on 'The Message of the Church to Labouring Men'. The sermon was a scathing indictment of an industrial society that, amid all its wealth and engineering marvels, consigned a large proportion of its labourers to poverty and squalor. 'How dare you', he proclaimed to Christian propertied classes, '. . . keep God's children exposed to filth, brutality, and temptation, which festers in your courts and alleys, making cleanliness impossible – drunkenness all but excusable – prostitution all but natural – self-respect and decency unknown?'[59] It was, he insisted, a sacred duty of the clergy to work for a more just social order:

I assert that the business for which God sends a Christian priest in
a Christian nation, is to preach and practice liberty, equality, and
brotherhood, in the fullest, deepest, widest, simplest meaning of these

three great words: that in so far as he does, he is a true priest, doing his Lord's work . . . that in so far as he does not, he is no priest at all, but a traitor to God and man.[60]

As Kingsley finished, the incumbent of the parish church rose up to denounce the sermon as false and dangerous. The newspapers attacked Kingsley as the 'Apostle of Socialism' and the bishop of London forbade him to preach in the diocese. Kingsley's supporters, however, published the sermon, and working people demonstrated in his support on Kennington Common.[61]

The Christian Socialist movement drew to a close in 1854. There were by now serious disagreements among the leaders over the extent to which the movement should become involved in promoting socialism. The producers' co-operatives were not having much success and their example was not spreading. In 1853, Maurice was dismissed from his chair at King's College, London – primarily for questioning the doctrine of eternal punishment, although his socialist pronouncements were also a factor. He now distanced himself from the movement. Economic conditions, moreover, were improving, and Chartism, socialism and the threat of revolution faded in the early 1850s. The need to Christianise socialism no longer seemed so imperative. Some of the initiatives of the movement, among them the consumers' co-operatives and the educational activities, continued, but the brotherhood came to an end. Over the coming decade, Maurice and Kingsley would recant many of their socialist views. None the less, the Christian Socialist movement of 1848 to 1854 had been pioneering and it would be remembered. It had shown that some members of the Church of England were prepared to challenge many of the assumptions of the political economists. They had demonstrated through their co-operative associations that there were alternative ways of organising the production and distribution of goods, apart from competitive industrial capitalism. And they had shown working people that there were members of the clergy and educated upper classes who were prepared to work with them in reforming the social order.

Anglican sisters and Bible women

Perhaps equally profound in their long-term impact on church and society were the Anglican sisterhoods and the Bible women who emerged in the later 1840s. These were associations of women who were committed to serving God through alleviating the social suffering of urban-industrial society. Women, of course, were active in church work throughout the nineteenth century, visiting the poor and the infirm, distributing charity, collecting signatures for anti-slavery petitions, raising money for overseas missions, and teaching Sunday schools. What was distinctive about the sisterhoods and Bible women was that they were made up exclusively of women and controlled by women. Some 90 Anglican sisterhoods were founded between 1845 and 1900, and perhaps a total of 10,000 women served within these communities. There were about 3,000 to 4,000 active members of Anglican sisterhoods in 1900. The Bible women numbered in their hundreds, and touched the lives of thousands.

As their historian, Susan Mumm, has shown, the early Anglican sister-hoods were inspired by the Oxford Movement.[62] In 1845, a small group of Anglo-Catholic women, supported by a committee of Anglican laymen, including Lord John Manners and William Gladstone, formed the first Anglican sisterhood as a memorial to the high church romantic poet and essayist, Robert Southey. This was the Sisterhood of the Holy Cross, founded in Park Village, London, for the work of visiting the poor and educating children in the slums of Somers Town and Camden. The Park Village sisterhood was short-lived, but other sisterhoods soon appeared, with women themselves now taking the leading role in founding and governing their communities. By 1851, ten Anglican sisterhoods had been founded and a number of influential leaders had emerged. In 1848, the formidable Lydia Sellon, daughter of a naval commander, founded the Devonport Sisters of Mercy to visit the poor and sick, and distribute charity in impoverished districts of Plymouth and Devonport. Over the next two years, her sisterhood established an orphanage, several ragged schools, a home for old sailors, model lodging houses, and a soup kitchen providing 80 meals a day.[63] Another prominent figure in the early move-ment was Harriet Monsell, daughter of an Irish MP and baronet, sister of the Young Ireland leader, William Smith O'Brien, and widow of a Church of England clergyman. In 1851 she formed the Community of St John Baptist, with its main house at Clewer, near Windsor. Still another was Harriet Day, the daughter of a Sussex farmer, who became the superior of the Community of St Mary the Virgin at Wantage from 1850 and proved herself a leader of great practical ability.

Anglican sisters visited the poor, cared for the sick, and taught and fed neglected children in ragged schools. They set up orphanages, and organ-ised day care for the children of working mothers. From the beginning, the sisterhoods became particularly involved in rescue work among prostitutes in London and other large towns. Prostitution was widespread in Britain. While there are no accurate figures, the metropolitan police estimated that there were about 10,000 full-time prostitutes in London alone.[64] Many more women were casual prostitutes, forced on the streets in times of crisis to feed their families. Others were kept mistresses. While young prostitutes might have been reasonably healthy and well off, it was not long before venereal disease, violence, alcohol and psychological breakdown brought physical degeneration. The Anglican sisterhoods created houses of refuge, or 'penitentiaries' (places of penance), where women wishing to give up prostitution could undergo a two-year programme of recuperation and retraining, leaving with certificates and assistance with finding employment, usually as domestic servants. Prostitutes entering the homes could leave at any time, and some would enter for a warm bed and regular meals during the winter and return to the streets in the spring. But many others were enabled by the homes to make a new start. Two of the earliest and fastest growing communities, those located at Wantage and Clewer, were founded especially for work among prostitutes.[65] In the mid-1850s, there were an average of 22 'penitents' residing in the home at Wantage, and another 38 in Clewer.[66]

The sisterhoods encountered some opposition from bishops and parish clergy, who bristled at the idea of women conducting social service work outside of male control. There was also popular hostility, often fomented by ultra-Protestant agitators, who portrayed the sisterhoods as steeped in Roman Catholic devotional practices, and also as representing a challenge to male-dominated family life. The sisters were portrayed by such critics as 'stolen daughters', women who had been seduced away from their proper place in the home and from the subordinate role assigned to their gender by providence. Despite this opposition, however, the sisterhoods persevered. Hostile bishops, such as Blomfield of London, discovered to their dismay that they had no legal power to deny sisterhoods entry into their dioceses, and parish clergy found that they had no legal authority over sisterhoods within their parishes. Many of the urban poor were won over by witnessing the sisters' willingness to live among them and share their poverty, or by experiencing the sisters' readiness to nurse the sick and dying during the cholera epidemics of 1849 or 1866. Public opinion, moreover, had been impressed when, during the Crimean War of 1854–56, over 100 Anglican sisters had served as volunteer nurses to the sick and wounded in Turkey. By the 1860s, leading clerics, especially A. C. Tait, bishop of London from 1856 and archbishop of Canterbury from 1868, were giving the sisterhoods guarded support.[67]

Within the evangelical wing of the Church of England, women organised and directed another form of association. In 1857, Mrs Ellen

Ranyard, a successful author of devotional works, founded the London Bible and Domestic Female Mission. The Mission involved the recruitment of working-class women to serve as full-time, paid church workers, who would visit the homes of the urban poor, talking with the women and reading the Bible to them. The Mission was interdenominational, but dominated by Anglican evangelicals. One of its strengths was that its women workers came from the same social class as the women they helped, and therefore had an understanding of their circumstances and problems. The Bible woman, as Frank Prochaska has observed, was to be 'a "native agent", at home in the courts and alleys'.[68] As one early Bible woman, the daughter of a drunken sailor, wrote: 'I know nothing of the customs and manners of the rich; I could not undertake the most menial service in a gentleman's house; but I can talk to the poor outcasts among whom I dwell; [and] my deepest sympathy is secured to them by the sad history of my own early days'.[69]

Ranyard initially had no intention that her 'Bible women' would engage in any kind of social work. However, in their visits, the Bible women often felt called to offer guidance on cooking, hygiene, child care and minor ailments, and to provide material assistance in cases of desperate poverty. Ranyard soon agreed that the Bible women could provide advice and charity, as well as Bible readings, during their visits. Some Bible women began conducting women's meetings in homes, at which women would sew, discuss practical problems and provide mutual support. By November 1859, there were 35 full-time Bible women; this number increased to 137 by November 1860. By now, the women were being given three months of training on the poor law, Scripture and hygiene. Increasingly they were asked for medical help, and from 1868, Ranyard arranged for the training of some of her working-class Bible women as itinerant nurses at Guy's Hospital. These nurses were soon making regular rounds through the urban slums, dispensing medicines and providing basic health care, while carrying with them in their handbags a Bible, a copy of Florence Nightingale's *Notes on Nursing*, some basic utensils, and a bar of soap. Between 1868 and 1874, Guy's Hospital trained 78 such nurses, while other London hospitals also provided assistance. In 1874 alone, Bible women nurses made 111,601 visits to 4,392 patients in London. Twenty years later, in 1894, the London Mission's 82 nurses made 215,000 visits to some 10,000 patients. Their medical training was greatly augmented during the 1880s, and they provided essential medical care at a time when there were few trained doctors in deprived districts. The Mission also set up residences for single working women and a rescue home for prostitutes, and the movement spread from London to English provincial cities and also to the empire.[70]

Ranyard's evangelical Bible Mission, meanwhile, inspired Mrs Jane Talbot, the daughter of a duke and the mother of the future bishop E. S. Talbot, to found in 1861 a similar society (though with a high Anglican ethos): the Parochial Mission Women. The Bible women movement also spread to Scotland, where by the 1850s the Presbyterian churches were employing Bible women for work both among the urban poor, and among women labourers with the fishing industry along the coasts.[71] The Bible women, moreover, had connections with the new deaconess movement, which had come to Britain from Germany and which involved the use of trained women health workers for service to the poor. Deaconess institutions appeared in London from the late 1850s. In the mid-1860s, William Pennefather, an evangelical Anglican curate, and his wife Catherine, established a major Christian deaconess training institution at Mildmay in North London, with an attached dispensary and hospital.[72] By the mid-1860s, there was a growing number of trained, disciplined, efficient and often uniformed Christian women workers – Anglican sisters, Bible women and deaconesses (not to mention Roman Catholic nuns) at work among the urban poor. They encountered hostility from some quarters, but they also contributed to changing attitudes regarding the capabilities of women and their social role outside the home.

Theological controversy within the Church of England

The Church of England in the mid-nineteenth century was not only the largest church in the United Kingdom, it was also becoming the centre of a world-wide Anglican communion. In 1841, supporters of Anglican missions had established the Colonial Bishoprics Fund, to raise money for the creation of new bishoprics in the empire. In 1848, the Church of England founded St Augustine's College in Canterbury for training colonial clergy. By 1850, there were 23 colonial bishoprics in Canada, the West Indies, India, Africa, Asia and Australasia, and hundreds of Anglican clergymen were serving in the colonies. Taking together the United Church of England and Ireland (and its colonial branches), the Episcopal Church of Scotland, and the Episcopal church of the United States, there was by mid-century a world-wide Anglican communion comprising 125 bishops and 23,000 clergy.[73] At home, the mid-nineteenth-century church was benefiting from the leadership of a number of energetic bishops, including Charles James Blomfield of London, John Kaye of Lincoln and Samuel Wilberforce of Oxford. Such bishops promoted diocesan societies for church and school building, home mission work and charitable activity, and demanded more regular services and pastoral visiting from the parish clergy. The Church of England retained a substantial degree of control over the ancient universities of Oxford and Cambridge. It also dominated instruction in the public schools, both the older establishments – Eton, Rugby, Harrow, Winchester, Marlborough and the others – and the newer establishments being formed in the mid-nineteenth century. The public schools had been reformed in part through the example of the celebrated liberal Anglican headmaster of Rugby, Thomas Arnold, and they were increasingly conveying an Anglican ideal of social service to a new generation of civil and military leaders serving the Victorian imperial state at home and abroad. The popular hostility to the church, which had been so pronounced in the 1830s and early 1840s, had waned by 1860, in part through the influence of such sincere Anglican social activists as Lord Ashley, the Christian Socialists or the Anglican sisterhoods and Bible women.

All these efforts to restore the influence and authority of the established Church of England, however, were weakened by deep factional divisions within the church – the legacy of the ecclesiastical strife of the 1830s and 1840s. The two main parties, the High Church party and the Evangelical party, continued to hold very different views of the Christian faith and the nature of the church, to the extent that they could seem scarcely part of the same communion. The High Church party, although weakened by the secession of many prominent Tractarians in 1845–46, remained a significant force. There was a large body of high churchmen – 'church and king' Anglicans who venerated the traditions of the church and authority of the bishops, but who had been uncomfortable with Tractarian excesses and had been glad to see the 'Romanisers' depart. Some leading Tractarians, moreover, most notably John Keble and Edward Pusey, had not left the church and continued to represent high views of the apostolic succession, sacramental grace and the authority of the visible church. A number of younger high Anglicans, who had come under the influence of the Tractarian Movement while students at Oxford or Cambridge, now held parish livings, where they often combined selfless devotion to the pastorate with high views of church authority. The Evangelical party, on the other hand, continued to emphasise the importance of the conversion experience, individual Bible study, and the godly life, and they viewed the high church teachings on apostolic succession and sacramental grace with deep suspicion. The high church emphases, they believed, led to over-reliance on external authority and ceremonial, at the expense of personal faith and Christ in the heart. And high church views, they feared, could lead susceptible persons along the path to Rome.

Between 1847 and 1850, the High Church and Evangelical parties became locked in a struggle which, for a time, threatened to break up the Church of England. This was the Gorham controversy, which first emerged as a dispute over the doctrine of the Church of England, and then came to involve the nature of episcopal authority and the relationship of church and state. George Cornelius Gorham (1787–1857) had been a fellow of Queen's College, Cambridge, until in 1846, at the age of nearly 60, he was appointed vicar of the mining parish of St Just in Cornwall. He had been installed into the parish by the combative high churchman, Henry Phillpotts, bishop of Exeter. However, the relations between Phillpotts and Gorham had soon deteriorated, especially after Gorham, an evangelical, had advertised in the *Ecclesiastical Gazette* for a curate who would be 'free from Tractarian error'. In 1847, the Whig Lord Chancellor, acting for the crown, presented Gorham to the parish living of Brampford Speke, near Exeter. Phillpotts now insisted upon subjecting Gorham to an examination of his orthodoxy before he would institute him to Brampford Speke. The examination was highly unusual, to say the least, lasting for 38 hours in December 1847 and another 14 hours in March 1848: for Gorham, it was a 'penal inquisition'. Phillpotts put to him no fewer than 149 questions. These focused mainly on the doctrine of baptismal regeneration, a long-standing issue of contention between the high church and evangelical schools of thought. In the high church view, which they based on both the Thirty-nine Articles and the Prayer Book, baptism conferred regeneration, or spiritual rebirth, unconditionally upon infants (although not necessarily on adults). In the evangelical view, which they based on the Thirty-nine Articles, the sacrament of baptism did not in itself confer regeneration on either infants or adults, because faith and repentance were necessary conditions before regeneration could take place.

Unsatisfied with Gorham's answers, Phillpotts refused to institute him to Brampford Speke. Believing he had been unfairly treated, Gorham appealed against Phillpotts' decision to the Court of Arches, the ecclesiastical court of the province of Canterbury. In August 1849, however, the Court of Arches decided that Phillpotts's interpretation of baptismal regeneration was the orthodox one and that Phillpotts had been correct to refuse to institute a cleric whose doctrine was unsound. With this decision, the position of most evangelicals within the established church was put at risk; if their view of baptism was indeed defined as heresy, they would have to leave the church – and if they did so, it would be a mass exodus similar to that which took the evangelicals out of the Church of Scotland at the Disruption of 1843.[74] Gorham's fellow evangelicals convinced him to appeal against the decision of the Court of Arches to the Judicial Committee of the Privy Council, which was the highest court of appeal in ecclesiastical cases. It was unusual for a civil court to adjudicate on a doctrinal matter, but the Judicial Committee agreed to hear the case. By now there was considerable public concern within the church over the outcome. In the event, the Judicial Committee, in March 1850, reversed the decision of the Court of Arches. It decided that Gorham had not contradicted the teaching of the Church of England and that he should be installed at Brampford Speke.

This time it was the High Church party that was outraged, both at the Judicial Committee's decision that Gorham's view of baptism was allowable in the Church of England, and even more at a civil court reversing the decision of an ecclesiastical court on a theological question. The High Church party was already incensed over the crown's appointment of the liberal theologian, R. D. Hampden – denounced by high churchmen as a heretic – to the bishopric of Hereford in late 1847. Now a civil court was instructing the church to give the cure of souls in Brampford Speke to a man whom the ecclesiastical Court of Arches had determined to be unsound in doctrine. 'How can a priest', asked the high church archdeacon of Chichester, Henry Manning, of a friend, 'twice judged unfit for the cure of souls by the church, be put in charge of souls at the sentence of the civil power without overthrowing the divine office of the church?'[75] Tempers grew overheated; high churchmen denounced the Judicial Committee's action and prepared to secede from the Church of England. In a public letter, Phillpotts took the extraordinary step of threatening to excommunicate the archbishop of Canterbury if the latter upheld the Gorham judgement. At a meeting on 23 July 1850, over 2,500 high churchmen loudly protested the Gorham judgement.

A number of high Anglicans did depart. They formed a second wave of converts to the Roman Catholic Church, following the path taken in the mid-1840s by Newman, Ward and the Oxford converts. The converts over the Gorham judgement included individuals of talent and influence, including James Hope-Scott, a prominent lawyer and son-in-law of Sir Walter Scott, Henry Wilberforce, the son of the evangelical anti-slavery champion, and T. W. Allies, a gifted theologian and historian. They also included Henry Manning, a widowed Anglican priest of great energy and ability, who within 15 years would rise to the primacy of the Roman Catholic Church in England. Most high Anglicans, to be sure, did not depart and the Church of England was spared a major disruption over the Gorham case. None the less, the church remained deeply divided. For many high Anglicans, the evangelicals were heretics, denying the teachings of the church on baptismal regeneration, and relying on the power of the civil state to maintain their influence within the church. For evangelicals, the high Anglican views of the sacraments and church authority were highly dangerous, threatening to corrupt the Protestant establishment from within and open England to fresh assaults from Rome.

The revival of Convocation

For some, the greatest lesson of the Gorham judgement had been that the Church of England needed an independent governing synod. The judgement had highlighted what for many was an unpalatable truth – that the established Church of England was effectively governed by Parliament. This might have been acceptable in the past, when virtually all the members of Parliament had been members of the Church of England and when Parliament could be rightly viewed as the lay synod of the Anglican Church. But Parliament now included Roman Catholics, Scottish Presbyterians, and English Dissenters, and the Church of England's doctrine and discipline were ultimately decided upon by men who had no theological training and in some cases no sympathy for Anglicanism. For George Anthony Denison, the high church vicar of East Brent, the 'great fact' of the Gorham controversy had been the 'unfaithfulness of [the Parliament of] England in exercising the trusteeship of the Church of England'.[76] And why should the Church of England be without a national synod? The Church of Scotland, after all, had its General Assembly, while the Roman Catholic Church in Ireland was strengthened in 1850 by the work of the Synod of Thurles. The calls for independent church government came primarily from the High Church party, those who had been most outraged by the Gorham judgement.

When its advocates spoke of a governing synod for the church, they meant reviving the Convocations, that is, the medieval synods of the provinces of Canterbury and York. Although the Convocations had not been permitted to deliberate on church matters since 1717, they did continue to have a formal existence. They convened briefly at the beginning of each new Parliament (following a general election) to adopt an address of loyalty to the crown. They then immediately disbursed. They were archaic bodies, with an upper house of bishops, and a lower house made up mainly of church dignitaries. Whatever their weaknesses, the two Convocations had the advantage for high churchmen of being part of the centuries-old constitution of the church.

The calls for the revival of Convocation were resisted by evangelicals and liberals within the church.[77] For them, a revived Convocation would take the discussion of church matters out of Parliament, and this would serve to weaken the connection of church and state. The Church of England would become little more than another denomination, while the state would become increasingly secularised. Further, opponents of Convocation suspected that the High Church party would try to use a revived Convocation to condemn evangelical and liberal beliefs as heresy, and drive all who did not accept high church views out of the church. Convocation in its medieval form, moreover, was not representative of the church as a whole: the laity, in particular, was not represented, and evangelicals and liberals feared it would become a means to fasten a rigid clerical control upon the church. There were also fears that a revived Convocation, by stirring ecclesiastical debate and rancour, would only serve to deepen divisions within the church. Such synods, warned Bishop Kaye of Lincoln, would become 'the means of multiplying disputes, and increasing contention'.[78] The archbishop of Canterbury, the evangelical J. B. Sumner, firmly opposed reviving the Convocations, arguing that the various church building, educational, missionary and philanthropic societies attached to the church already provided ample representative government.[79]

None the less, the advocates of Convocation persisted. When Convocation convened briefly after the general election of 1852, high Anglicans managed to insert a petition in the customary address to the crown, asking that Convocation be allowed to meet as a deliberative assembly. Later that year, there was another general election, and a new Parliament meant another brief convening of Convocation. At this meeting, however, the archbishop of Canterbury reluctantly allowed the lower house to meet for three days in order to discuss clerical grievances and disciplinary matters. The evangelicals were alarmed at the experiment, while the new prime minister, Lord Aberdeen, feared that a revived Convocation in such a divided church 'would only hasten the inevitable smash'.[80] Yet the deliberations in 1852 were conducted with such moderation and forbearance that several bishops, including Sumner, became convinced that a revived Convocation might be useful for the church. By 1855, the province of

Canterbury had restored a regular annual meeting of its Convocation, and its example was followed by the province of York in 1861. Far from hastening the 'smash', the revival of the two Convocations probably eased tensions, by bringing the parties together each year and allowing them to debate their differences with a degree of decorum, rather than to denounce each other in the press and at public meetings.

Papal aggression

In late September 1850, Pope Pius IX, having 'invoked the assistance of Mary the Virgin, Mother of God, and of those Saints who illustrated England by their virtues', solemnly restored the territorial hierarchy of the Roman Catholic Church in England.[81] Since the early seventeenth century, Rome had treated England as a missionary province, with its priests under the authority of vicars apostolic, who were in turn directed by the Congregation of Propaganda in Rome. But now, for the first time since the Reformation, England was to be organised into regular territorial dioceses under the authority of resident bishops, including an archbishopric of Westminster who would be the Roman Catholic Primate of All England. For Roman Catholics, this act recognised the permanency of their church in England and provided more effective ecclesiastical government. For many English Protestants, however, it was an act of 'papal aggression', aimed at reimposing a Roman ecclesiastical tyranny in England – and it led to one of the greatest religious storms of the century.

The restoration of the hierarchy had been planned for a number of years, and this reflected the growing confidence of the English Catholic Church in the years following Catholic emancipation. The Oxford Movement had brought a number of wealthy, well-connected converts into the Catholic Church – men and women drawn to what they viewed as the true catholic and apostolic church, its authority preserved through the centuries by the apostolic succession and its catholicity represented by the throne of St Peter. Other well-connected converts, such as the wealthy landowner Ambrose Phillipps de Lisle, had been drawn to Catholicism through the culture of Romanticism, with its celebration of medievalism, chivalry, gothic architecture, monasticism, and the beauty of holiness. The growing confidence within the Catholic Church was reflected during the building of A. W. Pugin's gothic cathedral of St George's in Southwark. When the foundation-stone for the new building had been laid in 1840, only a small service was held early in the morning to avoid alarming Protestant opinion. At the actual opening of the gorgeous building in

1848, however, 13 bishops, 240 priests, a massed choir and a huge congregation joined in the celebration, while the event was fully reported in the press.[82]

The restoration of the hierarchy was also a response to need for greater episcopal supervision of the growing numbers of Catholics in England – numbers that had been swollen by the massive migration of Irish Catholics into Britain. The migration had begun on a large scale from about 1820 with the demand for cheap labour to dig canals, work in the mines and mills, and later lay the railways. It became a flood during the famine years in Ireland, as tens of thousands of half-starved Irish made their way into Liverpool, London, Glasgow and other cities, crowding into cellars and garrets. By 1851, there were approximately 520,000 Irish-born people, the vast majority of them Catholics, living in England and Wales. These migrants needed priests, chapels, schools, teachers, and charitable foundations. Only a restored hierarchy, it was believed, could provide the required organisation and supervision.

The papacy had first formulated its proposals for the restoration of the hierarchy in 1847, but the actual decision on restoration was delayed by the revolution in Rome and the pope's flight from the city. Only when the revolutionaries had been defeated and Pius IX returned to the Vatican could the plans proceed. To minimise political difficulties, the papacy agreed that the new ecclesiastical titles would not duplicate those of the established Church of England: thus there would not be a Roman Catholic archbishop of Canterbury, Roman Catholic bishop of London and so forth. Shortly before the announcement of the restoration, Nicholas Wiseman, the leading figure in the English Catholic Church, was summoned to Rome, where he was made a cardinal and appointed the first archbishop of Westminster and primate of England.

Scholarly, aloof and imperious, Wiseman sought to inspire English Catholics with a proper sense of the magnitude of the historic occasion, and he announced the restoration to English Catholics with a flamboyant pastoral letter, 'Out of the Flaminian Gate of Rome', issued on 7 October 1850. The tone was triumphalist. 'The great work, then', Wiseman proclaimed, 'is complete . . . Catholic England has been restored to its orbit in the ecclesiastical firmament, from which its light had long vanished'. The 'Saints of our country' looked down from their 'seats of bliss, with beaming glance, upon this new evidence of the faith and Church which led them to glory'. The martyrs, who had long 'mourned . . . over the departure of England's religious glory' were now filled with joy that the 'silver chains' binding England to Rome had been 'changed into burnished gold'.

It was the language of a man who waited long for this moment and who believed that his prayers for England were at last answered. Wiseman made his way homewards in an ostentatious procession through Europe, returning to England in early November 1850.

His pastoral letter, meanwhile, had raised a storm in Britain. There was outrage over Wiseman's language about Protestant England being 'restored' to the 'orbit' of Rome. *The Times* proclaimed war on this 'papal aggression' in a series of angry editorials, and other newspapers took up the cry, fanning popular rage to a white heat. The usual bonfires and processions on that fifth of November drew enormous crowds, and brought more than the usual thuggish attacks on Catholic priests and chapels. Public meetings were hastily called to protest this new threat to the traditional liberties and Protestant faith of Britain. On reading Wiseman's extravagant claims of England now bound to Rome, the young queen was said to have asked, 'Am I Queen of England, or am I not?'[83] 'An agitation, perhaps unparalleled in our times', admitted Wiseman after his return to England, 'has been raised by the constitution of a Catholic Hierarchy in this island. The violence had been that of a whirlwind'.[84] In many minds, the restoration of the hierarchy was closely connected with the Oxford Movement; many were certain that Edward Pusey and his high Anglican supporters within the Church of England were secretly spurring Wiseman and the Catholics on. There were clearly covert plots and devious machinations directed at undermining the great Protestant empire at the peak of its power.

On 7 November, the Whig prime minister, Lord John Russell, published a letter to Edward Maltby, bishop of Durham, in which he denounced 'the aggression of the Pope upon our Protestantism' and expressed contempt for the 'mummeries of superstition' and Catholic efforts 'to confine the intellect and enslave the soul'. He noted with particular scorn those Romanising 'clergymen of our own Church' who, despite their outward and formal subscription to the Protestant standards, were 'most forward in leading their flocks "step by step to the very verge of the precipice" '.[85] Russell had been a leading proponent of Catholic emancipation and a supporter of the Maynooth grant. His Durham letter seemed a volte-face, and the reasons behind it are still not fully understood. He seems to have nurtured a deep-seated personal hostility to Tractarianism within the Church of England, combined with a belief that a more militant Catholic Church, under the leadership of Wiseman in England and Paul Cullen in Ireland, was becoming a threat to religious liberty and intellectual progress. He was also angered by what he perceived as Catholic ingratitude. 'For thirty years', he wrote to Lord Clarendon on 10 November 1850, 'the Whigs have sacrificed power to maintain their opinion that the Roman Catholics ought to be admitted to power. The cause was gained, and the Pope applied himself to thwart the English government in every way he can imagine – to insult our Queen – to supplant our religion'.[86] In the coming months, over 2,600 petitions bearing nearly 900,000 signatures were sent to the queen protesting against papal aggression. Of these, about 30 per cent linked papal aggression to Tractarianism within the Church of England.[87] New societies were formed to combat the papal aggression – including the Scottish Reformation Society, formed in Edinburgh in December 1850, and the Protestant Alliance, formed in London in June 1851. In mid-1851, the populist Free Church clergyman, James Begg, and members of the Scottish Reformation Society founded a new journal, the virulently anti-Catholic *Bulwark*, to stoke the fires of Protestant resentment.

To understand the fervent reaction to Wiseman's letter, it is necessary to consider the extent to which most early Victorians perceived their liberties and their identity as inextricably connected with their Protestantism. For people nurtured on stories of the Marian martyrs, the Armada, the gunpowder plot, and the 'Protestant Wind' of 1688, Britain was a Protestant state, preserved by providence to represent religious truth, responsible government and liberty of conscience. Only recently, Protestant Britain had triumphed over revolutionary and Napoleonic France, abolished slavery within its colonies, opened India and China to Protestant missionary activity, and championed free trade. In June 1850, Viscount Palmerston, the Whig foreign secretary, delivered his celebrated Don Pacifico speech in the House of Commons. In this speech, he defended his decision to take military action to compel the Greek government to compensate a Jewish British subject, David Don Pacifico, who had experienced loss at the hands of an anti-Semitic mob. In doing so, he portrayed the British empire as the heir to the ancient Roman empire, ushering in a new world order, a *pax Britannica*. For Protestant patriots, this rising empire – representing free trade, anti-slavery, justice, liberty and progress – must not come under the sway of the Roman Catholic Church. Lord John Russell, in his Durham letter, may well have sought to capture some of the patriotic spirit of Palmerston's Don Pacifico speech.

Also contributing to the public reaction was the fear and hostility aroused in Britain by the massive influx of migrants from Ireland. Destitute and desperate, traumatised by the famine, and filled with a justifiable sense of grievance, the Irish in Britain tended to keep to themselves, while they viewed their British neighbours with hostility. Many spoke only Irish. They were prepared to work for lower wages than their British neighbours and accept living conditions that could seem to English, Scottish and Welsh people to be barbaric. In his *Chartism* of 1840, Carlyle had portrayed the Irish migrant as:

the sorest evil this country has to strive with. In his rags and laughing savagery, he is there to undertake all work that can be done by mere strength of hand and back; for wages that will purchase him potatoes. He . . . lodges to his mind in any pighutch or doghutch, roosts in outhouses; and wears a suit of tatters, the getting off and on of which is said to be a difficult operation, transacted only in festivals and the hightides of the calendar.[88]

For many in Britain, the degradation of these Irish migrants was the result, not of the famine or of an unjust social system, but of their Catholicism, which had enslaved them to superstition and priestcraft.

A further aspect of the anti-Catholic ferment of 1850–51 was the revulsion aroused in many Protestants by Roman Catholic devotional practices. For Protestants, there seemed to them something dangerously sensual, lurid and foreign in Catholic ritual, incense, plainsong and church decoration. There were also dark rumours of secretive sexual practices among priests and nuns. It was all somehow unwholesome. Protestant fathers and husbands often felt threatened by priests, who under the guise of celibacy and their 'feminine' cassock were believed to insinuate themselves into the confidence of women, coaxing them to reveal in the confessional the secrets of the marriage bed, and seducing them – in thought, if not in deed – by softly whispered intimacies. There was also an unhealthy fascination with convents and what were viewed as the 'unnatural' lives of nuns. The middle years of the nineteenth century witnessed a stream of novels in which young women were lured by false promises into Catholic convents, which turned out to be places of gothic torment and sexual depravity, where they either mouldered away, or from which they had daring escapes, often aided by former Protestant lovers. Among such works was the *Awful Disclosures of Maria Monk*, with its grisly tales of rape, infanticide, torture and murder supposedly taking place within the dark recesses of a convent – with bodies buried in lime in the cellar. First published in the United States in 1836, it proceeded through numerous editions on both sides of the Atlantic.[89] Thus for many Protestants, Roman Catholics, and the no less dangerous Tractarians, were a threat not only to liberty and progress, but also to their families and homes.

With popular anti-Catholic fury aroused, Russell's Whig government turned to drafting legislation in response to the papal aggression. Its Bill, introduced on 7 February 1851, was a piece of penal legislation. The first clause made it a crime, punishable by fines and imprisonment, for any cleric outside the established church to assume a territorial title within the United Kingdom (with the exception of bishops of the Scottish Episcopal church). The second clause declared that any ecclesiastical action taken by a Roman Catholic cleric claiming an illegal territorial title was null and void, and the third clause ordered that any property held by such a cleric was to be forfeited to the crown. For probably most British MPs, the Bill did not go far enough. 'Is this all?' asked Benjamin Disraeli in the Commons on 8 February. 'Is a piece of petty persecution the only weapon we can devise on a solemn political exigency of this importance?'[90] The Bill was in difficulties from the beginning. The problem was that it was hard to frame a new penal law for Roman Catholics in England without also imposing the same penal law on those in Ireland. Indeed, the proposed Bill would make the government of the Catholic Church in Ireland illegal: its bishops (who held territorial titles) would be subject to imprisonment and its endowments would be subject to seizure by the crown. The proposed Bill was inconsistent with previous policy in Ireland. Since the mid-1840s, state officials, including members of Russell's own government, had been addressing the Irish Catholic bishops by their ecclesiastical titles. Was a Whig-Liberal government now to cease talking to Irish bishops, abandon Catholic emancipation, and revive the spirit of the seventeenth-century Irish penal laws? The government considered excluding Ireland from the Bill, but decided that this would undermine the Union. The sensible course would have been to drop the proposed legislation. Passions, however, were aroused, and Russell's government would not back down.

The Bill, of course, created outrage in Catholic Ireland. It alienated those Irish Catholic bishops, such as Daniel Murray, archbishop of Dublin, who had been seeking accommodation with the state. More important, it greatly strengthened the position of Archbishop Paul Cullen, who had been working since his return to Ireland to assert the independence of the Catholic Church from any connection with the 'British' state. The Bill gave added credence to Cullen's insistence that the Catholic Church could expect no real benefits from co-operation with this state. It also bolstered his claims that the education of young Catholics could not be entrusted to the new Queen's Colleges. What could the Catholic Church expect from a government, Cullen asked, that portrayed its teachings as mere 'mummeries' and that threatened to imprison its bishops? In Ireland, support for the Whig government plummeted. The Bill, complained Lord Clarendon to Russell on 13 February, 'has lowered Whig popularity twenty fathoms deep and we shall not live to see it dug up again'.[91] The Catholic Church organised a national agitation in Ireland against the Ecclesiastical Titles Bill, which culminated on 11 May 1851, when meetings were held simultaneously in nearly all the parishes in Ireland.[92]

In Parliament, a group of Irish liberal and Catholic MPs came together as an independent 'Irish Brigade' to oppose the Bill. They were joined by a number of British Liberal and Radical MPs, who maintained a steady and effective opposition (despite the large majority which supported it), and the debates were prolonged month after weary month. In late March 1851, William Gladstone condemned the Bill as not only unjust, but as contrary to the spirit of progress. 'Are you going to spend the latter half of the nineteenth century', he asked, 'in undoing the great work which with so much pain and difficulty your greatest men have been achieving during the former?'[93] For the liberal Quaker MP, John Bright, speaking in the Commons in May 1851, Russell's Bill 'had separated Ireland from this country, had withdrawn her national sympathies from us, and done an amount of mischief which the legislation of the next ten years could not entirely, if at all, abate'. 'The noble lord', he added, 'had drawn up an indictment against eight millions of his countrymen'.[94]

The Ecclesiastical Titles Bill was finally passed by both Houses at the end of July 1851, having occupied Parliament for six months and forming almost the only piece of legislation passed that session. By now the popular anti-Catholic agitation in Britain had died away, as public attention focused on the Great Exhibition and the wonders of modern science and industry housed in the Crystal Palace. The Roman Catholic Church simply ignored the Act, which was never enforced. (It was quietly repealed by Gladstone's first government in 1871.) The whole affair had severely weakened Russell's government, which fell several months after the passage of the Act. While popular Protestantism and anti-Catholicism remained strong, there was no real support for a renewal of penal laws.[95]

In Ireland, the affair helped Paul Cullen to consolidate his ascendancy over the Catholic Church and to shape it into a well-organised institution under a unified leadership – a church that was capable of giving vigorous leadership to the ongoing 'devotional revolution' in Irish national life. In August 1851, Irish Catholics formed a Catholic Defence Association, under Cullen's patronage, to promote independent Irish political activity in response to Catholic grievances. In 1852, Cullen was made archbishop of Dublin, moving from Armagh to the administrative centre of Ireland.

He pursued, meanwhile, his plan for the creation of a great Catholic university in Dublin, which would, he believed, overshadow the Queen's Colleges and establish Ireland as a European centre for Catholic higher education. The plan had been approved by the Synod of Thurles in September 1850, and substantial donations were coming in from the Irish faithful, both the well-off and the poor. To head the new university, Cullen took the controversial step, in July 1851, of inviting the celebrated Oxford convert, John Henry Newman, and Newman accepted the appointment.[96] In May and June 1852, Newman presented a series of six lectures in Dublin, outlining his ideas about university education and the role of theology in a liberal education. The lectures were published later that year as *Discourses on University Education* and would later form the first part of Newman's *The Idea of a University*, a profound statement of the case for a broad-based university curriculum aimed at shaping the intellect rather than simply imparting knowledge. Newman's lectures revealed an educational ideal for the Catholic Church that encompassed all the arts and sciences, including theology. His eloquence and learning made the talk of Catholic 'mummeries of superstition' seem all the more misguided. The Catholic university opened in 1854. Tensions soon developed between Cullen and Newman, largely over the amount of time the latter was willing to spend in Ireland, and Newman resigned his position as rector in 1858. By now, Cullen's ascendancy was secure, and the church he led was a powerful force, with a unified body of bishops, a largely disciplined and professional clergy, and a laity that was becoming regular in its attendance at mass. It was a church that expressed the spirit of the post-famine devotional revolution. It was a church, moreover, that felt little loyalty to the United Kingdom Parliament that had legislated against its ecclesiastical titles and threatened a renewal of the penal times.

The religious census of 1851

In 1851, the state had conducted its first religious census of the population of England, Wales and Scotland – as part of the statutory decennial census taken that year.[97] The religious census was conducted partly in response to continuing calls by members of the established churches for state grants to support church extension for Britain's rapidly growing population. Before any further consideration could be given to church extension, Parliament needed to know how many churches there were in the country, how many people attended them, and thus how many people did not attend church and might require additional churches. Ireland was not included in the religious census, partly because there was no real possibility that Parliament would extend the Protestant Church of Ireland, and partly because there was little likelihood that the Catholic Church would co-operate in any census.

The religious census form was sent to ministers or representatives of all churches in Britain – established, Dissenting and Roman Catholic. It asked for information on three points: the number of buildings used for worship, the number of sittings provided in each building, and the number of persons attending worship on a given census Sunday (30 March 1851). There were serious difficulties in collecting the statistics. As the government had decided not to impose penalties for refusal to co-operate, a number of ministers did not complete the form and census officials had to estimate the number attending their religious services. In many churches, moreover, ministers submitted only rough estimates of the numbers attending their services. There were also difficulties in counting people who attended more than one service, and a formula had to be developed to try to ensure that such people were not counted more than once. Despite the difficulties, the report of the religious census, prepared by a young civil servant, Horace Mann, formed a reasonably accurate description of the patterns of religious worship. Parliament published Mann's report for England and Wales in January 1854 and for Scotland in March 1854.

According to the report for England and Wales, 7,261,032 persons had attended worship on the census Sunday in March 1851, while 10,666,577 had not. Mann estimated that of the non-attenders, approximately 32 per cent had been unable to do so for good reason – they were in poor health, or were caring for someone in poor health, or were young children, or were involved in essential domestic or public services. This left 5,288,294 people who could have attended worship, but did not. Surprised and disturbed by this large number of non-attenders, in a state that viewed itself as Christian, Mann devoted much of his report to seeking to explain the non-churchgoing. The levels of non-attendance, he observed, were highest in the large industrial towns and cities, indicating a failure on the part of the churches to attract the industrial working classes to regular churchgoing. For Mann, the root of the problem was not, as the advocates of church extension tended to argue, an insufficient number of churches. To be sure, there were not enough churches to accommodate all who could have attended worship, especially in the large towns and cities: Mann estimated that at least 2,000 more churches were required. But it was also the case that many urban churches in working-class districts, including many churches built since 1818, were half empty. The problem, Mann argued, was that the working classes had become alienated from the churches.

They might be taught in church-maintained schools, but 'no sooner do they mingle in the active world of labour than . . . they soon become as utter strangers to religious ordinances as the people of a heathen country'.[98] There were, he maintained, a number of reasons for this – long and overly-intellectual sermons, expectations of proper Sunday clothing (which working class families could not afford), high pew rents, and the class snobbery exhibited by many middle- and upper-class worshippers. Whatever the causes, working-class irreligion was a serious problem. In Scotland, the levels of church attendance were slightly higher than in England and Wales, but there were similar concerns over the high levels of non-attendance among the industrial workers.

What struck contemporaries with still greater force were the numbers who attended non-established churches. According to Mann's report, of those who attended church in England on census Sunday, only about 52 per cent attended the established church. The numbers attending Roman Catholic worship were very small, perhaps 4 per cent of the total, which was an embarrassment to those who had recently made so much of papal aggression. On the other hand, the numbers attending Protestant Nonconformist churches were substantial, representing about 44 per cent of worshippers in England and Wales. Taking Wales alone, the figures were still more striking, as nearly four out of every five worshippers attended a Nonconformist chapel. In Scotland, where the religious establishment was still reeling from the Disruption of 1843, only about 32 per cent of worshippers attended the established church. Thus, the established churches had been reduced to minority status in Ireland, Wales and Scotland, and were close to minority status in England as well. The English Voluntary leader, Edward Miall, was delighted by the report, which, he maintained, at last recognised the true place of Nonconformity in the United Kingdom. It was, he wrote in the *Nonconformist* in January 1854, 'as if the son of a peer, treated from birth as a menial by his own relatives . . . should find himself all at once in the saloon of his ancestral residence . . . receiving the attention due his birth'.[99]

Protestant Nonconformity

The report on the religious census gave a much needed boost to the Nonconformist churches, after what had been for most of them several very lean years. On the whole, the late 1840s and early 1850s were a time of stagnation and even decline in the main Nonconformist denominations. The stagnation was in part a result of the economic recession of the 1840s, which had placed heavy financial strains on all Voluntary churches. The difficulties proved especially acute for the Wesleyan Methodists, the largest of Britain's Nonconformist denominations. After decades of astonishing growth, the numbers of Wesleyans had, in the 1840s, ceased to expand, and then, by the late 1840s, began to decline. This led to much agonised soul-searching and recriminations. Some Wesleyans called for a return to the revivalist methods of the eighteenth century, when itinerant preachers had scoured the highways and byways for sinners, and made passionate appeals for conversion. They blamed the decline on what they viewed as excessive centralisation and bureaucracy, on the emphasis upon respectability and income-levels among the clergy, and above all on the dictatorial manner of Jabez Bunting, the venerable leader of the denomination. Between 1845 and 1849, these criticisms found powerful expression in a series of anonymous publications, entitled the *Fly Sheets*. The Methodist governing conference responded to the criticisms in a heavy-handed manner, requiring all ministers to repudiate the *Fly Sheets* and, in 1849, expelling three ministers believed to be in sympathy with the publications. This proved catastrophic for the denomination. The expulsion of three dedicated ministers for no clear infraction inspired widespread revulsion, and it was followed by a mass secession of reform-minded members – representing nearly 23 per cent of the total Wesleyan Methodist membership – between 1850 and 1852.[100]

The Congregationalists also experienced internal dissension and a significant slowing of growth during these years. The Congregationalists had formed a Union in 1831, bringing the independent congregations under a degree of central organisation concerning such matters as publication of tracts, education, and pensions for retired ministers. There were, however, serious tensions between those who wanted to tighten still further the central control, and those who wanted to retain a considerable degree of independence for individual congregations. In the late 1840s, the growing influence of John Campbell, minister of the London Tabernacle and editor of the two official Congregational newspapers, was arousing intense opposition which threatened to lead to schism. A moderate, Campbell had alienated Congregationalist Voluntaries, such as Edward Miall, by his refusal to support disestablishment and by his open dislike for the Evangelical Alliance. Congregational growth, meanwhile, had slowed or come to a halt – the result, some argued, of its membership growing too staid and respectable, overly influenced by moderates like Campbell, and too prepared to invest in expensive buildings for middle-class congregations rather than to support evangelising among the working classes. The

Baptists, both General and Particular, also experienced slow growth after 1845. The Particular Baptists, moreover, became divided between the more liberal congregations, which were prepared to share the Lord's Supper with all those professing an evangelical faith, and the Strict Baptists, who insisted on restricting communion to church members.[101] These internal conflicts within the main Nonconformist bodies also contributed to a slowing of political activity. The Anti-State Church Association, formed amid great excitement in 1844, achieved very little in the later 1840s. At the general election of 1847, only 13 English Nonconformist MPs and one Scottish United Presbyterian MP were returned to Parliament; of these, only five were members of the Anti-State Church Association.[102]

This situation began to change in 1852, as the improving economy and easing of internal dissension led many Nonconformists to take up again the struggle for religious equality and the separation of church and state. At the general election of 1852, 27 Nonconformist MPs were returned from England and Wales, and another six United Presbyterian or Free Church MPs were returned from Scotland. Significantly, Edward Miall was returned for Rochdale and entered Parliament for the first time. The Anti-State Church Association, meanwhile, experienced a metamorphosis. In 1853, it changed its name to 'The Society for the Liberation of Religion from State Patronage and Control' and subsequently became known simply as the 'Liberation Society'. It formed a parliamentary committee in 1854, and developed its political organisation and tactics, pioneering the 'whipping system' to ensure Nonconformist MPs would be present at key parliamentary votes.[103] It also began forming Nonconformist political organisations in the parliamentary constituencies.[104] In 1855, it introduced a monthly journal, *The Liberator*, as an organ of the Society. The religious census published in early 1854, meanwhile, emboldened both the Liberation Society and the Nonconformist MPs with its revelations of the real numerical strength of Nonconformity in Britain.

Nonconformists won a significant victory in 1854 over the right to attend Oxford University. That year, Lord Aberdeen's government introduced an Oxford University Reform Bill, which proposed changes in the governance and financial arrangements of the University. In the Commons, the Unitarian MP, James Heywood, introduced two amendments to the Bill, one to end the requirement that students had to subscribe to the Thirty-nine Articles at matriculation, and the other to make it possible for Nonconformists to receive non-theological bachelor degrees. The government accepted the amendments and the Bill passed. As William Gladstone, who drafted the original Bill, explained to a friend, it was difficult to resist the amendments – in view of the large numbers of Nonconformists now known to inhabit the United Kingdom.[105] Two years later, a similar Bill made it possible for Nonconformists to be admitted to non-theological degrees at Cambridge University. Nonconformists, to be sure, continued to experience discrimination at the ancient universities, and it would not be until 1871 that fellowships and non-theological advanced degrees would be opened to them. None the less, in 1854 and 1856 Nonconformists had achieved significant victories, which went far towards eliminating a long-standing grievance and which enabled growing numbers of Nonconformists to educate their sons for careers in the civil and imperial service.

Nonconformists also directed their attention to another long-standing grievance, the legal requirement in England and Wales to pay the church rate, where it was still levied, for the maintenance of the parish church. The church rate had been under threat since the early 1830s, while the right of vestries to stop the payment of the rate had been confirmed by the House of Lords in 1853 in a judgement involving the Braintree parish church in Essex. From 1853 to 1858, bills for the abolition of the church rate were introduced annually in the Commons, while by 1864 nearly 5,000 of the 12,000 parishes in England and Wales had ceased levying any church rate.[106] From the mid-1850s, then, Nonconformity was recovering its confidence and renewing its political campaign for religious equality, while some even began talking of reviving the agitation for disestablishment.

Jewish emancipation

In 1858, Parliament agreed to permit Jews to sit in the House of Commons. It was the culmination of nearly 30 years of struggle. For its supporters, it was a logical development of the movement for religious equality. The repeal of the Test and Corporation Acts in 1828 had ensured full political rights to Dissenters, and Catholic emancipation in 1829 had granted nearly full political rights to Roman Catholics. With Jewish emancipation, political rights were extended yet again, now bringing a non-Christian community within the pale of the constitution.

Expelled from the territories of the English crown in 1290, Jews had been permitted to resettle in Britain from 1656, and their numbers had steadily increased in the eighteenth century. By the 1850s, there were an estimated 35,000 Jews living in England and Wales. The largest concentration, about 20,000, resided in London, where they formed about one per cent of London's population.[107] Ireland and Scotland each had populations of only a few hundred Jews. Unlike many Continental states, the Jews in Britain did not form a separate corporate estate, governed by special laws; rather, from an early date they were subject to the same laws as other British subjects. They had the right to raise legal actions in the civil courts and they could appear as witnesses. They owned property from the eighteenth century, and their legal right to do so was confirmed by Parliament in 1846. Legislation in 1825 made it possible for Jews to become naturalised subjects, and in 1826 the repeal of the Aliens Act removed restrictions on Jewish immigration. Many Jews, meanwhile, were achieving commercial success, often developing business connections with Protestant Dissenters, especially Quakers. With the opening of the non-denominational University College, London, in 1828, Jews in England were given access to higher education, and they began entering the legal profession from 1833.[108] Along with Protestant Nonconformists, Jews were also allowed to qualify for lower non-theological degrees at Oxford in 1854 and at Cambridge in 1856. Jews had been disqualified from voting in parliamentary elections by their inability as electors to take the Abjuration Oath 'upon the true faith of a Christian'. In 1835, however, new election procedures dispensed with the requirement of administering the oath to voters, and this meant that Jews who met the property qualifications could vote. However, newly elected MPs and peers were still required to take the Abjuration Oath before taking a seat in Parliament, and this disqualified Jews.

By the 1830s Jews viewed themselves as the third major non-established religious community in Britain (after Protestant Nonconformists and Roman Catholics). Following the repeal of the Test and Corporation Acts and Catholic emancipation, there was thus a strong feeling within the Jewish community that their political emancipation should follow. Their exclusion from Parliament, they insisted, was 'a degrading stigma fastened upon us by the Laws of our country', and they wanted it removed.[109] In 1830, Robert Grant, MP for Inverness and a future governor of Bombay, brought forward a bill in the House of Commons for Jewish emancipation, which would have permitted Jews to sit in Parliament and removed nearly all remaining civil disqualifications. Although it received support from such leading Whigs as Lord John Russell and Lord Holland, the bill was defeated by 228 votes to 165. Three years later, in 1833, Grant introduced a second bill for Jewish emancipation. This time the bill was passed by the Commons, only to be rejected by the House of Lords, where the opposition was led by the bishops. During the next 25 years, 11 more Jewish emancipation bills would be passed by the Commons, only to be rejected by the Lords. The arguments did not change much over this period. For the supporters of Jewish emancipation, it was a logical step in the onward march towards religious liberty and equality, a recognition that religious tests in public life were a relic of the past and that the state should not impose penal restrictions on people for their religious beliefs. As Timothy Larsen has shown, most Nonconformists strongly supported Jewish emancipation, viewing it as part of their own struggle for religious equality.[110] For opponents of Jewish emancipation, the admission of Jews to Parliament would undermine the Christian basis of the British state. The liberal Anglican, Thomas Arnold, supported the admission of Nonconformists and Roman Catholics to Parliament, but drew the line there. 'I would thank Parliament', he wrote in 1836, 'for having done away with distinctions between Christian and Christian'. But, he added, 'I would pray that distinctions be kept up between Christians and non-Christians'.[111] For the Anglican clergyman, Julius Hare, Jewish emancipation was not part of the movement towards religious equality, but was rather a 'totally different course' that would destroy 'the Christian character of the State and Nation'.[112] For some, it was God's will that Jews should not become settled subjects of the United Kingdom. One of the most vehement opponents of Jewish emancipation was Lord Ashley, who insisted that Jews were destined to be restored to the Holy Land in the series of events that would culminate in Christ's return.[113]

In 1847, the campaign for Jewish emancipation took a new turn when Lionel de Rothschild, eldest son of a successful German-born banker, was elected to Parliament by the City of London. Rothschild – said to be the model for the character of the cultivated Jewish aristocrat, Sidonia, in Disraeli's novel, *Coningsby* (1844) – ran on a platform that included freedom of religion, free trade and the extension of the franchise. In his election address, he professed his belief that 'religion is a matter solely between man and his Maker, that faith, like love, is free, that it never can be the result of constraint'. It was wrong, he added, 'to punish men for not doing that which they cannot do', and this included believing what they could not believe.[114] Although there were allegations that he bribed voters, he was a genuinely popular figure in London, warmly received on the hustings. Rothschild's election in 1847 evoked memories of Daniel O'Connell's election to Parliament for county Clare nearly 20 years earlier – the event that had led to the passing of Catholic emancipation. Rothschild could not swear the Oath 'upon the true faith of a Christian' and therefore was not permitted to take his seat, denying his constituency its full representation in Parliament. In 1849, after two further emancipation bills had been rejected by the Lords, Rothschild retired from his unoccupied seat and ran at a by-election, to allow his constituents the opportunity of electing another candidate. But he was re-elected on this occasion, and again in the general elections of 1852 and 1857. In 1851, a second Jew, the tempestuous agitator David Salomons, was elected to Parliament at a by-election in Greenwich. Salomons attempted to take his seat in the Commons without swearing the Oath, and even managed to vote in a division before being forcibly ejected.

Finally, in 1858, under the Conservative government of Lord Derby, a compromise was reached over the Jewish question. Despite the continued opposition from the majority of bishops in the Lords, Parliament agreed that the House of Commons and the House of Lords should each be allowed to determine separately the form of oath to be administered to Jewish persons. The House of Commons immediately adopted a form of words acceptable to Jews, omitting the phrase 'upon the true faith of a Christian' and in July 1858, 11 years after his first election, Lionel de Rothschild was at last allowed to take his seat.[115] The House of Lords continued to insist on the old oath, until, in 1866, Parliament enacted a new form of oath, acceptable to Jews, for admission to both Houses. In 1886, Lionel de Rothschild's son was raised to the peerage and became the first Jew to sit in the Lords. Jewish emancipation, although long in coming, marked yet another victory for toleration and religious equality. It was also a blow to the edifice of the Christian state, and for some it raised further questions about the idea of the providential Christian empire.

Missions and empire

For one section of British society, however, there were few doubts about the Christian nature and destiny of the British imperial state. This was the 'missionary public', a large and influential body of opinion. The missionary public, as Catherine Hall has observed, was made up of men and women from both the established churches and the Nonconformist denominations, who were committed to the conversion of the world, and who often viewed the expanding British empire as one of God's instruments for this great work.[116] These men and women attended lectures and meetings in support of missions, relished the articles on missions in the religious press, supported anti-slavery efforts, donated money and signed petitions for missionary causes, and joined in circles of prayer for world conversion. They drew support from the skilled artisan classes, as well as the middle- and upper-classes. They thrilled to the heroic exploits of missionaries, who traversed the globe and preached to heathen peoples in exotic settings – sometimes to receive the martyr's crown, sometimes to gain the trust of those they hoped to save, and sometimes to see their fortitude rewarded with converts. Members of the missionary public were appalled (and sometimes titillated) when they read missionary accounts of the heathens – including tales of cannibalism, polygamy, nakedness, promiscuity, child sacrifice and idolatry – and they were genuinely horrified by the image of African and Asian souls being daily lost to the eternal torments of hell.

For the missionary public, there was little doubt that Britain was an elect nation, chosen and raised up by providence for the work of Christianising the globe. This was the reason for Britain's world pre-eminence in commerce and manufactures, and for the success of British arms in subduing vast and distant territories. And nowhere was the hand of providence more visible than in the establishment of British dominion over the vast subcontinent of India – India, the jewel of the empire and the gateway to Asia, with its ancient civilisation and its hundreds of millions of inhabitants, located half a world away. The belief in Britain as elect nation, with a special mission to India, received eloquent expression in 1849 in the episcopal charge of Daniel Wilson, the pre-millenarian evangelical bishop of Calcutta and metropolitan of India. During the past 60 years, Wilson observed, Britain had not only triumphed over revolutionary and Napoleonic France, but it had also been raised 'to the possession of the most wonderful empire, and the widest influence which the world has ever seen, either in ancient or modern times'. 'And', he asked, 'for what purpose. Why has India been given to us, as it were by miracle?' 'The answer', he continued:

can be but one – that we may be put upon our probation – that it may be seen whether we will communicate to India and the world the immense blessings of the Gospel which have been committed to our trust. If not, the same hand which has raised us to such a summit, can in one moment sink us to the lowest depth, as the fates of Tyre, of Nineveh, and of Babylon of old, have so many centuries been proclaiming to each succeeding age.[117]

Britain's election was thus a blessing, but also a responsibility, which brought with it grave dangers if the nation did not respond faithfully to its divine calling.

The decades after the opening of India to missionary activity in 1813 had witnessed, as we have seen, the gradual expansion of Britain's Protestant missions in the subcontinent. By the 1850s, the number of

Protestant missionaries in India had increased to about 400, representing 25 Protestant churches or societies.[118] Much of the mission work was focused on education, as missionaries believed that a Western education, especially training in science and logic, would undermine faith in traditional Hindu cosmologies and open young minds to Christian influence. By 1852, there were an estimated 14,000 boys and 11,500 girls attending mission schools in India.[119] The relations between the missionaries and the government in India had been cool in the years immediately following the opening of the subcontinent to missionary activity. However, they grew more co-operative under two reform-minded governors-general – the evangelical Anglican, Lord William Bentinck (1828–35), and the Scottish Presbyterian, Lord Dalhousie (1848–56). As we have observed in Chapter 2, there was a growing tendency in the 1830s for the state to intervene in India society – acting to suppress *sati*, *thuggee* and child sacrifice, and providing grants to English-language schools that taught Western forms of learning. In the 1830s, the missionary interest convinced the British government in India that it should, as soon as possible, cease collecting the pilgrim tax for the support of Hindu temples. Protestant missionaries also called on the state to abolish caste restrictions.[120] More and more wives and families began joining the missionaries, and women grew increasingly active in the missions, teaching in the schools, visiting the poor, and making efforts to reach Indian women, who were generally shielded by custom and their families from the male missionaries.

The attention of the mission public in the 1850s was increasingly directed eastwards. The economy of the sugar islands in the Caribbean had stagnated since the abolition of slavery, and public interest in the mission to the former slaves of Jamaica and the Caribbean islands was flagging. However, India was absorbing more and more public attention. India supplied trendy consumer goods – fashionable Kashmir shawls, lightweight printed muslins and silks, chutneys, pickles and condiments, brass work and wood carvings, ornate rugs and tapestries, and especially teas. There was fascination with Dalhousie's successful military campaigns in the Punjab, and over the accounts of Indian buildings, dress, customs and wildlife. Surely the conversion of such a vast and diverse subcontinent, and of such varied peoples and cultures, would be a glorious achievement and a sign that the millennium was near.

In 1854, the Britain went to war in alliance with France and Turkey against Russia – in what was the first major conflict involving the great powers of Europe since the close of the Napoleonic Wars. In the Crimean War, Britain's major aims were to shore up the Ottoman empire and thus to protect the Mediterranean route to India against Russian advances. The main theatre of the war was the Black Sea region, and one of the most celebrated episodes was the struggle of Florence Nightingale to improve the appalling conditions at the British military hospital at Scutari, near Istanbul, where she was joined by a number of Anglican and Roman Catholic sisters. This was the last British war to open with the proclamation of a day of fasting and prayer, and on the whole the British churches, both established and Nonconformists, supported the conflict as a 'just war', fought to protect the Ottoman state from Russian aggression and to maintain the international order.[121] Despite some early military disasters – which brought the proclamation of a second day of fasting and supplication – Britain and its allies were victorious over Russia by 1856, ending the perceived threat to British India. Providence, it seemed, had blessed British arms in the Near East and ensured the permanence of British dominion in India.

Then in May 1857, north-central India was swept by a series of mutinies among the Indian sepoy troops, which very quickly developed into a general uprising, aimed at the elimination of British rule in India and the restoration of the Mughal emperor and the time-honoured local princes. The rising was accompanied by some large-scale murders of Europeans, most notoriously at Cawnpore, where several hundred men, women and children were massacred after they had surrendered on the promise of safe treatment. The 'Indian Mutiny', as it became known in Britain, caught the authorities by surprise. Although resentments against the Westernising and Christianising policies of the British state had been simmering among Hindus and Muslims for decades, no one in Britain had anticipated a mass rising of such magnitude, while the massacres of Europeans indicated a depth of popular hatred that was as unexpected as it was distressing. For a time, it seemed that Britain would lose control of India; this might well have been the case had the rising spread to the south and to the Punjab. However, it remained localised, and in India as a whole most sepoy troops remained loyal to their British commanders. There were months of hard struggle, with pitched battles, in which both sides fought with courage and determination. Gradually the discipline of the British forces, aided by telegraph communication, prevailed, and the victors took their revenge for the killings of Europeans through large-scale killings of Indians.

In Britain, the public followed the campaigns closely in the newspapers. There was horror over the massacres of Europeans, and cries for retribution. There was also fevered excitement, as the public scanned the press reports to learn whether besieged enclaves would be relieved and spared massacre. The war brought forward new military heroes, many of them devoted Christians, whose lives reflected the spread of evangelical piety and practice in the early Victorian army. Of the Christian heroes, the most celebrated was General Sir Henry Havelock. An evangelical Baptist, who had converted from Anglicanism in 1823 and married a daughter of a prominent Baptist missionary, Havelock had been active in promoting prayer meetings, Sunday schools, and regimental temperance societies within the army. He was not a narrow sectarian, and his was a broad, inclusive evangelicalism. He died immediately after leading the successful action to relieve Lucknow, and became an iconic figure – an ideal Christian warrior and a martyr to the faith, who had fallen in the act of rescuing others. A grateful nation placed his statue in Trafalgar Square, his image appeared on thousands of prints, while preachers extolled his virtues and the leading Baptist William Brock wrote one of his many popular biographies.[122] For Nonconformists, he symbolised their patriotism and participation in the British imperial mission.

For the mission public, the bloodshed of the Mutiny came as a particular shock after all the confident claims that Christianity had been steadily advancing in India. The queen called for a 'day of national humiliation' on 7 October 1857, and special services were held in all places of worship connected with the established churches and in large numbers of Nonconformist chapels.[123] For probably most preachers on this day, and in sermons, addresses and pamphlets issued in the coming months, the Mutiny – so unexpected, so seemingly inexplicable, so terrible – was a visitation from God. As such, it was, like the Old Testament visitations, both punitive and remedial. It was on the one hand a divine punishment visited upon Britain for not having been sufficiently zealous in the work of converting India. Despite all the evidence of God's real purpose in giving Britain dominion over the country, too many people in Britain had persisted in viewing India as primarily a source of material wealth and power. Britain had been too slow in opening it to missionary activity and too moderate in its support for missions. For one preacher, the slaughtered Europeans had died in atonement for Britain's sins in not doing more to Christianise India. 'They have suffered innocently', he insisted, 'for their country's guilty misrule. THEY ARE INDIA'S MARTYRS FOR ENGLAND'S SINS'.[124] The visitation on the other hand was also remedial, intended to call Britain to corporate repentance for its sins in India. It was a warning of the consequences of God's displeasure, and a summons to Christian Britain to embrace with new commitment the sacred responsibility of rule over the country. 'Who can doubt', observed Samuel Wilberforce, bishop of Oxford, in November 1857, 'that God has so dealt with us, in order that we may . . . act, as we never yet have acted, with true Christian zeal and courage in the administration of our Eastern empire'.[125] If Britain would heed the warning, there was the promise of success in the Christianisation of India, and a glorious future for the empire. Through the 'blood of our martyred fellow-countrymen and countrywomen', proclaimed the Earl of Chichester, president of the Church Missionary Society, at a special meeting on the Mutiny in January 1858, 'in God's good time some of us – or if not ourselves, our children – will be permitted to witness the precious fruits of a wise repentance, will see that great territory occupied from one end to the other by a Christian population, will see the peaceful kingdom of Christ established there, and we shall then see the native Indians gratefully acknowledging our justice, and cheerfully submitting to our sway'.[126]

What the India mission now needed, insisted its supporters, was increased commitment and support. At home, public donations to the mission must increase. In India, the missionaries must move out of the cities, where they had for too long been concentrated, and into the villages. They must expand their educational work, with the aim of bringing all the children of India, poor as well as rich, into English-language Christian schools. The missions must disregard caste, work for improved conditions for women, openly confront both Hinduism and Islam, and use all legitimate means to spread the gospel. They must move forward in the spirit of Havelock and those other stalwart Christian warriors who suppressed the Mutiny. While the government in India should not seek to impose conversion by force, it should end any appearance of religious neutrality and openly give its support to the Christian missions. It must make the peoples of India understand that the imperial state expected their conversion. Britain must publicly recognise that it was 'the will of Providence' that 'alone constitutes our charter to govern India'.[127] The suppression of the Mutiny, insisted one Anglican clergyman, must be followed by 'the reconquest of India, not for our glory or pecuniary aggrandisement, but for the real extension of the kingdom of Christ, and of the annihilation of Satan's kingdom there'.[128] 'This is the revenge I covet', proclaimed the Anglican evangelical clergyman, Hugh Stowell, in October 1857, 'that every idol should be cast to the moles and the bats, every pagoda changed into a house of prayer, every Mahommedan mosque into a temple of the living God'.[129]

Among those responsible for governing India, however, few would support such a Christianisation policy. From the onset of the Mutiny, influential voices in Britain insisted that a major cause of the rising had been the resentments that the Christian missionaries had created among Hindus and Muslims. For these critics, the presence of missionaries in India was not only divisive and dangerous, but their work was also largely futile. Their converts represented only a tiny proportion of India's huge population and came mainly from the lowest classes, while their efforts to convert the upper classes through their English-language schools had brought few results. For the state now to promote missions would, the critics claimed, only lead to further rebellion and bloodshed. 'The religious people who now tell us that we must hold India to convert it', observed the free trader, Richard Cobden, to his colleague, John Bright, in October 1857, 'ought, I should think, to be convinced by what has passed that sending red coats as well as black to Christianize a people is not the most likely way to insure the blessing of God on our missionary efforts'.[130]

In 1858, following the suppression of the Mutiny, the queen issued a royal proclamation, defining her state's future religious policies in India. While she affirmed her own Christian faith, she also disclaimed 'alike the right and desire to impose our convictions on any of our subjects'. In 1858, Parliament ended the East India Company's role in governing India and brought British territories in India under direct crown rule. Parliament did not, however, provide additional funds for an enlarged church establishment in India nor did it increase state support for the Christian missions. It was all very disappointing for those who believed the Mutiny had been a divine call to the state to Christianise the country. The mission public grew uncertain about the subcontinent, and giving to the India missions stagnated. The total number of missionaries supported by the five major missionary societies actually decreased from 262 to 234 in the decade 1861–71.[131]

In 1857, meanwhile, a new missionary hero came into the public gaze. His exploits served to shift the imagination of the mission public from mutinous India to what appeared a more promising mission field – one that could stir the imaginations of free traders as well as the proponents of mission. In December 1856, the Scottish missionary-explorer, David Livingstone, arrived in Britain after an astonishing journey in which, as a solitary European travelling with a band of Kololo tribesmen, he had traversed Africa from the eastern to the western coasts, and explored much of the course of the Zambesi river. The newspapers had given extensive coverage to the exploit, and Livingstone was already famous on his return home. Invited to lecture across the United Kingdom, he was received with enthusiasm by large audiences. He drafted his own account of his astonishing journey in the first six months of 1857. Published in November 1857, his book, *Missionary Travels and Researches in South Africa*, sold over 70,000 copies.[132]

There was much in Livingstone and his message to attract the mid-nineteenth-century Christian public. Like Havelock, Livingstone was a Nonconformist, and like Havelock he also had a broad, non-sectarian faith that could appeal to members of the established churches. Born in humble circumstances in 1813 in Blantyre, in southwest Scotland, Livingstone had gone to work in a local cotton mill at the age of ten, and had pursued his education at night school. He attended the Congregational church with his family in nearby Hamilton. Stirred by an appeal for medical missionaries, he had studied at the Andersonian Medical School in Glasgow, supporting himself by working in a cotton mill during the vacation periods. He was accepted for service by the London Missionary Society, and received theological training and further medical training in London. He was, as we have seen, present at the great public meeting of June 1840 that inaugurated the ill-fated Niger expedition, with its aim of uprooting the slave trade at its source, by bringing Christianity and commerce into the interior of Africa. On completing his training, he travelled to South Africa, where he began work at a mission-station in the bush. From there he conducted his explorations into the interior of central Africa.

His public lectures and his *Missionary Travels and Researches* were presented in a simple, clear and direct style, without rhetorical adornment; they conveyed the image of a practical man of science, providing objective descriptions of the fauna, wildlife, geography, geology, rainfall, climate, and peoples of the African interior. They combined adventure and discovery with Christian mission; his maxim was to 'view the end of the geographical feat as the beginning of the missionary enterprize'.[133] Until Livingstone's explorations, most people in Britain had believed that while the African coasts were marshy and fever-ridden, the interior of central Africa was parched desert, similar to the Kalahari or the Sahara, and was inhabited by brutal savages. Livingstone, however, presented a very different vision. While much of the African interior was dense jungle, there were also grassy and wooded uplands, where the climate was moderate and which were suitable for cultivation and European settlement. There were, he insisted, rich mineral deposits, including seams of coal and iron ore near the surface. The Zambesi river, as he described it, was a great inland waterway, navigable by steamship for most of the year, which could be used to transport cotton and other agricultural products. Above all, the peoples of the interior were on the whole intelligent, friendly and sociable, with often sophisticated tribal cultures and traditions. They suffered grievously, to be sure, from the slavers – and among Livingstone's most moving passages were his descriptions of captives, yoked with forked sticks, being marched by the slavers to the coasts.[134] But there could be another future for central Africa. In what was the climax of his lecture tour, a public lecture in Cambridge on 4 December 1857, Livingstone appealed to the peoples of the United Kingdom to follow up his explorations, and bring Christianity and commerce to central Africa. 'I beg', he proclaimed at the close of his lecture, 'to direct your attention to Africa. I know that in a few years I shall be cut off in that country, which is now open; do not let it be shut again! I go back to African to try to make an open path for commerce and Christianity; do you carry out the work which I have begun. I LEAVE IT WITH YOU.' As he spoke these words, he looked up to the galleries, which were crowded with undergraduates, to whom he spoke his message directly. There was prolonged and deafening applause.[135]

How could anyone resist the appeal? The words echoed the noble sentiments of Buxton and the anti-slavery activists who had planned the Niger expedition 17 years before. They were also a promise, from a pragmatic man of action, who had actually traversed the ground, that the lofty aims of 1840–41, of eradicating slavery and bringing the benefits of Christian civilisation to the African interior, could be achieved. Livingstone's confidence in the beneficial effects of commerce and Christianity might have seemed to some observers a little simplistic, in the aftermath of the Irish famine and the revelations of conditions in the mines, mills and sweated workshops of industrial Britain – but then Livingstone had been away from Britain for most of the period since 1841. He was able to speak of free trade and providence with an absolute conviction that many in the later 1850s found attractive. Nor did he seem to have any self-interested aims. He had never supported the expansion of European rule in Africa, insisting that it was the impact of missions, education and commerce alone that would transform the Continent.

At the close of 1857, with Livingstone's words resounding through the land, Palmerston's government announced in the House of Commons that it would finance an expedition up the Zambesi, to be led by Livingstone, to explore further the possibilities for cotton cultivation and commercial development. It evoked memories of the government's financial support of the Niger expedition in 1841, and the new plan had the warm support of Prince Albert, the great champion of the Niger venture. Livingstone now resigned from the London Missionary Society so that he could devote himself to the work of exploration. His appeal to Christianity and commerce, meanwhile, had, as we have seen, inspired members of both Cambridge and Oxford Universities, and they now undertook to organise a religious and scientific mission up the Zambesi. The organisers, mainly high Anglicans, were soon joined by members of the University of Durham and Trinity College, Dublin, to form the Universities' Central African Mission. It was a sign, supporters claimed, that missionary zeal was now winning support in the very heart of the Anglican establishment.[136] To head the mission, the Church of England took the innovative step of appointing a bishop. High Anglicans hailed the decision as marking a return to the apostolic practice of bishops leading missions into heathen lands. Charles Mackenzie, a Cambridge-educated clergyman with pastoral experience in Natal, was consecrated bishop of Central Africa. He arrived at the head of a small band of missionaries in January 1861 in East Africa at the Kongone mouth of the Zambesi. There they met with Livingstone and his state-supported expedition of explorers, and the two groups advanced together to bring commerce and Christianity into the African interior.

The mission and expedition, however, were soon shadowed by tragedy. The Zambesi proved to be far less navigable than Livingstone had believed, while malaria was a constant danger. The Portuguese, who claimed the region, were hostile to what they viewed as unfriendly intrusion. Livingstone, meanwhile, left Mackenzie's mission party in the uplands while he continued his explorations up river. The missionaries, inexperienced with African ways, soon began using force to free bands of slaves. This seemed proper in light of the aims of the mission: for how could they turn a blind eye to the dreary processions of enslaved men, women and children? However, as the slaves they freed had been captured through intertribal warfare, the missionaries found themselves caught up in this fight, firing upon and killing Africans they had come to convert. In January 1862, Mackenzie died of malaria, and the leaderless mission was soon adrift. Others also died of fever, including Livingstone's wife, Mary, who had joined him on the expedition. Reports of the mission's involvement in tribal warfare, meanwhile, reached England and led to a wave of denunciations in the religious press, where it was argued, quite sensibly, that missionaries should not wage war. There was also a growing chorus of criticism of Livingstone, who many believed had deceived the British public with false impressions of the climate and natural resources to be found along the Zambesi. By November 1863, the survivors of the mission had withdrawn from the Zambesi to Zanzibar, and a few months later

Livingstone's expedition came to a disappointing end. Prince Albert, the patron of the expedition, had died of typhus in December 1861, plunging the queen into a prolonged period of mourning. A curtain seemed again to fall upon the vision of redeeming the African interior and ending slavery.

Conclusion

'His death', observed the *British and Foreign Evangelical Review* of Bishop Mackenzie's martyrdom, 'is the pledge of the continuance of his mission, the sacrifice, out of which there shall yet arise life to Africa'.[137] The Zambesi expedition, like the Niger expedition 20 years before, had been a costly failure. None the less, many continued to believe in the mission to Africa. They retained their faith in the providential destiny of the United Kingdom to bring commerce, civilisation and Christianity to the African interior. They knew that God often acted through apparent defeats, apparent evil, to achieve His grand designs. The evil of the Opium War of 1840–42, after all, had led to the partial opening of China to missionary activity. A second Opium War in 1856–60 had opened the country still further to Christian missions. In India, despite the bloodbath of the Mutiny, the empire had survived and the missions continued. Many retained their belief in providential empire, and viewed the setbacks as part of the providential plan. By 1857, some were even looking back upon the Irish famine as a providential event, one which was now bringing lasting benefits to Ireland in the form of improved agriculture and a smaller population.[138] 'Without canvassing the separate steps by which we ascended the summit of empire', wrote the LMS missionary to India, Edward Storrow, in 1859, 'it may be averred confidently that we have been led upward to the giddy height by God himself'.[139]

Yet others were having doubts about Britain's providentialist role in the world. The failures of the Niger and Zambesi expeditions, the horrors of the Irish famine, the Indian Mutiny – the cumulative effect raised serious questions about whether the empire was in truth God's agent. Adding to the unease, there was the new strength and confidence of the Roman Catholic Church in Ireland and in England, the bitter conflicts between high Anglicans and evangelicals that threatened the unity of the established Church of England, the revival of tensions between Nonconformity and the established church, and the opening of Parliament to Jews. By the later 1850s, educated public opinion was becoming less convinced by providentialist interpretations of free trade or imperial expansion. Boyd Hilton, for example, has discerned a waning confidence in Christian political economy by about 1860, while Andrew Porter has noted during the same period a 'drift of . . . mainstream missionary thinking' away from the slogan of commerce and Christianity.[140] By the late 1850s, Peter Gray has observed, 'wholehearted assurance in the benign governance of human affairs was more problematic for public intellectuals'.[141] The evangelical minister, Baptist Noel, sounded a sombre tone in his account of the India mission in 1859. In India, he observed, 'Protestantism is on its trial before Catholic nations; and Christianity is put to the proof before Mahomedans and Hindoos'.[142] Noel was uncertain how Britain's Protestant empire would perform in this trial.

Notes

1 E. Longford, *Victoria R. I.* (London, 1964), 82.

2 W. L. Arnstein, 'Queen Victoria and Religion', in G. Malmgreen (ed.), *Religion in the Lives of English Women 1760–1930* (London, 1986), 90–8.

3 H. Thomas, *The Slave Trade: The History of the Atlantic Slave Trade 1440–1870* (London, 1997), 653.

4 Rice, *Rise and Fall of Black Slavery*, 239.

5 Quoted in A. Porter, ' "Commerce and Christianity": The Rise and Fall of a Nineteenth-Century Missionary Slogan', *Historical Journal*, 28 (1985), 613.

6 Cited in C. P. Groves, *The Planting of Christianity in Africa*, 4 vols (London, 1948–1958), vol. 2, 6.

7 Quoted in C. Buxton, *Memoirs of Sir Thomas Fowell Buxton* (London, 1848), 515.

8 J. Gallagher, 'Fowell Buxton and the New African Policy, 1838–1842', *Cambridge Historical Journal*, 10 (1950), 47.

9 D. H. Maynard, 'The World's Anti-Slavery Convention of 1840', *Mississippi Valley Historical Review*, 47 (1960), 452–71.

10 Groves, *Planting of Christianity in Africa*, vol. 2, 10.

11 C. Hall, *Civilising Subjects: Metropole and Colony in the British Imagination 1830–1867* (Cambridge, 2002), 338.

12 P. W. Fay, 'The Protestant Mission and the Opium War', *The Pacific Historical Review*, 40 (1971), 145–61.

13 Ibid., 159–60.

14 B. Stanley, ' "Commerce and Christianity": Providence Theory, the Missionary Movement, and the Imperialism of Free Trade, 1842–1860', *Historical Journal*, 26 (1983), 79.

15 Ibid., 78–9.

16 K. T. Hoppen, *The Mid-Victorian Generation 1846–1886* (Oxford, 1998), 156.

17 Arnstein, 'Queen Victoria and Religion', 95.

18 Hilton, *A Mad, Bad, and Dangerous People?*, 502–3.

19 M. Lynn, 'British Policy, Trade and Informal Empire in the Mid-Nineteenth Century', in *The Oxford History of the British Empire*, vol. 3: *The Nineteenth Century*, ed. A. Porter (Oxford, 1999), 104.

20 Quoted in J. A. Hobson, *Richard Cobden: The International Man* (London, 1919), 38.

21 N. McCord, *The Anti-Corn Law League 1838–1846* (London, 1958), 103–7; R. G. Cowherd, *The Politics of English Dissent* (New York, 1956), 134–6.

22 'Christianity and the Corn Laws', *Church of England Quarterly Review*, vol. x (1841), 432, 444

23 Quoted in Hilton, *The Age of Atonement*, 249.

24 B. Hilton, 'Peel: A Reappraisal', *Historical Journal*, 22 (1979), 585–614.

25 J. C. Hare, 'The Unity of Mankind in God' (1848) in J. C. Hare, *Miscellaneous Pamphlets on Some of the Leading Questions Agitated in the Church* (Cambridge, 1855), 19.

26 A. Tyrrell, 'Making the Millennium: The Mid-Nineteenth Century Peace Movement', *Historical Journal*, 20 (1978), 75–95.

27 C. T. Longley, *A Charge, addressed to the Clergy of the Diocese of Ripon* (London, 1850), 8.

28 P. Gray, 'Potatoes and Providence: British Government's Response to The Great Famine', *Bullán: An Irish Studies Journal*, 1; 1 (Spring 1994), 75–90; P. Gray, 'Ideology and the Famine', in C. Póirtéir (ed.), *The Great Irish Famine* (Cork, 1995), 86–103; P. Gray, *Famine, Land and Politics: British Government and Irish Society 1843–1850* (Dublin: Irish Academic Press, 1999), 96–125.

29 Gray, *Famine, Land and Politics*, 231–2, 253–4; J. Hart, 'Sir Charles Trevelyan at the Treasury', *English Historical Review*, 75 (1960), 99–102.

30 Mary E. Daly, 'The Operations of Famine Relief', in Póirtéir (ed.), *The Great Irish Famine*, 123–34.

31 James S. Donnelly, Jr, 'Mass Eviction and the Great Famine', in Póirtéir (ed.), *The Great Irish Famine*, 155–73.

32 D. Kerr, *'A Nation of Beggars'? Priests, People, and Politics in Famine Ireland 1846–1852* (Oxford, 1994), 137.

33 [T. Chalmers], 'Political Economy of a Famine', *North British Review*, vol. 7 (May 1847), 247–90, quotations on 271, 282.

34 Gladstone to Manning, 9 March 1847, in D. C. Lathbury (ed.), *Correspondence on Church and Religion of William Ewart Gladstone*, 2 vols (London, 1910), vol. ii, 274–6.

35 D. Bowen, *Souperism: Myth or Reality* (Cork, 1970), 202–3.

36 Gray, *Famine, Land and Politics*, 259.

37 Bowen, *Souperism: Myth or Reality*, 183–234; Kerr, '*A Nation of Beggars'?*, 210–11; I. Whelan, 'The Stigma of Souperism', in Póirtéir (ed.), *The Great Irish Famine*, 143–54.

38 J. H. Murphy, 'The Role of Vincentian Parish Missions in the "Irish Counter-Reformation" of the Mid Nineteenth Century', *Irish Historical Studies*, 24 (Nov. 1984), 152–71.

39 E. Larkin, *The Making of the Roman Catholic Church in Ireland, 1850–1860* (Chapel Hill, North Carolina, 1980), 27–57.

40 Quoted in Kerr, '*A Nation of Beggars'?*, 229–30.

41 E. Larkin, 'The Devotional Revolution in Ireland, 1850–75', *American Historical Review*, 77 (June 1972), 625–52.

42 Larkin, *Pastoral Role of the Roman Catholic Church in Pre-Famine Ireland*, 189–258.

43 Larkin, 'Devotional Revolution in Ireland', 645.

44 Ibid., 626, 644.

45 R. Foster, *Modern Ireland 1600–1972* (London, 1988), 340.

46 Hilton, *The Age of Atonement*, 36–162.

47 T. Carlyle, *Chartism* (London, 1840), 51, 59.

48 C. Whibley, *Lord John Manners and his Friends*, 2 vols (Edinburgh, 1925), vol. I, 63–74, 96–156; R. Faber, *Young England* (London, 1987); R. Blake, *Disraeli* (London, 1966), 168–75.

49 B. Disraeli, general preface to the Young England trilogy of novels, 1870, quoted in W. F. Monypenny and G. E. Buckle, *Life of Benjamin Disraeli*, 2nd edn in 2 vols (London, 1929), vol. I, 873.

50 Recent biographies of Shaftesbury include G. B. A. M. Finlayson, *Shaftesbury* (London, 1981); G. Battiscombe, *Shaftesbury: A Biography of the Seventh Earl* (London, 1974); and G. Best, *Shaftesbury* (London, 1964).

51 E. R. Norman, *Church and Society in England 1770–1970* (Oxford, 1976), 171.

52 C. Kingsley, *A Sermon preached at Hawley Church, April 30, 1848* (Wokingham, 1848), 6.

53 *Politics for the People*, no. 1 (6 May 1848), 1.

54 D. E. Hall, 'On the Making and Unmaking of Monsters: Christian Socialism, Muscular Christianity, and the Metaphorization of Class Conflict', in D. E. Hall (ed.), *Muscular Christianity: Embodying the Victorian Age* (Cambridge, 1994), 47–54.

55 *Politics for the People*, no. 4 (27 May 1848), 58–9.

56 C. Kingsley, *Sermons on National Subjects* (London, 1852), 195.

57 F. Maurice, *Life of Frederick Denison Maurice*, 2 vols (London, 1884), vol. ii, 34–5.

58 P. N. Backstrom, *Christian Socialism and Co-operation in Victorian England: Edward Vansittart Neale and the Co-operative Movement* (London, 1974), 9–52.

59 C. Kingsley, *The Message of the Church to Labouring Men* (London, 1851), 23.

60 Ibid., 8.

61 F. E. Kingsley, *Charles Kingsley: His Letters and Memories of his Life*, 8th edn, 2 vols (London, 1880), vol. I, 229–32.

62 Most of the discussion that follows is based on S. Mumm, *Stolen Daughters, Virgin Mothers: Anglican Sisterhoods in Victorian Britain* (London, 1999).

63 Chadwick, *Victorian Church, Part One*, 506.

64 Hoppen, *The Mid-Victorian Generation*, 322.

65 Mumm, *Stolen Daughters, Virgin Mothers*, 100.

66 S. Wilberforce, Bishop of Oxford, *Charge delivered at the Triennial Visitation of the Diocese* (Oxford, 1857), 33–8.

67 R. Kollar, 'A Death in the Family: Bishop Archibald Campbell Tait, the Rights of Parents, and Anglican Sisterhoods in the Diocese of London', *Journal of Religious History*, 27 (2003), 198–214.

68 F. Prochaska, *Christianity and Social Service in Modern Britain: The Disinherited Spirit* (Oxford, 2006), 74.

69 Quoted in F. Warre Cornish, *The English Church in the Nineteenth Century*, 2 vols (London, 1910), vol. ii, 79–80.

70 Prochaska, *Christianity and Social Service*, 129–39; K. Heasman, *Evangelicals in Action: An Appraisal of their Social Work* (London, 1962), 36–7, 236–7; Lewis, *Lighten their Darkness*, 221–3.

71 L. A. Orr Macdonald, *A Unique and Glorious Mission: Women and Presbyterianism in Scotland 1830–1930* (Edinburgh, 2000), 85–6.

72 S. Gill, *Women and the Church of England from the Eighteenth Century to the Present* (London, 1994), 163–7.

73 C. T. Longley, *A Charge addressed to the Clergy of the Diocese of Ripon, at the Triennial Visitation* (London, 1853), 27–8.

74 P. Toon, *Evangelical Theology 1833–1856* (London, 1979), 90.

75 Quoted in Chadwick, *Victorian Church, Part One*, 263–4.

76 G. A. Denison, *An Appeal to the Clergy and Laity of the Church of England, to Combine for the Defence of the Church and for the Recovery of her Rights and Liberties* (London, 1850), 11.

77 For the revival of Convocation, see Chadwick, *Victorian Church, Part One*, 309–24; P. J. Welch, 'The Revival of an Active Convocation of Canterbury (1852–1855)', *Journal of Ecclesiastical History*, 10 (1959), 188–97.

78 J. Kaye, *Charge delivered at the Triennial Visitation in 1852*, in J. Kaye, *Nine Charges delivered to the Clergy of the Diocese of Lincoln* (London, 1854), 461.

79 J. B. Sumner, *The Charge of John Bird, Lord Archbishop of Canterbury, to the Clergy of his Diocese* (London, 1852), 11–30.

80 A. R. Ashwell and R. G. Wilberforce, *Life of Samuel Wilberforce*, 3 vols (London, 1881), vol. ii, 162.

81 Quoted in M. Wheeler, *The Old Enemies: Catholic and Protestant in Nineteenth-Century English Culture* (Cambridge, 2006), 6.

82 Chadwick, *Victorian Church, Part One*, 287–8.

83 Wheeler, *The Old Enemies*, 8.

84 N. Wiseman, *An Appeal to the Reason and Good Feeling of the English People on the Subject of the Catholic Hierarchy* (London, 1850), 7.

85 *The Times*, 7 November 1850.

86 Quoted in Kerr, '*A Nation of Beggars*'?, 253.

87 D. G. Paz, *Popular Protestantism in Mid-Victorian England* (Stanford, 1992), 11; D. G. Paz, 'Popular Anti-Catholicism in England, 1850–1', *Albion*, 11 (1979), 349.

88 Carlyle, *Chartism*, 28.

89 G. F. A. Best, 'Popular Protestantism in Victorian Britain', in R. Robson, ed., *Ideas and Institutions of Victorian Britain* (London, 1967), 125–32; Paz, *Popular Protestantism*, 59–66.

90 Quoted in Larkin, *Making of the Roman Catholic Church in Ireland*, 82.

91 Quoted in Kerr, '*A Nation of Beggars*'?, 271.

92 Larkin, *Making of the Roman Catholic Church in Ireland*, 92.

93 Quoted in Machin, *Politics and the Churches in Great Britain 1832 to 1868*, 220.

94 Quoted in Kerr, *'A Nation of Beggars'?*, 278.

95 Machin, *Politics and the Churches in Great Britain 1832 to 1868*, 227–8.

96 For Newman and the Catholic University, see C. Barr, 'Paul Cullen, John Henry Newman and the Movement to Create a Catholic University in Ireland, 1845–60' (Univ. of Cambridge, unpublished D.Phil., 2000).

97 K. S. Inglis, 'Patterns of Religious Worship in 1851', *Journal of Ecclesiastical History*, 11 (1960), 74–86; W. S. F. Pickering, 'The 1851 Religious Census – a Useless Experiment?', *British Journal of Sociology*, 18 (1967), 382–407; D. J. Withrington, 'The 1851 Census of Religious Worship and Education: with a Note on Church Accommodation in Mid-19th-Century Scotland', *Records of the Scottish Church History Society*, 18 (1974), 133–48.

98 [H. Mann], 'Report of the Census, 1851 – Religious Worship', *Parliamentary Papers*, vol. lxxxix (Session 1852–53), clviii.

99 *Nonconformist*, 4 Jan. 1854, quoted in Watts, *The Dissenters*, vol. ii, 568.

100 R. Currie, *Methodism Divided* (London, 1968), 65–76; Watts, *The Dissenters*, vol. ii, 614–25.

101 G. R. Breed, *Particular Baptists in Victorian England* (Didcot, 2003), 29–70.

102 Watts, *The Dissenters*, vol. ii, 552.

103 D. M. Thompson, 'The Liberation Society, 1844–1868', in Hollis (ed.), *Pressure from Without in Early Victorian England* (London, 1974), 221–2.

104 R. J. Helmstadter, 'The Nonconformist Conscience', in G. Parsons (ed.), *Religion in Victorian Britain: IV, Interpretations* (Manchester, 1988), 76.

105 W. E. Gladstone to C. Marriott, 12 July 1854, in Lathbury (ed.), *Correspondence on Church and Religion of Gladstone*, vol. i, 218–19.

106 Watts, *The Dissenters*, vol. ii, 587.

107 M. C. N. Salbstein, *The Emancipation of the Jews in Britain* (London, 1982), 38.

108 Ibid., 17–53; D. Englander, 'Anglicized Not Anglican: Jews and Judaism in Victorian Britain', in G. Parsons (ed.), *Religion in Victorian Britain: I, Traditions* (Manchester, 1988), 240–6.

109 G. Alderman, *Modern British Jewry*, 2nd edn (Oxford, 1998), 57.

110 Larsen, *Friends of Religious Liberty*, 127–32.

111 Stanley, *Life of Dr Arnold*, vol. ii, 27.

112 J. C. Hare, *The Duty of the Church in Times of Trial* (London, 1848), 33–4.

113 Salbstein, *The Emancipation of the Jews*, 147–8.

114 Quoted in Ibid., 143.

115 Machin, *Politics and the Churches in Great Britain 1832 to 1868*, 292–4.

116 Hall, *Civilising Subjects*, 292–301.

117 D. Wilson, *A Charge delivered to the Clergy of the Four Dioceses of Calcutta, Madras, Bombay, and Colombo, at the Second Metropolitical Visitation* (London, 1849), 10.

118 E. Storrow, *India and Christian Missions* (London, 1859), 43.

119 C. K. Robinson, *Missions Urged upon the State on Grounds both of Duty and Policy* (Cambridge, 1852), 118.

120 D. B. Forrester, *Caste and Christianity: Attitudes and Policies on Caste of Anglo-Saxon Protestant Missions in India* (London, 1980), 37–43.

121 O. Anderson, 'The Reactions of Church and Dissent towards the Crimean War', *Journal of Ecclesiastical History*, 16 (1965), 209–20.

122 O. Anderson, 'The Growth of Christian Militarism in Mid-Victorian Britain', *English Historical Review*, 86 (1971), 49–52; Larsen, *Friends of Religious Equality*, 219.

123 B. Stanley, 'Christian Responses to the Indian Mutiny of 1857', in W. J. Sheils (ed.), *The Church and War, Studies in Church History*, 20 (Oxford, 1983), 277–89.

124 Anon., *England's Sins and India's Martyrs* (London, 1857), 11.

125 S. Wilberforce, *Speeches on Missions*, H. Rowley (ed.) (London, 1874), 106.

126 *The Indian Crisis: Special General Meeting of the Church Missionary Society at Exeter Hall* (London, 1858), 23.

127 G. F. MacLear, *The Christian Statesman and our Indian Empire* (Cambridge, 1859), 14.

128 R. Croly, *The Night, the Dawn, and the Day: The Reformed Church bringing India to Christ* (London, 1859), 179.

129 Quoted in L. James, *Raj: The Making and Unmaking of British India* (London, 1997), 292.

130 J. Morley, *Life of Richard Cobden*, 9th edn (London, 1903), 670.

131 T. R. Metcalf, *The Aftermath of Revolt: India, 1857–1870* (Princeton, 1965), 96–7.

132 A. C. Ross, *David Livingstone: Mission and Empire* (London, 2002), 107–15; T. Jeal, *Livingstone* (London, 1973), 163.

133 Quoted in 'Bishop Mackenzie and African Missions', *British and Foreign Evangelical Review*, 13 (October 1864), 723.

134 D. Livingstone, *Missionary Travels and Researches in South Africa* (London, 1857); O. Chadwick, *Mackenzie's Grave* (London, 1959), 14–16.

135 D. Livingstone, *Dr Livingstone's Cambridge Lectures*, ed. W. Monk, 2nd edn (London, 1860), 168; H. Goodwin, *Memoir of Bishop Mackenzie* (Cambridge, 1864), 205–6; Ross, *Livingstone*, 121.

136 'Bishop Mackenzie and African Missions', 722.

137 Ibid., 746.

138 P. Gray, 'The Making of Mid-Victorian Ireland? Political Economy and the Memory of the Great Famine', in Gray (ed.), *Victoria's Ireland: Irishness and Britishness, 1837–1901* (Dublin, 2004), 151–66.

139 E. Storrow, *India and Christian Missions* (London, 1859), 110.

140 Hilton, *The Age of Atonement*, 255–339; Porter, 'Commerce and Christianity', 617.

141 Gray, 'The Making of Mid-Victorian Ireland?', 166.

142 B. W. Noel, *England and India* (London, 1859), 216.

CHAPTER 4

Revivalism, Ritualism and Authority, 1859–1876

Reasserting the faith: the revival of 1859–62

As the 1850s drew to a close, much of the United Kingdom was swept by religious revival. Thousands experienced conversion, often amid scenes of extreme emotional excitement; tens of thousands more attended revival meetings and had their faith renewed. The revivals occurred with greatest intensity on the 'Celtic fringe' of the United Kingdom, in northern Ireland, Scotland and Wales – among communities for whom the social dislocations of the expanding industrial and commercial economy had come rather late. They also occurred mainly outside the established churches. The revivals were communal events, characterised by collective activity – prayer meetings, prolonged religious services, outdoor meetings, the singing of hymns and gospel songs. They were also deeply personal, with direct emotional preaching aimed at confronting individuals with a sense of their sin, the threat of eternal damnation, and their need to accept Christ as their personal saviour immediately. The emotional intensity of the revival meetings led in some cases to so-called 'physical manifestations' – prostrations, exaggerated movements, convulsions, uncontrollable utterances and trances, with those affected often claiming special gifts of the spirit, including gifts of 'tongues', prophecy and visions. While the early revivals were promoted largely by local Christians, the later phases of the movement witnessed the growing influence of professional revivalists, including James Caughey, Walter and Phoebe Palmer, Brownlow North, H. Grattan Guinness, E. Payton Hammond, and Charles G. Finney – who travelled about the country using well-honed methods for arousing and sustaining revival activity.

The British revival movement was connected with one in the United States. There, the so-called 'prayer meeting' revival emerged in late 1857 in the cities of the northeastern seaboard (which were experiencing an economic crisis), and then swept across much of the country. It was characterised by interdenominational prayer meetings, intense emotion, physical manifestations, and the work of professional revivalists. The American revival of 1857–58 claimed perhaps half a million converts and it had a profound impact on a nation that was deeply divided over the slavery question, and where the clouds of civil war were gathering.

The revival in Ulster

By 1858, reports of the American revival were reaching Ireland, where they found a warm reception among the Presbyterian communities of Ulster. The Ulster Presbyterians, descendants of seventeenth-century Scottish settlers, had preserved a distinctive communal identity, keeping themselves separate from both Roman Catholics and Anglicans. Until the middle of the nineteenth century, Ulster Presbyterians were mainly small farmers or handloom weavers, who lived in villages or market towns, worshipped in simple meeting houses, sang psalms without musical accompaniment, read their Bibles regularly, led disciplined lives under the watchful eyes of the elders, married within the community, and respected an educated ministry.[1] During the eighteenth century, a significant minority of Ulster Presbyterians had embraced a rational, non-Trinitarian faith, and in the 1790s some had taken up republican politics in alliance with liberal Irish Catholics. However, following the bloody rising of 1798, most Presbyterians had renounced both rationalism and republicanism, and under the leadership of the conservative Belfast minister, Henry Cooke, had returned to the strict Calvinist orthodoxy of the Westminster Confession of Faith.

These Ulster Presbyterians were feeling under threat by the 1850s. The industrialisation of textile production was bringing an end to the traditional handloom weaving in their rural communities. Industrialisation also contributed to the rapid growth of the manufacturing towns, especially Belfast, where growing numbers now found employment in large textile mills. In the towns, the old communal ties broke down, and Presbyterian ministers no longer exercised the same authority. The Presbyterians also felt threatened by the increasing confidence and assertiveness of the Roman Catholic Church, as expressed at the Synod of Thurles in 1850 and in the emerging 'devotional revolution'. Growing sectarian tensions led to serious rioting in Belfast in the summer of 1857, when Catholics, now representing a third of the city's population, responded violently to the traditional Protestant marches on 12 July to commemorate the battle of the Boyne. Many Presbyterians feared that the state was no longer committed to maintaining its Protestant identity. It had, after all, made no effort in 1843 to prevent the breakup of the Presbyterian Church of Scotland (which Ulster Presbyterians had revered as their 'mother' church), while it had increased the endowment to Maynooth in 1845 and declined to take decisive action against the 'papal aggression' of 1850.

At its annual meeting in July 1858, the General Assembly of the Presbyterian Church in Ireland held at special conference on revival. It agreed to send two ministers to the United States to gather information on the movement there, and it dispatched a pastoral letter to all congregations, asking them to pray for revival. The first incident of revival came in March 1859 at Ahoghill, in county Antrim, where thousands had gathered for the biannual celebration of communion at the Presbyterian Church of David Adams, a zealous evangelical minister. Amid great excitement, many were 'struck down' (physically prostrated) in the process of being converted. News of the extraordinary events at Ahoghill spread rapidly, and revivals broke out in a number of villages during the spring. Observers compared its spread to an epidemic, and spoke of people 'catching' the revival as they might a contagion. Concentrated in the areas of Presbyterian settlement, the rural revival affected entire communities, and was accompanied by prolonged prayer meetings, dramatic conversions, and a decline of heavy drinking, gambling, disorder and crime.

The revival reached the towns of Coleraine, Derry and Belfast early in June. In the urban areas, the revival became more multidenominational, with Methodists, Baptists, Congregationalists and members of the Church of Ireland joining the Presbyterians in holding 'union' prayer meetings. In Belfast, a mass meeting was held in the Botanical Gardens on 29 June, attracting an estimated 35,000 – many of them brought into the city from outlying districts on special trains. A second mass meeting in the Gardens in August attracted 20,000, while a meeting in Armagh in September also attracted 20,000. Along with these 'monster' meetings, there were numerous smaller neighbourhood gatherings. The Ulster revival attracted international attention, and during the summer, a number of celebrated preachers made their way to Ulster, including the American Methodist lay preachers, Phoebe and Walter Palmer, and the 'gentleman' lay preacher, Brownlow North. These preachers employed methods that had been developed among revivalists in the United States, including prolonged meetings, direct conversionist preaching, the use of emotional gospel songs, gentle calls for the unconverted to come forward, and special meetings for the 'anxious inquirers'.

The revival was also characterised by lay activism. Throughout much of the province, there was a multiplication of prayer meetings, organised mainly by lay men and women, and held in houses, barns or schoolhouses. With the coming of the revival to Connor, in county Antrim, the local minister reported that over 100 separate prayer meetings were held regularly in the parish, all of them conducted by lay members.[2] The prayer meetings enabled lay people to proclaim publicly their religious beliefs, and farmers, millworkers and housewives often emerged as powerful lay preachers. In a Presbyterian religious culture that had placed great stress on the authority of the ordained clergy, the prayer meetings and lay preaching were liberating experiences. 'For the first time in the history of Ulster Presbyterianism', noted one historian, 'laymen became prominent as preachers'.[3]

A notable feature of the Ulster revival was the prevalence of the 'physical manifestations'. These included a variety of phenomena – prostrations, convulsions, bodily rigidity, uncontrollable weeping or trembling, unnatural utterances, temporary blindness or deafness, trances and visions. The manifestations appeared with the beginning of the revival in Ahoghill and continued throughout the course of the movement. Defenders of the revival often played down the importance of the phenomena, claiming that only a minority of the converts – perhaps only one in ten – experienced the manifestations. None the less, hundreds did so. After one outdoor meeting in county Antrim, an observer noted that 'the lawn was literally strewed like a battlefield with those that were stricken down in this mysterious manner'.[4] Such manifestations appeared almost exclusively among the lower social orders. Young unmarried female millworkers were particularly susceptible – perhaps, as Peter Gibbon has suggested, because of their vulnerable position in society and their diminished prospects of marriage and a family, at a time when young men were emigrating in large numbers from the province.[5] Most physical manifestations were probably the result of extreme emotion, combined with the physical pressure of crowds or the overheating of halls. There was also an element of sympathy with those experiencing the signs and a desire to share their experience; many came to view the manifestations as a symbol of group belonging. 'I have seen', observed a Church of Ireland minister, '[affected] females rush forward to kiss each other. They express the greatest delight when their friends are visited in the same way, and frequently pray for them that they may have an attack'.[6] Some of those experiencing the manifestations claimed to have received prophetic powers, and these powers brought them new status and respect within their communities.

The physical manifestations attracted considerable interest from the newspapers and the scientific establishment, as well as from the curious. In keeping with the growing scientific spirit of enquiry in mid-Victorian Britain, newspaper reporters, physicians, clergymen, students of religion and religious sightseers made their way to the revival scenes in Ulster to observe the phenomena at first hand. Individuals who had been struck down or who claimed prophetic gifts were often repeatedly visited by these 'scientific' observers and encouraged to describe their prostrations or visions. They were also frequently paid for their trouble, which could, of course, encourage fraudulent claims. In September 1859, a Scottish religious periodical described the procession of British spiritual tourists along the now well-trodden route from Belfast to Ballymena and Coleraine:

In each town or village they procure a list of converts there, and make the round of them, regarding them with a curiosity such as might be evinced at the sight of some singular phenomenon – Tom Thumb, for example, or the Siamese Twins. Having exhausted their last list, they return to report what they have seen and heard to their expectant friends at home.[7]

There was soon a considerable public controversy over the manifestations. For sympathisers, they demonstrated the working of the Holy Spirit upon sinful human nature. Such phenomena, they observed, had been part of the Christian experience since Paul was struck down and temporarily blinded on the road to Damascus. For sceptics, the phenomena were physical reactions to conditions of extreme emotional stress, and if unchecked would lead to 'hysteria' and other forms of mental derangement.

The Ulster revival drew to a close in the early months of 1860. There were by now claims of 100,000 converts across the province, and the Presbyterian Church in Ireland added 10,696 new communicants to its rolls during what it termed 'the Year of Grace'. The revival gave a new confidence to the Ulster Protestants, and especially the Presbyterians, who could now perceive of themselves as an integral part of a larger trans-Atlantic evangelical Protestant culture. It promoted more emotional forms of piety, including gospel songs, prayer meetings and conversionist preaching, and it gave an enhanced role to the laity. There was less focus on doctrinal orthodoxy, and more on religious experience and feeling. There had not, to be sure, been many converts among the Roman Catholics, but there had not been much effort to evangelise among them. Unlike the previous 'New Reformation' campaigns, the revival had been mainly concerned with strengthening Protestant, and especially Presbyterian, identity.

The revival in Scotland and Wales

The revival movement in the United States, meanwhile, had also aroused considerable interest in Scotland, where many began praying for a similar outpouring of the Spirit. After months of expectation, a revival began in the city of Aberdeen in November 1858 (four months before the outbreak in Ulster). Over the next three years, there were instances of religious revival across much of the country, in what became arguably Scotland's first *national* revival movement. At the meeting of the General Assembly of the Free Church in May 1861, no fewer than 42 of the 66 Free Church presbyteries reported a 'decided awakening and revival' within their boundaries, while the remaining ones all reported heightened excitement. 'The revival', concluded the convener of the Free Church Religion and Morals Committee, 'with which God has been pleased to bless us, extends over the length and breadth of the land'. 'The general aspect of the town and country', he added, 'is morally and spiritually changed – absolutely revolutionised'.[8] The revival came to a nation that was experiencing rapid industrialisation and urbanisation, including the formation of an urban working class that was drifting away from regular church attendance. It also came to a Scotland that was deeply divided ecclesiastically, with three main Presbyterian denominations, a number of smaller Protestant denominations and the Roman Catholic Church competing for influence and showing precious little Christian charity towards one another.

The denomination most active in promoting the revival in Scotland was the Free Church – formed at the Disruption of 1843. With several hundred churches and schools, the Free Church provided pastoral care across most of Scotland. It was, on the whole, conservative in theology, firmly committed to the maintenance of the Westminster Confession. For many in the Free Church, the revival of 1859 promised to renew the spiritual fervour of 1843 and restore the hopes of Chalmers and the Disruption Fathers that Scotland would become a godly commonwealth, a harmonious Protestant society in which individuals and social classes would be united by shared religious beliefs and moral values. The established Church of Scotland was less prominent in the movement, though its General Assembly did give a guarded welcome to the revival and some congregations and ministers took an active role.

The revival movement in Scotland was characterised by local diversity. As Kenneth Jeffrey has observed, there were three main types of revival activity.[9] In the cities and large towns, including Aberdeen, Glasgow, Edinburgh and Dundee, the revival centred on prolonged prayer meetings, which often continued for several hours or more. These urban revivals also made use of the new methods developed in North America, including direct and emotional preaching, the use of lively gospel songs, prayers for individual sinners, and special gatherings for anxious inquirers. A number of professional revivalists made their way to the Scottish cities, among them the celebrated American proponent of new method revivalism, Charles G. Finney. The second type of revival occurred in the inland rural districts. These revivals normally centred upon an existing congregation, usually a Free Church congregation. They frequently began at the celebration of communion, which in rural congregations normally took place twice a year and involved four or five days of prayer, examination and preaching. These rural revivals were generally led by the local ministers and elders, and physical manifestations were discouraged. The converted were usually nominal church members, and the spread of conversions was often assisted by the existence of extended kinship groups – with cousins and other relatives 'catching' the revival from one another. There were some mass revival meetings in the rural districts, such as the meeting among the miners at Dreghorn, in Ayrshire, which was reported to have attracted 15,000.[10] However, such 'monster' meetings were rare in the countryside.

A third type of revival centred on the fishing villages of the eastern coast, especially the Moray Firth and the districts around Eyemouth in the southeast. These revivals were largely led by the laity, and included the proliferation of impromptu prayer meetings and prolonged revival meetings led by lay preachers, among them James Turner, a converted fisherman, and Duncan Matheson, a former stonemason and former missionary to the soldiers outside Sevastopol during the Crimean War. These men proclaimed a simple gospel message in direct, homespun language. 'In most of the villages that stud the Banffshire coast', noted one observer, 'a stranger in those days had but to signify his willingness to preach the gospel, when suddenly, as if by magic, the whole population, men, women and children, would assemble to hear the Word of God'.[11] The revivals in the fishing communities were characterised by intense emotion and physical manifestations. The intensity may have reflected the dangers of the seafaring life, with the North Sea claiming hundreds of lives each year and the fishing villages filled with the widows and orphans of fishermen. Indeed, revivals sometimes followed losses at sea. At Footdee, a fishing

village near Aberdeen, the drowning of four men in January 1860 left
15 children orphaned and the community in considerable distress. Shortly
after, the whole village was caught up in a revival.[12]

The revival movement continued in Scotland through most of 1862,
and had a lasting impact on Scottish religion. Nearly all the denominations
of Scotland registered increases in membership, while united prayer meetings contributed to a lessening of denominational warfare. The revival
brought an increased element of emotion to Scottish religion. This included
a taste for hymns and gospel songs, and for direct conversionist preaching,
aimed at securing a personal decision for Christ. There was also an
increased emphasis on lay leadership in religion. The denomination in
Scotland that experienced the largest growth during the 1859 revival were
the Brethren, with their pre-millenarian teachings and their rejection of
an ordained clergy.[13] Mission churches or stations, often organised by lay
converts and independent of any denomination, began appearing in the
working-class neighbourhoods of Scottish towns and villages, offering
informal, rousing services, which people could attend in their working
clothes.[14] Carrubber's Close Mission in Edinburgh's Old Town was one
such product of the revival.

In Wales the revival had its initial stirrings well before the coming of
news of the American revival, but the reports from America served to
transform those stirrings into what would become known as the 'Great
Revival', a movement which spread rapidly through the principality and
claimed to add 80,000 new church members out of a Welsh population of
about a million.[15] In the later 1850s Wales was, as we have seen, overwhelmingly Nonconformist, with about four-fifths of the churchgoing
population attending Dissenting chapels. Their identity was defined by
chapel life, including Sunday schools, temperance societies, and congregational singing. However, perhaps half the Welsh population, especially in
the mining and industrial districts in mid- and south Wales, did not attend
church regularly, and there was concern that rapid industrialisation in the
south and the commercialisation of agriculture in the north were weakening Welsh piety and chapel culture.

The leading figure in the Welsh revival was Humphrey Jones, an
eloquent, gifted, but emotionally unstable young Calvinistic Methodist
preacher, who returned to his native county of Cardiganshire in September
1858, after four years as a minister in the United States. Jones had been
active in the North American revival, and he brought with him its
methods, especially the united prayer meeting. Linking up with a fiery
Calvinistic Methodist preacher, David Morgan, Jones helped to initiate a

revival movement in Cardiganshire which claimed thousands of converts during the winter of 1858–59. From Cardiganshire, the revival spread. Revival preaching, nearly always in the Welsh language, placed emphasis on the fires of hell and the coming judgement, and the dangers of being at ease in Zion. The movement had particular impact within the coal, slate, lead and iron mining communities, where men were drawn together by their need to rely upon one another in dangerous work, and where people lived in constant fear of deaths through mining accidents. Revivals in these districts included prayer meetings underground in the mines and frequent physical manifestations. For example, virtually all 200 workers at the Frongoch lead mines in Cardiganshire embraced the revival, and turned their work-breaks into prayer meetings. The revivals in the mines were encouraged by some mine owners, who were themselves practising Nonconformists, and who probably believed that a converted labour force would be less prone to strike action.[16] While there was some involvement by members of the established church, the movement was overwhelmingly dominated by Nonconformists, especially Calvinistic Methodists.

Humphrey Jones's role in the revival came to an abrupt end in June 1859 in Aberystwyth. He had been preaching once or more daily since the previous November, and was now showing signs of nervous exhaustion. One day, he announced in chapel that the Holy Spirit would descend in a visible form at 11 am in a few days' time. On that day, a vast crowd gathered in the chapel. The hour came, Jones kept exclaiming that 'He is coming', but nothing happened. The crowd grew impatient, and Jones broke into tears and fled the scene. His role in the revival now ended and he subsequently returned to America.[17] The movement, however, continued for several months more, renewing and strengthening the hold of Nonconformity in Welsh society.

The revival in England

The revival in England was closely connected with the work of professional revivalists, many of whom had direct experience with the American revival methods. They included the powerful Irish-born American Methodist revivalist preacher, James Caughey, whose emotional style of preaching had aroused great controversy during his visit in the 1840s. Tall, cadaverous and dark complexioned, Caughey added to his dramatic appearance with a sweeping, long black cloak. He returned to England in July 1857, and conducted a revival campaign in 1858–59 in Sheffield and the Midlands, claiming 8,000 converts before his return to America in the summer of 1859. The veteran American revivalist, Charles G. Finney, arrived in England in December 1858. Now 66-years-old, he no longer had the old energy, and his meetings in the north of England and Scotland did not have much success. Then in Bolton, between December 1859 and April 1860, Finney recaptured some of the old magic, and his meetings there claimed some 1,200 converts.

In June 1859, two American lay Methodist evangelists, Phoebe and Walter Palmer, arrived in Britain. Walter Palmer was a successful New York physician; his wife Phoebe, the daughter of a Yorkshire Methodist, was the leading proponent of the doctrine of Christian 'perfection' or 'holiness'. This was perceived as a divine state of perfect love, and a gift from God, in which the Christian was elevated above all sinful desires. The Palmers' meetings were carefully structured, with gentle gospel music, frequent prayer, a Bible reading and interpretation given by Walter, and a sermon by a local minister. The high point of each meeting, however, came when Phoebe Palmer would walk modestly to the communion rail to talk directly to the congregation in her calm and musical voice about the individual's duty to seek holiness. They were 'to lay their all upon the altar' and then to have faith that God would accept and sanctify their offering – bringing them to a second conversion and a state of Christian perfection. To avoid controversy with those opposed to women preaching, her supporters would insist that she was not preaching, but simply giving a heartfelt talk. When she had finished, the congregation would sing hymns, while Walter gently invited those anxious about their souls to come forward and give their names, for follow-up visits by mission workers. It all had a powerful effect, and the Palmers remained in Britain until 1864, planting their holiness teachings within British evangelicalism.

There were also native revivalists who took a prominent role in the English revival. They included Reginald Radcliffe, a lay preacher and tract-seller with a loose connection to the Church of England, and Brownlow North, a gentleman of independent means who had experienced conversion following what he claimed had been years of hedonism and vice. Both Radcliffe and North had participated in the Scottish revival, before coming to London in December 1859. They were joined by Richard Weaver, a former coal miner and prize-fighter from Shropshire, who had been converted after years of hard drinking and fighting. He revelled in his status as a lay preacher. 'You see on the bills', Weaver would tell his revival congregations, 'I'm called the converted collier: that's better than Reverend'. Or again, 'I have not been ordained; no Bishop's hand has been on my head: but I have got the Blood upon me'.[18]

Still another leading evangelist of the English revival was the New Connexion Methodist preacher, William Booth, a largely self-taught former apprentice pawnbroker, who had begun lay preaching to the poor of Nottingham in 1848, at the age of 17. With a simple message of salvation through Christ's blood, Booth proved highly effective as an itinerant preacher among the unwashed poor. In 1860, his intelligent and energetic wife, Catherine, embraced both the holiness teachings of Phoebe Palmer and the belief that women, no less than men, could be called by the Spirit to preach. Catherine defended Phoebe Palmer's vocation to preach in a powerful pamphlet, and then, in 1860 she began preaching herself at revival meetings. Her husband supported her calling, and she emerged as a highly effective preacher who was soon in great demand. In 1861, the Booths left the Methodist New Connexion in order to have greater freedom as revivalist preachers, and in 1862 they founded the 'Christian Society' to support their evangelical mission among the destitute in London's East End, holding emotional meetings in rented rooms, struggling to meet expenses, gaining converts with their simple gospel message, and gathering a team of devoted supporters. From the beginning, the Booths' Christian Society gave women active roles as evangelists and administrators.

The revival also contributed to the fame of a young Baptist preacher who had already established himself as a leading London evangelist. Charles Haddon Spurgeon was born in 1834 in Essex, the son of a Congregational minister. Converted at the age of 15, he had gained local notoriety as the 'boy preacher of Cambridgeshire'. Invited to become pastor of a small Baptist congregation in London in 1853, he experienced a meteoric rise to fame as a preacher, winning a huge lower middle-class and working-class following. During the revival years, Spurgeon preached regularly to gatherings of 10,000 in the Music Hall, Surrey Gardens, while his supporters raised money to build a suitably large church for him in south London. Opened in 1861, at a cost of £31,000, the Metropolitan Chapel was a massive preaching hall, in the form of a round domed amphitheatre, with semicircular tiers designed to accommodate a congregation of 5,000 people. For the next 30 years, Spurgeon would preach here twice each Sunday to a packed house – it was said to be the largest congregation in the world. He became a London celebrity, and his services were one of the tourist attractions of the capital. His was essentially the old gospel message of sin, eternal punishment, redemption through the blood of Christ, and the perseverance of the redeemed through the travails of the world – which he proclaimed in direct, simple, businesslike, vigorous and natural language, making abundant use of humour and wit, as well as pathos, to captivate his hearers. It was a message that inspired urban dwellers struggling to maintain respectability in an unforgiving social and economic environment. 'Mr. Spurgeon', observed one admirer, 'always made salvation a wonderful, a supernatural thing – won through battle and agony and garments rolled in blood'. It was a precious gift to offer to those who otherwise 'had missed all the prizes of life'.[19] A large, rotund man with the appearance of a successful Victorian businessman, he declined to wear a clerical gown, and enjoyed cigars and a good meal. His Metropolitan Chapel included a preachers' college, at which over 1,000 preachers were trained under Spurgeon's influence.[20]

The revival in England did not have the same mass impact that it had in Northern Ireland, Scotland and Wales. This was in large part, as John Kent has argued, because of serious division within English evangelical circles over the revival movement, and especially over the role of the professional revivalists. Many English evangelicals were put off by the physical manifestations; others were unhappy with the coarse language of such revivalists as the former boxer, Richard Weaver, with their emphasis on instantaneous conversion and their lack of respect for the ordained clergy. None the less, despite much opposition, the English revival added significantly to the number of professed Christians, especially among the working classes. It helped the Nonconformist churches to recover their numbers after their unhappy divisions of the late 1840s and early 1850s. The revival also went some way towards diminishing the alienation of the working classes from Christianity that had raised such concern in Horace Mann's report on the 1851 religious census. While many of those working men and women converted during the revival would later lapse from regular attendance, they would often retain their Christian beliefs, remember the gospel songs, and ensure their children attended Sunday school.

A significant aspect of the revival movement was the marked role taken by women – including the appearance of a number of effective women preachers. One of the early 'manifestations' of the Ulster revival was the manner in which women would often lead public prayer at the prayer meetings. As the movement spread through Ulster and Britain, there was a sense that something extraordinary was shaking the Christian world, and that old conventions concerning women's subordinate role in public worship were being overruled by the Holy Spirit. Women preachers and prophets, as we have observed, had been prominent during the spread of evangelical Dissent in the 1790s and early 1800s. But they had been largely silenced by the 1820s. Then, beginning about 1860, women began preaching with considerable impact at revival services. Olive Anderson has identified about 40 women preachers in the mid-Victorian years, and there were undoubtedly more.[21] They included, as we have seen, the American revivalist, Phoebe Palmer, and the Methodist revivalist, Catherine Booth. There was also Jessie MacFarlane, a Scottish Presbyterian, who began preaching in Edinburgh in 1862 under the encouragement of the Plymouth Brethren; Isobel Armstrong, an Ulster woman converted in 1859, who began preaching in the west of Scotland in 1863; and Geraldine Hooper, an English Anglican, who was lauded in the press as the 'female Spurgeon' and who had an ability to control the largest and most unruly of meetings. These women came from the middle classes, dressed with decorum and were in some cases married with children. They generally directed their appeal to the emotions and their preaching reflected the mid-Victorian stereotypes of feminine tenderness and selfless devotion to family and the home. But these women were also preaching in public and exercising religious leadership. As the fires of revival cooled in the mid-1860s, many meeting houses, mission halls and churches were again closed to women. But a precedent had been established of middle-class women speaking in public and taking leadership roles. Moreover, within one group, the 'Christian Mission' of William and Catherine Booth, the practice of female preaching continued.[22]

Questioning the faith

'What is boasted of at the present time as the revival of religion', wrote the philosopher and political economist, John Stuart Mill, in 1859, 'is always, in narrow and uncultivated minds, at least as much the revival of bigotry.' Such minds, he added, were intolerant by nature, and 'it needs but little to provoke them into actively persecuting those whom they have never ceased to think proper objects of persecution.'[23] In Britain, many were unhappy with the revival movement. They looked disdainfully on the revivalist preachers, with their simple old-fashioned gospel and their eager, semi-literate converts. They viewed the revival as a threat to individual freedom, including the freedom not to believe Christian teachings and not to attend church. And some went further and viewed the revivalists not only as vulgar and bigoted, but also as deluded fanatics, whose gospel of salvation through the blood of Christ was a fiction.

During the 1840s and 1850s, a number of otherwise 'respectable' people in Britain had begun openly professing non-belief in many of the basic doctrines of orthodox Christianity. They rejected the faith in which they had been raised and withdrew themselves from the Christian communion. They experienced what has become known as 'the Victorian crisis of faith'. This growth of unbelief, certainly, was not without precedent. The natural religion of the eighteenth-century, for example, had ignored or down-played certain fundamental doctrines of Christianity, including the Trinity and the atonement, in an effort to emphasise the essentials of religious faith. Early nineteenth-century Radicals, such as Jeremy Bentham, James Mill or Richard Carlile, had made non-belief a part of their assault upon the established churches and the Christian foundations of the monarchy. There was, however, something unprecedented about the scope of the Victorian crisis of faith, which was not connected to any particular philo-sophical movement or political ideology, and which included a number of strands of unbelief. From about 1840, many influential thinkers from respectable middle- and upper-class backgrounds were rejecting Christianity. They included the novelist, Mary Ann Evans (George Eliot), who renounced her evangelical Christian faith in about 1840; the philo-sopher, Herbert Spencer, who lost his faith during the 1840s; the man of letters and former Tractarian, James Anthony Froude, who published an autobiographical novel about his loss of belief, *The Nemesis of Faith*, in 1849; the poet, Arthur Clough, who resigned his Oxford fellowship because of his loss of faith in 1849; Francis Newman, the brother of the celebrated Oxford convert, whose autobiographical *Phases of Faith*, an account of his loss of Christian faith, appeared in 1850; the former Tractarian and Oxford historian of ideas, Mark Pattison, who struggled to hold his faith but in the 1860s felt it drop off him like 'a husk which I had outgrown';[24] or the art historian and critic, John Ruskin, who had dis-covered suddenly in 1858 that he now longer believed in Christianity.

These were earnest people, who did not view their rejection of Christianity as in any way frivolous or immoral. For them, the greatest virtue was the pursuit of truth, and they felt compelled to be honest and open about their religious doubts. These 'honest doubters' had usually held a sincere Christian faith in their youth, and most found the process of losing their religion to be a painful experience, which often led to agonised breaks with family and friends. The causes for the loss of Christian faith varied, and were intensely personal for each individual. Some were influenced by ethical concerns about Christianity. They had found it difficult to reconcile their moral sense with certain passages in Scripture, especially the massacres and slavery in the Old Testament, or with the doc-trine that a wrathful God had demanded the sacrifice of the innocent Christ to atone for the sins of the guilty. Some embraced a faith in progress in this world, and were unable to accept the Christian view of the world as steeped in sin and evil.[25] Some were influenced by the biblical and historical scholarship emanating from the Continental, and especially the German, universities. The so-called 'higher criticism' represented the effort to discover, through careful scholarship, the dates and historical context – social, political, cultural – in which the books of the Old and New Testaments had been written, and to identify the authorship. In the later eighteenth and early nineteenth centuries, German scholars, including J. G. Herder, W. de Wette, and J. G. Eichhorn, had made great strides toward understanding the context and content of the Scriptures. However, in the process they also raised awkward questions about the inspiration of the Scriptural authors and the historical truth of the Scriptural accounts. The fruits of this biblical scholarship were becoming known among educated people in Britain during the 1840s and 1850s, and for some individuals this undermined their belief in the inspiration of Scripture.

Along with the new biblical scholarship was a growing knowledge, through the imperial experience, of other world faiths, including a recognition that Christians formed only a minority of the world's population. Was it to be believed that God elected particular peoples for His special favour, whether the ancient Hebrews, or, as some would now have it, the British people? Was it really to be believed that a just God would relegate such a vast proportion of the world's population to eternal damnation, for not having professed their faith in Christ? There were also growing moral doubts about the existence of hell as a place of eternal punishment. This was the case even among many Christians. In 1853, the liberal Anglican and Christian Socialist, F. D. Maurice, had been dismissed from his chair at King's College, London, for publicly questioning the doctrine of eternal punishment for sinners and non-believers. Honest doubters could not accept that a God who was just and good could impose eternal torment upon any creature. 'I will call no being good', John Stuart Mill wrote in 1865, 'who is not what I mean when I apply that epithet to my fellow creatures; and if such a being can sentence me to Hell for not so calling him, to Hell I will go'.[26]

The 1840s and 1850s also brought new interpretations of geology and the natural sciences which challenged the truth of the Genesis narrative of creation. There was a movement away from belief in a fixed and harmonious natural order, and towards the vision of a nature that underwent continued change and evolution. The 'testimony of the rocks', as it was conveyed in the numerous editions of Sir Charles Lyell's seminal text, *Principles of Geology* (first published 1830–33), demonstrated that the world was millions of years old, far older than had been indicated in Genesis, and that it had been subject to continual changes. Lyell's geological evidence discredited the idea of a universal flood; indeed, after the publication of his great work the number of natural philosophers who referred to the catastrophic events in Genesis to explain geological formations rapidly declined.[27] As well as the fascination with geology, there was also growing interest in the variations in the species of plants and animals, and how those variations had come to be. In 1826, the Edinburgh professor of natural history, Robert Jameson, concluded a course of lectures with a discussion of the 'Origin of Species'. During the 1820s and 1830s, some scholars of comparative anatomy, among them Robert Grant and Hewett Watson of Edinburgh, came to reject the orthodox Christian notion of a single creation and to suggest instead the progressive transformation of the species. Grant, who moved south in 1827 to become the first professor of comparative anatomy at the newly formed London University, did much to undermine confidence in providential design in the scientific world, and to promote ideas of the self-generated 'metamorphoses', or evolution, of life forms under the influence of long-term climate change.[28] In his lectures published in 1855, the Scottish anatomist John Knox insisted that this was 'a self-created, self-creating world – ever alive, never decaying, never old'.[29]

In 1859, Charles Darwin – a naturalist of independent means who had explored the fauna and animal life of South America on a government-sponsored expedition in the early 1830s – published his celebrated *The Origin of Species*. Darwin's achievement was to describe, with a wealth of supporting evidence, a plausible process by which evolution could have occurred. This process involved mutation and natural selection. Out of the millions of new plants or animals being continually produced each year, some experienced mutations. Most of these mutations left the individual creature weakened and less able to survive. Such creatures perished without reproducing, and left no trace. But some mutations made the plant or animal better able to compete for nourishment and safety. These life forms reached maturity and reproduced, passing their mutation on to their offspring. Nature, in Darwin's conception, was brutal. With far more new creatures born into the world than could be supported by nature's resources, the world was a place of continual struggle, in which only the strongest survived. It was this grim struggle for existence that drove the process of natural selection, and ensured that some mutations were passed on and preserved. When the actions of mutation and natural selection were repeated over millions of years, they produced variations that accounted for the existing species in all their manifold diversity.

Darwin's *Origin* was an immediate best-seller and found rapid accept-ance within the scientific community and among much of the educated public. While Darwin had avoided any mention of humankind in *Origin*, it was not long before his supporters began applying his theory to humans, and suggesting that humankind was also part of the evolutionary process. A few years earlier, in 1856, the German palaeontologist, Hermann Schaaffhausen, had discovered an ancient skull in the valley of the Neander. Although identifiably human, the skull also had a shallow brain cavity and heavy ridges over the eye sockets, suggesting an ape-like appear-ance. The appearance of Darwin's *Origin* now offered an explanation for this skull; the 'Neanderthal man' might be a link in the evolution of humans from the ape. In February 1862, the anatomist, T. H. Huxley, offered a series of lectures on 'The Relation of Man to the Rest of the Animal Kingdom', which attracted a large and enthusiastic audience, with their message that humans had evolved from lower life forms. 'By next Friday', he joked to his wife, 'they will all be convinced that they are mon-keys'. Huxley's *Evidence of Man's Place in Nature* appeared in January 1863, and found a large readership.[30]

And if humankind had evolved through a series of stages, what of the present-day division of races? In 1864, the natural philosopher Alfred Wallace presented a paper entitled 'The Origin of Human Races and the Antiquity of Man deduced from the Theory of "Natural Selection"' to the recently founded Anthropological Society of London, arguing that the dif-ferent races had evolved through the process of natural selection, by which certain characteristics, physical and mental, rendered some racial groups more successful in the constant struggle of tribe against tribe, race against race.[31] By the mid-1860s, anthropologists were beginning to categorise races according to an evolutionary hierarchy, and speaking of lesser or more primitive races. This type of thinking would be taken up by social commentators, with tragic results, and become known as 'social Darwinism'. Anthropologists were also undermining the divine claims of Christianity, by suggesting that theistic belief and religious doctrines of 'sacrifice' and 'atonement' had their origins in the fears and 'fetishes' of primitive man. E. B. Tylor, who would become the first professor of anthropology at Oxford, published two seminal works, *The Early History of Mankind* (1865) and *Primitive Culture* (1871), in which he portrayed religious ritu-als, folklore and superstition in modern society as 'survivals' of the beliefs of our primitive ancestors. The implication was that as humans continued to evolve, their religious urges would fade away, like vestiges of organs in evolving life forms, as those vestiges were no longer functional.[32]

The new evolutionary ideas challenged traditional Christian teachings both about the natural world as reflecting a divine purpose and about humans as uniquely created in the image of God. They challenged notions of providential design and chosen peoples. Despite some beautiful passages in *Origin* about evolution reflecting the divine wisdom of the creator, Darwin's book revealed a natural order evolving through a series of random and accidental mutations that had no apparent purpose or ethical grounding. Further, human society was part of this blind and purposeless evolutionary process, and had no special place in the universe. As the high church bishop of Oxford, Samuel Wilberforce, summed up Darwin's theory in the *Quarterly Review* in 1860: 'Man, beast, creeping thing, and plant of the earth, are all the lineal and direct descendants of some one individual *ens* [entity]'.[33] Wilberforce, who had maintained an interest in natural philosophy alongside his busy clerical work, now emerged as the leading clerical critic of Darwinism, providing a reasoned assault in the *Quarterly* on the evidence for Darwin's theory. In June 1860, he continued his assault on Darwin's theory at the annual meeting of the British Association for the Advancement of Science in Oxford. However, on this occasion he allowed himself to use flippant language about the Darwinians and their claims of human evolution from the ape, which earned him a sharp and well-deserved rebuke from T. H. Huxley, who chastised him for using mocking rhetoric rather than reasoned argument in a serious scientific forum. In truth, as Frank Turner has argued, science was now emerging as a distinct 'profession', with its own experimental methods, systems of peer review, sources of funding and patterns of career progression, and scientists had little patience with clergymen, like Wilberforce, who sought to intrude their version of truth, based on Scriptural authority, into scientific discussions.[34] As relatively few clergymen had the time or the training to keep up with the latest scientific literature, they were increasingly marginalised from serious investigations of the natural world.

Educated people in mid-Victorian Britain began seeking truth less in sacred texts and more and more in the scientific method and the free interchange of ideas. In 1859, the year that Darwin's *Origin* was published, another, no less revolutionary work appeared – John Stuart Mill's essay *On Liberty*. Mill was in many respects an oddity in Britain. Raised according to the plan of his father, James Mill, and his father's friend, Jeremy Bentham – both leading philosophic Radicals – Mill had from earliest childhood believed that Christianity was false, and this had placed him outside the mainstream of British society. His *On Liberty* was an extended essay on the benefits of toleration, including toleration for non-believers.

In it, Mill insisted that society advanced in knowledge through the free exchange of ideas. It was in this free market-place of ideas that the truth of some ideas was demonstrated and the falsehood of others exposed. Social progress was an incremental process, achieved through the competition of ideas, and it therefore followed that each individual should have the maximum freedom of speech and action, so long as they did no harm to others. The similarities of Mill's *On Liberty* with Darwin's *Origin*, and indeed with *laissez faire* economics, were clear. Society was in a constant state of change and development, and new ideas emerged and flourished through a version of 'natural selection' within a competitive natural environment or free market-place. There was, moreover, for many people, no longer any clear providential purpose in this constant change, no certainty of where social and intellectual change was leading.

Within the established Church of England, with its claims to represent the spiritual aspect of national life, there was consternation over the widening gap between orthodox Christianity and these intellectual developments. The two main parties within the church – the High Church party and the Evangelical party – both seemed powerless to bridge this gap. The High Church party was firmly committed to the absolute authority of both the ancient apostolic church and of the Bible. The Evangelical, or Low Church party (as it was becoming known), while less committed to the authority of the church, was zealous in defence of the authority of Scripture as the infallible word of God. Both ecclesiastical parties were appalled by the sceptical spirit of the higher criticism, by the ethical questioning of Christian doctrines, by the rejection of eternal punishment (which seemed to threaten the foundations of morality), by the new developments in natural science, and by the calls for unrestricted intellectual freedom. Despite their differences on some issues, the High and Low Church parties shared a consensus that Scriptural authority was absolute, and that there could be no dialogue with those who rejected this authority.

In the 1840s and 1850s, some more liberal adherents of the Church of England sought to preserve the influence of Christianity by promoting a spirit of greater accommodation with the intellectual movements of the times. The church no longer had the power to silence sceptics and unbelievers, and simply to ignore the new scientific and ethical thought, or to hurl epithets at it, could leave it appearing out of touch, or even ridiculous. Far better would be to promote dialogue, in the hope of finding common ground between Christianity and the new thought. Those liberal Anglicans who took this view became known as the 'broad church' movement – the name given them by W. J. Conybeare in an influential article on 'Church Parties' that appeared in the *Edinburgh Review* in 1853. The broad church movement was never a party in the sense of being a unified body pursuing a defined set of objectives; rather, as one historian described it, broad church referred to 'a tendency of mind common to assorted individuals or small groups'.[35]

The nineteenth-century broad church movement had its roots in eighteenth-century latitudinarianism and in the liberal Anglican thought of Samuel Taylor Coleridge and Thomas Arnold and their efforts in the 1820s and 1830s to revive the ideal of an inclusive national church. Supporters of the broad church approach sought to shape a comprehensive Christianity, with emphasis on the essentials of the faith and especially the moral teachings of Christ. They wished to make the established church, in the words of Richard Shannon, once again 'co-extensive with the nation at large, liberal and comprehensive in doctrine, tolerant and inclusive in its formularies, rooted in the nation's past and expressive of its historic continuity'.[36] Such an inclusive national faith would play down the dogmatic aspects of Christianity. It would be open to the higher criticism of the Bible, and not insist on the infallibility of every passage or view Scripture as providing an accurate historical narrative. The truth of Christianity, they argued, did not depend upon Scripture as an exact record of events; rather, Christian truth was discerned through the poetry, parables, portraits and stories in Scripture. Broad churchmen believed that revelation was ongoing, and that as all truth was of God, there was no cause to fear new discoveries in history, anthropology or the natural sciences. By 1860, some broad churchmen believed that another 'Reformation' – to be based on the new understanding of Scripture and of an ongoing process of revelation – was approaching. 'That a second Reformation is in store for us', wrote the broad churchman, A. P. Stanley, to a friend in 1865, 'and that the various tendencies of the age are preparing the way for it, I cannot doubt, unless Christianity is doomed to suffer a portentous eclipse'.[37]

The broad church movement included among its adherents Connop Thirlwall, bishop of St David's in Wales, and Julius Charles Hare, who had both been active in introducing the fruits of German theology and biblical scholarship to Britain. It also included Benjamin Jowett, professor of Greek at Oxford University, whose contributions to biblical scholarship in the mid-1850s suggested that divine revelation had not been confined to the Jews and Christians, and thus that religion should be studied comparatively. One of the most prominent figures in the movement was A. P. Stanley, son of the bishop of Norwich and author of a best-selling biography of Thomas Arnold. Cultured, well-connected, well-travelled, humane and sensitive, Stanley became professor of ecclesiastical history at Oxford in 1856. A fluent rather than profound author, he promoted through his varied writings toleration and charity for those of different beliefs, and confidence in the moral progress of the human race. In Scotland, a similar broad church movement developed under the influence of Norman MacLeod, a burly, good humoured and pragmatic Church of Scotland minister in Glasgow who combined a liberal Reformed theology with a keen social commitment, John Tulloch, the learned and eloquent professor of ecclesiastical history at St Andrews University, and John Caird, a humane and cultivated Church of Scotland minister in Perthshire and later professor of divinity at Glasgow University. All three of these men were favourite preachers of Queen Victoria and Prince Albert, who now spent part of each year at their Highland estate at Balmoral. After Albert's untimely death in 1861, the queen turned largely to broad church leaders, especially Stanley, MacLeod and Tulloch, for consolation.

Essays and Reviews

In March 1858, three Anglican broad churchmen – Henry Bristow Wilson, Rowland Williams and Mark Pattison – met in London to plan a volume of essays that would express the broad church spirit of enquiry.[38] They recruited four more authors to join them in contributing to the volume, which appeared in April 1860 under the title *Essays and Reviews*. There was no editorial control, and each author was allowed complete freedom to develop his theme. Frederick Temple, headmaster of Rugby school, submitted a sermon in which he portrayed the progressive nature of revelation through history, and argued that in its present maturity, Christendom had advanced beyond the need of divine law or divine example in Scripture, and was now guided by the Holy Spirit as expressed through conscience and reason. Williams, of St David's College, Lampeter, wrote favourably of the German higher criticism. Baden Powell, professor of geometry at Oxford University, submitted an essay which rejected miracles as evidence for Christian truth. Wilson, an Anglican vicar, advocated a comprehensive national church, in which the clergy would have the maximum freedom to respond to new ideas. He denied that there could be no salvation outside the Christian faith, insisted that portions of the Bible should be viewed as myth, and questioned the doctrine of eternal punishment. C. W. Goodwin of Cambridge University, the only layman among the authors, wrote of how recent discoveries in geology and natural science undermined the literal truth of the creation story in Genesis. Mark Pattison of Lincoln College, Oxford, provided a pioneering essay on the theological debates in eighteenth-century England, in which he suggested that historical theology was another form of intellectual history and could be examined without reference to divine truth. Finally, in the last and longest essay in the volume, Benjamin Jowett wrote on the interpretation of Scripture, arguing that it should be studied with the same critical methods as any other form of literature. Taken as a whole, the essays formed a manifesto for the broad church movement. They were a call to the church to embrace the new critical approaches to Scripture and church history, to adapt its teachings to the developments in natural science, and to strive for less dogmatic, more ethical formulations of the ancient faith.

The volume aroused revulsion and outrage from the large majority of British Christians, most of whom never read it, but who none the less saw it as an attack on God and the church. In the months after its appearance, *Essays and Reviews* received hostile reviews from both Anglican and Nonconformist journals. Most reviewers were convinced that the volume would encourage doubt and infidelity, and that its authors were enemies of God who sought to subvert Christianity from within. *Essays and Reviews*, insisted the lead article in the evangelical Anglican *Record* of 21 May 1860, 'if unchallenged, will produce more evil than anything which has issued from the press for a long period . . . their direct and necessary tendency is to subvert all faith'.[39] The temperature was further raised in October 1860, with the appearance of an anonymous review – provocatively entitled 'Neo-Christianity' – in the Radical *Westminster Review*.[40] The author, Frederic Harrison, was a young barrister who had lost his Christian faith while a student at Oxford, and would go on to become one of the leading British proponents of a non-Christian positivist philosophy. Harrison opened his review by praising the volume as marking 'an epoch in the history of opinion'. Its seven authors, he insisted, wrestled courageously with the great questions confronting Christianity. They represented the best among church members, and he applauded their honest effort. And yet, he continued, although their aim had been to defend Christianity in the new intellectual climate, the effect of their volume had been just the opposite. Their work undermined the very foundations of Christianity. Instead of preserving the faith, their critical approach was simply dissolving the Christian faith for the simple believer, like the action of the sea on a crumbling cliff:

All the basis of his creed are undermined; the whole external authority on which it rests is swept away; the mysterious book of truth fades into an old collection of poetry and legend; and the scheme of Redemption in which he has been taught to live and die turns out to be a demoralizing invention of men.[41]

Harrison's review was widely read and discussed, and in turn greatly increased the sales of *Essays and Reviews*. At the same time, such a review was also a challenge to the church. How could it now not act against the subversive authors within its midst?

Yes, the Church of England had to act – both to demonstrate its continued commitment to its Scriptural and doctrinal beliefs and to show that it possessed the will to uphold its doctrinal standards. With the revival movement still running strong (and with many lay preachers criticising the clergy for being lukewarm towards the Bible and the old gospel), the church needed to show where it stood. The High Church and Evangelical parties were for once united in condemning *Essays and Reviews*. In December 1860, a group of Church of England clergymen organised a petition against the essayists, and during the next three months over 8,000 clergymen signed. Under pressure from their clergy, the Church of England bishops issued a pastoral letter in February 1861, affirming the church's belief both in the Bible as the infallible word of God and in everlasting punishment for the damned.

However, petitions and pastoral letters were not enough for some within the church: to demonstrate that it was really serious about its beliefs, surely there must be judicial proceedings, and severe punishment, for the offending authors. The church must show that it would not allow its clergy openly to flaunt their disbelief in teachings which they were bound by their ordination oaths to uphold. But disciplinary action against all the authors proved difficult. One of the authors, Baden Powell, died in 1860, and was thus removed 'to a higher tribunal'. Jowett, an Oxford professor, and Pattison, rector of an Oxford college, were both subject to academic discipline, and not to discipline by the bench of bishops. Temple was a royal chaplain, and therefore outside normal episcopal jurisdiction. Goodwin was a layman, and was no longer a college fellow, and thus was not subject to clerical discipline. All these legal complications were immensely frustrating, but could not be helped. In the event, it was possible to pursue disciplinary action within the ecclesiastical courts against only two of the essayists, Williams and Wilson, both of whom were clergymen holding pastoral livings. As it happened, they had also written the essays that caused greatest offence.

Formal charges were brought against both clergymen, and they were tried together in the Court of Arches (the court of the archbishop of

Canterbury) beginning in December 1861. The presiding judge, the learned octogenarian Stephen Lushington, delivered the judgment in June 1862. As Lushington explained, he was called not to judge the theological soundness of the two essayists' views, but merely whether they were at variance with the doctrines of the Church of England, as stated in its Articles and Formularies. On this basis, he dismissed a number of the charges against the two, but found that they had contravened some doctrines. In its final judgment, given in December 1862, the Court of Arches suspended Williams and Wilson for one year from their church livings, and imposed court costs on them. The orthodox, however, were outraged by both the moderate language of the judgment and the leniency of the sentences. Was this all that could be done against two clerics who had set themselves against Christ and His Church? For the orthodox, worse was to come, for Williams and Wilson immediately appealed against the Court of Arches judgment to the Judicial Committee of the Privy Council, the highest court of appeal in such cases. The result was a virtual repeat of the Gorham judgment of 1850. After a lengthy legal process, Lord Westbury delivered the judgment of the Judicial Committee in February 1864. Despite the presence of three bishops (all of whom dissented from the decision), the Judicial Committee found for the two essayists. Neither author, Westbury insisted, had explicitly denied that Scripture was the word of God, while it was nowhere stated in the church's Articles or Formularies that every part of the Bible was inspired by the Holy Spirit. As for the charge that Wilson had denied the doctrine of eternal punishment, Westbury noted that Wilson had simply expressed the humane hope that the punishment of the wicked would not be everlasting.

It was a victory for the essayists, though by now their broad church supporters were weary of the lengthy legal struggle and felt no sense of triumph. Within the Church of England as a whole, there was much bitterness. In late February 1864, a declaration of protest against the Judicial Committee decision, drafted by the veteran high churchman, E. B. Pusey, was circulated among the clergy of the established church in both England and Ireland: it gathered 11,200 signatures out of a total of 24,800 clergymen. A similarly worded lay protest gathered some 137,000 signatures. In June 1864, moreover, the Convocation of Canterbury issued a formal synodical condemnation of *Essays and Reviews*. It was clear that the decision of the Judicial Committee was opposed by probably the large majority within the Church of England. There were no secessions from the church, such as those that had followed the Gorham judgment 14 years earlier. There was, however, a gnawing sense of doubt, felt by many, about whether the benefits of establishment were worth the humiliation of being thus bound by the civil courts in matters of faith and discipline.

John William Colenso

While the conflict over *Essays and Reviews* was raging, a second controversy emerged over the writings on theology and biblical criticism by an Anglican bishop of a distant colonial bishopric. This was the case of John William Colenso, bishop of Natal.[42] Colenso was born in 1814, and grew up in poverty in Cornwall. Attending Cambridge University as a sizar (assisted student) and helping support himself by what he could earn by private teaching, prizes and exhibitions, he distinguished himself in mathematics, and was ordained priest in the Church of England. After some years of teaching mathematics at Harrow, he received a rural church living in Norwich. Here he came under the influence of the liberal theologian and Christian Socialist, F. D. Maurice. Colenso began questioning certain Christian teachings, including God's anger with sinful humanity and the eternal punishment of those who did not profess belief in Christ. At the same time, he began taking an active role in supporting Anglican overseas missions, editing reports of the Anglican Society for the Propagation of the Gospel. In 1853, just short of his 40 birthday, he was appointed by the crown to the newly formed colonial bishopric of Natal, in South Africa, on the recommendation of the high church bishop of Cape Town, Robert Gray, who had been impressed by Colenso's enthusiasm for overseas missions and was probably unaware of his unorthodox theological speculations.

In Natal, Colenso established a mission centre at Bishopstowe, outside the town of Pietermaritzburg – setting up a model farm and schools for agricultural and mechanical training. He learned the Zulu language and began translating the Bible with the help of Zulu assistants. An earnest, hard-working man, he was also something of a loner, with a highly-strung, prickly personality. He believed that his primary responsibility was to the Africans, and this served to alienate white settlers. His broad church views, moreover, brought him into conflict with many of his clergy. Even his former supporter, Bishop Gray, grew concerned. 'We . . . feel very anxious about the views and state of mind of the Bp. of Natal', Gray confided to Samuel Wilberforce in January 1861. 'He has a very strong will, and an able mind . . . which has already led him into speculations of the future state, and vicarious sacrifice, and Scripture which are I fear not in accordance with the Spirit of the Ch. of England's teaching'.[43] Later that year,

Colenso published a commentary on the Book of Romans, which was his attempt to express a missionary gospel. In this work, he denied that God felt anger towards sinful humanity, and insisted that all humankind had been redeemed by Christ's death and resurrection. To preach Christ to the heathens, he insisted, meant informing them of their redemption and of God's universal love; it was to proclaim a joyous gospel of liberation. This was too much for Bishop Gray of Cape Town, who referred the work to the archbishop of Canterbury for disciplinary proceedings. Then, in October 1862 – before the archbishop had taken any decision on *Romans* – there appeared in the English bookshops another work by Colenso, which many found far more subversive of the faith. This was part one of *The Pentateuch and Book of Joshua Critically Examined*.

It was a curious work of higher biblical criticism. According to Colenso's preface, the idea of writing the book came to him while he had been translating the Scriptures into Zulu. While translating the story of the flood, one of his Zulu assistants had apparently put to him the question, 'Is all that true? Do you really believe that all this happened thus?' Colenso, familiar with Lyell's work in geology, could not say that he believed in the universal flood.[44] In truth, he had been wrestling with doubts about the historical accuracy of the Old Testament for many years. He now felt compelled to express his views and he wrote *Pentateuch and Joshua* at considerable speed between January 1861 and April 1862. He had only a limited knowledge of the biblical scholarship in Britain and the Continent, and no access to key books in the field. His study was based largely on his powers of observation and reason. It was a work of negative criticism, which focused on the inconsistencies and improbabilities in the Old Testament narratives. Noting, for example, that the Book of Numbers states that the Israelites had 600,000 fighting men on leaving Egypt, Colenso calculated that this would have meant a total population (adding women, children, older men) of over 2,000,000, moving across the Sinai in a vast camp that would have occupied some 24 square miles. It was not difficult to demonstrate the absurdity of such a picture. Indeed, the whole work aimed at demolishing the idea that the early books of the Bible were an accurate historical record.

Such a work, appearing in the midst of the controversy over *Essays and Reviews*, was bound to stir ferment. The fact that the author was a bishop of the Church of England – a mere colonial bishop, to be sure, but a bishop none the less – added to the offence. As Edward Pusey observed to the bishop of London on 17 December 1862, 'Had he been *Mr.* Colenso still, his book would have been still-born. Now it is read by tens of thousands because he is a Bishop. It is his office of Bishop which propagates infidelity'.[45] Some less devout observers found something ludicrous in the picture of a bishop, sent out to convert the heathen, being himself converted to disbelief. A limerick was soon going the rounds:

> A bishop there was of Natal
> Who took a Zulu for a pal,
> Said the Kaffir, 'Look 'ere,
> Ain't the Pentateuch queer?'
> And converted My Lord of Natal.[46]

The English bishops were almost unanimously agreed that they must officially condemn the work. In February 1863, 41 of their number, English, Irish and colonial, signed a letter, drafted by Bishop Tait of London, advising Colenso to resign. A few months later, the Convocation of Canterbury adopted resolutions which declared Colenso's *Pentateuch* to be subversive of the faith. However, Convocation declined to take further action, as it understood Colenso's case would be brought before the ecclesiastical courts.

A trial, however, proved problematical. This was because of certain ambiguities in the nature of Colenso's appointment. Bishop Gray of Cape Town claimed to exercise metropolitan jurisdiction over all the bishops of southern Africa, including Colenso, and he now convened an ecclesiastical court of South African bishops to try Colenso for heresy. But Colenso insisted that Bishop Gray had no jurisdiction over him, and did not appear for the trial. The latter's ecclesiastical court then tried him in his absence and in December 1863 it deposed him as bishop of Natal on nine counts of heresy – while allowing him a four-month period in which to recant his errors. Colenso did not respond, and he was formally deposed. Colenso, meanwhile, had appealed to the crown against Bishop Gray's claims of authority over him. His case was heard by the Judicial Committee of the Privy Council, which in March 1865 ruled in Colenso's favour – deciding that the colonial bishop of Natal had been appointed by the crown and that only the crown could remove him. The sentence of Bishop Gray's court deposing Colenso was therefore null and void. For many Anglicans, high churchmen and evangelicals alike, the Judicial Committee had once again intervened in a spiritual matter, undermining the church's efforts to discipline heretical clergy and threatening its spiritual independence.

The Church of England took the position that, regardless of the Judicial Committee's decision, Colenso had been deposed. This was the view taken by the Convocation of Canterbury in June 1865. The clergy of Natal, moreover, with only one exception, no longer recognised Colenso as their bishop. When, in November 1865, Colenso returned to Natal and resumed his episcopal functions, the bishop of Cape Town formally excommunicated him. At this point, the issue was taken up by the world Anglican communion, which until now had been a nebulous entity. A number of Canadian Anglicans, concerned over the doctrinal difficulties emerging from the controversies over both *Essays and Reviews* and the Colenso case, asked the archbishop of Canterbury to convene a council of bishops to express the mind of the whole Anglican Church. The archbishop was supportive, and in September 1867 the first Lambeth Conference was held at the archbishop's palace in London. It was attended by 76 bishops from Anglican/Episcopal churches throughout the world. After a prolonged and heated discussion, 55 bishops signed a declaration in support of the sentence of excommunication imposed on Colenso by Bishop Gray and the other South African bishops. Further, by a vote of 40 to 3, the Lambeth Conference recommended that a new bishop be appointed to the see of Natal. Accordingly, in 1869, W. K. Macrorie was consecrated bishop of Natal by the bishop of Cape Town. There were now two Anglican bishops of Natal – the one recognised by the church and the other by the imperial state – both uneasily occupying the same colonial see. The result was a schism within the diocese.

Colenso, meanwhile, continued his biblical scholarship, eventually completing the seventh and final volume of *The Pentateuch and Book of Joshua Critically Examined* in 1879. Perhaps more important, he devoted himself to the mission to the Zulus, working for their welfare, fighting for their rights and earning their respect, even through the dark period of the Zulu war of 1879. He became the advocate of the Zulu people. His mission theology very much reflected the broad church ideal of an undogmatic, ethical Christianity, with an emphasis on the love of God for all His creation. Colenso died in 1883. While revered by many Zulus as a 'father to His people', however, he was distrusted by most white settlers and viewed as a heretic by most of the Anglican communion, and he spent his last years as a lonely and, in many respects, a tragic figure.

The growth of the broad church movement

The broad church movement expanded its influence in the 1860s and 1870s, despite the attacks it experienced over *Essays and Reviews* and Bishop Colenso. Liberal Christians continued seeking to define an inclusive faith that would encompass the new intellectual forces of the day and the higher criticism of the Bible. They shifted their emphasis away from the dogmatic aspects of the faith, and focused instead on what they viewed as the essentials of Christianity, which they found in the ethical teachings and moral example of Christ. Some sought to strip away the dogmatic accretions of the centuries and recover the humanity of the 'historical' Jesus, that is, Jesus the man who had lived, loved and taught in Palestine at a particular moment in history. In 1865, a young professor of Latin at King's College, London, John Robert Seeley, published a biography of Jesus under the title of *Ecce Homo*. He published the book anonymously in order to protect the reputation of his father, a publisher of religious works. Drawing inspiration from the efforts of Continental scholars to reconstruct the life of the historical Jesus, Seeley portrayed Jesus as essentially a moralist, who was filled with an 'Enthusiasm for Humanity', and who showed people how to shape an ethical society. Some orthodox Christians were outraged by this portrayal of Christ more as a good man and moral teacher than as the son of God who died to propitiate divine justice; they objected to its emphasis on the incarnation over the atonement. The evangelical Lord Shaftesbury, growing more crusty as he aged, famously declared *Ecce Homo* to be 'the most pestilential book ever vomited, I think, from the jaws of hell' – and in so doing aroused curiosity and helped ensure the book sold more than 10,000 copies.[47] Many others, however, were attracted by Seeley's human Christ, so accessible, so sympathetic, so unlike the warring ecclesiastics and heresy hunters. 'From the moment when I opened that volume', wrote William Gladstone, 'I felt the touch of a powerful hand drawing me on', and he published a highly favourable review of the work in the broad church periodical, *Good Words*.[48] Seeley's book resonated with the pre-Raphaelite Holman Hunt's painting, *Light of the World* (1853), with its portrayal of a very human, suffering Christ, knocking at a door covered in brambles, asking for admission into each life, in Victorian Britain no less than ancient Palestine. Reproduced on a massive scale, prints of the painting hung in thousands of homes, schools, churches and chapels.

Many broad church thinkers shared Colenso's conviction that Christ's ethical message had to be restored in order to breathe life into the overseas mission. There was a sense in the later 1860s and early 1870s that the much of the overseas missionary movement was stagnating. The slow progress of the Christian mission in India, where there were relatively few converts from Hinduism and Islam, was especially disturbing. It raised difficult questions. If the peoples of India were not being converted, was there in truth a providential purpose behind Britain's imperial control of the subcontinent? Had the mission public simply been deluded about Britain's real role, and had the bloody suppression of the Mutiny been merely to preserve power and ensure profits? Here broad church thinkers provided some fresh approaches. For them, the lack of success in the India mission resulted in large part from the missionaries' emphasis on dogma, and their insistence that non-Christians must accept the truth of Christian doctrines and hence view all other faiths as false. Perhaps it was time for Christians to rethink their approach to mission, as Colenso had been trying to do in Natal. Broad churchmen advocated dialogue with unbelievers at home. Might there not be dialogue with other religions abroad?

In December 1872, the learned biblical scholar and regius professor of divinity at Cambridge University, Brooke Foss Westcott, delivered an influential sermon before the University, in which he suggested that Britain's providential mission might be not so much to Christianise the world, as to promote understanding and reconciliation between the major religious faiths of the East and West.[49] 'God', he insisted, 'has fitted us as a people and as a church . . . to be the interpreters of the East to the West, and of the West to the East, to be the witnesses and heralds of truth recognised as manifold'.[50] British Christians should seek to learn from the faiths of the East, and to recognise that all religions were continually evolving and developing in their apprehension of spiritual truths. They should welcome the emergence of reform movements within Hinduism, such as the Brahmo Samaj movement with its emphasis on promoting Hindu social ethics. Westcott envisioned the establishment in India of a community of learning, in connection with Cambridge University, that would promote religious and cultural dialogue. Such a community would be, he insisted, a 'new Alexandria', a melting pot of theologies, in which Christians would come to a fuller understanding of their own faith by learning more about other faiths. Inspired by Westcott's vision, members of the University formed in 1876 the Cambridge University Missionary Brotherhood in Delhi.[51] From the beginning, its work included, as well as education and dialogue with Hindus and Muslims, social service in the slums of Delhi – following Christ's moral example.

In December 1873, a year after Westcott's mission sermon at Cambridge, F. Max Müller, the broad church professor of comparative philology at Oxford University (and a native of Germany), presented a lecture on missions before a large and distinguished audience at Westminster Abbey in London.[52] The lecture had been organised by the broad churchman, A. P. Stanley, who had been appointed dean of Westminster, largely through the queen's influence, in 1864. Müller opened his address with an overview of the religious map of the world. All the great religions, he maintained, were works of God. They were living things, which evolved over time and which developed in relation to each other, influencing one another through their proximity or their missionary outreach. For too long, he argued, British missionaries had approached the other great world religions in a controversial spirit, seeking to convince their adherents that their beliefs were false and that the Christian system alone was true. There was an element of violence in this approach, and controversial missions tended to arouse resistance and hostility from those they sought to convert. What was needed, Müller continued, were Christian missionaries who would seek to influence others by their moral example, who would strive to live Christ-like lives of selfless service among the poor and outcast, who would be more concerned with doing good than with dogma. Such missionaries would not attempt to convert others to a set of creeds or doctrinal formulas, certain that their formula was right and all others were wrong. 'What are all these formulas', he asked, 'but the stammerings of children, which only a loving father can interpret and understand?'[53] These ethical missionaries might not achieve the conversion of peoples of other faiths to Christianity. Rather, they might encourage reform movements within Hinduism or Islam, which, inspired by the missionary's moral example, might lead to purer, more ethical versions of those faiths.

Other broad church thinkers directed their attention to the church at home, arguing that a major role of a national church was to provide moral education, encourage intellectual cultivation and promote national unity through a shared spiritual culture. In late 1866 and early 1867, Viscount Amberley, son of the Whig Lord John Russell and Liberal MP for Nottingham (and father of the philosopher, Bertrand Russell), published two articles on the Church of England in the *Fortnightly Review*, in which he argued for the broadest possible terms of membership in the national church. 'It ought', he asserted of the church, 'to represent the religious feelings of the whole community; no one should feel himself utterly excluded from it; no theological faction should be permitted to use it for the exclusive promotion of its own opinions'.[54] He portrayed Colenso as the heroic champion of freedom of thought, and insisted that the church could not afford to expel such men from the ranks of its clergy. Amberley maintained that there should be no doctrinal tests imposed on the clergy: so long as they fulfilled their liturgical and pastoral obligations and embraced the ethical precepts of Christ, they should be free to follow where their intellectual enquiries took them. The church must make no attempt to enslave the intellects of its clergy. 'Intellectual freedom is the highest privilege of a rational man. The sacrifice of that freedom is one which he ought never to make, nor we to accept'.[55] Further, as society was advancing rapidly in knowledge, so the clergy must be free to develop their minds, in order to continue to speak to a society experiencing rapid intellectual change. Similar views were expressed by J. R. Seeley in an influential essay published in 1868 on 'The Church as a Teacher of Morality', in which he advocated the broad church ideal of a national Christianity.[56] The national church, he argued, should be inclusive of the whole nation and should strive to elevate national life through its ethical teachings. Its clergy should endeavour to keep pace with the intellectual advances in liberal Britain, 'at a time when society moves with a speed like that of the planet itself through space'; they should familiarise themselves with 'political economy and the principles of political and social science'. The national church should strive in all things for 'comprehension and union'.

In 1867, the poet, essayist and literary critic, Matthew Arnold – son of the liberal Anglican educator, Thomas Arnold – published a collection of *New Poems*, which included the melancholy musings of 'Dover Beach', in which he contemplated the weary waning of the Christian faith that had once shaped Western civilisation, and spoke of the need for humans to love one another in a world 'swept with confused alarms of struggle and flight'. The collection also included 'Rugby Chapel', his tribute to his father. Here, he contrasted those embracing the stern puritanical spirit, who, 'with frowning foreheads, with lips firmly compressed', struggle forward alone to their personal salvation, with his father, an early broad churchman, whose higher aim was to encourage, through compassion and cheerfulness, others on the path to truth, and to keep the church united against the 'factions' that divide and dissolve, and to help all souls to reach truth and salvation. Two years later, in 1869, Arnold published *Culture and Anarchy* – extolling the benefits of a unified, comprehensive national culture, embracing a shared social ethic and insisting that what Britain needed was not more 'fire and strength' but rather the cultivation of 'sweetness and light'. He ridiculed the exclusive spirit of those modern Puritans, the Nonconformists, who, he claimed, set their private consciences and strict conceptions of sin against the broader culture. Theirs, he insisted, was a mindset of envy, grievance and self-righteousness that would lead only to anarchy. The Nonconformist, he averred, needed to be persuaded 'that his time spent in agitating for the abolition of church-establishments would have been better spent in getting worthier ideas of God and the ordering of the world'.[57] The ideal of culture, he insisted, was a balance between what he termed the spirit of 'Hebraism', or zeal to fulfil the will of God, and 'Hellenism', or celebration of human reason and creativity. What were needed were institutions, including a national church, that would nurture a unifying culture.

In predominantly Calvinist Scotland, there were movements within the Presbyterian churches away from rigid Sabbatarianism, from strict adherence to the Westminster Confession of Faith and from literal interpretations of Scripture. In 1865, there was a loud public outcry against a railway company's decision to run Sunday trains between Glasgow and Edinburgh. In response, Norman MacLeod, the broad church minister of the Barony church in Glasgow and editor of the popular magazine *Good Words*, delivered a speech in the presbytery of Glasgow in which he denounced the strict Sabbatarianism then prevailing in Scotland. There was, he insisted, no New Testament warrant for refusing to allow activity or outdoor recreation on Sundays. MacLeod was widely attacked for his speech, and there were moves to have him deposed from the ministry. Yet others took up his call for Sunday opening of parks, museums and galleries, noting that while middle- and upper-class families worked shorter hours and had the leisure to frequent them during the week, Sunday afternoons were the only time that most working-class families could enjoy those facilities.[58] The public came to admire MacLeod for his courage, and only four years later, he was elected moderator of the General Assembly in the Church of Scotland. The broad church John Tulloch of St Andrews University fought against the tendency to make an idol of the Calvinist Westminster Confession, as though it were divine inspiration. 'The [Westminster] Confession of Faith', he observed in 1865, 'in its origin and its principles was the manifesto of a great religious party which, after a fierce conflict, gained a temporary ascendancy in England and Scotland'.[59] Such an assertion would have been unimaginable coming from a minister of the Church of Scotland 20 years earlier.

Even the theologically conservative Free Church was moving in liberal directions during the 1860s, as the Fathers of the Disruption were one by one removed by death or infirmity. By the 1860s, professors at the Free Church's New College in Edinburgh were introducing students to the fruits of Continental scholarship. This included German higher criticism, which was taught at New College by the formidable scholar A. B. Davidson, who was from 1863 professor of Hebrew and Old Testament Exegesis. One of the Davidson's most able students was William Robertson Smith, who entered New College in 1866 and four years later became professor of Old Testament at Aberdeen Free Church College. Smith had studied in

Germany and his outspoken advocacy of the more advanced conclusions of the higher criticism soon antagonised Free Church conservatives. Formal charges were brought against him in 1876. After a prolonged and bitter struggle in the Free Church courts, Smith was deposed from his chair in 1881 – his belligerence, refusal to suffer fools, and youthful arrogance making matters difficult for his supporters. But for many Free Church students who crowded the galleries of the General Assembly during Smith's trial, he was a hero. Moreover, liberal leaders in the Free Church, most notably Robert Rainy, principal of New College, fought hard to ensure that while Smith might have to go, the principles of free enquiry and the higher criticism would become accepted within the Free Church.[60] Smith went on to an illustrious career as professor of Arabic at Cambridge, helping to shape the modern discipline of cultural anthropology before his early death in 1894. Biblical criticism, meanwhile, thrived in the Free Church colleges, with such scholars as George Adam Smith and Marcus Dods making significant contributions.

During the 1860s, a number of broad churchmen gained positions of influence within the established churches and the universities. They benefited from the favour of Queen Victoria and from the patronage of governments which preferred their open, tolerant faith. In 1864, as we have noted, A. P. Stanley became dean of Westminster Abbey. Charles Kingsley became regius professor of modern history at Cambridge (a part-time post) in 1860 and a canon of Westminster Abbey in 1873. The broad church bishop of London, A. C. Tait, became archbishop of Canterbury in 1868. The following year, in 1869, one of the contributors to *Essays and Reviews*, Frederick Temple, was consecrated, against considerable opposition, bishop of Exeter, and in 1870, another *Essays and Reviews* contributor, Benjamin Jowett, was elected master of Balliol College, Oxford. F. D. Maurice became Knightsbridge professor of moral philosophy at Cambridge in 1866, F. Max Müller became professor of comparative philology at Oxford in 1868, J. R. Seeley became professor of modern history at Cambridge in 1869 and Brooke Foss Westcott became professor of divinity at Cambridge in 1870. In Scotland, the leading broad church preacher and theologian, John Caird, was appointed professor of divinity at Glasgow University in 1862 and then principal of Glasgow University in 1873. His gifted younger brother, Edward Caird, a leading proponent of Hegelian idealism, became professor of moral philosophy at Glasgow University in 1866, while the broad churchman A. H. Charteris was appointed professor of biblical criticism at the University of Edinburgh in 1868. Under broad church influence, the established churches not only grew more open to biblical scholarship, Darwinian evolution and dialogue with other religions, they also grew more attached to the broad church ideal of an inclusive, comprehensive national church, expressing the spiritual aspirations of the nation in an increasingly democratic age.

Disestablishment

Many, however, did not share this ideal of a comprehensive national church. In the 1860s, there was a renewed assault on the established churches of England, Ireland and Scotland – on their influence in society, their privileged status and the alliance of church and state which they represented. A large portion of the British and Irish population – Nonconformists, Roman Catholics and Radicals – refused to accept the idea that the established churches could define, in any real sense, *their* national identity and aspirations. Protestant Nonconformists in particular bristled at the suggestion that not to be a member of the established church was not to fully participate in national culture. They were deeply offended by Matthew Arnold's *Culture and Anarchy*, with his depictions of Protestant Nonconformists as small-minded provincials, nurturing a sense of grievance, opposed to intellectual progress and spiritual cultivation. This, they insisted, was simply untrue. Had not Dissenters been in the vanguard of the century's movement toward greater liberty and equality? If they were to continue to be subject to such attacks, perhaps it was time to end forever the stigma attached to Dissent, by ending the established churches. Disestablishment, argued R. W. Dale, Congregational minister of Carr's Lane, Birmingham, in a response to Arnold, 'would make the Church less worldly and the State more Christian'. This, he added, would be 'genuine spiritual "development"'.[61] In Ireland, the Catholic majority continued to view the established Protestant church as one of their chief grievances under the Union. Although it now exercised little national influence, it remained a symbol of the Protestant ascendancy and a continual reminder of the humiliations suffered by the Catholic majority in the past. Its endowments and properties were viewed as national resources properly belonging to the Irish people as a whole, but which had been unjustly diverted to benefit a small and wealthy Protestant minority. So long as the established Church of Ireland existed, the Irish majority would have no confidence in Parliament's claims to govern Ireland justly and impartially. Protestant Nonconformists and Irish Catholics had little love for one another. But they shared the view that the established churches were a nuisance and had to be removed.

In 1862, the Nonconformist denominations in England and Wales commemorated the bicentenary of the ejection of some 2,000 Puritan ministers from the established Church of England in 1662. Public meetings were held across the country. Although some leaders, in their celebrations of the history and achievements of Dissent on this occasion, sought to avoid any reference to the establishment question, many others, including R. W. Dale, insisted that the ejections had demonstrated the fundamental unsoundness of religious establishments, while they argued that the spirit of persecution lived on within them. Dale was a self-professed 'Puritan', committed to achieving the godly society. He saw nothing wrong with Nonconformists being active in politics; on the contrary, he viewed political participation as a sacred duty. And disestablishment, he was certain, would make a more just society for all the inhabitants of the United Kingdom.[62]

The Liberation Society followed up the bicentenary commemorations by renewing their campaign to secure the abolition of religious establishments. The Society, it will be recalled, had been founded in 1844, and had been struggling for almost two decades for disestablishment. Their cause now began to find increased support. Subscriptions increased from £4,413 in 1860–61 to £8,913 in 1868–69, with the number of subscribing members reaching 10,000 by 1869.[63] The Society's journal, *The Liberator*, launched in 1855, achieved a circulation of about 6,000 by 1863. After 1862, the Society commenced a new plan of campaign. Lecturers were sent out on circuit around the country. In December 1864, the Society appointed a full-time electoral agent, who focused his activities on marginal parliamentary constituencies, where there was a good chance of getting pro-disestablishment candidates elected. In the year 1868 alone, the Society distributed 825,000 tracts and 57,000 placards.[64] From 1866, they began a campaign in Wales, issuing tracts in the Welsh language and holding regional conferences around the country. Wales, with its overwhelming Nonconformist majority, proved to be particularly fertile soil.[65] Much of the Liberation Society's agitation was directed against the church rate, which formed one of the chief remaining grievances of Nonconformists in England and Wales. But the Society was not mainly concerned with removing specific grievances; they focused on the larger principle of disestablishment and pursued this goal with zeal. 'Our one great object in this Society', proclaimed Edward Miall of the Liberation Society in early 1867, 'is simply this, to give to Christianity a clear stage and no favour. Nay, we go farther than this – to give not to Christianity only, but to every man, a clear stage and no favour for the dissemination of those religious principles and views which he holds'.[66]

The prospects for disestablishment were aided by a further instalment of parliamentary reform. From the 1850s, there had been growing calls for redistribution and extension of the franchise to recognise both the expansion of urban centres and the improved status of the skilled working classes. In October 1865, the death of the aristocratic Whig leader, Lord Palmerston, who had led the Whig–Liberal government for the past decade, provided the occasion for action on reform. The veteran Whig, Lord John Russell, succeeded Palmerston as prime minister, and under his leadership the Whig–Liberal government brought forward an ill-conceived reform measure in 1866, which failed to get through Parliament. Russell's government resigned in June and the Conservative party under Benjamin Disraeli formed a minority government. By now popular zeal for reform was aroused, and there were public disturbances at an illegal reform demonstration at Hyde Park in July 1866, with the crowd famously damaging the railings and trampling the flowerbeds. Much to everyone's surprise, Disraeli now brought forward a far more sweeping reform bill than the Liberals, taking a 'leap in the dark' towards greater democracy. Parliament passed the Reform Act for England and Wales in 1867, and this was followed by separate Reform Acts for Ireland and Scotland in 1868. The Acts enlarged the electoral representation of the boroughs relative to the counties, and significantly increased the number of voters, especially among the lower middle-classes and skilled artisans – adding another million voters in England and Wales alone. Of adult males over the age of 21, about a third now had the vote in England, Wales and Scotland and about a sixth had the vote in Ireland.[67] The Acts increased the electoral influence of the Nonconformists and encouraged their hopes for disestablishment.

The Nonconformists now found an unexpected ally in the former Peelite Tory, William Ewart Gladstone. A man of deep Christian faith, financial acumen, broad intellectual interests and political astuteness, Gladstone had in his youth thought of becoming a clergyman, and he now believed that his career as a politician included bringing Christian influence to bear on public life. Described by Macaulay in 1839 as 'the rising hope of those stern and unbending Tories', he had become a Liberal only in 1859, at the age of 50. In the early 1860s he had begun speaking at mass political meetings, transforming himself into a popular leader, the 'People's William'. His lofty rhetoric and eloquent appeals to justice and morality appealed to working-class crowds that were often accustomed to long sermons and were flattered by a politician who refused to speak down to them. Rejected by his long-term parliamentary constituency of Oxford University in 1865, Gladstone was elected that same year for the industrial constituency of South Lancashire, which had a large Nonconformist population. During the 1850s, as David Bebbington has shown, Gladstone, while a high Anglican, developed broad church sympathies, which included openness to biblical criticism, emphasis on Christ's ethical example, respect for sincere Christians of various hues and a desire to unite the nation through an inclusive Protestant faith.[68] He became convinced, as he explained to his friend, Samuel Wilberforce, in October 1862, that 'part of the special work of this age ought to be to clear the relations between church and state', and that this could only be achieved if members of the established church were prepared to work 'liberally and even sometimes boldly' to conciliate the Nonconformists.[69] From about 1864, he cultivated friendly relations with leading Nonconformist clergymen, including R. W. Dale.[70] And, in the mid-1860s, he became convinced that the Church of Ireland would have to be disestablished.

The disestablishment of the church in Ireland

In the decennial census of 1861 there was, for Ireland only, a question about religious affiliation. This census indicated that out of a total Irish population of 5,798,967, no fewer than 4,505,265, or 77.6 per cent, were Roman Catholics. A further 523,291, or just over 9 per cent, were Presbyterians, who were concentrated mainly in Ulster. Only 693,357, or 11.9 per cent, were adherents of the established church in Ireland. Supporters of the Irish establishment pointed out that the percentage of established church members in the Irish population had increased slightly, from 10.7 per cent in 1834 to 11.9 per cent in 1861.[71] But few were favourably impressed.

The Irish Protestant establishment consisted of two provinces and 12 dioceses. Its income, since the abolition of the Irish tithe in 1838, was derived partly from the rentals of church lands and partly from a rent-charge, which was levied on landowners and certain categories of lease-holders. This income in 1868 totalled £616,840. Out of 1,414 parishes with an incumbent clergyman, 486 had fewer than 100 established church members, and 92 had fewer than 20 church members.[72] The general standards of the Church of Ireland clergy had improved since the early years of the nineteenth century. There was less non-residence and pluralism, and many of the established clergy were exemplary pastors, showing concern for the welfare of all their parishioners, Catholic as well as Protestant. Supporters of the Irish Protestant establishment denied that Irish Catholics had any real grievance against the established clergy. The Irish Catholic peasantry, insisted the Protestant archbishop of Dublin, R. C. Trench, in 1865, respected the Church of Ireland clergy – for they knew the parish clergyman was 'one in their midst, who, if nothing more to *them*, is a country gentleman, bound to almost constant residence among them; often, indeed, with most moderate means, but dispensing these on the spot'.[73] In truth, this line of defence, while it might have appealed to the governing classes in the 1820s, no longer found much support with the expanded British and Irish electorate of the later 1860s. It was glaringly obvious that the established church had not the remotest claim to be the national church of the Irish people, and that its sizeable endowments and rent-charges were being employed for the benefit of a small minority, which included the wealthiest members of Irish society. For many in Ireland, the Irish establishment was an abomination, and its existence an affront to the Irish people. 'The Protestant Church', observed Archbishop Paul Cullen in the *Dublin Post* in August 1864, 'founded as it has been in the lust of a brutal king, propagated by fire and sword, and supported by robbery and confiscation of property, has no power to resist those dangerous encroachments of error and infidelity'.[74]

Catholic Ireland remained largely disaffected from the United Kingdom. Irish Catholics, haunted by the famine memories, did not share the providentialist views of the state as having a mission to spread the benefits of free trade and liberal institutions to the world. In 1859–60, for example, while the most of the United Kingdom supported the unification of Italy as a 'progressive movement' – and British popular opinion hailed the Italian nationalists, Garibaldi and Mazzini, as freedom fighters – most Irish Catholics supported the pope's possession of the papal states and therefore opposed Italian unification. Indeed, Irish Catholics had raised an Irish brigade to fight for the papal states and against the Italian nationalists.[75] In 1860, 1861 and 1862, there was a run of ruinous harvests in Ireland, and outbreaks of sheep-rot and foot-and-mouth disease devastated the livestock. The result was mass destitution and fears of a return to famine conditions. The government, however, refused to provide extraordinary relief, and this, for many, revived memories of its indifferent response to the great famine. Irish distress and anger contributed to popular support for the Fenians, revolutionaries dedicated to the creation of a democratic Irish republic. Emerging in the late 1850s with support in Ireland and from Irish emigrants who had settled in Britain and North America, the Fenian brotherhood was made up of secret and self-contained groups of activists. Its recruits often felt guilt and shame over the famine, and vowed that the masses would never again die passively, like sheep.

During the American Civil War of 1861–65, hundreds of Irish-Americans gained military training and experience while serving in the armies of both the North and the South, and many of these hardened veterans embraced the Fenian cause. In 1865, the Fenians launched a campaign of violence, including bombings and murders, in Ireland and England. The state managed to infiltrate the Fenian cells with informers and made a number of arrests. In September 1867, a botched Fenian attempt to free two of their comrades from police custody in Manchester resulted in the unintended shooting of a policeman. Three Fenians were convicted of the policeman's murder, and hanged, despite widespread pleas for clemency. Outrage over these 'Manchester martyrs' united much of Catholic Ireland and increased popular support, including the sympathy of many priests, for the Fenian cause.

Paul Cullen and most of his fellow Catholic bishops in Ireland opposed the Fenian movement. This was not out of loyalty to the United Kingdom. Rather, they believed that the Fenian campaign of violence would prove futile in the face of British military power and that the Fenian republican ideal threatened the influence of the Catholic Church. In response to the Fenian challenge, Cullen and the majority of Catholic bishops supported the creation of a National Association of Ireland, to provide an alternative, constitutional means of redressing Irish grievances. The National Association was inaugurated in December 1864 in Dublin, at a public meeting attended by seven Catholic bishops, including Cullen; indeed, the new Association was popularly viewed as 'Cullen's Association'. The Association was to advance Catholic and national interests along three lines. First, it would seek legislation to secure rights for tenant farmers, especially the right to receive compensation from landowners for improvements the tenants made to their farms. Second, it would seek state support for Catholic and other denominational schools, on the principle that education must have a firm Christian basis. Finally, the National Association would agitate for the disestablishment and disendowment of the established Protestant church in Ireland. In an unexpected development, the Protestant Nonconformists of Britain's Liberation Society entered into an alliance with Cullen's National Association, largely through the efforts of the Irish reformer, William O'Neill Daunt. 'It was', Daunt later confided to his journal, 'no easy task to get Irish ecclesiastics to place confidence in the Liberation people whose anti-Catholic bigotry in theological matters was notorious'. There was, however, a shared commitment to bring an end to the established church in Ireland, which the Liberation Society hoped would be the first step towards general disestablishment in Britain.

With economic distress, Fenian violence and Cullen's National Association, the situation in Ireland was highly volatile. There was a growing sense, felt even by many Anglicans, that disestablishment of the Church of Ireland was the price to be paid for peace. The Irish would remain disaffected, wrote the high Anglican London priest, Malcolm MacColl, to Gladstone in September 1866, so long as they had 'the religion of a fraction of the population established over them, with all its hateful reminiscences'. 'Abolish the Established Church', MacColl advised, 'and I believe that the Irish will gradually, though not all at once, regard themselves as a free people, and will come, in time, to be as proud of their connection with England as the Scotch . . . now are'.[76] In late 1867, Gladstone decided to embrace the three-part programme of Cullen's National Association – pledging himself in a speech in Southport to take up the issue of the Irish church, Irish tenant rights, and Irish education.[77] The first and most pressing issue was the Irish church. In March 1868, he brought before the House of Commons resolutions calling for Irish disestablishment, and these were adopted despite the opposition of Disraeli's Conservative government. The resolutions were not binding, but they did indicate that the Commons was now prepared to legislate for disestablishment.

Taking up the cause of Irish disestablishment was a bold move on Gladstone's part. The Liberal party was by no means united in support of the action. Gladstone, moreover, had opened himself to the charge of inconsistency. In his first book, *The State in its Relations to the Church*, published in 1838, he had argued that the state had a collective conscience and was responsible, under God, to maintain the true Protestant church. Now he was proposing to leave Ireland without an established Protestant church, and to make the state in Ireland effectively secular. To many, his move to disestablish the Irish church was unjust: it had submitted to reform by Parliament in 1833, and since then it had made significant improvements in its organisation and clerical discipline. Further, had not the Church of Ireland been united to the Church of England 'for ever' by the Act of Union of 1800? Could the Irish portion of the United Church of England and Ireland be disestablished, without threatening the establishment of the church in England as well? The Liberals, declared Disraeli in a public letter in March 1868, meant to destroy 'that sacred union between church and state which has hitherto been the chief means of our civilization and is the only security of our religious liberty'.[78]

The general election in the late autumn of 1868 was largely a plebiscite on the Irish church. Liberal candidates promised at the hustings that disestablishment in Ireland would not only strengthen the Union, but would also free the established church in England from its unhealthy association with the Irish church. Some suggested that disestablishment might even help the Protestant cause in Ireland. The Liberation Society was active, distributing over a million pamphlets in support of Irish disestablishment, while its paid speakers gave over 500 lectures across the country.[79] In this first general election under the new franchise, the Liberals achieved an overwhelming victory, and were returned to office with a majority of 112 in the Commons. The new House also included 63 Nonconformists. On 1 March 1869, Gladstone introduced his government's bill for the disestablishment and disendowment of the Irish church in a masterful speech of three and a half hours. The Irish church would be disestablished from 1 January 1871; the Irish ecclesiastical courts would cease to exist from that date; Irish bishops would no longer sit in the House of Lords; and the Act of Union would be amended to reflect the changes. The disestablished church in Ireland would be deprived of most of its endowments. It would be permitted to retain its church buildings, and properties given by private donors after 1660. However, the tithe rent-charge and all properties given to it before 1660 would be taken and diverted to other uses, most notably to improve conditions for the Irish poor. The church would have to purchase from the state the residence houses of its clergy. The incomes of the existing clergy would be protected during their lifetimes, but these properties would be taken by the state on the death of the benefice-holder. In ending the endowments of the Church of Ireland, the state would also cease all other religious endowments in Ireland. This meant that the annual grant for the support of the Roman Catholic college at Maynooth, and the modest annual *regium donum* grants to the Presbyterian clergy in Ireland, would cease – though both churches would be compensated with substantial, one-off grants of money.[80] With a large Liberal majority behind it, the bill passed easily through the Commons by the end of May.

In the House of Lords, however, there was strong opposition to the bill. This included most of the English and Irish established bishops, who believed it would weaken the place of Protestantism within the United Kingdom. Many peers, moreover, viewed the disestablishment of the Irish church as a blow to the Act of Union, to the constitution, and to the place of religion in society. They also saw the provisions for disendowment as a fundamental threat to all property. For if the state could seize the property of the Church of Ireland in order to appease popular agitators, the state might also one day seek to placate other agitators by seizing landed estates and country houses. Archbishop Trench was intransigent and refused to negotiate with Gladstone's government. The Irish Protestant bishops must not, Trench explained to Samuel Wilberforce in January 1869, become 'active agents and accomplices' in the 'overthrow' of their church.[81] On 8 June, 150 Conservative peers met and pledged to oppose the bill at all costs. With a constitutional crisis now looming, the queen appealed to the new archbishop of Canterbury, A. C. Tait, to find a compromise.

Tait was a Scot and in some senses an outsider within the English ruling elite. Raised as a Presbyterian, he had joined the Church of England on entering Oxford University. Following a distinguished career at Oxford, he succeeded Thomas Arnold as headmaster of Rugby in 1842. In 1849, he became Dean of Carlisle cathedral, and here, in the spring of 1856, five of his six daughters, ranging in age from eighteen months to ten years, were swept away in a scarlet fever epidemic. It was an appalling tragedy and Tait was devastated. Deeply moved by his story, the queen actively supported his appointment as bishop of London later that year. A moderate broad churchman, he threw himself into his work and proved an exemplary bishop, with strong pastoral commitments and an ability to communicate with people of all ecclesiastical parties. The queen subsequently pressed for his appointment as archbishop of Canterbury and primate of England in 1868. She shared his broad church theology, and felt united with him in shared grief following the death of Prince Albert in 1861.[82]

During the early summer of 1869, Tait struggled for a solution to the Irish church crisis. His position was a delicate one. He could not, of course, openly support the disestablishment and disendowment of a portion of the United Church. And yet he recognised that the people of the United Kingdom had made it clear in the general election of 1868 that they wanted Irish disestablishment. The House of Lords, he argued, should not seek to thwart the will of the people, though it might try to modify the bill in order to minimise the damage to the Irish church. With the queen's support, Tait hosted a series of meetings with leading conservative peers, pressing them to seek to amend rather than reject the bill. His intervention was effective and in the event, the peers voted by a narrow margin to amend rather than reject. Although unable to accept most of the peer's proposed amendments, Gladstone did agree to increase the financial compensation to the Irish church.[83] This was enough, and the Lords reluctantly accepted the bill, which received the royal assent in late July 1869.

The disestablishment of the Irish church was a landmark event. It ended the formal connection of church and state in one of the three historic kingdoms forming the United Kingdom, and it set a constitutional precedent that might be followed elsewhere. In Ireland, religion would now be entirely voluntary, and the state would be essentially secular. The Roman

Catholic primate of Ireland was triumphant. 'The poor Protestants', Cullen wrote to Alessandro Barnabó, cardinal prefect Propaganda in Rome, on 31 July, 'are all very irritated. They never did imagine that England would have abandoned their cause'.[84] 'I intend', he wrote to Tobias Kirby, rector of the Irish College in Rome, on 13 August 1869, 'to have a Te Deum for the downfall of the old church of Elisabeth. The people who mix with Protestants think we ought to say nothing about the matter but I think it will do good to return thanks to God'.[85] The Protestant Church of Ireland felt abandoned not only by the state, but also by the Church of England. In truth, as the high Anglican, G. A. Denison, later observed of the events of 1869, 'English Church-people did not care much about the Irish Church'.[86] This indifference was felt deeply by Irish Protestants. The Church of Ireland was stripped of much of its property and thrown upon its own resources. It now set about the difficult work of reconstructing itself as an independent Episcopal church, governed by a General Synod.

Hopes that Irish disestablishment would strengthen Irish loyalty to the Union were soon disappointed. The disendowment of the church did not, as had been anticipated, create a large surplus income that could be used for national purposes. There was no downpouring of ecclesiastical wealth upon the Irish poor. The modest sums that were generated became simply an 'emergency reservoir' from which Chancellors of the Exchequer drew to supplement spending on such mundane Irish matters as roads and fisheries.[87] Gladstone had intended disestablishment to be only the first instalment of a programme of Irish reforms. However, his legislative effort to improve conditions for the hard-pressed tenant farmers proved largely unsuccessful. His government's Land Act of 1870, which provided compensation to tenants for improvements, might have satisfied Cullen's National Association back in 1864. However, by 1870 the demands of Irish tenants had grown more strident, and the Land Act did not go nearly far enough to satisfy them. There was widespread Irish protest against the Act, and much of the goodwill among Catholics generated by disestablishment was now dissipated. Rural unrest and Fenian violence continued. Even many Irish Protestants lost confidence in the Westminster Parliament to govern their country. In 1870, Isaac Butt, the son of a Church of Ireland clergyman and a prominent Conservative Protestant barrister, formed in Dublin a Home Government Association, with the aim of securing home rule for Ireland, with a separate Dublin parliament and a loose federal connection to United Kingdom. The Association worked to educate public opinion and to secure the election of home rule candidates at parliamentary by-elections. Initially

Butt's Association attracted support from Protestant Conservatives who were furious over disestablishment, as well as from liberal Protestants, Catholics and Fenians. However, it moved steadily in a nationalist direction over the coming years, as Irish Catholic disillusionment with Gladstone's Liberal government grew. In 1873, it was rechristened as the Home Rule Association. At the general election of 1874, no fewer than 59 MPs were elected on the Irish Home Rule platform, marking a new era in Irish politics. The following year, in April 1875, a young Irish Protestant landlord, Charles Stewart Parnell, was elected to Parliament in a by-election for county Meath, and joined the Home Rulers at Westminster. A new era for politics and religion in Ireland had begun.

The Education Act of 1870

The 1860s also witnessed growing calls for improved primary education for the masses. For the Christian public, it was vital for their eternal salvation that children of all social orders receive basic religious instruction and be taught to read the Bible and other Christian literature. Education was also seen as vital for public order. Many suspected, moreover, that the United Kingdom was falling behind the other leading states, especially Prussia, in the education of its population, and that this was dangerous in an era of intensifying industrial and commercial competition. The report of the Royal Commission on popular education in England and Wales, published in 1861, estimated that of a school-age population of about two and a half million, only one and a half million children were in school. Of these, about 750,000 attended state-aided, inspected schools, while several thousand more middle- and upper-class children attended public schools or elite day schools. The remainder were taught in non-inspected private venture schools, often 'by pathetic old women or spiritless and disheartened men who had failed in other walks of life'.[88] Most of the state-aided, inspected schools were denominational schools, which were supported by either the predominantly Anglican National Society or the predominantly Nonconformist British and Foreign Society. There were in the late 1860s approximately 8,000 state-aided denominational schools in England and Wales, of which about 6,000 were National Society schools, and about 1,500 were British and Foreign Society schools, while the Roman Catholics maintained another 350 state-aided schools. The problem was that the number of these denominational schools fell far short of the need. There were not nearly enough schools, and those that did exist tended not to be located in the poorer districts. According to the magistrates in

Liverpool, there were in 1869 some 30,000 children wandering the streets of the city, 'learning habits of vagrancy, mendicancy and crime'.[89]

In 1869, a group of advocates of educational reform, mainly Nonconformists, founded the Birmingham Educational League, which quickly expanded and was renamed the National Education League. The guiding principle of the League, as stated by one of its leading lights, the Congregational minister, R. W. Dale, was 'that every child has a right to be educated as well as to be fed, and that it is the duty of the state to protect this right'.[90] In order to achieve this, the League called for the creation of a national system of education, to be supported by local rates on property. Primary education, they argued, should be compulsory for all school-age children, free for all children and 'unsectarian' in character. There were differences among League members about what unsectarian should mean. For most, it meant a nondenominational form of Christian teaching – that is, including Bible reading and moral instruction, but free of any creeds and catechisms. Some Radicals, however, went further, and called for a completely secular education, arguing that any religious instruction, including Bible reading, should be provided by families and churches outside school hours.

Another group of educational reformers, meanwhile, began agitating for a national system of education that would be based on denominational Christian teaching, and that would include the teaching of creeds and catechisms. In the autumn of 1869, they formed in Manchester the National Education Union, which was made up largely of members of the established Church of England, as well as some Roman Catholics and Methodists. What was needed, they argued, were additional state grants to the churches, to encourage them to build more schools where needed. For members of the Union, education must have a Christian content, and this would be best provided by schools that provided doctrinal instruction. The League and the Union carried on a vigorous public debate over the respective benefits of nondenominational and denominational education.

Amid growing public pressure for educational reform, Gladstone's government prepared an educational bill in late 1869. The bill was largely drafted by the vice-president of the Council, William Edward Forster. Born into a Quaker family, Forster had joined the Church of England on marrying in 1850 the daughter of the liberal Anglican, Thomas Arnold. Forster was thus the brother-in-law of the broad churchman, Matthew Arnold, and like him, believed that religion could help to shape a unified and inclusive national culture. The bill, which Forster introduced in the Commons on 17 February 1870, represented an effort to find a compromise between the denominational and the nondenominational positions. According to the bill, each district of the country would conduct a survey of its educational provision and its educational needs. There would then be a year of grace, in which the churches and denominational societies would be allowed to attempt to meet the need by erecting new schools or enlarging existing schools. After a year, if there was still a clear need for additional schools in a locality, a school board would be appointed. The new school board would have considerable powers to levy rates on property holders within the district and to use the money as it saw fit – either to build and maintain additional schools, or to support the enlargement of existing denominational schools. The school board would also have discretion to determine the religious content of the schools it supported. The state, meanwhile, would continue its policy of making grants to the schools provided by the denominational societies. The bill, in short, was an attempt to fill the gaps in the denominational system.

Despite its moderate nature, the bill encountered intense opposition. Advocates of a nondenominational education vehemently opposed the continued payment of state grants to the older denominational schools. They suspected, moreover, that the new school boards would be dominated by members of the established church and would use their powers to promote Anglican religious instruction in the board schools. Under pressure, the government made a number of amendments to the bill. The grace period during which the denominational societies would be permitted to meet the existing educational need was reduced from a year to six months. It was also agreed that the new school boards, which were originally to be appointed by town councils or rural vestries, would be elected by ratepayers to ensure they were representative of the range of religious opinion in society. Finally, the government agreed to an amendment to the bill proposed by the MP for South Hampshire, William Cowper-Temple. The Cowper-Temple clause, as it became known, prohibited the use of any 'catechisms or religious formularies distinctive of any particular denomination' in the rate-supported schools. With these amendments, the bill passed through both Houses and became law in August 1870.

For its supporters, the Education Act of 1870 was flawed and untidy, but it did represent a step towards the goal of universal elementary education in England and Wales. The Act was essentially broad church in nature, calling for the education of children in an inclusive, undogmatic and biblical faith, which, its supporters hoped, would lead in time to a waning of sectarian animosities. This was certainly Forster's view. 'Surely the time will come', he asserted, in defending the religious aspects of the bill, 'when we shall find out how we can agree better on these matters – when men will find out that on the main questions of religion they agree, and that they can teach them in common to their children'.[91] Much of the population seemed to accept the intentions of the Act.[92]

Many Nonconformists, however, bitterly opposed the Education Act. They remained convinced that the new board schools would be Anglican in tone, and would work to convert their children to Anglicanism. They objected to the continued state grants to Anglican schools, and they were especially unhappy with a clause in the Act which permitted school boards to pay the fees of children from poorer families who wished them to attend a denominational school. They felt betrayed by the Liberal government which their votes had helped to bring to power. 'Once bit, twice shy', the veteran Voluntary, Edward Miall, exclaimed to Gladstone on behalf of the Nonconformists in the Commons on 22 July 1870: 'We can't stand this sort of thing much longer'.[93] The National Educational League carried on a vigorous agitation against the Act, and a Unitarian screw manufacturer of Birmingham, Joseph Chamberlain, emerged to national prominence as a vehement League speaker. In November 1871, an angry R. W. Dale lectured on 'The Politics of Nonconformity' before huge audiences in Manchester and Birmingham.[94] For too long, he argued, Nonconformists had been content to hold a subordinate place in the Liberal party. The hated Education Act highlighted the need for Nonconformists to organise for independent political action aimed not simply at the redress of grievances within an Anglican state, but at reshaping that social and political order according to their vision of the Christian commonwealth. 'We are Nonconformists', he proclaimed, '– we are political Nonconformists – not because we wish to make the political life of England less religious, but because we wish to make it more religious; and we intend, God helping us . . . to pursue it until the time shall come – it is not far distant – when the principles of which it is our glory to be the representatives and the guardians shall control the legislation and the policy of our country'.[95] In January 1872, some 1,900 Nonconformist delegates met at a conference in Manchester, agreeing to withhold support from any parliamentary candidate who would not pledge to work to change the Education Act.[96]

Incensed by the Act and encouraged by Irish disestablishment, some Nonconformists worked with renewed vigour for the disestablishment of the Church of England. In October 1870, the Congregational Union passed a resolution for disestablishment, and in the following months the Liberation Society held well-attended public meetings in Bradford, Manchester, Liverpool and London in support of disestablishment. In May

1871, Miall introduced a motion in the House of Commons for the disestablishment of the Church of England. An established church, he maintained, was an anachronism in modern society. 'It continues to stand among us', he continued, 'for no other reason than that it has stood for so long. Logically speaking, the spring and the stay of its life is gone'.[97] But Gladstone's government firmly opposed English disestablishment and after a seven-hour debate Miall's motion was overwhelmingly defeated by a vote of 374 to 89. Undaunted, the Liberation Society continued its agitation, holding 100 meetings in the second half of 1871, then 222 meetings in 1872 and 269 meetings in 1873 – mainly in the Midlands, North and West of England. Miall brought forward further disestablishment motions in 1872 and 1873, which were also defeated by substantial margins.[98]

Although opposed to English disestablishment, the government did take significant steps to remove remaining Nonconformist grievances. In 1868, it secured the passage of legislation to end compulsory church rates, thus ending a long-standing source of strife in the localities.[99] In 1871, the government carried the Universities Test Act, which opened all lay positions – fellowships, tutorships, college headships – as well as non-theological advanced degrees to qualified persons regardless of religious persuasion.[100] With these grievances now largely addressed, English Nonconformist interest in disestablishment began to wane.

The disestablishment campaign in Scotland

Scotland, however, took a different path. While the disestablishment campaign in England was faltering, in Scotland, an intense, hard-fought disestablishment campaign emerged in the early 1870s. It was led by members of the two main non-established Presbyterian denominations – the Free Church and the United Presbyterian Church – and it aroused broad public support. By the mid-1870s, disestablishment had become the major political issue in Scotland and the established Church of Scotland was under serious threat.

To understand the vehemence of the campaign, some attention must be given to Scotland's distinctive religious circumstances. There were in mid-Victorian Scotland three major Presbyterian denominations. The largest of these was the established Church of Scotland. This church had lost much of its membership at the great Disruption of 1843, and for the next decade its fortunes had fallen very low. Some compared it to the established Church of Ireland, and predicted its demise. However, largely under broad church leadership, it began to experience a recovery in its numbers and

pastoral commitment from the 1850s. It gained support from the upper-
and middle-classes, who venerated the 'auld kirk' as a time-honoured
institution. It also recovered a sense of itself as the 'poor man's kirk', with
a particular mission to the poor. By 1870, it possessed 1,254 churches,
and according to marriage and educational statistics, its membership represented about 44 per cent of the Scottish population. This was a marked
improvement from the religious census of 1851, when its adherents had
been estimated at a mere 32 per cent of the population.

The main rival of the established church was the Free Church, which
had been formed by those who had followed Thomas Chalmers out of the
established church at the Disruption. The Free Church had 873 churches in
1870, and according to the marriage and educational returns, its adherents
represented about 25 per cent of the population. This was a decline from
an estimated 32 per cent in 1851, and suggested that the Free Church was
losing some of its vibrancy. Both the Church of Scotland and the Free
Church shared a common Reformed theology, Presbyterian organisation
and liturgy. Both churches believed that in an ideal commonwealth there
would be a close legal alliance of church and state. But the legacy of the
Disruption kept them apart; even after 30 years the wounds were still raw
and animosity between the two churches ran deep. The third major
denomination in Scotland was the United Presbyterian Church, made
up of congregations which had originally seceded from the Church of
Scotland in the eighteenth century. It was also Reformed in theology,
with a Presbyterian organisation and liturgy. Unlike the Church of
Scotland and the Free Church, however, the United Presbyterian Church
was a Voluntary denomination, opposed in principle to any connection
of church and state. In 1870, it possessed about 600 churches and its
adherents represented between 11 and 14 per cent of the population,
which was a slight decline from their estimated 19 per cent in 1851.[101]

The nature of the divisions between the main Presbyterian denominations – so similar in doctrine, organisation and liturgy – was perplexing to
those who were unfamiliar with Scotland's complex religious history.
Outsiders could poke fun at the divisions, as when Disraeli suggested in
his novel *Lothair* (1870) that the United Presbyterian Church was in truth
nothing more than the invention of a mischievous Jesuit, aimed at sowing
such confusion among Presbyterians that they would have no choice
but return to Rome. For Scottish Presbyterians, however, the divisions
were real, heartfelt and no laughing matter. These divisions also had a
political dimension. Church of Scotland clergy voted overwhelmingly
Conservative, and Free Church and United Presbyterian clergy voted

overwhelmingly Liberal. The laity of the three churches probably voted in a broadly similar manner.[102] In villages, towns and urban neighbourhoods across Scotland, rival Church of Scotland, Free Church and United Presbyterian congregations eyed one another suspiciously, nurtured their historic grievances and competed for members. They erected impressive, neo-Gothic churches that were often too large for their congregations, built more to impress onlookers, show up their rivals and attract new members with their grandeur, than to meet real need. As a result, many of these churches remained half empty, and burdened their congregations with heavy debts.

At the same time, there was also by the 1860s a growing sense among many Presbyterians that these divisions were becoming less and less acceptable. The divisions had left much of Scotland 'over-churched', with too many half-empty buildings which would never be filled and too many ministers struggling to maintain respectability on small stipends. The effort to maintain so many small congregations, especially in the depopulated rural districts, meant that the denominations lacked the needed resources for their ministry in the rapidly expanding urban districts, where much of the working class had no church affiliation. There was also a sense that the divisions were a scandal to their communities and a mockery of their professed Christian beliefs. In 1870, the Church of Scotland minister and Edinburgh University professor, A. H. Charteris, gave an address in Glasgow on the religious costs of Presbyterian division. He noted that taking all the Presbyterian denominations together, there was now one Presbyterian minister for every 1,200 inhabitants of Scotland. With such a ratio, it would seem that the country would be thoroughly Christianised. However, this was far from the case, and there were some 500,000 people in Scotland who had no church connection whatsoever. 'There must surely', he observed, 'be something wrong. So many ministers, so many churches, and so much heathenism'. 'Can it be', he continued, 'that they are contending more with one another than with the common foe?' Were not the warring Presbyterian denominations more concerned with their 'sectarian squabbles' and with 'hating one another' than with advancing a common front against the growing irreligion. Clearly it was time to work for reunion.[103]

In 1869, the General Assembly of the Church of Scotland took a bold initiative to promote reunion – agreeing to petition Gladstone's Liberal government to abolish the law of patronage in the Scottish church. Patronage had, it will be recalled, been the main cause of the conflict that had culminated in the Disruption of 1843. Before that, it had also been the main cause of the eighteenth-century secessions from the established church. Thus, by securing the end of patronage, established church leaders hoped to open the way for the Free Church and the United Presbyterians to return to the national church. The established Church of Scotland would once again be the church of the large majority of the Scottish people and a reunited church would be able to conduct a more effective home mission. The decision to approach the Government was largely the idea of broad churchmen within the Church of Scotland, including Charteris, Norman Macleod, and John Tulloch. They were, however, disappointed. Gladstone politely received their deputation, but he declined to act on their petition.[104] This seemed to the deputation a curious attitude for a Liberal prime minister. Would not the abolition of patronage increase the popular voice in the selection of ministers and thus be more democratic? Gladstone, however, responded that his government would not abolish patronage at the sole request of the established Church of Scotland. The Free Church and the United Presbyterians, he noted, had been forced out of the established church because of their conscientious opposition to patronage. For many years, their ministers and members had suffered and sacrificed for their anti-patronage principles. Those two Presbyterian churches would have to be consulted and would have to give their support to any Liberal legislation to end patronage.

As Gladstone was aware, the leaders of the Free Church and the United Presbyterian Church were in fact incensed by this anti-patronage initiative of the established church. They viewed it as little more than an unprincipled attempt to poach their members. Further, Free Church leaders insisted that the abolition of patronage would not address the real legacy of the Disruption. Patronage had certainly been a major factor in it, but the real cause of that event had been the state's claim to control the established church, and thus deny the church's spiritual independence. Parliament might now decide to end the grievance of patronage, but the established church would still be under the control of the state. Further, it would not undo the injustices of the past. Too much damage had been done, too much pain inflicted, for the simple abolition of patronage now to bring the Free Church and United Presbyterians back to the fold.

In January 1872, Arthur Stanley, the broad church dean of Westminster, travelled to Scotland to try to calm the troubled waters with a series of lectures on Scottish church history, which he delivered before large crowds in Edinburgh. Stanley, who loved Scotland, called for an end to the divisions that plagued Scottish Presbyterianism, and a revival of the united national Church of Scotland that represented so much that was good and admirable in the Scottish character. His intentions were no doubt honourable, but the condescending way in which he referred to 'the littleness and minuteness of the points' over which Scottish Presbyterians had deserted their national church was deeply offensive to members of the non-established churches. They also resented the intervention of this English dean in a Scottish controversy. Stanley's lectures were immediately answered in three public lectures by the Free Church's Robert Rainy, who provided a masterly criticism of Stanley's account. While Scotland's religious divisions, he observed, might look ridiculous from the perspective of Westminster Abbey, they none the less involved theological and moral principles that the people of Scotland held to be worth struggle and sacrifice. Those who stood outside the established church might appear to be stubborn and combative, but they sincerely believed that adherence to truth was more important than religious unity based on compromise and concession.[105]

In May 1872, the General Assembly of the United Presbyterian Church decided the time had come to launch a fully-fledged disestablishment campaign, and they invited the Free Church to join them in bringing an end to the established church. More moderate elements in the Free Church, however, resisted the invitation. They remembered that Chalmers, even after the Disruption, had hoped that one day a purified established church might be restored to Scotland, and they hesitated to abolish the establishment forever. Then in 1874, a Conservative government headed by Benjamin Disraeli responded to the Church of Scotland's petition and sponsored legislation which abolished patronage in Scotland. For most Free Church leaders this amounted to a declaration of war, and in May 1875 its General Assembly agreed by a vote of 397 to 84 to join the United Presbyterians in the campaign for disestablishment.[106] Free Church and United Presbyterian leaders claimed that their campaign aimed not simply at bringing down a rival church; rather, they insisted it would bring real benefits to Scotland. It would promote freedom of opinion and religious equality. It would also be the one sure path to the Presbyterian reunion, for once all the Presbyterian churches were equal before the law, those churches could reunite solely on the basis of their shared theology, liturgy and organisation.[107]

Soon Scotland was on fire with the disestablishment agitation, and the country was swept with meetings, pamphlets, tracts, broadsheets, and petitions. Robert Rainy of the Free Church and John Cairns of the United Presbyterians emerged as leaders in the campaign, which had a particular appeal to Scotland's democratic and national sentiment. For many Scots, disestablishment meant the liberation of their national religion from control by a 'British' state. The Church of Scotland was initially surprised by the onslaught, and its leaders hoped that it would die away. When it did not, they gradually organised their own movement for church defence, and the warfare intensified. The established church proved, under its able broad church leadership, to be a formidable adversary and found that it too could mobilise considerable popular support in the country, largely by appeals for the preservation of the historic Church of Scotland as a venerated national institution. Patriotic sentiment, then, was enlisted on both sides of this conflict. Scotland was not the same as Ireland, and the struggle over the Scottish established church proved to be prolonged and hard-fought.

Roman Catholicism and the Vatican Council

While the Protestant churches had been carrying on their controversies over biblical criticism, science, education and disestablishment, the Roman Catholic Church in Britain had been quietly working to strengthen its provision of worship and pastoral care among its members. The hopes of 1850 that the restoration of the territorial hierarchy would bring the return of Britain to the Roman Catholic fold had faded by the 1860s – and the triumphalist spirit of Nicholas Wiseman's 'From the Flaminian Gate' had been replaced by more modest and realistic ambitions. The Roman Catholic Church in Britain faced profound challenges. The popular Protestant fury over the Ecclesiastical Titles Act had left British Catholics feeling alienated, marginalised and defensive. Most of the Catholic population in Britain was working class and poor, made up largely of post-famine Irish migrants. The church was hard-pressed to provide churches, schools, pastoral care and charitable relief for these largely impoverished Catholics. None the less, significant efforts were made. Between 1851 and 1870, the number of priests in England and Wales increased from 826 to 1,536, and the number of churches from 586 to 947.[108] There were by 1860 about 600,000 Roman Catholics in England and Wales, representing about 3.5 per cent of the population. In Scotland, there were about 350,000 Roman Catholics by 1878, making up some 9 per cent of the population.

Roman Catholic chapels, schools, priests and nuns were becoming a more familiar presence in the land. Among the governing classes, there were few individuals who did not know someone who had converted to Catholicism. William Gladstone's sister Helen had joined the Roman Catholic Church and her Protestant father allowed her a place for her private devotions in the family home at Fasque. Three of the brothers of Samuel Wilberforce, Anglican bishop of Oxford, had become Catholics. In the more liberal political atmosphere of the later 1850s, Catholics gained a number of political concessions. The Ecclesiastical Titles Act was never enforced. In 1858, Parliament ended the official church service of national thanksgiving that had been conducted on 5 November to mark the thwarting of Roman Catholic designs. From 1858, Catholic priests could be appointed as army chaplains, and from 1863 they could also be appointed as prison chaplains.[109] The 1860s and 1870s witnessed a renewed stream of conversions to Catholicism among the upper classes. Among the converts were Elizabeth, Lady Herbert of Lea, widow of Sidney Herbert and a prominent philanthropist, who converted in 1866; Lord Ripon, a member of the Liberal government and future viceroy of India, who converted in 1874; and Lord Albemarle, a former treasurer of the queen's household, who converted in 1879. The conversion in 1868 of the wealthy young third Marquis of Bute, with his vast estates in Scotland and Wales, had aroused considerable national interest and inspired Disraeli's novel, *Lothair*. A liberal Catholic school of thought emerged in the late 1850s, which centred on the Catholic literary review, *The Rambler* (which in 1862 was transformed into the *Home and Foreign Review*), and its leading contributor, the historian and man of letters, Lord Acton.

The improving status of Catholics was illustrated by a celebrated exchange between John Henry Newman and Charles Kingsley. Late in 1863, Kingsley had published an offhand remark in an article in *Macmillan's Magazine* – observing that Newman maintained Catholics need not be truthful, when deceit would serve their political ends. Newman, who had been living quietly in the Birmingham Oratory, saw the remark and, after first asking Kingsley to retract it, felt that he had to deny the allegation in public. There followed a spirited public controversy, in the course of which Kingsley accused Newman of dishonesty during his Anglican period – alleging that he had been a secret Roman Catholic for years before his formal conversion and had thus abused a position of trust in order to subvert the Church of England from within. Newman responded to this challenge to his integrity in the only way he thought he could: he published in 1864 a beautifully crafted autobiographical account of his conversion to Catholicism, the *Apologia pro Vita Sua*, in which he claimed to give expression to his innermost beliefs and feelings, and he invited the British public to judge him. The educated public was moved by his prose and judged favourably. The book became a best-seller, and was favourably reviewed even in Nonconformist journals. It was, Gladstone wrote to Samuel Wilberforce, 'one of the most touching, transparent, and profoundly interesting narratives I have read in my whole life'. 'It certainly gives me', he added, 'the impression of a great nobleness, and fills me with reverence for the man'.[110] Its success marked a public recognition that it was possible to be both a Roman Catholic and a truth-telling gentleman.

But not everyone welcomed the assimilation of Roman Catholics into British society. For many British Protestants, Catholics remained unwanted, foreign, volatile and disloyal. Catholics, many believed, could never become part of a British national culture, which owed its liberties, its progress, and its highest achievements, to its Protestantism. Protestant societies, such as the Evangelical Alliance, Protestant Alliance or Scottish Reformation Society, steadily turned out tracts, leaflets and magazines directed against Catholicism. They supported lecturers, who travelled about the country 'exposing' the superstition and iniquities of Rome. The London-based Protestant Evangelical Mission and Electoral Union, for example, was sponsoring 350 anti-Catholic lectures and 150 sermons at year by the late 1860s. One of its lecturers was William Murphy, an Irish-born convert to Protestantism from County Limerick, who by the mid-1860s was attracting large audiences with lurid attacks on priest-craft and the confessional, which bordered on the pornographic and were deeply offensive to Catholics. In June 1867, Murphy's lectures in Birmingham sparked off three days of sectarian riots, as working-class Irish Catholics broke up his meetings and Protestant supporters retaliated by ransacking Catholic neighbourhoods. His lectures led to further sectar-ian riots in 1868 in the Midlands.[111]

Protestant agitators continued to make allegations of dark practices in convents, including the imprisonment, abuse and starvation of young women who wished to renounce their vows. In 1869, public opinion was shocked and titillated by the Saurin case, in which an Irish-born Catholic nun brought a suit against her mother superior for libel. The trial, which was extensively reported in the newspapers, brought out lurid stories of systematic physical and mental abuse of the plaintiff, as well as of theft, cruelty and slander among the sisters. In the spring of 1870, the conserva-tive MP for North Warwickshire, Charles Newdegate, successfully moved for the creation of a parliamentary select committee to inquire into condi-tions within Catholic conventual and monastic institutions. Some were uncomfortable with the idea of inspectors forcing their way into women's personal living space and interrogating nuns about their private affairs, but others believed the convents were beyond the pale of respectability. In the event, the enquiry came to little, but there was clearly considerable public concern over the convents, which many persisted in viewing as grim, secre-tive, unwholesome and medieval institutions, out of place in a progressive nineteenth-century society. From platforms across the country Protestant campaigners thundered the message that the Roman Catholic Church was fundamentally opposed to human freedom, progress, and the spirit of the age, and intent upon enslaving people to priestcraft and superstition.

The opponents of Catholicism found additional reason for concern in the growing influence of ultramontanism, or the tendency within the Roman Catholic Church to seek to centralise all influence and authority within the papacy. The papacy was growing more assertive in the 1860s. It had recovered from the shock of the revolutions of 1848 and the loss of the papal states by 1860, and it was now striking back at the forces of modern society, including science, biblical scholarship, materialism, nationalism, socialism and liberalism, which Pope Pius IX believed were undermining the faith of simple believers. In 1864, the pope issued the Syllabus of Errors, a set of 80 theses which condemned many aspects of modern thought and concluded by rejecting the proposition that there must be any accommodation of the church 'with progress, liberalism and modern civilisation'. The following year, the primate of the English Catholic Church, Cardinal Wiseman, died after a long period of poor health. He was replaced as primate and archbishop of Westminster by Henry Manning, the former Church of England archdeacon of Chichester, who had entered the Roman Catholic Church during the Gorham controversy 14 years earlier. Lean, ascetic, able, ambitious and disciplined, Manning was at the height of his intellectual and administrative powers. He had been a close friend of Gladstone before becoming a Roman Catholic. But while Gladstone's thought had evolved to include broad church sympathies, Manning was one of the most uncompromising ultramontanes in England. He worked tirelessly to strengthen the church for its urban mission among the largely Irish Catholic working classes in England. He had little time for the type of cultivated English Catholicism represented by Newman, which he derided in a letter of February 1866 as 'the old Anglican, patristic, literary, Oxford tone transplanted into the Church'. 'It takes the line', he continued, 'of deprecating exaggerations, foreign devotions, Ultramontanism, anti-national sympathies. In one word, it is worldly Catholicism'.[112]

The ultramontanist commitment to strengthening papal authority led Pope Pius IX as early as 1864 to envisage holding a great ecumenical council in Rome. Its main business would be to promulgate the doctrine of papal infallibility, or the belief that the pope, when pronouncing *ex cathedra* on matters of faith and morals, was infallible, preserved against error by the Holy Spirit. Although the idea of papal infallibility had a long history in the church, it had never been formally declared as an article of faith for all Catholics. Pius IX believed that the moment had come to proclaim the doctrine and that it would strengthen and preserve the church in an era of growing uncertainty and doubt. In 1868 the papacy issued the summons to bishops from throughout the world Roman Catholic communion to attend the Vatican Council. Many, Catholics as well as non-Catholics, viewed the prospect with foreboding. Papal infallibility, they believed, represented a threat to civil liberties, by placing far too much authority in the hands of a pope whose infallible pronouncements could not be questioned by the faithful. Further, for such liberal Catholics as Lord Acton, the doctrine would require Catholics to place faith above reason, denying clear historical evidence that popes had erred and even contradicted one another.[113] Archbishop Manning, on the other hand, supported the doctrine with passion. In December 1869, some 600 bishops convened in the Vatican and over the next several months, the Council deliberated, though there was little doubt of what it would decide. On 18 July 1870, amid a summer thunderstorm, the crucial vote was taken and the bishops overwhelmingly adopted the doctrine of papal infallibility.

In Britain, Manning and the ultramontanes felt new confidence. The Roman Catholic Church would now have the authority that people needed so desperately in unsettled times; papal authority would provide the faithful with the true spiritual 'liberty' which mere freedom of speech and assembly – liberty in John Stuart Mill's sense – could never provide. 'Obedience to the Church', Manning insisted in a pamphlet published early in 1874, 'is liberty, and it is liberty because the Church cannot err or mislead either men or nations'. 'This', he continued, 'is Ultramontanism, or the liberty of the soul divinely guaranteed by an infallible Church'.[114]

The Liberal prime minister, Gladstone, grieved over what he termed in 1870 'the rampancy of Ultramontanism'.[115] The Vatican decrees, he believed, would stifle liberal Catholicism and raise up new barriers between Protestants and Catholics. In Ireland, the decrees would complicate his government's efforts to bring Catholics fully within the United Kingdom's liberal political order. So long as he was prime minister, Gladstone felt it was inappropriate for him to speak out publicly against the Vatican Council. However, with the fall of his government in 1874 – a fall which he attributed in part to the intransigence of the Irish Catholics after the Vatican Council – he let loose his indignation in a fierce pamphlet, *The Vatican Decrees in their Bearing on Civil Allegiance: A Political Exposition*, which appeared in November 1874. In the work, Gladstone maintained that papal infallibility represented a new doctrine – a 'policy of violence and change in faith'. It was aimed at ending the 'moral and mental freedom' of Catholics, placing them under the absolute authority of an infallible pope – a pope who had, in the Syllabus of Errors, 'condemned free speech, free writing, a free press, toleration of nonconformity, [and] liberty of conscience'.[116] Papal infallibility undermined the allegiance of Catholics to the civil state, by insisting that they give their absolute obedience in politics and social ethics to the pope. Supporters of the doctrine evidently hoped one day to subordinate all governments to papal dominance. 'Individual servitude', he insisted, 'however abject, will not satisfy the party now dominant in the Latin Church; the State must also be a slave.'[117] Such a pamphlet coming from the leader of the Liberal party and former prime minister aroused intense public interest, and 145,000 copies had been printed by the end of the year.[118]

Gladstone's pamphlet was met by a barrage of ultramontane pamphlets and articles. Of these, one of the most influential came from his former close friend, Manning. Gladstone and Manning had been estranged for a decade after the latter left the Church of England in 1851, and while they had renewed their relations in 1861, there was no longer the same intimacy. Beneath the 'external smoothness', Gladstone confided to his diary, there was a 'chill indescribable'.[119] This chill certainly permeated Manning's *The Vatican Decrees, in their Bearing on Civil Allegiance*, which appeared early in 1875. In the pamphlet, Manning expressed dismay that such a respected statesman should enter the field of theological controversy, a field of which he had little knowledge, and seek to foment sectarian suspicion and strife. Gladstone's pamphlet, Manning's observed, threw a shadow over a friendship of 45 years.[120] Manning then proceeded to insist that in proclaiming the doctrine of papal infallibility, the Vatican Council had not created a new doctrine, but had simply defined a belief that had been part of Catholic teaching since the beginning – since Christ had first promised divine assistance to the apostle Peter.[121] The Council had not discussed church–state relations, and papal infallibility did not affect the church's teachings about the obedience due to the civil authority. Those teachings remained what they had always been, and the six million Catholic subjects of the United Kingdom were loyal to the civil state, not in spite of their religion, but because of their church's teachings and because they had good reason to be loyal to a liberal state which respected religious freedom.[122] The Vatican Council had decided that a definition of the pope's infallibility in matters of faith and morals was needed at this time, not because it sought political dominion, but because of a conviction that Christian Europe was losing its moorings. Biblical criticism, historical studies of the early church, rationalism, science and materialism, were all threatening the faith for Catholics, as well as for Protestants. 'If I were asked to say what is the chief intellectual malady of England and of the world at this day', Manning observed:

I should say, ubiquitous, universal doubt, an uncertainty which came in like a flood after the rejection of the Divine certainty of Faith. This uncertainty has already led multitudes to an entire rejection of Christianity; and they have not rested even in Deism. They have gone on to the rejection even of natural religion. They have no certainty that they have a conscience, or a will, or a soul, or a law of morality, or that there is a God.[123]

In short, for Manning, the Vatican Council was part of the larger move-ment within Christendom to define the foundations of the faith and find a firm ground for belief in an era of scientific innovation and encroaching materialism. His church was not declaring war upon Protestantism or the liberal state; it was declaring war upon the unbelief that was becoming more pervasive every day.

Newman also answered Gladstone with a reasoned pamphlet that argued that Catholics shared the values of liberal Britain and had no tri-umphalist ambitions. Gladstone responded with a second pamphlet on the Vatican degrees in April 1875, and there were further answers to this – but then the controversy drew to a close. Gladstone had, not for the first time, allowed himself to become overexcited and to overstate his case, while the responses, especially those by Manning and Newman, appeared calm and reasoned. Neither Gladstone nor any other leading British politician was seriously willing to recommend legislative action against the decrees; there would be no revival of the penal laws or repeat of the Ecclesiastical Titles Act. The controversy served to highlight the fact that the Roman Catholic Church was independent of the state, that it could determine its doctrine as it pleased, and that while non-Catholics might not like its doctrines or practices, it was now too well embedded in British society to be seriously threatened. The Roman Catholic Church, indeed, now had a spiritual independence, a confidence in its mission and a sense of unity that many in the Church of England envied.

Ritualism and the Public Worship Regulation Act of 1874

While the Roman Catholic Church was strengthening its internal discipline and asserting its independent spiritual authority, the Church of England continued to be distracted by internal division and strife. In the later 1860s, this focused increasingly upon certain devotional practices being promoted by high church clergymen and lay people. These practices, referred to collectively as 'ritualism', had been gradually taking shape and gaining support within the Church of England since the 1840s. Ritualism had developed out of the Tractarian movement, and especially the Tractarian concern to recover a sense of the Church of England as part of the ancient Catholic and Apostolic church, and to revive the rich devotional life of the pre-Reformation centuries. Ritualists were concerned to restore the beauty and poetry of ancient liturgical practices and church decoration. Christian truth, they believed, was not only conveyed through Scripture and doctrinal formulations; it also took material forms through ceremony, church architecture, church decoration and clerical dress. These material forms were important because, in taking human form at the incarnation, Christ had sanctified the material world. The ceremonies, images and practices were symbols of higher spiritual truths, they were material expressions of God's grace, and were thus to be approached with reverence and with scrupulous regard.

Ritualists sought to bring more colour, light, music, poetry and drama to public worship, and to beautify the interiors of their churches, removing high pews and high pulpits, installing stone altars decorated with candles, colourful covers and flowers, decorating the chancel, erecting rood screens, hanging tapestries, placing crucifixes and ornaments, and multiplying stained glass windows. In this, they reflected the tastes of many mid-Victorians, who liked their sitting rooms lavishly furnished and filled to overflowing with prints, objects of art, overstuffed chairs and lavish drapery. By 1870, most English cities had at least one ritualist church. Ritualist clergy, moreover, emphasised their priestly character. They adopted distinctive dress outside of church, including white 'dog-collars', long black coats and what evangelicals dubbed 'Mark of the Beast' black waistcoats (so-called for their similarity to the dress of Roman Catholic priests). Many remained celibate. They heard private confessions. Some were dedicated pastors, accepting difficult curacies in deprived urban districts and gaining support through selfless service. Ritualist priests had frequently embraced the high conception of their office while students at one of the new diocesan training colleges. Cuddesdon, the high church theological college founded in 1853 in the diocese of Oxford, became, through the influence of its first vice-principal, the Anglo-Catholic H. P. Liddon, a particular nursery of ritualist clergy. The protégé and biographer of Pusey, Liddon was one of the more eloquent preachers of the Victorian era and exercised a profound influence over aspiring priests at Cuddesdon and at Oxford University, where he became professor of exegesis in 1870. Ritualist clergy frequently came from aristocratic or upper-middle-class backgrounds. Some had private incomes, which gave them the self-assurance and independence needed to persist in their practices against opposition.[124] In worship, ritualist practices varied, but ritualist priests broadly agreed upon six main points of ceremony: they wore vestments when performing church services; adopted the eastward position when celebrating the eucharist; mixed water and wine in the chalice; used unleavened wafer bread at Holy Communion; placed lighted candles on the altar; and burned incense.

These practices were contentious and divisive within Church of England congregations. Evangelicals and liberal Anglicans believed the ritualists were intent on Romanising the Anglican Church through sensual, foreign and superstitious practices. At the same time, ritualist priests had their supporters, including many working-class people who enjoyed the colour, incense and poetry of ritualist services within beautifully decorated churches. Working people could be attracted to ritualist services for many of the same reasons they were attracted to revivalist services – for the drama and spectacle. Many labouring families, moreover, had experienced at first hand the pastoral commitment of the ritualist clergy. For example, the ritualist priests, Alexander Mackonochie and Charles Lowder, visited regularly among working-class victims of the cholera epidemic of 1866 in the London docklands, working closely with the Anglican sisters and helping raise money for the victims and their families.[125]

Both the ritualists and their opponents organised associations to represent their views. Beginning in the later 1840s, Tractarians and Anglo-Catholics formed local Church Unions, for the purpose of defending a range of high church principles. In 1860, an English Church Union was created, with the aim of co-ordinating the work of local Church Unions in defending ritualist practices. The English Church Union was a mainly lay society, with about 200 branches and nearly 7,000 members by 1870. It supported a weekly journal, the *Church Review*, founded in 1861.[126] The Anglo-Catholic *Church Times*, founded in 1863, had a circulation of some 10,000 by 1865.[127] From the early 1850s, Anglo-Catholics had also begun forming confraternities and parish guilds for the laity, to promote ritualism and a better understanding of the sacraments, to encourage the leading of disciplined spiritual lives, to conduct general church work or to assist the parish clergy. In 1871, a number of these guilds joined to form the Church Guilds Union.

The opponents of ritualism responded in 1865 by forming the Church Association, for the purpose of counteracting 'the efforts now being made to pervert the teaching of the Church of England on essential points of the Christian faith, or assimilate her services to those of the Church of Rome'. By 1869, the Church Association had 138 branches and over 8,000 members.[128] It decided on a policy of bringing private prosecutions in the courts against ritualist priests for breaking the laws regulating worship within the established church. The aim was to secure legal judgments that would clarify the law and force ritualist priests to desist from illegal practices. Although denigrated by its opponents as 'The Persecution Society, Limited', the Church Association was convinced that it had no other course of action. Its prosecutions led to a series of legal cases, in the course of which the Judicial Committee of the Privy Council ruled that a number of ritualistic practices were unlawful. The prosecutions, however, proved to be lengthy, bitterly contested and expensive. For example, the case involving the Revd John Purchas, vicar of St James, Brighton, lasted over three years and cost nearly £7,700.[129] Even when expensive prosecutions did result in Privy Council decisions that certain ritualist practices were unlawful, there was no guarantee that all ritualist priests would cease the actions. Many simply ignored the ruling. The only way to suppress the illegal practices, it seemed, was to bring expensive prosecutions against each individual ritualist clergyman, and even then there was no certainty that the offender would submit to the law. For its critics, the established church was in process of breaking in two. 'In philosophy, in dogma, in ecclesiastical sympathies, in ritual', observed the Congregationalist minister, J. Guinness Rogers, of the two factions in 1869, 'they are as wide as poles asunder'.[130] For Guinness Rogers, this was further reason to disestablish a church which had no claim to be national. By February 1871, even Gladstone suspected, as he informed his friend, H. P. Liddon, that the ritualist controversy was 'too likely to end not only in disestablishment but in schism'.[131]

Beginning in 1865, the evangelical Lord Shaftesbury introduced a series of parliamentary bills aimed at controlling ritualism, all of them unsuccessful.[132] In 1867, the government appointed a Royal Commission to enquire into the ritualist controversy. The Commission, however, was soon divided. A majority of the commissioners recommended legislation to curb ritual, including the creation of a new court to judge ritual cases. But a substantial minority opposed legislation, which they feared would strengthen the state's control over the church and would drive many ritualists, who were often exemplary pastors and people of blameless moral lives, out of the church. As the controversy continued to rage, the pressure for action increased. Finally in early 1874, the archbishop of Canterbury, A. C. Tait, brought forward a parliamentary bill aimed at facilitating prosecutions of ritualists. Tait had no love for them. Nor did the queen, who informed Tait on 15 January 1874 that 'Something *must be done*' to stop their 'Romanizing tendencies'.[133] Widespread Protestant opposition to the Vatican decrees contributed to the demand for action. Disraeli's Conservative government came to office in February 1874, and although the cabinet included moderate ritualists, most notably the high church Lord Salisbury, the government supported the archbishop's bill. Disraeli, indeed, defended it in the Commons as a bill 'to put down Ritualism' and bring an end to the 'Mass in masquerade'.[134] The Public Worship Regulation Act became law in August 1874.

The Act did not change the law regarding ritual, but rather tried to improve its enforcement – by creating a new court to try ritual cases. The court was presided over by a single judge appointed jointly by the archbishops of Canterbury and York. Formal complaints against alleged violations of the law governing ritual were to be made to the bishop of the diocese, who would then have three options. He could veto the proceedings, try the case himself, or allow the case to be tried in the new ritual court. If a case went to the court, the judge had the power to suspend a clergyman from his benefice or even deprive him of it – although the offender would have the right to appeal against the judgment to the Judicial Committee of the Privy Council. The Public Worship Regulation Act found little support within the church as a whole. Many objected that it weakened the role of the bishops, and strengthened the control of the state over the church. The first judge of the ritual court to be appointed was Lord Penzance, and it did not help that he had been a former judge in divorce cases.

The Public Worship Regulation Act did not end the strife over ritual. On the contrary, it probably strengthened the resolve of ritualist priests to resist what they viewed as efforts by the civil power to suppress ancient Christian practices and persecute the faithful. There were soon martyrs. In 1876, Revd Arthur Tooth, incumbent of St James, Hatcham, in the diocese of Rochester, was charged under the Public Worship Regulation Act with 18 offences, including the wearing of improper vestments, the use of incense and the mixture of water and wine in the chalice. Refusing to recognise Lord Penzance's court, Tooth was imprisoned for contempt of court on 22 January 1877. For his supporters, he was a martyr to conscience, and he was visited in prison by leading Anglo-Catholics. Those who had brought the charges against him had not wanted him imprisoned, and they now asked for his release. Tooth was let out on 17 February, though he was barred from entering his church. Far from feeling contrite, Tooth broke into the church through a window and conducted worship. Further legal proceedings were only avoided when Archbishop Tait convinced Tooth, a man of independent wealth, to resign his living. During the next decade, four more ritualist priests were imprisoned for contempt of court, with the Revd S. F. Green, of St John's, Miles Platting, Birmingham, locked up for the longest period – 20 months between March 1881 and November 1882. The imprisonment of these committed ritualist clerics made the Public Worship Regulation Act appear odious and oppressive – a blunt instrument of state control. In consequence, bishops became increasingly unwilling to allow cases within their dioceses to be tried before Lord Penzance's court. The ritualist clergy, meanwhile, came to see themselves as godly rebels resisting an unjust order in church and state, prepared to suffer in obedience to a higher spiritual authority. They saw themselves as followers of the Christ who had challenged the established order of His day, and was crucified by the Roman state. Their sense of being rebels brought some ritualists to identify with other opponents of the established order, including land reformers, Irish nationalists and socialist activists.

Revivalism again

In June 1873, with the religious life of the three kingdoms distracted by conflicts over biblical authority, Darwinism, national education, disestablishment, the Vatican council and ritualism, two American lay evangelists arrived quietly in Liverpool. They had come at the invitation of two English evangelical Nonconformists, who had promised to cover their expenses. However, when the Americans arrived, they learned that their prospective hosts had both died several weeks earlier, and no arrangements had been made for them. Stranded, they decided to do some itinerant preaching in the north of England before returning home.

Dwight L. Moody was a former shoe salesman from Chicago with five years of primary schooling, who had become involved with the Young Men's Christian Association. He served with the Christian Commission during the Civil War and became a professional evangelist a few years after the end of the war. He was 37 years old, a short, stocky man with a heavy black beard and piercing eyes. He presented a simple gospel message in a direct, straightforward manner of speaking, full of American slang and homely anecdotes. His partner, Ira D. Sankey, had worked at his father's bank in Pennsylvania, served with the Union army during the war, and met Moody in 1870 through his involvement in the YMCA movement. Sankey provided musical accompaniment at evangelical meetings, singing sentimental gospel songs in a deep baritone voice and playing a small portable organ. After some months of conducting meetings, with only moderate success, in the north of England, the Americans were invited by some ministers of the Scottish Free Church to come to Edinburgh and lead a revival campaign there.

Arriving in Edinburgh in late November, they soon made an extraordinary impact and began drawing immense crowds. 'Our American brethren', reported the Edinburgh *Daily News* on 29 November 1873, '. . . have shaken Edinburgh out of its genteel propriety this week'. Moody and Sankey would regularly conduct three meetings a day, including a noon prayer meeting in the Free Church Assembly Hall which attracted an average attendance of about 2,000. Their meetings were carefully orchestrated, with a programme of Bible readings, gospel songs and short, racy addresses. The message in Moody's addresses was a simple one – what he termed the 'three Rs', 'Ruin by Sin, Redemption by Christ, and Regeneration by the Holy Ghost'. Many meetings closed with an appeal to the anxious to come forward and stay for an inquiry meeting. Here lay volunteers would converse earnestly with each inquirer, generally male volunteers with males, and female volunteers with females. Names and addresses would be taken and given to local ministers, who would arrange follow-up visits. For much of Edinburgh, Moody and Sankey brought a new approach to religion. People enjoyed Sankey's gospel songs, grounded in the flourishing American popular music industry, with catchy tunes and sentimental themes. They responded warmly to Moody's addresses, which were given in simple language with familiar illustrations. Moody told Bible stories as though they involved everyday people and might have occurred in any Edinburgh neighbourhood. He had a store of humorous stories. He also had a great number of poignant anecdotes – about dying children, suffering mothers, prodigal sons, repentant drunkards – which could reduce his audiences to tears.

To Scots accustomed to sedate Presbyterian services and intellectual sermons, the American revivalists were refreshing and full of life. Their meetings were, moreover, respectable, without the outbursts and prostrations that had accompanied meetings during the 1859 revival; middle-class people could attend without being embarrassed. 'The singular quietness and orderliness' of the meetings, observed an Edinburgh Free Church College professor, 'have struck every one. There has been no sensationalism, no undue excitement, no prostrations, no screaming, no fondness for late meetings'. 'It is', he added, 'revival without revivalism'.[135] This calmness resulted in part from the careful orchestration of the meetings. When Moody sensed that his preaching might be overexciting some hearers, he would quietly signal to Sankey, and from the corner of the stage would come soft chords from the harmonium, and Sankey's deep bass voice would intone a gentle gospel song to calm the mood. Moody and Sankey were not identified with any social class or any particular denomination, and they seemed refreshingly unconcerned with the issues of patronage, disestablishment or Vatican decrees, which so absorbed the minds of the Scottish clergy. Instead, they proclaimed an old-fashioned gospel in a language ordinary people could understand.

In February 1874, Moody and Sankey proceeded to Glasgow, where they remained for some months, experiencing similar success. Their final Glasgow meeting was conduced on 17 April in the Botanical Gardens, and attracted an estimated 20,000, with 2,000 remaining for the inquirers' meeting. After a preaching tour of the north and west of Scotland, they crossed to Ireland, spending the autumn of 1874 in Belfast and Dublin, where their packed meetings attracted Catholics as well as Protestants. Indeed, Cardinal Cullen felt obliged to issue a pastoral letter condemning 'itinerant preachers or singers'.[136] At the end of November they crossed to England, and for the next several months they conducted revivals in the great commercial and industrial cities of the North and Midlands – Liverpool, Manchester, Sheffield, Birmingham. There were careful preparations in each city in advance of their arrival; local supporters formed committees, raised funds, rented halls, prepared advertisements, organised choirs, gained support among the clergy and visited households. In Birmingham, the Congregational pastor and political activist, R. W. Dale, surprised many when he threw his support behind the ungainly 'two American strangers', whose success he believed was divinely inspired. 'I told Mr Moody', Dale reported in the *Congregationalist* for March 1875, 'that the work was most plainly of God, for I could see no real relation between him and what he had done'. 'He laughed cheerfully', Dale added, 'and said he should be very sorry if it were otherwise'.[137]

In March 1875, Moody and Sankey began a London mission that continued until July. Supporters booked the Agricultural Hall in Islington, the largest enclosed space in the city. They installed 15,000 chairs, expanded the gas-lighting system and hung huge crimson banners, emblazoned with Scriptural passages. In addition to the nightly meetings at Islington, meetings were held at Exeter Hall, and at churches around the city. There were an estimated 2,500,000 attendances at the Moody and Sankey meetings in London, although this number included many who attended more than once. The crowds included people of all social classes. Many who came out of curiosity or for the entertainment found themselves won over. In the tense religious atmosphere of 1875, the Americans offered their hearers a return to a simple gospel and a simpler time. Gladstone looked in on one of the Islington meetings, and was impressed by Moody's power to hold so many spellbound.

There was, however, also much opposition. Broad church clergy and liberal Nonconformist ministers fastened on Moody's lack of theological learning and biblical literalism, which, they argued, could not meet the intellectual challenges to the faith. 'I do not think', observed the liberal Dundee United Presbyterian minister, George Gilfillan, of the revivalists in March 1874, 'that the Doubt of the Age is such a shallow matter after all as can be disposed of by a few well-played tunes and a good many earnest but not very well digested harangues'.[138] High church and even many evangelical Anglicans were unhappy with the revivalists' lack of due reverence for ecclesiastical forms and episcopal leadership. There was also much condemnation of Moody's efforts to popularise divine truths and biblical stories by presenting them in everyday language; surely this was vulgar and disrespectful. Complaints were made about the confused state of the inquirers' meeting, where the gospel workers often appeared as ignorant about basic Christian doctrines as the inquirers. In May 1875, Archbishop Tait published a letter in the press in which he refused to give the revival movement 'any direct sanction'; he was especially unhappy with the inquirers' meetings, in which untrained persons tried to provide spiritual guidance to often troubled individuals. When pressed to attend one of the revival meetings, the queen declined, observing that 'this sensational style of excitement like the revivalists is not the religion which *can last*'.[139] Some critics claimed that the revivalists failed to reach the working classes, and that those who packed their meetings were largely female middle-class churchgoers.

Yet many working people did attend the meetings, and many were as a result drawn to an active Christian life. As John Coffey has argued, labouring people were attracted to the egalitarian and democratic atmosphere of the meetings.[140] Moody presented himself as an ordinary man, without much formal education and without pretensions, who had a common-sense approach to religion. He never spoke down to people. Behind his biblical literalism was the Reformation ideal that ordinary people should read and interpret Scripture for themselves. While he sought the co-operation of local clergy in campaigns, he did not defer to their authority, social status or education. As the *Daily Telegraph* observed in May 1875, Moody's message brought to all 'a sense of personal worth, and proclaimed the equality of the poor with the rich'.[141] Nor was Moody's message simply one of personal salvation. He had a social conscience, and was distressed by urban poverty. He took his meetings into deprived districts, and encouraged his supporters to follow up his revival meetings with philanthropic work. Moody would later grow more conservative in his social attitudes, but between 1873 and 1875 he believed in social progress through the influence of Christian moral and spiritual teachings. He appealed to the moral sense of common people in the increasingly democratic society that followed the Parliamentary Reform Acts of 1867 and 1868, and many labouring men and women responded to that appeal.

The Moody and Sankey campaign coincided with a revival of the holiness teachings that had played such an important role in the revival of 1859–62. These teachings, with their roots in Methodist doctrines of Christian perfection, had been nurtured after 1856 by a series of annual conferences for Christian workers held first at Barnet and then at Mildmay Park in north London. The conferences were major events in the evangelical calendar – the conference in 1869 had attracted over 1,000 participants – and they reflected the desire among Christians to transform their lives in a practical sense. In 1873, another pair of American lay revivalists arrived in Britain, bringing with them vivid new expressions of the holiness teachings. They were Robert Pearsall Smith, a prosperous glass manufacturer, and his wife Hannah, who had been raised by Quakers and retained Quaker dress and modes of speech. For the Pearsall Smiths, the true Christian life was characterised by a complete triumph over sin. This triumph was not simply to be achieved in the next life; it could be experienced by the Christian in this world. The power to overcome the temptations of sin, they insisted, was a free gift from God to the faithful. It came through a sudden, post-conversion experience, bringing immediate sanctification. The believer experienced a second baptism by the Holy Spirit, which brought with it a fulfilling 'Higher Life' of happiness and peace of mind, free from any conscious sense of sin. Some spoke of it as a second conversion experience. The Pearsall Smiths carried their gospel of holiness through England, speaking at well-attended conferences and numerous smaller meetings. Their teachings resonated with the mid-Victorian emphasis on the vital importance of individual moral character, as well as with the desire of many Christians to experience Christ within, independently of the external evidences of Christianity. But Robert, it appeared, was not himself totally free of the temptations of the flesh. In the early summer of 1875, he evidently attempted to seduce a young female admirer in a London hotel, and the Pearsall Smiths were hustled by their promoters back to America. The reason for this hurried departure was successfully kept quiet, and the holiness teachings continued to spread.[142]

In July 1875, supporters of the new teachings held an interdenominational 'Convention for the Promotion of Practical Holiness', gathering together some 400 participants at Keswick, in the English Lake District. The summer Keswick conferences became annual events and the number of participants grew to several thousand by the end of the century. The conferences served both to promote the holiness teachings and to provide the movement with an institutional base. They offered participants the prospect for the 'Higher Life' amid the fellowship of like-minded Christians. The Keswick influence spread to the universities, making a particular impact at Cambridge. In 1877, the evangelical Cambridge Inter-Collegiate Christian Union was formed, and about the same time evangelicals began preparations for a new residential hall for the training of clergy. Ridley Hall was opened in 1881; its first principal was the Anglican clergyman, H. C. G. Moule, who was a regular participant in the Keswick conferences and deeply influenced by the holiness teachings. Under Moule's leadership, Ridley Hall became a major training college not only for evangelical clergymen at home but also for missionaries, sending out nearly 200 ministers to the mission fields or colonies between 1881 and 1899. As Andrew Porter has shown, the holiness teachings of Keswick, communicated through such educational institutions as Ridley Hall, exercised a profound influence upon British overseas missions.[143] They promoted an increased emphasis on the 'Higher Life' in the character and conduct of mission workers. The formation of individual moral character was increasingly viewed as the key to success in the mission field, and evangelicals noted the evidence of the indwelling of Christ and the Higher Life in such Christian heroes as David Livingstone and, as we shall see, General Charles Gordon. Emphasis was placed on the faithfulness of the individual mission worker more than on the supporting missionary organisation, and on zeal for gospel more than on knowledge of other cultures and religions. This focus on individual character resonated with the growing emphasis within the schools and universities upon team sports and physical training in character formation. Indeed the Evangelical world was ecstatic when, in 1885, the famed 'Cambridge Seven' – seven well-connected students and sportsmen of the highest moral and spiritual character – became missionaries in China. What Moule described as the 'uncompromising spirituality and unworldliness' of such Keswick-influenced missionaries of the 1880s could also lead to highhanded and intolerant attitudes towards non-Western Christians in the mission fields. At the same time, the enthusiasms awakened by the revivals of the 1870s contributed to a renewed commitment to Christian Britain's mission to spread both Christianity and civilisation to the wider world.

The revival movement of the 1870s found still another expression. In the later part of the decade, the holiness revivalists William and Catherine Booth began dressing the members of their Christian Society in uniforms, giving them military titles, and making use of brass bands to call attention to their open-air meetings on the streets of London and other cities. Reflecting the growing public fervour for military and imperial heroes, they rechristened their Society in 1878 the 'Salvation Army', and declared war upon home heathenism. In 1879, they began a new magazine, *The War Cry*, which had a circulation of 110,000 within a year. They continued the commitment to the holiness theology that they had embraced in the early 1860s. Their pretensions to military titles and uniforms, meanwhile, aroused anger from urban mobs. Encouraged by local pub owners (who viewed the Salvationists as a threat to business) and often emboldened with free drink, local thugs frequently attacked the Salvationists' meetings, physically assaulting both men and women. In 1882 alone, William Booth claimed that 669 Salvationists (including 251 women) had been injured in mob attacks. The Salvationists, however, viewed the attacks as the ragings of Satan, and accepted the blows as wounds for the Lord. Gradually, the authorities began acting to protect their meetings, while the public grew to respect their courage and refusal to return the blows. By 1882, there were 440 Salvation Army corps, and 1,019 officers; this had increased to 910 corps and 2,332 officers by 1884. Women took a leading role in the movement, serving as officers and often exercising authority over men, and the 'hallelujah lasses', as the women Salvationists were known, became a frequent sight on the streets of urban Britain.[144]

Conclusion

The religious life in the United Kingdom had grown increasingly diverse between the late 1850s and the late 1870s. A multitude of religious denominations and movements flourished in the liberal environment of the mid-Victorian years. The religious revival movements of 1858–62 and 1873–78 had not succeeded in reimposing an evangelical faith upon the whole of the United Kingdom. But they had strengthened religious feeling, especially among the labouring orders, and they had promoted varied and lively forms of religious expression – mission halls, revival services, holiness teachings, Keswick conferences and the Salvation Army.

The mid-Victorian years saw intense religious strife – between religious liberals and conservatives, Nonconformist churches and established churches, Protestants and Catholics, ritualists and anti-ritualists. And yet the strife did not lead to many new schisms or to much actual violence, and there was a growing consensus among educated men and women that toleration was a virtue – and that even honest doubters and Roman Catholics could be respectable members of civil society. This consensus was reflected in the growing influence of the broad church movement. Moreover, since the failure of the Ecclesiastical Titles Act of 1851, the parliamentary state had grown less prepared to promote any particular religious creed or practices. Parliament, to be sure, maintained the established churches in Britain. However, it disestablished the Church of Ireland in 1869 when there was a clear electoral mandate to do so, and it was becoming evident that it would also disestablish the Church of Scotland, and even the Church of England, should it receive a similar mandate. In the Education Act of 1870, Parliament had agreed that the new board schools would not provide instruction in the creeds or formularies of any particular Christian denomination. Further, very soon after the passing of the Public Worship Regulation Act in 1874, it had become clear to many that the legislation had been misguided, and that the state should not have put itself in a position in which it had to imprison conscientious ritualist clergymen. Individual politicians, certainly, had strong religious opinions, and expressed them in public debate – as Gladstone had done over the Vatican decrees. But Parliament as a whole was becoming less prepared either to promote any particular denomination, or to suppress or persecute any group for its religious opinions. Even amid the furore over the Vatican decrees, there had been no serious consideration of reviving the anti-Catholic penal laws, which most would have viewed as a backward step and an undoing of the achievements of the century.

The controversies of these years had aroused great passion. Many Christians were prepared to speak out against what they believed were false religious teachings or dangerous practices; they attended meetings and demonstrations, signed petitions, and loudly denounced Romanists, ritualists, revivalists, Salvationists, women preachers, Darwinists, biblical critics, established churches or disestablishers. Behind much of this passion was a profound insecurity in the face of the new scientific and biblical scholarship, and a longing for certainty and authority – which could lead to hostility against those seen as undermining religious truth. Still, it is also important to note that these controversies were only a part of religious life. Millions of mid-Victorians attended church Sunday after Sunday, heard sermons, read the Bible and religious periodicals, sang hymns, gave generously to religious causes, and practised Christian virtues because they found spiritual fulfilment in doing so, and because they hoped for eternal life. Further, amid the conflicts, there also remained for many a strong sense of Britain as a fundamentally Christian nation, with a collective responsibility before God. This was especially true as British Christians contemplated their power and influence in the wider world.

Notes

1 A. Holmes, *The Shaping of Ulster Presbyterian Belief and Practice, 1770 to 1840* (Oxford, 2006).

2 J. Weir, *The Ulster Awakening* (London, 1860), 15–17.

3 W. T. Latimer, *A History of Ulster Presbyterians*, 2nd edn (Belfast, 1902), 492.

4 W. Steuart Trench, *Realities of Irish Life*, 5th edn (London, 1870), 332.

5 P. Gibbon, *The Origins of Ulster Unionism* (Manchester, 1975), 58–62.

6 G. Salmon, *The Evidences of the Work of the Holy Spirit* (Dublin, 1859), 47.

7 *United Presbyterian Magazine*, new series, vol. iii (September 1859), 400.

8 *Proceedings and Debates of the General Assembly of the Free Church of Scotland* (1861), 75–86.

9 K. S. Jeffrey, *When the Lord Walked the Land: The 1858–62 Revival in the North East of Scotland* (Carlisle, 2002), 254–6.

10 C. Brown, *Religion and Society in Scotland since 1707* (Edinburgh, 1997), 116.

11 J. Macpherson, *Life and Labours of Duncan Matheson* (London, 1871), 152–3.

12 Jeffrey, *When the Lord Walked the Land*, 185.

13 N. T. R. Dickson, *Brethren in Scotland 1838–2000* (Carlisle, 2003), 72–111.

14 Brown, *Religion and Society in Scotland since 1707*, 116.

15 R. Carwardine, *Transatlantic Revivalism: Popular Evangelicalism in Britain and America 1790–1865* (Westport, Conn., 1978), 173.

16 D. Gareth Evans, *A History of Wales 1815–1906* (Cardiff, 1989), 237–8; P. Jenkins, *History of Modern Wales* (London, 1992), 201.

17 Watts, *The Dissenters*, vol. ii, 667.

18 J. Kent, *Holding the Fort: Studies in Victorian Revivalism* (London, 1978), 115.

19 W. Robertson Nicoll, *Princes of the Church* (London, 1921), 50.

20 R. J. Helmstadter, 'Spurgeon in Outcast London', in P. T. Phillips (ed.), *The View from the Pulpit: Victorian Ministers and Society* (Toronto, 1978), 161–85; H. Davies, *Worship and Theology in England: From Newman to Martineau, 1850–1900* (Princeton, 1962), 333–41.

21 O. Anderson, 'Women Preachers in Mid-Victorian Britain: Some Reflexions on Feminism, Popular Religion and Social Change', *Historical Journal*, 12 (1969), 467–84.

22 P. J. Walker, *Pulling the Devil's Kingdom Down: The Salvation Army in Victorian Britain* (Berkeley, 2001), 22–34, 109–113.

23 J. S. Mill, *On Liberty* (1859), D. Spitz (ed.) (New York, 1975), 31.

24 M. Pattison, *Memoirs of an Oxford Don*, 1885 (London, 1988), 164.

25 H. R. Murphy, 'The Ethical Revolt against Christian Orthodoxy in Early Victorian England', *American Historical Review*, 60; 4 (July 1955), 800–17.

26 From *An Examination of Sir William Hamilton's Philosophy*, quoted in G. Rowell, *Hell and the Victorians* (Oxford, 1974), 3.

27 C. C. Gillespie, *Genesis and Geology* (New York, 1959), 121–48.

28 A. Desmond, *The Politics of Evolution: Morphology, Medicine and Reform in Radical London* (Chicago, 1989), 41–100.

29 Ibid., 60.

30 W. Irvine, *Apes, Angels and Victorians: A Joint Biography of Darwin and Huxley* (London, 1956), 107–11.

31 J. Oppenheim, *The Other World: Spiritualism and Psychical Research in England, 1850–1914* (Cambridge, 1985), 308–11.

32 J. W. Burrow, *The Crisis of Reason: European Thought, 1848–1914* (New Haven, Conn., 2000), 80.

33 [S. Wilberforce], 'Darwin's *Origin of Species*', *Quarterly Review*, vol. 108 (July, 1860), 231.

34 F. Turner, 'The Victorian Conflict between Science and Religion', in F. Turner, *Contesting Cultural Authority* (Cambridge, 1993), 171–200.

35 J. L. Altholz, *Anatomy of a Controversy: The Debate over Essays and Reviews 1860–1864* (Aldershot, Hants., 1994), 5.

36 R. T. Shannon, 'John Robert Seeley and the Idea of a National Church', in R. Robson (ed.), *Ideas and Institutions of Victorian Britain* (London, 1967), 236.

37 Cited in A. Crowther, *Church Embattled: Religious Controversy in Mid-Victorian England* (Newton Abbot, Devon, 1970), 39.

38 Much of the following discussion is based on Joseph Altholz's definitive recent study, the *Anatomy of a Controversy*.

39 Cited in Altholz, *Anatomy of a Controversy*, 35.

40 [F. Harrison], 'Neo-Christianity', *Westminster and Foreign Quarterly Review*, new series, no. 36 (October 1860), 293–332.

41 Ibid., 296.

42 J. Guy, *The Heretic: A Study of the Life of John William Colenso 1814–1883* (Johannesburg, 1983); P. Hinchcliff, *John William Colenso: Bishop of Natal* (London, 1964). For a brief overview of the controversy, see T. Larsen, 'Bishop Colenso and his Critics: The Strange Emergence of Biblical Criticism in Victorian Britain', *Scottish Journal of Theology*, 50 (1997), 433–58.

43 R. Gray, Bishop of Cape Town, to S. Wilberforce, Bodleian Library, Oxford, Wilberforce Mss, d.39, fos 1–8.

44 J. W. Colenso, *The Pentateuch and Book of Joshua Critically Examined*, Part I, 5th edn (London, 1863), vii–ix.

45 Cited in T. R. Davidson and W. Bentham, *Life of Archibald Campbell Tait*, 2 vols, 3rd edn (London, 1891), vol. i, 337.

46 Quoted in Guy, *The Heretic*, 133.

47 Chadwick, *Victorian Church*, part ii, 65.

48 Gladstone to Macmillan and Co., 25 December 1865, in *Correspondence on Church and Religion of William Ewart Gladstone*, D. C. Lathbury (ed.), 2 vols (London, 1910), vol. ii, 87–8.

49 B. F. Westcott, 'The Universities in Relation to Missionary Work', in B. F. Westcott, *On Some Points in the Religious Office of the Universities* (London, 1873), 25–44.

50 Ibid., 68.

51 J. Cox, *Imperial Fault Lines: Christianity and Colonial Power in India, 1818–1940* (Stanford, CA, 2002), 47–8, 136–7; A. Westcott, *Life and Letters of Brooke Foss Westcott*, 2 vols (London, 1903), vol. i, 383–4, 422–3.

52 F. Max Müller, 'Westminster Lecture on Missions', in F. Max Müller, *Selected Essays on Language, Mythology and Religion*, 2 vols (London, 1881), vol. ii, 46–86.

53 Ibid., 73.

54 Lord Amberley, 'The Church of England as a Religious Body, Part I', *Fortnightly Review*, 6 (1 December 1866), 778.

55 Lord Amberley, 'The Church of England as a Religious Body, Part II', *Fortnightly Review*, new series, 1 (1 February 1867), 199.

56 J. R. Seeley, 'The Church as a Teacher of Morality', in J. R. Seeley, *Lectures and Essays* (London, 1870), 245–89.

57 M. Arnold, *Culture and Anarchy* (1869), in *The Complete Prose Works of Matthew Arnold*, R. H. Super (ed.), 11 vols (Ann Arbor, Mich., 1960–77), vol. v, 226.

58 R. D. Brackenridge, 'The "Sabbath War" of 1865–66: The Shaking of the Foundations', *Records of the Scottish Church History Society*, 16 (1969), 23–34.

59 A. C. Cheyne, *The Transforming of the Kirk: Victorian Scotland's Religious Revolution* (Edinburgh, 1983), 74.

60 P. Carnegie Simpson, *Life of Principal Rainy*, 2 vols (London, 1909), vol. I, 306–403.

61 R. W. Dale, 'Mr Arnold and the Nonconformists', *Contemporary Review*, 14 (July 1870), 569.

62 Skeats and Miall, *History of the Free Churches of England*, 569–73; A. W. W. Dale, *Life of R. W. Dale of Birmingham* (London, 1902), 164–78; J. Kenyon, 'R. W. Dale and Christian Worldliness', in Phillipps (ed.), *View from the Pulpit*, 187–209.

63 M. J. D. Roberts, 'Pressure-group Politics and the Church of England: the Church Defence Institution 1859–1896', *Journal of Ecclesiastical History*, 35 (Oct. 1984), 564.

64 S. M. Ingham, 'The Disestablishment Movement in England, 1868–71', *Journal of Religious History*, 3 (1964), 39.

65 P. M. H. Bell, *Disestablishment in Ireland and Wales* (London, 1969), 19–21; Machin, *Politics and the Churches in Great Britain 1832 to 1868*, 345–6; J. Vincent, *The Formation of the British Liberal Party* (New York, 1966), 73–4.

66 Quoted in Larsen, *Friends of Religious Equality*, 92.

67 Hoppen, *The Mid-Victorian Generation*, 253.

68 D. Bebbington, *The Mind of Gladstone: Religion, Homer, and Politics* (Oxford, 2004), 105–41.

69 W. E. Gladstone to S. Wilberforce, 2 October 1862, 'Most Private', Bodleian Library, Oxford, Wilberforce Papers, d. 37, fos 51–4.

70 Morley, *Life of William Ewart Gladstone*, vol. I, 768–71.

71 N. D. Emerson, 'The Last Phase of the Establishment', in W. A. Phillips (ed.), *History of the Church of Ireland*, 3 vols (Oxford, 1933), vol. iii, 314–5.

72 Bell, *Disestablishment in Ireland and Wales*, 29–41.

73 R. C. Trench. Archbishop of Dublin, *A Primary Charge delivered to the Clergy* (Dublin, 1865), 71.

74 Quoted in E. R. Norman, *The Catholic Church and Ireland in the Age of Rebellion 1859–1873* (London, 1965), 12.

75 E. Larkin, *The Consolidation of the Roman Catholic Church in Ireland, 1860–1870* (Dublin, 1987), 3–50.

76 MacColl to Gladstone, 15 September 1866, British Library, Gladstone Papers, Add Mss 44242, fos 366–71.

77 Morley, *Life of Gladstone*, vol. i, 877.

78 Monypenny and Buckle, *Life of Benjamin Disraeli*, vol. ii, 360.

79 J. P. Parry, *Democracy and Religion: Gladstone and the Liberal Party 1867–1875* (Cambridge, 1986), 276.

80 Hansard's Parl Deb., 3rd series, vol. 194, cols 412–66.

81 R. C. Trench to S. Wilberforce, 11 January 1869, Bodleian Library, Oxford, Wilberforce Mss, c.6/2, R. C. Trench Corr. II, fos 235–9.

82 P. T. Marsh, *The Victorian Church in Decline: Archbishop Tait and the Church of England 1868–1882* (London, 1969), 15–17.

83 Ibid., 18–37; Davidson and Bentham, *Life of A. C. Tait*, vol. ii, 1–43.

84 Quoted in Norman, *The Catholic Church and Ireland in the Age of Rebellion*, 382.

85 Quoted in Larkin, *The Consolidation of the Roman Catholic Church in Ireland, 1860–1870*, 639.

86 G. A. Denison, *Notes of my Life, 1805–1878* (Oxford, 1878), 339.

87 Bell, *Disestablishment in Ireland and Wales*, 218–9.

88 M. Cruickshank, *Church and State in English Education, 1870 to the Present Day* (London, 1964), 19.

89 Ibid., 11.

90 R. W. Dale, 'The Nonconformists and the Education Policy of the Government', *Contemporary Review*, 22 (September 1873), 646.

91 T. Wemyss Reid, *Life of William Edward Forster*, 2 vols (London, 1888), vol. i, 489.

92 Parry, *Democracy and Religion*, 306.

93 Morley, *Life of Gladstone*, vol. i, 939.

94 Dale, *Life of R. W. Dale*, 285–6.

95 R. W. Dale, *The Politics of Nonconformity* (Manchester, 1871), 32–3.

96 Dale, *Life of R. W. Dale*, 286–8; D. Bebbington, *The Nonconformist Conscience: Chapel and Politics 1870–1914* (London, 1982), 131.

97 Skeats and Miall, *History of the Free Churches of England*, 631–2.

98 W. H. Mackintosh, *Disestablishment and Liberation: The Movement for the Separation of the Anglican Church from State Control* (London, 1972), 242–9; Ingham, 'Disestablishment Movement in England', 52.

99 O. Anderson, 'Gladstone's Abolition of Compulsory Church Rates: A Minor Political Myth and its Historiographical Career', *Journal of Ecclesiastical History*, 25 (April 1974), 185–98.

100 W. R. Ward, *Victorian Oxford* (London, 1965), 254–62.

101 R. Wallace, 'Church Tendencies in Scotland', in A. Grant (ed.), *Recess Studies* (Edinburgh, 1870), 187–239; H. A. Page, 'Church Tendencies in Scotland', *Contemporary Review*, 14 (June 1870), 377–403.

102 J. G. Kellas, 'The Liberal Party and the Scottish Church Disestablishment Crisis', *English Historical Review*, 79 (1964), 32.

103 A. Gordon, *Life of Archibald Hamilton Charteris* (London, 1912), 214–8.

104 Gordon, *Life of Charteris*, 197–226.

105 S. J. Brown, 'Dean Stanley and the Controversy over his History of the Scottish Church', *Records of the Scottish Church History Society*, 31 (2001), 145–72.

106 A. L. Drummond and J. Bulloch, *The Church in Late Victorian Scotland 1874–1900* (Edinburgh, 1978), 101–9.

107 J. Cairns, *On the Disestablishment of the Church of Scotland* (Edinburgh, 1872), 20–1; R. Rainy, *Disestablishment in Scotland* (Edinburgh, 1874), 14–15; Carnegie Simpson, *Life of Principal Rainy*, vol. I, 279–82.

108 J. D. Holmes, *More Roman than Rome: English Catholicism in the Nineteenth Century* (London, 1978), 102.

109 W. L. Arnstein, *Protestant versus Catholic in Mid-Victorian England: Mr Newdegate and the Nuns* (Columbia, Missouri, 1982), 74; J. L. Altholz, 'The Political Behavior of the English Catholics, 1850–1867', *Journal of British Studies*, 4 (November, 1964), 89–103.

110 W. E. Gladstone to S. Wilberforce, 23 May 1864, Bodleian Library, Oxford, Wilberforce Mss, d.37, Gladstone Letters, fos 94–6.

111 Arnstein, *Protestant versus Catholic in Mid-Victorian England*, 88–97.

112 H. E. Manning to George Talbot, 25 February 1866, quoted in E. S. Purcell, *Life of Cardinal Manning*, 2 vols (London, 1895), vol. ii, 323.

113 O. Chadwick, *Acton and History* (Cambridge, 1998), 70–1.

114 H. E. Manning, *Caesarism and Ultramontanism* (London, 1874), 25.

115 Gladstone to Lord Acton, 8 January 1870, in *Correspondence on Church and Religion of Gladstone*, Lathbury (ed.), vol. ii, 51–2.

116 W. E. Gladstone, *The Vatican Decrees in their Bearing on Civil Allegiance: A Political Exposition* (London, 1874), 12, 42.

117 Ibid., 40.

118 Morley, *Life of Gladstone*, vol. ii, 127.

119 H. C. G. Matthew, *Gladstone 1809–1874* (Oxford, 1988), 155.

120 H. E. Manning to the Editor of *The New York Herald*, 10 November 1874, cited in Purcell, *Life of Cardinal Manning*, vol. ii, 476.

121 H. E. Manning, *The Vatican Decrees in their Bearing on Civil Allegiance* (London, 1875), 28–9.

122 Ibid., 135–8.

123 Ibid., 173.

124 J. Bentley, *Ritualism and Politics in Victorian Britain: The Attempt to Legislate for Belief* (Oxford, 1978), 20–4.

125 L. E. Ellsworth, *Charles Lowder and the Ritualist Movement* (London, 1982), 74–85.

126 N. Yates, *Anglican Ritualism in Victorian Britain 1830–1910* (Oxford, 1999), 150–1.

127 J. S. Reed, *Glorious Battle: The Cultural Politics of Victorian Anglo-Catholicism* (Nashville, 1996), 91.

128 K. Hylson-Smith, *Evangelicals in the Church of England 1734–1984* (Edinburgh, 1988), 128–9.

129 Bentley, *Ritualism and Politics*, 39.

130 J. Guinness Rogers, *The Ritualist Movement in the Church of England* (London, 1869), 9.

131 W. E. Gladstone to H. P. Liddon, 26 February 1871, copy, Gladstone Papers, BL, Add Mss 44237, fos 51–2.

132 Yates, *Anglican Ritualism in Victorian Britain*, 223.

133 Quoted in Bentley, *Ritualism and Politics*, 42.

134 Monypenny and Buckle, *Life of Benjamin Disraeli*, vol. ii, 665.

135 W. G. Blaikie, 'The Revival in Scotland', *British and Foreign Evangelical Review*, 23 (1874), 482–3.

136 J. Coffey, 'Democracy and Popular Religion: Moody and Sankey's Mission to Britain, 1873–1875', in E. F. Biagini (ed.), *Citizenship and Community: Liberals, Radicals and Collective Identities in the British Isles, 1865–1931* (Cambridge, 1996), 109.

137 Quoted in Dale, *Life of R. W. Dale*, 318.

138 *Glasgow Herald*, 23 March 1874.

139 Quoted in J. C. Pollock, *Moody Without Sankey* (London, 1963), 145.

140 Coffey, 'Democracy and Popular Religion', 93–119.

141 Quoted in ibid., 104.

142 D. Bebbington, *Evangelicalism in Modern Britain* (London, 1989), 151–80; K. Hylson-Smith, *Evangelicals in the Church of England 1734–1984* (Edinburgh, 1988), 190–4.

143 A. Porter, 'Cambridge, Keswick, and late-nineteenth-century Attitudes to Africa', *Journal of Imperial and Commonwealth History*, 5 (Oct. 1976), 5–34; Porter, *Religion versus Empire?*, 243–53.

144 Walker, *Pulling the Devil's Kingdom Down*, 94–129, 206–34; R. Hattersley, *Blood and Fire: William and Catherine Booth and their Salvation Army* (London, 1999), 221–84.

CHAPTER 5

Overseas Crusades and the New Christian Social Conscience, 1875–1896

Gladstone and the Bulgarian atrocities

In January 1875, some months after the devastating Liberal defeat in the general election of 1874 that had brought down his government, William Gladstone retired as leader of the Liberal party. His late administration had been dogged by religious conflicts with Nonconformists over disestablishment and the Education Act of 1870, with Irish Catholics over the Catholic University, and with Anglicans over Irish disestablishment and ritualism – all of which had left the Liberal party divided, weary and distracted.[1] Gladstone had turned 65, and now planned to devote his remaining years to theological scholarship and his beloved studies of Homer. In a letter to his wife on 6 April 1874, he observed that the 'welfare of mankind' no longer depended so much on 'the state of the world of politics'. Rather, the 'real battle' for the future of humankind was taking place in the 'world of thought', where atheists and agnostics now mounted 'a deadly attack . . . with great tenacity of purpose and over a wide field upon the greatest treasure of mankind, the belief in God and the Gospel of Christ'.[2] It was to the intellectual defence of the faith that he would devote his final years. He also took an interest in ecumenical initiatives, including the Bonn Reunion Conferences of 1874 and 1875, which were sponsored by his old friend, the German church historian, Johnann Ignaz von Döllinger, and which brought together Old Catholics (those opposed to papal infallibility), high Anglicans and representatives of the Eastern Orthodox churches for discussions on church union.[3]

The new Conservative government was led by Benjamin Disraeli, now ill and world-weary. He lacked Gladstone's high Christian moral tone, but believed he had a more realistic conception of the United Kingdom's real interests. In November 1875, he astonished the world by purchasing, on behalf of the United Kingdom, 40 per cent of the shares of the recently completed Suez Canal from the bankrupt Khedive of Egypt. Control of the canal, Disraeli maintained, was vital to securing communications with British India. However, many feared that by acting alone and not in concert with the other powers, the United Kingdom was arousing international envy and ill-will that it would in time regret. In 1876, Disraeli's government secured parliamentary legislation to give Queen Victoria the title of Empress of India. This was a symbolic gesture, redolent with the romance of the East. The queen was pleased, as was a substantial portion of the public; for many Liberals, however, this was another expression of imperialist hubris.

In July 1875, various Orthodox Christian populations in the Ottoman territories in the Balkans rose up in rebellion, after suffering long years of misgovernment and oppression. Disraeli's government feared Russia would provide military assistance to the Orthodox Christians, leading to war between Russia and Turkey. Russia would then revive its efforts to gain control of the Balkans, Constantinople and the eastern Mediterranean, and would thus threaten the Suez Canal and Britain's Mediterranean route to India. Britain had expended blood and treasure in the Crimean War 20 years before to defend the Ottoman empire against Russian expansion, and its preservation remained fundamental to British strategic thinking. In May 1876, Russia, together with the other Continental powers, issued the Berlin Memorandum, demanding sweeping reforms in the Ottoman administration of the Balkans. Disraeli's government treated this as an aggressive act and responded with a show of force in support of the Ottomans, sending a fleet of ironclads to the Dardanelles.

At this point, the Orthodox Christian Bulgarians in eastern Rumelia also rose in rebellion against Ottoman rule. The Ottomans moved to crush the rising, employing both regular troops and local Muslim militias. These forces acted with extreme cruelty – massacring an estimated 15,000 Bulgarian Christian men, women and children, and destroying some 70 villages, 200 schools and 10 monasteries. There was widespread rape and torture, and large numbers were sold into slavery.[4] In early June 1876, the first reports of the Bulgarian atrocities appeared in the British press. Public opinion was appalled. It was not simply that the atrocities were an affront to the nineteenth-century belief in moral progress or that the massacres took place in a region supposed to be subject to European conventions of moral behaviour. Still more galling, the presence of the British fleet in the Dardanelles meant that Britain appeared complicit in the massacres. Further, if Russia intervened militarily to help Bulgaria, there was a real prospect that Britain would go to war, as in 1854–56, in support of the Ottomans and their brutal policies.

Beginning in July, there was a mass agitation to protest the Bulgarian massacres; within six weeks, 500 meetings were held across Britain. Nonconformists, including R. W. Dale, J. Guinness Rogers and the young Welsh Methodist preacher, Hugh Price Hughes, took a prominent role in the movement. The recent Moody and Sankey revival had contributed to a reawakened Christian social conscience, and many Christians now embraced the protests in the spirit of the anti-slavery campaign: it was a religious crusade for international righteousness. An idealistic young Congregationalist journalist, W. T. Stead, editor of the Darlington *Northern Echo*, joined the protest campaign after he heard what he described as the 'clear call of God's voice'.[5] Within the Church of England, high church clergymen – especially H. P. Liddon, canon of St Paul's Cathedral and professor of exegesis at Oxford University, Malcolm MacColl, a London parish priest, and R. W. Church, dean of St Paul's – were at the forefront of the protest campaign. The High Church party had long been attracted to the theology and liturgy of the Orthodox church, and this gave them a special sympathy for the suffering Orthodox Christians of Bulgaria.

Disraeli had not been impressed with the reports of massacres, believing them to be greatly exaggerated. His Jewish background may have also been a factor in his decision to support the Ottoman empire, as he viewed the Ottomans as broadly tolerant of Jews.[6] Many British Christians declined to take up the Bulgarian cause. Archbishop Tait stayed aloof from the controversy, along with most supporters of the Broad Church and Evangelical parties within the Church of England. Tait would have nothing to do with the 'unholy alliance' formed by Nonconformists and Anglo-Catholics in response to the atrocities. Other broad churchmen, such as Jowett and Stanley, disliked the crusading rhetoric and also felt it was improper for the national church to denounce its government's handling of foreign affairs. Many Church of England evangelicals, meanwhile, suspected that Anglo-Catholics were using the campaign to promote their project of union with the Orthodox church, which they opposed.[7] The Roman Catholic Church, on the whole, declined to support the agitation. Roman Catholics were concerned about the fate of their co-religionists within the Ottoman empire, and they would not support Russia against the Ottomans – as they had bitter memories of Orthodox Russia's brutal suppression of the rising of Catholic Poland in 1863. In a sermon in early October at Kensington Cathedral, Cardinal Manning threw the blame for the Bulgarian atrocities on agitators and secret societies.[8]

Gladstone's was one Christian conscience that did become deeply troubled. He had served in the Aberdeen government during the Crimean War, and felt a personal responsibility for having helped preserve Ottoman control of the Balkans. On 6 September 1876, he burst forth from his retirement with an impassioned pamphlet on *The Bulgarian Horrors and the Question of the East*. Written in white heat, the pamphlet condemned the atrocities and criticised Britain for complicity in the crimes of its Ottoman ally. Britain, he insisted, must now end its support for the Ottoman presence in southeast Europe. By its crimes against humanity, the Ottoman state had forfeited all moral claim to govern the region and would have to depart. 'This thorough riddance', he insisted, 'this most blessed deliverance, is the only reparation we can make to the memory of those heaps on heaps of dead; to the violated purity alike of matron, of maiden, and of child; to the civilisation which has been affronted and shamed'.[9] He called for united action by the Concert of Europe, the great powers which he viewed as the custodians of Christian standards of morality. The pamphlet sold approximately 200,000 copies by the end of September.

On 9 September 1876, Gladstone addressed an open-air demonstration in the rain at Blackheath, in his southeast London parliamentary constituency of Greenwich. Despite a torrential downpour, 10,000 gathered to hear the Grand Old Man condemn the atrocities in one of his most moving speeches. The protest movement, he proclaimed, was founded 'on grounds, not of political party, not even of English nationality, not of Christian faith, but on the largest and broadest ground of all – the ground of our common humanity'.[10] 'It was', reported Stead in the *Northern Echo*, 'as if the High Priest of humanity were pronouncing the doom which was impending over a guilty empire'. 'The address', he continued, 'was throughout permeated by a religious spirit, in its lofty appeal to man's better nature, in its earnest pleading for the cause of the oppressed, in its constant recognition of the superintendence and government of the Almighty'. In the 'tempest of applause' on the rain-swept heath, Stead claimed to hear the masses crying out to Gladstone to 'Lead us! Lead us!'[11] On 8–9 December 1876, the protestors held a great national conference at St James's Hall in London. As well as Gladstone, speakers included the Anglo-Catholic Liddon and the evangelical Lord Shaftesbury. The historian and high Anglican, E. A. Freeman, captured the mood of the conference when he proclaimed: 'Perish the interests of England, perish our dominion in India, rather than that we should strike one blow or speak one word on behalf of the wrong against the right'.[12]

The first Midlothian campaign

Russia declared war on Turkey in April 1877, and public attention shifted from the Bulgarian atrocities to the war. By 1878, the Russian army was approaching Constantinople, and it seemed that Britain would enter the war in order to save the Ottoman empire from disintegration. Some in Britain were enthusiastic for war against Russia, and a pro-war music hall song brought a new word into the language – 'jingoism'. For 'jingos', the pro-Bulgarian agitators were unpatriotic, and in February 1878, a jingo mob, hot for war, attacked Gladstone's London house. In the event, Disraeli secured a meeting of the Concert of Europe powers in Berlin in 1878, and peace between Russia and the Ottomans was negotiated. Britain had again rescued the Ottoman empire, and this time without going to war. In return, the Ottomans promised to reform their system of government, particularly regarding the treatment of non-Muslim minorities.

Disraeli's government followed up its triumph in the Conference of Berlin with an assertive foreign policy. The Cyprus Convention in 1878 permitted Britain to station troops on the island. Wars, widely regarded as unnecessary, against the Zulus in southern Africa and the Afghans in Central Asia, followed. For Gladstone, this 'forward' imperialism was both immoral and dangerous. Although no longer leader of the Liberal party, he now carried on a very personal crusade against the policies of Disraeli (elevated to the peerage as Lord Beaconsfield in 1876). For Gladstone, 'Beaconsfieldism' stood for an aggressive foreign policy that placed national interest above Christian morality, that pursued territorial expansion at the expense of small nations, and amassed national wealth through the economic exploitation of the poor and vulnerable. Against this, Gladstone maintained that the state possessed a moral conscience, and had a responsibility before God to conduct its policies in accordance with Christian ethics.

In his righteous fury, Gladstone received ardent support from much of the British public, including many working-class and lower middle-class Christians who had responded with such fervour to the Moody and Sankey revival of 1873–75. Nonconformists, who had opposed Gladstone's policies over education and disestablishment and who had prided themselves on their role in bringing down his government in 1874, now fervently took up his campaign against the iniquities of Beaconsfield-ism. According to Richard Shannon, Nonconformists hailed Gladstone 'as the incarnation of the virtuous passion of the English people'.[13] Gladstone returned the praise. 'The cause of humanity, of mercy, of right, of truth for many millions of God's creatures in the East of Europe', he proclaimed in November 1877, 'has found its best, its most consistent, and its most unanimous supporters in the Nonconformist churches of the land'.[14] It was a righteous crusade, a struggle of light against darkness (though the hostil-ity to Beaconsfield also had, for some, an anti-Semitic aspect.) 'The English people', Gladstone later observed, 'decided the Eastern Question in a Christian sense'. The agitation, he added, was 'pre-eminently a Christian revolution'.[15] Some pre-millenarian Christians prophesied that the upheavals in the East were leading to the collapse of the Ottoman empire, British control of Palestine and the restoration of the Jews to the Holy Land – to be followed by Christ's return.[16]

Large crowds began coming to Gladstone's Hawarden estate, as though on a pilgrimage; when he indulged in his passion for chopping down trees, the woodchips were collected by these admirers as mementoes. Gladstone grew convinced that he could hear God calling him to restore the nation to its providential purpose. In his diary on his 69 birthday, in December 1878, he reflected on the extraordinary activity of the past three years, and how he had been sustained in such an 'unusual manner'. '[It] appears to me', he observed, 'to carry the marks of the will of God. For when have I seen so strong the relation between my public duties and the primary purposes for which God made and Christ redeemed the world'.[17]

In 1878, Gladstone decided that he would not stand again for his parliamentary constituency of Greenwich. It was proving too expensive for him, and, with its large munitions industry, was vulnerable to the seductions of Beaconsfieldism. Instead, he accepted the invitation to stand for the Scottish county of Midlothian, which surrounded the city of Edinburgh. Late in November 1879, Gladstone travelled north to intro-duce his policies. The speeches of this Midlothian campaign would become famous, not so much for their content, as for the manner in which he addressed large crowds of Scottish artisans, miners and farm labourers on matters of public finance, domestic reforms and imperial policy.[18] He spoke to them as intellectual equals, and they – accustomed to long ser-mons from learned Presbyterian ministers – responded warmly. He gave many of his speeches in churches, and once, indeed, spoke from the pul-pit.[19] Normally staid Edinburgh now showed much the same enthusiasm for Gladstone's lay sermons that it had shown for Moody and Sankey six years previously. A crowd of 20,000 people packed into the Waverley Market in Edinburgh for Gladstone's public address on 28 November; those who fainted had to be handed out over the heads of the crowd.

Gladstone did not introduce new policies in the Midlothian campaign; his message was one of restoring the United Kingdom to peace, free trade, balanced budgets and ordered progress.[20] It was a revival of the providentialist language of free traders and Peelites of the 1840s, a revival of the belief that Britain had a responsibility before God to spread the benefits of peaceful commerce, Christianity and civilisation that would unite the world in mutual dependence and shared values. Above all, he denounced Beaconsfield's forward imperialism as a moral disease that weakened the state by extending its territories beyond what it could govern, overburdened public finances with the spiralling costs of imperial defence, and corrupted the morals of the people with false claims of racial and cultural superiority. He bade his audiences consider the human costs of imperial conquest; he bade them 'remember that the sanctity of life in the hill villages of Afghanistan among the winter snows, is as inviolable in the eye of Almighty God as can be your own'. Foreign policy, he insisted, should reflect 'the best and most fundamental interests of Christian society', and Britain's world mission within the 'sisterhood of nations' should be – echoing the great anti-slavery language of Wilberforce, Buxton and Livingstone – the spread of 'freedom'.[21]

Many Nonconformists now agreed they must subordinate their demands for disestablishment or educational reform to the greater need to unify the Liberal party for its struggle for the soul of the Christian empire.[22] At the general election of 1880, the Liberals, who strained every nerve to defeat Beaconsfieldism, gained an overwhelming majority, and Gladstone was called, at the age of 70, to form a government. It was a relatively conservative one, dominated by peers and Whigs. However, two leading Nonconformists were given Cabinet posts – the veteran Quaker free trader and peace activist, John Bright, and the ambitious Birmingham screw manufacturer and Unitarian, Joseph Chamberlain. Nonconformists were especially encouraged by the appointment of Chamberlain, who in 1877 had formed the National Liberal Federation as a Radical pressure group to press for disestablishment, an end to state subsidies for Anglican schools, and land reform – under the slogan of 'Free church, Free Schools and Free Land'. His appointment to the Cabinet seemed a sign that Gladstone had received new light on the disestablishment question. Although the Nonconformists of England, Wales and Scotland had not pressed this issue during the election campaign, they had good reason to believe that their loyal support of Gladstone over Beaconsfieldism would be rewarded.

Gladstone's second government, however, would give scant attention to disestablishment. It was instead forced to respond to violent unrest in two very different parts of the world, and to seek ethical paths of national policy where probably none was to be found. The first of these regions was Egypt, where a train of events set in motion by Disraeli's purchase of the Suez Canal shares gradually drew Christian Britain into the exercise of sovereignty over a vast and largely Muslim state. This in turn contributed to a religious rising, with a strong nationalist dimension, among Muslims residing in the Egyptian province of the Sudan, and then to the ill-fated mission of the evangelical General Charles Gordon. The second region was Ireland, where a series of poor harvests in the late 1870s resulted in the mass evictions of tenant farmers. Irish resistance in turn helped to promote a nationalist movement under the leadership of Charles Stewart Parnell, a movement that gained the support of the Roman Catholic hierarchy.

Egypt and the 'martyrdom' of General Gordon

Gladstone came to power in 1880 pledged to halt the 'forward' imperialism of Beaconsfield and return to mid-century policies of peace, free trade and balanced budgets. But the Liberals soon found it was one thing to denounce Beaconsfieldism, it was something else to try to bring Christian morality to bear in a practical manner on Britain's imperial policy, as the crisis in Egypt demonstrated.

Although nominally part of the Ottoman empire, Egypt was in practice an autonomous state which claimed a vast territory, including the Sudan and the lakes region of Central Africa. It was also deeply in debt to Western bondholders, as a result of costly public works projects and governmental corruption. In 1876, the Egyptian ruler, or Khedive, was forced to suspend his government's debt payments. This brought prompt retaliatory action by the European powers. By 1878 they had imposed a system of dual British and French control of the Egyptian economy. To safeguard the bondholders, the British and French commissioners demanded severe cuts in Egyptian public spending – cuts that had devastating effects on an impoverished population. In 1881, the army, under the leadership of an Egyptian officer, Colonel Arabi Pasha, seized effective control of the state and imposed a new constitution. The British and French governments responded by sending fleets to Alexandria to protect their financial interests. In June 1882, anti-Western resentments in Alexandria boiled over into riots, and 60 Europeans, including the British consul, were killed. Gladstone's government decided that military action was now necessary to protect both Western investments and the Suez Canal. It hoped for joint action with the French, but when they declined to co-operate, Britain acted alone. In July, its fleet bombarded Alexandria, and in September, a British military force invaded Egypt, defeated Arabi's army, and imposed British control over the country.

Not surprisingly, many of those Liberals who had rallied to Gladstone's crusade against the Bulgarian atrocities strongly opposed the invasion of Egypt. Was this not the same 'forward imperialism' that Liberals had recently condemned as Beaconsfieldism? The consciences of Gladstone's Nonconformist supporters were sorely tried. R. W. Dale was 'grievously distressed', while John Bright resigned from the government in protest. 'Mr Gladstone', Bright wrote to a friend in January 1883, 'is a religious man & has said & thought much, I do not doubt, against war – but . . . he feels no difficulty, or seems to feel none, in defending the recent deplorable war in Egypt'.[23] Other Nonconformist leaders, among them Hugh Price Hughes and J. Guinness Rogers, concluded after anguished mental struggle that Britain had had no choice but to act.[24] The occupation profoundly changed the religious nature of Britain's empire. With its forty million Muslim subjects in India, and now millions more in Egypt, Christian Britain had become ruler over more Muslims than any other state in the world. The British empire, noted a Russian observer in 1895, had 'in reality become a Mahomedan empire' ruled by a 'Christian minority'.[25]

In the Sudan, the disintegration of Egyptian control became the occasion for a popular rising – led by Mohammed Ahmed ibn Abdullah, the son of a Sudanese sharif. In May 1881, Mohammed Ahmed proclaimed himself to be the Mahdi, or 'expected one', drawing upon Islamic eschatological tradition that the Mahdi would come at a low point in Islamic civilisation – in the year 1300 of the Hegira, or in 1882 according to the Christian calendar – to defeat the forces of the unbelievers and usher in a new world order.[26] The Mahdi gathered support from Arab tribes which had long resented Egyptian rule, while the fact that Christian Britain now controlled Egypt further swelled his following. The Mahdists overran isolated Egyptian garrisons and seized arms. In November 1883, they annihilated an Egyptian army of 10,000 commanded by a British officer, Colonel William Hicks, and now controlled most of the Sudan, with the exception of several garrisoned towns, including the provincial capital of Khartoum. Following the Hicks disaster, Gladstone's government decided to withdraw all Egyptians and Europeans from the Sudan. The difficulty was how to safely evacuate these people – some 6,000 soldiers and 15,000 civilians (men, women and children) – through hundreds of miles of desert and an inflamed Sudanese population.[27] Early in 1884, the journalist, W. T. Stead, now editor of the *Pall Mall Gazette*, began promoting the notion that only one man could lead the garrisons to safety – the evangelical Christian mystic, General Charles Gordon. Although the government had doubts about Gordon, there could be no question about his knowledge of the region, and in January 1884, he was sent to the Sudan.

Charles George Gordon was renowned as a Christian soldier, explorer and opponent of slavery. Born in 1833 into a prominent military family, he had served in the Crimean War and then in China, where he had assisted the imperial Chinese government in crushing the Taiping rebellion. Returning to Britain, he supervised the construction of fortifications in Gravesend. There he also embraced the work of Christian philanthropy, teaching deprived children in a ragged school and giving out charity and tracts. He had embraced evangelicalism in his youth, and he developed a highly personal evangelical Christian theology, emphasising the indwelling of the Holy Spirit, an overwhelming sense of providence, and a respect for other religions, including Islam, as representing different paths to God. In 1874, he accepted the invitation from the Khedive of Egypt to become governor of the Egyptian province of Equatoria, in the tropical region to the south of the Sudan. His instructions included the suppression of the slave trade in the heart of Africa.

In late 1874, just a few days before Gordon left London for Africa, reports reached the capital that David Livingstone had died several months before in the African interior.[28] Livingstone's sun-dried body was carried 1,500 miles overland by loyal Africans, and then returned by ship to England and buried in Westminster Abbey in April 1874, with an epitaph that asked God's blessing on those who would continue the struggle against slavery and help 'heal this open sore of the world'. For many, Gordon now inherited Livingstone's mantle as Christianity's leading opponent of the slave trade in Africa's interior. Gordon served for three years as governor of Equatoria, and another two years as governor of the Sudan – traversing the region, combating slave raiders and breaking up slave caravans. However, he also grew increasingly despondent over his inability to end the slave trade, or to ease the growing exactions of the Western bondholders on an impoverished people. In 1879, he resigned. He spent most of 1883 in Palestine, writing theology and exploring bib-lical sites; his placing of the site of Christ's crucifixion is still known as

'Gordon's Calvary'. He was back in England when Gladstone's government called on him to hasten to the Sudan and supervise the evacuation of the garrison populations.

Once in the Sudan, Gordon changed his mission. On arriving in Khartoum in February 1884, he announced to the welcoming crowd, in messianic tones, that 'I come without soldiers, but with God on my side, to redress the evils of the Soudan'. He publicly burned the taxation records, freed political prisoners, destroyed the implements of torture, and improved the care of the poor and the sick. But as the weeks passed, he made no serious attempt to evacuate the garrisons. In truth, he lacked the means to do so. He also believed that the Mahdi's revolt could be 'smashed' and humane government brought to the Sudan, if Britain would send a military force. By May, Gordon was cut off in Khartoum, while in Britain there was a growing clamour for a military expedition to be sent to crush the revolt and rescue him. Gladstone resisted. He knew that crushing the Mahdists would mean British occupation of the Sudan. 'These are people', he assured the Commons on 13 May, in words that evoked his Bulgarian campaign, 'struggling to be free, and they are struggling rightly to be free'.[29]

The public clamour, however, continued to grow. Gladstone was accused of abandoning Gordon, and leaving the Sudan to be ravaged by fanatics and slave traders. At the end of July, the government bowed to public pressure and reluctantly agreed to send a relief expedition, led by Gordon's friend, General Garnett Wolseley. There were now months of mounting national excitement, as the British people followed the slow progress of the relief expedition up the Nile, struggling with both the desert and Mahdist forces. Churches held special prayer services. Finally, on 28 January 1885, two gunboats sent in advance of the main force came within sight of Khartoum. But smoke was wafting up from charred buildings and the Egyptian flag no longer flew. Two days earlier, the city had fallen and Gordon had been killed. The expedition made no effort to retake the city, and withdrew back to Egypt.

There was grief and anger when in early February news of the fall of Khartoum reached Britain. Thousands had perished when the city fell, but for the British public only Gordon's death seemed to matter. Gladstone was widely condemned for having delayed too long the relief expedition. The queen sent Gladstone an unencrypted telegram to express her moral outrage. She later placed Gordon's battered Bible, from which he had taught his ragged children at Gravesend, in an enamelled glass case at Windsor Castle. Some feared that the Mahdi's triumph would send a signal to Muslims everywhere that 'the Cross is yielding to the Crescent', and be the occasion for a rising of Muslims throughout Britain's empire.[30] 'There never has been', Edward White Benson, the archbishop of Canterbury, noted in his diary on 19 February, 'so universal a sense of loss and danger in England'.[31] At the end of February, there was a motion in the Commons to censure the government over Gordon's death, and the motion was defeated by only 14 votes. On 13 March, the Church of England, fulfilling its role as the expression of national Christianity, held memorial services for Gordon in its cathedrals and in many parish churches. The churches were full for the services, and a National Gordon Memorial Fund was instituted. Numerous sermons, addresses, poems, biographies, collections of Gordon quotations, and other publications now poured from the presses.

In much of this literature, Gordon was portrayed as a martyr and saint, and his final lonely months at Khartoum were cast in the form of Christ's passion. He was envisaged as going to the Sudan as a servant to the people, to free the slaves and bring succour to the needy. His triumphant entry into Khartoum was compared to Christ's entry into Jerusalem; the people, according to one Anglican preacher, 'crowded around Gordon, kissing his very feet, and hailing him as their saviour'.[32] His time of lonely vigil when he felt forsaken by his country was compared to Christ's vigil in the garden.[33] A story circulated widely that a Sudanese whom Gordon had loved and trusted had opened the gates to the Mahdists. Thus he had been betrayed by the 'Judas kiss'.[34] According to many accounts, Gordon had died unresisting, refusing to shed the blood of his assailants.[35] When Khartoum burned around him, it was, lamented the future Church of England bishop, H. Hensley Henson, 'a flaming martyr's pile against the deep, dead blackness of the surrounding barbarism'.[36] But his martyrdom was not in vain, and he now lived with the saints. If this were not so, asked Ernest Roland Wilberforce, bishop of Newcastle, at the Gordon memorial service at St Paul's cathedral, 'what meant this thrill . . . that was running through the life-blood of the nation, what this lifting of the heart and the strong resolve to live and work for Christ that was kindling many a soul?'[37] (Wilberforce was the grandson of the great anti-slavery campaigner, William Wilberforce, and thus his selection as preacher on this occasion had an added significance.) The journalist Stead believed that in pressing the government to send Gordon to Khartoum, he had served a divine purpose. The martyr's death, he wrote to Gordon's sister on the last day of 1885, had come at a time when 'the key idea of the Christ was dying out in many hearts'. The country was drifting away from its Christian moorings, and needed the martyr's light:

*'It needed that one man should die for the people, that Khartoum should
remind men of Calvary, and that your brother should recall to the soul
of man and woman everywhere the Divine call to each one of us to be
another Christ, a living sacrifice for the feeblest and most forsaken of
Christ's brethren'.*[38]

Conservatives used the image of the martyred Gordon as a means of
attacking Gladstone's anti-imperialist policies. Gladstone had demanded
action on behalf of the suffering Bulgarians, but had been unwilling to rescue
Gordon and save the Sudanese from Mahdist fanatics and slave traders.
Had it not been Gladstone himself who delivered the 'Judas kiss', by fatally
delaying the relief expedition? The popular fervour aroused by Gordon's
death, and encouraged by the churches, included a reviving belief in the moral
and civilising mission of empire. Gladstone had condemned Beaconsfield's
forward imperialism as immoral and unchristian. In the person of Gordon,
however, there was an imperialist hero who was a 'suffering servant' –
who sought, not his nation's worldly interests, but to end slavery and
spread the benefits of civilisation to the 'backward' regions of the world.
Gordon represented a Christian ethic of imperial service, a willingness to
go into the world and take up the burden of the cross in freeing the slaves,
healing the sick or feeding the hungry; it was an ideal that would later find
expression in Rudyard's Kipling's poem of 1898 on 'The White Man's
Burden'.[39] For Gordon's admirers, a forward imperialism could be a
Christian duty, aimed at relieving suffering and extending humane government, and they revived the idea of the providential mission of empire.

The Gordon episode also reflected growing concerns in Britain about a
resurgent Islam, and the belief that Christian Britain was called by providence to confront Islam, not necessarily with physical force, but with
moral force, as missionaries, physicians and teachers. The Gordon cult
inspired new British missionary ventures to the Islamic world. For example, the Gordon-admirer and Cambridge-educated Semitic scholar,
Ion Keith-Falconer, travelled in 1886 to Aden as a Church of Scotland missionary.[40] Two friends, Douglas Thornton and William Temple Gairdner,
inspired by their shared hero-worship of Gordon, became missionaries
in Egypt in the late 1890s.[41] Graham Wilmot Brooke, encouraged by
Gordon's 'martyrdom' and driven by a pre-millenarian belief in Christ's
imminent return, formed the Sudan Mission Party, in association with the
Church Missionary Society, and sought from 1889 to penetrate the Sudan
from the south, before dying of fever in central Africa in 1892.[42] The 1880s
witnessed a new surge of British imperial expansion, associated with the

'scramble for Africa', in which the Continent was divided up among the European powers. British Christians largely supported this imperial expansion, believing it would bring the benefits of Christianity and civilisation to the 'Dark Continent'.

Ireland and the forging of the Roman Catholic–nationalist alliance

During the early and mid-1870s, the Irish Home Rule party had attracted broad support from substantial farmers and the urban middle classes for its political campaign for an Irish Assembly to legislate on domestic matters. Under the leadership of the Protestant barrister, Isaac Butt, the Home Rule party employed moderate political methods and at first had some support from Irish Conservatives alienated from Westminster by the disestablishment of the Irish church and the Land Act of 1870. Irish Home Rule, like Irish disestablishment, was to be sought through constitutional means. By Irish standards these were good years. Agricultural production was improving, prices were steady and there was relative prosperity and social peace. Public support for the Fenian ideal of armed struggle waned. But then, as the decade grew to its close, the good years came to an abrupt end. Beginning in 1877, Ireland experienced two uncertain harvests, followed by a disastrous harvest in 1879, when there was also a return of the potato blight. Tenant farmers were unable to pay their rents and there were large-scale evictions: the number evicted grew from 553 in 1876 to 1,238 in 1879.[43] In response, some tenants turned to violence to resist evictions and protect their families – striking at landlords, at their agents, and at those who took over the farms of evicted tenants. There was a resurgence of agrarian terrorism, with night raids to maim livestock, burn barns and houses, inflict savage beatings and commit murder. The Fenians gained renewed support and revived the language of armed struggle for an independent Ireland.

Isaac Butt died in May 1879 and a more militant figure, Charles Stewart Parnell, moved to assert his control over the Home Rule movement. An Irish Protestant landlord from county Wicklow, Parnell was young, tall, handsome, capable, aloof and ambitious – able to move with ease among the landlord class, as well as to speak with passion to large crowds against the injustices inflicted on the Irish poor. From his American mother, Parnell had imbibed a dislike of the English, and he did not shy away from violent language. (His mother's father, Charles Stewart, had been the American naval hero who commanded the *Constitution*, or 'Old Ironsides', when in a single engagement it captured two British frigates during the war of 1812.) In June 1879, he travelled to the west of Ireland to show his solidarity with the tenants struggling against the evictions. 'You must not', he proclaimed, referring to the famine memories, 'allow yourselves to be dispossessed as you were dispossessed in 1847'.[44] In October 1879, Michael Davitt – a one-armed Fenian gunrunner, son of an evicted tenant farmer, and convict on parole – founded the Irish National Land League to help tenants resist evictions and to agitate for land reform. Parnell accepted the presidency of the Land League.

There now emerged what was termed the 'New Departure' in Irish politics, aimed at securing an autonomous Irish state. Parnell and Davitt united the Land League agitation and the Home Rule agitation into a national political movement. Many Fenians agreed to halt their armed struggle and support this national political movement (though reserving the prerogative of returning to bullets should the ballot not bring results). The Irish Catholic community in America, made up largely of famine migrants and haunted by famine memories, embraced the 'New Departure' (which was an American label) and provided significant financial contributions. The New Departure transformed Irish politics, creating a broad-based political movement with a nationalist ethos. At the general election of 1880, some 63 Irish Home Rulers were returned to Parliament. Parnell became leader of this enlarged Irish Party in Parliament, as well as of the Land League. He also developed a cruel but effective means for tenants to resist evictions. This was the practice of 'boycotting', enunciated by Parnell in a speech at Ennis in September 1880, by which communities were to cut off all relations with anyone who would take over the farm of an evicted tenant – 'isolating him from the rest of his kind as if he was a leper of old'.[45] This could include refusal to allow the moral 'leper' a decent burial. In response to boycotting, landlords grew reluctant to force people out, and evictions fell from 3,447 in the three months from July to September 1880 to 954 in the three months from October to December 1880.[46]

The Catholic clergy in Ireland were divided in their responses to the New Departure. Paul Cullen, after his long ascendancy over the Catholic Church in Ireland, had died in 1878 and the church was initially bereft of strong leadership as it confronted the agricultural crisis of the late 1870s. Many parish priests were sympathetic to the Land League. They were themselves often the sons of tenant farmers. They had to minister to hard-pressed rural communities and knew the pain that eviction brought to families. When the Land League was created, 13 priests, including the dean of Cashel, allowed themselves to be appointed to the executive committee of 53. Other parish priests, however, condemned the Land League and its boycotting policy as Socialistic and revolutionary. The Catholic bishops were also divided. Of the 28 bishops and archbishops in 1879, five bishops were prepared publicly to encourage the League, five were quietly sympathetic, nine were neutral, while nine were openly hostile.[47] League supporters included the compassionate but excitable Thomas Croke, archbishop of Cashel. Among those hostile to the League were conservatives like Edward McCabe, the new archbishop of Dublin, and Patrick Moran, bishop of Ossory. In December 1879, Moran denounced the Land League as 'Atheist', 'Socialist', Fenian', and 'Protestant'.[48] But the League was also denounced by the veteran Irish nationalist, Archbishop John MacHale of Tuam.

Gladstone's government responded to the renewed Irish unrest by securing a parliamentary Land Act in 1881, which was meant to give Irish tenants a more secure tenure at fair rents, with compensation paid for the improvements they made to their farms. Along with help to tenants, the government also took coercive measures aimed at ending agrarian terrorism and restoring public order. The coercive measures included the arrest of Parnell in October 1881, and his incarceration without trial in Dublin's Kilmainham prison. At the same time, the government sought to influence the Roman Catholic Church in Ireland – by employing quiet diplomacy in Rome to convince the papacy to denounce the Irish Land League and its agitation. The government's agents in Rome portrayed the League as a revolutionary organisation, an enemy to private property, political authority and social order. They also held out the possibility that if the pope denounced the Land League, the United Kingdom might establish formal diplomatic relations with the Vatican for the first time since the Reformation. This proved tempting to Pope Leo XIII, whose church was threatened by nationalism in Italy and revolutionary activity across Europe. He well understood that diplomatic relations with the British empire could strengthen the Vatican's influence, both in Europe and in the wider world. In response to the British inducements, then, the Vatican began to discourage support for the Irish Land League. In 1882, the pope made the fiercely anti-Land League Archbishop McCabe a cardinal, and he expressed his displeasure with those Irish bishops and priests who supported the land agitation.

Parnell was released from Kilmainham prison in early May 1882, after he promised to work to curb agrarian violence and co-operate with the Liberal government. Then, only a few days after Parnell's release, an Irish terrorist gang, the Invincibles, hacked to death with surgical knives the newly appointed Irish chief secretary, Lord Frederick Cavendish, and his under-secretary, T. H. Burke, in broad daylight in Phoenix Park, Dublin. Parnell denied any involvement in the atrocity, which shocked opinion in both Ireland and Britain. But many did not believe his denials and held him responsible for the murders, and indeed for most of the bloodshed afflicting Ireland. Rome grew more alarmed over the Parnellite agitation. On 1 August 1882, the pope sent a public letter to Cardinal McCabe, warning the Irish clergy against involvement with agitators 'who stained themselves with atrocious murders, as if it were possible to find hope for national happiness in public disgrace and crime'. 'We are confident', the pope added (with reference to Gladstone's government), 'that the statesmen who preside over the administration of public affairs will give satisfaction to the Irish when they demand what is just'.[49] Several months later, in May 1883, the office of propaganda in Rome issued a circular which forbade the faithful from making financial contributions to the Parnellite movement. The apostolic teachings of the church, the circular proclaimed, 'condemn such collections as are got up in order to inflame popular passions, and to be used as the means for leading men into rebellion against the laws'. It noted that, even if not directly implicated in atrocities, the Parnellites fomented a climate of 'hatred and dissensions', while they never censured 'the crimes and murders with which wicked men stain themselves'.[50]

By this circular, however, Rome went too far. Most Irish Catholics condemned the Phoenix Park murders. But they were incensed that Rome should now censure their national movement – a movement that was striving, however imperfectly, to protect Irish tenant farmers, to save the Irish people from another great famine, and to secure Irish political rights. They were further enraged that Rome should appear to take the side of the 'British' state against the Irish national movement. The influence of the Roman Catholic Church in Ireland was considerable, but this influence was based upon the voluntary obedience afforded it by the Irish people. This obedience was not unconditional, but was rooted in the belief that the Roman Catholic Church was the church of the Irish people – that it stood with the people amidst their suffering and that it denounced, with a prophetic voice, all those who oppressed and persecuted the people. 'If Rome', the Catholic and nationalist journal, the *Nation*, proclaimed on 19 May 1883, 'will enter into an unholy alliance with England against us, then trusting in the help of the good God, we shall stand for the national rights and liberties of Ireland against Rome and England'.[51]

Most of the Irish Catholic clergy seemed to agree. They would stand, as they had in the past, with the Irish people. Most priests believed that without the Land League's agitation, there would have been no land legislation by Parliament, and in consequence thousands more families would have been evicted from their farms and driven to ruin and starvation. The anti-Parnellite Roman circular was received with sullen silence by the Irish clergy (when it was not defied by their public subscriptions for Parnell), and the anti-Parnellite Cardinal McCabe's leadership within the Irish church was seriously weakened. The Vatican began paying the cost of openly opposing the Irish nationalist movement, while its policy of supporting the Westminster government against Irish nationalism was not bringing any tangible benefits. Gladstone's government had made no real effort to establish diplomatic relations with the Vatican, or to promote the Vatican's international interests.

Parnell, meanwhile, worked shrewdly to build more bridges between the nationalist movement and the Roman Catholic Church. The Home Rule party in Parliament supported Catholic efforts for increased state support for Catholic higher education. Parnell became more moderate in his language, distancing himself from agrarian violence, from 'Captain Moonlight' and the rural 'hillside men' who inhabited barren upland regions and committed brutal acts in the dead of night. The Irish Catholic clergy drew closer to Parnell, and a clerical-nationalist alliance began to take shape, which would have profound consequences for Ireland's future. On 11 February 1885, Cardinal McCabe died after a brief illness. For his successor as archbishop of Dublin, both the clergy of the see and the Irish bishops nominated William J. Walsh, the president of Maynooth College. Then 44 years of age, able and energetic, Walsh was an Irish nationalist who supported both the Land League and the Home Rule movement. Walsh was thus viewed by the Liberal government as 'a violent and dangerous man' and it made strenuous efforts in Rome to block his appointment.[52] After some months of procrastination, however, the pope appointed Walsh as archbishop of Dublin on 23 June 1885, thus signalling a new, more favourable Vatican stance towards the Irish nationalist movement. Two weeks earlier, meanwhile, Gladstone's government, weakened by the Gordon affair and distracted by internal dissensions, had resigned office. The Conservatives under Lord Salisbury formed a minority government and a few months later, in the autumn of 1885, called a general election. At this election, Parnell's Home Rule party won no fewer than 86 seats in the House of Commons, including every Irish seat outside the Protestant heartland of eastern Ulster and the two Irish university seats. Parnell's nationalist movement and the clerical–nationalist alliance were now ascendant in Ireland.

Between 1878 and 1885, as Emmet Larkin has shown, Parnell forged a new political order in Ireland. He gained the confidence of the Irish Catholic tenant farmers – the backbone of the political nation – and he shaped the Home Rule party in Parliament into a disciplined political force. He drew upon financial support from the Irish immigrant communities in North America. Moreover, his movement gained the support of the Catholic Church in Ireland, and benefited from the church's dominance over national education and the influence of its pulpits. By 1885, Parnell's movement was well positioned to achieve its goal of Home Rule for Ireland. With the forging of the clerical–nationalist alliance, it was also clear that a Home Rule Ireland would be a Roman Catholic state, one in which the Catholic Church would expect to build upon its post-famine 'devotional revolution' and exercise decisive influence over Irish education and public morality. This, in turn, threatened to have very serious consequences for Ireland's Protestant minority.

The election of 1885 and the disestablishment movement

While in Ireland the general election of 1885 provided a mandate for Parnellism, in Britain, it was fought largely on the issue of disestablishment. In 1880, Nonconformists had agreed that disestablishment would not play an important part in the general election, as they must concentrate all their efforts on opposing Beaconsfieldism. In 1885, however, they returned to the old cause of religious equality. They insisted that disestablishment must be prominent in the election, so that the next Liberal government would have a clear popular mandate to end the established churches. Conditions for disestablishment, they believed, were now ripe. Their churches were growing in numbers; between 1870 and 1901, the membership of the Baptist churches in England had increased by 51 per cent, of the Wesleyan Methodists by 27 per cent and of the Primitive Methodists by 23 per cent.[53] In 1884, moreover, Parliament had passed a further Franchise Act, granting the vote to male householders in the county constituencies and increasing the electorate for the United Kingdom as a whole from about 3,153,000 to some 5,675,000.[54] The people as a whole, the liberationists had long maintained, wanted an end to religious oppression and privilege; now a more democratic electorate could give effect to the people's will.

With Gladstone's resignation in June 1885, the Liberation Society began a well-planned election campaign – supporting lecture tours, issuing pamphlets and broadsheets, and working on behalf of Liberal candidates who were committed to disestablishment. By September, the Society confidently claimed that no fewer than 462 Liberal parliamentary candidates were committed to support disestablishment, while only 33 were opposed.[55] Joseph Chamberlain and his Radical wing of the Liberal party also championed disestablishment. In mid-July 1885, they issued a booklet, *The Radical Programme*, with a collection of papers outlining their legislative programme. The longest of the papers was that on 'Religious Equality' by the agnostic journalist and politician, John Morley, who outlined a detailed plan for the disestablishment of the Church of England and the nationalisation of church property and endowments. 'The march of legislation for the last half century', he insisted, 'has faithfully registered the conviction that the installation of the Episcopal Church in the seat of privilege . . . is a political injustice, a social mischief, and a hindrance to the full sense of equal citizenship in a united community'.[56] Chamberlain echoed these sentiments in a speech before the Scottish National Liberal Federation in September. 'I am', he proclaimed, 'an English Nonconformist – born and bred in dissent.' 'I would free the Church from State control', he continued, 'whether in England, in Scotland or in Wales'.[57]

The Conservative leader, Lord Salisbury – a high Anglican and strong supporter of religious establishments – took up the liberationist challenge, and the Conservatives fought the 1885 election under the banner of 'the Church in danger'. Leaders of the Church of England took an active role in the election – denouncing the motivations behind disestablishment and warning of dire consequences should the liberationists have their way. For the bishop of Bath and Wells, the disestablishment campaign was 'an infidel, democratic and socialist upheaval against religion and against our Lord Christ'.[58] Disestablishment and disendowment, insisted J. C. Ryle, the evangelical bishop of Liverpool, would close two-thirds of the rural Anglican churches, which could not exist without the tithes; disestablishment would also shut down Anglican schools and deprive the poor of Anglican charity. More important, he warned, were Parliament to disestablish the Church of England, 'the State will risk incurring the displeasure of Almighty God, on whom alone our prosperity depends, when she deliberately chooses to ignore Christianity'.[59] For a group of Anglican Cambridge-based Liberals, including the biblical scholar, F. J. A. Hort and the ecclesiastical historian, Mandell Creighton, disestablishment challenged the very heart of Christian society, and if successful it would both marginalise religion and undermine social morality.[60]

While the church struggle was hard fought in England, it was Scotland that provided the main arena for the forces of disestablishment and establishment in 1885. As Lord Salisbury observed in July, it was 'in Scotland that the battle of the State Church will be fought' – not only for Scotland but for the United Kingdom as a whole.[61] In Scotland, as we have seen, the two main non-established Presbyterian churches – the Free Church and the United Presbyterian Church – had been jointly conducting a disestablishment campaign since 1874. They had conducted meetings, collected statistics, issued broadsheets and pamphlets, and petitioned Parliament. In October 1885, a total of 1,475 Scottish Liberal clergymen issued a public manifesto calling for disestablishment. They included all but 58 of the nearly 600 United Presbyterian ministers, and all but 200 of the approximately 1,000 Free Church ministers.[62] Principal Robert Rainy of the Free Church College, Edinburgh, was the acknowledged leader of the Scottish disestablishment campaign. Cultivated, intelligent, self-controlled and aloof, with a pale, marble-like visage, Rainy was a true prince of the church and a commanding presence in Scotland, arguably the leading Scottish public figure of the 1880s. Like his cousin, William Gladstone, Rainy was a Liberal through and through – a champion of individual freedom in the religious as well as secular realms. For Rainy, according to a long-time friend, 'the Church is not so much a corporate body as a mass of individuals . . . and the progress of the Church is the progress . . . in the life of progressive individuals'.[63] In 1885, Rainy was determined that these 'progressive individuals' would have their say, and secure the election of a Parliament that would end forever established religion and the alliance of church and state in Scotland.

The established Church of Scotland, however, was well prepared to defend itself against Rainy and the Scottish liberationists. A few years before, in 1882, the Church of Scotland General Assembly had formed a Church Interests Committee, to co-ordinate a vigorous response to the disestablishment campaign. This Committee was assisted by a national Church Defence Association, which conducted pro-church meetings, issued tracts and canvassed parliamentary candidates. In 1884, the church organised petitions against disestablishment, and 1,258 petitions, with 688,195 signatures, were sent to Parliament.[64] The leading intellectual force in this church defence movement was the broad church historian, John Tulloch of St Andrews University, who, despite suffering from depressive illness, was a match for Rainy in both intellect and political acumen. In developing the case against disestablishment, Tulloch portrayed the established Church of Scotland as a venerable national institution, rooted in Scotland's national history and expressing Scotland's highest spiritual aspirations. While Rainy appealed mainly to individual liberty, Tulloch appealed to national sentiment. The church question, he had insisted in a speech before the General Assembly in May 1883, involved the very identity of the Scottish nation. 'Is our national life', he asked, 'to be Christian or not? Is the State a moral and not merely a secular reality?' 'These are', he added, 'the real questions that underlie Establishment or Disestablishment'.[65] Tulloch was a Liberal in politics, but he insisted that Liberalism did not mean disrespect for venerable national institutions or support for extreme individualism at the expense of national purpose. Tulloch's great moment came at the General Assembly of May 1885, when in the face of the disestablishment threat, he evoked Martin Luther's celebrated 'Here I stand' speech. 'The Church of Scotland', Tulloch proclaimed:

is an Established Church. Because it is so it is a witness for the great principle of a Christian State, and of the maintenance of national religion, and it cannot forego that principle. It would forego its very existence if it did. It would forego all for which many hold it dear – nay, for which all who intelligently belong to it must hold it dear. We must stand somewhere. We stand here. We cannot give up the principle of national religion, or parley with assaults on that principle.[66]

With these words, 'the walls rang with the shout of response'.[67] For Tulloch and his supporters, the established Church of Scotland represented both the religious aspect of Scottish nationhood and Scotland's role in the mission of the Christian imperial state; it stood for a Scotland that was proud of its national identity and also of its place in the United Kingdom and the empire. In the face of Tulloch's vision of the providential Scottish political order, the Scottish disestablishers could appear as malcontents, wreckers, motivated by envy of a national church that was reviving its mission to bring religious and moral instruction to all the people of Scotland. 'Disestablishment', observed the Liberal *Scotsman* on 21 May 1885, 'could not be made acceptable to the people when it was presented, not as a wise and safe political principle, but as a shabby ecclesiastical expedient. Honest men do not care to associate themselves with a movement which looks like an attempt on the part of one whose business is failing to pull down another whose business is prospering exceedingly'.[68]

As the electoral campaign of 1885 proceeded, it soon became evident that the plans of the English, Scottish and Welsh Nonconformists were going terribly wrong. Much of British public opinion was proving either indifferent to disestablishment, or opposed to it. In a number of constituencies, church Liberals brought forward their own Liberal candidate to run against a previously declared pro-disestablishment Liberal candidate – thus splitting the Liberal vote. Soon Liberal candidates, discovering there were large numbers of pro-church voters in their constituencies, began giving pledges that they would not vote for disestablishment in the next Parliament. Among those giving this pledge was John Morley, who had written the chapter promoting disestablishment in *The Radical Programme*.[69] Even Chamberlain now distanced himself from it as an electoral issue. In Scotland, disestablishment was failing to gain much popular support. 'I have made enquiries in all directions', Charles Cooper, the editor of the *Scotsman*, informed the Earl of Rosebery on 31 August 1885, 'and I am convinced that the people of Scotland do not care a straw about Disestablishment. It is mainly a minister's question'.[70] In October 1885, opponents of Scottish disestablishment held a public meeting in Glasgow, which attracted many prominent Liberals, including the Duke of Argyll, a former member of Gladstone's Cabinet, and the earl of Stair, a former president of the Scottish Liberal Association.[71] On 11 November, Gladstone addressed a large public gathering of Liberals in the Free Church Assembly Hall in Edinburgh. He had been widely expected to declare his support for Scottish disestablishment. However, in the days before the meeting, he learned that a majority of voters in his Midlothian constituency did not want it. At the Edinburgh meeting, he insisted that the most important thing was to preserve the unity of the Liberal party, and this meant disestablishment would have to be set back, as he put it, to 'the end of a long vista'.[72] Rainy and his fellow liberationists sat in the hall in sullen silence; they felt betrayed by the Liberal leader, but there was little they could do.

'The Radical attack on the Church', observed *The Times* on 2 December, 'has proved a complete failure. There is no popular response to the demand for Disestablishment'.[73] When the general election closed on 18 December 1885, the Liberals had won 334 seats and the Conservatives 250 seats.[74] This meant that the Liberals would form the next government. It also meant, however, that 86 Irish Home Rule MPs could, if they combined with the Conservatives, bring down the Liberal government. The election of 1885 was, according to one historian, 'probably the high water mark of the movement for general disestablishment'.[75] It was also as close as campaigners for disestablishment in England and Scotland would come to achieving their goal. While they would continue their campaign and supporters in Parliament would bring forward the periodic motion or bill,

English and Scottish public support for the cause steadily waned. In part, this was because of the skilful defence of the establishment principle by such figures as J. C. Ryle or John Tulloch, who effectively portrayed the established churches as forming the foundations of national religion, public morality and the Christian empire – as opposed to the narrow individualism of the Nonconformists. In part, disestablishment failed in 1885 because most people in England and Scotland no longer felt serious grievances relating to the established churches. This was especially true of the voters newly enfranchised by the Reform Act of 1884, many of whom were artisans and industrial workers, for whom the principles involved in the establishment debates seemed overly intellectual, abstract and sterile. Labouring people could be far more interested in whether a local clergy-man was a committed pastor and effective preacher, than whether he belonged to an established or Nonconformist denomination.

Further, many Nonconformists were becoming more interested in assimilating into British society than in perpetuating their separateness through the old disestablishment warfare. Nonconformists, especially from the 1880s, were growing self-conscious over what some portrayed as their exclusiveness and lack of broad culture. In 1881, William Hale White published *The Autobiography of Mark Rutherford*, a fictional account of a Congregational and later Unitarian minister, which provided harsh depictions of Nonconformist provincialism, narrow-mindedness, cant, hypocrisy and incessant dreariness. Among the novel's characters was the odious Mr Snale, a deacon in the church who 'hardly ever spoke to a "leedy" [lady] without a smirk and some faint attempt at a joke' and whose vicious gossip drove the young Rutherford from his first ministerial charge. It was this world and these caricatures that many Nonconformists wanted to put behind them. Socially, they were now reading novels, attending con-certs, joining gentlemen's clubs, smoking, taking holidays and, from the 1880s, going to the theatre in significant numbers. In their social thinking, they were moving away from economic individualism towards a greater social conscience.[76] They took a keen interest in the empire and, whether they called for intervention to halt atrocities in Bulgaria, criticised the occupation of Egypt, thrilled to the exploits of the non-denominational Christian hero General Gordon, or contributed money to Christian mis-sions, they did so as patriots. Such Nonconformists as W. T. Stead, Joseph Chamberlain and R. W. Perks were strong imperialists. The old call for the separation of church and state seemed less important when set against the appeals for the co-operation of all churches with the imperial state in the spread of Christian civilisation within the empire.

There was one notable exception to the waning disestablishment fervour. This was Wales, where Liberals began a major campaign for the disestablishment of the Church of England in Wales *after* the election of 1885 – a campaign that found broad Welsh popular support. There were motions for Welsh disestablishment in the House of Commons in 1886, 1889 and 1891, and bills for Welsh disestablishment were introduced in 1894 and 1895. The disestablishment cause was embraced by the overwhelming majority of Welsh MPs: in 1892, the number of Welsh MPs who supported disestablishment of the church in Wales was 31, and only 3 were opposed. The emergence of the campaign reflected the distinctive religious circumstances in Wales, where the large majority were Nonconformists. According to figures compiled in 1893, there were 381,795 Nonconformist communicant members, as opposed to only 114,885 Church of England communicants. Many Nonconformists viewed the Church of England as not only as privileged and wealthy, but also as an alien presence, the 'English' church in Wales, 'an exotic and a foreign weed', or a church 'introduced at the point of a sword'.[77] Resentments were also stirred by the collapse in cereal prices from the later 1870s, which forced many Welsh farmers into debt, making it difficult for them pay the tithe rent-charge to the church. Although the charge was shifted from the tenants to the landlords by the Tithe Act of 1891, the legacy of resentment and grievance continued to rankle.[78]

Perhaps most important, the disestablishment campaign reflected a growing sense of national identity in Wales. As it became clear in 1885 that most English voters did not want disestablishment, Welsh Liberals insisted that the Welsh people, who *did* want disestablishment, should be allowed to decide the issue for themselves, independently of England. Just as the Irish people had been permitted to disestablish their portion of the United Church of England and Ireland in 1869, so the Welsh people should be permitted to disestablish their portion of the Church of England. Disestablishment became a national cause, championed by the 'Young Wales' movement of Thomas E. Ellis and David Lloyd George, and by Cymru Fydd ('Wales of the Future'), the cultural society founded in 1887, which soon established branches across Wales. Disestablishment in Wales, insisted the Liberal MP for Montgomeryshire, Stuart Rendel, in 1892, was 'inextricably linked to the question of Welsh national identity'.[79] For Lloyd George, writing in 1895, 'the treatment our ecclesiastical grievances have received at the hands of the Imperial Parliament would constitute the most potent argument one could ever use in support of Welsh Home Rule'.[80]

The first Home Rule bill and Ulster Unionism

In late December 1885, following the general election, there came one of the most astounding announcements of the century: Gladstone went public with his decision to introduce a Home Rule bill for Ireland. He would respond – some said, surrender – to the demands of the Parnellites in Ireland by supporting the creation of a semi-autonomous Ireland, in which the Roman Catholic majority would be ascendant. Gladstone's conversion to Irish Home Rule sent a seismic shock through the politics of the United Kingdom; and nothing would ever be the same. Suddenly disestablishment receded as an issue for most of the country; Ireland now absorbed the public attention. The Conservative government was defeated on a confidence vote shortly after the new Parliament convened. In February 1886, the queen nearly caused a constitutional crisis by refusing to entrust her government to a man she viewed as a half-mad demagogue who would break up her United Kingdom – but then reluctantly, very reluctantly, she called Gladstone to form a government. On 8 April, Gladstone introduced his government's Home Rule bill in the House of Commons.

He had drafted the Home Rule bill almost single-handedly; it was his bill, and he called on the party to trust him. That said, the bill was probably unworkable. He proposed the creation of an elected Irish assembly that would meet in Dublin and legislate on Irish domestic matters, including land policy and education. Ireland would remain part of the United Kingdom, and the imperial Parliament at Westminster would continue to legislate on all matters regarding imperial defence and the regulation of trade. But Ireland would have no representation in that body, although it would be expected to pay taxes for defence as determined by the imperial Parliament. Many within his party, although willing to concede a degree of self-government to Ireland, could not support this bill. By March, Lord Hartington and Chamberlain had resigned from the Cabinet, and in the following months a substantial portion of the Liberal party came to oppose the bill. Gladstone persevered. 'The G.O.M. [Grand Old Man]', wrote his friend, R. W. Church, dean of St Paul's, on 7 April 1886, '[is] persisting in his heroic enterprise in the teeth of everything and everybody, sure that he is right, and apparently sure that he knows best the conditions of success. I cannot conceive how it will all end'.[81]

Within the established churches of England and Scotland, most clergymen could not support Gladstone's Home Rule bill. They could not condone placing part of the United Kingdom under a separate parliament that would be dominated by Roman Catholics. The United Kingdom, they maintained, was a Protestant state, its empire had a providential purpose, and the unity of both must be preserved. Frederick Temple, bishop of London and a Liberal in politics, owed much to Gladstone, who had nominated him to his first bishopric in 1869 against widespread opposition. Nonetheless, Temple viewed Home Rule as a blow directed at the Protestant state and empire, and he now distanced himself from the Liberal leader. Gladstone, he lamented in August 1886, 'does not feel with us when we talk of our Empire as a gift from God, to be used for the good of mankind'.[82] Most British Nonconformists, on the other hand, supported Home Rule – though with little enthusiasm and mainly out of loyalty to the Liberal leader.[83] The Congregationalist minister and journalist, J. Guinness Rogers, admitted to having difficulties with the bill, but would not desert Gladstone.[84] Hugh Price Hughes, editor of the *Methodist Times*, stood by Gladstone on Home Rule, as he had supported him over the Bulgarian atrocities. However, some leading Nonconformists could not bring themselves to support it. The influential Birmingham Congregationalist leader, R. W. Dale, opposed the bill because he was convinced that the exclusion of Irish representatives from the imperial parliament would lead inevitably to Irish separation from the United Kingdom.[85] The Quaker MP, John Bright, and the celebrated Baptist preacher, C. H. Spurgeon, both opposed the bill, in part because it would mean placing the Irish Protestant minority under an Irish parliament controlled by Catholics. For them, 'Home Rule meant Rome Rule'.

While British Protestant opinion was divided over Home Rule, in Ireland, Protestants were virtually unanimously against the measure. 'It was only Mr Gladstone', exclaimed the Tory MP, Lord Randolph Churchill, at a public meeting in London on 13 February, 'who could for a moment imagine the Protestants of Ireland would . . . recognize the powers or would satisfy the demands of a parliament in Dublin – a parliament of which Mr Parnell would be the chief speaker and Archbishop Walsh the chief priest'.[86] Irish Protestants represented almost a quarter of Ireland's population in 1881. Some 75 per cent of these Protestants lived in Ulster, concentrated mainly in the eastern part of the province – the result of settlement patterns dating back to the seventeenth century (much strengthened by industrial migration in the nineteenth century).[87] The Protestant communities of Ulster, as we have seen, had been greatly affected by the revival of 1859 – which had helped to forge a common evangelical identity, combined with a sense that Catholics had rejected the gospel. For most Ulster Protestants, moreover, their links to industrial Britain were more important than those to the agrarian South. Belfast and the Lagan valley were experiencing rapid industrialisation in the second half of the nineteenth-century, first in textile production, and then in heavy engineering, especially shipbuilding. Belfast was the fastest growing major city in the United Kingdom, with a population of 122,000 in 1861 growing to 350,000 by 1901. By 1911, 74 per cent of Belfast's workforce was industrial.[88]

Irish Protestants feared for their religious freedom and religious identity in an Ireland governed by a parliament dominated by the Catholic-nationalist alliance forged by Parnell. They suspected that a Home Rule parliament would sooner or later demand the entire separation of Ireland from Britain, and that its Catholic majority would then use its power to ensure that state funding only went to Catholic education, to claim the remaining property of the Church of Ireland, and to make Roman Catholicism the established religion in Ireland. It would expropriate the property of the Irish landowners, and erect tariff barriers to protect small farmers. These tariff barriers, in turn, would severely weaken Irish industries, drive away capital, and leave industrial Belfast facing ruin. 'Behind the claim for Home Rule', proclaimed Lord Plunket, Protestant archbishop of Dublin, at a special general synod of the Church of Ireland in March 1886, '. . . there lurks the demand for entire Separation, and for a very advanced form of Socialism'.[89] Liberal Irish Presbyterians had supported Gladstone in the late 1860s and 1870s because they believed that he was committed to bringing religious freedom and equality to Ireland. Gladstone had disestablished the Church of Ireland and brought an end to the old Episcopalian ascendancy, making all denominations equal before law. Presbyterians had responded with gratitude: according to one estimate, 338 out of 550 ministers of the Presbyterian Church in Ireland had supported Gladstone in 1885.[90] However, for them Gladstone had then betrayed his Liberal ideals and proposed to erect a new church ascendancy in Ireland, now a Roman Catholic ascendancy, undoing the progress of recent decades.[91] Such an ascendancy, Protestants believed, would not only be a retrograde step for religious liberty, but would also be a blow to religious truth. 'Home Rule for Ireland', insisted the Irish Methodist *Christian Advocate* on 8 January, 'means not only war against the Crown rights of England, but war against the Crown rights of Christ . . . its inspiration is religious antipathy, its methods plunder, its object Protestant annihilation'.[92]

Home Rule, Protestants believed, would lead inexorably to the separation of Ireland from the United Kingdom. Ireland would cease to be part of the beating heart of empire. 'Irishmen have for ages', observed William Pakenham Walsh, Protestant bishop of Ossory, 'shared the glory, and the honour, and the advantages of the Imperial connexion'. 'Are we ready,' he asked, 'to separate ourselves from the glorious history of the Empire, and sink down to the level of a petty state?'[93] And it was not simply the glory and profits of empire that Ireland would forfeit by separation. There was also, observed Charles Graves, Protestant bishop of Limerick, the moral and spiritual privilege of participating in the imperial mission, which was 'diffusing throughout the world the humanising influences of civilization and religion'.[94] Ireland, insisted the *Presbyterian Churchman* in early 1886, must remain 'an integral and loyal portion of the greatest Protestant Empire that has as yet existed in the world'.[95] In early March, a special meeting of the General Assembly of the Presbyterian Church unanimously resolved to oppose the bill. There was, to be sure, a small but influential body of Irish Protestant support for Home Rule. But on the whole, the Ulster Protestant Unionist, Major Edward Saunderson, was not far off the mark when he stated in February 1886 that: 'all Protestants might now be considered to be ranged on one side of the question, and all Catholics on the other'.[96] A distinctive Ulster Protestant identity was taking shape, based on self-reliance, opposition to Catholic nationalism and loyalty to the British connection.

In late February 1886, Lord Randolph Churchill famously 'played the Orange card', travelling to Ulster for a brief visit to show his solidarity with the opponents of Home Rule and convey the message that Ulster Unionists did not stand alone. Audacious, ambitious and gifted, Lord Randolph claimed to represent the ethos of Tory democracy. In Belfast, he received a rapturous welcome – what his recent biographer has described as 'an ecstasy bordering on hysteria'.[97] Addressing a mass rally, Churchill observed that Ulster's opposition to Home Rule was likely to go beyond political action, and he promised that in the event of civil war, there were those in England 'who would be willing to cast in their lot with you' and 'share your fortunes and your fates'.[98] In a published letter on 7 May, he coined that ominous phrase 'Ulster will fight; Ulster will be right' – while in Ulster itself, Unionist leaders claimed to be preparing an army of 100,000, which some claimed would be led by the veteran Christian soldier and friend of the late Charles Gordon, General Wolseley.[99] Then between 7 June and 15 August 1886, Belfast was shaken by a series of sectarian riots that left 25 dead and 130 wounded, along with large-scale destruction of property. Such demonstrations were not new to Belfast – there had been major sectarian riots in the city in 1864 and 1872 – nor was the violence of 1886 directly related to the Home Rule agitation. None the less, the tensions associated with the crisis were contributing factors. 'Had there been no Home Rule Bill', observed the *Fortnightly Review* in September, 'there would have been no riots'.[100] For some, belief in the providential nature of the empire found expression in the form of house-burnings and ethnic cleansing in the working-class districts of industrial Belfast.

Gladstone's Home Rule bill was defeated in the House of Commons on 8 June, and the government called a general election. The result was an overwhelming electoral defeat for the Gladstonian Liberals and Home Rule. In July 1886 Lord Salisbury formed a government with a Conservative and Liberal Unionist majority of 118. The prospects for Home Rule for Ireland faded for the next several years. Salisbury, moreover, would give no countenance to disestablishment, and the disestablishment agitation also cooled. Unrest in Ireland continued, and some Nonconformists, especially in Scotland and Wales, sought to keep the disestablishment cause alive. But the year 1886 marked the close of a decade of intense political activity. Gladstone had returned from retirement in 1876 to direct public attention to the horrors in Bulgaria and the dangers of a forward imperialism. For the next decade, the political life of the nation had been absorbed with imperial and Irish affairs, and particularly with the moral and religious aspects of empire.

While Christian opinion was by no means united on all aspects of imperial policy, probably most British Christians continued to view the empire as part of the providential plan for the diffusion of Christianity, commerce and civilisation to the larger world. Certainly, this imperial Britain had now become ruler over more Muslims than any state in the world, while there was a real prospect that the next Liberal government would establish a Catholic Irish state, and very likely foment religious civil war in the heart of this Christian empire. Yet perceptions do not always mirror reality. British and Irish Protestants continued to view their empire as a gift from God which existed for the purposes of God.

Combined with this view was the belief that the people of the United Kingdom were a chosen nation – chosen by God not to be an insular people secure in their own righteousness, but to play a world role. One of the most famous oil paintings of the time was Thomas Jones Barker's 'The Secret of England's Greatness', completed in about 1863, which depicted Queen Victoria handing a Bible to a kneeling and grateful African. As Andrew Walls has noted, there was a perceptible change in attitudes towards empire in nearly all the British churches after about 1880, with an enhanced sense of responsibility towards what were viewed as the 'child races', those peoples who were at a lower stage of development and needed to be protected from the slave traders and nurtured under imperial tutelage.[101] In 1887, the British people marked the Golden Jubilee of Queen Victoria's accession to the throne. This was an opportunity to celebrate the growth and consolidation of the empire during those 50 years, and churches throughout Britain also held special services. The pageantry culminated on 21 June with an imperial service in Westminster Abbey presided over by the archbishop of Canterbury, and attended by hundreds of foreign dignitaries. A hymn composed for the Jubilee by the Wesleyan minister, Henry Burton, conveyed the ideal of the providential empire:

> Our bounds of empire thou hast set in many a distant isle
> And in the shadow of our throne the desert places smile
> For in our laws and in our faith it's thine own light they see
> The truth that brings to captive souls the wider liberty.[102]

It was a glorious vision, redolent with the spirit of Livingstone and Gordon. Yet there was also a disturbing aspect to this great Christian empire, which raised questions about its real religious and moral foundations. It was the largest empire the world had seen, and it represented great wealth and power. It gave the United Kingdom the capacity to do much good in the world, and to promote the aims of providence for the spread of Christianity, commerce and civilisation. And yet there was also something dark at the centre of that empire. In the sprawling industrial and commercial cities, there were nether-regions of appalling poverty, atrocious housing, crime, drunkenness, prostitution, and irreligion, where the divine 'light' never seemed to shine and millions of 'captive souls' were without the 'truth' that brought 'wider liberty'. Despite the presence of tens of thousands of churches, the great Christian empire permitted a large portion of its own citizens, especially in the large urban slums, to live in squalor and to die outside the Christian faith. Despite the great revivals of 1859–62 and 1873–75, countless inhabitants of Britain seemed as far from Christianity as the heathens of the 'distant isles' and 'desert places'. Was there not something deeply wrong with a Christian society that permitted such conditions to persist in its midst? And was there not something dangerous to the Christian empire in the existence of a large and disaffected urban underclass, prey to revolutionary teachings? The later 1870s and 1880s had witnessed an awakened Christian moral conscience in overseas and imperial affairs. The same period also saw an awakened Christian moral conscience in matters relating to Britain's social order. It brought a revival of social Christianity, a renewed effort to bring the moral teachings of Christ to bear upon Britain's industrial and commercial society.

Matthew Arnold and social Christianity

On 22 February 1876, the biblical scholar and man of letters, Matthew Arnold, delivered a public lecture on 'The Church of England' at Sion College, an educational and conference centre for the London-area clergy.[103] Arnold was, as he admitted to his audience, an unusual choice for a speaker on such a theme. His published writings on the Bible – most notably *St Paul and Protestantism*, published in 1870 – were regarded by many orthodox Christians as deeply suspect. Some viewed him as an unbeliever; for others, he was 'one of the worst enemies the Church has'.[104] Arnold denied that he was either. Rather, he insisted, he was a true son of his father (the liberal Anglican Thomas Arnold), and a warm friend of the established Church of England. He appeared before them to fulfil a long standing personal aspiration – to encourage the national church's mission in an industrial society deeply divided by social class and sectarian strife.

The Church of England, Arnold asserted, was, in its essence, 'a great national society for the promotion of what is commonly called *goodness*'. It existed for the purpose of teaching people to do their moral duty. Its teachings were rightly rooted in biblical precepts, because only the Bible touched the human condition at its deepest level. In saying this, however, Arnold did not mean the Bible as it was commonly understood – that is, as a book containing a set of doctrines about original sin, election, justification and so forth. Rather, he meant the original teachings of the Bible, and especially the teachings of Jesus of Nazareth, as these teachings were now being rediscovered in their historical context through the work of modern biblical scholars. In particular, Arnold focused on what scholars were now recognising as Jesus's central teachings about the kingdom of God. What Jesus had proclaimed during his time on earth was an ideal of social reform – 'the ideal of popular hope and longing, an immense renovation and transformation of things'. For Arnold, when Jesus had spoken of the coming of the kingdom of God, he had meant a transformation of this world; he had proclaimed 'a kingdom here on earth, not in some other world unseen'.[105] He had meant a new social order of peace, compassion and righteousness.

After Jesus had died in humiliation, Arnold continued, his disillusioned followers had changed Jesus's message of the kingdom. They had reinterpreted it as referring not to this world, which had crucified him, but to another world, a spiritual realm, which would be a place of eternal reward for his followers. This became the gospel that the church proclaimed through the centuries. The church taught the common people to accept inequality, poverty and oppression in this world – to defer to existing social hierarchies and traditional rulers – in the hope of a future reward in a heavenly kingdom. The church became in time 'a stronghold of stolid deference to the illusions of the aristocratic and propertied classes'.[106] But this, insisted Arnold, was not what Jesus had taught. Jesus had proclaimed the kingdom of God on earth, a gospel of social liberation in this world. What was needed now was a new Reformation, to strip away the centuries of corrosion from Christian doctrine and restore Jesus's original social teachings.

This, Arnold maintained, should be the mission of the national Church of England – to revive and proclaim Jesus's original message of the kingdom. In doing so, the national church would lay the foundation for a new social gospel, and declare a message that would have real meaning for the urban working classes, who were largely alienated from the church. It would provide the basis for an ethical culture of mutual responsibility. The church, Arnold insisted, should cease preaching submissiveness to the poor, or to see its role as one of preserving the existing social hierarchy. It must not be 'an institution devoted above all to the landed gentry' and 'to the propertied and satisfied classes generally'.[107] A national church proclaiming the kingdom of God on earth would gain the support of the working classes. It would also eventually win back most of the Nonconformists – perhaps not of the present generation, so much immersed in religious strife – but of future generations.[108]

Writing to his sister two days after his lecture, Arnold claimed that he had, somewhat surprisingly, carried the mainly clerical audience with him, and that many who had 'come to curse, remained to bless'. His success had become clear in the discussion that had followed his talk. Piers Claughton, the former Anglican missionary bishop of Colombo, in Ceylon, had stood up to protest that Arnold was heretical in claiming that Christ's original gospel had proclaimed the kingdom of God on earth. This was false doctrine, and the church must reject Arnold's claim. Christ's kingdom, Claughton insisted, was a spiritual kingdom and was not of this world. However, the majority of the clergy in the audience seemed to support Arnold's position. As Arnold explained to his sister, 'clergyman on clergyman . . . turned upon Claughton and said they agreed with me far more than they did with him'. Even the prominent Anglo-Catholic clergyman, Malcolm MacColl, could find little to criticise and much to praise in Arnold's address.[109] The Sion College address was published in *Macmillan's Magazine* for April 1876, and republished a year later in Arnold's *Last Essays on Church and Religion*.[110]

Arnold had articulated an idea that would increasingly shape the think-ing of the Church of England, and indeed of all the churches of the United Kingdom after 1876 – the idea that the church should work for the coming of the kingdom of God on earth, and that it should revive Jesus's message of liberation to the poor. In the view of those clergy who had rallied to the support of Arnold at Sion College, and of thousands more around the country, the church must align itself with the progressive forces in society in order to work for practical social reforms. It must proclaim a 'social gospel'. It must seek to Christianise the social structures, relationships and attitudes in Britain's industrial state. It must strive, not only for the conversion and salvation of individuals in the life to come, but also for the establishment of a righteous Christian commonwealth in this world. Of course, there was nothing new in calling upon the church to Christianise society. But there was a new sense of urgency in the 1870s and 1880s, a sense that urban industrial society was hurling away at a railway pace from its historic Christian foundations, and that class conflict, industrial unrest, poverty, prostitution, alcoholism, crime, domestic violence, athe-ism, scientific materialism, and revolutionary ideologies were threatening social cataclysm.

New social criticism in Britain

Late Victorian Britain was the wealthiest society the world had ever seen. With its early lead in industrialisation, its policies of free trade after 1846, its engineering achievements and its entrepreneurial spirit, Britain domi-nated the emerging global economy. It was indeed the world's workshop: Britain's imports were almost exclusively raw materials, and its exports almost exclusively finished goods. Textile production remained a vital part of the industrial economy, and consumption of raw cotton by Britain's tex-tile mills increased from 266,800 metric tons in 1850 to 565,100 metric tons in 1873.[111] But economic activity was spread across a broad range of industries – shipbuilding, locomotives, railway rolling stock, cutlery, cook-ing pots, chinaware, sewing machines, leather goods, tinplate, iron and steel. Between 1876 and 1885, Britain's exports of manufactured goods represented nearly 40 per cent of the world's total.[112] In 1880, British steel output, at 1,020,000 tons, was one-third of the world's total.[113] While eco-nomic historians had at one time referred to a 'long depression' beginning about 1873 and lasting until 1896, it is now generally accepted that the economy as a whole maintained healthy rates of growth for most of this period, despite periodic recessions in certain industries. Certainly, by the

1870s Britain faced increasing industrial competition from other nations, most notably Germany and the United States. However, Britain's industries continued to grow and compete, while British ownership of most of the world's shipping and its large overseas investments ensured a further flow of income.

The labour force in late Victorian Britain was diverse and becoming more so – forming what one historian has termed 'a patchwork quilt of almost infinite variety'.[114] The percentage of people employed in agriculture declined steadily, and increasing numbers lived in cities or substantial towns, or in new suburbs that were steadily pressing outwards, linked to the urban centres by tramways and commuter railways. Despite the prevalent image of an industrial working class employed in large-scale urban textile mills, foundries and factories, most manufacturing labourers were in fact employed in small workshops employing 20 or so labourers. There was, moreover, a growing army of white-collar office workers – clerks, bookkeepers, and from the 1880s, typists; such employment rose from about 100,000 in 1861 to some 750,000 by 1911.[115] Conditions for most labouring people were improving. Sanitary reforms were bringing infectious diseases under control and mortality rates were declining – though in 1870, the life expectancy of a male at birth was still only 41 years and a female 43.5 years, and relatively few lived past the age of 60.[116] Skilled and semi-skilled labouring men in full employment could support their families in relative comfort – with their children in one of the new board schools, new shoes for the children every year, a house of three or more rooms, a spot of garden, perhaps a parlour with a piano, a Sunday suit of clothes, and a little money in a friendly society to cover funeral costs.

However, large numbers of working people were not so fortunate, and there were pockets of extreme deprivation. The continual development of mass production meant that skilled craftsmen were often thrown out of work. In the competitive free market economy, businesses regularly failed, putting large numbers of manual and clerical workers into unemployment each year, and not all, especially older workers, could find new jobs. Unskilled casual labourers – dockworkers, builders' assistants – were vulnerable to frequent and prolonged periods of unemployment. The earnings of women, who formed an estimated 30 per cent of the labour force, were less, often far less, than those of men, and women living on their own or single mothers with children were hard-pressed. Some were forced into prostitution to make ends meet. A study of social conditions in London, privately funded and conducted between 1889 and 1903 by Charles Booth, a wealthy Liverpool shipowner, concluded that about 30 per cent of the population lived in poverty. They experienced poor diet, weak health and overcrowded housing. Moreover, family breakdowns, ill-health, alcoholism or old age could drive people still further downwards into what was termed the 'submerged tenth', the 10 per cent of the population on the lowest incomes, for whom living conditions could be truly appalling.

In October 1883, there appeared an anonymous penny pamphlet, *The Bitter Cry of Outcast London*, which shocked the public with its graphic descriptions of life for the submerged tenth in the slums of London. It was published under the auspices of the London Congregational Union, and was written by two Congregational ministers, Andrew Mearns and W. C. Preston, with much of its evidence dawn from the reports of agents of the London City Mission. *The Bitter Cry* portrayed a dark underworld of overcrowding, disease, filth, despair and human degradation – all within the metropolis of the wealthiest country in the world. It called attention to appalling conditions in the heart of the great empire – an empire that prided itself on bringing Christianity and civilisation to the world and combating the slave trade. With growing residential segregation, the better-off members of London society were increasingly spared the sight of the worst slums and many had no knowledge of conditions there. 'Few who will read these pages', observed the authors:

have any conception of what these pestilential human rookeries are, where tens of thousands are crowded together amidst horrors which call to mind what we have heard of the middle passage of the slave ship. To get into them you have to penetrate courts reeking with poisonous and malodorous gases arising from accumulations of sewage and refuse scattered in all directions and often flowing beneath your feet . . . You have to ascend rotting staircases, which threaten to give way beneath every step . . . You have to grope your way along dark and filthy passages swarming with vermin. Then, if you are not driven back by the intolerable stench, you may gain admittance to the dens in which these thousands of beings who belong, as much as you, to the race for whom Christ died, herd together.[117]

The pamphlet presented through a number of individual case studies the destructive impact of poverty, overcrowding and despair upon those making up the submerged tenth. Most disturbing to many Christian readers were the accounts of widespread sexual promiscuousness. 'Incest is common', insisted the authors, 'and no form of vice or sensuality causes surprise or attracts attention'.[118]

The revelations of *The Bitter Cry* were taken up by the newspapers, and especially the *Pall Mall Gazette*, edited by W. T. Stead, the zealous, red-bearded son of a Congregational minister, a member of the Wimbledon Congregational church, and a pioneer of the sensationalist New Journalism of the 1880s. (The 'New Journalism' was a term coined by Matthew Arnold to refer to a style of popular journalism that aimed at manipulating public opinion and mobilising support for moral and political causes, often through shocking and scandalous stories.[119]) 'What a satire it is upon our Christianity and our civilization', proclaimed Stead in the *Pall Mall* in October 1883, 'that the existence of these colonies of heathens and savages in the heart of our capital should attract so little attention'. The *Pall Mall* placed much of the blame on the churches, which it insisted were so absorbed with their disestablishment agitations and theological 'wranglings' that they ignored the poverty, misery and immorality surrounding them. Too many Christians, moreover, focused their religion on doctrines of personal salvation while neglecting the pressing human need around them in this world. 'Why all this apparatus of temples and meeting houses', Stead asked, 'to save men from perdition in the world which is to come, while never a helping hand is stretched out to save them from the Inferno of their present life.'[120] In the summer of 1885, Stead published a series of articles in the *Pall Mall Gazette* on the sordid world of child prostitution, under the title 'The Maiden Tribute of Modern Babylon'. Learning that the child victims suffered in silence, he reportedly exclaimed, 'Then *I* will raise hell!'[121] To show how easily it could be done, he purchased a young girl from her mother in a London slum; he was in consequence arrested, tried and briefly imprisoned, but public opinion was awakened.

Five years after his 'Maiden Tribute' articles, Stead collaborated with William Booth, the venerable founder of the Salvation Army (now deep in grief over the recent death of his wife, Catherine), in writing a graphic account of conditions among the submerged tenth.[122] *In Darkest England and the Way Out*, published under Booth's name in 1890, opened with a comparison between the social conditions in 'darkest Africa', as described in the explorer Henry Stanley's recent book of that title, and the social conditions in the slums of England. It linked memories of the great Christian campaigns of Buxton, Livingstone and Gordon to eradicate slavery in the heart of Africa, with revelations of the similar horrors for the poor in the heart of London. 'Hard it is, no doubt', observed the authors of *In Darkest England*:

to read in Stanley's pages of the slave-traders, coldly arranging for the surprise of a village, the capture of the inhabitants, the massacre of all who resist, and the violation of all the women; but the stony streets of London, if they could be speak, would tell of tragedies as awful, of ruin as complete, of ravishments as horrible . . . only the ghastly devastation is covered, corpselike, with the artificialities and hypocrisies of modern civilisation.[123]

The prospects for life were indeed bleak for children born in central Africa, surrounded by fetid swamps and disease and under constant threat of the slave raiders. But were prospects any better for many children in Britain's urban slums? 'For', as *Darkest England* maintained of the slum children, 'thousands of these poor wretches are . . . not so much born into this world, as damned into it'.

The bastard of a harlot, born in a brothel, suckled on gin, and familiar from earliest infancy with all the bestialities of debauch, violated before she is twelve, and driven out into the streets by her mother a year or two later, what chance is there for such a girl in this world – I say nothing of the next. Yet such a case is not exceptional. There are many such differing in detail, but in essentials the same.[124]

The book sold over 200,000 copies within a year, and made a profound impact with its descriptions of life for the 'people of the abyss'.[125] Some people were drowning, *Darkest England* acknowledged, because they were weak or vicious or self-indulgent, but even the most degraded human beings had a spark of the divine, and must not be left by Christian society to perish, in the manner of the social Darwinists. There was a strong sense that the churches, established, Nonconformist and Roman Catholic – which claimed to be the keepers of the nation's conscience – must take more responsibility for addressing such conditions. The work brought increased public support and financial contributions to the Salvation Army, and especially to their urban rescue homes for the victims of strong drink or for women who had been driven into prostitution.

The religion of Socialism

The atrocious conditions of *The Bitter Cry* or of *Darkest England* were not general for the working classes. Yet all working people were vulnerable: illness, old age, or loss of employment could suck them down into the whirlpool of poverty and despair. In their concern over such conditions, a number of men and women, mainly from the middle classes, were drawn in the 1880s to embrace forms of socialism, as a path to a more humane and egalitarian society. If, some believed, the system of industrial capitalism, with all its generated wealth, could leave such a large proportion of the population in dire poverty, it was time to consider another system. There was resentment over the gross inequalities of society, in which a quarter of the land of England and Wales was in the 1870s owned by 710 individuals, in which 10 per cent of the adult population in the 1890s owned 92 per cent of the nation's wealth, while 768,938 people, nearly 3 per cent of the population of England and Wales, were dependent on poor relief.[126] In 1881, a mixed group of radicals, secularists, republicans, anarchists, Irish nationalists and land reformers, united by a common commitment to fundamental social change, came together to form the Democratic Federation. Adopting the revolutionary socialism of the German émigré, Karl Marx, whose writings were being translated into English from the later 1870s, the group changed their name to Social Democratic Federation in 1884. The Federation soon split, with the socialist artist and author, William Morris, leading a breakaway to form the Socialist League. In January 1884, a group of middle-class intellectuals founded the Fabian Society, with the aim of preparing the ground for the reconstruction of society along collectivist lines. Branches of these societies, and of other socialist organisations, sprang up in towns and cities across Britain, drawing together the disaffected, the discontented and the dreamers of a better world. With small memberships and large hopes, the socialist societies held meetings, sponsored lectures, issued tracts, organised marches and demonstrations, enjoyed close comradeship, and often fell out in bitter disputes and mutual recriminations.

In the 1880s and early 1890s, then, many looked to a socialist future with glistening eyes and fervent expectations. Was not socialism – with its slogan of 'from each according to his abilities, to each according to his needs' – a revival of the original teachings of the historical Jesus and the early church, and a truer version of Christianity than that presented in many contemporary churches? These decades, as Stephen Yeo has observed, saw the flourishing of a 'religion of socialism', as enthusiasts looked to socialism to usher in a new world of co-operation and communal responsibility, in which all would have fulfilling lives.[127] Early socialist societies behaved like evangelical sects, but proclaiming a this-worldly gospel of social redemption. They sang socialist hymns and found a sense of belonging in their meetings. Socialist pioneers used the familiar language

of Christianity to express their personal journeys. They spoke of the sin of
being part of a system of industrial capitalism that brought undeserved
misery to so many, both in Britain and abroad. This consciousness of capitalist sin was often followed by a sudden conversion experience, as they
embraced the socialist cause. Men and women were frequently converted
under the influence of a powerful socialist speaker – a William Morris,
Katherine Conway, Bruce Glasier, or Carrie Martyn. The religion of
socialism, like the Salvation Army, gained particular strength from its use
of women preachers. Under socialist influence, converts saw the world dif-
ferently, and were consumed by an inner compulsion to share the socialist
message with others through evangelistic activity – preaching on street cor-
ners or in public parks, marching in groups through the streets singing
socialist songs. In speaking of the 'religion of socialism', the Scottish artist,
Bruce Glasier, noted in 1890 'that Socialism gives us our highest ideal of
the conduct of life, and calls from us the highest service of thought, emotion, and deed – that it is our aim and prophecy, and to it is due the utmost
and gladdest devotion of all our gifts and powers'.[128]

Socialists would often claim Jesus of Nazareth as a prophet of socialism, even if they did not accept the doctrine of eternal life. In a sense, this
religion of socialism mirrored Matthew Arnold's vision of Jesus's gospel of
a this-worldly kingdom of God. Some socialists were drawn to the labour
church movement, founded in 1891 by John Trevor, a Unitarian minister
in Manchester, who left the Unitarian Church in order to form a new
movement that would, in his words, 'develop the religious life inherent in
the Labour movement' and strengthen it for the 'great work of personal
and social regeneration that lies before it'. The Labour church appealed to
many of those who had abandoned the Christianity in which they had been
raised, but wished to retain an element of religious worship and practice.
There were 54 Labour church congregations by 1895. A Socialist Sunday
School movement began in 1892 in Glasgow, and had particular strength
in Scotland and the north of England.[129]

Secularism and the Bradlaugh affair

Some visionaries, reformers and 'enthusiasts for humanity' were drawn to
the secularist movement, which experienced a surge of growth in the early
1880s. The movement had its origins in the atheist crusade of the early
nineteenth century, when radicals, republicans and Owenite socialists,
influenced by the materialism of the later Enlightenment, had begun
mounting attacks on Christianity. These propagandists had rejected both

the truth of Christian teachings and the idea that belief in an afterlife was necessary for either happiness or morality. In the late 1850s, a dynamic young lecturer and journalist, Charles Bradlaugh, rose to leadership in the anti-Christian movement, which had by now adopted the name 'secularist'. The son of a legal clerk, Bradlaugh had grown up in poverty and was largely self-educated. A large, powerful and charismatic figure of great energy and sharp intellect, Bradlaugh had been elected President of the London Secular Society in 1858 and then in 1866 had founded the National Secular Society, which held its meetings in the Hall of Science in London, where his lectures would regularly attract audiences of 1,000 or more. Secularists carried on a steady assault on Christianity through lectures, pamphlets and periodicals, of which Bradlaugh's weekly, *The National Reformer*, emerged as most influential.

In 1874, Bradlaugh formed a partnership with Annie Besant. Highly intelligent, attractive and an effective speaker, Annie had left her husband, Frank Besant, Anglican vicar of Sibsey, after losing her Christian faith. In the mid-1870s, Bradlaugh and Besant took up the cause of promoting the knowledge of devices for birth control – in the belief that large families were imposing crippling burdens on the labouring poor and often destroying the health of women. For most Christians, however, artificial forms of birth control thwarted God's purpose of procreation within marriage and promoted sexual promiscuity. In 1877 Bradlaugh and Besant republished a birth control manual, *The Fruits of Philosophy; or, the Private Companion of Young Married People*, written by the American physician, Charles Knowlton (1800–1850), and first published in 1832: the two were in consequence arrested and prosecuted in the civil courts for obscenity. Bradlaugh narrowly escaped imprisonment, while Besant was now shunned by respectable society and lost custody of her daughter. But the publicity promoted sales of the book, and by 1879 some 185,000 copies of *The Fruits of Philosophy* were in circulation.

In 1880, Bradlaugh fulfilled a lifetime ambition when, in the general election of that year, he was returned to Parliament as Liberal MP for Northampton. There followed a prolonged controversy, which over the next six years chipped away at the Christian foundations of the parliamentary state.[130] In order to take his seat in the Commons, Bradlaugh asked to be allowed to affirm his loyalty, as was permitted for Jews and Quakers, rather than to take the oath on 'the true faith of a Christian'. His request was denied. He then agreed to take the oath, but Parliament refused to allow him to do so, because, as an avowed atheist, the oath would for him be meaningless. The Liberals under Gladstone were now in office, and although Gladstone had no sympathy for Bradlaugh's atheism, he also had no wish to see him made into a martyr for conscience. He therefore argued that Bradlaugh should be allowed to affirm. But a majority of MPs were adamant that he must not be permitted to sit in the Commons. They must not, Lord Randolph Churchill insisted, incur the 'indelible stain' of placing in the Commons 'an avowed atheist and a professedly disloyal person'.[131] Bradlaugh was equally determined to take his seat, and a prolonged legal and political struggle ensued. Parliament refused to allow him to sit and declared the seat vacant. But in no fewer than five subsequent elections, the Northampton constituency voted to return him as their MP. At one point, Bradlaugh sought to force his way into the House, and was briefly imprisoned in the clock tower.

The issue became the subject of national debate, in which the Christian public was deeply involved. For many, what was at stake was nothing less than the Christian nature of the state and empire. For how could the state represent the providential purpose, and spread the benefits of Christianity and civilisation, if it permitted avowed atheists to sit in Parliament and determine its laws and policies? One of the leading evangelical Anglican journals, the *Rock*, viewed the controversy as a struggle for the soul of the state. 'It is', the journal asserted in June 1880, 'not a mere political test. It is a national, an imperial question involving the stability of the throne, and the very existence of the empire'.[132] The churches were, in fact, divided on the issue. The established churches of England and Scotland, with their commitment to the connection of church and state, were on the whole opposed to Bradlaugh's admission. The Roman Catholic Church was also adamantly opposed, and in Ulster Catholics and Orangemen co-operated in gathering petitions against his admission. Many British Nonconformists, however, argued that Bradlaugh should be permitted to affirm. Finally, after six years of weary struggle and following the general election of 1886, the speaker of the House simply refused to hear any further challenges to Bradlaugh's right to take his seat, and he did so. Two years later, in 1888, Parliament passed the Affirmation Act, allowing new MPs with no religious belief to affirm their loyalty rather than take the oath. Atheists now had the right to sit in Parliament, and the foundations of the Christian state were further eroded.

Bradlaugh, meanwhile, was exhausted and suffering acute financial strain. He retired from public life in 1889, and died two years later. Although a republican, he had never been a socialist, but was rather a life-long champion of economic individualism and self-reliance. The numbers of secularists, meanwhile, had swelled during the early 1880s, as public attention had fastened on the drama of the Bradlaugh case. By 1886, there were 29 secularist societies in the London area. Secularists were drawn into a number of progressive causes, including republicanism, land reform, and Irish Home Rule.[133] Many secularists, moreover, did not share Bradlaugh's radical individualism, and embraced socialism. Among them was Annie Besant, who in 1884 joined both the Social Democratic Federation and the Fabian Society, and in consequence distanced herself from Bradlaugh. In the 1880s, secularism, birth control, women's rights, socialism and labour organisation were, for many, combining into a new vision of the future.

Enthusiasts for humanity

In February 1888, there appeared a new three-volume novel, which explored the now pressing themes of religious doubt, secularism and enthusiasm for humanity, and which would become one of the best-selling works of the nineteenth century. The novel was *Robert Elsmere* and the author was Mary Ward, the granddaughter of the famed liberal Anglican headmaster of Rugby, Thomas Arnold, and the niece of Matthew Arnold. *Robert Elsmere* tells the story of an idealistic young Oxford-educated clergyman and his marriage to Catherine, a devout evangelical and daughter of a clergyman from the Lake District. After their marriage, the couple settle in a rural parish in the south of England, where Robert serves as Anglican vicar and Catherine engages in regular visiting among the parish poor. Their idyllic life is shattered, however, when Robert loses his belief in Christianity, in part through reading rationalist works provided for him by the local squire. Although their marriage is shaken, it survives the blow. Robert, however, resigns his Church of England living and he and Catherine move to London's East End, where Robert now commits himself to educational work among the London poor. He dreams of a new religion of humanity, based on the moral example of the historical Jesus and his work of social regeneration. He forms a religious society, the New Brotherhood of Christ, that would put aside miracles, and proclaim Jesus as risen, not in the old sense of a bodily resurrection, but in the hearts and minds of all those who dream and struggle for a most just and caring world. Elsmere dies shortly after, in part of exhaustion, a martyr to a new, this-worldly faith. The novel captured the public imagination, selling 80,000 copies in Britain and another 100,000 in North America within a decade.[134]

The novel was semi-autobiographical. Mary Ward had drawn upon the memories of her childhood, when her father, Thomas Arnold, an author and educator, had drifted in and out of the Christian faith, with damaging consequences for his marriage, his teaching career and his ability to support his large family.[135] Gladstone was profoundly moved by the novel, going out of his way to meet Mary Ward and contributing a 10,000-word review to the *Nineteenth Century*.[136] While Gladstone found much to praise in the novel, he was distressed at the manner in which the younger generation embraced the book and apparently felt they could throw off Christian belief while retaining a Christian moral vision. Too many seemed to believe that an enthusiasm for humanity was sufficient for building a new society. But this, Gladstone insisted, would not do. Western morals, he maintained, were rooted in the Judaic–Christian tradition and they could not live and grow apart from the transcendental faith that had borne and nurtured them. 'We have before us', he observed of the secularist enthusiasts for humanity, 'a huge larcenous appropriation, by the modern schemes, of goods which do not belong to them. They carry peacocks' feathers, which adorn them for a time, and which they cannot reproduce'.[137] Despite this critique, Gladstone's review helped the soaring sales of the novel. It is not clear what Mary Ward's uncle, Matthew Arnold thought of the book, and whether he would have recognised in Elsmere's religion of social regeneration similarities to the religion he had extolled in his address on the Church of England in 1876. Arnold died suddenly of heart failure on 15 April 1888; he had only finished reading the first volume of his niece's novel before his death.[138]

Tens of thousands of late Victorian readers, however, were stirred by Elsmere's pilgrimage from the Christian religion to the religion of humanity, from a supernatural faith to a faith in social improvement in this world. Beatrice Potter, the future Beatrice Webb, Fabian Socialist, author and reformer, lost her childhood faith and went through a prolonged spiritual quest before finding in 1883 a faith in scientific social reform; she would later describe her conversion as 'the flight of emotion from the service of God to the service of man'.[139] The new religion could seem more noble than the old, because there was no element of selfishness. Those who, like Elsmere, had no belief in an afterlife and yet struggled to help the poor and shape a better world, were not doing so in hope of gaining a heavenly reward. As the agnostic journalist and politician, John Morley, wrote of the unbeliever, John Stuart Mill, following Mill's death in 1873: 'Why . . . do you not recognise the loftiness and spirituality of those who make their heaven in the thought of the wider light and purer happiness that, in the immensity of ages, may be brought to new generations of men, by long force of vision and endeavour?'[140]

The churches and the changing society

In the charge delivered at his regular visitation of 1876, the archbishop of Canterbury, A. C. Tait, presented two apparently contradictory images of the Church of England, and indeed of all the British churches in their rapidly changing society. On the one hand, he portrayed the churches as seriously threatened and beleaguered. They were challenged by 'a growing power which resists all Christianity and which would establish some empire of merely human reason in place of divine truth'. The forces of 'materialistic atheism' were on the march, capturing hearts and minds, and many now viewed 'the cause of Christ as worn out'. On the other hand, however, he noted that the churches were growing in numbers and confidence. There were unprecedented levels of church building, and growing congregations of worshippers. 'We live in an age', he observed, 'of restored churches, of increased services, of vastly increased numbers of communicants'.[141]

Tait was correct in noting the ambiguity. The secularist and socialist challenges to the faith were serious and growing. None the less, the churches – established, Nonconformist and Roman Catholic – were on the whole healthy and expanding in the 1870s and 1880s. The revivals of 1859–62 and 1873–75 had added thousands of new members and strengthened the church adherence of tens of thousands more. The United Kingdom remained an overwhelmingly Christian country. The last quarter of the nineteenth century was a time of substantial church building, as both the established churches of England and Scotland, and the Nonconformist denominations erected new churches for the expanding urban and suburban populations. Between 1841 and 1876, the established church had added 3,199 new churches or chapels in England and Wales, increasing its total number by 25 per cent. Then between 1876 and 1911, it added another 2,159 churches and chapels, increasing the total by a further 13.5 per cent. According to Home Office statistics, over twenty million pounds were expended in building and restoring established churches between 1873 and 1891 alone.[142] There was also considerable Nonconformist church building. Between 1860 and 1901, the number of Congregationalist churches and chapels in England and Wales increased from 2,236 to 4,579; and the number of Baptist churches or chapels rose from 1,150 to 6,313. During the same period, the number of Roman Catholic churches and chapels in England and Wales increased from 798 to 1,536, as that church made largely successful efforts to extend its pastoral ministry to the large numbers of post-famine Irish migrants to Britain.[143]

In some regions, church building in the latter part of the century was astounding. S. J. D. Green discovered in his study of industrial Yorkshire that 'probably two-thirds of all those churches, chapels and mission-churches *ever built* in [the municipal boroughs of] Halifax and Keighley were constructed between the passing of the Second Reform Act and the death of Queen Victoria'.[144] In the four years between 1880 and 1884, the energetic evangelical bishop of Liverpool, J. C. Ryle, consecrated nine new churches in the diocese, while during the same period two other churches were rebuilt and enlarged, and a further eight new churches were under construction.[145] In Scotland, between 1870 and 1890, the established church added 151 new churches, the Free Church 112 new churches and the United Presbyterians 69 new churches.[146] Many of the new churches built across Britain had church halls, and often more than one hall, to accommodate the wide range of church-based activities that were now becoming part of church life, including Young Men's Guilds, Women's Guilds, choirs, literary societies, Bands of Hope (for the encouragement of temperance), and especially Sunday schools. In the last decades of the century, an estimated 50 per cent of children under the age of 14 attended Sunday school in England, and the percentage was probably higher in Scotland and Wales. In 1895, there were some 50,000 voluntary Sunday school teachers in the Scottish Presbyterian churches alone.[147] With the expansion of state-supported primary education after 1870, the Sunday schools gradually ceased providing basic teaching in literacy, and tended to focus exclusively on Christian instruction.

The late Victorian churches were, on the whole, more committed to social work than churches in the early decades of the nineteenth century, and more prepared to adopt a variety of forms of social engagement in their effort to shape Christian communities, especially in the towns and cities.[148] As Frederick Temple, bishop of London, wrote in October 1896, the work of the church now 'meant far more than the visiting of the sick, the instruction of the young, the conduct of the services of the Church, and the preaching of God's blessings'.[149] The amount of social involvement varied from church to church, with much depending on the personality of the clergyman, and the level of commitment and social composition of the congregation. In many churches, the minister, assisted by teams of voluntary lay visitors, conducted regular house-to-house visiting in the surrounding district, encouraging church attendance, seeking to ensure that children attended school, providing religious instruction and moral advice, distributing tracts and Bibles, and identifying cases of material need. In meeting with cases of genuine distress, the district visitors would provide clothing, blankets, meal tickets, coals or money. There were visits to the sick and elderly. Lay visitors now tended to be mainly women, in part because women were seen as more nurturing and concerned with domestic arrangements, and in part because it was seen as more proper for women to visit homes when the men might be out. Churches often provided medical clinics on one or more days each week, with local physicians volunteering their time and helping to dispense medicines. While it is difficult to quantify, the churches were clearly major contributors of poor relief at a time when local poor relief boards were often working to discourage rate-supported charity. According to an estimate by the social commentator, James Greenwood, the total monetary value of private charity – most of it church-based – distributed in 1868 in London was about £2,000,000 while that expended on rate-supported relief was about £1,317,000.[150]

Many churches conducted mothers' meetings, which offered mainly working-class women with opportunities to socialise outside of their overcrowded homes and to make clothing for their families in sewing circles, while the meetings often provided parcels for the mothers' families at Christmas and material help to new mothers. In 1876, Mary Sumner, wife of an Anglican archdeacon and daughter-in-law of the former bishop of Winchester, founded the Mothers' Union to build upon the success of the mothers' meetings. By 1914, the Mothers' Union had some 400,000 members and was one of the most active organisations in the Church of England.[151] Other churches, meanwhile, provided needy families and individuals with thrift clubs, savings banks, temperance clubs, sewing meetings, crèches, working men's clubs, soup kitchens, and Christmas dinners. Most churches, as we have seen, supported Sunday schools, and these usually included an annual Sunday school excursion to the seaside or country park, which for many urban children was their only opportunity for a day out of the city. From the 1880s, churches began providing special organisations for young people. The Boys' Brigade movement began in Glasgow in 1883 and spread rapidly among the Presbyterian churches in Scotland and the Nonconformist churches in England. It provided boys with an opportunity to drill, wear uniforms and play group games. The Church of England responded in 1891 with the Church Lads' Brigade, while a Jewish Lads' Brigade followed in 1895 and a Catholic Lads' Brigade in 1896.[152] From the 1880s, moreover, many churches supported, usually through the Boys' Brigade or Church Lads' Brigade, cricket teams and football teams. To help support their charitable outreach, churches held bazaars and tea parties, organised and conducted mainly by the women of the congregations.

Wealthier congregations also supported separate mission halls in working-class neighbourhoods. These missions often held their worship, led perhaps by a divinity student or an ordinand, in rented rooms, storefronts, or rooms formed in the arches under railway embankments. The mission halls were not expected to be self-supporting, but rather survived through the charity of other congregations. Working people were encouraged to attend in their working clothes, and the services often included fervent gospel preaching and rousing gospel songs, drawn perhaps from Ira D. Sankey's popular *Sacred Songs and Solos*. Women formed the majority of the mission hall congregations – many in the hope of receiving forms of charitable help for their families. Such halls proliferated in late Victorian Britain. There were virtually no mission halls at the time of the religious census of 1851. By 1888, the Nonconformist *British Weekly* counted 873 mission halls in London alone.[153] They provided a significant conduit through which charity was sent from more prosperous congregations to the poor of deprived urban parishes – from West End to East End parishes. In the multiplicity of churches, chapels and mission halls, the *British Weekly* discerned a lively urban religious market-place, full of opportunity for the energetic clergyman. 'There never was a time', it wrote of London in 1895, 'when so many great chapels were thronged, and that in almost every part of the city. Put a good minister in the midst of a large population, and give him fair play; in no long time he is at the head of a powerful and flourishing organisation'.[154]

Across urban Britain, new clergymen were pursuing a range of pastoral programmes with enthusiasm, becoming social workers and managers of charity as well as pastors of souls. In 1886, for example, a young Church of Scotland minister, David Watson, received his first charge, a 'chapel-of-ease' (or mission hall), in Glasgow's East End. As a divinity student, Watson had been deeply moved by *The Bitter Cry of Outcast London* and he had made the acquaintance of the crusading journalist, W. T. Stead. In 1885, while a probationer minister, he published a series of vivid articles – emulating the style of *The Bitter Cry* and Stead's journalism – in the *Paisley Gazette* entitled 'How the Paisley Poor Live!' In Glasgow, he threw himself into his pastoral ministry. As well as regular house-to-house visiting, he delivered regular weeknight lectures for young men and women who resided in lodging houses, held neighbourhood evening social gatherings, and gave lunch-time talks at local factories and foundries. He co-operated with the Glasgow Workmen's Dwelling Company in building attractive and affordable working-class housing in his parish. He established an evening club for young people, with games and magazines, to get them off the streets, and a rambling club to enable urban dwellers to enjoy Saturday walks in the countryside. He served as local chairman of the Charity Organisation Society. Within a few years, he had gained a membership of over 1,000, rebuilt and enlarged his church building, added a church hall, and elevated his former 'chapel-of-ease' into a thriving working-class parish church.[155] Jesus, Watson wrote, 'was the supreme Social Worker, the peerless philanthropist, the unwearied servant of man', and Watson sought to emulate this example.[156] Watson was, to be sure, a man of extraordinary energy, but thousands of ministers were demonstrating a similar zeal for social work.

Amid all this activity, however, there was also a gnawing sense within the British churches that charitable giving and the church-based charitable societies were not in themselves a sufficient response to the horrendous conditions suffered by many in Britain's maturing industrial society – conditions rightly portrayed as an offence to Christian civilisation. In the face of mass deprivation, exploitation, sweated labour, child prostitution, and 'the people of the abyss', the social and philanthropic efforts of the churches could seem little more than ambulance work, aimed at patching up some of the individual victims of urban-industrial society, but doing little to change the conditions that were producing those victims. A real test of the morality of any society was how it treated its most vulnerable members, and the revelations of conditions for the submerged tenth in the urban heart of the empire were a serious, some might say damning, indictment upon Britain's Christian society – an indictment that raised questions about any claims of a providential mission for the United Kingdom and its empire. Secularists and socialists made use of the revelations of mass deprivation to portray Christian society as fundamentally selfish, callous and hypocritical. Many middle- and upper-class Christians were finding themselves hard-pressed to respond to such criticisms, especially as their own large and handsome stone churches, with lofty spires, rose up in the new leafy middle- and upper-class suburbs, accentuating the separation of wealthier Christians from their poorer brethren left behind in decaying inner cities.

Despite the charitable activities of the different churches, moreover, many labouring people believed that churchgoers viewed them as inferiors and they resented the way in which better-off churchgoers could afford Sunday clothing and attend grand churches, while the unwashed, shabby and often lice-ridden poor were directed to dreary little mission halls. 'It was unusual in my young days', recalled David Kirkwood, the trade unionist and Labour politician, of his working-class childhood in Glasgow in the

1880s, 'for those of the labouring class to go to church. The church was regarded by them as a place for the "well aff folks wi' guid claes". The church regarded itself in that light and provided "missions" for the poor'.[157] The Glasgow Presbyterian clergyman, Donald MacLeod, observed in 1886 that most self-respecting labouring people had disdain for the mission halls with their assumptions of inferiority. They 'stand aloof', he noted, 'and refuse to be "missionised"'.[158] Some of the charitable relief provided by the churches, moreover, might have done more harm than good, promoting dependency on handouts, transforming inner city clergymen into little more than distributors of upper-class alms, while also stirring resentment among people who felt obliged to be incessantly demanding, or to feign piety, gratitude and remorse for their 'sins', in order to get a share of church charity. Such charity, observed the East London clergyman, Samuel Barnett, was simply 'fostering the spirit which "bullies or cringes"'.[159] Edward Denison, a wealthy young layman (and son of the bishop of Salisbury) chose to live in a deprived district of Stepney in the 1860s, and grew highly critical of the 'bread and meat doles' sent to the East End slums from prosperous West End parishes. These doles served, he maintained, only to degrade some and alienate others.[160]

In any event, such doles were perceived as no longer sufficient. 'The sin of the Church', wrote the west of Scotland Presbyterian minister, A. Scott Matheson in 1893, 'has been to care more for distributing charity than for distributing wealth . . . Charity is good, but far better is the justice which quenches the need for it'.[161] While the churches were providing their ambulance work, meanwhile, secularist and socialist activists were proclaiming grand visions of social regeneration, and claiming the high moral ground of disinterested commitment to real social reform. Surely what was needed was for the churches to become active in the new movements for social reform – with it to be conceived not simply in terms of well-maintained parish or church-based clubs and societies, or in the well-managed distribution of charity, but rather in terms of new structures for industrial and capitalist society.

Stewart Headlam and the Guild of St Matthew

One of the pioneers of a new Christian social reform ethos was the Anglo-Catholic Church of England priest, Stewart Headlam, the stubborn, opinionated, combative, but dedicated promoter of Christian Socialism.[162] Headlam was born in 1847, the son of a wealthy Liverpool underwriter. He was educated at Eton and Cambridge, where he came under the influence of the Christian Socialist theologian, F. D. Maurice. In 1870, Headlam became Anglican curate of the parish of St John's, Drury Lane, in the heart of London's theatre district. He proved conscientious in pastoral visiting, but was soon under suspicion within the church. For he extended his ministry to actors, dancers, playwrights and stage people – men and women who were suspected of being morally lax and sexually promiscuous. His sermons, moreover, suggested the possibility of universal salvation. In 1873, he was asked to leave St John's. He became curate in the parish of St Matthew's in a largely impoverished part of Bethnal Green. After a life of privilege, he now confronted at first hand the grim reality of grinding East End poverty. He developed friendships with trade union organisers and also with secularists, among them Charles Bradlaugh; he grew to understand the anger that many felt toward a church which, despite its professed commitment to the poor, seemed to sanction an unjust social order. He publicly supported Bradlaugh and Annie Besant at their 1877 trial for promoting birth control, and gave evidence for the defence. In the East End, he was also impressed by the selfless ministry of the ritualist slum priests and was drawn to the ritualist movement. He came to embrace the sacraments as corporate symbols of the kingdom of God – Christ, he believed, had sanctified the material life when he became flesh, and had called his disciples to serve the needy and the outcast. Ritualist churches, he also held, brought beauty, light, music and drama into the drab lives of the urban poor.

In 1877, Headlam founded the Guild of St Matthew in the Bethnal Green parish. As we have seen, confraternities and parish guilds, which gathered together lay parishioners to assist the clergy in promoting church interests, were proliferating within the Church of England at this time. The Guild of St Matthew had three main objects: first, to combat popular prejudices against the church; second, to promote more fervent worship and practical piety; and third, to encourage the study of social and political questions in the light of the incarnation.[163] The incumbent of St Matthew's, meanwhile, was by now unhappy with Headlam's universalist theology, secularist friendships, and defence of the theatre, and in 1878 Headlam was dismissed from his curacy. He held a few more London curacies until 1882; after that he never held an official cure within the Church of England. With his ample private means, he now devoted himself to various social reform causes of his own choosing. In 1879, he formed the Church and Stage Guild, 'to assert and vindicate the right of religious people to take part in theatrical amusements': this further antagonised conservative Christians. He promoted the radical land taxing ideas of the American socialist, Henry George, and gave public support to Bradlaugh's struggle to enter Parliament. In 1882, at Annie Besant's request, he even became convener of the educational committee of the National Secular Society.

His main interest, however, was the Guild of St Matthew, which he developed into a national organisation for promoting social reform. In 1884, with his own money he purchased the *Church Reformer*, a monthly Anglo-Catholic journal, which he made the organ of the Guild. His aim for the Guild was to respond to the secularist and working-class critics of Christianity by reviving the teachings of the historical Jesus. This Jesus, Headlam proclaimed in 1883, was 'a Carpenter who became a Radical reformer both in social and economic matters . . . the social and political *Emancipator*, the greatest of all secular workers, the founder of the great Socialistic society for the promotion of righteousness, the preacher of a Revolution, the denouncer of kings, the gentle, tender sympathiser with the rough and outcast, who could utter scathing, burning words against the rich, the respectable, the religious'.[164] During the 1880s and 1890s, Headlam and the Guild embraced a number of reform programmes – the extension of popular education, increased public funding for the arts, the adoption of a national minimum wage, restriction of working hours, full legal rights for women, land reform, subsidised housing, Irish home rule, and the nationalisation of public houses (with the aim of making them less inviting). Guild membership remained relatively small, reaching its peak in 1895 with 364 members, of whom about a quarter were Anglican priests.[165]

In 1895 the Guild of St Matthew was dealt a severe blow, from which it never really recovered, as a result of Headlam's involvement in the Oscar Wilde affair. That year, while at the height of his fame, the celebrated playwright was arrested and tried for his homosexual relationship with Lord Alfred Douglas. The nation was scandalised, and the mob bayed for Wilde's blood. Headlam had met Wilde only once or twice through his work with the Church and Stage Guild, and scarcely knew him. He was, however, familiar with members of Wilde's circle, many of whom he entertained at his fashionable Bloomsbury home in evening gatherings that the author Edgar Jepson portrayed as the real beginnings of the Bloomsbury Group – that is, the circle of artists, authors and critics who led the revolt against Victorian cultural restrictions in the early years of the twentieth century.[166] Headlam felt called by his Christian faith to offer assistance to one who had become a reviled outcast. He also had a personal understanding of Wilde's situation: his own marriage had dissolved, as his wife was a lesbian. He helped pay Wilde's bail, and accompanied him to and from court through the jeering crowds. After the conviction, he regularly visited Wilde in prison. For much of the British public, Headlam and the Guild were now identified with Wilde's homosexuality. Indeed, the affair seemed to confirm suspicions regarding Headlam's involvement with stage people and Anglo-Catholic ritualism. Membership in the Guild fell by nearly half and mounting debts forced the closure of the *Church Reformer*. The Guild survived into the next century, continuing to call for radical social reform initiatives, but its influence was greatly curtailed. In its early years, however, the Guild had made significant advances toward a revival of Christian Socialism and it had inspired many idealistic younger clergymen and lay people to work for social transformation. Such younger social critics as H. W. Massingham and the playwright George Bernard Shaw frequently attended Guild events. 'Shaw', recalled one Guild member, 'used our meetings as a training ground for public speaking and debate'.[167] Headlam had the power to stir controversy and make the comfortable uncomfortable. His Guild convinced a significant number that the best Christian response to their secularist and socialist critics was to take up the work of social reform.

Samuel and Henrietta Barnett, and the settlement movement

Another seminal figure in the social Christian movement, Samuel Barnett, was born in 1844, the son of a prosperous manufacturer. Raised within an upper-middle-class Tory home, he attended Wadham College, Oxford, and taught for two years at Winchester public school. Ordained in 1867, he served for five years in a London curacy. Here the gentle, reserved young curate came under the influence of the formidable social reformer, Octavia Hill, who was organising and managing the provision of decent housing for the London labouring poor. Through Hill, Barnett met one of her equally tough-minded young rent-collectors, the 18-year-old Henrietta Rowland. These women helped direct him toward social work. Barnett married Henrietta, and in 1873, helped by Octavia Hill's influence, he became vicar of St Jude's parish, Whitechapel, in London's East End. Here, amid a largely impoverished parish population of 6,000, crowded into a rabbit warren of unsanitary courts and alleys, rife with prostitution and crime, the Barnetts conducted a socially committed ministry, visiting regularly the homes in the parish, setting up education classes, a parish library, a savings bank, and a maternity society. They worked to make St Jude's charitable endeavours more systematic, efficient and discerning. In this, they adopted the methods, including careful social investigation, the keeping of statistics, and the maintaining of individual case studies of relief recipients, which were being promoted by Octavia Hill and by the recently formed Charity Organisation Society.

In the later 1870s, the Barnetts became frequent visitors to Oxford, speaking to groups of students about the social conditions in their East End parish. They developed a friendship with Arnold Toynbee, an able young economic historian, Christian socialist, and fellow of Balliol College, who is credited with having first used the term 'industrial revolution'. Toynbee challenged the prevalent belief that the economy was governed by inexorable natural laws and ultimately by the design of providence. The economy, he insisted, was a human creation, and as such its structures and laws could be altered for human ends; he argued for increased state intervention in the economy in the interest of shaping communities and protecting the vulnerable.[168] Despite his precarious health, he occasionally stayed with the Barnetts in Whitechapel, seeking to learn more about East London social conditions. He died, aged only 31, in 1883. The Barnetts also became friendly with the broad churchman Benjamin Jowett, one of the contributors to the notorious *Essays and Reviews*, and now the revered master of Balliol. Jowett believed that a well-rounded university education should include the development of an ethos of disinterested civic service. Balliol was also the college of the influential idealist philosopher, T. H. Green, who had died in 1882 but whose intellectual legacy lived on in the generation of students he had inspired with social service idealism. For Green, Christ was indeed risen, in the sense that he now 'realised himself in all the particulars of a moral life'.[169]

In the autumn of 1883, amid the public outcry caused by the publication of *The Bitter Cry of Outcast London*, Barnett presented a paper in Oxford, in which he argued that one way to begin changing conditions in the urban slums would be for educated and well-connected Oxford men to go and live there. A major cause of slum conditions was residential segregation. The wealthy were moving to fashionable West End neighbourhoods or leafy suburbs, while the poor were concentrated into decaying inner-city areas of overcrowded, dilapidated housing and industrial pollution. Parishes such as Barnett's were made up almost exclusively of the lowest social classes. There was no 'resident gentry' to use their political influence and knowledge in helping to shape local communities. What was needed was for Oxford men to settle in 'outcast London', if only for a time, and share in the lives of the people there. 'This', Barnett insisted, 'will alleviate the sorrow and misery born of class division and indifference. It will bring classes into relation; it will lead them to know and learn of one another, and those to whom it is given will give'.[170] The Oxford audience was moved by the appeal, and a number of those present resolved to create a settlement. A committee was formed and money raised. They purchased a disused school in Barnett's Whitechapel parish and reconstructed it to include residential accommodation for 17 residents, as well as classrooms, communal dining hall and meeting rooms. On Henrietta Barnett's suggestion, it was called Toynbee Hall, in honour of Arnold Toynbee, and the first Oxford 'settlers', all young men, moved in at the end of December 1884. Barnett was appointed warden. Toynbee Hall did not have a religious test for its settlers, nor did it maintain a defined Christian ethos.

The main work of the settlement community was educational. Barnett believed that the most effective way to empower people was to educate them, and Toynbee Hall settlers taught classes on a variety of subjects for people of different ages, as well as organising public lectures, discussion groups, literary clubs, and art exhibitions. In its physical appearance, Toynbee Hall resembled an Oxford college, and the settlers were, of course, engaging in the activities they knew best. For a time Barnett held out the hope that it might become the nucleus of a great democratic East End university, providing affordable higher education for the labouring poor.[171] This was not to be, but education, self-improvement and the dissemination of culture remained its main purposes.

Settlers were encouraged to entertain people from the surrounding community. The initial contacts were difficult, with stiff tea parties in the drawing room, local people uncomfortable and bored, and the settlers fumbling to make conversation. However, in time connections were made and the gatherings grew more relaxed and natural. In 1888, Whitechapel was the scene of the infamous 'Jack the Ripper' murders, with one of the murdered prostitutes found only a few yards from Toynbee Hall. Settlers joined in the street patrols organised by a local vigilance committee, and they also sought through writings and lectures to educate the wider British public about the causes of prostitution – poverty, atrocious housing and the exploitation of women.[172] During the strike of the London dockworkers in 1889, Toynbee settlers gave support to the strikers, and in 1892 they organised a 'Toynbee Commission' to study the social effects of a trade depression – which led to the setting up of a public works scheme for unemployed dockers.[173] Settlers also became involved in local politics, becoming Poor Law guardians, getting elected to school boards, providing legal advice, conducting campaigns for the establishment of a public library and for improvements in sanitation. There was, to be sure, no great transformation of social conditions, but there was a change in attitudes. 'It would obviously be absurd', wrote Barnett in 1899, 'to expect that twenty men living in Whitechapel should make any evident mark on the public opinion of half-a-million people, but for my part I am convinced that, as a result of their settlement, there is an increase of good will'.[174]

Toynbee Hall captured the imagination of the nation, and other settlements soon followed. In 1885, members of Keble College, Oxford, established Oxford House as a settlement in Bethnal Green. It was decidedly high Anglican in orientation and less political than Toynbee Hall. Nonconformists began forming settlements, with Congregationalists founding Browning Hall Settlement in Walworth, followed by Mansfield House in 1890. Wesleyans founded the Bermondsey Settlement that same year. Roman Catholics established St Phillip's House in East London, and Newman House in Southwark in 1891. The successful novelist Mary Ward founded University Hall in 1890, to give practical expression to the ideal of selfless social service expressed in her novel *Robert Elsmere*.[175] A Women's University Settlement was founded in Southwark in 1886. The settlement movement was particularly strong in London, but gradually expanded across the United Kingdom. By 1913, there were 27 settlements in London, another 12 elsewhere in England, five in Scotland and one in Belfast. Of these, only 32 were decidedly religious in orientation.[176] The settlements did much good in their neighbourhoods, particularly through their educational and youth programmes. But the greatest benefit of the movement was in bringing future clergymen, teachers, journalists, politicians and civil servants – as a part of their education – to experience at first hand conditions in the urban slums and to learn to value the humanity of those who struggled under those conditions. The settlers carried with them from the settlements a new sense of the importance of community. Most also came to believe in the need for collectivist action in confronting the problems of bad housing, bad schools and bad drains. Not all settlers became socialists, but most became advocates of the social welfare state. The settlement movement played a major role in changing social and economic attitudes among the clergy. There was a shift away from the belief, so prevalent in the mid-Victorian years, that the economic laws were divinely ordained and that the free market-place, if left alone, would bring progress and prosperity for the population as a whole. Instead, there was a growing recognition among Christians of the need for state intervention in the economy to ensure basic human rights, including freedom from hunger, cold, disease, and overwork. Through the settlement movement, collectivist ideas were entering into the mainstream of Christian social thought.

Lux Mundi and the Christian Social Union

In the mid-1870s, a group of young Oxford dons began meeting regularly for shared reading and discussion. The group shared the high sacramental piety of Anglo-Catholicism, combined with the social concerns of the broad church movement. They included Henry Scott Holland, senior student of Christ Church, J. R. Illingworth, fellow of Jesus College, E. S. Talbot, the first warden of Keble College, and Charles Gore, fellow of Trinity College and the first warden of Pusey House (the Edward Pusey memorial library), and they called themselves, in jest, the 'Holy Party'. Their radicalism, they joked, was indicated by the fact that most of them sported red beards – those unable to grow one, including Scott Holland, remained clean shaven.[177] Able, well-connected and devout, this group saw themselves as successors to the Oxford Tractarians. They were influenced by the idealist philosophy of T. H. Green and the ethos of disinterested social service as represented by Jowett and Balliol College. Gore also served for a time with the Oxford University Mission in Calcutta, where he engaged in dialogue with Hindus. From the late 1870s, the Holy Party took a growing interest in questions of economics and social ethics. They were drawn to the thinking of Arnold Toynbee.[178] 'Theirs was a Catholicism', one historian has noted, that 'leaped with confidence into the questions of the hour'.[179] They were also dismayed that the church as a whole seemed so unadventurous. 'We do so need to know', Holland wrote to R. W. Church in 1882, 'that the Church of England . . . will not always seem afraid of all that is not sensible, prudent, tame: that she will *sometimes*, and, above all, at hours of crisis, find favourable place for those higher factors of spiritual power, which move with splendour, which enlighten, and quicken, and dominate, and brace'.[180]

They endeavoured to find a connection between the rituals of the ancient Catholic and apostolic faith and the new social teachings, and found this connection in the doctrine of the incarnation. When the Christ had become flesh, they argued, He had sanctified the material world and ended forever the division between the holy and profane, the spiritual and the material, the religious and the secular. The incarnate Christ called upon His followers to work for a more just and equitable social order, in which all might have fulfilling lives. He came into the world, not to spirit His followers away to some ethereal paradise, but to inspire them for the work of transforming the world. As the Balliol fellow, W. H. Fremantle, proclaimed in his Bampton lectures of 1883, 'the Christian Church is designed, not to save individuals out of the world, but to save the world itself'.[181]

In 1887, the Oxford group decided upon a volume of essays to give expression to their common theological views. Twelve individuals prepared essays, which the group then collectively revised. The volume was edited by Charles Gore and published in 1889 under the title *Lux Mundi: A Series of Studies in the Religion of the Incarnation*. It was an attempt to restate the ancient faith for the changing needs of the modern world. A common theme running through the essays was that of development. Christian truth was in the process of unfolding: as human understanding of the material world grew, it brought new insights which contributed to a fuller perception of Christianity. This process was integral to the life of the church. As Gore wrote in the preface, theological development was the process by which the church 'standing firm in her old truths, enters into the apprehension of the new social and intellectual movements of each age'. The church, he added, was thus able 'to throw itself into the sanctification of each new social order'.[182] In his own essay, Gore took up the challenge of biblical criticism. The modern church, he wrote, had learned though the work of the biblical critics that the Old Testament narratives were not to be taken as a literal historical record. Rather, they were largely allegorical and poetic expressions of belief, which had to be understood partly as myth. The New Testament narratives, he continued, provided more accurate historical accounts of the life of Christ and the early church, but even here there were difficulties: for example, what was the church to make of Christ's erroneous claims about the authorship of the Psalms? The Scriptures were 'the most conspicuous of the modes in which the Holy Spirit has mercifully wrought for the illumination and encouragement of our race'.[183] But they were not the only mode. For the Holy Spirit was immanent in the world, sanctifying all of nature and all social relations, and guiding social development, perhaps even inspiring the new collectivist modes of social thought in industrial Britain.

Lux Mundi excited immense public interest. Many were appalled by its use of such terms as 'myth' in reference to the Scriptures – just as readers had been appalled by the language of 'myth' in *Essays and Reviews* almost 30 years previously. H. P. Liddon, the biographer of Pusey and leading embodiment of the ethos of the Oxford Movement, was deeply distressed, insisting that the work was 'a proclamation of revolt against the spirit and principles of Dr. Pusey and Mr. Keble'. He was especially disappointed in Gore, who had been seen as a future leader of the Anglo-Catholic movement.

Lux Mundi was denounced in much of the religious press and its editor became known as 'that awful Mr. Gore who doesn't believe the Bible'. The combative veteran high churchman, G. A. Denison, sought to rouse the English Church Union against Gore, and there was pressure for him to be dismissed as warden of Pusey House.[184] Others, however, spoke favourably of the volume as inaugurating a new Oxford movement, one combining the sincere Anglo-Catholic faith of Pusey and Keble with a new openness to modern biblical criticism and a new commitment to social reform.

In 1889, while the controversy over *Lux Mundi* raged, members of the Oxford group formed a new society, the Christian Social Union (CSU), which represented an effort to bring their theological views to bear on social conditions. The purpose of the CSU was to study in common the social and economic problems of the day, and promote Christian social teachings. There was some question about the need for a new Anglican society for Christian social reform, when the Guild of St Matthew was already at work in the field. Certainly, Stewart Headlam was privately unhappy about the CSU. But the founders apparently had no wish to connect themselves with Headlam's radicalism and eccentricities. Gore, Scott Holland, Illingworth, Talbot and the other founders of the CSU were men of influence, position, connections and prospects within the church and universities, and they sought to use their status to convince the different parties within the Church of England – High, Evangelical and Broad – to embrace the cause of social reform. In November 1889, the CSU elected as its first president Brooke Foss Westcott, the eminent broad church biblical scholar and regius professor of divinity at Cambridge University – who a few months later was elevated to the episcopal bench as bishop of Durham. Westcott remained president until his death in 1901; his reputation encouraged many 'good Conservatives' to join the CSU, and helped to ensure that its influence 'thoroughly permeated the Church of England, especially the hierarchy'.[185]

The Christian Social Union expanded rapidly, establishing branches across England and Wales. By 1897, there were 27 branches, with a membership of about 2,600.[186] The CSU was primarily involved in propagating ideas of social reform among Christians. It produced numerous leaflets and pamphlets, and made use of various journals, including the scholarly *Economic Review* based in Oxford, the outspoken *Goodwill* which was established in 1894 and claimed a circulation of 28,000 by 1896, and *Commonwealth*, a popular monthly edited by Scott Holland from 1896. Beginning in 1894, the London CSU sponsored courses of sermons during Lent at different city churches; some of the sermon series were later published as books. CSU members took prominent roles in discussions of social issues at Church Congresses, meetings of Convocation, Lambeth Conferences and other forums. At the Church Congress of 1890, for example, Westcott gave an address on socialism, in which he contrasted the selfishness of individualism with altruism of socialism. 'The aim of Socialism', he insisted, 'is the fulfilment of service, the aim of Individualism is the attainment of some personal advantage'. He denied that socialism necessarily meant violent revolution or class conflict. Rather, it represented the evolving understanding of society 'as an organic whole, a vital unity formed by the contributory members mutually independent'.[187] Such language from a bishop helped diminish suspicions among the clergy that socialism meant class war or atheism.

In 1892, Westcott brought the CSU national attention when, as bishop of Durham, he intervened in an industrial dispute in the Durham coalfields which had thrown nearly 100,000 people out of work.[188] He brought the representatives of the mine owners and the miners' union together for negotiations at his episcopal palace, and helped to arbitrate a settlement that brought the miners back to work (although with a 10 per cent reduction in their wages). While many miners were far from happy with the agreement, within the church and much of British society there was ringing praise for Westcott's arbitration. Here, it seemed, was a role for the established church in the emerging era of collectivist politics – it would serve as a mediator between the forces of capital and the forces of labour, using its ethical authority to gain the confidence of both sides and to represent and promote the common good. In the following year, the Oxford CSU introduced a new form of Christian economic activity, when it published a 'white list' of 20 local businesses which paid acceptable union wage-rates and maintained healthy working conditions. Consumers were encouraged to buy only from firms included on the list. Businesses soon responded by endeavouring to follow good practice, and within a year, the Oxford CSU white list had increased to 80 firms. Other CSU branches now compiled and published their own white lists, creating a form of 'Christian shopping'.[189]

Social Christianity among English Nonconformists and Scottish Presbyterians

The commitment to social reform represented in the Church of England by the Christian Social Union found expression in other denominations as well. As the historian David Thompson has shown, by the 1880s such leading Nonconformists as R. W. Dale of Birmingham, A. M. Fairbairn, principal of Airedale College in Bradford, and J. B. Paton, principal of the Congregational Institute in Nottingham, came to accept the fundamental importance of environmental factors in the formation of character and to support increased state intervention in the economy to protect vulnerable members of society.[190] For Fairbairn, writing in 1894, the primary aim of the church was to establish the kingdom of God on earth – a kingdom that was 'ethical in character'. In 1886, a group of Nonconformist socialists in London formed the Christian Socialist Society, an interdenominational forum for the promotion of socialism. Its organ was the *Christian Socialist*, and branches were established around Britain. The Society, however, failed to agree on the Christian element in its social ideal, and it dissolved in 1892. In 1894, the London Baptist preacher and Fabian Socialist, John Clifford, founded the Christian Socialist League, a larger and more influential body, which carried on the interdenominational ethos of the Christian Socialist Society. The Christian Socialist League metamorphosed into the Christian Social Brotherhood in 1898, continuing its call to the free churches of Britain to work for social reform. Among the Methodists, the eloquent, cultivated and passionate London-based minister, Hugh Price Hughes, emerged as a leading proponent of Christian socialism by 1884.[191] Hughes founded the weekly *Methodist Times* in 1885, calling on Methodists to move forward in their social and political attitudes. Two years later he founded the West London Mission and became the leading light of what was termed the 'Forward Movement' in English Nonconformity. In 1887–88, Hughes delivered in London a series of addresses on social and political questions, which were published under the title of *Social Christianity*. 'The social failure of Christianity', he insisted in this work, 'is not the fault of Christianity, but of Christians who have been selfishly individualistic'. For Jesus 'was the greatest social reformer the world has ever seen'. He had come 'into this world to save human society as well as to save individuals' and Christians were bound to follow in His great work of social regeneration.[192]

In Scotland, a growing number of Presbyterians – from the established church, the Free Church and the United Presbyterian Church – embraced the new social Christianity during the 1880s and 1890s. Industrial and urban Scotland faced the same problems of poverty, inequality, class resentments, prostitution and crime as did England, and Scots were influenced by English social writings. Scots also had their own traditions of social protest, expressed in the stories of the seventeenth-century Covenanters, the poetry of Robert Burns, and, more recently, in condemnations of the nineteenth-century Highland Clearances through which tens of thousands of Highlanders had been forced from their ancestral lands in order to make room for sheep pastures and hunting preserves. In 1885, several younger Free Church ministers, among them the Old Testament scholar, George Adam Smith, delivered a set of public lectures, which were published under the title *Christianity and Social Life*.[193] The lecturers denounced the Scottish churches for treating the suffering of the poor as though it were God's will and the teachings of political economy as though they were holy writ. These ministers emphasised instead the contemporary relevance of the social teachings of the Old Testament prophets and the historical Jesus, and the need to work for the kingdom of God in this world.

There was new interest in the effects of social environment. In May 1888, Donald MacLeod, a venerable Church of Scotland minister in Glasgow, addressed the General Assembly on the evils of slum housing. Many claimed to be concerned, MacLeod observed, about the 'lapsed masses', the large numbers of working people who were outside church influence. In Glasgow, he observed, there were an estimated 120,000 who attended no church. There were also, he added, 126,000 people condemned to live in overcrowded single-room dwellings, and the statistical correlation was no accident.[194] The church had to work to improve housing conditions, if it ever hoped to reach the 'unchurched'. The church must admit, he insisted, that 'it has more to do for these so-called 'lapsed masses' than to assault them with armies of district visitors, and shower upon them tracts and good advices, while we are leaving them to swelter in dens, and under conditions where Christian life is so difficult, if not impossible, to realise'.[195] In response to MacLeod's appeal, the presbytery of Glasgow appointed a commission to investigate the housing of the poor, which issued a comprehensive report in 1891. That same year, the General Assembly of the Church of Scotland appointed a commission to enquire into the religious condition of the Scottish people, including the social factors affecting church attendance. Reporting in 1896, the commission concluded that social deprivation was a major cause of non-churchgoing, and that the church would have to work for 'a more equitable distribution of wealth' through 'combined action along the whole line of social life'.[196]

Cardinal Manning and Social Catholicism

The Roman Catholic Church, with its separate hierarchies in England and Wales and in Scotland, also underwent a reorientation in its views towards industrial society in the 1870s and 1880s. In the early and mid-nineteenth century, the attitudes of the Roman Catholic Church towards the problems of urban industrial society had been conservative, portraying the social hierarchy as divinely ordained, proclaiming the rights of property to be both sacred and absolute, and condemning socialist and democratic movements as not only misguided but sinful. To the poor, the church preached that poverty was a holy condition, if accepted in a proper spirit of humility; to the wealthy, it taught the obligation of giving alms. The Catholic Church was largely silent on matters of social reform, despite the dire poverty of the post-famine Irish migrants crowded into the slums of London, Liverpool, Glasgow and other cities.

The leading force in promoting a change in Catholic social attitudes was the Roman Catholic primate of England, Archbishop Henry Manning. He began taking an active interest in social reform in the early 1870s, following the great Vatican Council, which had raised him to a new international prominence (he became a cardinal in 1875). In December 1872, he appeared at a conference at Exeter Hall called to promote the unionisation of English agricultural labourers, and proposed the first resolution. His support for agricultural labour grew in part out of his early experiences while Anglican rector of Lavington in rural Sussex and in part from his concern over conditions for Catholic tenant farmers in Ireland. Commitment to the cause of agricultural labour led to an acquaintance, and then a friendship, with the English Radical politician, Sir Charles Dilke. In 1884, Manning was appointed to the Royal Commission on the Housing of the Working Classes, which was chaired by Dilke and instructed to investigate social conditions. Manning was by now convinced that poor housing had a destructive effect on morals, and at the first meeting, he proposed sweeping reforms, including the removal of industry to the outskirts of cities. The first report of the Commission was largely drafted by Manning and Dilke. Amid the severe trade depression of 1887–88, Manning served on the Committee on the Distress in London, and led a deputation to the prime minister, pressing for short-term relief works combined with long-term social reforms.[197]

Manning expressed his views on labour and industry in a pamphlet entitled *The Rights and Wrongs of Labour*, which was first given as an address to the Leeds Mechanics' Institute in 1874 and reissued in 1887. In this work, he supported trade union organisation and advocated a degree of state intervention in the economy to improve conditions for the labouring orders, ensure decent housing, provide adequate leisure time for family life, and reduce child labour. 'We must', he insisted, '. . . put labour and the profits of labour second – the moral state and the domestic life of the whole working population first'.[198] In 1887, he argued in an article in the *American Quarterly Review* that the natural right to life prevailed over the rights of private property, and that a starving man committed no crime if he took sufficient food from his neighbour to sustain his life or that of his family. For many critics, Manning was advocating socialism. This was untrue: he was never a socialist. He called for limited state intervention to ensure decent domestic conditions for labouring families in the free market economy, and he sought to broaden the appeal of the Catholic Church in a more democratic age. In an autobiographical note written near the end of his life, he observed that 'if the Church is to be spread in England, it will be by its large popular sympathies identifying it, not with the governors, but with the governed'.[199]

He established his reputation as a champion of labour during the London Dockers' Strike of the late summer of 1889, when the dockers and supporting unions closed the port of London for several weeks. Manning decided to intervene in the fourth week of the strike, on learning that the employers planned to import foreign labour, with the potential of violent clashes and loss of life. He was now 81 years of age and physically frail, but with patience and perseverance he managed to mediate a settlement and bring a peaceful end to the strike. The dock workers were grateful, while the press noted that the Roman Catholic cardinal had arbitrated a settlement while the archbishop of Canterbury was enjoying a holiday in Wales. The end of the strike was, for many, 'the Cardinal's Peace'.[200] One of Manning's aims in his social activism was to overcome the popular perception of Roman Catholics as foreigners and their church as 'the Italian mission'. He had deeply felt his own ostracism by former friends after his conversion to Rome in 1845, and longed to end the alienation of Catholics. When asked in 1889 how he felt when the dockers cheered him, he replied simply, 'An Englishman'.[201] Two years later, Pope Leo XIII issued an encyclical on labour and industry, *Rerum Novarum*, which offered scathing criticisms of the exploitation of industrial workers. While hostile to socialism, it did promote Catholic trade unions and state intervention to ensure a living wage for all workers. Manning warmly welcomed the encyclical as an expression of compassion for the masses. He died in 1892, and the dockers turned out in their thousands to join the vast numbers thronging the streets at his London funeral.

By the mid-1890s, collectivist attitudes were becoming widespread among Christians across the United Kingdom. There was a fundamental shift in attitudes away from the belief, so prevalent in the mid-nineteenth century, that the economic laws of classical political economy were instituted by God. Christians now were more likely to view the economic laws as human constructions. 'Economic laws', insisted Bishop Westcott in 1895, were simply 'generalisations from the observations of the conduct of average men at particular times and places under a particular aspect'.[202] There was an increased emphasis on the role of environment in shaping individual character, and growing acceptance that atrocious housing, poor sanitation, and long working hours could form impassable obstacles to the spread of the gospel. With this came a recognition that the free market-place was all too often characterised by 'jungle law' and the devouring of the weak by the strong. The wealthy, insisted the Scottish Free Church professor, George Adam Smith, in 1896, were 'feeding upon the poor', by paying them inadequate wages, charging them extortionate rents, and degrading them with alcohol: 'the truth is clear that many families of the middle class, and some of the very wealthiest of the land, are nourished by the waste of the lives of the poor'.[203] Finally, late Victorian Christians came to believe that society was evolving in a collectivist direction, and that the individualism so important to the providentialist thought of early Victorian Christian free traders and political economists would not survive.

Ireland, the churches and the fall of Parnell

For most of the British population, the Victorian era was perceived as one of material progress and the growth of liberal values; the queen's jubilee year, 1887, had been an opportunity to reflect on the providential blessings of her reign. For most Irish Catholics, however, Victoria's jubilee brought no such grateful reflections. 'The present Queen's reign', observed Patrick McAlister, the Catholic bishop of Down and Connor, to the rector of the Irish College in Rome on 7 July 1887:

has been to Ireland the most disastrous since that of Elizabeth. During her reign there have died of Famine in Ireland 1,228,000 persons; the number of Emigrants was 4,186,000; there were evicted 3,667,000. The number of evicted equals 75 percent of the actual population. In 1885, there were 15,423 persons evicted; in 1884, 20,025 persons evicted; in 1883, 17,855 evicted; in 1882, 26,836 evicted and so on, for the last half century.[204]

For McAlister and many other Catholic clerics, this saga of misery would have to end. Ireland would have to gain its autonomy through the influence of Parnell and the clerical–nationalist alliance.

Following the defeat of the Home Rule bill and the fall of the Liberal government in 1886, the focus of the Irish nationalist movement had shifted to the agrarian struggle. The agricultural depression in Ireland continued, aggravated by growing imports of cheap American grain and frozen meat. With falling agricultural prices, farmers were hard-pressed to pay their rents, and families continued to be evicted from their farms. In 1886, a poor harvest threatened to bring a return to mass evictions and famine across rural Ireland.

Late in 1886, the leadership of the agrarian wing of the nationalist movement responded to this crisis by inaugurating the 'Plan of Campaign'. By this plan, the tenant farmers on each estate were encouraged to band together and offer the landlord what they decided was a fair and affordable rent for their farms. If the landlord refused to accept their offer, the tenants would not pay them any rent, but would instead place the proffered rent in an 'estate fund', to be held by trustees selected by the tenants. This fund would then be used to assist tenant families who were evicted. The local community, moreover, would boycott anyone who took over the farm of an evicted tenant. Parnell had misgivings about the Plan, which he suspected would antagonise British opinion and harm prospects for Home Rule. None the less, he allowed the Plan to go forward, and meetings were held across rural Ireland to promote it. Parnell proved correct about British opinion, which largely viewed it as an attack on the rights of property and the sanctity of contracts – a form of revolutionary socialism. In early 1887, Salisbury's government secured coercive legislation empowering the authorities in Ireland to suppress any associations deigned to be 'illegal in their intent and operation'.

Rural Ireland was again engulfed in conflict, with refusals of rent, arrests of League organisers, protest meetings, defiant speeches, boycotting – then more arrests, more meetings, more defiance.[205] In July 1887, police fired on a crowd in Mitchelstown, killing three; 'Remember Mitchelstown' now became a watchword for the movement. Many Catholic priests joined the agitation, while Archbishops Croke and Walsh gave the Plan of Campaign their public support. The Salisbury government, meanwhile, assisted by some leading English Catholics, convinced the Vatican to intervene in an attempt to curb the agrarian violence. In April 1888, after sending a representative to investigate the situation in Ireland, the pope issued a rescript, condemning the Plan of Campaign and the boycotting, as 'altogether foreign to natural justice and to Christian charity'. The United Kingdom, the pope noted, had established land courts to arbitrate disputes peacefully. Aggrieved tenants should look for justice within these courts, rather than through unlawful means.[206]

The papal rescript sparked outrage in Ireland. The papacy, it seemed, was following the orders of the 'British' state. Irish nationalists condemned the rescript and launched a protest campaign that opened with a great public meeting in Dublin in May. 'Our religion', exclaimed the Irish Catholic MP, Thomas Sexton, at this meeting, 'is independent of England, and our politics are independent of Rome'. 'The feeling throughout the country', T. A. O'Callaghan, bishop of Cork, reported to the rector of the Irish College in Rome on 2 June, 'was most intense. Cursing the pope was quite common. Women threw his likeness out of their houses and the excitement extended even to the children'.[207] The Catholic clergy in Ireland were caught in a dilemma. They were bound to obey the pope. However, if they openly supported his condemnation of the Plan of Campaign, they would set themselves against the Irish national movement. In the event, the clergy decided their place was with the Irish people. In a joint letter signed by 28 of the 30 Irish bishops, they informed the pope that they were more familiar with the situation in Ireland than he or his advisors, and that the church must not set itself against the Irish nationalist movement. Over the coming months, the Vatican came to accept this view. The cost of alienating the millions of Irish Catholics living in Ireland or abroad was not to be contemplated. The Vatican ceased its criticism of the Plan of Campaign and the clerical–nationalist alliance in Ireland was preserved. However, the influence and authority of the Catholic Church in Ireland had been damaged. The place of the church in the national movement was becoming a subordinate one; nationalists had made it clear in 1888 that in any conflict of loyalty between Catholicism and nationalism, nationalism must come first.

The prospects for Irish Home Rule, meanwhile, were improving. By 1890, Salisbury's Unionist government was in serious difficulties. Its coercive policies in Ireland were not proving effective, while there was high unemployment and social unrest in Britain. Gladstone, contrary to expectations, had not retired as Liberal leader. Although now in his eighties, he was determined to head the next Liberal government and introduce another Home Rule bill. He held to the cause of Irish Home Rule with a righteous fervour. After hearing Gladstone speak on the Irish question in 1887, the Baptist pastor, John Clifford, could not avoid being swept up in the 'moral momentum'. 'The hearer felt', Clifford confided to his diary, 'he was witnessing a fight for righteousness, for humanity, for God'.[208] Meanwhile, an attempt by *The Times* newspaper to link Parnell with violent crime in Ireland, including the Phoenix Park murders of 1882, had collapsed in 1889, when it was proved that the allegations were based on forged letters. Parnell emerged from the affair with his reputation enhanced.

Then in November 1890 came a bombshell from a London divorce court. Captain William O'Shea, MP, a Catholic former member of

Parnell's Home Rule party, had filed for divorce from his English Catholic wife Katherine, naming Parnell as co-respondent. The unmarried Parnell had been Mrs O'Shea's lover for several years, and had fathered at least two of her children. In the trial, Parnell was portrayed as a man devoid of moral scruples, who had abused the friendship and trust of one of his political supporters in order to seduce the man's wife and had then carried on the deception for years for his own sexual gratification. While the relationships between the three people were far more complex than this, Parnell's behaviour appeared to the public as deceitful, manipulative, treacherous, and contemptuous of family values. Despite the damaging revelations, many Irish nationalists remained loyal to their chief. They believed his assurances that his behaviour had not been dishonourable, or they accepted that great leaders must be excused some human failings, or more pragmatically they thought that only Parnell could deliver Home Rule.

Many others, however, insisted that Parnell must now resign the leadership of his party. How, they asked, could a man, shown to be dishonest in his personal relations, be trusted with political negotiations or the exercise of government? Opposition to Parnell was especially intense among those English Nonconformists who stood loyally by Gladstone over Home Rule. Hugh Price Hughes decided that Parnell must go. 'We have sacrificed much for Ireland', he exclaimed in late November at a public meeting in London:

She is entitled to many sacrifices at our hands. But there is one thing we will never sacrifice, and that is our religion. We stand immovably on this eternal rock: what is morally wrong can never be politically right; and we are certain that any politician who is the acknowledged enemy of God and social purity can, under no circumstances, be the true friend and rightful leader of men.

'*He must go*', insisted the Baptist John Clifford in the *Star* newspaper, 'British politics are not what they were. The conscience of the nation is aroused. Men legally convicted of immorality will not be permitted to lead in the legislation of the kingdom'.[209] It was amid the calls for Parnell's resignation that the phrase 'Nonconformist conscience' came into general use, initially as a term of abuse, but then quickly taken up as a badge of honour by leading Nonconformists. Gladstone – like most leading politicians – had known of Parnell's relationship with Katherine O'Shea for years. None the less, he could not afford to alienate his English Nonconformist support, and he now publicly called for Parnell's resignation.

In Ireland, Catholic leaders professed to be shocked by the revelations; they could hardly allow themselves to appear less morally appalled than the British Nonconformists. For some Catholic priests, Parnell's personal immorality related to the larger problem of the church's subordinate place within the clerical–nationalist alliance. Such a scandal, they insisted, would never have gone this far if the church had been an equal partner in the alliance and had been better able to ensure the highest levels of morality among Ireland's political leaders. The scandal was the result of placing nationalism above the church and its moral teachings, of allowing the Home Rule party and its Protestant leader to lord it over the clergy. 'I have flung him [Parnell] away from me forever', wrote the nationalist archbishop of Cashel, Thomas Croke, to Archbishop Walsh, on 22 November. 'His bust which for some time has held a prominent place in my hall I threw out yesterday. And as for "the party" generally, I go with you entirely in thinking that they make small, or no, account of the bishops and priests now, as independent agents, and only value them as money gatherers and useful auxiliaries in the agitation'.[210] The bishops as a body called for Parnell's resignation. Parnell, however, refused to go quietly. He turned upon his assailants, and fought desperately to hold on to the leadership of the movement that he had created. When the parliamentary party at Westminster removed him as leader, he returned to Ireland and appealed to the Irish people, holding public meetings, making effective use of those newspapers he controlled, putting forward his supporters in parliamentary by-elections, threatening the renewal of agrarian violence – fighting, in the words of one observer, like 'a tiger in the frenzy of its rage'.

But over the coming months, the anti-Parnellite politicians, supported by the Catholic clergy, gradually wore him down. They must not be led, insisted a priest in Mitchelstown, 'by a man reeking with the filth and corruption of a London divorce court. Parnell stood a withered and blasted thing before the eyes of the world'. The Irish people, he added, would now 'write him down as politically dead'.[211] In the destruction of Parnell, Emmet Larkin has argued, the role of the bishops and their clergy 'was more than central – it was decisive'.[212] Parnell died of rheumatic fever, aged 45, on 6 October 1891, and he was buried in Dublin. An estimated 100,000 turned out for the funeral. His followers now separated from the Irish Home Rule party and the divisions between Parnellites and Anti-Parnellites would embitter Irish political life for a generation. For the Parnellites, there could be no mistaking the real villains in the tragedy: their chief had been hounded to his death by the priests. But for the Anti-Parnellite majority, as Larkin has observed, the clerical–nationalist alliance that Parnell had helped forge was greater than the man, and it was clear that the Catholic church would have a central place in any Home Rule state.

Several months after Parnell's death, in the summer of 1892, the government called a general election. As expected, the Liberals won a narrow victory and Gladstone, at the age of 83, formed his fourth government. But its majority in the Commons, including the Irish Home Rule party, was only about 40, and Gladstone's physical powers were fading. The historian Alvin Jackson has also suggested that Gladstone's belief in his providential call to achieve Home Rule may have been fundamentally shaken by the Parnell affair.[213] He fulfilled his promise of introducing a Home Rule bill, but the bill, while better than its predecessor, was still not well conceived and inspired little confidence. The Liberal MPs dutifully stood by their leader and the bill passed through the Commons by a narrow majority – only to be decisively rejected by the House of Lords on 8 September 1893 by a vote of 419 to 41. Gladstone suggested bringing the Home Rule measure forward again in 1894, but his Cabinet would not have it. Cabinet attention was now directed to pressing imperial matters – tribal warfare and anarchy in Uganda which threatened the lives of missionaries and called for either occupation or evacuation, continued unrest and insecurity in Egypt, and growing demands by the Admiralty for major new expenditure on the navy. Gladstone resigned as prime minister in March 1894, and was replaced by Lord Rosebery. The Liberal Cabinet then quickly lost cohesion, and Rosebery resigned in June 1895. Lord Salisbury returned to office, the Unionists won an overwhelming majority in the general election of 1895, Protestant Ulster breathed a sigh of relief, and the prospects for Irish Home Rule receded for a time.

The Armenian massacres

In 1894, the Eastern Question again forced itself upon the public mind, as reports began reaching Britain of widespread massacres of Armenian Christians within the Ottoman empire. As with the reports of the Bulgarian atrocities nearly 20 years before, the accounts of Armenian massacres shocked and horrified the British public, and stirred a national agitation of protest. There were again calls for British military intervention, and Gladstone again came out of retirement to speak for the nation's conscience. In the event, Britain failed to halt the massacres, a failure that indicated the limits of its power and influence, and raised further questions about the action of providence in world affairs.[214]

The Armenian massacres of 1894–96 were carried out over the course of approximately two and half years and, according to the most recent estimate, claimed some 100,000 lives.[215] They began in the summer of

1894 in the province of Sasun, in eastern Anatolia, where Armenian Christian communities refused to continue paying both protection money to local Kurds and taxes to the Ottoman state. The Ottomans treated this as rebellion and unleashed local Kurdish tribesmen, supported by Ottoman troops, on the largely defenceless Armenians. The result was a wave of local massacres that continued for several months. When some Armenians tried to form a resistance movement, further waves of massacres followed, now spreading across Anatolia and decimating the scattered Armenian populations. The massacres were perpetrated by local mobs, with the apparent collusion of Ottoman officials, and were accompanied by torture, rape and the destruction of Armenian homes, churches and businesses. Ottoman troops and police either stood by, or participated in the killing.

The British public learned of the massacres through harrowing firsthand accounts by journalists and consulate officials. As was the case during the Bulgarian atrocities of 1876, many in Britain believed their country was partly responsible for the Armenian massacres. Britain had threatened to go to war against Russia in 1878 to preserve the Ottoman state. In return for this support, the Ottomans had given pledges for the humane treatment of Armenians and other minorities – but Britain had then made no real effort to ensure these pledges were honoured. Because of this history, many now argued that it was incumbent upon Britain to force the Ottomans to stop the killing – acting along with the other powers in the Concert of Europe if possible, but acting alone if necessary.

Beginning in the autumn of 1894, there was a national agitation to protest the massacres. It continued over the next two years, reaching peaks of intensity in the autumn of 1895 and the autumn of 1896. The clergy were active and many meetings were held in churches. As in the agitation against the Bulgarian atrocities, high Anglicans and Nonconformists now took a leading role. Among the high Anglicans, Malcolm MacColl, a veteran of the Bulgarian atrocities agitation and now canon of Ripon cathedral, was especially prominent in the cause. He was joined by Charles Gore and Henry Scott Holland from the Christian Social Union. The 'Nonconformist conscience' was also thoroughly roused, with Hugh Price Hughes and John Clifford as frequent speakers, and W. T. Stead joining the fray.[216] The protest meetings expressed outrage over the massacres of Christians, called for outside intervention, and collected funds to help with relief for the survivors. Combined with the painful revelations of Armenian deaths and suffering, there was a galling sense that Britain was held being held in contempt by the Ottomans and humiliated before all the world. 'The tide of indignation is rising', wrote MacColl to Lord Salisbury in September 1896, 'and I don't think it will be possible to stem it'.[217]

In December 1894, Gladstone came out of retirement to speak at Hawarden on the Armenian Question. All reports, he observed sadly, indicated that 'the scenes and abominations of 1876 in Bulgaria have been repeated in 1894 in Armenia'. If this were proved to be true, the Concert of Europe would have to intervene. He spoke again on the Question in August 1895 at Chester. The reports of massacres, he noted, had been confirmed, 'in all their horrible substance, in all their sickening details', and he now called for combined action by the Concert powers. In late September 1896, at the age of almost 87, he spoke yet again at a protest meeting in Liverpool. Eighteen months had passed, he observed, since the killings began, and in response to the protests 'the Sultan has added massacre to massacre'. As it was now clear that the Concert of Europe would not act, he called for unilateral British action, including the withdrawal of the British ambassador from Constantinople and military measures.[218] There were by now growing Christian calls for military action to protect the Armenians. While war was undoubtedly evil, insisted Clifford in December 1895, 'this wholesale butchery and robbery, this ravishing of maidens that was going on against the Armenians was worse than war'.[219] Speaking on 19 October 1896 at the national rally at St James Hall in London, Edward Talbot, the bishop of Rochester, declared, amid rapturous applause, 'that the sword which is so often waved needlessly when British interests are at stake, should not be ostentatiously placed in the scabbard when a great question of humanity arises'.[220] The Nonconformist *British Weekly* insisted in October 1896 that the British people were prepared for war. 'If ever a war were popular in this country', it observed, 'it would be a war of disinterestedness waged on behalf of an afflicted Christian race'.[221]

The high Anglican Lord Salisbury was personally troubled by the massacres. But when his government looked to its military options, it found them severely limited. Russia had reversed its previous stance towards the Ottoman empire and now posed as its champion against British 'bullying'. France, which still bristled over Britain's occupation of Egypt, had entered into an alliance with Russia in 1894. No power would join Britain in military intervention, and unilateral action against the Ottomans might well lead to war with both Russia and France. Further, it was not clear that any British military action could help the Armenians, who resided mainly in eastern Anatolia. Salisbury briefly contemplated naval action against the Ottomans, but it became clear that a naval demonstration would not help the Armenians and would likely be followed by their extermination. There was, meanwhile, another reason Salisbury believed Britain must not act. As ruler of a vast multi-faith empire, Britain should not appear to favour Christians over Muslims. 'The Queen', Salisbury proclaimed in his speech at the Guildhall Banquet in November 1895, 'is the mistress of more Mohamedans than the Sultan of Turkey, and we should have been neglecting our duty if we had allowed ourselves to appear as the partisans of one religion against the other'.[222]

So in the event, Britain did little beyond hold protest meetings. The Ottoman state ended the massacres in 1896 only when it decided that Armenians had been taught a sufficient lesson. By then, the British Christian public had learned the harsh truth that the Concert of Europe, which they had viewed as the custodian of Christian ethical values, no longer existed, and that Britain could not look to international support to resist oppression, as it had over the Bulgarian atrocities 20 years before. Other nations now viewed Britain as an oppressor, with blood on its hands in Egypt and in Ireland, and disdained its moral appeals. Britain's failure to act over the Armenian massacres raised questions not only about the extent of its real power, but also about its role as a Christian state. The belief in the providential empire, to be sure, was still potent in the 1890s, and this was reflected in the speeches and petitions of the Armenian agitation. But as the months passed and appeals to providence, chivalry and morality yielded little, some of the conviction began to drain away. A national rally held in St James Hall, London, on 19 October 1896, was, in the words of one historian, 'a pale reflection of its predecessor in the same place twenty years earlier'.[223]

For some, Britain had failed to act upon its Christian principles or view its empire as a gift from God and a sacred trust. It had been tested, and found wanting. According to the journalist, E. J. Dillon, who had investigated the massacres at first hand, Armenian men and women had refused to convert to Islam to save themselves, but had 'unhesitatingly . . . laid down their lives for their religious belief'. And yet, he continued, 'it is a melancholy fact that we have not alleviated the sufferings of these woe-stricken people by a single pang'.[224] 'I cannot believe,' Lord Rosebery exclaimed in the House of Lords in February 1896, 'and there are millions and millions of my fellow-countrymen who cannot believe, that all has been done that might have been done'.[225] The Christian faith, it seemed, was becoming less central to British interests by the mid-1890s, while there were 'ominous signs', as MacColl observed in 1895, that British policy was being determined by 'the lust of empire, regardless of moral considerations'.[226] The providentialist conceptions regarding the United Kingdom and its place in the world, which for many had been revived in the mid-1870s amid the agitation against the Bulgarian atrocities, began to fade. His address of late September 1896 on the Armenian massacres, meanwhile, was Gladstone's last public speech; within a year and a half, he was dead and his passing removed a great advocate of the providential ideal in politics.

Notes

1 J. P. Parry, 'Religion and the Collapse of Gladstone's First Government, 1870–1874', *Historical Journal*, 25 (1982), 71–101.

2 Quoted in P. Magnus, *Gladstone: A Biography* (London, 1954), 229.

3 H. C. G. Matthew, *Gladstone 1809–1898* (Oxford, 1997), 264–5.

4 R. Shannon, *Gladstone and the Bulgarian Agitation 1876*, 2nd edn (Hassocks, Sussex, 1975), 22.

5 Ibid., 71.

6 A. Pottinger Saab, 'Disraeli, Judaism, and the Eastern Question', *International History Review*, 10 (1988), 564–72.

7 Shannon, *Gladstone and the Bulgarian Agitation*, 171–90.

8 J. P. Rossi, 'Catholic Opinion on the Eastern Question, 1876–1878', *Church History*, 51 (1982), 54–70.

9 W. E. Gladstone, *Bulgarian Horrors and the Question of the East* (London, 1876), 31.

10 Quoted in Matthew, *Gladstone 1809–1898*, 294.

11 Quoted in E. W. Stead, *My Father* (London, 1913), 68–9, 69, 70.

12 Quoted in A. J. P. Taylor, *The Trouble Makers: Dissent over Foreign Policy*, 2nd edn (London, 1993), 76.

13 Ibid., 170.

14 F. Whyte, *The Life of W. T. Stead*, 2 vols (London, 1925), vol. i, 52.

15 Quoted in E. Bar-Yosef, *The Holy Land in English Culture 1799–1917: Palestine and the Question of Orientalism* (Oxford, 2005), 204.

16 Ibid., 205–10.

17 Quoted in Shannon, *Gladstone: Heroic Minister*, 229–30.

18 R. Kelley, 'Midlothian: A Study in Politics and Ideas', *Victorian Studies*, 4 (December 1960), 164.

19 Matthew, *Gladstone 1809–1898*, 301.

20 D. Brooks, 'Gladstone and Midlothian: The Background to the First Campaign', *Scottish Historical Review*, 64 (April 1985), 64.

21 Kelley, 'Midlothian: A Study in Politics and Ideas', 127, 134–9.

22 D. A. Hamer, *The Politics of Electoral Pressure: A Study in the History of Victorian Reform Agitations* (Hassocks, Sussex, 1977), 147–8; Machin, *Politics and the Churches in Great Britain 1869 to 1921*, 97–8.

23 Quoted in K. Robbins, *John Bright* (London, 1979), 246–7.

24 Dale, *Life of R. W. Dale*, 436–7; Bebbington, *Nonconformist Conscience*, 109; Hughes, *Life of Hugh Price Hughes*, 546.

25 Olga Novikoff, 'The Eastern Question II', *Nineteenth Century*, 38 (December 1895), 1007.

26 W. Jukes, 'Imâm Mândy, and Dajjâl, the Muhammadan Antichrist', *Church Missionary Intelligencer*, 8 (October 1883), 596–601; 'The Mahdi', *Pall Mall Gazette*, 'Extra', 7 February 1884; C. C. Trench, *Charles Gordon: An Eminent Victorian Reassessed* (London, 1978), 187–90.

27 J. Marlowe, *Mission to Khartoum: The Apotheosis of General Gordon* (London, 1969), 154–5.

28 H. Montagu Butler, *Ten Great and Good Men* (London, 1909), 238.

29 Quoted in Shannon, *Gladstone: Heroic Minister*, 332.

30 Sir Richard Temple, 'The Mahdi and British India', *Contemporary Review*, 47 (March 1885), 305–14.

31 A. C. Benson, *Life of Edward White Benson*, 2 vols (London, 1900), vol. ii, 49.

32 W. M. Sinclair, *Gordon and England: A Sermon preached at St Stephens, Westminster, on Sunday, February 22, 1885* (London, 1885), 9.

33 [D. MacLeod], 'General Gordon', *Good Words* (1885), 235; J. Fleming, *The Forsaken Hero: A Sermon, preached at St Michael's Church, Chester Square* (London, [1885]), 3.

34 Bishop of Newcastle, sermon at Gordon Memorial Service, St Paul's cathedral, *The Times*, 14 March 1885.

35 D. H. Johnson, 'The Death of Gordon: A Victorian Myth', *Journal of Imperial and Commonwealth History*, 10 (1981–82), 302–4.

36 H. Hensley Henson, *Gordon: A Lecture* (Oxford, 1886), 31.

37 *The Times*, 14 March 1885.

38 W. T. Stead to Augusta Gordon, 6 February 1885, British Library, Moffitt Collection, Add Mss 51300, fo. 69.

39 G. R. Searle, *A New England? Peace and War 1886–1918* (Oxford, 2004), 32.

40 R. Sinker, *Memorials of the Hon. Ion Keith-Falconer* (Cambridge, 1903), 100–1.

41 C. E. Padwick, *Temple Gairdner of Cairo*, 2nd edn (London, 1930), 65–8.

42 Porter, *Religion versus Empire*, 197–200, 221–4.

43 F. S. L. Lyons, *Charles Stewart Parnell* (London, 1977), 84.

44 Ibid., 92.

45 Ibid., 134.

46 E. Larkin, *The Roman Catholic Church and the Creation of the Modern Irish State 1878–1886* (Philadelphia, 1975), 47.

47 Ibid., 24.

48 Ibid., 27–8.

49 Ibid., 175–6.

50 Ibid., 185–6.

51 Ibid., 190.

52 The phrase was that of the government's unofficial representative in Rome, George Errington. T. J. Morrissey, *William J. Walsh, Archbishop of Dublin 1841–1921* (Dublin, 2000), 47, also 49–55.

53 J. Munson, *The Nonconformists: In Search of a Lost Culture* (London, 1991), 10.

54 Hoppen, *Mid-Victorian Generation*, 265.

55 A. Simon, 'Church Disestablishment as a Factor in the General Election of 1885', *Historical Journal*, 18 (1975), 794–5.

56 [J. Morley], 'Religious Equality', in J. Chamberlain, et al., *The Radical Programme* [1885], D. A. Hamer (ed.) (Brighton, Sussex, 1971), 127.

57 J. L. Garvin, *Life of Joseph Chamberlain*, vol. ii (London, 1933), 66.

58 Simon, 'Church Disestablishment', 804.

59 J. C. Ryle, *Our Position and Our Dangers: An Address delivered at the Fourth Diocesan Conference of the Diocese of Liverpool* (London, 1885), 20–1.

60 L. Creighton, *Life and Letters of Mandell Creighton*, 2 vols (London, 1904), vol. i, 349.

61 Quoted in Machin, *Politics and the Churches in Great Britain 1869 to 1921*, 155.

62 A. R. MacEwen, *Life and Letters of John Cairns* (London, 1895), 733–6.

63 A. Taylor Innes, *Chapters of Reminiscence* (London, 1913), 192.

64 J. G. Kellas, 'The Liberal Party and the Scottish Church Disestablishment Crisis', *English Historical Review*, 79 (1964), 35.

65 M. Oliphant, *Memoir of Principal Tulloch* (Edinburgh, 1888), 421.

66 Ibid., 451.

67 Ibid., 453.

68 *The Scotsman*, 21 May 1885.

69 Simon, 'Church Disestablishment', 813.

70 Charles Cooper to Earl of Rosebery, 31 August 1885, National Library of Scotland, Rosebery Papers, Ms 10011, fos 111–12.

71 Kellas, 'The Liberal Party and the Scottish Church Disestablishment Crisis', 35.

72 Carnegie Simpson, *Life of Principal Rainy*, vol. ii, 30–48; Gordon, *Life of A. H. Charteris*, 399–403.

73 Quoted in Simon, 'Church Disestablishment', 815.

74 The numbers as given in Hoppen, *The Mid-Victorian Generation*, 680.

75 Bell, *Disestablishment in Ireland and Wales*, 230.

76 R. J. Helmstadter, 'The Nonconformist Conscience', in G. Parsons (ed.), *Religion in Victorian Britain*, 4 vols (Manchester, 1988), vol. iv, 86–91.

77 Morgan, *Wales in British Politics*, 67; W. B. George, 'Welsh Disestablishment and Welsh Nationalism', *Journal of the Historical Society of the Church in Wales*, 20 (1970), 86.

78 Ibid., 85–7; Bell, *Disestablishment in Ireland and Wales*, 239–40.

79 Quoted in R. Tudur Jones, *Faith and the Crisis of a Nation: Wales 1890–1914*, S. Prys Jones (trans.), R. Pope (ed.) (Cardiff, 2004), 378.

80 D. Lloyd George, 'Welsh Disestablishment', *British Weekly*, 7 November 1895, 34.

81 R. W. Church to Edward Talbot, 7 April 1886, quoted in B. A. Smith, *Dean Church: The Anglican Response to Newman* (London, 1958), 223.

82 F. Temple to H. Lee Warner, 16 August 1886, quoted in Sandford, *Memoirs of Archbishop Temple*, vol. ii, 641.

83 D. Hempton, ' "For God and Ulster": Evangelical Protestantism and the Home Rule Crisis of 1886', *Studies in Church History*, Subsidia 7: *Protestant Evangelicalism*, K. Robbins (ed.) (Oxford, 1990), 238.

84 Bebbington, *Nonconformist Conscience*, 85–8.

85 Dale, *Life of R. W. Dale*, 451–69.

86 Quoted in R. F. Foster, *Lord Randolph Churchill: A Political Life* (Oxford, 1981), 253–4.

87 Hempton and Hill, *Evangelical Protestantism in Ulster Society*, 162–3.

88 A. C. Hepburn, 'Work, Class and Religion in Belfast, 1871–1911', *Journal of Irish Economic and Social History*, 10 (1983), 35.

89 *The Church of Ireland and the Present Crisis: Report of the Special Meeting of the General Synod . . . Dublin, March 23, 1886* (Dublin, 1886), 10–11.

90 H. Hanna, *Scotland, Ulster, and Home Rule for Ireland* (Dublin, 1888), 6.

91 G. Walker, 'Thomas Sinclair: Presbyterian Liberal Unionist', in R. English and G. Walker (eds), *Unionism in Modern Ireland: New Perspectives on Politics and Culture* (Basingstoke, 1996), 19–36.

92 Quoted in Hempton, ' "For God and Ulster": Evangelical Protestantism and the Home Rule Crisis of 1886', 236.

93 *The Church of Ireland and the Present Crisis*, 37–8.

94 Ibid., 15.

95 Quoted in Hempton, ' "For God and Ulster": Evangelical Protestantism and the Home Rule Crisis of 1886', 234.

96 Foster, *Lord Randolph Churchill*, 255.

97 Ibid., 255.

98 H. Montgomery Hyde, *Carson* (London, 1953), 59.

99 Foster, *Lord Randolph Churchill*, 258.

100 'The Riots in Belfast', *Fortnightly Review*, new series, vol. xl (1 Sept. 1886), 288.

101 Walls, *The Cross-Cultural Process in Christian History*, 188–9.

102 Ibid., 190.

103 I am grateful to Owen Chadwick for directing attention to this episode. See Chadwick, *The Victorian Church, Part 2*, 272–3; M. Arnold, 'The Church of England', in *The Complete Prose Works of Matthew Arnold*, R. H. Super (ed.), 11 vols (Ann Arbor, Michigan, 1960–77), vol. 8, 63–86.

104 Ibid., 64.

105 Ibid., 76.

106 Ibid., 73.

107 Arnold, 'The Church of England', 71.

108 Ibid., 83.

109 Matthew Arnold to Frances Whately, 24 February 1876, in *Letters of Matthew Arnold, 1848–1888*, G. W. E. Russell (ed.), 2 vols (London, 1895), vol. 2, 127–8.

110 [M. Arnold], 'The Church of England', *Macmillan's Magazine*, vol. 33 (April, 1876), 481–94; M. Arnold, *Last Essays on Church and Religion* (London, 1877), 108–36.

111 D. Landes, *The Unbound Prometheus: Technological Change and Industrial Development in Western Europe from 1750 to the Present* (Cambridge 1972), 194.

112 Hoppen, *The Mid-Victorian Generation*, 293.

113 K. Hutchison, *The Decline and Fall of British Capitalism* (Hamden, Connecticut, 1966), 23.

114 J. Harris, *Private Lives, Public Spirit: Britain 1870–1914* (London, 1993), 125.

115 Ibid., 129.

116 T. C. Smout, *A Century of the Scottish People 1830–1950* (Glasgow, 1986), 119; Searle, *A New England?*, 45–6.

117 [A. Mearns and W. C. Preston], *The Bitter Cry of Outcast London* (London, 1883), 4.

118 Ibid., 7.

119 J. O. Baylen, 'The "New Journalism" in Late Victorian Britain', *Australian Journal of Politics and History*, 18 (1972), 367–85.

120 [W. T. Stead], 'Is it Not Time?', *Pall Mall Gazette*, 16 October 1883.

121 Whyte, *Life of W. T. Stead*, vol. i, 161.

122 K. S. Inglis, *Churches and the Working Classes in Victorian England* (London, 1963), 202–3.

123 William Booth, *In Darkest England and the Way Out* (London, [1891]), 13.

124 Ibid., 47.

125 Inglis, *Churches and the Working Classes*, 204–6.

126 Searle, *A New England?*, 83.

127 S. Yeo, 'A New Life: The Religion of Socialism in Britain, 1883–1896', *History Workshop: A Journal of Socialist Historians*, no. 4 (Autumn 1977), 5–56.

128 Katherine and J. Bruce Glasier, *The Religion of Socialism: Two Aspects* (Glasgow, [1890]), 10.

129 G. C. Binyon, *The Christian Socialist Movement in England* (London, 1931), 182–4; S. Budd, *Varieties of Unbelief: Atheists and Agnostics in English Society 1850–1960* (London, 1977), 72–6; Yeo, 'Religion of Socialism', 33–4, 37.

130 W. L. Arnstein, *The Bradlaugh Case: Atheism, Sex, and Politics among the Late Victorians* (Oxford, 1965).

131 Ibid., 44.

132 Ibid., 169.

133 H. McLeod, *Piety and Poverty: Working-Class Religion in Berlin, London and New York 1870–1914* (New York, 1996), 44–5.

134 J. Sutherland, *Mrs Humphry Ward: Eminent Victorian, Pre-eminent Edwardian* (Oxford, 1991), 125–31.

135 Arnold's movements between Anglicanism, Roman Catholicism and agnosticism, and their effects on his family, are explored at length in B. Bergonzi, *A Victorian Wanderer: The Life of Thomas Arnold the Younger* (Oxford, 2003).

136 Ibid., 126–8; Bebbington, *The Mind of Gladstone*, 246–7.

137 W. E. Gladstone, '*Robert Elsmere* and the Battle of Belief', *Nineteenth Century*, 23 (May 1888), 783.

138 L. Trilling, *Matthew Arnold* (London, 1939), 314–16.

139 J. Rose, *The Edwardian Temperament 1895–1919* (Athens, Ohio, 1986), 23–4.

140 J. Morley, 'Mr. Mill's *Autobiography*', in J. Morley, *Critical Miscellanies*, vol. iii (London, 1909), 83.

141 A. C. Tait, *Some Thoughts on the Duties of the Established Church of England as a National Church, being Seven Addresses delivered at his Second Visitation* (London, 1876), 18–19, 28, 41.

142 C. Brooks, 'Introduction', in C. Brooks and A. Saint (eds), *The Victorian Church: Architecture and Society* (Manchester, 1995), 9–10.

143 Chadwick, *The Victorian Church, Part 2*, 241.

144 S. J. D. Green, *Religion in the Age of Decline: Organisation and Experience in Industrial Yorkshire 1870–1920* (Cambridge, 1996), 91.

145 J. C. Ryle, Lord Bishop of Liverpool, *A Charge* (London, 1884), 15–16.

146 A. L. Drummond and J. Bulloch, *The Church in Late Victorian Scotland 1874–1900* (Edinburgh, 1978), 164.

147 H. McLeod, *Religion and Society in England, 1850–1914* (London, 1996), 79; C. Brown, *Religion and Society in Scotland since 1707* (Edinburgh, 1997), 128–30.

148 For a seminal account of the churches and their late nineteenth-century urban social and relief work, see J. Cox, *The English Churches in a Secular Society: Lambeth, 1870–1930* (New York, 1982), 48–89.

149 Quoted in E. G. Sandford (ed.), *Memoirs of Archbishop Temple by Seven Friends*, 2 vols (London, 1906), vol. ii, 124.

150 J. Greenwood, *The Seven Curses of London* (London, [1890]), 421–7.

151 Prochaska, *Christianity and Social Service*, 99–100.

152 McLeod, *Religion and Society in England, 1850–1914*, 79, 153.

153 Cox, *English Churches in a Secular Society*, 57.

154 *British Weekly*, 3 October 1895, 371.

155 D. Watson, *Chords of Memory* (Edinburgh, 1938), 37–81.

156 D. Watson, *The Church at Work* (Edinburgh, 1926), 43.

157 D. Kirkwood, *My Life of Revolt* (London, 1935), 23.

158 D. MacLeod, 'The Parochial System', in *The Church and the People*, St Giles Lectures, 6th series (Edinburgh, 1886), 131.

159 S. A. Barnett, 'University Settlements', *Nineteenth Century*, 38 (December 1895), 1016.

160 S. Meacham, *Toynbee Hall and Social Reform 1880–1914: The Search for Community* (New Haven, Conn., 1987), 4–5.

161 A. Scott Matheson, *The Church and Social Problems* (London, 1893), 58.

162 For Headlam's life, see especially J. R. Orens, *Stewart Headlam's Radical Anglicanism: The Mass, the Masses, and the Music Hall* (Champaign, Illinois, 2003).

163 P. d'A. Jones, *The Christian Socialist Revival 1877–1914: Religion, Class and Social Conscience in Late-Victorian England* (Princeton, 1968), 114–15.

164 S. D. Headlam, *The Sure Foundation: An Address given before the Guild of S. Matthew, at the Annual Meeting, 1883* (London, 1883), 6.

165 Jones, *The Christian Socialist Revival*, 129.

166 Orens, *Stewart Headlam's Radical Anglicanism*, 119.

167 Quoted in D. O. Wagner, *The Church of England and Social Reform since 1854* (New York, 1930), 192.

168 Meacham, *Toynbee Hall and Social Reform*, 16–17.

169 Quoted in D. Boucher and A. Vincent, *British Idealism and Political Theory* (Edinburgh, 2000), 37.

170 H. Barnett, *Canon Barnett: His Life, Work, and Friends*, 2 vols (London, 1919), vol. i, 310.

171 Meacham, *Toynbee Hall and Social Reform*, 48.

172 Barnett, *Canon Barnett*, vol. ii, 302–9; J. A. R. Pimlott, *Toynbee Hall: Fifty Years of Social Progress* (London, 1935), 81–2.

173 Inglis, *Churches and Working Classes in Victorian England*, 163.

174 Ibid., 169.

175 Sutherland, *Mrs Humphry Ward*, 217–29.

176 Inglis, *Churches and Working Classes in Victorian England*, 162.

177 G. L. Prestige, *The Life of Charles Gore* (London, 1935), 98.

178 Jones, *Christian Socialist Revival*, 167–74.

179 D. L. Edwards, *Leaders of the Church of England 1828–1944* (Oxford, 1971), 259.

180 H. S. Holland to R. W. Church, [1882], British Library, Gladstone Papers, Add Mss 44127, fols 267–70.

181 W. H. Fremantle, *The World as the Subject of Redemption*, quoted in Jones, *Christian Socialist Revival*, 173–4.

182 C. Gore (ed.), *Lux Mundi: A Series of Studies in the Religion of the Incarnation*, 12th edn (London, 1891), viii.

183 Ibid., 266.

184 Prestige, *Charles Gore*, 102–15.

185 E. Norman, *The Victorian Christian Socialists* (Cambridge, 1987), 162–3.

186 Wagner, *Church of England and Social Reform*, 227.

187 Quoted in Binyon, *Christian Socialist Movement in England*, 162.

188 A. Westcott, *Life and Letters of Brooke Foss Westcott*, 2 vols (London, 1903), vol. ii, 115–33.

189 Jones, *The Christian Socialist Revival*, 183–4.

190 D. Thompson, 'The Emergence of the Nonconformist Social Gospel in England', *Studies in Church History*, subsidia 7: *Protestant Evangelicalism*, K. Robbins (ed.) (Oxford, 1990), 255–80.

191 R. F. Wearmouth, *Methodism and the Struggle of the Working Classes 1850–1900* (Leicester, 1954), 147–8.

192 H. Price Hughes, *Social Christianity* (London, 1889), xi–xii, 54–5.

193 A. B. Bruce, et al., *Christianity and Social Life: A Course of Lectures* (Edinburgh, 1885); D. C. Smith, *Passive Obedience and Prophetic Protest: Social Criticism in the Scottish Church 1830–1945* (New York, 1987), 268–73.

194 D. MacLeod, *Non-Church Going and the Housing of the Poor* (Edinburgh, 1888), 8.

195 Ibid., 13.

196 *Reports on the Schemes of the Church of Scotland* (Edinburgh, 1896), 808, 814.

197 V. A. McClelland, *Cardinal Manning: His Public Life and Influence 1865–1892* (Oxford, 1962), 129–39.

198 H. Manning, *The Rights and Dignity of Labour*, 2nd edn (London, 1887), 23.

199 Quoted in McClelland, *Cardinal Manning*, 129.

200 Ibid., 140–8; Purcell, *Life of Cardinal Manning*, vol. ii, 658–61.

201 Inglis, *Churches and the Working Classes*, 311.

202 B. F. Westcott, *The Christian Social Union* (London, 1895), 9.

203 Quoted in Smith, *Passive Obedience and Prophetic Protest*, 272.

204 Quoted in E. Larkin, *The Roman Catholic Church and the Plan of Campaign 1886–1888* (Cork, 1978), 107.

205 C. C. O'Brien, *Parnell and his Party 1880–1890*, 2nd edn (Oxford, 1968), 207–11.

206 Larkin, *Roman Catholic Church and the Plan of Campaign*, 201–2.

207 Ibid., 221–4, 235–6.

208 Quoted in J. F. Glaser, 'Parnell's Fall and the Nonconformist Conscience', *Irish Historical Studies*, 12 (1960–61), 120.

209 Quoted in ibid., 128, 123.

210 O'Brien, *Parnell and his Party*, 291.

211 E. Larkin, *The Roman Catholic Church in Ireland and the Fall of Parnell 1888–1891* (Liverpool, 1979), 240.

212 Ibid., 263.

213 A. Jackson, *Home Rule: An Irish History 1800–2000* (London, 2004), 94.

214 D. Bloxham, *The Great Game of Genocide: Imperialism, Nationalism and the Destruction of the Ottoman Armenians* (Oxford, 2005), 51–61; R. Douglas, 'Britain and the Armenian Question', *Historical Journal*, 19 (1976), 113–33; P. Marsh, 'Lord Salisbury and the Ottoman Massacres', *Journal of British Studies*, 11 (May 1972), 63–83.

215 Bloxham, *Great Game of Genocide*, 51.

216 Bebbington, *Nonconformist Conscience*, 116–18.

217 G. W. E. Russell, *Malcolm MacColl* (London, 1914), 159.

218 *The Times* (London), 31 December 1894, 7 August 1895, 25 September 1896.

219 Quoted in Bebbington, *Nonconformist Conscience*, 117.

220 *British Weekly*, 22 October 1896, 9.

221 *British Weekly*, 1 October 1896, 375.

222 *The Times* (London), 11 November 1895, 6.

223 Marsh, 'Lord Salisbury and the Ottoman Massacres', 76.

224 E. J. Dillon, 'Armenia: An Appeal', *Contemporary Review*, 69 (January 1896), 2–3.

225 *Parliamentary Debates*, 4th series, vol. 37 (11 February 1896), col. 48.

226 M. McColl, *England's Responsibility towards Armenia* (London, 1895), 127.

CHAPTER 6

Religious Diversity, Identities and Conflicts, 1896–1914

The 1890s were a time of unsettlement. The Victorian era, with its faith in unremitting work, unceasing progress, and a providential world order was drawing to a close; and artists, novelists, poets, fashionable prophets, dilettantes and dreamers welcomed the approaching *fin de siècle*, the end of the century. Everywhere there was discontent with the social and political order. Hitherto marginalised social classes or groups – unskilled labourers, women, the unemployed – were finding their political voice, and were dismissive of established institutions, values and beliefs. The sensationalist New Journalism, pioneered by such figures as W. T. Stead, came into full flow in the 1890s, exposing corruption and sexual scandal, and undermining public trust in institutions and leaders. For some, perceptions of the Christian, moral and civilising mission of empire were giving way to darker views of imperialism as an exercise of naked power for the exploitation of colonised peoples – views that would find expression in the publication of Joseph Conrad's *Heart of Darkness* in 1899. In his recessional written for the occasion of the Queen's Diamond Jubilee in 1897, Rudyard Kipling prophesied that all the pomp of Britain's empire would in time become 'one with Nineveh and Tyre'. 'Judge of the Nations', he prayed, 'spare us yet'.

Science was transforming conceptions of the physical universe and of humanity. Wireless telegraphy emerged in 1887; by 1901 the British-based Italian inventor, Guglielmo Marconi, was sending wireless messages across the Atlantic. Science was dissolving the Newtonian conception of the universe, with its building blocks of matter and its absolutes of time and space. The atom was shown to be divisible and matter to be made up of energy; the electron was discovered in 1897 and this led to theories of the atomic disintegration of matter. X-rays (discovered 1895) and radio-activity (discovered 1896) entered the vocabulary of modern physics. The development of the quantum theory after 1901 introduced new levels of uncertainty and relativity into physics. There were similar revolutions in biology. In 1899, the rediscovery of Abbot Gregor Mendel's experiments on heredity led to the development of new work in the discipline of 'genetics' and to new notions of biological determinism. Cultural anthropology, particularly the work of J. G. Frazer of Cambridge University (whose multi-volume *Golden Bough* began appearing in 1890), suggested that the origins of all religion would be found in the myths of primitive peoples and their efforts to propitiate unseen forces with sacrifices. Psychology was portraying human personality as multi-layered, subject to dark impulses from the subconscious or 'subliminal self'. Along with the often over-whelming new conceptions, there was also an element of pessimism in this new science. The physics of thermodynamics was positing a universe in which heat flowed towards the cold, and energy tended to dissipate, stars to burn out, planets to whirl off into infinite space, and a cold, empty silence was to be the future. In time, observed the politician and philo-sopher, A. J. Balfour, in 1888, 'the energies of our system will decay, the glory of the sun will be dimmed. The uneasy consciousness, which in this obscure corner has for a brief space broken the contented silence of the Universe, will be at rest. Matter will know itself no longer'. This, Balfour continued, raised questions about worldly progress. In time, all traces of humanity's presence in the universe would be gone. 'Imperishable monu-ments and immortal deeds', he observed, 'death itself, and love stronger than death, will be as though they had never been'.[1] H. G. Wells's futur-istic novel, *The Time Machine* (1895) climaxed on a vision of a future, more than thirty millions years hence, when the world had descended into a cold and lifeless silence, gripping the time traveller with horror.

For many thinkers, these new scientific visions, even with the darker shadows, brought a sense of liberation from old beliefs in fixed natural and moral laws. 'Not a little of *fin de siècle* attractiveness', observed Holbrook Jackson in his classic study of the 1890s (first published in 1913), 'was the result of abandonment due to internal chaos'.[2] Some artists and thinkers abandoned themselves to 'decadence'. Great art, they believed, grew out of dying civilisations, and Britain was now in the evening of its day. Amid gathering shadows would come introspection, reflection, spiritual insight, and new forms of expression. The 1890s witnessed much deliberate flout-ing of moral conventions – this was the time of the exotic images of *The*

Yellow Book and the *Savoy*, of Aubrey Beardsley's erotic drawings, Oscar Wilde's *Picture of Dorian Gray* and *Salome*, of the 'naughty nineties', of affectation, artificiality, 'art for art's sake' and the aesthetic movement, self-indulgence, absinthe and opium, sexual experiment and West End vice. Some, like the poet Ernest Dowson, who died in 1900 of consumption and alcohol, aged 33, 'cried for madder music and for stronger wine' and relished feelings of 'desolation' as night shadows fell.

Others, influenced by the French philosopher Henri Bergson, were drawn to a search for vitalism, or the life force. They sought the unifying principles behind all existence, they embraced creativity and the active life, celebrated the versatility, energy and mystery of nature, and elevated expressions of the human will.[3] Some were drawn to Friedrich Nietzsche's ideal of the 'superman', who embraced a will to power that transcended traditional morality, including what he portrayed as the 'slave ethic' of Christianity. Others, like the author Samuel Butler, perceived of life itself as a form of divinity. As G. K. Chesterton observed, theirs was a time when people grew weary of conventional morality, when heretics alone were regarded as 'clear-headed and courageous', and when the leading playwright George Bernard Shaw could pen the epigram that the only 'golden rule is that there is no golden rule' (the doctrine of John Tanner, hero of Shaw's *Man and Superman* of 1905). 'All previous ages', Chesterton wrote in 1905, 'have sweated and been crucified in an attempt to realize what is really the right life, what was really the good man. A definite part of the modern world has come beyond question to the conclusion that there is no answer to these questions'.[4] Along with this questioning of moral conventions, however, went an openness to new expressions of spirituality and an often intense religious searching.

The Victorian Age came to its formal end on 22 January 1901, the day the old queen died. Her health had been failing in the latter months of 1900, and she was seriously ill from 15 January. Mainly inert in her last days, she left no pious deathbed scenes to inspire her people. Her quiet passing had been watched over by the empathetic and kindly Randall Davidson. Despite her 81 years, her death had been curiously unexpected, and many were profoundly shaken by what seemed yet another sign of the 'great silent collapse' in the old moral order. As a leading minister in the Scottish United Free Church observed of her passing, 'there was the sense of a great blank in the order of things'.[5] She had died, in the phrase of the popular novelist, Charlotte M. Yonge, as 'The Mother of the Homes of the Nation'. Hers had been a broad church Christianity, with a strong sense of the providential role of Britain and her empire in the world. In the sermon preached in Westminster Abbey on the occasion of her death, Hensley Henson, had compared her faith and her sense of imperial responsibility under God to that of her beloved General Gordon.[6] But now she was gone and many in her United Kingdom were harkening after a different spiritual music. The new king, Edward VII, did not share her Christian convictions.

Spiritualism

In the closing decades of the nineteenth century, growing numbers were drawn to new forms of religious expression. While the large majority in Britain and Ireland remained within the Christian tradition, a significant number looked outside the churches for spiritual truths that would make sense of the universe, affirm the value of human love and sacrifice, and offer hope of life beyond the grave. They sought new paths to spiritual knowledge or fulfilment, often with the same fervour that had been shown a century before, when in the 1790s society had pulsated with the prophecies of Richard Brothers and Joanna Southcott, and when the religious landscape had included Swedenborgians, Muggletonians, and others dreaming of a coming millennium. Now in the 1890s came new religious beliefs – associated with ancient wisdom, Eastern religions, Celtic spirituality, magic and the occult, alternative medicines, reincarnation, theosophy and mysticism. As Jackson observed, 'all the cynicisms and petulances and flippancies of the decadence, the febrile self-assertion, the voluptuousness, the perversity were, consciously or unconsciously, efforts towards the rehabilitation of spiritual power'. The decadents, he added, were 'the mad priests of that new romanticism whose aim was the transmutation of vision into personal power'.[7] Of the new religious movements of the late nineteenth century, one of the most influential was modern spiritualism, or the belief in communication with the spirits of the dead.

Efforts to communicate with the dead are, of course, as old as humankind. Modern spiritualism in the English-speaking world had its beginnings in the United States in the late 1840s, where the claims by some individuals to receive messages from the spirits of the departed through rappings had created a sensation. These gifted individuals, or mediums, served as channels of communication for the spirits – either through private sittings or at evening parties. They were usually offered gifts of money by those who attended their sessions, and some prospered. The first mediums arrived in London from the United States in the early 1850s. They won the patronage of prosperous members of the upper and middle classes, and attracted the interest of the British intelligentsia. A number of prominent public figures attended group sessions or séances. Among them was the socialist, Robert Owen, who embraced spiritualism in his eighties, and published a book describing his conversations with the spirits of historic figures. Partly through his influence, the movement spread among labouring people, with mediums emerging in working-class neighbourhoods and spiritualism becoming a popular subject for lectures and demonstrations at mechanics' institutes, temperance halls and workingmen's clubs. Working-class spiritualism was especially strong in the north of England, where it had connections with secularism, socialism, and other forms of radical social criticism. There were a number of spiritualist socialists, including William Phillips, J. T. Ward, C. Allen Clarke, and Ernest Marklew, who were drawn to the movement in part because it was an alternative faith to Christianity.[8]

Interest continued to grow in the second half of the century, with numerous private circles, many upper- and middle-class (as well as working-class) devotees, and some mediums rising to national prominence. The séances were generally conducted in darkened rooms, with participants seated in a circle, sometimes holding hands. The medium communicated with the spirit world through a control, or a spirit who acted as a guide to the other world and would bring forward other spirits. Communication occurred through rappings, the movement of objects, playing of musical instruments – or sometimes the spirits would enter the medium, whose voice and behaviour would become that of the departed. Mediums were often skilled illusionists. A majority were women. Mediumship offered women the prospect of respectable incomes, improved social status, and access to the homes of rich and influential people. It was an occupation, moreover, that fitted in with the mid-Victorian ideal of women as passive, spiritual beings, whose moral influence came through their renunciation of self. The medium, like the 'ideal' woman, became the passive vehicle through which the dead communicated with the living. Her role was to support and nurture. But the female medium was not simply passive; she was also the leader of the spirit circle and the active communicator between the two worlds. Mediumship, as Alex Owen has observed, 'promoted a species of feminine power whilst at the same time interacting with contemporary concepts of acceptable womanhood'.[9] In the 1870s, a number of younger female mediums appeared on the scene – among them the renowned Florence Cook, with her spirit control 'Katie King' – who combined physical beauty and playful flirtatiousness with elaborate theatrical displays, including full-figure spirit manifestations. Most of these mediums had their illusions exposed at one time or another, but that did not deter the curious from enjoying their performances, and many continued to believe.

Spiritualism took on the form of a religion, claiming to offer proof of the existence of an afterlife that could be 'empirically tested'. It rejected the doctrine of eternal punishment, which was causing Victorians such moral difficulties, and offered a new vision of the afterlife – characterised by a prolonging of human aspirations and continued improvement. The spirits suffered over the misdeeds of their worldly lives, but out of this suffering came new wisdom and an eternity of individual spiritual growth.[10] Spirits of infants grew into adults and flourished in an afterlife of endless summer. Spiritualists did not see a need for a Christ-figure to atone for human sins before God, but rather viewed each individual as responsible for their own development. Spiritualist societies emerged, often from informal spirit circles. From the late 1860s, these societies began forming local 'lyceums', holding Sunday services, adopting rituals and hymns, and organising spiritualist Sunday schools. There were also national organisations and publications. The British National Association of Spiritualists was founded in 1873; it was reconstituted as the London Spiritual Alliance in 1883. The National Federation of Spiritualists was formed in 1891; it changed its name to the Spiritualists' National Union in 1902, and had 120 affiliated spiritualist societies by 1910. Among the spiritualist journals were *Light*, which began publication in 1881 and *Two Worlds*, which began in 1887. An important aspect of the movement was spiritualistic healing, with many mediums claiming the power to heal. A disproportionate number of them were women – harkening back to the tradition of village 'wise women' and white witchcraft.[11]

The spiritualist movement was generally viewed as an alternative faith to Christianity. In 1890, for example, an article in *Two Worlds* dismissed orthodox Christianity as 'a monstrous scarecrow invention of priestcraft' while the following year it dismissed what it called 'Ecclesiastical Circusdom'.[12] None the less, some Christians were drawn into the movement, and they insisted that it was possible to combine Christianity and spiritualism. Christian spiritualists included the Anglican clergymen, Hugh Reginald Haweis, for whom spiritualism was a logical development of Christianity, Charles Maurice Davies (also a journalist), who brought to his explorations a sense of fun, and Stainton Moses, who became a medium and developed a form of spirit-controlled 'automatic writing' in the 1870s. Moses claimed his automatic writing was directed by a cohesive group of spirits, the 'Imperator Band', who were using him to warn of an impending crisis of Western civilisation.[13] 'We are receiving', he insisted in his presidential address to the London Spiritualist Alliance in 1887, 'new developments of truth now as certainly as in olden days it was revealed to our forefathers'.[14] The high Anglican Gladstone participated in a séance in 1884, and was 'satisfied' when he witnessed automatic writing in Greek and Spanish.[15]

A number of prominent scientific figures became keen believers in spiritualism – among them Alfred R. Wallace, who had developed a theory of biological evolution at the same time as Darwin. For Wallace, spiritualism was a higher form of the development of the species, transcending physical evolution.[16] The eminent physicist, Sir Oliver Lodge, principal of the University of Birmingham from 1900, believed that spiritualist communication occurred through a universal fluid he termed 'ether', in a manner similar to radio waves, x-rays, radiation and other unseen forces.[17] Many found spiritualist communication to be credible in a universe where matter itself was discovered to be composed of energy. In his short story, 'Wireless' of 1902, Rudyard Kipling juxtaposed the new wireless communication with an episode of 'automatic writing', suggesting that the one was no less believable than the other.[18] Converts also included W. T. Stead, who became deeply involved in spiritualism in the 1890s, began practising automatic writing in 1892, and in 1895 founded a journal, *Borderland*, to spread popular awareness of spiritualism, or, as he put it, 'to democratise the study of the spook'.[19] In 1897, he published a volume of his automatic writings, *Letters from Julia*, which he believed to be communications from his deceased friend, Julia A. Ames, and in 1909, he opened a 'surgery' of mediums, called 'Julia's Bureau', to help the bereaved. Three years later, he was travelling to America, on an eclectic mission both to address a Christian revivalist meeting and to meet a prominent medium, Mrs Etta Wriedt (who was to assist him with 'Julia's Bureau'), when he perished in the sinking of the *Titanic*.[20]

Eastern religion and Theosophy

As well as spiritualism, growing numbers in later nineteenth-century Britain and Ireland began turning to the religions of the East, especially Hinduism and Buddhism, and to occult practices believed to have their roots in the ancient Near East. While most people in Britain viewed Asians as backward, and in need of Western civilisation and conversion to Christianity, a significant number began to be attracted by Eastern faiths as an alternative to Christianity. Their gaze was drawn eastwards in part by a fascination with the exotic. They were also attracted by faiths that seemed uncorrupted by the rationalist, empiricist, scientific and materialist thought of the West. In the East, they believed, ancient wisdom had been preserved among peoples who lived simpler, more spiritual lives. In the East would be found liberation from the desire to accumulate, master and control. Some were attracted by faiths that taught the immanence of God in all creation and that 're-enchanted the universe'.[21] As Janet Oppenheim observed, 'if Christianity had been hopelessly compromised by its concessions to science, the Hindu and Buddhist faiths might still be studied for their ageless spiritual teachings'.[22] Some may have turned to these faiths as a way of protesting against Britain's imperialism in the East, an imperialism viewed by many as inextricably linked to Christian missions. Theirs was, to be sure, a romanticised version of Eastern religion, but it had a broad appeal none the less.

The lure of the East found expression in Theosophy, a movement that claimed to be based on ancient teachings that formed the essence of all the great world religions. In its modern guise, the Theosophical movement emerged in the 1870s, and was associated with the Russian, Helena Petrovna Blavatsky, and her American collaborator, Colonel Henry Steele Olcott.[23] These two founded the Theosophical Society in 1875 in New York. In a series of what she claimed were inspired writings, most notably the two-volume *Isis Unveiled* (1877), Blavatsky described the ancient 'wisdom-religion', which included belief in a deity that infused the whole of the universe, in a universe that evolved through a cycle of emanations of the deity, in the reincarnation of the soul, in the capacity of magi to harness the vital forces through occult practices, and in the existence of a higher self within each individual.[24] For her, all world religions were offshoots of this original wisdom-religion, of which the inspired religious prophets of history – the Buddha, Zoroaster, Jesus and others – had conveyed only partial insights to their followers. But now at last she had been given the ancient truths, and the spread of this original wisdom-religion would lead to world unity and peace. As her movement reached Britain in the later 1870s, many spiritualists moved into theosophical circles.

In 1879, Blavatsky travelled to India, where she and her followers developed new forms and institutions for their religion. Although having no knowledge of the languages of India, she claimed to be instructed in an esoteric version of Buddhism by a mysterious lodge of superhuman mahatmas, higher beings who had evolved through a series of reincarnations and who resided high in the Himalayas; they communicated with her through letters that wafted through space. These mahatma letters conveyed the esoteric doctrines that formed the origins of all religions, and she expressed their teachings in *The Secret Doctrine* (1888). In India, she and her follow-ers were highly critical of the Christian missions and published reports of missionary misdeeds – which helped them to gain a considerable follow-ing on the subcontinent. By 1886, the Theosophical Society had issued 121 charters for separate lodges, 106 of them in British-controlled India or Burma; Theosophy was becoming very much an imperial movement.[25] Among Blavatsky's disciples was an English journalist resident in India, A. P. Sinnett, who published two books based on the mahatma teachings – *The Occult World* (1881) and *Esoteric Buddhism* (1883) – both of which went through numerous editions and were widely read in the English-speaking world. For Sinnett, the mahatmas were 'wondrously endowed representatives of occult science, whose mortal nature has been so far elevated and purified that their perceptions range over other worlds and other states of existence, and commune directly with beings as much greater than ordinary mankind, as man is greater than the insects of the field'.[26] Their teachings, he mused, far transcended those of the churches, and resolved all tensions between science and religion. Sinnett returned to London in 1883, and established his dominance over the English Theosophical movement. Writing in 1893, the broad church Sanskrit scholar, F. Max Müller, insisted that the Theosophist claims were largely absurd. None the less, he was heartened by the growing popular interest in Buddhism. His own great editorial project, a collection of the *Sacred Books of the East* – to which he had devoted 16 years of his life – was now nearing completion, with 48 volumes published.[27]

Theosophy had a particular appeal to women, offering opportunities for religious leadership denied them in churches and proclaiming the equality of the sexes.[28] Blavatsky herself was impulsive, excitable and plagued by ill-health, a chain-smoker who died in 1891, aged 58. She was also a charismatic figure, who could inspire intense loyalty from her fol-lowers. Among those drawn to Theosophy was Annie Besant, former evan-gelical Christian of Irish parentage, former Church of England clergyman's wife, former secularist and colleague of Bradlaugh, and committed social-ist and feminist.[29] Besant had grown dissatisfied with socialist materialism, and from about 1886, partly through the influence of her friend, W. T. Stead, she began exploring psychic and spiritualist phenomena, holding séances in her home. In 1889 she joined the Theosophical Society, where she found spiritual teachings that she believed gave deeper meaning to her socialist ideals. She settled in India in 1893, founded the Central Hindu College in Benares in 1897, became President of the Theosophical Society in 1907, was elected the first woman President of the Indian National

Congress meeting in 1917 in Calcutta, and played a leading role in both Theosophy and Indian nationalism until her death in 1933. While early and mid-Victorians had viewed the British empire as a vehicle for the spread of Christianity to the larger world, Besant believed that the empire and the English-speaking world were now becoming vehicles for the world-wide dissemination of Indian religion and philosophy. 'India', she wrote in 1900, 'is a conquered nation'. But from India, a religion was now spreading, much as Christianity had once spread from a conquered province to win the Roman empire. Though India was a subject nation:

her thought, her teaching, her ancient literature [are] translated into the English tongue, which is the most widely spread tongue on the earth, and is fast becoming the world language, which is spreading in every direction, which is talked by the foremost nations of the world. Thus, while politically she is subject, her thought is beginning to dominate the whole of that Western civilization.[30]

The growing fascination with both spiritualism and Eastern religions was reflected in the popularity of literature presenting supernatural tales from Asia and Africa, which some literary scholars have described as 'imperial gothic'.[31] A number of writers, among them Rider Haggard, Bram Stoker, Rudyard Kipling, Arthur Conan Doyle, and the young John Buchan, portrayed the East as a realm of secret wisdom, ritualistic magic, reincarnation, otherworldliness, and spiritualist visitations, which defied Western rationalism and conventional Christian teachings. For example, in Rider Haggard's *She* of 1886, two English explorers discover an ancient Egyptian priestess in central Africa; she has discovered the fountain of eternal youth and beauty, and exercises a severe rule over a savage cannibal people. She aims to usurp Victoria's imperial throne, and use the British empire to establish her endless world dominion. In Kipling's short story, 'The Mark of the Beast', an Englishman desecrates a Hindu temple and is turned into a werewolf. Doyle's 'The Ring of Thoth' of 1890 and Stoker's *Jewel of the Seven Stars* of 1903 portray ancient Egyptian mummies coming back to life. Such literature also included Stoker's *Dracula* of 1897, in which the Transylvanian count, from the frontier between Europe and the Near East, holds a grim secret of prolonging life, and envisages an empire of the undead. Much of this literature had a humorous side – unicorns summoned forth in séances that proceed to wreck the furnishings, dabblers in Eastern levitation teachings, who find they must wear lead underwear to keep from floating into space. The popularity of such literature, as Patrick

Brantlinger has argued, reflected the widespread fascination with spiritualism and Theosophy. A generation before, the majority in Britain had looked upon the empire as a providential instrument for the Christian conversion of the East; now growing numbers were enthralled with spiritual powers, real or imaginary, coming from the Eastern provinces of the empire home to Britain.

Late Victorian society also witnessed a revival of ritualistic magic, through which initiates studied ancient ceremonies and symbols with the aim of attaining spiritual wisdom and supernatural power. The original magi and their teachings were believed to have had their origins in the Near East, and the new vogue for ritualistic magic was connected with interest in Near Eastern religious expressions, including the kabbalah and freemasonry. The most prominent of these societies was the Hermetic Order of the Golden Dawn, founded in 1888 in London. By 1896 the Order claimed some 315 initiates, with 'temples' in London, Edinburgh and Paris. Its initiates advanced through degrees of knowledge of the occult. By training their senses, they had out-of-body experiences, engaged in astral travel, explored other worlds, and encountered beings that either aided or hindered their quest for esoteric enlightenment. In one sense, the initiates were aware that their journeys were taking them through different layers of human consciousness, and that their occult experiences were manifestations of the little understood powers of the mind. In another sense, they believed that they were gaining insights into the world soul, or *spiritus mundi*, the spiritual reality that underlay the physical universe and all its life forms. The Order took a particular interest in the legends and symbolism of the Holy Grail, viewed as an ancient symbol of occult power that had been taken up by the Christians.[32] The most prominent figure within the Golden Dawn was the Irish poet, W. B. Yeats – a Theosophist and a spiritualist – who was initiated into the Order in March 1890. The Order was fragmented in 1900 as a result of sexual scandals and infighting, but Yeats maintained his connection, finding inspiration for his poetry in its ritual and symbolism.[33]

Seekers after occult wisdom and unseen worlds were also drawn to Celtic mythology and folklore. Yeats' first major work, *The Wanderings of Oisin*, published in 1889, portrayed the pre-Christian hero's visits to three magic lands, and his recognition, after a dialogue with Ireland's patron saint, Patrick, that truth would be found, not in Christianity, but in the ritualistic magic of his own pagan and Celtic past.[34] In *The Celtic Twilight* of 1893, Yeats brought together tales of Irish ghosts, spirits and supernatural visions, many from his native Sligo in the west of Ireland. Yeats was not the only voice in the revival of Celtic spirituality during the 1890s. In Ireland, Douglas Hyde and Augusta, Lady Gregory collected ancient Celtic legends, songs and incantations. George Russell linked Theosophy and Celtic magic, and insisted that Ireland was known as the 'sacred isle' because 'the Gods lived there'.[35] There was an active Theosophical Lodge in Dublin from 1886, and Theosophy and Celticism became intertwined in many minds. Besant was a frequent speaker at the Dublin Lodge, and her claim that 'Ireland is to the West what India is to the East' became a refrain of the *fin de siècle* Irish literary revival.[36] In Scotland, William Sharp, who wrote under the name Fiona MacLeod, discovered and preserved pre-Christian myths and legends from the Highlands and Islands, and in 1892 founded a short-lived *Pagan Review*. In 1897, Yeats, Russell, Sharp and the passionate Irish spiritualist and nationalist Maude Gonne, established the Order of Celtic Mysteries to promote investigations into Celtic occult symbols and rituals.[37]

Psychic research and the psychological approach to religion

One important group of late nineteenth-century thinkers approached spiritualism and the occult, not as devotees, but in a spirit of scientific enquiry. They became convinced that, while there was much fraud and deception among professional mediums, there were also phenomena for which existing science had no explanation. Those drawn to the investigation of spiritualist and other psychic phenomena were often 'honest doubters', who had lost their faith in Christianity, but who craved evidence of a spiritual dimension. They hoped that the systematic study of spiritualism would provide incontrovertible proof of a higher intelligence governing the universe and of personal immortality. Among those undertaking such psychic investigations was Henry Sidgwick, Knightsbridge professor of moral philosophy at Cambridge University and brother-in-law to Edward White Benson, archbishop of Canterbury. The son of an Anglican clergyman, Sidgwick had lost his Christian faith while in his twenties, though he remained a theist. He was drawn to spiritualism from 1860 in his search of evidence for personal immortality, which he hoped would form the basis for a new system of ethics. In 1874, he gathered a circle of like-minded individuals at Cambridge for the systematic study of psychic phenomena. They included the young Arthur Balfour, Sidgwick's brother-in-law and the future prime minister, and Balfour's sister, Eleanor, an able mathematician and later principal of Newnham College, Cambridge. The group experimented with séances and hypnotism. Several years later, in 1882, Sidgwick's circle joined with other investigators to form the Society for Psychical Research – which sponsored studies of telepathic communications, hypnotism, spiritualism and automatic writing, among other phenomena.

A leading figure in the Society for Psychical Research was Frederic Myers.[38] The son of an Anglican clergyman, Myers had a brilliant student career at Trinity College, Cambridge, where he was a fellow from 1865 to 1874. He lost his Christian faith by 1870 and while he associated with Mary Ann Evans (George Elliot) he was unsatisfied with the position of the 'honest doubters'. From 1873, he was drawn into Sidgwick's circle of psychic research. About the same time, he also fell in love with Annie Marshall, the wife of his mentally-ill cousin; she returned his affection and shared his interest in spiritualism, but their love remained platonic. When she committed suicide in 1876, he was devastated, and struggled to communicate with her spirit, while he desperately sought scientific proof for the existence of life after death. He co-published a two-volume study of apparitions, *Phantasms of the Living*, in 1886 and participated in séances. He was drawn to the study of hypnotism, which, he came to believe, revealed different layers of consciousness existing within each individual personality. Hypnotism, and related phenomena such as automatic writing, provided for Myers glimpses into what he termed the 'deep-sea world' of human personality.[39] At the depths of personality was the unconscious 'subliminal self', which expressed the essence of the individual; here, Myers believed, would be found the realm of psychic experience, and the root of all religious stirrings. It was the subliminal self that represented the spiritual nature of the individual; it was the subliminal self that formed the immortal soul. It was at the subliminal level, moreover, that individuals experienced the purest form of love, which was platonic, like the love Myers had known for Annie Marshall. It was here that the individual self touched what mystics and occultists described as the 'world-soul'.[40] For Myers, psychical research provided new insight into the religious sense. 'Our duty', he told the Society for Psychical Research in 1900, 'is not the founding of a new sect, nor even the establishment of a new science, but is rather the expansion of Science herself until she can satisfy those questions which the human heart will rightly ask, but to which Religion alone has thus far attempted an answer'.[41] Myers's grand synthesis of his life's work, *Human Personality and its Survival of Bodily Death*, was published two years after his death, in 1903.

Others were similarly drawn to the new science of psychology in their explorations of spiritual phenomenon and religious experiences. Of these, the most influential was the American philosopher and psychologist, William James, who presented a celebrated series of Gifford Lectures at the University of Edinburgh in 1901–02. Published under the title, *Varieties of Religious Experience*, they went through 12 large editions by 1906. James was a member of the American branch of the Society for Psychical Research and had a long-standing commitment to psychical research, especially into automatic writing and trance voices. In the *Varieties*, James approached the subject of religion through a study of the religious feelings and impulses of a number of personalities. He presented a wide array of individual religious experiences, drawn from different Christian denominations and different world faiths. He concluded that all religions were rooted in common experiences and a common longing to connect with divine powers. He professed a belief in God, but his was an immanentist view of the divine; for him, God infused the world, speaking to different individuals in a variety of ways. James shared Myers' belief that religious impulses originated in the 'subliminal consciousness' and that it was here, in the depths of consciousness, that God touched the individual. In this sense, he believed, theologians were correct when they claimed that all religious communication came from God – for God touched the subconscious and the subconscious then influenced the conscious mind and human action.[42]

His reflections on the varieties of religious experience led James to commend the fullest possible religious tolerance. Individuals had their own distinctive spiritual experiences. Most individuals interpreted their spiritual experiences according to the religious tradition and culture in which they had been raised. But each individual's experience yielded only a partial insight into 'human nature's total message', and none had the whole truth. 'Unquestionably', he maintained, '. . . for each man to stay in his own experience, whate'er it be, and for others to tolerate him there, is surely best'.[43] His work denied that Christianity had an exclusive claim to knowledge of God's will, and affirmed that truly religious individuals would be found in mosques or Hindu temples, in spirit circles or Theosophical societies, as well as in Christian churches. James's *Varieties* did much to promote the psychological approach to religion in Britain. Religious faith, he suggested, was subjective and relative, a unique expression of the complex and multilayered individual self. Individuals should not be held culpable for having 'wrong' religious beliefs.

The psychological approach to religion, as well as the fascination with spiritualism and other religions, was also reflected in a renewed interest in mysticism. James had claimed in the *Varieties* that 'personal religious experience had its root and center in mystical states of consciousness'.[44] Such a view was shared by other thinkers drawn to the psychological approach, for whom mysticism and the mystical path united the variety of religious experiences and offered a sound basis for devotional life. In his Gifford Lectures of 1892, delivered at the University of Glasgow and published under the title of *Theosophy and Psychological Religion*, F. Max Müller had maintained that his long years of research into comparative religion had convinced him that the essence of all religions was 'the yearning for union or unity with God'. This yearning, he insisted, 'had always been the deepest spring of all religions'.[45] Further, because human nature was essentially the same across cultures, the symbols used by the various world faiths to describe the paths to union with God were also similar. Indeed, he suggested that memories of ancestral striving for mystical union with God survived as layers of religious consciousness, which formed the religious psychology of each individual and which were shared by individuals as a collective consciousness. The study of comparative religion, then, was also a process of self-discovery, of exploring the psychical deposits in these different layers of the collective consciousness and finding that the ancestral beliefs of our remote past continued to influence us. 'Nothing', he averred, 'seems more delightful than to be able to discover how by an unbroken chain our thoughts and words carry us back from century to century, how the roots and feeders of our mind pierce through stratum after stratum, and still draw their life and nourishment from the deepest foundations'.[46]

In his Bampton Lectures at Oxford in 1899, published under the title *Christian Mysticism*, W. R. Inge insisted that there was a need to return 'to the fundamentals of a spiritual religion'. 'As the old seats of authority, the infallible church and the infallible book, are fiercely assailed', we must look for support in 'the depths of the religious consciousness itself'.[47] Other writers on mysticism portrayed it as a means to transcend the 'subliminal consciousness'. In her *Mysticism: A Study of the Nature and Development of Man's Spiritual Consciousness* of 1911, Evelyn Underhill accepted the teaching of 'modern psychology' that 'the unconscious or subliminal personality' was the realm both of the individual's 'most spiritual intuitions' and of 'all those "uncivilized" instincts and vices, those remains of the ancestral savage'.[48] However, it was not in this realm of the 'unconscious' that the individual would find true union with God. Rather, she insisted, the mystical path lay through training what she termed the 'transcendental sense' and soaring above the instincts and intuitions of the unconscious.[49]

The New Theology

The growing interest in the psychology of religious experience, in other world religions and in mysticism contributed to the New Theology movement associated with the Congregational minister, R. J. Campbell (1867–1956).[50] The New Theology represented an effort to adapt the language and imagery of Christianity to the new psychological insights and approaches. Campbell, the son of a United Methodist minister, had spent part of his youth living in Ireland, where he had what he termed 'supernormal spiritual experiences'.[51] He studied at Oxford in the early 1890s, coming under the influence of Charles Gore and the *Lux Mundi* group. But then he turned from Anglo-Catholicism, joined the Congregational church, and became a Congregational minister in Brighton. There he read widely in Hegelian philosophy, in Max Müller's *Sacred Books of the East*, and in William James's psychology of religion, while he established a reputation as a powerful and original Christian preacher.[52] In 1903, he was appointed, amid great fanfare, minister of the City Temple, the most prominent Congregational church in London; over 7,000 people attended the services on his first Sunday. He gathered a large following through his stirring pulpit oratory, compelling personality, calls for social reform, and efforts to adapt Christianity to modern thought. Soon, however, serious doubts were being expressed about his eclectic beliefs and his Christian orthodoxy.

In response to his critics, Campbell wrote at 'great speed' a theological work, *The New Theology*, which he published in mid-1907. In this book, he presented a mystical vision of Christianity, with emphasis on the unity of all creation and the immanence of God in all things. The universe, he argued, was infused with the divine; it was 'God's thought about Himself'.[53] Humans should strive to transcend their individualism, selfishness and narrow concerns in order to achieve unity with God and all creation. Campbell drew upon the psychology of Frederic Myers, with its emphasis on the 'subconscious mind, or subliminal consciousness' as the 'seat of inspiration and intuition'. He suggested that it was at this level of 'subliminal consciousness' that individuals would discover their ultimate unity with one another and with God.[54] Believers should learn to 'trust the voice of God within'.[55] Campbell sought to give new meanings to traditional Christian language. The story of Adam's fall represented humanity's temporary loss of its consciousness of the infinite. The real nature of human sin was blindness to the true divine nature that lay within each person. Christ had shown humans the way to overcome this blindness, recover their consciousness of the infinite and realise their divine nature. Thus Christ's atonement referred to his 'assertion of the fundamental unity of all existence'.[56] The Bible, Campbell believed, contained inspired writings but was it not uniquely the word of God, for inspiration was ongoing and 'we are writing a Bible with our own lives to-day'.[57] Jesus, he insisted, had come into the world not to found a 'church', but to establish the kingdom of God, that is, to achieve the unity of all humankind.

Campbell's ideas found considerable support among people who wanted a more modern Christianity. His followers founded a New Theology League, which was later renamed the Progressive League. Campbell and other proponents of the New Theology lectured and published widely, seeking to win support for their 'modern' version of Christianity. Campbell developed his views on the kingdom of God in a second book, *Christianity and the Social Order*, also published in 1907, in which he argued that the socialist movement was now taking over from the churches in proclaiming the kingdom of God.[58] He made Christian socialism an integral part of the New Theology movement, and he spoke on labour platforms, joined the Independent Labour Party and was elected to the executive of the Fabian Society. By early 1909, the Progressive League had over 3,000 members and some 100 branches.

However, there was also growing Christian opposition to Campbell's movement. For these opponents, the New Theology was nothing more than a vague pantheism, which sought to infuse humanity and nature with divinity, but which downplayed both the existence of real evil in the world and God's transcendence. They resented Campbell's use of Christian language to convey non-Christian ideas – or what the Scottish United Free Church theologian, James Denney, called Campbell's 'systematic debasement of the Christian currency'.[59] Criticisms of the New Theology grew louder, until soon the chorus of condemnation was affecting Campbell's health and creating tensions within his City Temple congregation. The controversy convinced him to study anew the Bible and Church Fathers, and as he did so, he began to moderate his theological views and expressions. The onset of the Great War in 1914 forced him to confront the radical evil of sin, and then shattered his belief in his New Theology. In late 1915, he resigned his ministry in the Congregational church, and under the influence of Charles Gore, he was received into the Church of England, where he would close his career as an Anglican priest. The New Theology movement ended.

While the New Theology movement was an extreme attempt to adapt Christianity to modern thought, other denominations experienced similar movements from about 1890. Preachers and theologians sought to adapt Christian language to scientific thought and biblical criticism, to emphasise individual religious experience, and to claim that revelation was ongoing. Within Western Roman Catholicism, there was the significant movement known as 'Modernism', which in Britain became associated with the Jesuit priest, George Tyrrell, and the lay theologian, Baron von Hügel. Catholic Modernists accepted the approaches of critical biblical scholarship, turned from scholastic theology, and were sceptical about orthodox views of the origins of Christianity. Concerned over where such ideas would lead, Pope Pius X condemned Modernism in 1907, and in the years that followed a number of leading Modernists, including Tyrrell, were dismissed from teaching positions and effectively silenced. In 1910, meanwhile, Christianity in Britain was further unsettled by the English translation of Albert Schweitzer's *Quest of the Historical Jesus*, in which the young Continental scholar challenged the prevalent views of the founder of Christianity. In a work of exacting scholarship, Schweitzer concluded that Jesus was a visionary, who had wrongly believed that the end of the world was near and whose moral teachings had been intended for only the short duration before the end. Discussion of this work dominated much of the annual Church Congress held at Cambridge in September 1910 – so much so, that it became known as the 'Schweitzer Congress'.[60] The psychological approaches, Christian mysticism, the New Theology, Catholic Modernism and Schweitzer's eschatological claims about the founder of Christianity all contributed to the ferment of theological ideas, and raised deep questions about theological truth. Was there a body of religious truth, rooted in historic events in the ancient Hebrew world, and now to be communicated to the modern world, or were there simply diverse narratives of personal spiritual journeys?

Jewish immigration and Zionism

Adding to the unsettled religious mood in late nineteenth-century Britain was a social phenomenon – the massive immigration of the descendants of the ancient Hebrew people. Between 1881 and 1914, upwards of three million Jews from Russia and Eastern Europe moved westwards. This migration had been sparked by waves of pogroms, or massacres of Jews, which began following the assassination of the Russian Tsar Alexander II in 1881 and which continued into the twentieth century. These pogroms were combined with anti-Semitic legislation in the Russian empire. Once the flood of political refugees began, they were joined by large numbers of economic refugees, seeking a better life in the West. Most of the migrants sought new homes in North America. However, tens of thousands of Russian and eastern European Jews immigrated to Britain between 1881 and 1914. Mainly impoverished and unskilled, they settled largely in the East End of London, which had an estimated 120,000 Jews by 1899.[61] Some neighbourhoods became exclusively Jewish, with Hebrew shop signs, Yiddish theatres, kosher shops, Saturday sabbaths and chapels turned into synagogues. 'The whole district', according to Charles Booth's account of Whitechapel in 1902, 'has been affected by the increase of the Jewish population. It has been like the slow rising of a flood. Street after street is occupied'.[62] Immigrants also settled outside London, and Manchester, Leeds, Glasgow and Liverpool gained substantial Jewish populations. In 1880, there were an estimated 60,000 Jews in Britain. By 1914, that number had increased to some 250,000.[63]

The Jewish immigrants were very different in ethnic background and economic status from the existing Anglo-Jewish population, which had benefited from Jewish emancipation in 1858 and which had largely assimilated into British culture. Many British Jews had come to view their religion as another Nonconformist denomination. They often prospered in commerce or finance within Britain's imperial economy, sent their children to prestigious public schools and then to Oxford and Cambridge, where they encountered relatively little overt prejudice. The elite society of the Cambridge 'Apostles' had Jewish members, and the Oxford Union had Jewish officers. Seven Jews were raised to the peerage between 1881 and 1914, Lord Rosebery, the Liberal leader, was married to a Jew (Hannah Rothschild), Queen Victoria frequently visited Jewish country homes later in her reign, while under her son, King Edward VII, Jewish participation in court life became 'a renowned symbol of the whole reign'.[64] This largely assimilated and well-off Anglo-Jewish community was, not surprisingly, uncomfortable with the new immigrants – with their poverty, ragged clothing, overcrowded housing, 'foreign' ways, Yiddish language, and noisy congregations. Established Jewish families feared that the East End Jewish immigrants would stir nativist resentments that might undermine the achievements of the era of emancipation.

These fears were not unfounded. By the turn of the century, there was growing popular opposition to the new Jewish immigrants. Britain, it is true, did not experience the large-scale virulent anti-Semitism that became prevalent in parts of the Continent (in part because the Jewish percentage of the overall British population remained small). But there were simmering resentments, especially in the East End of London, where there was a concentrated Jewish population and where impoverished Jewish immigrants, often from rural peasant backgrounds, could ignore sanitation, work for starvation wages, bring increased crime and prostitution, engage in exclusive dealing with other Jews, and flout sabbatarian conventions by trading on Sundays. One Liberal MP spoke of 'the scum of Europe' being dumped in Britain.[65] In response, the Conservative government secured the passage in 1905 of an Aliens Act, which tightened immigration procedures and authorised immigration officers to withhold permission to land from 'undesirables', including the diseased, infirm and criminals. While the Aliens Act found some support among the Anglo-Jewish establishment, it was deeply disliked by the new immigrants of the East End. For them, it was a sign that they would always be unwelcome – that, as the *East London Advertiser* expressed it in 1899, 'a Jew is always a Jew' and could never assimilate.[66]

In the 1890s, some British Jews, especially in the East End, turned to the new Zionist movement. The aspiration of a collective Jewish return to Jerusalem was as old as the dispersal of the Jews following the second-century destruction of the temple. Through the centuries, this aspiration had been enshrined in Jewish liturgy and symbolism. But the modern Zionist movement for a Jewish national homeland in Palestine only emerged among the Jews of Eastern Europe following the first wave of pogroms in the early 1880s. The movement reached Britain by 1890, and a series of visits by the dynamic Viennese Jew, Theodor Herzl, to London from 1895 onwards aroused large-scale enthusiasm among British Jews for the idea of a Jewish state in Palestine. The first Zionist Congress was held in Basle, Switzerland, in 1897, and Herzl and the Congress then launched a campaign to mobilise mass support for the movement across Europe. In 1899, Herzl's English supporters founded the English Zionist Federation, which had a membership of 7,000 by 1902.[67] The movement spread beyond London, and soon Manchester became a major centre for Zionism, with Chaim Weizmann, an immigrant Russian Jew and a chemistry lecturer, emerging as the leader of Manchester Zionism by 1906.

Zionists cultivated support outside the Jewish community. They argued that a restored Jewish state in Palestine would not only benefit Jews, but would serve as a beacon, lighting the way for the advancement of all humanity.[68] Such ideas proved attractive to a section of conservative

Christians – especially evangelicals with pre-millenarian beliefs – for whom the restoration of the Jews to the Holy Land was part of the providential plan for the world, and would lead to the return of Christ in glory. We have seen how the Eastern Question of 1876–78 had revived among some Christians the prophecies relating to the restoration of the Jews to Palestine. As Eitan Bar-Yosef has shown, a rich Christian Zionist literature also emerged in the early years of the twentieth century, including a number of melodramatic novels portraying Zionist endeavours to establish the Jewish state.[69] These novels included M. P. Shiel's *The Lord of the Sea* (1901), Winifred Graham's *The Zionists* (1902) and Violet Guttenberg's *A Modern Exodus* (1904) – all with larger-than-life hero-adventurers who lead Jews to the promised land. Such literature reflected the lure of the East, and revived for some the providentialist visions of the British empire. A number of influential non-Jews were attracted to Zionism, among them Joseph Chamberlain, David Lloyd George, and Arthur Balfour.[70] Active support for the movement was restricted to a minority in Britain before the Great War. None the less, Zionism had taken hold of some imaginations.

Declining Christian influence in Britain

There was a sense in *fin de siècle* Britain that the public influence of Christianity was beginning to recede, slowly but perceptibly. The nineteenth century had been a great century for Christian endeavour, as reflected in the building of thousands of new churches, a vigorous home mission among the labouring classes, the extension of popular education, the campaign against slavery, and the spread of overseas missions. Yet now, as the century drew to its close, the churches were, it seemed, failing to inspire the same commitment and activism, and church attendances began to fall.

Some, as we have seen, were attracted to non-Christian religious movements or had developed doubts about Christian teachings. But probably more important were the new mass leisure industries that increasingly competed with traditional religious observances.[71] Large numbers of people were deciding that they could find fulfilling lives apart from regular church attendance. Some were finding a substitute for churchgoing in the leisure industries. The end of the nineteenth century witnessed the explosive growth of professional sport. Many loyal fans would spend their Saturdays at the match and their Sundays reading about sporting events in the Sunday newspapers. The Football League had about 450 players in 1891, but some 5,000 players a decade later. First division matches were drawing average crowds of 13,000 by 1905–06, while international matches could attract 80,000 or more; a crowd of 113,000 attended the Cup Final in 1901. Grand stadiums were erected to accommodate the growing crowds. Cricket, rugby and horse-racing also had their mass followings.

There was also a growth in participatory sports, especially lawn tennis and golf; England had about 1,200 golf clubs by 1912. The development of the modern bicycle led to a cycling craze in the 1890s, with men and women of all social classes devoting their weekends, including their Sundays, to exploring the countryside. Some 750,000 bicycles were being produced annually by the late 1890s. Growing numbers were enjoying weekend holidays to seaside resorts – with their piers, sea-bathing, donkey rides, and Punch and Judy shows. The Victorian music halls were, during the 1890s, being transformed into variety theatres, often seating more than 2,000 and employing highly paid entertainers. Then came the cinema, which had its first British public screening in 1896. By 1914, there were over 3,500 picture houses in Britain. The traditional British Sabbath, as a day when people were expected to be in church or to stay indoors, was increasingly broken – initially because it was seen as unjust to deny the working classes healthy amusements on their one day of leisure. Public parks began to be opened on Sunday afternoons, while from the late 1890s, the main London museums, including the British Museum and National Gallery, also had Sunday afternoon openings.

The churches were finding it more difficult to maintain their influence, and there was much statistical evidence of declining church attendance. Studies of religious life in London by the *British Weekly* in 1886–87 and the *Daily News* in 1902–03 provided a picture of decline for both the established church and the Nonconformist denominations. In inner London, total church attendances relative to population fell from 28.5 per cent in 1886 to 22 per cent in 1903. A study of eight towns in the North Midlands showed a fall in total attendances from 44 per cent in 1851 to 27 per cent in 1902–04. The crucial decade for the onset of decline seems to have been the 1890s. While evidence for rural churchgoing is sketchy, a study of rural Oxfordshire suggests that attendances there may have fallen to 25 per cent in 1913, a significant decline from the 45 per cent attendance in 1851.[72] In the early nineteenth century, low levels of church attendance among the labouring orders had been blamed on insufficient church accommodation; build more churches, it had been argued, and the people would attend. Now, after decades of building, the churches in many places were largely empty. At their evening services, Nonconformist churches in London had been on average 53.6 per cent full in 1851 but were only

34.6 per cent by 1903. The evening services at Anglican churches were on average only 30.3 per cent full in the same year. And even at the morning services, most churches had far from a capacity congregation. Of those who did attend services, an estimated two-thirds were women.[73]

As some churches grew emptier, their barren pews and darkened spaces could appear bleak and uninviting to the visitor. Here, it seemed, was a remnant of usually older worshippers that a busy world was passing by. For churches in difficulty, there could be a downward spiral. The cost of maintaining a large, half-empty structure and paying accumulated debts could place an intolerable financial burden on a dwindling congregation, and discourage new members from joining. As the author of a study of Liverpool Nonconformist churches in 1908 put it: 'people are afraid to attend a church where there are constant appeals for money to which they feel themselves unable to respond'.[74] By 1907, total memberships of the largest English Nonconformist denominations were showing significant decline.[75] The novelist, Hall Caine, observed of London in 1897 that 'of the five millions of people in this vast city, not one million cross the threshold of church or chapel'.[76] 'There are those', noted Herbert Ryle, the Anglican bishop of Winchester, in 1904, 'who look for the overthrow and destruction of the Church. They believe she is powerless in the strength of modern forces'.[77]

In Scotland, there was also a widespread perception that more and more people, especially of the urban working classes, were deserting the pews. As early as 1887, John Marshall Lang, Church of Scotland minister of the Barony church in Glasgow, observed of the Scottish people in a sermon before the synod of Glasgow and Ayr:

They are departing. Men in thousands and tens of thousands . . . The drift is representative of different attitudes of mind . . . But at one point all these attitudes meet: people decline to enter within the gates of any ecclesiastical society.[78]

'It is a terrible tho' true confession', observed another Church of Scotland minister in Glasgow in 1893, 'that there is in every city and town in this country, whole sections of the community . . . to whom it would make little practical difference were we tomorrow to close every church in the land'.[79] An investigation of Scottish religion in 1900, prepared by the respected statistician, Dr Robert Howie, concluded that some 1,600,000 people in Scotland – fully 37.5 per cent of the country's total population – had no church affiliation.[80] The prominent Church of Scotland minister,

John White, would later describe the 1890s as marking the general movement of Scotland 'from an unquestioning acceptance of the orthodox message of the Church to a secular rationalism, Hedonism, and the New Psychology which appeared to succeed in their attacks on religion'. During the 1890s, he recalled, 'the new rationalist was out-thinking the old champion of orthodoxy'.[81] In Wales, too, there was a sense of stagnation in the churches from the 1890s. While Welsh ministers had long expressed concerns about a lack of real faith among their congregations, these concerns, as R. Tudur Jones has noted, took on a new urgency. 'One concern that was voiced time and time again by religious leaders', Tudur Jones observed, 'was that Christian Wales was rapidly losing its grasp of the divine'. The influence of the great Welsh-language preachers, who had held chapelgoers spellbound for over a century, was waning in the 1890s; the spell was broken, and the style and manner of the great preachers now often became the subject of parody. Speaking in 1888, Thomas Charles Edwards, principal of the Calvinistic Methodist College at Bala, sensed that his nation's faith was fading. 'It is not impossible', he observed, 'for Wales again to become religionless and faithless'.[82]

It is true that many of those who no longer regularly attended church still retained their Christian faith. They believed in God, viewed Christ as their personal saviour, and sought to live according to Christian ethical precepts. They remembered the hymns, gospel songs and Bible stories they had learned in Sunday school. In times of personal difficulty or crisis, they might return to church, pray, or search their Bible for answers. Most wanted to be married in church, to have their children baptised, and to have a Christian funeral. They could be roused to action by religious causes and most viewed themselves as part of a Christian nation. As Callum Brown has observed, well into the twentieth century, 'a vibrant Christian identity remained central to British popular culture' and this identity retained 'a capability to explode in fulsome self-expression'.[83] But more and more people did not see church membership or regular attendance to be necessary to their Christian identity, and this was having an impact upon the institutional churches.

The sense of malaise in the churches was reflected in growing difficulties in recruitment for the clergy. Within the Church of England, fewer candidates came forward for ordination. The numbers of newly ordained clerics had peaked in 1886, and then declined rapidly, falling from 777 in 1889 to 752 in 1897, to 569 in 1901.[84] This was at a time when the population of England and Wales was growing at a rate of 300,000 a year, and when the colonies were still recruiting many clergymen from the mother country. The result was an insufficient number of clergy, especially in the cities and in the North. In the Nonconformist churches and the Presbyterian churches of Scotland, the decline in the numbers of new ministers was less pronounced, but by 1914, nearly all denominations were experiencing difficulties in recruiting. Along with the falling number of ordinands, there was evidence that the most able men were no longer entering the clergy. The percentage of Church of England ordinands with Oxford or Cambridge degrees remained fairly constant, at about 60 per cent. However, there was a decline in the number of ordinands who received the best degrees. In 1841–43, of Cambridge graduates who earned first-class honours, 65 per cent went on to be ordained. In 1881–83, the number of Cambridge Firsts going on to ordination had fallen to 18 per cent.[85] While in the mid-nineteenth century half of all graduates of Oxford's Balliol College had become clergymen, by the 1890s only one in 25 did so.[86] 'We want to induce the best class of men to take Holy Orders', fretted a clerical author in the *Nineteenth Century* in 1898, 'and not those who properly would have been failures in any other profession'.[87] One cause of the falling number of young men coming forward for ordination was the declining value of clerical livings, relative to rising incomes in other professions. At the end of the 1890s, perhaps half of the parish clergy had incomes of less than £200 a year, which was hardly sufficient to maintain a middle-class standard of living. For many families, the investment of money in the education of a future clergyman – which normally meant several years at public school, three years at university and one or two years of seminary training – was simply not likely to bring an adequate return.

Another reason for the declining numbers was the doubt about Christianity that now permeated the universities. Writing in 1901, F. W. Head, fellow of Emmanuel College, Cambridge, believed that many sons of clergymen came up to university planning to follow their father's calling, but when confronted with the new scientific and philosophic thought, the brightest of them developed religious doubts, and gave up their plans for the ministry. 'The abler men from the clerical homes', he observed, 'drift off, and their places are not supplied by able converts'. 'The more able and more thoughtful men', he added, 'the men who will count for most in their day, are being thinned out from the ranks'.[88] Fifty years before, the common-rooms of the Oxford and Cambridge colleges had been dominated by earnest discussions of the role of the sacraments, the nature of the apostolic succession, and the prospects of Christianising the world. The best and the brightest planned to enter holy orders. Now those common-rooms resounded with the language of physics, medicine, psychology and historical research, the dominant mood was agnosticism, and the best and the brightest planned to enter the medical professions, the civil or imperial service, and, increasingly, commerce and finance. As the historian David Newsome poignantly observed, 'these men closed their Bibles, and . . . for them and for their generation – the angels lost their wings'.[89]

The Church of England and the ritualist controversy

But the Church of England still remained the established church in England and Wales, and for millions of inhabitants, it expressed the spiritual identity of the nation. It was the church in which the queen worshipped, and the church that provided the lion's share of chaplains to the army and navy. Its cathedrals provided worship on a grand scale, surrounded by funereal monuments, battle-flags and other emblems of the nation's past. Westminster Abbey provided the final resting place for the nation's great and good. The parish churches were prominent in many communities, representing continuity with past generations, marking out the seasons with the ancient Christian holidays, and providing baptisms, confirmations, marriages and burials. With their incomes derived in part from rent charges and endowments, the parish churches were more financially secure than most Nonconformist churches. The Church of England was by far the largest church in the United Kingdom: in 1901 it included 17,368 churches or chapels, and 23,679 clergy. It maintained thousands of schools, and was educating some two million pupils in England and Wales in 1887.[90] There had been an increase in the episcopate to meet the needs of a growing population. Several new bishoprics were created after 1875. The church also found it could make use of sixteenth-century legislation to create suffragan, or assistant, bishops, and there were some 30 suffragan bishoprics created in England and Wales between 1870 and 1910. Twenty-six bishops sat in the House of Lords, selected from what was now a much larger number. Bishops and clergy were prominent in national ceremonies and commemorations. The queen was the supreme governor of the church, and Parliament controlled many aspects of ecclesiastical organisation, discipline and even liturgy.

Some devout Anglicans were uncomfortable with the element of state control, and said openly that the church would be healthier if disestablished. But probably most supported the principle of a national religious establishment, and wished to preserve the Church of England as 'the spiritual organ of the nation'. 'The confession of the national faith through the National Church may be imperfect', observed Brooke Foss Westcott, bishop of Durham, in a public address in 1893, 'but it is increasingly powerful as a witness and rich in promise for the future'. 'It witnesses', he continued, 'that religion is not an accident of human nature, but an essential element in every true human body. It brings all the great crises of national life into direct connexion with the unseen and the eternal . . . It is progressive, because it is living. It has proved from age to age that it can embody the spirit of the people'.[91] There was disquiet in the church, but also much commitment to its national mission.

The archbishop of Canterbury, Edward White Benson, died suddenly of heart failure in October 1896 at Hawarden parish church, while he was visiting Gladstone. Benson had been primate for 14 years. Cultivated, outwardly self-composed (though inwardly subject to depression), distinguished in appearance and moderately high church, he had been quietly effective. His primacy had been devoted to a vigorous defence of the established church, especially in Wales, where he promoted parochial and diocesan missions that helped revive the Welsh church.[92] He was succeeded as archbishop and primate by Frederick Temple, one of the contributors to the notorious *Essays and Reviews* in 1860. A gruff, plain-speaking broad churchman who had known poverty in his youth, Temple saw himself as a man of the people. Hard-working and self-reliant, he was reluctant to delegate administrative responsibilities. 'Temple', according to one observer, 'worked like a horse himself and he let everyone else work in the way they liked'.[93] But he was 75 years of age when raised to the archbishopric, and his prodigious energy was soon failing. As archbishop, Temple played a leading role in the celebrations of the queen's Diamond Jubilee in 1897, presided over the fourth Lambeth Conference of world Anglicanism in 1897, and served at the coronation of Edward VII in 1901, though by now his sight was going and he managed to put the crown on backwards. As well as failing health, Temple's years as primate were plagued by a revival of the bitter controversy over ritual.

The ritualist controversy, it will be recalled, had been a smouldering fire within the Church of England since the 1840s, a fire that flared up periodically in disruption of worship, riots and even bloodshed. Following the passing of the Public Worship Regulation Act of 1874, there had been a series of highly publicised trials of ritualist priests. These culminated in 1890 when Edward King, the high church bishop of Lincoln, was tried before an ecclesiastical court presided over by Archbishop Benson. Although King was instructed to desist from a few of his ritualist practices, the judgment had gone mainly in his favour and his trial was widely seen as a ritualist victory. The Anglo-Catholic party, meanwhile, was growing in confidence and in numbers. The theological colleges had become predominantly Anglo-Catholic in orientation, and produced ordinands who were steeped in ancient rituals and symbolism. At a time of growing interest in the mystical elements in religion, many lay people were drawn to this ritual – with its incense, lighted candles in procession, mixing of water and wine in the chalice, eastward position, reserving of the elements, and celebration of mass rather than the Lord's Supper. According to one recent estimate, the number of Anglican churches that could be classified as ritualist increased from about 200 in 1875 to over 2,000 in 1904.[94] In 1901, membership of the Anglo-Catholic English Church Union was about 39,000, including approximately 4,000 clergy. Other societies were committed to reviving liturgical practices, among them the Confraternity of the Blessed Sacrament, the Guild of All Souls, and the Society of the Holy Cross. Although a minority within the established church as a whole, ritualists were highly committed and growing in numbers.

Many Anglo-Catholics within the Church of England longed for reunion with the Roman Catholic Church. In 1894, Charles Wood, second Viscount Halifax, the president of the English Church Union and son of Lord John Russell's chancellor of the exchequer, initiated discussions between some Anglican leaders, French Catholics and eventually the Vatican over a plan for the corporate reunion of the Anglican and Roman Catholic churches. Wealthy, cultivated, and with a deep sense of the supernatural (including a fascination with ghost stories), Halifax dreamed of a restored Catholic Christendom. Pope Leo XIII initially showed interest in the plan, and the discussions, which continued for over two years, found fervent support among many Anglo-Catholics. But the reunion prospects were brought to an abrupt end in September 1896, when the pope, in the bull *Apostolicae Curae*, declared the Anglican orders to be invalid and the Church of England not to be a true church.[95] It was a devastating blow to Anglo-Catholic hopes. None the less, many continued to hope and pray that the pope would receive new light on this question.

A number of prominent *fin de siècle* British poets, artists and literary critics, meanwhile, were being drawn to Roman Catholicism in part through attraction to religious ritual and symbolism.[96] These included Robert Hugh Benson, the son of the Anglican primate and a talented author, who converted to Rome in 1894. They also included several artistic figures associated with the decadent movement. The poets Ernest Dowson and Lionel Johnson both converted to the Roman Catholic

Church in 1891. The poet John Gray, Oscar Wilde's intimate friend and wrongly believed to be the model for Wilde's decadent novel, *The Picture of Dorian Gray*, converted to Roman Catholicism in 1890, and was ordained to the priesthood in 1901, serving for the remainder of his life in an Edinburgh parish. Gray's friend, the homosexual Jewish poet and critic, Marc-André Raffalovich, followed him into the Roman Catholic Church in 1896, and helped finance church restorations in Edinburgh. Together they raised funds and oversaw the erection of the sumptuous St Peter's church in Edinburgh, with its Italianate design and décor. The artist Aubrey Beardsley was received into the Roman Catholic Church in 1897, a year before his death. Oscar Wilde had found strength and consolation after his imprisonment for homosexuality through his Roman Catholic faith. His *Ballad of Reading Gaol*, published in 1898, was a haunting evocation of Christ's redeeming love for torn and sinful humanity – redolent with the symbolism of blood and wine, fire and torment, new life from death. Frederick Rolfe, called Baron Corvo, who converted to Rome in 1886, wove an English pope into his autobiographical and decadent novel, *Hadrian the Seventh* (1904). These artists of the decadence, often souls in pain, found comfort in the ancient rituals, imagery and symbolism of the Christian faith. As Halévy put it, 'there are many rooms in the spacious mansion of Rome, and one in particular, somewhat retired and comfortably furnished, for artists who have learned that penitence is a pleasure, and a pleasure whose intensity is in proportion to the depth of their falls'.[97]

But many Protestants viewed all this with profound distaste, especially the attraction of decadent poets and artists to ritualism and Romanism. For them, this was further proof – if proof were needed – of the unwholesome, fetid, 'unmanly', and corrupting nature of the rituals, whether of the Roman Catholic Church or the Anglo-Catholics. Protestants were alarmed over the growing numbers of ritualist clergy, and the Anglo-Catholics' longing for union with Rome.[98] Some detected a papal plot to capture the Church of England; others viewed ritualism as contributing to the moral degeneration of the younger generation. In 1897, the evangelical journalist, Walter Walsh, published a sensationalist book, *The Secret History of the Oxford Movement*. Collecting documentary evidence from a number of groups on the fringes of the Anglo-Catholic movement, Walsh wove the material into a plausible account of a dark conspiracy against English Protestantism, beginning with the Tractarians of the 1830s and continuing to the present. The book had considerable influence and 32,000 copies were in print by 1899.[99]

In January 1897, an evangelical bookseller, John Kensit, gained notoriety when he disrupted the confirmation ceremony of the new bishop of London, the moderate high churchman and historian of the papacy, Mandell Creighton – protesting against Creighton's wearing of the cope and mitre. Kensit, who had founded the Protestant Truth Society in 1889, was fanatically anti-ritualist and anti-Catholic. He condemned the ritualism so prevalent in the Church of England, and championed a robust Protestantism. He railed against 'clergymen in petticoats', insisting that ministers should be 'manly men'.[100] In 1898, he and his followers began systematically disrupting what they defined as illegal ritualist services in Anglican churches, and they demanded that bishops institute proceedings to remove the ritualist clergy in their dioceses. Kensit recruited a group of anti-ritualist agitators, called the 'Wycliffites', who travelled about the country preaching against ritualist practices and disrupting ritualist services. By 1903, there were some 30 'Wycliffite' agitators on circuit, conducting hundreds of meetings.[101] While their methods and language were crude, Kensit and his Wycliffites found broad support, including support from Orangemen and others with a deep hatred for Irish Catholics. In 1898, the Liverpool-based Protestant activist, George Wise, founded the British Protestant Union, to combat the 'trinity of evils – Romanism, Ritualism and infidelity'. The Imperial Protestant Federation, also founded in 1898, united 21 existing Protestant organisations, including the evangelical Church Association and the Orange Order, in opposition to ritualism and Romanism.[102]

The anti-ritualist movement was not confined to bigoted extremists like Kensit. There was a growing feeling among moderate evangelicals and liberals that ritualist clergymen were going too far, openly flouting the laws governing worship within the established church, corrupting it with sensual, impure and foreign practices, and driving many sincere Protestant believers away from the parish churches. There was also a widespread belief that the bishops were not fulfilling their responsibility to suppress illegal ritualist practices. Beginning in late 1898, Sir William Harcourt, leader of the Liberal party and a broad church Anglican, denounced the illegal ritualist practices in a series of letters in *The Times*, which he published in 1899 under the title of *Lawlessness in the National Church*. The struggle over ritual, Harcourt insisted, involved not only the future of the Church of England as a Protestant church, but also its future as the national church of the English people. The aim of the ritualist clergy, Harcourt maintained, was mainly their own 'glorification and aggrandisement'. They sought 'to convert the minister of the gospel into the priest of the sacrifice'. They aimed to destroy the Reformation achievement of empowering the laity, and to transform the established Church of the English people into a sacramental, authoritarian and clerically-dominated body. The ritualists, Harcourt further argued, were often aided and abetted by the bishops, who not only declined to act against the lawless clergy, but also abused the powers given them by the Public Worship Regulation Act in order to veto legal proceedings initiated by others against ritualist abuses. 'They have', he insisted, 'for years shut the gates of ecclesiastical justice; they have deprived the laity of the protection which the law has provided'.[103]

The bishops resented such criticisms. They insisted that it was not their place to act as ecclesiastical policemen, dragging ritualist clergy before the civil courts or threatening them with civil punishments. Rather, as spiritual fathers to their clergy, they should seek to persuade the ritualists to act within the law. The ritualist clergy, after all, were conscientious men of God, fully convinced that their practices were rooted in the ancient traditions of the church. They were also prepared to be martyrs – and did anyone seriously want to return to the practice of imprisoning ritualist clergy? For most bishops, moreover, it seemed clear that protests against ritualist priests were initiated largely by outside agitators, and not by the parishioners who were allegedly alienated by ritual.

All this sounded reasonable, but Parliament was growing impatient with both the ritualist excesses and the bishops' excuses about why they did not enforce the law. In April 1899, the House of Commons adopted a motion, by a vote of 200 to 14, to censure the lawlessness of ritualist clergy and recommend that the crown refuse such clerics future church preferment. A month later, the Commons unanimously adopted a government motion that if the bishops would not bring the ritualist clergy to order, Parliament would do so through new legislation. Confronted by this ultimatum, the two archbishops conducted their own enquiry into the legality of certain ritualist practices. They agreed in July 1899 that incense and processional lights in Anglican worship were illegal and would have to cease; the following year, the archbishop of Canterbury ruled that the practice of reserving the sacrament was also illegal. Some ritualist clergy now desisted from those practices, but many did not.

Meanwhile, the anti-ritualist agitation out in the streets, and the related anti-Catholic and anti-Irish violence, grew uglier. Protestant extremists broke into the churchyard at Hickleton in Yorkshire and destroyed a monument Lord Halifax had raised to his dead sons.[104] During the summer of 1901, militant Protestant crowds in Liverpool attacked Roman Catholic churches and priests, as well as disrupting Anglican ritualist services. Kensit rushed to Liverpool to lead the agitation. In late September 1901, he was struck with an iron file during a fracas between Protestants and Roman Catholics and died ten days later. A young Roman Catholic artisan was tried for murder, but the jury did not convict. Kensit was now widely viewed as a martyr to the Protestant cause. His son assumed the leadership of the movement, and the street violence continued.[105] By early 1903, the Conservative prime minister, A. J. Balfour, writing to the bishop of Rochester, confessed to having 'the gloomiest apprehensions as to the future of the Church of England'. An 'ignorant, fanatical, reckless' Protestant faction battled daily with a ritualist faction that was every bit 'as ignorant, as fanatical and as reckless'. Meanwhile, the laity were 'divided from the clergy by an ever deepening gulf, and exercised by religious problems which the clergy cannot help them to solve'.[106]

Archbishop Temple had died in 1902, and he was succeeded as archbishop of Canterbury by Randall Davidson, the bishop of Winchester. An Oxford-educated Scot, Davidson was an efficient administrator and smooth politician. Constant pain from a boyhood hunting accident instilled him with a genuine empathy for human suffering, and this had endeared him to the queen in her final years. As bishop of Winchester, Davidson had famously confronted the well-loved Anglo-Catholic Portsmouth slum priest, Robert Dolling, denying him permission to erect an altar in his mission church for saying prayers for the dead. Dolling had responded by resigning from the Anglican priesthood; and while he professed the greatest sympathy for the ritualist's scruples, Davidson had readily accepted his resignation.[107] Davidson had thus gained a reputation as a bishop who was prepared to stand firm against illegal ritual. Within a month of becoming archbishop, he was waited on by a deputation of over 100 Conservative MPs, appealing for firm action to end the ritualist crisis.[108]

In 1904, Balfour's government, with Davidson's support, appointed a Royal Commission to investigate the whole ritualist controversy. The Commission met 118 times, examined scores of witnesses, and produced in 1906 a long and rather tedious report, which effectively steered a middle course. On the one hand, the report called for greater clerical discipline and insisted that certain practices, including processions with the sacrament, the invocation of saints, and special devotion to the Virgin, must be suppressed. On the other hand, it acknowledged that public worship in the Church of England should not be too narrowly defined by law, and that 'modern thought and feeling' were 'characterised by a care for ceremonial, a sense of dignity in worship, and an appreciation of the continuity of the church'. Just as there were many varieties of religious experience, so the established church should be legally permitted to accommodate a variety of worship. While the report did not satisfy the extremists on either side, it was accepted by more moderate ritualists and Protestants and the controversy subsided. This was no small achievement. The unity of the church had been preserved, and extremists on both sides had been contained. None the less, the ritualist crisis of 1898–1906 had been damaging for the social influence of the Church of England, making it seem that many of its clergy were more absorbed with 'bells and smells' than with ministering to society at large.

The Roman Catholic Church

The Roman Catholic Church in Britain, meanwhile, had been growing in numbers and in confidence. By the mid-1890s, there were an estimated 1,500,000 Roman Catholics in England and Wales, and about 365,000 in Scotland. There were some 1,500 Catholic churches in England and Wales, 1,000 Catholic schools, and 3,000 priests. The Catholic population was concentrated mainly in the urban districts and to a considerable extent it was made up of labouring people of Irish birth or descent. However, there was also a significant aristocratic element in English Catholicism. According to the *Catholic Year Book* of 1900, there were 41 Catholic peers, 54 Catholic baronets, and 28 knights.[109] Drawn largely from old Catholic families, this Catholic social elite was led by Henry Fitzalan-Howard, the influential 15th Duke of Norfolk, who succeeded to his title in 1860 and died in 1917. A prominent Conservative who sat in the third Salisbury government, Norfolk was renowned for his charity and his English patriotism. There was, moreover, a growing Catholic middle class of lawyers, bankers, businessmen, civil servants and doctors, who were moving into suburban villas and sending their children to boarding schools. Catholics were increasingly prominent in political and cultural life. The convert, Lord Ripon, the first Catholic to hold cabinet rank, served in the Liberal governments of 1886, 1892–95 and 1906. From 1886 to 1892, the Catholic Henry Matthews, later Lord Llandaff, was home secretary in Salisbury's Conservative government. Long before his death in 1890, John Henry Newman was recognised by Protestants as well as Catholics as a national literary treasure. His poem, 'The Dream of Gerontius' was set to music by the Catholic composer, Edward Elgar, and received its first performance in 1900; it remains the greatest British oratorio. In 1895, Lord Acton, one of the founders of the *English Historical Review*, was appointed to the regius chair of modern history at the University of Cambridge. The foremost advocate at the English bar, Sir Charles Russell, an Ulster Catholic, became lord chief justice the same year. In 1896, the Roman Catholic authorities lifted their ban (operational since 1865) on Roman Catholics attending Oxford and Cambridge Universities.

The 'Englishness' of the Catholic communion was emphasised in the appointment of Herbert Vaughan as archbishop of Westminster following Manning's death in 1892. From an old Catholic landed family, Vaughan had an aristocratic bearing that many found cold and remote. He had not been a popular choice. He had little sympathy for Irish causes and lacked both Manning's ease with working-class Catholics of Irish descent and his zeal for their interests as workers. Vaughan's was a confident, uncompromising Catholicism, with emphasis on the mission and the glory of the church. He had worked to thwart Lord Halifax's negotiations for union between the Church of England and the Roman Catholic Church, believing that Anglicans should convert to the one true church. Perhaps his greatest achievement was the imposing Westminster Cathedral in London. Planning for the building of a great cathedral 'proportionate to the chief diocese of the Catholic Church in England, and to the chief city of the British Empire' had begun in 1865. However, there had been difficulties in obtaining a suitable site and in raising funds, while Manning had not taken much interest in the project. It was Vaughan who oversaw the building of the great brick cathedral on a Byzantine basilica plan. The foundation stone was laid in 1895, money was raised from the faithful, including small donations from the very poor, and year after year the walls grew higher. Vaughan died as the shell of the building was being completed, and his funeral, in June 1903, was one of the first events held in the cathedral. It was consecrated, when the debt was cleared, in 1910.[110]

In September 1908, London hosted the Roman Catholic International Eucharistic Congress. The Eucharistic Congresses, which were large-scale celebrations of the faith, had begun in 1881 and had become annual events in 1885. The Congress of 1908 was the first to be held in an English-speaking country. Events were held in Westminster Cathedral and the Albert Hall. The culmination of the Congress was to be a great procession with the Host around the city, followed by a benediction at the Cathedral. A number of Protestant organisations, however, including the Protestant Alliance, raised a protest with the government, insisting that such a procession was illegal under the terms of the Catholic Emancipation Act of 1829.

There were threats that those carrying the Host would be physically attacked. The king made representations to the Liberal government, which at the last moment refused permission for the procession to carry the Host or for the priests to wear vestments. The church authorities were hurt, but reluctantly agreed, and the procession went forward without the Host and vestments; 150,000 Catholics were said to line the route. Although a handful of Protestant extremists tried to disrupt the procession, the event came off peacefully and was deeply moving for the faithful. It was, enthused the Catholic *Tablet*, 'the public and official return of Our Lord to England'. The Congress, meanwhile, coincided with the Vatican's decision – nearly 80 years after the passing of Catholic emancipation – that the Roman Catholic Church in England and Wales should no longer have 'missionary' status, but should now be perceived as settled and permanent.[111]

There continued to be tensions between Protestants and Catholics, and occasional sectarian violence, especially in Liverpool and Glasgow, with their large ethnic Irish populations. It is not always clear whether working-class Catholics experienced hostility because they were Catholics or because they were Irish, but for those bearing the brunt of the hostility, it did not much matter. The language of Catholics often sounded a triumphalist note, and this could exacerbate tensions. On the eve of the Eucharistic Congress of 1908, for example, the archbishop of Westminster, Francis Bourne, had referred in a pastoral letter to the parish churches of the established Church of England as 'cold and empty' and in a 'forlorn condition', waiting for a return of the true worship that had once given them life. Despite continued sectarian tensions, however, Roman Catholics were now a settled presence in Britain, taking an active role in national life, helping to shape national culture and insisting upon their full civil rights. While Catholics of Irish background generally supported Irish Home Rule, English, Welsh and Scottish Catholics were just as likely to be strong supporters of the Union.

The educational controversy

The early years of the new century also witnessed a hard-fought struggle over the place of the churches in national education. The struggle focused upon the Education Act of 1902 – a controversial piece of legislation which aimed to create a more comprehensive system of education in England and Wales, in part by giving church schools – which were overwhelmingly Anglican and Roman Catholic – financial support from the local rates. But granting rate aid to church schools aroused the fury of the

Nonconformists, and led to one of the most intense religious conflicts of the century.

To understand the early twentieth-century educational conflict, we must return to the Education Act of 1870. That Act, it will be recalled, had aimed to establish a national system of elementary education for England and Wales by providing rate-supported schools to supplement those provided by the churches. According to the Act, elected school boards were to be formed only in those areas where the church schools were inadequate for the needs of the population. The new school boards were empowered to levy local rates on property to enable them to build and maintain new schools. By the terms of the Cowper-Temple clause, moreover, the board schools were to provide a non-denominational religious instruction. The expectation was that most education would continue to be provided by the established church. The existing church-provided schools (which were overwhelmingly Anglican) continued to receive grants from the Education Department, and they were allowed to give a specific denominational and doctrinal Christian instruction. But they were also required to operate a conscience clause, by which Nonconformist children could remove themselves from the classroom during the times of religious teaching.

Anglicans had viewed the Education Act of 1870 as a measure to fill the gaps resulting from the established church's failure to provide enough schools. For Anglicans, the new board schools would provide primary education mainly for the very poor – the ragged children of dissolute parents – while Church of England schools would educate the children of the middle and respectable working classes. After 1870, Anglicans redoubled their efforts to provide additional schools for the growing population, so as to minimise the need for board schools. Between 1870 and 1880, the number of voluntary schools (of which the overwhelming majority were Church of England) increased from about 8,000 to 14,000, and the number of children attending them rose from roughly 1,200,000 to 2,000,000. The Anglican National Society spent £12.25 million in building new schools between 1870 and 1883, which was nearly as much as it had spent in the first 60 years of its existence between 1811 and 1870.[112] Meanwhile, in contrast to the expanding Anglican schools, the new school boards provided fewer than 4,000 schools by 1880, and were educating only about 750,000 children.

Initially, most Nonconformists had hotly opposed the Education Act. For them, the Act had left the Anglican schools with far too much state support. Some deeply disliked the form of non-denominational religious instruction that had to be provided in the board schools under the

Cowper-Temple clause. Leading Nonconformists, such as R. W. Dale of Birmingham, argued that it would be better to have no religious instruction at all in board schools, than to have a vague, watered-down non-denominational teaching. Although they hated the Act, however, Nonconformists decided that they would take part in the school board elections. They would work to gain control of the boards, and make the best of what they saw as a bad situation. The years after 1870 witnessed hotly contested school board elections in the towns and cities, with Nonconformist-dominated 'progressive' parties pitted against Anglican-dominated 'moderate' parties. The 'progressives' were committed to increasing public expenditure on the board schools, and expanding the range of subjects taught. The 'moderates', on the other hand, sought to limit spending on the board schools, insisting that most public education should be provided by the established Church of England.

Gradually, the Nonconformists underwent a sea-change in their attitude to the Education Act. From being its bitter opponents, they became its warm supporters. They grew to appreciate the Cowper-Temple clause, and became convinced that a non-denominational Christian religious instruction could be effective, especially in conveying to children a moral sense. Further, as the progressive parties gained control over the school boards in many towns and cities, Nonconformists found that having the power to set the local school rates at an appropriate level ensured that they would have the financial resources to provide high quality board schools – often superior in quality to their Anglican rivals. Progressive boards began erecting modern, spacious, well-ventilated and attractive school buildings. They could pay higher salaries to their teachers than the Anglican schools, which meant they could recruit the most able new teachers. They had the resources to initiate new teaching methods, develop school libraries and museums, and expand their curricula to include science, music and art. In the larger towns, school boards began establishing 'higher grade' schools, which were in effect secondary schools – despite the fact that the Act of 1870 had made no provision for secondary education. By 1895, there were 67 such higher grade schools, educating 25,000 children.[113] Some school boards also offered evening classes for young adults, including recreational classes in dancing or swimming.

Church of England schools found it increasingly difficult to compete with all this. During the later 1880s, as the school board system expanded and more people had to pay school rates, voluntary donations to the Anglican schools declined and they began to struggle. By 1890, the Church of England had been forced by financial pressure to surrender almost a thousand of its schools. In 1891, Parliament established free primary education, which it financed by providing a uniform state grant to all schools (based on the number of pupils) that would replace the fees. The state grant, however, did not fully cover the cost of educating a child. The board schools could readily meet the deficit from the rates, but the denominational schools could not, and their financial difficulties worsened. Anglicans increasingly complained of the 'intolerable strains' of having to pay to support their church schools while at the same time paying rates to support the rival board schools.[114] While the latter drew from the seemingly inexhaustible rates, the Anglican schools had only limited funds, and this led to inferior facilities, especially for teaching science and technology. 'Through no fault of her own', complained one clergyman in 1893, 'the Church is compelled to ask . . . about every improvement in the way of "plant", not "Is it wise?" but always "Can I afford it?"'.[115] By the 1890s, the number of children attending board schools was growing steadily. In 1895, a total of 1,848,000 children attended board schools, as compared to 2,446,000 in voluntary schools (including some 2,000,000 in Church of England schools). During the previous five years, the number of children in the board schools had increased by 422,000, while the number in the Anglican or voluntary schools had grown by only 185,000. The growth of board schools was most pronounced in the cities. In London, 513,000 children attended board schools by 1898, while only 224,000 attended Anglican or voluntary schools.[116]

Within the Conservative party, many grew convinced that fresh legislation was needed to help the Anglican and other denominational schools. Some supported the denominational schools because they provided a sound doctrinal Christian education, regarded as superior to the vague non-denominational religious instruction taught in the board schools. Some believed that it was right and proper that the established Church of England should continue to educate most English and Welsh children in shared religious and moral values. Some felt that it was a matter of fairness that the denominational schools, with their dedicated, hard-working teachers, should receive the same level of support as the board schools. Others, pragmatically, recognised that the Anglican and Roman Catholic schools continued to educate over half of the children of England and Wales. So long as large numbers of parents chose to send their children to denominational schools, it was vital to ensure that those institutions had the resources they required. Leaving the denominational schools starved of resources, especially for the teaching of science and technology, would mean that the children they taught would not be adequately prepared for modern life. There was a growing awareness that modern industry, modern armies, and modern navies rested on scientific and technological education, and that well-taught children were vital to the security, prosperity and 'national efficiency' of the United Kingdom.

In March 1902, the Conservative government introduced a bill for improving the schools in England and Wales. It was a bold and far-reaching measure which aimed at creating a comprehensive system of elementary and secondary schools, and also at providing additional resources to the hard-pressed denominational schools. The proposals to strengthen denominational education aroused intense opposition from Nonconformists, Radicals and many Liberals, and the bill's passage through Parliament was hard-fought – occupying 57 days of debate (as compared with only 22 days for the passage of the Education Act of 1870).[117] But the Conservative majority in Parliament prevailed and in December 1902 the new Education Act received the royal assent. The Act had two main provisions. First, it abolished the school boards and placed education (both elementary and secondary education) under the authority of the county councils and county borough councils. These were elected local government bodies that Parliament had created in 1888, and they were now to create local educational authorities with broad powers. Second, the Act brought the denominational schools (Anglican, Roman Catholic and Jewish) under the authority of the Local Educational Authorities, and made it compulsory for the councils to support the denominational schools – including the payment of teachers' salaries and operating costs – from the local rates. The Anglican, Roman Catholic and Jewish schools could continue to offer a doctrinal religious instruction. If they did so, Nonconformist children attending the school would be allowed, as in the past, to withdraw at the times of denominational teaching.

Anglicans, Roman Catholics and Jews were broadly content with the Act, which for the first time provided their schools with much needed support from the rates.[118] Nonconformists, however, were outraged. For them, to grant the schools of the established Church of England support from the rates was a retrograde step, a move towards reviving the authoritarian religious establishment of the past. It threatened to undo the nineteenth-century progress towards religious liberty and equality. The established Church of England, they feared, would now gain the financial resources needed to expand its schools across the country and to impose its beliefs upon more and more Nonconformist children. Anglo-Catholics would be enabled to spread their ritualist and Romanising doctrines among vulnerable young people. Rate support for Anglican schools,

Nonconformists further argued, was simply a new version of the church rate, which had been abolished after a prolonged struggle in 1868. Once again, Nonconformists would have to pay rates to support the work of an established church that they conscientiously opposed. They were especially concerned about the approximately 8,000 rural parishes in which there was only a single Anglican school, which Nonconformist children had to attend as there was no alternative nearby. Their children, they claimed, were uncomfortable about withdrawing themselves from religious instruction, which left them feeling odd and marginalised. Now, with rate support, these rural Anglican schools would be strengthened in the work of indoctrinating Nonconformist children. In such rural parishes, David Lloyd George observed, 'the clergyman would come down to the school like a roaring lion, seeking what little Nonconformists he could devour at the expense of the ratepayer'.[119] Nonconformists also objected to providing compulsory rate support for schools of the Roman Catholic Church, which some viewed as nothing less than the antichrist.

The Nonconformists mounted a massive national agitation against the Education Bill. Their newspapers and journals, especially the influential *British Weekly*, encouraged a public outcry. Meetings and demonstrations were held across the country, and gathered tens of thousands of demonstrators. It was a crusade for 'national righteousness', and the education question became connected with Nonconformist fury against Anglican ritualists and Roman Catholics. The veteran London Baptist minister, Dr John Clifford – his famous red beard now turned grey but his energy undiminished – took the lead in this national agitation, coining the phrase 'Rome on the rates' to condemn rate support for Roman Catholic schools, and rousing crowds with fiery appeals to the memory of Cromwell and Puritan righteousness.[120] Lloyd George denounced the Bill with passionate eloquence at public rallies and in the Commons. In September 1902, a great rally was held in Leeds, with an estimated 70,000 gathering on Woodhouse Moor to hear speeches delivered from six platforms. A huge procession and rally was held in November in London, with nearly 20,000 packing the building and terrace of the Alexandra Palace.[121]

The passing of the Education Act in December 1902 did not diminish the agitation, but only gave it new directions. 'The Education Bill is now numbered among the laws of the land', wrote the leading Congregationalist, A. M. Fairbairn, 'but whatever may be its fate as a law, it is certain that its enactment means the beginning rather than the end of controversy'.[122] And so it proved. Nonconformists now organised a campaign for the non-payment of rates. A National Passive Resistance

Committee, chaired by Clifford, was formed to co-ordinate the campaign, while local passive resistance committees – eventually as many as 648 of them – were created around the country. A new magazine, *The Crusader*, was founded to publicise the campaign, while the *British Weekly* also provided vigorous support.[123] The Education Act went into effect in April 1903, and the Nonconformist revolt then began in earnest. When a passive resister refused to pay their rate, the legal authorities could distrain (or seize) their personal goods in the amount of the unpaid rate, and auction them off. If the person resisted the distraint of their goods, they could be imprisoned. By November 1904, there had been 33,678 summonses for non-payment of rates and 1,392 auctions of distrained goods, while 53 resisters had been imprisoned. By March 1906, this had increased to 70,880 summonses, 2,568 auctions, and 176 imprisonments.[124]

In Wales, Lloyd George organised another form of protest. Here, where Nonconformists formed the overwhelming majority of the population and controlled the county councils, he encouraged the local education authorities 'to take possession of the enemy's cannons, and turn his own guns against him'. That is, they were to use local democracy to thwart the will of Parliament. Lloyd George advised the county councils to interpret the Education Act as rigidly as possible, and to find any possible excuse to refuse to share the rates with the Anglican schools. The result was strife across Wales, and the thwarting of the Act. Parliament responded in August 1904 by passing a new act empowering the Education Department to seize control of the rates from rebellious county councils and enforce the Education Act. But the Welsh county councils resisted, the education rebellion continued – and the growing public anger also contributed to a revival of calls for the disestablishment of the Anglican Church in Wales.[125]

The Welsh revival of 1904–05

Amid all this strife, meanwhile, a very different religious movement emerged in the troubled valleys of rural Wales. This was the great Welsh revival.[126] Initially, the revival was largely a reaction to the education struggle and to the increasing permeation of Wales by the influences of sport, science, modern psychology, 'promiscuous' literature, socialism and labour unrest. However, it became a powerful movement in its own right, renewing belief in the spirit gifts and physical manifestations, and spreading far beyond Wales.

Revival activity began in New Quay, in rural Cardiganshire, near the end of 1903, when chapelgoers, distressed by the ferment over education and the influences of modern culture, began holding evening prayer meetings. These meetings grew steadily longer and more intense, and then took unexpected directions, becoming punctuated with passionate personal confessions, prostrations, uncontrollable weeping, crying out, and dramatic conversions. The movement then spread across South Wales, assisted by young male and female lay converts. By the end of 1904, local revivals also began breaking out in North Wales. The revival was a genuinely popular movement, one that seems to have emerged spontaneously among the laity. Thousands of meetings, often lengthy and emotion-charged, were held across Wales.

In late September 1904, the movement gained a powerful leader in the form of a young Welsh-speaking, working-class candidate for the Calvinistic Methodist ministry, Evan Roberts. Born in rural Glamorgan in 1878, the son of a coal miner, Roberts had worked as a miner from 1890 to 1902 and then as an apprentice blacksmith before deciding to prepare for the ministry. He had just begun his training, when he was caught up in the movement. Although possessing only a primary school education, Roberts proved a compelling lay preacher, who exuded an absolute conviction of the presence of the Holy Spirit and exercised an almost hypnotic effect on his hearers. His meetings, which would sometimes continue for ten hours or more, were characterised by fearful depictions of lost souls and impending judgement, a compelling aura of spiritual power, and intense appeals to sinners to come forward before it was too late. He would walk up and down the aisles, exhorting individuals; sometimes he would stop the meeting, claiming that the unfaithfulness of some unnamed individual was blocking the work of the Spirit; he would only resume when that individual had openly or secretly repented. The long pauses on such occasions could be frightening, and individuals would cry out for the secret sinner to repent. He travelled with a group of devoted young women. Some believed that he possessed 'occult' powers to see into souls, and they spoke of his penetrating eyes, hypnotic presence and 'telepathic' gifts.

During 1905, the movement spread beyond Wales, initially among the Welsh migrants in Liverpool, but then across much of England and Scotland. In England, the revival movement was taken forward by two professional American revivalists in the Moody and Sankey mould – Reuben Torrey, who preached, and 'Charlie' Alexander, who 'sang' the gospel. Their mission between February and June 1905 in London's Albert Hall comprised 202 meetings, brought in 1,114,650 attendances, and claimed over 17,000 converts.[127] The English revival meetings were often similar to those in Wales, with prostrations, uncontrollable weeping and outcries, trances, and other physical manifestations. In Wigan, there were meetings of 5,000 people and reports of the revival spreading 'like a raging fire', while Methodists described Hull as a 'furnace of revival'.[128] In 1905, at the Keswick Convention, 300 Welsh delegates conducted an all-night prayer meeting that had a profound impact on British evangelicalism. Evan Roberts prophesied that the revival would win 100,000 converts. Many more than this professed to be saved. The revival made its way to India, spreading initially among Welsh missionaries and local people in the northeast. On the subcontinent, the revival was characterised by both heightened emotion and the gifts of the Holy Spirit, including faith healing, speaking in tongues, and prophecy. It contributed significantly to a new world-wide movement of spiritual renewal, termed the Pentecostal movement, which proclaimed a belief in the return of the Spirit gifts and which remains one of the largest movements in contemporary world Christianity.[129]

In Wales, the revival movement drew to a close in early 1906. The excitement drained away and attendance at the meetings dwindled. Evan Roberts was emotionally and physically exhausted, and he withdrew from public life altogether in 1906. During the revival, the combined membership of the Congregationalists, Baptists and Calvinistic Methodists in Wales rose from 429,486 to 509,269, or an increase of 18.6 per cent. While many of these fell away, others remained, and church membership in Wales was 10 per cent higher in 1912 than in 1903.[130]

The general election of 1906 and the Liberal Education Bill

In December 1905, the Conservative government resigned, after over a decade in power, and the Liberals under Sir Henry Campbell-Bannerman formed a government and promptly called a general election. The country went to the polls in January 1906. British Nonconformists, many of them reinvigorated by the revival, were mobilised for this election as perhaps never before in their history. They were determined to secure an overwhelming Liberal majority that would snuff out forever the hated Education Act of 1902. The National Council of Free Churches, which had been formed in 1897, now organised conferences and demonstrations through its 51 district federations and 900 local councils.[131] Wealthy Nonconformists, among them George Cadbury, the Quaker cocoa manufacturer, and William Hartley, the Primitive Methodist jam manufacturer, contributed generously to the campaign chests of Liberal candidates. The Nonconformists played a major role in what proved a landslide victory for the Liberals in 1906. Between 180 and 200 Nonconformists, nearly all Liberals, were elected to the House of Commons, a record number.[132] Many of these, to be sure, were not regular churchgoers, but even those who had lapsed found it useful during the election to parade their Nonconformist credentials. 'We have been put into power by the Nonconformists', acknowledged the new Liberal prime minister, Henry Campbell-Bannerman.[133] The election indeed seemed a triumph for Nonconformity, reminiscent for some of the days of Cromwell. 'I suppose', Balfour observed in May 1906, 'that this is the first time in the history of our country since the Commonwealth when the great Nonconformist party . . . are, or conceive themselves to be, supreme'.[134]

With their huge majority in the Commons, and with the Nonconformists demanding action, the Liberal government immediately took up the education question. The Liberal minister for education was Augustine Birrell, the son of a Baptist minister. The Nonconformists, he later recalled, were ecstatic: 'They had done their "bit" on the platforms and at the Polls; and now all that remained was for the new [minister], a dark horse but of godly parentage, to buckle on his armour and produce . . . a Bill as great as the Victory!'[135] Birrell quickly drafted the government's Education Bill, and in April 1906, he introduced it in the Commons. He was no Cromwell and his Bill was not really 'as great as the Victory'; rather it was a cautious measure, which he hoped would secure a broad consensus among moderate Anglicans and Nonconformists. Its main provision was to bring all schools, the former board schools and the former denominational schools, under full public control by the local education authorities. Most of the publicly controlled schools would provide non-denominational religious instruction. However, by clause four, the Bill permitted certain urban schools, where four-fifths of the parents were of the same religious faith, to provide denominational religious instruction. This clause was mainly meant to protect Roman Catholic and Jewish schools, though it would have protected many Anglican schools as well. Birrell's Bill proved far too moderate for many of the government's Nonconformist supporters, including the Free Church Council, which demanded the withdrawal of the clause. Most Nonconformists, however, acquiesced over clause four, and the Bill passed through the House of Commons with a substantial majority.

The Bill went to the House of Lords, where the large Conservative and Anglican majority, led by the archbishop of Canterbury, proceeded to mutilate it with amendments aimed at enhancing public provision for Anglican schools. When the amended Bill came back to the Commons, it was unrecognisable. Birrell described his child as 'a miserable, mangled, tortured, twisted, tertium quid', and the Commons voted overwhelmingly to reject the Lords' amendments.[136] In the ensuing negotiations between the two Houses, the Commons proved ready to compromise, but the House of Lords refused to budge. The Lords' behaviour was irresponsible; they flouted political convention and thwarted a Commons bill that had a clear electoral mandate behind it. An outraged Liberal government threatened to call another general election. But the Conservatives knew the government would not do so. For while a vocal Nonconformist core supported the Bill, the larger British public was growing bored with it and indeed with the years of sectarian bickering over education. 'Who can doubt', Campbell-Bannerman asked the House of Commons on 20 December, 'that a sense of weariness, and nausea, and a dislike of clerical and sectarian squabbles have spread from one end of the country to the other?'[137] In truth, the passions of the Nonconformist crusade against the Education Act of 1902 could not be sustained amid the complexities of trying to draft a new Education Bill and steer it through Parliament. The government dropped the Bill.

The government brought forward two further Education Bills for England and Wales in 1908, but withdrew them both, and the Liberal pledge to replace the Education Act of 1902 ended in ignoble failure. Nonconformists were deeply disappointed. But they now learned that their 'triumph' in the election of 1906 had been more apparent than real. While their crusade over education had undoubtedly swelled the size of the Liberal victory in 1906, there had been other factors behind the electoral result, including opposition to Conservative proposals for tariff reform. In truth, many Liberals simply did not share the Nonconformists' obsession with education. Moreover, for a large portion of the population, especially the working classes, the educational question could appear as a squabble between middle-class churchmen and Nonconformists over social status. There were, many believed, far more pressing problems – poverty, malnutrition, atrocious housing, labour unrest and unsafe working conditions – needing to be addressed. Significantly, the general election of 1906 had been a breakthrough for the new Labour party, which won 29 parliamentary seats and emerged for the first time as a serious political force. Labour politicians had little patience with the educational squabbles between church and Nonconformity, and began calling for a strictly secular system of education – with no religious instruction, nondenominational or otherwise. 'The bulk of the working class', asserted the Labour MP, Keir Hardie, in early 1907, 'were indifferent on the subject of religious instruction, because they saw what little good had come to the country from the religious instruction of church and chapel alike'.[138] The election of 1906 had been seen as a Nonconformist triumph. But the failure of the Education Bill of 1906 indicated that the crusading 'Nonconformist conscience' was becoming less effective in the emerging democratic politics. It was not that Anglicanism was victorious; more and more of its schools would fail and be brought under the state system. It was rather that the old political conflicts between the established church and Nonconformists were becoming less important. After 1906, as John Glaser has observed, 'for religious people, the vital issue was not church vs. chapel, but Christianity vs. unbelief'.[139]

Nonconformity did achieve one major victory after 1906. This was the disestablishment of the Anglican Church in Wales. Most Welsh Nonconformists, as we have seen, had embraced disestablishment by the 1870s, and the cause was also taken up by Welsh nationalists in the late 1880s. In the 1906 election, the Liberals won every Welsh parliamentary seat, and Nonconformists and nationalists now looked to the Liberal government to bring forward a disestablishment measure. The government first appointed a Royal Commission to investigate religious life in Wales. It reported in 1910, and in 1912 the government brought forward its Bill. However, Wales was now being shaken by strikes and labour unrest, and there proved to be little enthusiasm for the old cause of the chapels. The advocates of disestablishment, to be sure, tried to arouse public fervour. But most people believed their country had other, far more pressing needs, especially concerning the rights of labour and social reform. The local opposition to the Education Act of 1902 had by now died down, and the established church in Wales was no longer viewed as a threat. In truth, it had been quietly gaining support in much of the country, and was pursuing a socially-engaged ministry, with particular success among the working classes in industrial South Wales. The old arguments about it being a 'foreign weed', or the church of the wealthy landowners, no longer rang true. Some suspected that taking away much of its property would only weaken its home mission, and contribute further to the drift of the working classes away from Christianity.

None the less, the Liberals were pledged and the Act disestablishing the church in Wales was duly passed in September 1914. By then Britain had entered the Great War, and the operation of the Act was suspended for its duration – finally going into effect in 1920. The Act ended the connection of church and state in Wales. The original Act of 1914 would have also deprived the Welsh church of £102,000 in annual income. This was reduced by an amending Act in 1919 to £48,000 of annual income, which was still a significant loss.[140] But disestablishment did not revive the fortunes of Welsh Nonconformity, and the victory seemed hollow.

Social legislation and labour unrest

While middle-class Nonconformists were largely disappointed with the Liberal government, many labouring men and women were not. For if the Liberal majority in Parliament after 1906 did little for the old cause of 'religious equality', it did enact a remarkable programme of social legislation, aimed at improving the quality of life for working people, and diminishing the effects of illness, accidents, unemployment and old age. The Liberal social programme was motivated by a number of factors. There was a humanitarian commitment to improving conditions for the most vulnerable members of society. There was recognition that a large percentage of working men now had the vote, and that social legislation would be a way to win their support. Above all, there was an understanding that it was vital for the defence of the nation and empire to have a healthy, educated population. 'In the great cities', the Liberal Lord Rosebery famously observed in 1900, 'in the rookeries and slums which still survive, an imperial race cannot be reared'.[141] Within the Liberal party, there was a growing body of 'New Liberals', men and women who had been influenced by the social idealism of T. H. Green, and notions of 'national efficiency', and who had come to believe the state should intervene in the economy to ensure a decent standard of living for all citizens.

The government's social reforms began in 1906, when it secured an act authorising schools to provide hot lunches for schoolchildren. This was followed by acts providing regular medical examinations for children and the establishment of school clinics. In 1908, the government secured legislation to restrict the working day for miners to eight hours, and to establish the first old-age pension scheme. In 1909, Parliament established a national network of labour exchanges, to assist the unemployed in finding work, and it passed the Trade Boards Act, which set up procedures for regulating wages and hours in tailoring, lace-making, and other sweated trades. To pay for the social programmes, David Lloyd George, now chancellor of the exchequer, brought forward in 1909 his ambitious 'people's budget', with proposals for greatly increased taxation on incomes, land and inherited property. It was, Lloyd George insisted, 'a war

Budget. It is for raising money to raise implacable warfare against poverty and squalidness'.[142] Viewing the budget as a radical assault on property, the House of Lords rejected it – which sparked a constitutional crisis and a hard-fought battle that culminated in the Parliament Act of 1911. This Act enabled the Commons to pass legislation over the Lords' veto, marking a major advance towards full political democracy and opening the way to further social legislation. In 1911, Parliament passed the National Insurance Act, providing a comprehensive package of old age, health, accident and unemployment insurance for millions of working people.

Despite these achievements in social legislation, the period after 1910 was also one of bitter industrial strife. The economy was proving erratic, as the United Kingdom faced increasing overseas industrial and commercial competition. Periodic recessions threw large numbers out of work, and mass unemployment became a pressing issue. Many employers sought to compete in the global economy by reducing wages. Trade unions responded with widespread industrial strikes after 1910, which further weakened the economy and led to violent clashes between strikers and police, with a number of deaths. Within the larger socialist movement, Syndicalists dreamt of uniting all the trade unions and organising a general strike that would bring the capitalist order crashing down. Other socialists called for open class war to achieve the ideal workers' state.

Social Christianity in the Church of England

The Church of England was broadly supportive of the Liberal government's social reform programme. There was a growing consensus among church leaders that it was morally right for the state to intervene in the economy in order to protect vulnerable members of society and promote greater social equality. What had been the views of a small 'Christian socialist' minority within the church in the 1880s and early 1890s were, by 1906, becoming more widespread, especially among high Anglicans. The church, or at least its more vocal clergy, seemed to move steadily leftwards. In 1905, Randall Davidson, the archbishop of Canterbury, appointed a committee of Convocation, under the chairmanship of Bishop Charles Gore, to consider the 'Moral Witness of the Church on Economic subjects'. The committee's report was presented to Convocation in 1907. It was decidedly Christian socialist in tone, appealing to the communal ethics of the Old Testament prophets and the early church, insisting that the Christian ethic is essentially social in nature, and condemning much of the existing industrial system as dehumanising and unchristian. Convocation adopted the report, and then called on each diocese to appoint a standing Social Service Committee to promote the local study of social questions. More and more Church of England clergy were coming to accept the maxim, put forward by the Leicester Anglican clergyman, F. L. Donaldson, that 'Christianity is the religion of which socialism is the practice.'[143] Few, it seemed, now subscribed to the teachings of Christian political economy with their notion that the economic laws were ordained for the good of humanity by a benevolent God. Addressing the Pan-Anglican Congress in 1908, the high church Lord William Cecil confessed that he felt 'almost out of place in speaking as a person with no belief in socialism'. The Congress was described as a 'socialist field day', in which speaker after speaker condemned industrial capitalism, with its divisiveness, inequality and widespread poverty.[144]

A major force behind this growing Christian socialist consensus within the church was the Christian Social Union. This organisation, it will be recalled, had been formed by a group of Oxford-based academics and clergy in 1889, and it had then grown steadily, mainly in London and the south of the country. In 1897, there were 27 branches and a total membership of 2,600. By 1910, this had increased to nearly 50 branches and a membership of over 6,000. The Christian Social Union has been described as 'a form of "socialism" for bishops'.[145] Of 53 appointments to bishoprics in the Church of England between 1889 and 1913, there were 19 that went to Union members.[146] The Union disseminated a moderate Christian socialism through its journals – the *Economic Review*, *Commonwealth*, and *Goodwill* – and through meetings, conferences, lectures, sermons, pamphlets and reports. The strength of the Christian Social Union was its broad base, its theological learning, its respectability, and its moderation. It managed to recruit members who would not have dreamed of joining a socialist organisation, and membership of the Union did no harm to one's career prospects.

However, the Union's moderation was also a weakness. There was, insisted some critics, too much emphasis on talk, and not enough action. One Union branch was reported approvingly in an official publication as 'vigorously pursuing a policy of discussion'.[147] When a young Union member, William Temple, sought in 1912 to describe the kingdom of God, it looked remarkably like the New Liberal ideal for a moderate social welfare state.[148] Despite some sporadic efforts, the Union failed to recruit working-class members, while its leaders were drawn from the privileged, upper-middle class. Nor could the Union agree on any clear programme of political action. For G. K. Chesterton, who was for a time a member of the

Union, its well-intentioned moderation could appear ridiculous – as he conveyed in some doggerel describing a meeting in Nottingham:

> The Christian Social Union here
> Was very much annoyed;
> It seems there is some duty
> Which we never should avoid,
> And so they sing a lot of hymns
> To help the Unemployed.[149]

By the mid-1890s, the Christian Social Union had become divided into two factions – the 'respectables', who advocated gradual, piecemeal and moderate reforms, and the 'extremists', who pressed for radical socialism. The extremists included F. L. Donaldson, who in 1905 led a march of 440 unemployed men from Leicester to London: an estimated 100,000 turned out to see the marchers off. In 1908, the extremists submitted a manifesto declaring that in their view Christian socialism meant the common owner-ship of the means of production, distribution and exchange, and was not simply a vague expression of fellowship. Many members found the manifesto too extreme, and a schism in the organisation was only narrowly averted. Two years later, its most prominent member, Charles Gore, now bishop of Birmingham, resigned from the Union, which soon went into decline.[150]

The Church Socialist League and guild socialism

In 1906, some of those disappointed with the moderatism of the Christian Social Union formed a new, more radical movement, the Church Socialist League. The League was from the beginning a decidedly socialist organisa-tion, dominated by clergy and laity from the industrial north of England. Its stated goal was 'the political, economic, and social emancipation of the whole people, men and women, by the establishment of a democratic com-monwealth in which the community shall own the land and capital collec-tively and use them co-operatively for the good of all'.[151] Many members of Stewart Headlam's Guild of St Matthew now joined the new body, prompting Headlam to see the inevitable and bring the Guild to an end.

A leading figure within the new League was Conrad Noel (1869–1942), a tall, lanky Anglo-Catholic and socialist. The son of a prominent poet and the grandson of the earl of Gainsborough, Noel attended public schools and then studied briefly at Cambridge University. He was drawn to Anglo-Catholicism in part through his reading of the Church Fathers, who attracted him with their stern condemnations of the oppression of the poor. He trained for the Anglican priesthood and, following ordination, held several curacies, including work in the slums of Salford and Newcastle. In the latter, he preached passionately against the South African War, arousing the wrath of the local munitions workers, who threatened to blow up the church. His parish priest was the Christian socialist W. E. Moll, who told him to persevere. 'My dear Noel', Moll reportedly said of his anti-war preaching, 'by all means let it go on, as it is the truth; and if we lose our church, which is the ugliest structure in Newcastle, we can build a new one with the insurance money'.[152] Large-minded and eccentric, Noel enjoyed defying convention, not least in his clothing. 'He took great pleasure', his friend G. K. Chesterton recalled, 'in appearing in correct clerical clothes, surmounted with a sort of hairy or furry cap, making him look like an aesthetic rat-catcher'.[153] In 1910, Noel received the living of Thaxted in Essex – having been presented by its patron, the aristocratic Christian socialist and League member, Lady Warwick. Here he stayed for the remaining 32 years of his life, transforming Thaxted into a centre for Anglo-Catholic socialism, Morris dancing and much else besides.

Noel became organising secretary of the Church Socialist League and under his energetic lead, it expanded its national influence. By 1909 there were 1,000 active members and 25 branches, including branches in London and the South. In 1912, a significant section of the Church Socialist League embraced the teachings of guild socialism, as these were being formulated by the Anglo-Catholic political theorist and theologian, John Neville Figgis, the Anglican architect and social theorist, Arthur Joseph Penty, and the socialist politician and former Quaker, S. G. Hobson.[154] Guild socialism was rooted in the social ideals of Thomas Carlyle, John Ruskin, and William Morris, with their celebration of medievalism, community and handicraft traditions. Guild socialists proposed to reorganise much of the nation's industrial activity around revived craft guilds, in which artists, craftsmen and workers engaged in similar forms of production would be united in associations under their own leadership, making decisions in common and sharing equally the fruits of their labour. In such associations, relationships would become more personal and labourers would find satisfaction and a sense of fulfilment by practising craft skills. Guild socialists envisioned a new society made up of a plurality of close-knit associations – not only craft guilds, but families, churches, universities, boroughs, cultural societies, consumers' co-operatives, rural communes, and so forth. Their movement had connections with other efforts to revive a communal style of living – such as those of the former Church of England curate, socialist author, and campaigner for homosexual rights, Edward Carpenter, who led a movement for a return to the land, a simple style of living, and the wearing of traditional peasant dress and sandals. The guild socialist ideal was adopted by the League's main publication, the *Church Socialist*, in 1912, and was publicised by the League as an alternative to both a dehumanising large-scale industrial capitalism, and the prospect of an equally dehumanising large-scale state socialism.

Through such movements as the Church Socialist League, guild social-ism and Christian socialism, early twentieth-century radical Anglican social theorists were adapting their Christian message to the needs of a more pluralistic society. They were formulating ideals for a society that was beginning to appear post-Christian, or at any rate turning away from the institutional churches. Such radical Christian socialists as Conrad Noel or Lady Warwick seemed to relish challenging authority and con-vention. Many were, to be sure, part of England's governing elite, and this gave them the confidence to be rebels. That said, they did sincerely reach out to socialist and non-Christian movements and seek to identify the church with all those who worked for a better society. Radical Anglican thinkers were co-operating on an intellectual level with New Liberals, Fabian socialists and Labour theorists, and helping to preserve some Christian social influence in an era of emerging social welfare politics and mass democracy. None the less, it also must be noted that the social pronouncements of the Church of England, and indeed all the churches, were becoming less important after 1909, as Parliament took the initiative in social welfare provision. Not all Anglicans, moreover, subscribed to the Christian socialist message. Anglican conservatives such as Hensley Henson directed scorn at what they viewed as muddled Christian socialist thinking, and argued that the clergy should cease meddling in matters of social and economic policy which they did not really understand.

Social Christianity and Scottish Presbyterian reunion

In Scotland, it will be recalled, all three of the major Presbyterian denom-inations had embraced social reform commitments in the 1880s, which grew more urgent in the new century. Scotland's industrial heartland, with shipbuilding and heavy engineering firms along the Clyde, was especially vulnerable to world economic fluctuations, which could throw thousands out of work. Glasgow's housing remained among the worst in Europe. The Clydeside became home to a radical labour movement, with calls for class war and dreams of socialist revolution.

Scottish Presbyterians, who continued to represent the overwhelming majority of Scotland's churchgoing population, struggled to develop strategies and programmes for addressing the social misery and unrest, and for reaching the growing numbers with no church affiliation. In 1901, a Church of Scotland minister in Glasgow, David Watson, played a leading role in founding a Scottish Christian Social Union, modelled on the Anglican Christian Social Union. It hosted meetings and sponsored reports, giving particular emphasis to child welfare in the cities. Between 1899 and 1907, the Church of Scotland hosted four national church congresses on social conditions. In 1904, the General Assembly established a standing committee on social work. There was a broad consensus that the social gospel was vital to the work of the church. For the Highland Church of Scotland minister, Malcolm MacCallum, speaking in the summer of 1914, 'the main function of the Church, the Body of Believers in Christ, is to inspire and direct political action towards the eradication of social injustice'.[155]

It is not clear that these Scottish Presbyterian social reform initiatives had much impact on the country's grave social problems. They did, however, become associated with a major ecclesiastical movement – that for reuniting the branches of Scottish Presbyterianism.[156] A renewed movement for Presbyterian reunion began during the 1890s, in part as a result of growing public weariness with the old denominational conflicts. Although the Scottish Liberal Association remained officially committed to disestablishment, and there were periodic disestablishment motions in Parliament, there was no longer much popular interest. By the 1890s, few Scots viewed the established Church of Scotland as a threat to religious liberty or equality. If asked to identify the major problem with Presbyterian religion in Scotland, probably most would have pointed to the divisions between the denominations. Many Scots were becoming hard-pressed to understand the reasons for the existence of separate Presbyterian denominations that shared the same theology, liturgy and ecclesiastical organisation.

In 1895, the two main non-established Scottish Presbyterian churches – the Free Church and the United Presbyterian Church – entered into formal union negotiations. The initiative came largely from the venerable Free Church leader, Robert Rainy, and the negotiations quickly led to a corporate union of the two denominations in 1900. The united body was called the United Free Church, and its formation was widely viewed as marking a new beginning for Scotland's troubled religious life. The union was marked by a great ceremony in the Waverley Market of Edinburgh, where a large temporary hall was erected, its galleries bedecked with Covenanting flags and other symbols from the history of Scotland's national church. Some 7,000 people packed into the hall, and Rainy, the man of the hour, was elected as the first moderator of the General Assembly.[157] There was, however, a shadow over the celebrations. A small, conservative minority of the Free Church, based mainly in the Highlands, decided not to join the United Free Church. Dubbed the 'Wee Frees' by the newspapers, the minority raised a legal action in the civil courts, claiming the whole property of the former Free Church. It all seemed ridiculous to the British press, but these stalwart Calvinists were in deadly earnest. They based their claim on the law of trusts, arguing that the majority of the Free Church had given up vital principles by entering into the union of 1900, and that they alone now represented the original principles of the Free Church as it had been created at the Disruption of 1843. The case was eventually appealed to the House of Lords, which in 1904 found in favour of the 'Wee Frees', awarding their 30 small congregations all the former Free Church property, including over 700 church buildings. Some dark months followed for the United Free Church, as many congregations were forced to vacate their churches and many ministers' families had to leave their homes. Then in 1905, Parliament intervened, passing an act that provided for a more equitable distribution of the property. The pressures took their toll on Rainy's health, and he died in 1906, removing the leading light of Presbyterian liberalism in Scotland.

The events of 1904–05 did two things. First, they demonstrated that no church, whether non-established or established, was free from a degree of state control. The non-established status of the United Free Church had spared it neither the loss of its property by the House of Lords decision, nor the need to appeal to Parliament for redress. Second, the events led to friendly relations between the newly formed United Free Church and the established Church of Scotland. The latter might have sat back and gloated over the misfortunes of the United Free Church, made up, as it was, of denominations that had been its most bitter opponents. But instead, the Church of Scotland General Assembly had conveyed expressions of sympathy and support, and congregations had shared their buildings with dispossessed United Free congregations. The result was a further union initiative. In 1906, leaders of the United Free Church made approaches to the Church of Scotland for union discussions, and these approaches were welcomed. There were, it is true, deep divisions between the two bodies over the question of establishment. However, there was also a new desire for unity, including a belief that union would strengthen Scottish Presbyterianism in confronting the country's pressing social problems and reaching out to its unchurched masses. 'There had been', observed the convener of the Church of Scotland committee on reunion to the General Assembly in 1908, 'a great awakening of conscience in their own Church, and in all Churches, with reference to these gigantic evils, social, moral and religious, which confronted them during these opening years of the twentieth century'. The Scottish people, he insisted, would be 'grievously disappointed' if the churches did not embrace this opportunity for union.[158]

In 1909, each church appointed a negotiating committee of 100 members, and in November 1909, the two committees held their first joint conference in Edinburgh. By 1912, they had drafted a Memorandum of Agreement, according to which the united church would be 'national' and 'spiritually independent' – that is, it would seek to provide religious observances for the whole Scottish population, and it would be independent from state control in matters of doctrine and discipline. By now, the prospect of church reunion was exciting great hopes among Scottish Presbyterians. Many believed that a reunited national Church of Scotland would lead a spiritual and moral renewal of the Scottish people. Church reunion would heal the wounds of the Disruption of 1843, and direct the energies of Presbyterians away from the conflict over disestablishment to the great work of social reconstruction. 'A reunited Church of Scotland', proclaimed George Reith in his opening address as Moderator of the United Free Church General Assembly of May 1914, 'should present itself in the eyes of their fellow countrymen as one concentrated force, bent, in Christ's name, on grappling with and ending the social sores from which our beloved land had suffered'.[159] And it might do more. Many Scots hoped that their proposed church union might serve as an example to other churches throughout the world, and be a major step towards the reunion of the broken and bleeding body of Christ.

Overseas missions and the empire

The years between 1890 and 1914 were the high point of the British overseas mission movement. Despite the waning social and political influence of the British churches at home, large numbers of British Christians thrilled, as perhaps never before, to the work of spreading Christianity to the larger world, and especially to that part coloured an imperial red on the maps. It was a time when church hall presentations about missionaries and missions, often illustrated by projected photographic slides on screens, 'became the rage'.[160] Missionary exploits and heroism were also recounted in religious magazines, biographies, reports, Sunday school textbooks, and story-books. Christian hearts at home were warmed by the accounts of missionary schools and medical stations, by stories of the courage and faithfulness of Asian and African converts, and by the testimony of missionary martyrs. British Christians believed that they were under a divine command not only to carry the gospel to all people, but also to bring them the benefits of Western education, medicine and scientific agriculture. They raised money to maintain and supply a growing army of overseas missionaries. In 1899, British churches and mission societies were supporting some 10,000 overseas missionaries. There were, as Andrew Porter has noted, half as many missionaries as there were ordained Anglican clergy in England and Wales, while annually British missionary societies spent as much as the entire cost of civil service salaries in the United Kingdom.[161] In 1908, Britain's financial contributions represented approximately 40 per cent of the world's total expenditure on Protestant missionary work.[162]

The late nineteenth- and early twentieth-century overseas missions were varied in their character. There was the traditional missionary work of establishing new churches. There were medical missions, in some cases simply a travelling doctor or nurse with a dispensary for medicines, but also larger, well-staffed hospitals in larger towns and cities. There were orphanages, hostels and colonies for victims of leprosy. Missionaries were active in education, establishing thousands of primary schools for boys and girls across Asia and Africa, as well as high schools and colleges. The colleges were often of a high quality and played a leading role in educating future African and Asian leaders. Larger missions maintained teams of local translators, and printing presses for the production of Bibles and tracts. They promoted science, technology, road-building, and agriculture. Some missions comprised self-supporting communities on a large scale. For example, the Scottish Free Church's Livingstonia mission among the Tonga, Tumbuka and Ngoni peoples of northern Malawi, established in 1875, acquired 45,000 acres of land to support its work. By 1901, it was providing the surrounding district with six major mission stations, 112 preaching stations, and 142 schools with 11,000 pupils, while it was helping to support 531 African teachers and preachers.[163] A similar mission complex was established by the Church of Scotland at Blantyre in 1876. This included schools, a hospital, workshops, botanical gardens and model farms, all centred upon an impressive church built in an eclectic style, reflecting the global diversity of the Christian faith.[164] By the end of the century, older established missionary societies, such as the Anglican

Church Missionary Society or the Nonconformist London Missionary Society, were maintaining sizeable bureaucracies at home in order to raise funds and administer their global networks of churches, schools, colleges, dispensaries, hospitals, orphanages, and hostels. The Salvation Army was active in missions, with a presence in 58 countries by the time of William Booth's death in 1912. There were also numerous smaller, leaner missionary operations, including new 'Faith missions' that became prominent under evangelical and pre-millenarian influence in the last decades of the nineteenth century. The Faith missions, which were particularly active in China and Africa, supported small teams of itinerant preachers and Bible readers, including locally recruited evangelists, to carry a simple gospel message to as many people as possible.[165]

Along with this burgeoning British overseas mission movement, there was also a renewed enthusiasm for empire during the 1890s. Imperial themes and events found expression in exhibitions and spectacles, music hall acts, theatrical plays and operettas, popular songs, school textbooks, children's fiction, the new cinema, and advertisements of soap and other products.[166] This surge of popular imperialist fervour was in part a response to real and perceived threats to Britain's place in the world – especially the fear of military and industrial competition from other great powers. In imperialism, many sought a renewed sense of national purpose. Bernard Porter has recently argued that the effects of the imperialist propaganda were limited, and that most of the home population remained largely indifferent to the empire. This may well have been the case. But Porter also acknowledged that a substantial part of the middle class did warm to the appeal of imperialism in these years, and this included many middle-class Christians who contributed to the missionary movement.[167] The new imperial spirit found expression during the River War of 1896 to 1899 in Egypt and the Sudan, where British arms destroyed the forces of the Mahdi and avenged General Gordon's death at Khartoum. It also found expression in the celebration of the Diamond Jubilee of the queen's reign in June 1897, with its grand military procession of 50,000 troops from every part of the empire, and its great national service at St Paul's cathedral in London. 'History may be searched', enthused *The Times* of the spectacle, 'and searched in vain, to discover so wonderful an exhibition of allegiance and brotherhood among so many myriads of men . . . The mightiest and most beneficial Empire ever known in the annals of mankind'.[168] The new imperialism included an increased emphasis upon race and on the 'scientific' racial theories of the social Darwinists and eugenicists, with their claims of the natural dominance of the white race over the 'lesser races'.

Within the churches, many embraced the imperialist language. There was renewed talk of 'imperial Christianity' and Britain's divine mission to spread Christian civilisation.[169] For the high church bishop of Rochester, E. S. Talbot, writing in 1900, 'the voice of God through events in history is teaching Englishmen . . . the lessons of Imperial responsibility. It drives home the questions of why and for how long that Empire is given'.[170] G. A. Lefroy, the Anglican bishop of Lahore in India, wrote in 1907 of how he felt 'very deeply the splendour – unique in the world's history and solemn beyond words – of the position to which, in the providence and by the guiding hand of God, the British Empire have been called in the world to-day'.[171] Some combined providentialist language with racialist conceptions, proclaiming the particular mission of the Anglo-Saxon race in fulfilling God's purpose. Through such conceptions British Protestants linked the destinies of the British empire with those of the United States – their main partner in Protestant missions. In the preface to the report of the international missionary conference held in 1888 in London, the editor concluded that 'it is the race which is sending the blessings of Christianity to the heathen to which God is giving success as the colonisers and conquerors of the world'.[172] For G. H. S. Walpole, Anglican rector of Lambeth, God had entrusted his mission of converting the world first to the Semitic race, then to the Latin race, and finally to the Anglo-Saxon race, as represented by the British people and their empire. This providential role was 'clearly seen in the formation of our empire. It is of God, and not of man'.[173] Anglican imperialists spoke of religion as the only force that could 'weld into one great whole' the diverse peoples of the empire and they looked to the day when the Church of England would assume the title of 'the Church of the British Empire'.[174] Henry Montgomery, bishop of Tasmania, who became secretary of the Society for the Propagation of the Gospel in 1901, hoped to reinvigorate the Church of England by rousing its young people to the ideal of an imperial Christianity, a faith that would become the bond of empire.[175]

The enthusiasm for empire swelled at the outset of the South African War of 1899–1902, when imperial military might was directed to subjugating two small republics of Boers (or descendants of Dutch settlers) and incorporating them into a South African federation. For probably the large majority of the British people, the war was necessary to ensure the human rights of non-Boers residing within the Boer territories, and to bring the benefits of civilisation and progress to a backward region. There was much pro-war fervour at home, and victories were celebrated with riotous frenzy. The majority of the British clergy, it seems, warmly supported the conflict, at least in its early phase.[176] 'Is it not true', enthused the bishop of Stepney, Arthur Winnington-Ingram, in a sermon at St Paul's cathedral at the outset of the war, 'that as a nation we are feeling the joy of fighting for a great ideal?'[177] Pro-war Christian sentiment was promoted by some African missionaries, such as James Stewart of Lovedale (moderator of the Free Church of Scotland General Assembly in 1899–1900) who were distressed by Boer treatment of Black Africans and believed that the incorporation of the Boer republics into the empire would mean fairer treatment for all races. The president of the Church Missionary Society, Sir John Kennaway, insisted in the spring of 1900 that victory in South Africa would bring 'freedom and justice and equality between races black and white'.[178] Many clergy not only supported the war, but declared openly that God was on the side of the British forces. So much so, that the liberal anti-war journalist, J. A. Hobson, blamed the churches for inciting jingoism and bloodlust. 'From the conception of England', he opined in 1901, 'as a country with a special mission to "civilise" the world with blood and iron, to the conception of "England's God" as a tribal God of Battles who shall fight with our big battalions and help us crush our enemies, is a step taken with ease and confidence by most of our Churches'.[179]

Not all, however, believed the war was righteous. From the beginning, a sizeable minority of clergy criticised the war as unnecessary and immoral, fought mainly to provide British capitalists with control over a mineral-rich region. Such critics included the Baptist Christian socialist, John Clifford, the Anglican bishop of Hereford, John Percival, and the Scottish United Free Church minister, James Barr. The Liberal *Daily News* published a peace manifesto signed by no fewer than 5,270 Nonconformist ministers.[180] Initially these critics were widely denounced as unpatriotic and 'pro-Boer'. But as the conflict dragged on, opposition to the war within the churches grew steadily. Many were appalled by the conduct of the final phase of the war, as the British army resorted to scorched-earth tactics in order to crush the Boer guerrilla fighters – burning Boer farms and herding non-combatants into the so-called 'concentration camps' where thousands, especially children, died of illness and malnutrition. This revealed all too clearly the brutal side of imperial power.

Imperialism's 'heart of darkness' was further revealed through emerging accounts of extreme cruelty in the lucrative rubber trade in the Congo Free State. That state had been created by the great powers at the Congress of Berlin in 1885 and placed under the control of King Leopold II of Belgium. It had been intended as a great philanthropic endeavour that would end the slave trade and bring the benefits of commerce and civilisation to Central Africa. But it had soon degenerated into a brutal regime in which Western officials employed murder and mutilation – including the severing of hands and feet – to intimidate African villagers into supplying them with rubber without payment. From 1900, the atrocities were publicised by E. D. Morel and later Roger Casement, who drew upon the testimony of some individual British and American Protestant missionaries[181] (although both Morel and Casement were also critical of the official missionary societies for keeping silent for too long). British Christians then took a prominent role in the Congo Reform Association created in 1904 in Britain, and in the national agitation that followed. The former Congo missionaries, John and Alice Harris, gave over 300 public lectures in the first year of the Association's campaign, and they recruited other Congo missionaries as speakers. Their harrowing portrayals of terror and mutilation were illustrated with photographic slides.[182] The campaign aroused the same spirit of righteous indignation that was seen in the agitation against the Bulgarian or Armenian atrocities, only this time it was not the Ottomans, but a Christian European power, that was inflicting the horrors. According to the Foreign Secretary, Sir Edward Grey, speaking in 1908, 'no external question for at least thirty years has moved the country so strongly and so vehemently as this in regard to the Congo'.[183] To the accounts of Congo atrocities were added, from 1904, revelations of cruel and degrading conditions in the labour camps of Chinese men imported to work the South African mines, conditions that differed little from slavery and that raised questions about what the South African War had achieved. Many were losing all confidence in the old formula of Christianity, commerce and civilisation.

Faith in a providential Western imperialism was dealt a further blow in 1904–05 when Japan defeated the Russian empire in a war for dominance over Manchuria. This victory by an Asian power over a European empire sent a thrill through the populations of the East, and infused new confidence into nationalist movements in India, Egypt, Persia, Turkey and China. The *Hindustan Review* of India observed in September 1904 that 'the irresistible energy of the Japanese has shattered the flattering European theory entertained for centuries past that there can be no true civilisation unless it was of Christian, Greek or Roman origin'.[184] For some, these were the birth pangs of a new world order. It was at this juncture that a great World Missionary Conference met in Edinburgh to plan for combined action by Protestant denominations and mission boards in renewing the missionary movement.

The World Missionary Conference, Edinburgh 1910

Representatives of the various Protestant missionary societies and boards were accustomed to meeting in periodic conferences to discuss strategy and co-operation in the mission fields. There were regional missionary conferences in India and China. There were also world missionary conferences held in British or American cities in 1854, 1860, 1878, 1888 and 1900. The world conference of 1900 in New York City was conducted on a grand scale, with over 200,000 people attending its various events.[185]

Along with these conferences, a number of Protestant denominations also formed international bodies, to foster co-operation on the global level. In 1875, a World Presbyterian Alliance was formed in London; it held its first conference two years later in Edinburgh, with delegates from over 30 Presbyterian churches worldwide. This was followed by the first Methodist Ecumenical Conference in 1881, the first International Congregational Conference in 1891, and the first Baptist World Congress in 1905. The first Pan-Anglican Congress was held in London in 1908; a total of 17,000 people attended one or more of its sessions. Christian leaders of the various Protestant denominations were thus growing accustomed to meeting and reflecting in common on global challenges and opportunities. All these international denominational bodies had been formed in London, reflecting the apparent dominance of British imperial influence. However, as Keith Robbins has observed, the initiative had often come from the United States, which was now exercising an increasing leadership in international Protestantism.[186]

In July 1908, planning began for another world missionary conference. This conference was to be a smaller affair, with most sessions restricted to the invited delegates. It would be held in the Scottish city of Edinburgh, in honour of the prominent role take by Scots in the missionary movement. The aim of this conference would be to reflect upon the changing world order and plan for appropriate missionary action. The key figures behind the conference were the American Methodist, John R. Mott, and the Scottish Presbyterian, J. H. Oldham – the former a physically large, robust, confident and commanding figure, and the latter a young man of small stature and slight build, troubled with partial deafness, but highly effective at organisation. Eight commissions were appointed, each with approximately 20 members, and each with an assigned theme to explore. These commissions gathered evidence from mission workers around the world and produced eight substantial reports. Then in June 1910 for ten days,

1,216 delegates, representing approximately 160 missionary societies and boards from throughout the Western world, met in the United Free Church Assembly Hall in Edinburgh to discuss the commission reports and hear addresses from leading religious figures.[187] The conference proved one of the most important events in the history of the missionary movement, and indeed of twentieth-century Christianity.

It was not obvious why this should have been the case. To begin with, despite its claim to be a *world* missionary conference, the Edinburgh conference was by no means representative of the world church. There was no official representation from the Roman Catholic, Orthodox or ancient Eastern churches. Moreover, despite protests from North American evangelicals, it was agreed not to include Protestant missions to predominantly Roman Catholic or Orthodox Christian lands. This meant there was virtually no representation of the missions in South America or the Caribbean. Further, there was very little attendance from inhabitants of the non-Western world. Of the 1,216 delegates, only 17 were of non-Western origin, and all of these were Asians.[188] As the foreign secretary of the London Missionary Society informed Oldham in February 1910, 'I do not think the time is ripe for the inclusion of delegates appointed by the churches in non-Christian lands in any great Conference such as ours'.[189] The size of the representation of the various missionary boards and societies, moreover, was determined according to the funds they raised. As a result, the conference was dominated by the big British and North American societies – which provided five-sixths of the delegates.

What, then, was so significant about the conference? First, the delegates endeavoured to distance the missionary movement from Western imperialism. There was a genuine effort to separate the message of Christianity from Western culture, and to criticise many aspects of Western imperial influence in Asia and Africa. While the delegates agreed that missionaries should not join in movements of national liberation, they acknowledged, often with passion, that missionaries must confront the 'great national wrongs' of the opium trade, liquor trade and forced labour that were bitter fruits of imperialism.[190] The conference avoided the language of Christian imperialism or claims of the providential role of empire in the spread of Christianity. There were also some efforts to confront racism. One of the most memorable episodes of the conference occurred when a young Asian speaker, Revd V. S. Azariah of India, ventured to criticise the sense of racial superiority that separated Western missionaries from Asians. He noted that while European missionaries would co-operate with Asians, they rarely invited Asian colleagues to their home for a meal. There was, he insisted, a need for friendship as well as co-operation. The initial reaction from most conference delegates was resentment and denial that such condescension existed. But on reflection, many came openly to concede the truth in Azariah's remarks, and this acknowledgement contributed to a change in attitudes.[191] Secondly, the conference showed respect for other religious faiths. There was, to be sure, agreement that Christianity was superior to other world faiths. But one of the most sensitive and perceptive of the commission reports was that on *The Missionary Message in relation to Non-Christian Religions*, edited by the Scottish Presbyterian theologian, D. S. Cairns. This report sought to be fair to other faiths, and called for greater understanding and dialogue on the basis of what they shared in common.[192]

Thirdly, and perhaps most important, the Edinburgh conference contributed significantly to a spirit of interdenominational co-operation in the mission field. There was criticism of the divisions of the churches and calls not only for co-operation, but for Christian unity. Perhaps the most influential of the reports was that on *Co-operation and the Promotion of Unity*, which outlined a broad range of areas in which the different denominations were working together in the mission fields, and insisted that 'in the matter of unity, the mission field is leading the way'.[193] It expressed hope that this spirit might return to Europe and North America, promoting movements for the corporate unification of the churches. The report called for a standing international committee, to promote inter-church consultation and co-operation in the world mission, and to contribute to the achievement of Christ's intention 'that we should be one in a visible fellowship'. Inspired by this ideal, the Edinburgh conference agreed to form a Continuation Committee to carry on its interdenominational work. This marked a major departure from previous conferences, and the Committee contributed in time to the formation of an International Mission Council, which in turn led to the Life and Work movement, the Faith and Order movement, and eventually, in 1948, the World Council of Churches. The World Missionary Conference of 1910 thus formed a key moment in the modern ecumenical movement and was, some would argue, the defining event in that movement. For the British churches, it also contributed to the movement away from Victorian notions of the elect nation and the providential empire.

The women's revolt

In the early years of the new century, British political life was shaken by a new force – a determined national agitation, led by women, to achieve the vote for women in parliamentary elections. Large numbers of women embraced the campaign, not only because they believed they had a right to the vote, but also because they were convinced that their empowerment would lead to a more just, peaceful, egalitarian, and moral society. For many the agitation took on the fervour of a righteous crusade. While the movement was largely peaceful and constitutional, a minority of women turned to violent action after about 1906, including destruction of property and street fighting with police.

By the later nineteenth century, women in unprecedented numbers were working outside the home, in factories and shops, but also in clerical jobs and the professions, especially teaching. Here the number rose from about 70,000 in England and Wales in 1851 to 172,000 in 1901 – making up 74.5 per cent of all teachers in that year.[194] In 1875, Parliament passed an act permitting universities to confer degrees on women, and from the later 1870s one institution after another admitted them, including to medical courses. Combined with the opening of degrees and professions to women, there were changes in their legal status. Beginning in 1870, a series of parliamentary acts gave married women greater rights over their property, while it became easier for married women to leave abusive or unfaithful husbands. There were growing calls to liberalise the procedures for divorce, which led to the appointment of a Royal Commission on marriage and divorce in 1909. It reported in 1912, but the Great War intervened before legislation could be enacted. Attitudes towards sexual behaviour were changing. The 1890s witnessed the emergence of the 'new woman' novels, with independent, outspoken, highly intelligent female characters, who challenged social norms and conventional morality in their search for personal fulfilment.[195]

Women were more politically active. The late 1860s had seen the beginning of a national campaign led by Josephine Butler, an Anglican cleric's wife, against the Contagious Diseases Acts. Passed between 1864 and 1869, the Acts had been intended to combat the alarming spread of venereal disease among British soldiers and sailors by subjecting prostitutes to mandatory inspection and licensing. But many found the Acts morally abhorrent, and Butler and others worked tirelessly to convince the British public that they must be repealed. The campaigners condemned the Acts on a number of grounds: they denounced the immorality of state-licensed prostitution, the double standard of laws that subjected women but not men to forcible inspection, the violation and injury of women's bodies through the forcible inspections, and the frequent errors made in enforcing the legislation, with non-prostitutes taken up and forcibly 'inspected'.

Josephine Butler rooted her feminism in her liberal evangelical faith, viewed Christ as the 'liberator' of women and believed that women, as much as men, could be called to preach.[196] Her campaign had a high religious and moral tone, and Butler and her supporters demonstrated considerable courage in the face of violent mobs which were incensed by an agitation led by women for the goal of greater gender equality. Women gained valuable political experience, including experience in speaking on sensitive issues at large public meetings. After years of agitation, the Contagious Diseases Acts were suspended in 1883 and finally repealed in 1886. Butler and her supporters then took up campaigns against the international traffic in prostitutes, and the state licensing of prostitution in India. For an admiring W. T. Stead (writing in 1887), they were the 'New Abolitionists', struggling with a religious fervour to liberate women world-wide from the slavery of the sex trade and state-licensed prostitution.[197] It was through such crusades that many women came to see their need for the vote. As Butler observed in 1885, many people:

prate about women coveting power, and stepping out of their sphere; while what we are craving for, with aching hearts, is but to be able to protect ourselves and our children from male destroyers, not only from their deeds of shame but from their evil influence in the legislature. There is a French saying that it is 'women who make the morals of a country'. That is not true; it cannot be true, so long as MEN ALONE MAKE THE LAWS.[198]

The campaign to achieve the vote for women in parliamentary elections began in 1867, with the formation of the London National Society for Women's Suffrage. There was some progress in subsequent years. Women gained the right to vote and be elected in school board elections in 1870 (and in 1872 in Scotland), to vote for and be elected as Poor Law guardians, and to vote in elections for the new county councils in 1888. In 1897 the campaigners formed a new National Union of Women's Suffrage Societies, to co-ordinate efforts for the parliamentary vote; it employed moderate methods and avoided outdoor meetings or demonstrations. Then in 1903, Emmeline Pankhurst and her daughter, Christabel, founded the more militant Women's Social and Political Union (WSPU). They began actively recruiting young working-class women and holding out-door demonstrations. Following the Liberal triumph in the election of 1906, hopes ran high that the government would introduce a women's suffrage bill. When it failed to do so, the Pankhursts launched a campaign of violence to force the government's hand; women smashed windows, chained themselves to railings, and fought with police. The press dubbed the militants 'suffragettes' and the police often treated them brutally. When arrested, some suffragettes employed a new weapon: the hunger strike. The authorities responded with forced feedings, which sometimes caused lasting physical damage.

As Jacqueline deVries has observed, the Women's Social and Political Union was influenced by Christian revivalist movements, and especially the methods of the Salvation Army.[199] WSPU borrowings included 'parades, pamphlets, billboards, and soapbox speakers'; their rallies resembled revival meetings, with suffragette 'preachers' proclaiming 'a new life inspired by feminist ideals'. Some suffragettes, such as Annie Kenney or Lady Constance Lytton, used the language of Christian conversion to describe their decision to join the movement.[200] Many believed that women's suffrage would usher in the millennium, elevating politics with new moral and spiritual ideals and diminishing, if not bringing to an end, aggressive war, imperialism, sweated labour, prostitution, domestic violence, alcoholism, and a host of other social ills. For a young suffragette in H. G. Wells's 'new woman' novel of 1909, *Ann Veronica*, the women's suffrage movement was part of a flurry of ideas – 'the Higher Thought, the Simple Life, Socialism, Humanitarianism' and the ideas of 'Christ and Buddha' – that were remaking British society. It was 'the real dawn', and 'women were taking it up . . . the women and the common people, all pressing forward, all roused'.[201] 'It is not only political reform we are called to accomplish', wrote a WSPU member in 1913, 'but a moral revolution. We preach the glad tidings of a new gospel to humanity'.[202]

Such views could justify violence against those who opposed the new gospel, and some women claimed a religious sanction for their militancy. When Helen Crawford, the wife of a Presbyterian minister in Glasgow, was agonising over whether to travel to London to join in a window-breaking raid, she went to church in hope of finding guidance from her husband's sermon. 'His sermon', she later recalled, 'was about Christ making a whip of cords, and chasing money-changers out of the temple. This I took as warrant that my participation in the raid was right. If Christ could be Militant, so could I.'[203] Some suffragettes were prepared to become martyrs. The suffragette Emily Wilding Davison threw herself under the hoofs of the king's horse at Derby Day in June 1913. Her funeral procession numbered some 5,000, and was led by a tall, fair-haired woman, dressed in white and carrying a gold martyr's cross.[204]

Believing their struggle to be a righteous one, many advocates of women's suffrage looked to the churches for support – believing that they must appreciate the real contributions of women in society. Women were, after all, the most active church members, making up as much as three-quarters of church attendances, participating in church-related organisations, and doing most of the voluntary church work. They visited the poor, the elderly and the sick, distributed charity, taught Sunday schools, and raised funds for Christian causes. Women missionaries, including doctors and teachers, served the church overseas with courage and competence. Surely the churches must see the justice of equal rights for women? And many within the churches did embrace the cause. In 1909, a number of Anglicans, led by a university extension lecturer, Maude Royden, and a clergyman, Claude Hinscliff, founded the Church League for Women's Suffrage. The bishop of Lincoln, Edward Hicks, became President, and by 1914 the Church League had over 5,000 members, including 500 Anglican clergymen. Roman Catholic suffragettes founded the St Joan's Alliance, and women's suffrage societies appeared within the Nonconformist churches. In Scotland, supporters founded the Scottish Churches League for Woman Suffrage in March 1912. The first president was Lady Frances Balfour, daughter of the Duke of Argyll, and sister-in-law of Arthur Balfour, and the vice-presidents included several leading Scottish clergymen. When in March 1913, Emmeline Pankhurst addressed a large public meeting in Glasgow, there were 12 ministers on the platform, and a minister gave the vote of thanks.[205]

However, there were also many within the churches who opposed women's suffrage, and as institutions they were not forthcoming with support. Opponents, among them large numbers of women, believed that the parliamentary vote was unnecessary and that women would be debased by engaging in sordid parliamentary politics. Some conservative Christians believed that God intended women to be subordinate to men. Others were put off by suffragette militancy, which was so opposed to Victorian ideals of feminine virtue. It did not help that decision-making in the institutional churches was dominated by men. In the Church of England, women could not sit in Convocation. When in 1904, the Church of England created a Representative Church Council of elected lay delegates to advise on matters of church governance, women were not allowed to sit on it.[206] In Scotland, women could not serve as elders or ministers in the Presbyterian churches, and therefore could not sit on any of the church courts. Women did have greater representation in some Nonconformist churches; for example, women could serve as delegates on the annual assemblies of the

Congregational Union from the 1890s.[207] But even here the debates were dominated by men.

For advocates of women's suffrage, the churches' failure fully to support the cause was unconscionable. Were not the churches supposed to represent higher spiritual and moral values in society? Did not the clergy daily confront the human costs of male oppression of women? Was not, as the Scottish educator and advocate of women's suffrage, Louisa Lumsden, put it in April 1913, 'the root idea of Christianity . . . the value of the individual' and did it not regard 'women as full individuals, setting before them equally with men, its high and stern vocation and its glorious hope'?[208] Women could feel betrayed when their churches opposed the movement. When in late 1913 the Church of Scotland presbytery of Dundee passed, by a 'large majority', a motion critical of women's suffrage, May Grant, a former missionary and the daughter of a Church of Scotland minister, gave vent to her indignation in a local newspaper. The presbytery's position, she insisted:

was all the more reprehensible if we consider how much it owes to those who are struggling for freedom. Who fill the churches, so far as they are filled? Who do Sunday school work? Who raise church funds? Who visit the poor and the sick? The men? Nay, verily. As one who is deeply, passionately, attached to the Auld Reformed Kirk o' the Realm, and who has served her for ten years at home and for four and a half years abroad, I protest against the attitudes of the ministers – an attitude as banal as it is insulting.[209]

Early in 1913, the WSPU began militant action meant to awaken the churches to the justice of the women's cause. This took various forms – groups of women would stand and ostentatiously walk out of church services just before the sermon, or disrupt the services with shouts of 'votes for women' or loud prayers for imprisoned suffragettes. There were also demonstrations at church meetings, such as those at the Church Congress of October 1913 at Southampton, or at the United Free Church General Assembly in May 1913 and again in May 1914. Some militants went further and torched churches; more than 50 Anglican churches suffered arson attacks between April 1913 and the onset of the Great War. In Scotland, suffragettes burned down the parish church at Whitekirk in February 1914 as a response to Scotland's first forcible feeding of a hunger striker.[210] While the number of militants remained small, such acts of violence by women directed against churches and the Christian social order were deeply unsettling to many people. The violence challenged Victorian ideals of feminine piety and raised questions about the future role of women as nurturers of children in the Christian faith.

Religious war in Ireland?

In the spring and summer of 1914, Ireland was on the verge of civil war – one that also threatened all the horrors of religious conflict. In the North, Protestants were arming and training a citizens' army of approximately 100,000 recruits, the Ulster Volunteer Force, and apparently preparing for war to assert the right of the largely Protestant province of Ulster to remain firmly within the United Kingdom. Ulster Catholics feared they would be the ultimate enemy, and their southern fellow-Catholics armed and trained a citizens' army, the Irish (National) Volunteers, and prepared to defend the right of a united Ireland to have Home Rule. On both sides, there were many who longed for conflict, to end the decades of bitter political wrangling over Home Rule and settle the issue once and for all. On both sides, there were those who believed the shedding of blood in armed struggle would have a redemptive value – that a blood sacrifice would propitiate God and cleanse and redeem their people. Catholic nationalists and Protestant unionists harkened after the martyrs of their past, the glorious dead who had sacrificed themselves for their faith, land and people.

The prospects for Home Rule, embraced by Gladstone and most of the Liberal party in 1886 as the only means to bring peace to Ireland, had, as we have seen, been seriously damaged in 1890 by the fall of the Irish leader, Charles Stewart Parnell, and his death the following year. The Irish Home Rule party became bitterly divided between the anti-Parnellites, or those who had turned against Parnell over his long affair with Mrs O'Shea, and the Parnellites, who remained loyal to the memory of their chief. Gladstone's government had brought forward a second Home Rule bill in 1893, which had been narrowly passed by the House of Commons, only to be thrown out by the Lords. With the failure of this bill, and with the Home Rule movement torn by internecine conflict, Home Rule receded from practical politics. After 1895, the Conservative government pursued a policy of 'killing Home Rule by kindness'; that is, they enacted a series of reforms – including an increase in state loans to enable tenants to buy their farms – which were aimed at convincing the Irish that they did not need Home Rule. The Roman Catholic bishops in Ireland, meanwhile, had been widely denounced for their condemnation of Parnell in 1890; for many Irish Home Rulers, their chief had been 'hounded to his death by the priests'.

In response, most bishops, including the nationalist Archbishop Walsh, now distanced themselves from Home Rule, and from politics generally.

As the Home Rule prospects waned from the early 1890s, and 'a disillusioned and embittered Ireland turned from parliamentary politics', there was, as W. B. Yeats observed, an increasing public interest in Irish cultural life.[211] Intellectuals, largely from the old Anglo-Irish Protestant ascendancy and including Yeats and Lady Gregory, collected Irish folk-lore, and wrote English-language poetry and fiction around Irish themes. In 1904, Yeats and his associates founded the Abbey Theatre in Dublin, in order to promote an Irish national drama. They used the English language for their productions. Others, however, sought to make the Irish language the sole medium for national culture. In 1893, Douglas Hyde, Eoin MacNeill and others founded the Gaelic League, to promote Irish as the national language. They organised language classes, sponsored publica-tions, and hosted a national festival. Highly critical of those who wrote on Irish themes in the English language, they demanded an Irish Ireland. The language movement was linked with that for the revival of Gaelic sports, promoted by the Gaelic Athletic Association formed in 1884.

There was also from the late 1880s a revival movement within Irish Roman Catholicism. This included a movement of renewed devotion to the Sacred Heart of Jesus that was led largely by a Jesuit priest, James A. Cullen. The main organ of the movement was the monthly magazine, the *Messenger of the Sacred Heart*, which began publication in 1888, and had a circulation of 47,000 by 1894 and 73,000 by 1904. Devotion to the Sacred Heart became connected with a renewed temperance crusade that began in 1888 and gained over 250,000 pledges of total abstinence by 1890, while a parallel temperance movement conducted by the Capuchin brothers claimed over a million pledges by 1912. Some began linking an ascetic Roman Catholicism with Irish cultural nationalism. Archbishop Walsh and a number of his fellow Catholic bishops supported the Gaelic League and the Irish-Ireland movement.[212] 'Ireland sober, Ireland free' now became a popular Catholic slogan – and both Catholic temperance reformers and Irish nationalists claimed that the British promoted Irish dependence on alcohol as a means of keeping the country enslaved. Catholic revivalists and Irish nationalists joined in condemning proselytis-ing activities in Ireland, physically attacking Protestant street preachers and denouncing Protestant-supported schools and orphanages.[213] They promoted an idealised version of a pious Irish peasantry – in contrast to what they viewed as the secularism, materialism and hedonism of modern British society. They could attack those who questioned the holiness and chastity of the peasantry, as when in January 1907 they violently broke up performances of John Millington Synge's *Playboy of the Western World* at Dublin's Abbey Theatre. Irish Catholic priests saw industrialisation and urbanisation as threats to the faith; they preferred to see the Irish people working on the land, either on farms or in small cottage industries.[214] A resurgent Roman Catholicism began looking upon the Protestant North as a mission field. 'The day of missionary heroism is at hand', proclaimed the *Catholic Bulletin* in March 1912. 'To bring into the bosom of Holy Church the million of our separated brethren is a most attractive programme, and there is in it enough of the heroic to engage and claim the hearts of Irish Catholics'.[215]

Under the influence of cultural nationalism and Catholicism, some began calling for Ireland to throw off the British yoke altogether and assume its place as an independent nation. The centenary of the Irish rising of 1798 provided the occasion for nationalist commemorations of the 'glorious dead' and the formation of 'Ninety-eight Clubs'. In 1900, the nationalist journalist, Arthur Griffith, formed a new organisation to promote Irish cultural identity and political independence. Following a reorganisation in 1905, it took the name of Sinn Féin ('Ourselves'). In 1900, the Catholic nationalist, D. P. Moran, founded *The Leader*, a weekly periodical, which quickly became one of the most widely read papers in Ireland. *The Leader* championed temperance, chastity, the Irish language, Gaelic culture, and a Catholic Irish nationalism. It waged what Moran termed the 'battle of the two civilisations', denouncing Anglo-Irish cultural influence, and dismissing Irish Protestants as 'sourfaces' and members of an 'alien race'.[216] In language that mirrored the providentialism of the Victorian British churches, such publications spoke of the national mission of the Catholic Irish people.

The Parnellite and anti-Parnellite factions of the Home Rule party were reunited in 1900, and with the return of the Liberals to power in 1906, Home Rule once again became a matter of practical politics. The Liberal government initially showed little interest in reviving Irish Home Rule, but by 1910 this changed. First, the Liberal majority in the Commons was greatly reduced by two general elections held in 1910, and the Liberals could hold office only with the support of the Irish parliamentary party. Second, as we have seen, the Parliament Act of 1911 reduced the House of Lords' power of veto to a mere delaying power. Now, if the House of Commons voted for a bill in two consecutive sessions after it had been vetoed by the Lords, that bill would become law. In April 1912, the government introduced a third Home Rule bill; after prolonged debates, it was passed by the Commons in January 1913. The bill was immediately rejected by the Lords, but the Lords could now only delay its passage. There was every prospect that Home Rule would be enacted by the summer of 1914.

The Protestants of Ulster, however, would not have Home Rule. Since 1910, they had begun organising resistance to the Home Rule bill – with much more discipline than their resistance to the previous bills of 1886 and 1893. Their arguments for opposing Home Rule remained the same – it would weaken Ireland's industrial and commercial links with Britain and discourage investment in the Ulster economy; it would lead to a Roman Catholic ascendancy, and give the Roman Catholic Church authority over education and public morals; it would not be a final settlement but only a stepping stone to complete Irish separation; it would threaten the survival of the culture and traditions of Protestant Ireland. There was now a greater sense of urgency and alarm, in part because of the growth of Catholic cultural nationalism since the early 1890s. As C. F. D'Arcy, the Church of Ireland bishop of Down, Connor and Dromore, argued in 1912, 'the dread of Roman tyranny is now more vivid and, as a motive, far more urgent' than it had been in 1886 or 1893. 'Protestants', he continued, 'are now convinced, as never before, that Home Rule must mean Rome Rule, and that, should it be forced upon them . . . they will be face to face with a struggle for liberty and conscience such as this land has not witnessed since the year 1690'.[217] Such sentiments also found expression in Rudyard Kipling's vehemently pro-Protestant 'Ulster' of 1912:

> The terror, threats, and dread
> In market, hearth, and field –
> We know, when all is said,
> We perish if we yield.

As evidence of their vulnerability under a future Catholic ascendancy, Protestants directed attention to the papal *Ne temere* decree of 1908, which required that any children of mixed Protestant–Catholic marriages must be brought up in the Catholic faith. Theirs was a struggle, Ulster Protestants believed, for their survival as a people. Many nationalists, they knew, regarded Protestants as an alien presence, with no place in a future Catholic Ireland.

On 1 February 1912, Presbyterians held a large convention in Belfast to protest against Home Rule. It attracted to the city 40,000–50,000 men, half the adult male Presbyterian population of Ulster.[218] The Methodists followed with their own anti-Home Rule convention in March, and in

April, the General Synod of the Church of Ireland held a special session to affirm their attachment to the Union. On Easter Tuesday, a parade and religious service was held at Balmoral, outside Belfast, which attracted an estimated 100,000 anti-Home Rule Protestants. The gathering was addressed by the new leader of the Conservative party, Andrew Bonar Law (the son of a Presbyterian minister of Ulster-Scots background) who pledged that his party would support Protestant Ulster in its resistance to Home Rule. In a show of Protestant unity, the religious service was conducted jointly by the moderator of the Presbyterian General Assembly and the primate of the Church of Ireland. In the months that followed, Protestant clergy regularly denounced Home Rule from the pulpit. 'In those days', a Presbyterian minister later recalled, 'I often spoke and preached on the subject, and I urged the people to resist even unto death'.[219] Solidarity against Home Rule was reinforced through the numerous local organisations that shaped Protestant lives and identity – churches, Sunday schools, Orange lodges, temperance meetings, Scouts and Boys' Brigades, commemorative fraternities (such as the Apprentice Boys), Protestant friendly societies and Mothers' Unions.

Ulster unionist leaders decided to unite the anti-Home Rule movement by means of a solemn and binding oath. They modelled this on the seventeenth-century Scottish national Covenant, by which Scottish Presbyterians had covenanted with God and with each other in defence of their national religion. The Ulster Covenant was drafted largely by the Presbyterian layman, Thomas Sinclair, and employed sombre, almost Old Testament language to pledge resistance to Home Rule. On Covenant Day, 28 September 1912, adult male supporters were invited to sign the document at locations across Ulster. The day had a religious atmosphere. Protestant churches held special services of preparation, and people wore their Sunday clothing for the signing. As one participant in Belfast later recalled:

On the day itself, a magnificent morning of fine and durable weather that made the hills around the city look blue in the sunlight, Belfast suspended all its labours and became like a place of prayer. Very solemnly, the people went to church to prepare their minds for their responsibilities, as postulants prepare themselves for consecration.[220]

While only men signed the Covenant, women were invited to put their names to a Declaration, and a total of 471,414 men and women signed – many with their own blood.[221] In Belfast cathedral, Bishop d'Arcy (who was the first Church of Ireland bishop to sign the Covenant) spoke of the prospect of civil war. 'We must', he insisted, 'face the fact that there are things worse than war . . . Our trust is in God'.[222] Following the signing of the Covenant, unionists formed the Ulster Volunteer Force, and began military training. There were soon some 100,000 recruits, and weapons were brought into the country through a series of gunrunning operations, culminating in late April 1914, when 25,000 rifles and three million rounds of ammunition were brought into Larne near Belfast. Plans were made to declare a provisional government in Ulster once the Home Rule bill became law. Some seemed almost to relish a religious war. 'How could men die better', asked the Belfast Presbyterian *Witness* newspaper on 18 July 1913, 'than facing the forces of Rome for the faith and liberty of their fathers, for the life and liberty of their children?'[223]

In November 1913, Catholic nationalists formed and began arming their own citizens' militia, the Irish (National) Volunteers, for the defence of Home Rule and a united Ireland. Against the Ulster Protestants' seventeenth-century language of covenant, Irish nationalist authors and poets took up the language of messianic death and redemption. They spoke of blood sacrifice for the cleansing of Ireland. The Irish people, proclaimed the nationalist author, Patrick Pearse, in November 1913, must prepare for sacrifice: 'the people itself will perhaps be its own Messiah, the people labouring, scourged, crowned with thorns, agonising and dying, to rise again immortal and impassible'. 'Bloodshed', he added, 'is a cleansing and a satisfying thing, and the nation which regards it as a final horror has lost its manhood'.[224] Many of the young men of both sides had joined their volunteer forces for a bit of fun and companionship in the evenings, but it seemed their soldiering would soon become deadly. With civil and religious war looming, the Liberal government sought to negotiate a compromise, and proposals were made for the temporary exclusion of portions of Ulster from the Home Rule settlement. But passions ran high, the negotiations foundered and armed conflict loomed.

The outbreak of the Great War

Then, on 4 August 1914, the United Kingdom declared war on Germany. The immediate cause was Germany's invasion of Belgium, whose neutrality the United Kingdom was bound by treaty to protect. Its leaders also believed that Britain was honour-bound to support its allies, France and Russia, which several days earlier had taken up arms against Germany and Austro-Hungary. The threat of civil war in Ireland suddenly receded before the reality of European conflict. The Home Rule Act was passed in September 1914, but was then suspended for the duration of the hostilities.

Few within the churches had expected a general European war. There had, it is true, been concern over the formation of opposing military alliances, the arms race, imperial rivalries, and bellicose nationalism. Delegations of British and German church leaders had exchanged visits to work for peace, and 'The Associated Councils of the Churches in the British and German Empires for Fostering Friendly Relations' had been formed in 1910. It sponsored conferences, and believed it was having a positive impact. In the early summer of 1914, the international situation seemed calm and the prospects for peace appeared good. Then came the Great War, with 'terrible and unlooked-for swiftness', according to a Church of Scotland preacher on 9 August.[225] Once the United Kingdom had entered the fighting, a wave of patriotic fervour swept through the land, and clergymen from all the British churches rallied to the cause. Many preached fiery sermons, appeared on platforms at recruitment rallies, and published articles and tracts on the conflict as a moral crusade. There was little questioning of the reasons for war. British church leaders denounced Germany's aggression against Belgium, and condemned German militarism. They spoke of the righteousness of the British cause – of Britain's respect for treaties and for the rights of small nations, of its defence of its empire and its liberty. 'Surely', proclaimed a Church of Scotland minister, John Muir, in a sermon in Paisley on 9 August 1914, 'if ever in the history of mankind there has been a just war, it is this war'.[226]

For many, the War promised to revive the influence and authority of the churches. There was a renewed sense of national unity – so refreshing after the bitter disputes in recent decades between Anglo-Catholic and Protestant, church and chapel, Irish Catholic and Ulster Protestant. Churches were filled in the late summer and autumn of 1914. Congregations formed work parties (made up largely of women), to put together parcels of socks, mufflers, gloves, tobacco, and chocolate for the soldiers. They provided hospitality and homes for Belgian refugees. Ministers corresponded with the local young men in the armed services, and informed those at home of their movements. When ministers volunteered for service as chaplains at the front, creating vacancies in pulpits, the congregations of different denominations would often unite for joint Sunday services. Roman Catholic clergy rallied noisily to the cause of 'Catholic Belgium'. Sectarian tensions eased, as young men from established church, Nonconformist and Roman Catholic backgrounds volunteered, and their families at home were united in pride and anxiety and later, increasingly, in mourning.

As men rushed to enlist, there was a sense that the younger generation was putting behind it the materialism, decadence, divisiveness and pursuit of pleasure that had been so rife in the pre-war years, and returning to traditional Christian values. The coming of the War, observed the Church of Scotland minister, Norman Maclean, in early 1915 was 'like the sudden lifting of a curtain'. 'Everywhere', he continued, 'the sanctuaries filled, the eyes turned inward, for instinct is mightier than reason. The smoke of battle has revealed the face of God'. 'Under the shadow of the Cross now lifted up', he added, 'a nation that sought life's pleasures has suddenly thrilled with the glory of self-sacrifice'.[227] Many within the churches looked for a religious revival. Surely God would reward the United Kingdom for its faithfulness, and the Holy Spirit would pour forth. Soon there were reports of large-scale revival activity among the troops at the front, along with accounts of miraculous occurrences – sightings of angels fighting alongside the British troops at Mons and of Christ tending wounded British soldiers.

But as 1914 drew to a close, the claims of Christian revival at the front grew muted and then largely ceased. The Western front stabilised and soldiers suffered and died amid hellish conditions in the trenches. The population at home grew to fear the long daily casualty lists, and more and more houses were darkened in mourning. Many individuals found in their religion the strength to confront suffering and bereavement, and believed that God helped them through their trials. Less orthodox faiths prospered, such as the Salvation Army, whose relief efforts were greatly valued by exhausted troops, and spiritualists, who attracted many of those bereaved by the War. Others felt betrayed by religion, and turned from the churches. But the hopes that the war would bring a revival of national Christianity faded.

Conclusion

The years between 1896 and 1914 had been a time of unsettlement, but also of vitality and passion, in the religious life of the United Kingdom. Amid the new conceptions of the material universe, the fascination with psychology and cultural anthropology, artistic celebrations of decadence, and challenges to moral convention, growing numbers sought fresh religious experiences and expressions. Some harkened after new religious movements – spiritualism, Theosophy, esoteric Buddhism, Celtic religion, the occult. Others turned to novel formulations of Christianity – in Christian mysticism, the New Theology or Catholic Modernism. Some were drawn to ritualism, finding in the beauty of ancient symbols and rituals a sanctuary from the greyness of urban-industrial society. Some were drawn to Christian socialism, church socialism, the social gospel, or guild socialism, hoping to reshape the whole of society around Christian morality. Still others thrilled to the stories of missionaries or, inspired by the Edinburgh World Missionary Conference of 1910, they dreamed of a reunited Christendom advancing to convert the world. Tens of thousands were converted during the great revival of 1904–05, with its mesmerising figure of Evan Roberts and its claims that the gifts of the Holy Spirit had returned and a new Pentecostal day was dawning. The large-scale Jewish immigration after 1881 contributed to this diverse religious landscape, and the emergence of Zionism revived an eastward-looking pre-millenarian fervour. Many came to believe that equal rights for women would usher in a new moral era. In Ireland, religion largely shaped the Unionist and nationalist identities, and called many to sacrifice. It was a time of unsettlement in the religious world, but not of lack of belief, hope or spiritual searching. Religion was, in many respects, profoundly important in the United Kingdom of 1914. The overwhelming majority of the population still saw themselves as Christian, millions regularly attended church each Sunday, and religious questions generated great passion. Of those who did not attend church, most professed a belief in God.

And yet, there was also a sense that the role of religion in the life of the state was declining. To be sure, many were full of passionate intensity for religious causes. The conflicts between Protestants and Anglo-Catholic ritualists, between church and chapel, between Irish Protestants and Irish Catholics demonstrated that the old religious identities, and the old hatreds, remained powerful, and could inspire violence. But the churches had also lost much of their former influence over education, social welfare and public morals, and their social role was narrowing. Church attendances in nearly all denominations were falling off from the 1890s and there were difficulties in recruiting the most able young men into the clergy. The political influence of the 'Nonconformist conscience' declined significantly after the failures of the Liberal education bills between 1906 and 1908. Moreover, as the state expanded its social welfare legislation (especially after 1909), the role of all the churches in the distribution of charity declined, and fewer working-class families felt any need to listen to moral and spiritual guidance from the clergy. In a time of intensifying conflict between capital and labour, confidence in the old formula of Christianity, commerce and civilisation waned. With the rise of nationalist movements in the East (especially after 1905), there were fewer references to the

United Kingdom as an elect nation with a providential purpose to extend the boundaries of Christendom. Among the educated classes, more and more viewed religion in terms of personal experience; it was an aspect of human psychology, a form of aesthetic expression, a search after spiritual fulfilment, or a response to personal need. While in the 1880s to be a secularist or freethinker, in the manner of Charles Bradlaugh, was to be an outsider and not quite respectable, after the 1890s it was socially acceptable – even expected in some intellectual circles – to be a non-Christian. The clergy were seen less as the representatives of God's immutable law, and more as counsellors or doers of good in their communities; Scripture was seen less as the expression of divine law, and more as a guide to the fulfilling life.

By 1914, as Brian Stanley has noted, there were serious questions about what constituted a 'Christian nation' and whether such an entity existed following the nineteenth-century liberal legislation that had dismantled the semi-confessional state.[228] Certainly the United Kingdom of 1914 was not a Christian state in the sense that the United Kingdom of 1815 had been Christian. The established churches, while they survived in England and Scotland, no longer had much legal authority for the religious instruction of the people, and most citizens would have rejected the notion that it was their duty to conform to the worship, doctrine and discipline of the churches by law established. In both Ireland and Wales, the church had been legally disestablished. The different Christian and Jewish denominations were largely seen as equal under the law. Parliament was no longer exclusively Christian, and indeed after 1888 it included professed atheists and agnostics. The monarch, certainly, remained by law a member of the established church, and the churches played a ceremonial role in national commemorations. Many had, indeed, sought to portray the beginning of the Great War as a national Christian crusade. But such language soon paled with the draining of blood on the Western front. The peoples of the United Kingdom in 1914 were overwhelmingly Christian, and many were intensely religious. But the state was largely secular, and would become increasingly so in the aftermath of the War.

Notes

1 A. J. Balfour, *The Religion of Humanity: An Address delivered at the Church Congress, Manchester* (Edinburgh, 1888), 25.

2 H. Jackson, *The Eighteen Nineties: A Review of Art and Ideas at the Close of the Nineteenth Century* (London, 1913), 20.

3 Rose, *Edwardian Temperament*, 74–98.

4 G. K. Chesterton, *Heretics* (London, 1905), 12, 13, 32.

5 G. M. Reith, *Reminiscences of the United Free Church General Assembly (1900–1929)* (London, 1933), 79.

6 J. Wolffe, 'The End of Victorian Values? Women, Religion and the Death of Queen Victoria', in *Women in the Church, Studies in Church History*, vol. 20 (Oxford, 1990), 481–503.

7 Jackson, *Eighteen Nineties*, 84–5.

8 L. Barrow, *Independent Spirits: Spiritualism and English Plebeians 1850–1910* (London, 1986), 96–124.

9 A. Owen, *The Darkened Room: Women, Power and Spiritualism in Late Nineteenth Century England* (London, 1989), 9.

10 Oppenheim, *The Other World*, 94–5; G. K. Nelson, *Spiritualism and Society* (London, 1969), 137–9.

11 Owen, *The Darkened Room*, 107–35.

12 Quoted in Barrow, *Independent Spirits*, 105.

13 A. Goldman, 'Yeats, Spiritualism, and Psychical Research', in G. M. Harper (ed.), *Yeats and the Occult* (London, 1976), 110.

14 Quoted in Oppenheim, *The Other World*, 80.

15 E. Maitland, *Anna Kingsford: Her Life, Letters, Diary and Work*, 2 vols (London, 1896), vol. ii, 194.

16 F. Turner, *Between Science and Religion: The Reaction to Scientific Naturalism in Late Victorian England* (New Haven, Conn., 1974), 87–103.

17 Searle, *A New England?*, 641.

18 'Wireless' (1902), in R. Kipling, *Traffics and Discoveries* (London, 1904), 213–39.

19 Barrow, *Independent Spirits*, 134.

20 Goldman, 'Yeats, Spiritualism, and Psychical Research', 114–15; W. S. Smith, *The London Heretics 1870–1914* (London, 1967), 164–7.

21 M. Bevir, 'Annie Besant's Search for Truth: Christianity, Secularism and New Age Thought', *Journal of Ecclesiastical History*, 50 (January 1999), 85–6.

22 Oppenheim, *The Other World*, 162.

23 For an excellent brief study of the movement, see B. F. Campbell, *Ancient Wisdom Revived: A History of the Theosophical Movement* (Berkeley, California, 1980).

24 M. Bevir, 'The West turns Eastward: Madame Blavatsky and the
    Transformation of the Occult Tradition', *Journal of the American Academy
    of Religion*, 57 (1994), 747–65.

25 S. Guinness, 'Ireland through the Stereoscope: Reading the Cultural Politics
    of Theosophy in the Irish Literary Revival', in B. Taylor FitzSimon and
    J. H. Murphy (eds), *The Irish Revival Reappraised* (Dublin, 2004), 21–2.

26 A. P. Sinnett, *Esoteric Buddhism* (London, 1883), 177.

27 F. Max Müller, 'Esoteric Buddhism', *Nineteenth Century*, 33 (May 1893),
    767–88.

28 D. Burfield, 'Theosophy and Feminism', in P. Holden (ed.), *Women's
    Religious Experience: Cross-Cultural Perspectives* (London, 1983), 27–56.

29 Bevir, 'Annie Besant's Search for Truth', 83–92.

30 A. Besant, *Ancient Ideals in Modern Life*, quoted in E. Halévy, *Imperialism
    and the Rise of Labour: A History of the English People in the Nineteenth
    Century*, 2nd edn, vol. v (London, 1951), 183, footnote 2.

31 The discussion here draws from P. Brantlinger, *Rule of Darkness: British
    Literature and Imperialism, 1830–1914* (Ithaca, New York, 1988), 227–53.

32 A. Owen, *The Place of Enchantment: British Occultism and the Culture of
    the Modern* (Chicago, 2004), 51–84, 114–85; R. Barber, *The Holy Grail:
    The History of a Legend* (London, 2005), 290–7.

33 R. Foster, *W. B. Yeats: A Life*, vol. I, *The Apprentice Mage* (Oxford, 1997),
    103–7, 231–3.

34 Ibid., 84.

35 I. Bradley, *Celtic Christianity* (Edinburgh, 1999), 140.

36 Guinness, 'Ireland through the Stereoscope', 27–8.

37 Foster, *W. B. Yeats*, vol. I, 186–7, 196–7; Owen, *The Place of
    Enchantment*, 168.

38 Turner, *Between Science and Religion*, 104–33; Oppenheim, *The Other
    World*, 254–62.

39 F. W. H. Myers, 'Automatic Writing', *Contemporary Review*, 47 (February
    1885), 244.

40 Owen, *The Place of Enchantment*, 176–7.

41 Quoted in Turner, *Between Science and Religion*, 118.

42 W. James, *The Varieties of Religious Experience: A Study in Human Nature*
    (London, 1902), 512–13.

43 Ibid., 488.

44 Quoted in B. McGinn, *The Foundations of Mysticism* (London, 1992), 291.

45 F. Max Müller, *Theosophy and Psychological Religion* (London, 1893), 538.

46 Ibid., 522–3.

47 W. R. Inge, *Christian Mysticism* (London, 1899), 329–30.

48 E. Underhill, *Mysticism*, 12th edn (London, 1930), 52.

49 Ibid., 53–5.

50 Much of what follows is based on K. Robbins, 'The Spiritual Pilgrimage of the Rev. R. J. Campbell', in K. Robbins, *History, Religion and Identity in Modern Britain* (London, 1993), 133–47.

51 R. J. Campbell, *A Spiritual Pilgrimage* (London, 1916), 23.

52 Ibid., 49–53, 95–108.

53 R. J. Campbell, *The New Theology* (London, 1907), 26.

54 Ibid., 29–33.

55 Ibid., 201–2.

56 Ibid., 139–40.

57 Ibid., 185.

58 R. J. Campbell, *Christianity and the Social Order* (London, 1907), 17.

59 *Letters of Principal James Denney to W. Robertson Nicoll 1893–1917* (London, 1920), 85.

60 R. Lloyd, *The Church of England 1900–1965* (London, 1966), 82–9.

61 G. Alderman, *Modern British Jewry*, 2nd edn (Oxford, 1998), 110–11, 118.

62 C. Booth, *Life and Labour of the People in London*, 3rd Series: *Religious Influences*, vol. 2 (London, 1902), 3.

63 Alderman, *Modern British Jewry*, 102–3, 120.

64 W. D. Rubinstein, *A History of the Jews in the English-Speaking World: Great Britain* (Basingstoke, 1996), 120–31.

65 D. Vital, *Zionism: The Formative Years* (Oxford, 1982), 134.

66 Quoted in C. Holmes, *Anti-Semitism in British Society 1876–1939* (London, 1979), 17.

67 S. A. Cohen, ' "The Tactics of Revolt": The English Zionist Federation and Anglo-Jewry, 1895–1904', *Journal of Jewish Studies*, 29 (1978), 169–85; Alderman, *Modern British Jewry*, 225.

68 M. Berkowitz, *Zionist Culture and West European Jewry before the First World War* (Cambridge, 1993), 3.

69 Bar-Yosef, *The Holy Land in English Culture*, 232–43.

70 Rubinstein, *A History of the Jews in the English-Speaking World*, 164–5.

71 For the new leisure industry, see especially Searle, *A New England?*, 529–70.

72 H. McLeod, *Religion and Society in England, 1850–1914* (London, 1996), 170–2.

73 R. Gill, *The Myth of the Empty Church* (London, 1993), 172, 176.

74 Ibid., 159.

75 McLeod, *Religion and Society in England*, 173–4.

76 H. Caine, *The Christian* (1897), quoted in E. Halévy, *Imperialism and the Rise of Labour (1895–1905)*, E. I. Watkin (trans.), 2nd edn (London, 1951), 169.

77 H. E. Ryle, Bishop of Winchester, *On the Church of England: Sermons and Addresses* (London, 1904), 83, 89.

78 Quoted in D. J. Withrington, 'The Churches in Scotland, c.1870–c.1900: Towards a New Social Conscience?', *Records of the Scottish Church History Society*, 19 (1977), 163.

79 D. MacLeod, *Christ and Society* (London, 1893), 46.

80 J. R. Fleming, *A History of the Church of Scotland 1875–1929* (Edinburgh, 1933), 56.

81 A. Muir, *John White* (London, 1958), 440–1.

82 R. Tudur Jones, *Faith and the Crisis of a Nation: Wales 1890–1914* (first published as *Ffydd ac Argyfwng Cenedl*, 1981–82), Sylvia Prys Jones (trans.), R. Pope (ed.) (Cardiff, 2004), 60–76, quotation on 64.

83 C. G. Brown, *Death of Christian Britain: Understanding Secularisation 1800–2000* (London, 2001), 169.

84 Chadwick, *Victorian Church, Part 2*, 249.

85 McLeod, *Religion and Society in England*, 194.

86 Searle, *A New England?*, 658.

87 A. C. Deane, 'The Falling-Off in the Quantity and Quality of the Clergy', *Nineteenth Century*, 45 (June 1899), 1030.

88 F. W. Head, 'The Church and the People', in C. F. G. Masterman, et al., *The Heart of the Empire* (London, 1901), 271.

89 D. Newsome, *Godliness and Good Learning* (London, 1961), 27.

90 Gilbert, *Religion and Society in Industrial England*, 28; Chadwick, *Victorian Church, Part 2*, 189.

91 Westcott, *Life and Letters of Brooke Foss Westcott*, vol. ii, 172–3.

92 R. L. Brown, *Reviving the Clergy, Renewing the Laity: Archbishop Benson's Mission in Wales* (Welshpool, 1994), 21–51.

93 Quoted in Creighton, *Life and Letters of Mandell Creighton*, vol. ii, 286.

94 Yates, *Anglican Ritualism in Victorian Britain*, 278.

95 J. G. Lockhart, *Charles Lindley, Viscount Halifax*, 2 vols (London, 1935–36), vol. ii, 38–91.

96 Wheeler, *The Old Enemies*, 273–95.

97 Halévy, *Imperialism and the Rise of Labour*, 186.

98 For the revived ritualist controversy, see G. I. T. Machin, 'The Last Victorian Anti-Ritualist Campaign, 1895–1906', *Victorian Studies*, 25 (1982), 277–302.

99 Reed, *Glorious Battle*, 234.

100 J. E. B. Munson, 'The Oxford Movement by the End of the Nineteenth Century', *Church History*, 44 (1975), 387.

101 Ibid., 385.

102 P. J. Waller, *Democracy and Sectarianism: A Political and Social History of Liverpool 1868–1939* (Liverpool, 1981), 175, 185.

103 W. Harcourt, *Lawlessness in the National Church* (London, 1899), 23, 116.

104 Lockhart, *Charles Lindley, Viscount Halifax*, vol. ii, 135–6.

105 Waller, *Democracy and Sectarianism*, 192.

106 B. Dugdale, *Arthur James Balfour*, 2 vols (London, 1936), vol. ii, 284–5.

107 G. K. A. Bell, *Randall Davidson*, 2 vols (Oxford, 1935), vol. i, 263–80; the episode is also depicted in Compton Mackenzie's novel, *The Altar Steps*.

108 Bell, *Randall Davidson*, vol. i, 398–400.

109 Chadwick, *Victorian Church, Part 2*, 403–4.

110 J. G. Snead-Cox, *Life of Cardinal Vaughan*, 2 vols (London, 1911), vol. ii, 313–60.

111 T. Horwood, 'Public Opinion and the 1908 Eucharistic Congress', *Recusant History*, 25 (2000–01), 120–32; E. Oldmeadow, *Francis Cardinal Bourne*, 2 vols (London, 1940), vol. i, 369–98.

112 Cruickshank, *Church and State in English Education*, 47–8.

113 B. Simon, *Education and the Labour Movement 1870–1920* (London, 1965), 179.

114 Ibid., 188.

115 Quoted in A. Rogers, 'Churches and Children – A Study in the Controversy over the 1902 Education Act', *British Journal of Educational Studies*, 8 (November 1959), 46.

116 Halévy, *Imperialism and the Rise of Labour*, 165–6.

117 Simon, *Education and the Labour Movement*, 220.

118 D. R. Pugh, 'The Church and Education: Anglican Attitudes 1902', *Journal of Ecclesiastical History*, 23 (1972), 219–32.

119 Quoted in Rogers, 'Churches and Children', 40, footnote 1.

120 Bebbington, *Nonconformist Conscience*, 145–6.

121 Machin, *Politics and the Churches in Great Britain 1869 to 1921*, 265; Cruickshank, *Church and State in English Education*, 81; J. Grigg, *Lloyd George: The People's Champion 1902–1911* (London, 1978), 36–7.

122 W. B. Selbie, *The Life of Andrew Martin Fairbairn* (London, 1914), 279.

123 Machin, *Politics and the Churches in Great Britain 1869 to 1921*, 266.

124 Bebbington, *Nonconformist Conscience*, 144.

125 Tudur Jones, *Faith and the Crisis of a Nation*, 277–81.

126 The best account of the revival of 1904–05 is ibid., 283–369.

127 C. G. Brown, *Religion and Society in Twentieth-Century Britain* (Harlow, 2006), 61.

128 Tudur Jones, *Faith and the Crisis of a Nation*, 341.

129 A. Anderson, *Spreading Fires: The Missionary Nature of Early Pentecostalism* (London, 2007).

130 Tudur Jones, *Faith and the Crisis of a Nation*, 362–4.

131 S. Koss, *Nonconformity in Modern British Politics* (London, 1975), 70.

132 Ibid., 73, 228.

133 Ibid., 74.

134 Quoted in N. J. Richards, 'The Education Bill of 1906 and the Decline of Political Nonconformity', *Journal of Ecclesiastical History*, 23 (January 1972), 51.

135 A. Birrell, *Things Past Redress* (London, 1937), 184.

136 Cruickshank, *Church and State in English Education*, 99.

137 J. Wilson, *CB: A Life of Sir Henry Campbell-Bannerman* (London, 1973), 559.

138 Simon, *Education and the Labour Movement*, 262.

139 J. F. Glaser, 'English Nonconformity and the Decline of Liberalism', *American Historical Review*, 63 (1958), 362.

140 Bell, *Disestablishment in Ireland and Wales*, 297–317.

141 Lord Rosebery, *Miscellanies Literary and Historical*, 2 vols (London, 1921), vol. ii, 250.

142 Grigg, *Lloyd George: The People's Champion*, 192.

143 Jones, *Christian Socialist Revival*, 188.

144 Norman, *Church and Society in England*, 220; Jones, *Christian Socialist Revival*, 213–16.

145 Jones, *Christian Socialist Review*, 217.

146 Ibid., 164; Wagner, *The Church of England and Social Reform since 1854*, 227.

147 R. Groves, *Conrad Noel and the Thaxted Movement* (London, 1967), 30.

148 W. Temple, *The Kingdom of God* (London, 1912), 78–83.

149 G. K. Chesterton, *Autobiography* (London, 1937), 166–8.

150 Inglis, *Churches and the Working Classes in Victorian England*, 278–80; Prestige, *Life of Charles Gore*, 280–1.

151 Groves, *Conrad Noel*, 35.

152 Jones, *Christian Socialist Revival*, 246.

153 Chesterton, *Autobiography*, 163.

154 Rose, *Edwardian Temperament*, 60–1; Jones, *Christian Socialist Revival*, 275–95.

155 M. MacCallum, *Religion as Social Justice* (Glasgow, 1915), 135.

156 R. Sjölinder, *Presbyterian Reunion in Scotland 1907–1921* (Stockholm, 1962), 86–90; Muir, *John White*, 86–8.

157 Carnegie Simpson, *Life of Principal Rainy*, vol. ii, 248–9.

158 *Glasgow Herald*, 23 May 1908.

159 *Glasgow Herald*, 20 May 1914.

160 J. M. MacKenzie, *Propaganda and Empire: The Manipulation of British Public Opinion 1880–1960* (Manchester, 1984), 32–3.

161 A. Porter, 'Religion and Empire: British Expansion in the Long Nineteenth Century, 1780–1914', *Journal of Imperial and Commonwealth History*, 20 (1992), 372.

162 A. Porter, ' "Cultural Imperialism" and Protestant Missionary Enterprise, 1780–1914', *Journal of Imperial and Commonwealth History*, 25 (1997), 371.

163 E. G. K. Hewat, *Vision and Achievement 1796–1956: A History of the Foreign Missions of the Churches United in the Church of Scotland* (London, 1960), 215.

164 J. M. MacKenzie, 'Missionaries, Science, and the Environment in Nineteenth-Century Africa', in A. Porter (ed.), *The Imperial Horizons of British Protestant Missions, 1880–1914* (Grand Rapids, Michigan, 2003), 106–30.

165 A. Porter, 'Missions and Empire, c.1873–1914', in B. Stanley and S. Gilley (eds), *The Cambridge History of Christianity*, vol. 8, *World Christianities, c.1815–c.1914* (Cambridge, 2006), 561–2.

166 MacKenzie, *Propaganda and Empire*; J. Schneer, *London 1900: The Imperial Metropolis* (New Haven, Conn., 1999), 93–115.

167 B. Porter, *The Absent-Minded Imperialists: Empire, Society, and Culture in Britain* (Oxford, 2004), 164–254.

168 Quoted in J. Morris, *Pax Britannica: The Climax of an Empire* (New York, 1968), 31.

169 D. Bebbington, 'Atonement, Sin, and Empire, 1880–1914', in Porter (ed.), *Imperial Horizons*, 14–31.

170 E. S. Talbot, 'Preface', in G. Longridge, *A History of the Oxford Mission to Calcutta* (London, 1900), ix.

171 G. A. Lefroy, 'Our Indian Empire', in J. Ellison and G. H. S. Walpole (eds), *Church and Empire* (London, 1907), 69.

172 Quoted in Porter, *Religion versus Empire?*, 285.

173 G. H. S. Walpole, 'The Vocation of the Anglo-Saxon Race and England's Responsibility', in Ellison and Walpole (eds), *Church and Empire*, 21–41, 33.

174 B. Wilson, 'The Church and the Empire', in H. H. Henson (ed.), *Church Problems: A View of Modern Anglicanism* (London, 1900), 371–2, 393.

175 S. Maughan, 'Imperial Christianity? Bishop Montgomery and the Foreign Missions of the Church of England, 1895–1915', in Porter (ed.), *Imperial Horizons*, 32–57.

176 G. Cuthbertson, 'Pricking the "Nonconformist Conscience": Religion against the South African War', in D. Lowry (ed.), *The South African War Reappraised* (Manchester, 2000), 169–87; A. Davey, *The British Pro-Boers 1877–1902* (Cape Town, 1978), 145–56.

177 S. C. Carpenter, *Winnington-Ingram* (London, 1949), 279.

178 Quoted in D. Bebbington, 'Atonement, Sin, and Empire, 1880–1914', in A. Porter (ed.), *Imperial Horizons*, 19.

179 J. A. Hobson, *The Psychology of Jingoism* (London, 1901), 48.

180 H. MacLeod, 'Dissent and the Peculiarities of the English, c.1870–1914', in J. Shaw and A. Kreider, *Culture and the Nonconformist Tradition* (Cardiff, 1999), 132.

181 C. A. Cline, 'The Church and the Movement for Congo Reform', *Church History*, 32 (1963), 51.

182 K. Grant, 'Christian Critics of Empire: Missionaries, Lantern Lectures, and the Congo Reform Campaign in Britain', *Journal of Imperial and Commonwealth History*, 29 (2001), 27–58; W. R. Louis, 'Roger Casement and the Congo', *Journal of African History*, 1 (1964), 99–120.

183 Grant, 'Christian Critics of Empire', 53.

184 Quoted in D. O'Connor, *Gospel, Raj and Swaraj: The Missionary Years of C. F. Andrews 1904–14* (Frankfurt am Main, 1990), 37.

185 T. Yates, *Christian Missions in the Twentieth Century* (Cambridge, 1994), 8–9.

186 K. Robbins, *Foreign Encounters: English Congregationalism, Germany and the United States, c.1850–c.1914* (London, 2006), 5–8.

187 W. H. T. Gairdner, *Edinburgh 1910: An Account and Interpretation of the World Missionary Conference* (Edinburgh, 1910); K. Clements, *Faith on the Frontier: A Life of J. H. Oldham* (Edinburgh, 1999), 73–99.

188 B. Stanley, 'Edinburgh 1910 and the Oikoumene', in A. R. Cross (ed.), *Ecumenism and History* (Carlisle, 2002), 89–91.

189 Quoted in ibid., 93.

190 B. Stanley, 'Church, State, and the Hierarchy of "Civilization": The Making of the "Missions and Governments" Report of the World Missionary Conference, Edinburgh 1910', in Porter (ed.), *Imperial Horizons*, 69–78.

191 Stanley, 'Edinburgh 1910 and the Oikoumene', 100–1; World Missionary Conference, *History and Records of the Conference* (Edinburgh, 1910), 306–15; Gairdner, *Edinburgh 1910*, 109–11; Clements, *Faith on the Frontier*, 89–90.

192 Yates, *Christian Missions in the Twentieth Century*, 24–8; Gairdner, *Edinburgh 1910*, 135–53.

193 World Missionary Conference, *Report of Commission VII: Co-operation and the Promotion of Unity* (Edinburgh, 1910), 143.

194 E. Halévy, *The Rule of Democracy 1905–1914*, E. I. Watkin (trans.), 2nd edn (London, 1952), 500.

195 J. Eldridge Miller, *Rebel Women: Feminism, Modernism and the Edwardian Novel* (London, 1994), 10–38.

196 H. Mathers, 'The Evangelical Spirituality of a Victorian Feminist: Josephine Butler, 1828–1906', *Journal of Ecclesiastical History*, 52 (2001), 282–312.

197 W. T. Stead, *Josephine Butler: A Life Sketch* (London, 1887), 85–6.

198 Quoted in M. Phillips, *The Ascent of Women: A History of the Suffragette Movement and the Ideas behind It* (London, 2003), 93.

199 J. R. deVries, 'Transforming the Pulpit: Preaching and Prophecy in the British Women's Suffrage Movement', in B. M. Kienzle and P. J. Walker (eds), *Women Preachers and Prophets through Two Millennia of Christianity* (Berkeley, California, 1998), 318–33.

200 Ibid., 321–2.

201 H. G. Wells, *Ann Veronica*, 1909, S. Schutt (ed.) (London, 2004), 110–11.

202 E. Pethick Lawrence, *Women as Persons or Property* (1913), quoted in L. A. Orr MacDonald, *A Unique and Glorious Mission: Women and Presbyterianism in Scotland 1830–1930* (Edinburgh, 2000), 302.

203 Quoted in Orr MacDonald, *A Unique and Glorious Mission*, 296–7.

204 deVries, 'Transforming the Pulpit', 324–5.

205 L. Leneman, 'The Scottish Churches and "Votes for Women"', *Records of the Scottish Church History Society*, 24 (1991), 240.

206 B. Heeney, 'The Beginnings of Church Feminism: Women and the Councils of the Church of England 1897–1919, *Journal of Ecclesiastical History*, 33 (1982), 93–100.

207 Binfield, *So Down to Prayers*, 222.

208 Orr MacDonald, *A Unique and Glorious Mission*, 305.

209 Quoted in Leneman, 'The Scottish Churches and "Votes for Women"', 245.

210 O. Chadwick, *Hensley Henson* (Oxford, 1983), 117–18; Leneman, 'The Scottish Churches and "Votes for Women"', 242, 244, 250.

211 W. B. Yeats, *Autobiographies* (London, 1955), 559.

212 Ibid., 35.

213 P. O'Farrell, *Ireland's English Question: Anglo-Irish Relations 1534–1970* (London, 1971), 223–40; F. S. L. Lyons, *Culture and Anarchy in Ireland 1890–1939* (Oxford, 1979), 79–82.

214 D. Miller, *Church, State and Nation in Ireland 1898–1921* (Dublin, 1973), 72–3.

215 Quoted in O'Farrell, *Ireland's English Question*, 245.

216 C. Cruise O'Brien, *Ancestral Voices: Religion and Nationalism in Ireland* (Dublin, 1994), 32–43; Lyons, *Culture and Anarchy in Ireland*, 59–61.

217 C. F. D'Arcy, 'The Religious Difficulty under Home Rule', in S. Rosenbaum (ed.), *Against Home Rule: The Case for Union* (London, 1912), 205.

218 G. Walker, 'The Irish Presbyterian Anti-Home Rule Convention of 1912', *Studies*, 86 (1997), 71–7.

219 Quoted in A. Megahey, ' "God Will Defend the Right": The Protestant Churches and Opposition to Home Rule', in D. G. Boyce and A. O'Day (eds), *Defenders of the Union: A Survey of British and Irish Unionism since 1801* (London, 2001), 168.

220 Ibid., 169–70.

221 A. T. Q. Stewart, *The Ulster Crisis: Resistance to Home Rule, 1912–14* (London, 1969), 66.

222 Quoted in R. F. G. Holmes, ' "Ulster will Fight and Ulster will be Right": The Protestant Churches and Ulster's Resistance to Home Rule, 1912–14', in W. J. Sheils (ed.), *The Church and War, Studies in Church History*, 20 (1983), 331.

223 Ibid., 333.

224 P. Pearse, 'The Coming Revolution', in *Collected Works of Padraic H. Pearse: Political Writings and Speeches* (Dublin, 1922), 91, 99.

225 A. Wallace Williamson, sermon in St Giles, Edinburgh, 9 August 1914, *British Weekly*, 13 August 1914.

226 J. Muir, *War and the Christian Duty* (Paisley, 1915), 20.

227 N. Maclean, *The Great Discovery* (Glasgow, 1915), 13, 76–7.

228 B. Stanley, 'The Outlook for Christianity in 1914', in Stanley and Gilley (eds), *World Christianities c.1815–c.1914*, 596–7.

Select Bibliography

General

Akenson, D. H., *The Church of Ireland: Ecclesiastical Reform and Revolution, 1800–1885* (New Haven, Conn., 1971).

Alderman, G., *Modern British Jewry*, 2nd edn, (Oxford, 1998).

Bar-Yosef, E., *The Holy Land in English Culture 1799–1917: Palestine and the Question of Orientalism* (Oxford, 2005).

Bebbington, D. W., *Evangelicalism in Modern Britain* (London, 1989).

Binfield, C., *So Down to Prayers: Studies in English Nonconformity, 1780–1920* (London, 1977).

Brown, C. G., *Religion and Society in Scotland since 1707* (Edinburgh, 1997).

Brown, C. G., *The Death of Christian Britain: Understanding Secularisation 1800–2000* (London, 2001).

Brown, S. J., *The National Churches of England, Ireland and Scotland 1801–46* (Oxford, 2001).

Chadwick, O., *The Victorian Church, Part One 1829–1859* (London, 1966).

Chadwick, O., *The Victorian Church, Part Two 1860–1901* (London, 1970).

Cheyne, A. C., *The Transforming of the Kirk: Victorian Scotland's Religious Revolution* (Edinburgh, 1983).

Drummond, A. L. and J. Bulloch, *The Scottish Church, 1688–1843: The Age of the Moderates* (Edinburgh, 1973).

Drummond, A. L. and J. Bulloch, *The Church in Victorian Scotland, 1843–1874* (Edinburgh, 1975).

Drummond, A. L. and J. Bulloch, *The Church in Late Victorian Scotland, 1874–1900* (Edinburgh, 1978).

Gilbert, A. D., *Religion and Society in Industrial England: Church, Chapel and Social Change, 1740–1914* (London, 1976).

Gill, S., *Women and the Church of England from the Eighteenth Century to the Present* (London, 1994).

Gilley, S., *Newman and his Age* (London, 1990).

Hempton, D. M., *Religion and Political Culture in Britain* (Cambridge, 1996).

Hempton, D. M. and M. Hill, *Evangelical Protestantism in Ulster Society 1740–1890* (London, 1992).

Hilton, B., *The Age of Atonement: The Influence of Evangelicalism on Social and Economic Thought 1785–1865* (Oxford, 1986).

Knight, F., *The Nineteenth-Century Church and English Society* (Cambridge, 1995).

Machin, G. I. T., *Politics and the Churches in Great Britain, 1832 to 1868* (Oxford, 1977).

Machin, G. I. T., *Politics and the Churches in Great Britain, 1869 to 1921* (Oxford, 1987).

Norman, E. R., *Church and Society in England 1770–1970: A Historical Study* (Oxford, 1976).

Norman, E. R., *The English Catholic Church in the Nineteenth Century* (Oxford, 1984).

Pope, R. (ed.), *Religion and National Identity: Wales and Scotland c.1700–2000* (Cardiff, 2001).

Porter, A., *Religion versus Empire? British Protestant Missionaries and Overseas Expansion, 1700–1914* (Manchester, 2004).

Prochashka, F., *Christianity and Social Service in Modern Britain: The Disinherited Spirit* (Oxford, 2006).

Reardon, B. M. G., *Religious Thought in the Victorian Age: A Survey from Coleridge to Gore* (London, 1980).

Robbins, K., *History, Religion and Identity in Modern Britain* (London, 1993).

Stanley, B., *The Bible and the Flag: Protestant Missions and British Imperialism in the Nineteenth and Twentieth Centuries* (Leicester, 1990).

Watts, M. R., *The Dissenters, Volume II: The Expansion of Evangelical Nonconformity 1791–1859* (Oxford, 1995).

Wheeler, M., *The Old Enemies: Catholic and Protestant in Nineteenth-Century English Culture* (Cambridge, 2006).

Chapter 1 Evangelicalism, Empire and the Protestant State, 1815–1829

Best, G. F. A., *Temporal Pillars: Queen Anne's Bounty, the Ecclesiastical Commissioners and the Church of England* (Cambridge, 1964).

Clark, J. C. D., *English Society, 1660–1832: Religion, Ideology and Politics during the Ancien Regime*, 2nd edn (Cambridge, 2000).

Colley, L., *Britons: Forging the Nation 1707–1837* (New Haven, Conn., 1992).

Harrison, J. F. C., *The Second Coming: Popular Millenarianism 1780–1850* (London, 1979).

Holmes, A., *The Shaping of Ulster Presbyterian Belief and Practice, 1770 to 1840* (Oxford, 2006).

Howse, W. M., *Saints in Politics: The 'Clapham Sect' and the Growth of Freedom* (London, 1953).

Larkin, E., *The Pastoral Role of the Roman Catholic Church in Pre-Famine Ireland, 1750–1850* (Dublin, 2006).

Lovegrove, D. W., *Established Church, Sectarian People: Itinerancy and the Transformation of English Dissent, 1780–1830* (Cambridge, 1988).

Machin, G. I. T., *The Catholic Question in English Politics, 1820–1830* (Oxford, 1964).

Martin, R. H., *Evangelicals United: Ecumenical Stirrings in Victorian Britain, 1795–1830* (Metuchen, New Jersey, 1983).

O'Ferrall, F., *Catholic Emancipation: Daniel O'Connell and the Birth of Irish Democracy, 1820–30* (Dublin, 1985).

Stunt, T. C. F., *From Awakening to Secession: Radical Evangelicals in Switzerland and Britain, 1815–35* (Edinburgh, 2000).

Thompson, E. P., *The Making of the English Working Class* (London, 1963).

Valenze, D. M., *Prophetic Sons and Daughters: Female Preaching and Popular Religion in Industrial England* (Princeton, 1985).

Virgin, P., *The Church in an Age of Negligence* (Cambridge, 1989).

Walvin, J., 'The Rise of British Popular Sentiment for Abolition, 1787–1832', in C. Bolt and S. Drescher (eds), *Anti-Slavery, Religion, and Reform* (Folkestone, 1980), 149–62.

Ward, W. R., *Religion and Society in England 1790–1850* (London, 1972).

Waterman, A. M. C., *Revolution, Economics and Religion: Christian Political Economy 1798–1833* (Cambridge, 1991).

Whelan, I., *The Bible War in Ireland: The 'Second Reformation' and the Polarization of Protestant-Catholic Relations, 1800–1840* (Madison, Wisconsin, 2005).

Chapter 2 The Waning of the Church–State Connection, 1829–1845

Brent, R., *Liberal Anglican Politics: Whiggery, Religion and Reform, 1830–1841* (Oxford, 1987).

Broderick, J. F., *The Holy See and the Irish Movement for the Repeal of the Union with England 1829–1847* (Rome, 1951).

Brose, O. J., *Church and Parliament: The Reshaping of the Church of England 1828–1860* (Stanford, California, 1959).

Brown, S. J., *Thomas Chalmers and the Godly Commonwealth in Scotland* (Oxford, 1982).

Brown, S. J. and M. Fry (eds), *Scotland in the Age of the Disruption* (Edinburgh, 1993).

Burns, A., *The Diocesan Revival in the Church of England c.1800–1870* (Oxford, 1999).

Drummond, A. L., *Edward Irving and his Circle* (London, 1937).

Gash, N., *Reaction and Reconstruction in English Politics 1832–1852* (Oxford, 1965).

Kerr, D., *Peel, Priests and Politics: Sir Robert Peel's Administration and the Roman Catholic Church in Ireland, 1841–1846* (Oxford, 1982).

Lewis, D. M., *Lighten their Darkness: The Evangelical Mission to Working-Class London, 1828–1860* (New York, 1986).

Macintyre, A., *The Liberator: Daniel O'Connell and the Irish Party 1830–1847* (London, 1965).

Newsome, D., *The Parting of Friends: A Study of the Wilberforces and Henry Manning* (London, 1966).

Nockles, P. B., *The Oxford Movement in Context: Anglican High Churchmanship 1760–1857* (Cambridge, 1994).

Rowell, G., *The Vision Glorious: Themes and Personalities of the Catholic Revival in Anglicanism* (Oxford, 1983).

Soloway, R. A., *Prelates and People: Ecclesiastical Social Thought in England 1783–1852* (London, 1969).

Wolffe, J., *The Protestant Crusade in Great Britain 1829–1860* (Oxford, 1991).

Chapter 3 Commerce, Christianity and Civilisation, 1840–1863

Anderson, O., 'The Growth of Christian Militarism in Mid-Victorian Britain', *English Historical Review*, 86 (1971), 46–72.

Bowen, D., *Souperism: Myth or Reality* (Cork, 1970).

Chadwick, O., *Mackenzie's Grave* (London, 1959).

Cox, J., *Imperial Fault Lines: Christianity and Colonial Power in India, 1818–1940* (Stanford, California, 2002).

Gray, P., *Famine, Land and Politics: British Government and Irish Society 1843–1850* (Dublin, 1999).

Hall, C., *Civilising Subjects: Metropole and Colony in the British Imagination 1830–1867* (Cambridge, 2002).

Kerr, D., *'A Nation of Beggars'? Priests, People, and Politics in Famine Ireland 1846–1852* (Oxford, 1994).

Larkin, E., *The Making of the Roman Catholic Church in Ireland, 1850–1860* (Chapel Hill, North Carolina, 1980).

Mumm, S., *Stolen Daughters, Virgin Mothers: Anglican Sisterhoods in Victorian Britain* (London, 1999).

Norman, E. R., *Anti-Catholicism in Victorian England* (London, 1968).

Paz, D. G., *Popular Protestantism in Mid-Victorian England* (Stanford, California, 1992).

Porter, A., ' "Commerce and Christianity": The Rise and Fall of a Nineteenth-Century Missionary Slogan', *Historical Journal*, 28 (1985), 597–621.

Ross, A. C., *David Livingstone: Mission and Empire* (London, 2002).

Salbstein, M. C. N., *The Emancipation of the Jews in Britain* (London, 1982).

Chapter 4 Revivalism, Ritualism and Authority, 1859–1876

Altholz, J. L., *Anatomy of a Controversy: The Debate over Essays and Reviews 1860–1864* (Aldershot, Hants., 1994).

Arnstein, W. L., *Protestant versus Catholic in Mid-Victorian England: Mr Newdegate and the Nuns* (Columbia, Missouri, 1982).

Bell, P. M. H., *Disestablishment in Ireland and Wales* (London, 1969).

Bentley, J., *Ritualism and Politics in Victorian Britain: The Attempt to Legislate for Belief* (Oxford, 1978).

Budd, Susan, *Varieties of Unbelief: Atheists and Agnostics in English Society, 1850–1960* (London, 1977).

Carwardine, R., *Transatlantic Revivalism: Popular Evangelicalism in Britain and America 1790–1865* (Westport, Conn., 1978).

Cockshut, A. O. J., *The Unbelievers: English Agnostic Thought 1840–1890* (London, 1964).

Crowther, A., *Church Embattled: Religious Controversy in Mid-Victorian England* (Newton Abbot, Devon, 1970).

Guy, J., *The Heretic: A Study of the Life of John William Colenso 1814–1883* (Johannesburg, 1983).

Hattersley, R., *Blood and Fire: William and Catherine Booth and their Salvation Army* (London, 1999).

Jeffrey, K. S., *When the Lord Walked the Land: the 1858–62 Revival in the North East of Scotland* (Carlisle, 2002).

Kent, J., *Holding the Fort: Studies in Victorian Revivalism* (London, 1978).

Larkin, E., *The Consolidation of the Roman Catholic Church in Ireland, 1860–1870* (Dublin, 1987).

Marsh, P. T., *The Victorian Church in Decline: Archbishop Tait and the Church of England 1868–1882* (London, 1969).

Norman, E. R., *The Catholic Church and Ireland in the Age of Rebellion 1859–1873* (London, 1965).

Parry, J. P., *Democracy and Religion: Gladstone and the Liberal Party 1867–1875* (Cambridge, 1986).

Turner, F., 'The Victorian Conflict between Science and Religion', in F. Turner, *Contesting Cultural Authority* (Cambridge, 1993), 171–200.

Yates, N., *Anglican Ritualism in Victorian Britain 1830–1910* (Oxford, 1999).

Chapter 5 Overseas Crusades and the New Christian Social Conscience, 1875–1896

Arnstein, W., *The Bradlaugh Case: Atheism, Sex, and Politics among the Late Victorians*, 2nd edn (Columbia, Missouri, 1983).

Bebbington, D. W., *The Nonconformist Conscience: Chapel and Politics 1870–1914* (London, 1982).

Cox, J., *The English Churches in a Secular Society: Lambeth, 1870–1930* (New York, 1982).

Green, S. J. D., *Religion in the Age of Decline: Organisation and Experience in Industrial Yorkshire 1870–1920* (Cambridge, 1996).

Hempton, D., ' "For God and Ulster": Evangelical Protestantism and the Home Rule Crisis of 1886', *Studies in Church History*, Subsidia 7: *Protestant Evangelicalism*, K. Robbins (ed.) (Oxford, 1990), 225–54.

Inglis, K. S., *Churches and the Working Classes in Victorian England* (London, 1963).

Jones, P. d'A., *The Christian Socialist Revival 1877–1914: Religion, Class and Social Conscience in Late-Victorian England* (Princeton, 1968).

Kitson Clark, G., *Churchmen and the Condition of England, 1832–1885* (London, 1973).

Larkin, E., *The Roman Catholic Church and the Creation of the Modern Irish State 1878–1886* (Philadelphia, 1975).

Larkin, E., *The Roman Catholic Church and the Plan of Campaign 1886–1888* (Cork, 1978).

Larkin, E., *The Roman Catholic Church in Ireland and the Fall of Parnell 1888–1891* (Liverpool, 1979).

McClelland, V. A., *Cardinal Manning: His Public Life and Influence 1865–1892* (Oxford, 1962).

McLeod, H., *Religion and Society in England, 1850–1914* (London, 1996).

Meacham, S., *Toynbee Hall and Social Reform 1880–1914: The Search for Community* (New Haven, Conn., 1987).

Norman, E. R., *The Victorian Christian Socialists* (Cambridge, 1987).

Orens, J. R., *Stewart Headlam's Radical Anglicanism: The Mass, the Masses, and the Music Hall* (Champaign, Illinois, 2003).

Royle, E., *Radicals, Secularists and Republicans: Popular Free Thought in Britain, 1866–1915* (Manchester, 1980).

Shannon, R., *Gladstone and the Bulgarian Agitation 1876*, 2nd edn (Hassocks, Sussex, 1975).

Yeo, S., 'A New Life: The Religion of Socialism in Britain, 1883–1896', *History Workshop: A Journal of Socialist Historians*, no. 4 (Autumn 1977), 5–56.

Chapter 6 Religious Diversity, Identities and Conflicts, 1896–1914

Barrow, L., *Independent Spirits: Spiritualism and English Plebeians 1850–1910* (London, 1986).

Campbell, B. F., *Ancient Wisdom Revived: A History of the Theosophical Movement* (Berkeley, California, 1980).

Cruickshank, M., *Church and State in English Education, 1870 to the Present Day* (London, 1964).

deVries, J. R., 'Transforming the Pulpit: Preaching and Prophecy in the British Women's Suffrage Movement', in B. M. Kienzle and P. J. Walker (eds), *Women Preachers and Prophets through Two Millennia of Christianity* (Berkeley, California, 1998), 318–33.

Holmes, R. F. G., ' "Ulster will Fight and Ulster will be Right": The Protestant Churches and Ulster's Resistance to Home Rule,

1912–14', in W. J. Sheils (ed.), *The Church and War, Studies in Church History*, 20 (1983), 321–36.

Jones, R. Tudur, *Faith and the Crisis of a Nation: Wales 1890–1914*, Sylvia Prys Jones (trans.), R. Pope (ed.) (Cardiff, 2004).

Miller, D., *Church, State and Nation in Ireland 1898–1921* (Dublin, 1973).

Oppenheim, J., *The Other World: Spiritualism and Psychical Research in England, 1850–1914* (Cambridge, 1985).

Orr MacDonald, L. A., *A Unique and Glorious Mission: Women and Presbyterianism in Scotland 1830–1930* (Edinburgh, 2000).

Owen, A., *The Darkened Room: Women, Power and Spiritualism in Late Nineteenth Century England* (London, 1989).

Owen, A., *The Place of Enchantment: British Occultism and the Culture of the Modern* (Chicago, 2004).

Porter, A. (ed.), *The Imperial Horizons of British Protestant Missions, 1880–1914* (Grand Rapids, Michigan, 2003),

Reed, J. S., *Glorious Battle: The Cultural Politics of Victorian Anglo-Catholicism* (Nashville, 1996).

Rose, J., *The Edwardian Temperament 1895–1919* (Athens, Ohio, 1986).

Sjölinder, R., *Presbyterian Reunion in Scotland 1907–1921* (Stockholm, 1962).

Stanley, B., 'Edinburgh 1910 and the Oikoumene', in A. R. Cross (ed.), *Ecumenism and History* (Carlisle, 2002), 89–105.

Turner, F., *Between Science and Religion: The Reaction to Scientific Naturalism in Late Victorian England* (New Haven, Conn., 1974).

Waller, P. J., *Democracy and Sectarianism: A Political and Social History of Liverpool 1868–1939* (Liverpool, 1981).

Williams, S. C., *Religious Belief and Popular Culture in Southwark c.1880–1939* (Oxford, 1999).

Index